WE NOW KNOW

WE NOW KNOW

Rethinking
Cold War History

JOHN LEWIS GADDIS

A COUNCIL ON FOREIGN RELATIONS BOOK

UNIVERSITY PRESS

OXFORD

UNIVERSITY PRESS

Great Clarendon Street, Oxford OX2 6DP

Oxford University Press is a department of the University of Oxford.
It furthers the University's objective of excellence in research, scholarship,
and education by publishing worldwide in

Oxford New York

Athens Auckland Bangkok Bogotá Buenos Aires Calcutta
Cape Town Chennai Dar es Salaam Delhi Florence Hong Kong Istanbul
Karachi Kuala Lumpur Madrid Melbourne Mexico City Mumbai
Nairobi Paris São Paulo Singapore Taipei Tokyo Toronto Warsaw

with associated companies in Berlin Ibadan

Oxford is a registered trade mark of Oxford University Press
in the UK and in certain other countries

Published in the United States
by Oxford University Press Inc., New York

First published 1997
First issued in paperback 1998

British Library Cataloguing in Publication Data
Data available

Library of Congress Cataloging in Publication Data
Data available
ISBN 0-19-878070-2
ISBN 0-19-878071-0 (Pbk.)

7 9 10 8

Printed in the United States of America

For students, colleagues, and friends at Ohio University
with heartfelt thanks
1969–1997

PREFACE

Some years ago the electors of the Harold Vyvyan Harmsworth professorship at Oxford University invited me to spend a year at that venerable institution. My duties included conducting tutorials, participating in seminars, dining at high table, and delivering a set of eight fifty-minute lectures on a topic of my choice. It was the fall of 1992 and, as it had been for well over seven hundred earlier Michaelmas terms, Oxford was filled with attentive but soggy students, wheezing and coughing as the microbes they had imported got to know those endemic to the local mists and bogs. A respectable number of them—students and microbes alike—attended my presentations in the Examination Schools on High Street, which I was soon punctuating with my own sneezes, sniffles, and post-nasal drip.

The topic, appropriately enough, was the Cold War, a familiar one for me. But the circumstances, like the germs, were unfamiliar: this was the first full year of what everyone now agreed was the post-Cold War era and, as a consequence, my first opportunity to lecture on the Cold War from beginning to end. I therefore followed the example of Louis Halle's classic but premature book, *The Cold War as History*, and set about to treat that subject as he had sought to do during the 1960s,

as a phenomemon not without precedent in the long history of international conflict; as a phenomenon that, experience has taught us, has its own dynamics; as a phenomenon that, typically, goes through a certain cycle with a beginning, a middle, and an end.*

For all his prescience, I had two great advantages over Halle: I knew how the Cold War had come out, and I had access to at least a trickle of documents on it from the former Soviet Union, Eastern Europe, and the People's Republic of China. So I resolved to throw away my old lecture notes (yellowed and crumbling, they would not have survived the damp Oxford climate anyway); to prepare these new ones as international history, not just as United States diplomatic history; and to focus them on how knowing the Cold War's end might affect our understanding of what it was all about. Perhaps they might then become a short book.

By the time I left Oxford in the summer of 1993, the trickle of sources from the "other side" was becoming, if not a flood, at least a substantial inundation. I began to see that lectures, even in an expanded published form, would hardly do them justice. It seemed worth attempting a more comprehensive history of the Cold War that would incorporate as much of this new material as possible while relating it to what we already knew. Still more documents then appeared, making it clear that I would have to focus what was quickly becoming a lengthy manuscript on the first third of that conflict, where the new information exists in the

---

* Louis J. Halle, *The Cold War as History* (New York: Harper & Row, 1967), p. xii.

greatest abundance. Hence this book, which I have organized as a series of over-
lapping but interconnected narratives extending through the Cuban missile crisis.

Its title, *We Now Know*, deserves deconstruction. By "we," I mean post-Cold
War scholars of Cold War history as I have interpreted their findings. Every historian stands on the shoulders of those who have gone before; and in that sense
my conflation of "we" with "I" is not unusual. But it is normally youths who
benefit from the work of elders, and here the pattern has been reversed. The
"new" Cold War history is being written by a generation still mostly in its twen-
ties and thirties. Several of its practitioners, I am proud to say, have been my students. Whatever they and their contemporaries may have learned from me
pales in comparison to what I have learned from them, and I am delighted
herein to record my indebtedness. It remains to be seen what grade these new
teachers will think it appropriate to assign.

By "now," I seek to situate this book at a particular point in time, not to claim
timelessness for it. This is what I think we know *now* but did not know, or at
least did not know as clearly, while the Cold War was going on. With the passage of time we will surely know more, which may or may not accord with what
I have written here. Prefacing each pontification with "it seems," or "it
appears," or "based on currently available information" would have been
tedious in the extreme. Such qualifications apply throughout this book, though:
I reserve the right in the light of new evidence to change my mind, just as this
volume revises much of what I have previously thought and argued.

By "know," I assume the contingent nature of all historical interpretation.
Historians are products and prisoners of their own time and place. They can no
more escape their preconceptions than they can levitate benignly above their
word processors or their students. I have tried to approach this new evidence
with an open mind; but I will not claim—indeed I doubt that any historian can
ever honestly claim—to have allowed the chips to fall where they may. I have
arranged them, as most scholars do, in patterns that seem to me to make sense.
Readers will have to decide for themselves whether they agree.

I wish I could say I had researched this book by slogging dutifully through
archives in Moscow, Warsaw, Prague, Berlin, Budapest, Beijing, Hanoi, and
Havana, while simultaneously perfecting my already fluent Russian, Polish,
Czech, German, Hungarian, Chinese, Vietnamese, and Spanish. Alas it is not so.
Instead I have relied upon—and been almost overwhelmed by—what is already
available in English. I have drawn particularly from the *Bulletins* and working
papers of the Cold War International History Project at the Woodrow Wilson
Center in Washington, where James Hershberg and his colleagues have done a
truly heroic job of pulling this information together and getting it out in an easily accessible form. They in turn, and through them most practitioners of the
"new" Cold War history, have benefited from the support the John D. and
Catherine T. MacArthur Foundation has provided CWIHP. Without it this field
would hardly exist.

My method is no substitute for direct monographic research in the original
sources and languages. "Do as I say, not as I've done," I tell my students, who

now know the line well enough that they can chant it back, like something out of *The Rocky Horror Picture Show*. But few if any historians will master *all* of the archives and *all* of the languages required for comparative comprehensive Cold War international history. Much of it will continue to be written as this book has been: with a heavy reliance on the scholarship—and the linguistic skills— of others.

An unusually large number of people and institutions have helped to bring this volume about. Tim Barton of the Oxford University Press (Oxford) braved my germ-laden lectures and first suggested that I turn them into a book. My long-time Oxford University Press (New York) editor Sheldon Meyer strongly supported the idea. The provost and fellows of The Queen's College provided a congenial setting as I began to write: I am especially grateful to Alastair Parker and, among other Oxford friends, to Anne Deighton, John Dunbabin, Rosemary Foot, Timothy Garton Ash, Daniel Howe, Robert O'Neill, Adam Roberts, John Rowett, Avi Shlaim, and Ngaire Woods.

Jim Hershberg's assistance has been indispensable: as his *Bulletins* swelled from thirty to three hundred pages each, I developed grave doubts as to whether I could write as fast as he could seek out and scoop up new documents. I have also had help from the National Security Archive, where Tom Blanton, Malcolm Byrne, Christian Ostermann, and Vladislav Zubok have introduced me to much new material. Geir Lundestad and Odd Arne Westad offered me the hospitality of the Norwegian Nobel Institute as I was pulling together my conclusions; I also very much benefited from a fellowship year at the Woodrow Wilson Center that was to have been for another purpose but wound up being used chiefly to complete this book. Charles Blitzer, Samuel F. Wells, Jr., and Robert Hutchings all showed patience and understanding as I scrambled to do so.

I owe a particular debt to Nicholas Rizopoulos, who at just the right moment nominated me for the Whitney Shepardson Fellowship at the Council on Foreign Relations. This award—acknowledged gratefully on the title page— afforded me the opportunity to present drafts of each chapter before a group of tough but insightful critics at Harold Pratt House in New York. They included, at one time or another: Robert Beisner, Thompson Bradley, McGeorge Bundy, John C. Campbell, James Chace, Mark Danner, Keith Dayton, David Denoon, Robert Devlin, Michael Dunn, Fred Greenstein, David Hendrickson, Stanley Hoffman, John Iatrides, John Ikenberry, Miles Kahler, Ethan Kapstein, Daniel Kaufman, Kenneth Keller, Brooks Kelley, Paul Kennedy, Diane Kunz, Charles Kupchan, Melvyn Leffler, Robert Legvold, Michael Mandelbaum, Ernest May, Charles William Maynes, Karl Meyer, Linda Miller, Philip Nash, John Newhouse, Waldemar Nielsen, Michael Oppenheimer, Michael Peters, Edward Rhodes, Gideon Rose, Arthur Schlesinger, Jr., Marshall Shulman, Leon Sigal, Tony Smith, Jack Snyder, Anders Stephanson, William Taubman, Marc Trachtenberg, Henry Turner, Robert W. Tucker, Richard Ullman, Linda Wrigley, and Fareed Zakaria. As these names suggest, the 'Rizopoulos treatment' in the writing of books has become famous. I can only hope that this one does justice to it.

My thanks, as well, to my research assistants, Lu Soo Chun, D. J. Clinton, and (at the Woodrow Wilson Center) Rebekah Davis; to my Ohio University graduate students, who had large portions of this book imposed on them in draft form; to my colleagues Alonzo Hamby, Steven Miner, and Chester Pach, who read and critiqued portions of the manuscript; and to Hallie Willard and Kara Dunfee of the Contemporary History Institute who cheerfully helped with its preparation. Sophie Ahmad of the Oxford University Press was both patient and meticulous in handling the final stages of publication.

Others who read and commented on the manuscript include Matthew Connelly, Robert H. Ferrell, Alexander George, Hope Harrison, George F. Kennan, Geir Lundestad, Wilson D. Miscamble, Thomas Schoettli, Martin Smith, Nancy Bernkopf Tucker, Odd Arne Westad, Vladislav Zubok, and, not least, my son Michael, who took time from his own Princeton dissertation (and his Christmas holiday) to plough through it. I am most grateful to all of these people and institutions for the contributions they have made: the book is far better for them. None, though—not even Michael—bears the slightest responsibility for its final form. That is mine alone.

Finally, a word about the dedication. Ohio University has been my home for over a quarter of a century. I can think of no better place to have built a career, trained a generation of students, started a now-thriving institute, and—in the remarkable town of Athens—raised a family. The time has come, at last, to move on; but I cannot do so without at least trying to express how I feel about this rare, humane, and still slightly secret place whose influence will accompany me for as long as I live.

JLG

Athens, Ohio
August 1996

CONTENTS

ONE

Dividing the World

There are now two great nations in the world, which starting from different points, seem to be advancing toward the same goal: the Russians and the Anglo-Americans. . . . [E]ach seems called by some secret design of Providence one day to hold in its hands the destinies of half the world.

Alexis de Tocqueville, 1835[1]

With the defeat of the Reich and pending the emergence of the Asiatic, the African, and perhaps the South American nationalisms, there will remain in the world only two Great Powers capable of confronting each other—the United States and Soviet Russia. The laws of both history and geography will compel these two Powers to a trial of strength, either military or in the fields of economics and ideology. These same laws make it inevitable that both Powers should become enemies of Europe. And it is equally certain that both these Powers will sooner or later find it desirable to seek the support of the sole surviving great nation in Europe, the German people.

Adolf Hitler, 1945[2]

I T has become almost obligatory to begin histories of the Cold War with Tocqueville's famous prophecy, made more than a century before the events it foresaw had come to pass. Hitler's prediction, advanced even as these events were happening, is deservedly less well known. Still, the similarity in these two visions of the future, put forward 110 years apart by the greatest student of democracy and the vilest practitioner of autocracy, is striking: it is rare enough for anyone to anticipate what lies ahead, even in the most general terms. Was the division of the world that began in 1945 really the result of "some secret design of Providence," or, if one prefers the Führer's more secular formulation, of a set of laws derived from history and geography? Or was it an improbable accident? Or was it, as great events most often are, something in between?

Tocqueville made his forecast the way most people do: by projecting the past and the present into the future. At the time he wrote the United States and Russia occupied vast expanses of thinly populated but resource-rich continents. Each had a high birth rate, and therefore the potential for rapid growth. Each had been expanding across successive frontiers; neither faced rivals capable of impeding that process. But there the similarities ended. The United States was already, in 1835, the world's most democratic republic, and the Russian empire its most prominent example of monarchical authoritarianism. Tocqueville saw the contrast clearly: Americans relied "on personal interest and [gave] free scope to the unguided strength and common sense of individuals," while Russians concentrated "the whole power of society in one man."[3] Significantly, though, he said nothing about how this difference in systems of government might affect relations between the two countries or their dealings with the rest of the world. What a subsequent generation would call "bipolarity" would not have surprised Tocqueville, but whether conflict—hot or cold—would result from that condition remained shrouded, even from this most clairvoyant of observers.

Today it is for historians, not clairvoyants, to account for the rise, flourishing, and decline of Russian–American global hegemony. We are well beyond the distant horizon Tocqueville could only barely discern. We know that his prophecy did come to pass, in such a way as to exceed even Hitler's expectations: enormous power did combine with intense hostility, to the point of encompassing not just all of Europe and much of the rest of the world, but—some would say—the future of civilization itself. We are in a position now to see how this happened, to trace the process by which the Russian–American predominance Tocqueville and Hitler anticipated became the Cold War the world so greatly feared. We are also free to speculate on whether this *had* to happen: whether there might have been alternative paths from 1835—or even from 1945—to where we are today.

I

At the time Tocqueville wrote, the United States and Russia had about as many connections as exist now, say, between Paraguay and Mongolia. The Americans had attempted, after the Napoleonic wars and their own nearly disastrous War of 1812, to exclude themselves from further involvement in European affairs: the Monroe Doctrine of 1823 was as much a welcome withdrawal from an old continent as a brash assertion of authority over a new one. Russia issued no such self-denying ordinance, but it too turned inward after the death of Tsar Alexander I in 1825, playing only an occasional role in the maintenance of a European order that seemed stable enough in any event. The simultaneous shift of American and Russian concerns away from Europe and toward the development of continental empires meant that for decades to come citizens of the two countries would have little to do with one another. The world was still empty enough for empires to expand without intersecting.

Some contacts, to be sure, did take place. There had been a thin trickle of trade and travel since the days of the American Revolution, and this in turn had given rise, among educated minorities in both the United States and Russia, to a modest interest in each other's culture and institutions. Both states shared the parallel but not equivalent problem of managing conquered peoples within their territories. Both abolished involuntary servitude at almost the same time— Russian serfs won emancipation in 1861 and American slaves in 1863— although under very different sets of circumstances. Both strongly distrusted that era's most visible hegemon, Great Britain, an attitude reflected in American sympathy for the Russians during the Crimean War and in a Russian "tilt" toward the North during the American Civil War. And both cooperated in resolving a long series of disputes over territory and fisheries in the Pacific Northwest, a process that culminated in Russia's sale of Alaska to the Americans in 1867.[4]

Russia became no less authoritarian and the United States no less democratic during those years, but in the nineteenth century diplomacy rarely reflected the compatibility, or lack thereof, of domestic institutions. Otherwise, the United States would have had its most amicable relationship with Great Britain and its most antagonistic with tsarist Russia; the reality, however, was just the opposite. One reason was that Britain's naval superiority and remaining North American possessions threatened interests as seen from Washington. But there was also, in the early relationship between the United States and Russia, a mutually acknowledged tradition of non-interference in each other's internal affairs. It simply did not occur to Americans or Russians that either country might gain by attempting to alter the other, distinctly dissimilar though they were.[5]

The first departures from this pattern arose from the remarkable improvements in transportation and communication that took place during the final decades of the nineteenth century. The Russians built the Trans-Siberian railroad just as the Americans were modernizing their navy, a technological coincidence that allowed both states to project influence into northeast Asia at a time when China, the ancient empire that had long dominated that part of the world, seemed on the verge of collapse. Expansionist impulses directed toward opposite ends of the earth suddenly converged at a time and in a place where the major European powers, as well as an increasingly assertive Japan, also had important interests. The Russo-Japanese War of 1904–5 eventually followed, and President Theodore Roosevelt helped settle it in such a way as to preserve a diminished presence for the defeated Russians in Manchuria. But the United States had, during that conflict, openly aligned itself alongside its old adversary Great Britain in support of Japan and in opposition to tsarist imperial aspirations.[6]

A second source of Russian–American antagonism also grew out of the transportation and communication revolutions of that era. Cheap steamship fares greatly increased the flow of emigrants from Russia to the United States—the figures went from about 19,000 annually during the 1880s to around 200,000 a year during the decade preceding World War I[7]—and with them came gruesome tales of privation and officially sanctioned oppression. Meanwhile, Americans had begun travelling to Russia, albeit in far smaller numbers, to satisfy their curiosity about that still mysterious empire; some of them revealed what they found in lurid detail on the lecture circuit and in the mass circulation newspapers and magazines that had recently begun to flourish. The American public therefore became more aware of the tsarist government's repressive character just as that regime, following the assassination of Alexander II in 1881, seemed determined to confirm it. No one did more to shift American attitudes about Russia than the explorer and author George Kennan with his vivid exposé of the Siberian exile system.[8] He was by no means alone, however, in questioning whether a democracy could ever have "normal" relations with a government that treated its people as harshly as Russia did. The issue would have seemed hypothetical to Americans in Tocqueville's day, when the number of constitutional democracies could have been counted on the fingers of one hand. But that situation too was changing: by the beginning of the twentieth century democratic institutions had spread sufficiently that Russia and not the United States stood out as the anomaly.[9]

The conquest of distance, therefore, did not strengthen Russian–American friendship; instead it worsened matters by injecting disputes over geopolitics and human rights into a relationship in which remoteness had heretofore encouraged the appearance of complementary interests. Technology allowed Russians and Americans to get to know one another better; but in defiance of the conventional wisdom that communications ease conflicts, their governments found it *more* difficult to deal with one another as a result. By the time World War I broke out, official contacts had fallen into a pattern of deep distrust, despite the fact that American financiers indirectly—through the British and the French—supported Russian military operations. And although the United States would have entered the war on the side of Great Britain, France, and Russia in 1917 even if the February Revolution[10] in Petrograd had not deposed the Tsar, American involvement alongside the Romanovs in a fight "to make the world safe for democracy" would have been difficult to justify. As he himself knew, Woodrow Wilson was fortunate in not having had to make the effort.[11]

II

If, as is often said, World War II created a vacuum of *power* in Europe, then surely World War I left a vacuum of *legitimacy*. For not only did that cataclysm sweep away entire empires—the German, the Austro-Hungarian, the Ottoman, the Russian—it also discredited the old forms of diplomacy that allowed war to break out in the first place and that proved so ineffective in ending it. Neither imperial regimes nor imperial methods had many defenders left by time the Bolsheviks staged their *coup d'état* late in 1917. And much as the military strength of the United States and the Soviet Union would fill the European vacuum in 1945, so American and Russian ideologies did in 1918. These emerged, though, at least as much from *individuals* as from institutions and traditions. For the first time, personalities shaped the course of Russian–American relations, in such a way as to magnify vastly the differences contrasting national experiences had already produced.

The United States and the new Provisional Government in Russia fought on the same side, but only briefly. For the October Revolution soon replaced that indecisive regime with one committed, not just to a separate peace, but to nothing less than ending capitalism throughout the world. The new Soviet government drew its legitimacy neither from God nor from free elections but from science: it claimed to have identified the class struggle as the ultimate engine of history and to have harnessed its policies to that mechanism, thereby ensuring their success.[12] It was, therefore, as confident as any government has ever been about reaching its intended objective, which was in this instance—however improbable the odds—world revolution.[13] What Lenin promised was the ultimate form of interference in other states' internal affairs: overthrowing not just their governments, but their societies.

He did so, though, just as a gentler revolution was transforming the foreign policy of the United States. Wilson had not been content to justify American entry into the war for what it was—an effort to restore the European balance of power. Instead, he too imposed an ideological framework by proclaiming as war aims self-determination, open markets, and collective security. His purpose was not to spread revolution, as was Lenin's; but Wilson did seek to alter world politics by removing what he thought to be the causes of injustice, and hence of war.[14] This was, in its own way then, as ambitious an agenda as that of the Bolsheviks. Much of the subsequent history of the twentieth century grew out of the clash between these ideologies—Wilson's versus Lenin's—both of them injected into world politics within the two and a half months that separated the Bolshevik coup of November 1917 from the President's January 1918 Fourteen Points address.[15]

Despite their apparent novelty, these ideas reflected deeply-rooted national characteristics. Tocqueville would have found Wilson's liberal-capitalism familiar, and Lenin ran his party and his government with an authoritarianism at least as firm as that of the Russian tsars.[16] The *universalism* in Wilson's and Lenin's proclamations might well have surprised Tocqueville or any other nineteenth century observer, though: they were meant not just for internal application or external emulation, but for the widest possible implementation. They constituted, albeit in wholly different ways, fundamental challenges to the international state system itself: in Wilson's case through the appeal for a supranational League of Nations, and in Lenin's by way of his call for proletarians in all countries to arise and overthrow their oppressors. Nothing like this had happened since the most militant days of the French Revolution; certainly there was no precedent for such sweeping and urgent pronouncements in the prior record of either American or Russian foreign policy.

An important feature of ideological thinking is its determinism. Ideologists convince themselves, and seek to convince others, that history is on their side, that progress toward the goal they have chosen is inevitable and therefore irresistible. And yet the ideological confrontation between Wilson and Lenin arose more from coincidence than from predestination: for this, bumbling German diplomacy was largely responsible. Wilson took the United States into the war only because the Kaiser's government had unwisely resumed all-out submarine warfare and then even more foolishly proposed an alliance with Mexico—an offer the British intercepted and quickly leaked to the Americans—promising the return of "lost provinces" extending from Texas to California.[17] Meanwhile, and with equal imprudence, the Germans had arranged for Lenin to travel from his exile in Switzerland back to Petrograd, thus setting in motion the astonishing sequence of events that would so quickly place a tiny band of quarreling conspirators in charge of the largest nation on the face of the earth.[18]

Wilson and Lenin responded to the situations in which they found themselves with a combination of improvisation, eloquence, purposefulness, and sheer audacity that would have been striking enough in either of them but that seems remarkable for having occurred, simultaneously, in both. We cannot know what course events would have taken had the great reformer and the great revolutionary not reached their respective preeminences—from which they proclaimed their respective messages to the world—at just the same time. History could hardly have happened as it did, though, without these two most messianic of twentieth century leaders. The moment was one of what chaos theorists call "sensitive dependence on initial conditions:"[19] had things occurred differently on a personal scale at this particular time, vast differences on a collective scale would have followed from them. Contingency created circumstances in which Wilson and Lenin defined mutually hostile ideological visions, imposed them upon the countries they led, and then departed from their positions of leadership, leaving it to less visionary successors to determine what their legacies were to be.

III

The events of 1917–18 created a *symbolic* basis for conflict between communism and capitalism by setting the self-proclaimed objectives of the United States and Soviet Russia against one another in the most fundamental way. But this clash of ideas brought few *actual* conflicts over the next quarter-century. International rivalries aligned themselves less than one might have anticipated along the ideological polarities Wilson and Lenin had left behind.

Instead of leading the movement to eliminate the causes of war, as Wilson had hoped, Americans relinquished the global predominance their military exertions had earned them; they thereby violated a basic premise of international relations theory, which is that great powers, having attained that status, do not willingly give it up. Instead of provoking world revolution, as Lenin had desired, his government began its transformation into a stifling and bureaucratized tyranny, thereby violating Marxist theories about the withering away of the state and the liberation of the masses who lived within it. Europe was again left, for the most part, to its own devices, with neither Washington nor Moscow exerting influence commensurate with the globalist pretensions each had earlier advanced.

Americans by no means isolated themselves from Europe after World War I. The United States participated, along with the British, the French, and the Japanese, in a half-hearted occupation of Russian territory that lasted from 1918 to 1920; but the motives behind that enterprise were a confused muddle,[20] and its results were correspondingly ineffective. Intervention may even have helped the Bolsheviks by allowing them to pose as defenders of Russian nationalism. There is little reason to think that they would have been any less hostile toward the capitalist world if it had never taken place.[21] The United States also retained the expanded economic ties with Europe that grew out of its shift, during the war, from international debtor to creditor. American private capital, it is now clear, was almost as important to the Europeans' recovery during the 1920s as was the much more visible Marshall Plan after World War II.[22] But economic influence alone can neither reshape an international system nor determine everything that happens within it, and it was in the non-economic sphere that American actions fell short of Wilsonian aspirations.[23]

The most significant geopolitical development of the early postwar years was surely the fact that the United States, despite its abortive intervention in Russia and its involvement in European economic stabilization, made no significant attempts after 1920 to shape political-military developments on the Continent. It chose this self-effacing path, historians have variously argued, because the nation's long-standing tradition of peacetime isolationism reasserted itself, or because Wilson had asked too much of the American people during the war, or because he had obtained too little of his visionary plan for peace in the Versailles Treaty.[24] But there was a deeper reason as well: the United States withdrew from Europe's politics because it saw no obvious challenge to the balance of power there, and thus no threat to its own security. Germany had been defeated; Soviet Russia was torn by civil war and factional disputes; Great Britain and France had been "associates" during the war and could hardly, in the future, be enemies. To the extent that there was any perceived danger in the 1920s it came from Japan's growing navy, and inasmuch as Washington had a coherent national security policy during that decade, it focused on handling that problem.[25]

The consequences of this disengagement from Europe are bound to have been important, although scholars disagree as to what they were. Some have maintained that the United States's failure to assume Britain's role as global economic hegemon left an absence of managerial authority that intensified and prolonged the Great Depression.[26] Others have insisted that greater American assertiveness would have bolstered the European democracies' determination to resist Adolf Hitler, and hence might have prevented World War II.[27] One pattern is definite, though: Americans were reluctant to assume world responsibilities in the absence of clear and present danger. Despite the alarms suspected subversive activities set off inside the United States, most notoriously during the "Red Scare" of 1919–20, the Soviet Union in the interwar years failed to meet that standard. Indeed, the most significant Soviet–American contacts during this period involved the efforts of American corporations—all of them reliable bastions of capitalism—to increase trade with and investment in the world's only communist state.[28]

The Soviet Union too, in a sense, withdrew from Europe after World War I, but for a different set of reasons. Lenin was no isolationist: his internationalism combined conventional diplomacy with what were, at the time, the highly unconventional methods of the Comintern, the agency he created in 1919 to spread revolution throughout the world. But these approaches undercut more than they reinforced one another. Barely concealed attempts to overthrow capitalist governments made it difficult for Soviet diplomats to negotiate with them. Chilled relations, in turn, did little to discourage efforts to root out Comintern agents. Nor did the Bolsheviks free their proletarian internationalism from the parochial habits of Russian radicalism, a deficiency that made their appeal to European workers less successful than it might otherwise have been.[29] Meanwhile, as with most revolutions, the passage of time was shifting the goals of this one from the immediately attainable to the ultimately desirable. As Lenin's successor, Josef Stalin, consolidated his power during the latter half of the 1920s, he by no means abandoned the goal of world revolution, but he did place increasing emphasis on first building up the strength and security of the Soviet state.

The USSR would probably have become a great power even if Stalin had followed his mother's advice and become a Georgian priest, but the fact that he did not—that this deceptively unimpressive figure succeeded in outmaneuvering all other aspirants to the succession as well as Lenin's own attempts to deny it to him—very much affected the *way* in which that happened. It is possible to imagine a Trotsky or a Bukharin ordering the collectivization of agriculture and the large-scale industrialization this was to have made possible. It is not at all clear, though, that they or anyone else would have implemented these measures with the brutality Stalin relied upon, or that they would have followed them with massive purges against mostly imaginary enemies.[30] Paranoia—the tendency to "place sinister interpretations on events that may have no sinister bearing, and attribute hostile motives to acts that may have no hostile intent"[31]—need not be incapacitating: in Stalin's case it coexisted with, and no doubt also inspired, a most extraordinary administrative performance. The number of deaths resulting from Stalin's policies *before* World War II, it is now agreed in both Russia and the West, was between 17 and 22 million—substantially more than twice the number of Hitler's victims in the Holocaust.[32]

The scale of this disaster makes the words that characterize it seem bleached, like the bones of the dead. But one way of putting it is that Stalin had conflated the requirements of national with personal security in a completely unprecedented way. It is revealing that the historical figure he most sought to emulate was not Lenin—whose experiments with terror were bad enough—but Ivan the

Terrible.[33] Years later Stalin's successor, Nikita Khrushchev, would recall his old boss's "utter irresponsibility and complete lack of respect for anyone other than himself."[34] Stalin's choices, as much as Lenin's legacy or the requirements of Marxist ideology, transformed the government he ran and even the country he ruled, during the 1930s, into a gargantuan extension of his own pathologically suspicious personality.[35] This supreme act of egoism spawned innumerable tragedies: one was that it constrained the Soviet Union's ability to counter the bid of another great authoritarian egoist, Hitler, for dominance in Europe.

It did so, first, by undercutting potential resistance within Germany itself. Stalin's distrust of European socialism was so great that he forbade the German Communist Party from collaborating with the Social Democrats to oppose the Nazi assumption of power in 1933.[36] Alarmed by the results of this policy, he then allowed his foreign minister, Maxim Litvinov, to advocate collective security through the League of Nations, but just as the highly visible Moscow purge trials were getting underway. Stalin put his own terror on public display, therefore, at a time when Hitler's, for the most part, was still hidden: no wonder the European democracies, themselves ambivalent over whether to resist or appease fascism, responded tepidly to Litvinov's efforts.[37] Nor did they monopolize short-sightedness: Stalin himself had long hoped for some kind of cooperation with Nazi Germany, despite the ideological inconsistencies this would have involved.[38] His decision to sign a non-aggression pact with Hitler in August 1939, just days before Germany invaded Poland and less than two years before it would attack the Soviet Union itself, was entirely in keeping with the spirit, and the characteristic competence, of Stalinist diplomacy.

The eve of World War II, then, found the United States and the Soviet Union on the sidelines: they had chosen to exclude themselves, or had found themselves excluded, from the role their size and strength should have given them in European affairs. Despite a contrast in forms of government that could hardly have been greater, Soviet and American leaders shared a sense of impotence as war again approached. Neither country could control what was happening, nor did there seem to be the slightest prospect that they might in the future cooperate. An informed observer, as late as the end of 1939, would have had every reason to regard Tocqueville's 1835 prophecy about an eventual Russian and American domination of the world as, still, a wild improbability.

IV

There were important parallels, but equally important differences, in the careers of Hitler and Stalin. Both had risen from being outsiders in their respective societies to positions of unchallenged authority over them; both had been underestimated by potential rivals; both were prepared to use whatever methods were available—including terror—to achieve their purposes. Both exploited the fact that a harsh peace and the onset of a global economic crisis had stalled the advance of democracy in Europe, but not the technological means of controlling large populations; both made full use of the opportunities for propaganda, surveillance, and swift action provided by such innovations as the telephone, radio, motion pictures, automobiles, and airplanes. Both benefited, as a consequence, from the conviction of many Europeans that authoritarianism was the wave of the future. Both merged personal with national interests; both dedicated themselves to implementing internationalist ideologies.

But where Stalin looked toward an eventual world proletarian revolution, Hitler sought immediate racial purification. Where Stalin was cautiously flexible, Hitler stuck to his perverse principles through thick and thin: he never placed the security of his state or even himself above the task of achieving literally, and at whatever cost, his goals of Aryan supremacy and Jewish annihilation. Where Stalin was patient, prepared to take as long as necessary to achieve his ambitions, Hitler was frenetic, determined to meet deadlines he himself had imposed. Where Stalin sought desperately to stay out of war, Hitler set out quite deliberately to provoke it.[39]

Both authoritarians wanted to dominate Europe, a fact that placed them at odds with the traditional American interest in maintaining a balance of power there. But only Hitler was in a position to attempt domination: he therefore created, for the United States, the European democracies, and even the Soviet Union itself, a threat whose urgency, one might have thought, would have transcended whatever differences divided his potential victims.

It certainly did so in Washington and London. Franklin D. Roosevelt had long regarded Nazi Germany as the primary danger to American security and had sought, ever since extending diplomatic recognition to the Soviet Union in 1933, to leave the way open for cooperation with Moscow.[40] Winston Churchill loathed Marxism-Leninism at least as much as his predecessor Neville Chamberlain, but he shared Roosevelt's view that geopolitics was more important than ideology.[41] Both leaders foresaw the fragility of the Nazi–Soviet alliance and were prepared to accept Soviet help in containing Hitler whenever that became possible. They also repeatedly warned Stalin of the impending German attack in the winter and spring of 1941.[42] Only the Soviet dictator's misplaced faith in a fellow authoritarian—a kind of brutal romanticism, to which his own temperament and style of governing would allow no challenge—prevented the necessary defensive measures and made Hitler's invasion in June of that year such a devastating surprise.[43] "My people and I, Iosif Vissarionovich, firmly remember your wise prediction," NKVD chief Lavrentii Beria wrote to Stalin on the day before the invasion: "Hitler will not attack us in 1941!"[44]

The German Führer had no comparable illusions about his Soviet counterpart, but he too subordinated geopolitical logic to authoritarian romanticism. He struck because he had always believed German racial interests required *Lebensraum* in the east; but he paid little attention to what Napoleon's precedent suggested about the imprudence of invading Russia while Great Britain remained undefeated. It is even more difficult to account for Hitler's declaration of war on the United States the following December, four days after the Japanese bombed Pearl Harbor. Had he not acted, Roosevelt would have found himself under immense pressure to divert American resources—including the Lend Lease aid already flowing to Great Britain and even by then to the Soviet Union—to the Pacific. The best explanation of Hitler's behavior appears to be that excitement over Japan's entry into the war impaired his ability to think clearly, and in an autocratic system no mechanisms existed to repair the damage.[45]

Both Stalin and Hitler made foolish mistakes in 1941, and for much the same reason: their systems of government reflected and reinforced their own romanticism, providing few safeguards against incompetence at the top.[46] The effect turned out to be a fortunate one, because it eliminated any possibility of an authoritarian coalition directed against the United States and its democratic allies; instead, the democracies now aligned themselves, however uneasily, with one authoritarian state against the other. German statecraft had once again drawn Americans and Russians into Europe, but this time in such a way as to throw them, despite deep ideological differences, into positions of desperate dependence upon one another. For without the Soviet Union's immense expenditure of manpower against the Germans, it is difficult to see how the Americans and British could ever have launched a successful second front. But without the United States' material assistance in the form of Lend Lease, together with its role in holding the Japanese at bay in the Pacific, the Red Army might never have repelled the Nazi invasion in the first place.[47]

Tocqueville had long ago foreseen that the United States and Russia, if ever moved to do so, would command human and material resources on an enormous scale: their *potential* power exceeded that of any European state he could envisage. What neither Tocqueville nor anyone else could have anticipated were the circumstances that might cause Americans and Russians to apply this strength, simultaneously, beyond their borders, and in a common cause. Hitler's twin declarations of war accomplished that, giving the Soviet Union and the United States compelling reasons to re-enter the European arena with, quite literally, a shared sense of vengeance. Through these unexpectedly unwise acts, therefore, this most improbable of historical agents at last brought Tocqueville's old prophecy within sight of fulfillment.

V

When a power vacuum separates great powers, as one did the United States and the Soviet Union at the end of World War II, they are unlikely to fill it without bumping up against and bruising each other's interests. This would have happened if the two postwar hegemons had been constitutional democracies: historians of the wartime Anglo-American relationship have long since exposed the bumping and bruising that did take place, even among these closest of allies.[48] Victory would require more difficult adjustments for Russians and Americans because so many legacies of distrust now divided them: the distinction between authoritarian and democratic traditions; the challenge communism and capitalism posed to one another; Soviet memories of allied intervention in Russia after World War I; more recent American memories of Stalin's purges and his opportunistic pact with Hitler. It was too much to expect a few years of wartime cooperation to sweep all of this away.

At the same time, though, these legacies need not have produced almost half a century of Soviet–American confrontation. The leaders of great nations are never entirely bound by the past: new situations continually arise, and they are free to reject old methods in attempting to deal with them. Alliance in a common cause was as new a situation as one can imagine in the Russian–American relationship. Much would depend, therefore, upon the extent to which Roosevelt and Stalin could—in effect—*liberate* their nations' futures from a difficult past.

The American President and his key advisers were determined to secure the United States against whatever dangers might confront it after victory, but they lacked a clear sense of what those might be or where they might arise.[49] Their thinking about postwar security was, as a consequence, more general than specific. They certainly saw a vital interest in preventing any hostile power from again attempting to dominate the European continent. They were not prepared to see military capabilities reduced to anything like the inadequate levels of the interwar era, nor would they resist opportunities to reshape the international economy in ways that would benefit American capitalism. They resolved to resist any return to isolationism, and they optimistically embraced the "second chance" the war had provided to build a global security organization in which the United States would play the leading role.[50]

But these priorities reflected no unilateral conception of vital interests. A quarter century earlier, Wilson had linked American war aims to reform of the international system as a whole; and although his ideas had not then taken hold, the coming of a second world war revived a widespread and even guilt-ridden interest in them as a means of avoiding a third such conflict.[51] Roosevelt persuaded a skeptical Churchill to endorse Wilson's thinking in August, 1941, when they jointly proclaimed, in the Atlantic Charter, three postwar objectives: self-determination—the idea here was that people who could choose their own forms of government would not want to overthrow them, hence they would achieve, to use a Rooseveltian term, freedom from fear; open markets—the assumption was that an unrestricted flow of commodities and capital would ensure economic prosperity, hence freedom from want; and collective security—the conviction that nations had to act together rather than separately if they were ever to achieve safety.[52] To put it in language Mikhail Gorbachev would employ decades later, security would have to be a condition *common to all*, not one granted to some and withheld from others.[53]

Despite this public commitment to Wilsonian principles, neither Roosevelt nor Churchill ruled out more realistic practices. Had postwar planning been left to them alone, as in democracies it could not be, they might well have come up with something like what Roosevelt occasionally talked about: the idea of four great powers—the United States, Great Britain, the Soviet Union, and Nationalist China—operating as world policemen, using force or the prospect of it to keep smaller states in line.[54] But even this cold-blooded approach, like the Wilsonian constraints that kept the politically sensitive Roosevelt from insisting on it, implied a sense of *collective* security among the four: it would not have worked if any one of them had sought to maximize security for itself, while attempting to deny it to others.[55] There was, thus, little unilateralism in F.D.R.'s thinking, whether he was operating in his idealistic or his realistic mode.

The United States would seek power in the postwar world, not shy away from it as it had done after World War I. It would do so in the belief that only it had the strength to build a peace based on Wilsonian principles of self-determination, open markets, and collective security. It would administer that peace neither for its exclusive advantage nor in such a way as to provide equal benefits to all: many as yet ill-defined possibilities lay in between these extremes. Nor would Roosevelt assume, as Wilson had, public and Congressional approval; rather, the administration would make careful efforts to ensure domestic support for the postwar settlement at every step of the way.[56] There would be another attempt at a Wilsonian peace, but this time by the un-Wilsonian method of offering each of the great powers as well as the American people a vested interest in making it work. It was within this framework of pragmatism mixed with principle that Roosevelt hoped to deal with Stalin.

The Soviet leader, too, sought security after World War II: his country lost at least 27 million of its citizens in that conflict;[57] he could hardly have done otherwise. But no tradition of *common* or *collective* security shaped postwar priorities as viewed from Moscow, for the very good reason that it was no longer permitted there to distinguish between state interests, party interests, and those of Stalin himself. National security had come to mean personal security, and the Kremlin boss saw so many threats to it that he had already resorted to murder on a mass scale in order to remove all conceivable challengers to his regime. It would be hard to imagine a more *unilateral* approach to security than the internal practices Stalin had set in motion during the 1930s. Cooperation with external allies was obviously to his advantage when the Germans were within sight of his capital, but whether that cooperation would extend beyond Hitler's defeat was another matter. It would depend upon the ability of an aging and authoritarian ruler to shift his own thinking about security to a multilateral basis, and to restructure the government he had made into a reflection of himself.[58]

It is sometimes said of Stalin that he had long since given up the Lenin–Trotsky goal of world revolution in favor of "socialism in one country," a doctrine that seemed to imply peaceful coexistence with states of differing social systems. But that is a misunderstanding of Stalin's position. What he really did in the late 1920s was to drop Lenin's prediction that revolutions would arise spontaneously in other advanced industrial countries; instead he came to see the Soviet Union itself as the center from which socialism would spread and eventually defeat capitalism.[59] The effect was to switch the principal instrument for advancing revolution from Marx's idea of a historically determined class struggle to a process of territorial acquisition Stalin could control. "The idea of propagating world Communist revolution was an ideological screen to hide our desire for world domination," one of his secret agents recalled decades later.[60] "This war is not as in the past," Stalin himself explained to the Yugoslav communist Milovan Djilas in 1945: "whoever occupies a territory also imposes his own social system. . . . It cannot be otherwise."[61]

Stalin was fully prepared to use unconventional means to promote Soviet interests beyond the territories he ruled. He kept Lenin's Comintern in place but turned it to his own purposes: this became clear during the Spanish Civil War, when Stalin used Comintern agents as much to wipe out Trotskyists as to fight fascists.[62] One of his most far-sighted initiatives involved the recruitment of an elaborate network of youthful spies in Great Britain and the United States during the 1930s—most of them anti-fascist intellectuals—years before they could have risen to positions that would have given them anything significant to spy upon.[63] Nor did Stalin rule out war itself as a means of advancing the revolutionary cause. He would not, like Hitler, risk military conflict to meet some predetermined timetable. But he did see wars *among capitalists* as likely to weaken them and therefore speed "socialist encirclement:" that may be one reason why he failed to foresee the German attack in 1941.[64] And he by no means excluded the possibility of an eventual war with capitalism involving the Soviet Union itself. "Stalin looked at it this way," his foreign minister, Viacheslav Molotov recalled: "World War I has wrested one country from capitalist slavery; World War II has created a socialist system; and the third will finish off imperialism forever."[65]

It would be easy to make too much of Stalin's words, for reality always seperates what people say from what they are able to do. What is striking about Stalin, though, is how small that separation was. To a degree we are only now coming to realize, Stalin *literally* imposed his rhetoric upon the country he ran: this was a dictator whose subordinates scrutinized his every comment, indeed his every gesture, and attempted to implement policies—even the most implausible scientific doctrines—on the basis of them.[66] Not even Hitler ran so autocratic a system.[67] The result was a kind of self-similarity across scale,[68] in which the tyrant at the top spawned smaller tyrants at each level throughout the party and state bureaucracy: their activities extended down to the level of scrutinizing stamp collections for evidence that their owners might value the images of foreign potentates more than those of Lenin and Stalin.[69] It was typical of the Kremlin boss, the most consummate of narcissists,[70] that he thought very far ahead indeed about security. But it was always and only his own security that he was thinking about.

Here, then, was the difficulty. The Western democracies sought a form of security that would reject violence or the threat of it: security was to be a *collec-*

tive good, not a benefit denied to some in order to provide it to others. Stalin saw things very differently: security came only by intimidating or eliminating potential challengers. World politics was an extension of Soviet politics, which was in turn an extension of Stalin's preferred personal environment:[71] a zero-sum game, in which achieving security for one meant depriving everyone else of it. The contrast, or so it would seem, made conflict unavoidable.

VI

But is this not putting things too starkly? The United States and its democratic allies found ways to cooperate with the Soviet Union, after all, in fighting Germany and Japan. Could they not have managed their postwar relationship similarly, so that the safety Stalin demanded could have been made to correspond with the security the West required? Could there not have been a division of Europe into spheres of influence which, while they would hardly have pleased everybody, might have prevented an ensuing four and a half decades of superpower rivalry?

Stalin appears to have relished his role, along with Roosevelt and Churchill, as one of the wartime Big Three.[72] Such evidence as has surfaced from Soviet archives suggests that he received reassuring reports about Washington's intentions: "Roosevelt is more friendly to us than any other prominent American," Ambassador Litvinov commented in June 1943, "and it is quite obvious that he wishes to cooperate with us." Whoever was in the White House, Litvinov's successor Andrei Gromyko predicted a year later, the Soviet Union and the United States would "manage to find common issues for the solution of . . . problems emerging in the future and of interest to both countries."[73] Even if Stalin's long-range thinking about security did clash with that of his Anglo-American allies, common military purposes provided the strongest possible inducements to smooth over such differences. It is worth asking why this *practice* of wartime cooperation did not become a *habit* that would extend into the postwar era.

The principal reason, it now appears, was Stalin's insistence on equating security with territory. Western diplomats had been surprised, upon arriving in Moscow soon after the German attack in the summer of 1941, to find the Soviet leader already demanding a postwar settlement that would retain what his pact with Hitler had yielded: the Baltic states, together with portions of Finland, Poland, and Romania. Stalin showed no sense of shame or even embarrassment about this, no awareness that the *methods* by which he had obtained these concessions could conceivably render them illegitimate in the eyes of anyone else. When it came to territorial aspirations, he made no distinction between adversaries and allies:[74] what one had provided the other was expected to endorse.

Stalin coupled his claims with repeated requests for a second front, quite without regard to the fact that his own policies had left the British to fight Germany alone for a year, so that they were hardly in a position to comply. He reiterated his military and territorial demands after the Americans entered the war in December, despite the fact that they were desperately trying to hang on in the Pacific against a Japanese adversary against whom the Soviet Union—admittedly for good strategic reasons—had elected not to fight. This linkage of postwar requirements with wartime assistance was, as the Russians used to like to say, "no accident." A second front in Europe in 1942 would have been "a completely impossible operation for them," Molotov later acknowledged. "But our demand was politically necessary, and we had to press them for everything."[75]

On the surface, this strategy succeeded. After strong initial objections, Roosevelt and Churchill did eventually acknowledge the Soviet Union's right to the expanded borders it claimed; they also made it clear that they would not oppose the installation of "friendly" governments in adjoining states. This meant accepting a Soviet sphere of influence from the Baltic to the Adriatic, a concession not easily reconciled with the Atlantic Charter. But the authors of that document saw no feasible way to avoid that outcome: military necessity required continued Soviet cooperation against the Germans. Nor were they themselves prepared to relinquish spheres of influence in Western Europe and the Mediterranean, the Middle East, Latin America, and East Asia.[76] Self-determination was a sufficiently malleable concept that each of the Big Three could have endorsed, without sleepless nights, what the Soviet government had said about the Atlantic Charter: "practical application of these principles will necessarily adapt itself to the circumstances, needs, and historic peculiarities of particular countries."[77]

That, though, was precisely the problem. For unlike Stalin, Roosevelt and Churchill would have to defend their decisions before domestic constituencies. The *manner* in which Soviet influence expanded was therefore, for them, of no small significance.[78] Stalin showed little understanding of this. Having no experience himself with democratic procedures, he dismissed requests that he respect democratic proprieties. "[S]ome propaganda work should be done," he advised Roosevelt at the Tehran conference after the president had hinted that the American public would welcome a plebiscite in the Baltic States.[79] "It is all nonsense!" Stalin complained to Molotov. "[Roosevelt] is their military leader and commander in chief. Who would dare object to him?"[80] When at Yalta F.D.R. stressed the need for the first Polish election to be as pure as "Caesar's wife," Stalin responded with a joke: "They said that about her, but in fact she had her sins."[81] Molotov warned his boss, on that occasion, that the Americans' insistence on free elections elsewhere in Eastern Europe was "going too far." "Don't worry," he recalls Stalin as replying, "work it out. We can deal with it in our own way later. The point is the correlation of forces."[82]

The Soviet leader was, in one sense, right. Military strength would determine what happened in that part of the world, not the enunciation of lofty principles. But unilateral methods carried long-term costs Stalin did not foresee: the most significant of these was to ruin whatever prospects existed for a Soviet sphere of influence the East Europeans themselves might have accepted. This possibility was not as far-fetched as it would later seem. The Czechoslovak president, Eduard Beneš, spoke openly of a "Czech solution" that would exchange internal autonomy for Soviet control over foreign and military policy. W. Averell Harriman, one of Roosevelt's closest advisers and his ambassador to the Soviet Union after 1943, was keenly interested in such an arrangement and hoped to persuade the Poles of its merits.[83] F.D.R. and Churchill—concerned with finding a way to respect both Soviet security interests and democratic procedures in Eastern Europe—would almost certainly have gone along.

Nor was the idea out of the question from Stalin's point of view. He would, after all, approve such a compromise as the basis for a permanent settlement with Finland.[84] He would initially allow free elections in Hungary, Czechoslovakia, and the Soviet occupation zone in Germany. He may even have *anticipated an enthusiastic response* as he took over Eastern Europe. "He was, I think, surprised and hurt," Harriman recalled, "when the Red Army was not welcomed in all the neighboring countries as an army of liberation."[85] "We still had our hopes," Khrushchev remembered, that "after the catastrophe of World War II, Europe too might become Soviet. Everyone would take the path from capitalism to socialism."[86] It could be that there was another form of romanticism at work here, quite apart from Stalin's affinity for fellow authoritarians: that he was unrealistic enough to expect ideological solidarity and gratitude for liberation to override old fears of Russian expansionism as well as remaining manifestations of nationalism among the Soviet Union's neighbors, perhaps as easily as he himself had overridden the latter—or so it then appeared—within the multinational empire that was the Soviet Union itself.[87]

If the Red Army could have been welcomed in Poland and the rest of the countries it liberated with the same enthusiasm American, British, and Free French forces encountered when they landed in Italy and France in 1943 and 1944, then some kind of Czech–Finnish compromise might have been feasible. Whatever Stalin's expectations, though, this did not happen. That non-event, in turn, removed any possibility of a division of Europe all members of the Grand Alliance could have endorsed. It ensured that an American sphere of influence would arise there largely by consent, but that its Soviet counterpart could sustain itself only by coercion. The resulting asymmetry would account, more than anything else, for the origins, escalation, and ultimate outcome of the Cold War.

VII

The question is worth asking, then: *why* did the Czech–Finnish solution work only in Finland and nowhere else? Why did Hitler's victims not welcome the Russians—who had done more than anyone else to defeat him—as warmly as they did the Americans and their British and French allies? The answer, at its simplest level, has to do with how much one can expect from human nature.

Stalin as well as Roosevelt and Churchill miscalculated when they assumed that there could be *friendly* states along an *expanded* Soviet periphery. For how could the USSR absorb the Baltic States entirely and carve off great portions of Germany, Poland, Romania, and Czechoslovakia,[88] while still expecting the citizens of those countries to maintain cordial attitudes toward the state that had done the carving?[89] It is of course true that the Finns, who were also carved upon, did somehow manage it. But not everyone else was like the Finns: if allowed free elections, it was by no means certain that Poles and Romanians would show the same remarkable qualities of self-control for which their northern neighbor would become famous. Nor was it obvious, even where the Russians permitted other Eastern Europeans to make a choice, that Moscow would follow its own Finnish example and stay out of their internal affairs: these states did have Germany, not Sweden, on the other side of them, and that surely made a difference.

But there was more to the matter than just geography: compounding it was a growing awareness of the particular system Stalin had imposed upon his own people and might well export elsewhere. The war was ending with the defeat of fascism, but not authoritarianism. The price of relying upon one authoritarian to conquer another had been that both would not simultaneously disappear. However vast the moral capital the Soviet Union—and the European communist parties—had accumulated in fighting the Germans, it could not obscure the fact that Stalin's government was, and showed every sign of continuing to be, as repressive as Hitler's had ever been.[90] A movement that had set out, a century earlier, to free the workers of the world from their chains was now seeking to convince its own workers and everyone else that the condition of being in chains was one of perfect freedom. People were not blind, though, and victory over German authoritarianism brought fears of Soviet authoritarianism out into the open.[91]

Worried that this might happen, Roosevelt and Churchill had hoped to persuade the Europeans that Stalin himself had changed: that he meant what he said when he denied any desire to extend his own system beyond its borders; that they could therefore safely accept the boundary changes he demanded and the sphere of influence within which he proposed to include so many of them. But this strategy required Stalin's cooperation, for it could hardly succeed if the Soviet leader failed to match his deeds with the Atlantic Charter's words. Unless the Soviet Union could show that it had shifted from a unilateral to a multilateral approach to security, there could be little basis for consent from Europeans certain to fall under its control. That situation, in turn, would place the Americans and the British in the painful position of being able to cooperate with Moscow only by publicly abandoning principles they themselves had proclaimed, and that Stalin himself appeared to have endorsed.

Authoritarians tend to see ends as justifying means, and are generally free to act accordingly. Democracies rarely allow that luxury, even if their leaders might, in their darker moments, wish for it. What people think does make a difference, and yet nothing in Stalin's experience had prepared him for this reality. Thus it was that although the objective he sought *appeared* to correspond with what his allies wanted—a secure postwar world—the *methods* by which he pursued that goal proved profoundly corruptive of it. Poland best illustrates the pattern.[92]

Presumably Stalin had security in mind when he authorized the murder, at Katyn and elsewhere in the spring of 1940, of at least 15,000 Polish officers captured during the invasion that followed the Nazi-Soviet Pact. He apparently hoped to avoid disturbances that might endanger his relationship with Hitler, to clear out overcrowded camps, and perhaps also to eliminate potential leaders of a future Poland who might be unsympathetic to Soviet interests. He cannot have given the matter much thought, for he was only meting out to the Poles the kind of treatment he had already accorded several million Soviet citizens, and would extend to many others in the future.[93]

What Stalin did not anticipate was that he would need to repair his relations with the Poles after Hitler attacked the Soviet Union in 1941, that he would find it necessary to recognize the Polish government-in-exile in London and reconstitute a Polish army on Soviet soil to fight the Germans, and that the Nazis, in 1943, would reveal the Katyn atrocity to the world. Rather than admit responsibility, Stalin chose to break off relations with the London Poles, who had called for an international investigation. He then created a puppet regime of his own in Lublin and begin treating it as the legitimate government of Poland, a maneuver he backed with force as the Red Army moved into that country in 1944. Stalin subsequently failed to support, or even to allow the Americans and the British to supply by air, an uprising of the Polish resistance in Warsaw, with the result that the Germans wound up completing, on a far more massive scale, the purge of Polish anti-communists he himself had started at Katyn four years earlier. This tragic sequence of events reflected Stalin's tendency, when confronting the prospect of insecurity, to try to redesign the future rather than admit that his own past behavior might have contributed to the problem in the first place.

Stalin in the end got the acquiescent Polish government he wanted, but only at enormous cost. The brutality and cynicism with which he handled these matters did more than anything else to exhaust the goodwill the Soviet war effort had accumulated in the West, to raise doubts about future cooperation in London and Washington,[94] and to create deep and abiding fears throughout the rest of Europe. He also earned the enduring hostility of the Poles, thereby making their country a constant source of *insecurity* for him and for all of his successors.[95] The most effective resistance to Soviet authority would eventually arise in Poland—effective in the sense that the Kremlin never found a way to suppress it.[96] And in an entirely appropriate aftermath, the belated official acknowledgement of Stalin's responsibility for Katyn, which came only in 1990, turned out to be one of the ways in which the last Soviet government acknowledged, not only the illegitimacy of the sphere of influence Stalin had constructed half a century before, but its own illegitimacy as well.[97]

It used to be thought that authoritarian leaders, unfettered by moral scruples, had powerful advantages over their democratic counterparts: it was supposed to be a source of strength to be able to use all means in the pursuit of selected ends. Today this looks much less certain. For the great disadvantage of such systems is the absence of checks and balances: who is to tell the authoritarian in charge that he is about to do something stupid? The killings Stalin authorized, the states he seized, the boundary concessions he insisted upon, and the sphere of influence he imposed provided no lasting security for the Soviet Union: just the opposite. His actions laid the foundations for a resistance in Europe that would grow and not fade with time, so that when a Soviet leader appeared on the scene who was not prepared to sustain with force the system Stalin had constructed, the Soviet empire, and ultimately the Soviet Union itself, would not survive the experience.

VIII

Social psychologists make a useful distinction between what they call "dispositional" and "situational" behavior in interpreting the actions of individuals. Dispositional behavior reflects deeply rooted personal characteristics which remain much the same regardless of the circumstances in which people find themselves. One responds inflexibly—and therefore predictably—to whatever happens. Situational behavior, conversely, shifts with circumstances; personal traits are less important in determining what one does. Historians need to be careful in applying this insight, though, because psychologists know how tempting it can be to excuse one's own actions by invoking situations, while attributing what others do to their dispositions.[98] It would be all too easy, in dealing with so controversial a matter as responsibility for the Cold War, to confuse considered judgment with that most satisfying of sensations: the confirmation of one's own prejudices.[99]

By the end of 1945 most American and British leaders had come around— some reluctantly, others eagerly—to a dispositional explanation of Stalin's behavior. Further efforts to negotiate or compromise with him were likely to fail, or so it seemed, because success would require that he cease to be what he was. One could only resolve henceforth to hold the line, remain true to one's own principles, and wait for the passage of time to bring a better world. Such at least was the view of a new George Kennan, whose top secret "long telegram" from Moscow of 22 February 1946, would shape American policy over the next half century more profoundly than his distant relative's denunciations of tsarist authoritarianism had influenced it during the preceding one. Nor was "containment" just an American strategy: Frank Roberts, the British *chargé d'affaires* in the Soviet capital, was dispatching similar arguments to London even as former prime minister Winston Churchill, speaking at Fulton, Missouri, was introducing the term "iron curtain" to the world.[100] It was left to Kennan, though, to make the dispositional case most explicitly in a lesser-known telegram sent from Moscow on 20 March: "Nothing short of complete disarmament, delivery of our air and naval forces to Russia and resigning of powers of government to American Communists" would come close to alleviating Stalin's distrust, and even then the old dictator would probably "smell a trap and would continue to harbor the most baleful misgivings."[101]

If Kennan was right, we need look no further in seeking the causes of the Cold War: Stalin was primarily responsible. But how can we be sure that this perspective and the policies that resulted from it did not reflect the all too human tendency to attribute behavior one dislikes to the *nature* of those who indulge in it, and to neglect the *circumstances*—including one's own behavior—that might have brought it about? Is there a test historians can apply to avoid this trap?

One might be to check for evidence of consistency or inconsistency, within a particular relationship, in each side's view of the other. Attitudes that show little change over the years, especially when circumstances have changed, suggest deep roots and hence dispositional behavior. Trees may bend slightly before the wind, but they stay in place, for better or for worse, until they die. Viewpoints that evolve with circumstances, however, reflect situational behavior. Vines, after all, can creep, climb, adhere, entwine, and if necessary retreat, all in response to the environment that surrounds them. Roosevelt's vine-like personality is universally acknowledged, and needs no further elaboration here: there could hardly have been a *less* dispositional leader than the always adaptable, ever-elusive F.D.R. But what about Stalin? Was he capable of abandoning, in world politics, the paranoia that defined his domestic politics? Could he respond to conciliatory gestures, or was containment the only realistic course?

Stalin's behavior toward fellow-authoritarians did twist and turn. He gave Hitler the benefit of the doubt at several points, but viewed him as an archenemy at others. His attitudes toward Josef Broz Tito in Yugoslavia and Mao Zedong in China would evolve over the years, albeit in opposite directions.[102] But Stalin's thinking about democratic capitalists remained rooted to the spot: he always suspected their motives. "Remember, we are waging a struggle (negotiation with enemies is also struggle) . . . with the whole capitalist world," he admonished Molotov as early as 1929.[103] He dismissed Roosevelt's and Churchill's warnings of an impending German attack in 1941 as provocations designed to hasten that event.[104] He authorized penetration, by his spies, of the Anglo-American atomic bomb project as early as June 1942, long before his allies made the formal but by then futile decision to withhold such information from him.[105] He placed repeated obstacles in the path of direct military cooperation with the Americans and the British during the war.[106] He not only arranged to have Roosevelt's and Churchill's living quarters at the Tehran Conference bugged; he also had Beria's son, a precocious linguist, translate the tapes daily and report to him on what was said.[107] "Churchill is the kind who, if you don't watch him, will slip a kopeck out of your pocket," Stalin famously warned on the eve of the landings in Normandy in June 1944, surely the highpoint of allied cooperation against the Axis. "Roosevelt is not like that. He dips in his hand only for bigger coins."[108]

A compliment? Perhaps, in Stalin's grudging way, but hardly an expression of trust. The Soviet leader is on record as having expressed compassion—once, at Yalta—for the president's physical infirmity: "Why did nature have to punish him so? Is he any worse than other people?" But the very novelty of the remark impressed Gromyko, who heard it: his boss "rarely bestowed his sympathy on anybody from another social system."[109] Only a few weeks later the same Stalin astounded and infuriated the dying Roosevelt by charging that secret Anglo-American negotiations for the surrender of Hitler's forces in Italy were really a plot to keep the Red Army out of Germany.[110] Many years later a Soviet interviewer would suggest to Molotov that "to be paralyzed and yet to become president of the United States, and for three terms, what a rascal you had to be!" "Well said," the old Bolshevik heartily agreed.[111]

If anyone knew Stalin's mind it was Molotov, the ever-faithful *apparatchik* who came to be known, for the best of reasons, as "his master's voice."[112] Even into his nineties, Molotov's recollections of F.D.R. were clear, unrepentant, and unvarnished. A Roosevelt request for the use of Siberian air bases to bomb Japanese targets had been an excuse "to occupy certain parts of the Soviet Union instead of fighting. Afterward it wouldn't have been easy to get them out of there." The President's larger intentions were transparent:

Roosevelt believed in dollars. Not that he believed in nothing else, but he considered America to be so rich, and we so poor and worn out, that we would surely come begging. "Then we'll kick their ass, but for now we have to keep them going." That's where they miscalculated. They weren't Marxists and we were. They woke up only when half of Europe had passed from them.

"Roosevelt knew how to conceal his attitude toward us," Molotov recalled, "but Truman—he didn't know how to do that at all." Charm, though, could not hide facts: "Roosevelt was an imperialist who would grab anyone by the throat."[113]

If Stalin's wartime attitude toward Roosevelt was half as distrustful as Molotov's in retirement, then a significant pattern emerges: neither American nor British sources reveal anything approaching such deep and abiding suspicion on the Anglo-American side. Churchill subsequently credited himself, to be sure, with having warned of Soviet postwar intentions; but the archives have long since revealed a more complex pattern in which his hopes alternated with his fears well into 1945.[114] In the case of Roosevelt, it is difficult to find *any* expressions of distrust toward Stalin, public or private, until shortly before his death. If he had doubts—surely he had some—he kept them so carefully hidden that historians have had to strain to find traces of them.[115] Kennan first put forward his dispositional explanation of Stalin's actions in the summer of 1944.[116] But in contrast to Molotov, he found no sympathy at the top, nor would he for some time to come.

From this perspective, then, one has to wonder whether the Cold War really began in 1945. For it was Stalin's disposition to wage cold wars: he had done so in one form or another throughout his life, against members of his own family, against his closest advisers and their families, against old revolutionary comrades, against foreign communists, even against returning Red Army war veterans who, for whatever reason, had contacts of any kind with the West in the course of defeating Nazi Germany.[117] "A man who had subjected all activities in his own country to his views and to his personality, Stalin could not behave differently outside," Djilas recalled. "He became himself the slave of the despotism, the bureaucracy, the narrowness, and the servility that he imposed on his country."[118] Khrushchev put it more bluntly: "No one inside the Soviet Union or out had Stalin's trust."[119]

Roosevelt's death in April 1945, then, is not likely to have altered the long-term course of Soviet–American relations: if Stalin had never trusted him, why should he have trusted that "noisy shopkeeper" Harry S. Truman, or the harder-line advisers the new president came to rely upon?[120] The Labour Party's subsequent victory in the British general election produced no improvement in Anglo-Soviet relations either: Stalin was entirely ecumenical in the range of his suspicions, and if anything detested European socialists more than he did European conservatives. Khrushchev describes him going out of his way at the December 1945 Moscow Foreign Ministers' Conference to insult both Truman—who fortunately was not present—and British Foreign Secretary Ernest Bevin: "What caused Stalin to behave that way? This is difficult to explain. I think he believed he could run the policy of the whole world. That's why he behaved in such an unrestrained way toward representatives of countries that were our partners."[121]

If doubts remained about Stalin's disposition, he thoroughly dispelled them in his first major postwar address, made on the eve of his own "election" to the Supreme Soviet in February 1946. The speech was not, as some Americans regarded it, a "declaration of World War III."[122] It was, though, like Molotov's reminiscences, a revealing window into Stalin's mind. World War II, the Kremlin leader explained, had resulted *solely* from the internal contradictions of capitalism, and *only* the entry of the Soviet Union had transformed that conflict into a war of liberation. Perhaps it might be possible to avoid future wars if raw materials and markets could be "periodically redistributed among the various countries in accordance with their economic importance, by agreement and peaceful settlement." But, he added, "that is impossible to do under present capitalist conditions of the development of world economy."[123] What all of this meant, Stalin's most perceptive biographer has argued, was nothing less than that "the postwar period would have to be transformed, in idea if not in actual fact, into *a new prewar period*."[124]

"There has been a return in Russia to the outmoded concept of security in terms of territory—the more you've got the safer you are." The speaker was former Soviet foreign minister and ambassador to the United States Maxim Litvinov, who had personally negotiated the establishment of Soviet–American diplomatic relations with Franklin D. Roosevelt. The occasion was an interview, given in Moscow to CBS correspondent Richard C. Hottelet a few months after Stalin's speech. The cause, Litvinov explained, was "the ideological conception prevailing here that conflict between Communist and capitalist worlds is inevitable." What would happen, Hottelet wanted to know, if the West should suddenly grant all of the Soviet Union's territorial demands? "It would lead to the West's being faced, after a more or less short time, with the next series of demands."[125]

Litvinov managed, remarkably enough, to die in bed.[126] His views on the breakdown of wartime cooperation, though, had hardly been a secret: his colleagues regularly listened to recordings of his conversations acquired, as Molotov put it, "in the usual way." Why was the old diplomat not arrested, charged with treason, and shot? Perhaps his public advocacy of collective security and cooperation with the West, paradoxically, shielded him: Stalin did, from time to time, worry about how his regime looked to the outside world. Perhaps his boss kept Litvinov alive in case the Soviet Union ever again needed the West's assistance. Perhaps he was just lucky, an explanation his successor as foreign minister favored. "Litvinov remained among the living," Molotov recalled with his usual grim clarity, "only by chance."[127]

IX

Only a few months after Litvinov's death Stalin too died in bed, probably as a result of medical neglect stemming from the fact that he had come, by 1953, to see even his own doctors as mortal enemies.[128] That terminal but characteristic event provides a useful vantage-point from which to look back to see how the Cold War had come to pass, and to speculate on whether it might have been avoided.

One hundred and eighteen years earlier, Tocqueville had predicted bipolarity but not necessarily hostility. He was a careful enough historian to understand that the trends visible to him in 1835 would only *frame* future history. Individuals as yet invisible would *determine* it by what they did with the conditions they encountered. "Men make their own history," another keen long-term observer, Karl Marx, would later note, "but they do not make it just as they please; they do not make it under circumstances chosen by themselves, but under circumstances directly found, given and transmitted from the past."[129]

The role of the historian is, or ought to be, to focus exclusively neither on individuals nor on the circumstances they inherit, but on how they intersect. One way to do that is to think of history as an experiment we can rerun[130]—if only in our minds— keeping Tocqueville-like trends constant but allowing for Marx-like variations in the individuals who have to deal with them. If the result replicates what actually happened, then it seems safe to assume that, on balance, circumstances and not men determined the outcome. But if it appears that different individuals might have altered the course of events—if rerunning the experiment does not always produce the same result—then we should question deterministic explanations, for what kind of determinism empowers unique personalities at distinctive moments?

Certain aspects of the Russian–American relationship would change very little in an experiment rerun with 1835 as a starting point: geographical position,
demographic potential, contrasting traditions of social and political organization. It is difficult to conceive how the Americans might have evolved an autocratic form of government, or the Russians a democratic one. Neither country
was likely to remain inactive on the international scene; each would surely have
found cause, sooner or later, to intervene in European and East Asian affairs.

But could it have been foreseen that both would transform their respective
traditions of democracy and authoritarianism into globalist ideologies at precisely the same moment, as Wilson and Lenin did? Could it have been anticipated that Stalin would then shift the internationalism of the Bolshevik
revolution, not simply back to a form of Russian nationalism resembling that of
the tsars, but to a brutal variety of narcissism matched only by the contemporaneous leader of an antipathetic ideology? Could it have been expected that
Hitler would then forge a coalition of communism and capitalism directed
against himself, culminating with the fraternal embraces of victorious Soviet
and American troops in the center of Germany? Could it have been predicted
that this alliance would then fall apart, within a matter of months, leaving in
its wake almost half a century of cold war?

Geography, demography, and tradition contributed to this outcome but did
not determine it. It took men, responding unpredictably to circumstances, to
forge the chain of causation; and it took one man in particular, responding predictably to his own authoritarian, paranoid, and narcissistic predisposition, to
lock it into place.[131] Would there have been a Cold War without Stalin?
Perhaps. Nobody in history is indispensable.

But Stalin had certain characteristics that set him off from all others in
authority at the time the Cold War began. He alone pursued personal security
by depriving everyone else of it: no Western leader relied on terror to the extent
that he did. He alone had transformed his country into an extension of himself:
no Western leader could have succeeded at such a feat, and none attempted it.
He alone saw war and revolution as acceptable means with which to pursue ultimate ends: no Western leader associated violence with progress to the extent
that he did.

Did Stalin therefore seek a Cold War? The question is a little like asking: "does
a fish seek water?" Suspicion, distrust, and an abiding cynicism were not only
his preferred but his necessary environment; he could not function apart from
it. "Conciliation struck Stalin as trickery or naiveté," William Taubman has concluded, "and toughness only confirmed the Soviets' image of America as an
unreconstructed enemy."[132] The Americans would in time develop a similar
view of Stalin and his successors; some of their leaders would hold onto it long
after the reasons for it had begun to disappear. But that was not the prevailing
attitude in Washington, or in other Western capitals, in 1945. It was, consistently had been, and would remain Stalin's, until the day of his own medically
under-attended demise.

TWO

Cold War Empires: Europe

The Prime Minister then said that it was important that the nations who would govern the world after the war, and who would be entrusted with the direction of the world after the war, should be satisfied and have no territorial or other ambitions. . . . He said that hungry nations and ambitious nations are dangerous, and he would like to see the leading nations of the world in the position of rich, happy men.

Tehran Conference minutes, 30 November 1943[1]

[A] map with new borders of the USSR . . . was brought after the war to Stalin's dacha. The map was very small—like those for school textbooks. Stalin pinned it to the wall: "Let's see what we have here. . . . Everything is all right to the north. Finland has offended us, so we moved the border from Leningrad. Baltic states—that's age-old Russian land!—and they're ours again. All Belorussians live together now, Ukrainians together, Moldavians together. It's okay to the west." And he turned suddenly to the eastern borders. "What do we have there? . . . . The Kuril Islands belong to us now, Sakhalin is completely ours—you see, good! And Port Arthur's ours, and Dairen is ours"—Stalin moved his pipe across China—"and the Chinese Eastern railway is ours. China, Mongolia—everything is in order. But I don't like our border right here!" Stalin said and pointed to the Caucasus.

Felix Chuev[2]

BY 1947, it was clear that cooperation to build a new order among the nations that had vanquished the old one was not going to be possible. There followed the most remarkable *polarization* of politics in modern history. It was as if a gigantic magnet had somehow come into existence, compelling most states, often even movements and individuals within states, to align themselves along fields of force thrown out from either Washington or Moscow. Remaining uncommitted, in a postwar international system that seemed so compulsively to require commitment, would be no easy matter. The United States and the Soviet Union were now as close as any great powers have ever been to controlling—as Tocqueville had foreseen Americans and Russians someday would—"the destinies of half the world."

Theorists of international relations have insisted that in seeking to under-stand such a system we need pay little attention to the "units" that make it up. Because states exist within an anarchic environment, survival has to be their common objective; power is the means by which all of them—regardless of their internal makeup—seek to ensure it. Nations therefore behave like feature-less billiard balls: their collisions are significant, but their character is not.[3] Tocqueville's distinction between authoritarian and democratic traditions in the Russian-American relationship, from this perspective, would be quite irrel-evant.

The historian must point out, though, that however "great" the United States and the Soviet Union were during the Cold War, the "power" they obtained and wielded was rarely comparable. If these were billiard balls, they were not of the same size or weight or mass. Nor did the spheres of influence Washington and Moscow dominated resemble one another, whether from a military, economic, ideological, or moral perspective—a fact that has become obvious now that one of them no longer exists. Apples and oranges might be the better metaphor: at least it would allow for asymmetry, irregularity, and the possibility of internal rot.

But even this model has its deficiencies, because it leaves little room for the role of third parties—to say nothing of fourth, fifth, and nth parties—in shap-ing the Soviet–American relationship. It makes a big difference if great powers have to extend their authority against, rather than in concert with, the wishes of those subjected to it. The choice is between resistance and collaboration, and it falls to those incorporated within spheres of influence, not to those who impose them, ultimately to make it. If we are to grasp the nature of the post-World War II international system, then we will need an analytical framework capable of accounting for the rise and fall of great powers; but also one that incorporates variations in the nature of power and the influence it produces, as well as the limitations on power that permit peripheries to make a difference, even when things are being run from very powerful centers.

Such a framework exists, I think, in a more ancient method of governance than either democracy or authoritarianism: it is *empire*. I mean, by this term, a situation in which a single state shapes the behavior of others, whether directly or indirectly, partially or completely, by means that can range from the outright use of force through intimidation, dependency, inducements, and even inspi-ration.[4] Leaders of both the United States and the Soviet Union would have bris-tled at having the appellation "imperial" affixed to what they were doing after 1945. But one need not send out ships, seize territories, and hoist flags to con-struct an empire: "informal" empires are considerably older than, and contin-ued to exist alongside, the more "formal" ones Europeans imposed on so much of the rest of the world from the fifteenth through the nineteenth centuries.[5] During the Cold War years Washington and Moscow took on much of the char-acter, if never quite the charm, of old imperial capitals like London, Paris, and Vienna. And surely American and Soviet influence, throughout most of the sec-ond half of the twentieth century, was at least as ubiquitous as that of any ear-lier empire the world had ever seen.

Ubiquity never ensured unchallenged authority, though, and that fact provides yet another reason for applying an imperial analogy to Cold War history. For contrary to popular impressions, empires have always involved a two-way flow of influence. Imperializers have never simply acted upon the imperialized; the imperialized have also had a surprising amount of influence over the imperializers.[6] The Cold War was no exception to this pattern, and an awareness of it too will help us to see how that rivalry emerged, evolved, and eventually ended in the way that it did.

I

Let us begin with the structure of the Soviet empire, for the simple reason that it was, much more than the American, deliberately designed. It has long been clear that, in addition to having had an authoritarian vision, Stalin also had an imperial one, which he proceeded to implement in at least as single-minded a way. No comparably influential builder of empire came close to wielding power for so long, or with such striking results, on the Western side.

It was, of course, a matter of some awkwardness that Stalin came out of a revolutionary movement that had vowed to smash, not just tsarist imperialism, but all forms of imperialism throughout the world. The Soviet leader constructed his own logic, though, and throughout his career he devoted a surprising amount of attention to showing how a revolution and an empire might coexist. Bolsheviks could never be imperialists, Stalin acknowledged in one of his earliest public pronouncements on this subject, made in April 1917. But surely in a *revolutionary* Russia nine-tenths of the non-Russian nationalities would not *want* their independence.[7] Few among those minorities found Stalin's reasoning persuasive after the Bolsheviks did seize power later that year, however, and one of the first problems Lenin's new government faced was a disintegration of the old Russian empire not unlike what happened to the Soviet Union after communist authority finally collapsed in 1991.

Whether because of Lenin's own opposition to imperialism or, just as plausibly, because of Soviet Russia's weakness at the time, Finns, Estonians, Latvians, Lithuanians, Poles, and Moldavians were allowed to depart. Others who tried to do so—Ukrainians, Belorussians, Caucasians, Central Asians—were not so fortunate, and in 1922 Stalin proposed incorporating these remaining (and reacquired) nationalities into the Russian republic, only to have Lenin as one of his last acts override this recommendation and establish the multi-ethnic Union of Soviet Socialist Republics.[8] After Lenin died and Stalin took his place it quickly became clear, though, that whatever its founding principles the USSR was to be no federation of equals. Rather, it would function as an updated form of empire even more tightly centralized than that of the Russian tsars.

Lenin and Stalin differed most significantly, not over authoritarianism or even terror, but on the legitimacy of Great Russian nationalism. The founder of Bolshevism had warned with characteristic pungency of "that truly Russian man, the Great-Russian chauvinist," and of the dangers of sinking into a "sea of chauvinistic Great-Russian filth, like flies in milk." Such temptations, he insisted, might ruin the prospects of revolution spreading elsewhere in the world.[9] But Stalin—the implied target of Lenin's invective—was himself a Great Russian nationalist, with all the intensity transplanted nationals can sometimes attain.[10] "The leaders of the revolutionary workers of all countries are avidly studying the most instructive history of the working class of Russia, its past, the past of Russia," he would write in a revealing private letter in 1930, shortly after consolidating his position as Lenin's successor. "All this instills (cannot but instill!) in the hearts of the Russian workers a feeling of revolutionary national pride, capable of moving mountains and working miracles."[11]

The "Stalin constitution" of 1936, which formally specified the right of non-Russian nationalities to secede from the Soviet Union, coincided with the great purges and an officially sanctioned upsurge in Russian nationalism that would persist as a prominent feature of Stalin's regime until his death.[12] It was as if the great authoritarian had set out to validate his own flawed prediction of 1917 by creating a set of circumstances in which non-Russian nationalities would not even *think* of seceding, even though the hypothetical authority to do so remained. The pattern resembled that of the purge trials themselves: one maintained a framework of legality—even, within the non-Russian republics, a toleration of local languages and cultures considerably greater than under the tsars. But Stalin then went to extraordinary lengths to deter anyone from exercising these rights or promoting those cultures in such a way as to challenge his own rule. He appears to have concluded, from his own study of the Russian past, that it was not "reactionary" to seek territorial expansion. His principal ideological innovation may well have been to impose the ambitions of the old princes of Muscovy, especially their determination to "gather in" and dominate all of the lands that surrounded them, upon the anti-imperial spirit of proletarian internationalism that had emanated from, if not actually inspired, the Bolshevik Revolution.[13]

Stalin's fusion of Marxist internationalism with tsarist imperialism could only reinforce his tendency, in place well before World War II, to equate the advance of world revolution with the expanding influence of the Soviet state.[14] He applied that linkage quite impartially: a major benefit of the 1939 pact with Hitler had been that it regained territories lost as a result of the Bolshevik Revolution and the World War I settlement. But Stalin's conflation of imperialism with ideology also explains the importance he attached, following the German attack in 1941, to having his new Anglo-American allies confirm these arrangements. He had similar goals in East Asia when he insisted on bringing the Soviet Union back to the position Russia had occupied in Manchuria prior to the Russo-Japanese War: this he finally achieved at the 1945 Yalta Conference in return for promising to enter the war against Japan.[15] "My task as minister of foreign affairs was to expand the borders of our Fatherland,"

Molotov recalled proudly many years later. "And it seems that Stalin and I coped with this task quite well."[16]

II

From the West's standpoint, the critical question was how far Moscow's influence would extend *beyond* whatever Soviet frontiers turned out to be at the end of the war. Stalin had suggested to Milovan Djilas that the Soviet Union would impose its own social system as far as its armies could reach,[17] but he was also very cautious. Keenly aware of the military power the United States and its allies had accumulated, Stalin was determined to do nothing that might involve the USSR in another devastating war until it had recovered sufficiently to be certain of winning it. "I do not wish to begin the Third World War over the Trieste question," he explained to disappointed Yugoslavs, whom he ordered to evacuate that territory in June 1945.[18] Five years later, he would justify his decision not to intervene in the Korean War on the grounds that "the Second World War ended not long ago, and we are not ready for the Third World War."[19] Just how far the expansion of Soviet influence would proceed depended, therefore, upon a careful balancing of opportunities against risks. "[W]e were on the offensive," Molotov acknowledged:

They [presumably the West] certainly hardened their line against us, but we had to consolidate our conquests. We made our own socialist Germany out of our part of Germany, and restored order in Czechoslovakia, Poland, Hungary, and Yugoslavia, where the situations were fluid. To squeeze out capitalist order. This was the cold war.

But, "of course," Molotov added, "you had to know when to stop. I believe in this respect Stalin kept well within the limits."[20]

Who or what was it, though, that set the limits? Did Stalin have a fixed list of countries he thought it necessary to dominate? Was he prepared to stop in the face of resistance within those countries to "squeezing out the capitalist order"? Or would expansion cease only when confronted with opposition from the remaining capitalist states, so that further advances risked war at a time when the Soviet Union was ill-prepared for it?

Stalin had been very precise about where he wanted Soviet boundaries changed; he was much less so on how far Moscow's sphere of influence was to extend. He insisted on having "friendly" countries around the periphery of the USSR, but he failed to specify how many would have to meet this standard. He called during the war for dismembering Germany, but by the end of it was denying that he had ever done so: that country would be temporarily divided, he told leading German communists in June 1945, and they themselves would eventually bring about its reunification.[21] He never gave up on the idea of an eventual world revolution, but he expected this to result—as his comments to the Germans suggested—from an expansion of influence emanating from the Soviet Union itself. "[F]or the Kremlin," a well-placed spymaster recalled, "the mission of communism was primarily to consolidate the might of the Soviet state. Only military strength and domination of the countries on our borders could ensure us a superpower role.[22]

But Stalin provided no indication—surely because he himself did not know— of how rapidly, or under what circumstances, this process would take place. He was certainly prepared to stop in the face of resistance from the West: at no point was he willing to challenge the Americans or even the British where they made their interests clear. Churchill acknowledged his scrupulous adherence to the famous 1944 "percentages" agreement confirming British authority in Greece, and Yugoslav sources have revealed Stalin's warnings that the United States and Great Britain would never allow their lines of communication in the Mediterranean to be broken.[23] He quickly backed down when confronted with Anglo-American objections to his ambitions in Iran in the spring of 1946, as he did later that year after demanding Soviet bases in the Turkish Straits.[24] This pattern of advance followed by retreat had shown up in the purges of the 1930s, which Stalin halted when the external threat from Germany became too great to ignore, and it would reappear with the Berlin Blockade and the Korean War, both situations in which the Soviet Union would show great caution after provoking an unexpectedly strong American response.

What all of this suggests, though, is not that Stalin had limited ambitions, only that he had no timetable for achieving them. Molotov retrospectively confirmed this: "Our ideology stands for offensive operations when possible, and if not, we wait."[25] Given this combination of appetite with aversion to risk, one cannot help but wonder what would have happened had the West tried containment earlier. To the extent that it bears partial responsibility for the coming of the Cold War, the historian Vojtech Mastny has argued, that responsibility lies in its failure to do just that.[26]

Where Western resistance was unlikely, as in Eastern Europe, Stalin would in time attempt to replicate the regime he had already established inside the Soviet Union. Authority extended out from Moscow by way of government and party structures whose officials had been selected for their obedience, then down within each of these countries through the management of the economy, social and political institutions, intellectuals, even family relationships. The differentiation of public and private spheres that exists in most societies disappeared as all aspects of life were fused with, and then subordinated to, the interests of the Soviet Union as Stalin himself had determined them.[27] Those who could not or would not go along encountered the same sequence of intimidation, terror, and ultimately even purges, show trials, and executions that his real and imagined domestic opponents had gone through during the 1930s. "Stalin's understanding of friendship with other countries was that the Soviet Union would lead and they would follow," Khrushchev recalled. "[He] waged the struggle against the enemies of the people there in the same way that he did in the Soviet Union. He had one demand: absolute subordination."[28]

Stalin's policy, then, was one of imperial expansion and consolidation differing from that of earlier empires only in the determination with which he pursued it, in the instruments of coercion with which he maintained it, and in the ostensibly anti-imperial justifications he put forward in support of it. It is a testimony to his skill, if not to his morality, that he was able to achieve so many of his imperial ambitions at a time when the tides of history were running against the idea of imperial domination—as colonial offices in London, Paris, Lisbon, and The Hague were finding out—and when his own country was recovering from one of the most brutal invasions in recorded history. The fact that Stalin was able to *expand* his empire when others were contracting and while the Soviet Union was as weak as it was requires explanation.[29] Why did opposition to this process, within and outside Europe, take so long to develop?

One reason was that the colossal sacrifices the Soviet Union had made during the war against the Axis had, in effect, "purified" its reputation: the USSR and its leader had "earned" the right to throw their weight around, or so it seemed.[30] Western governments found it difficult to switch quickly from viewing the Soviet Union as a glorious wartime ally to portraying it as a new and dangerous adversary. President Harry S. Truman and his future Secretary of State Dean Acheson—neither of them sympathetic in the slightest to communism—nonetheless tended to give the Soviet Union the benefit of the doubt well into the early postwar era.[31] A similar pattern developed within the United States occupation zone in Germany, where General Lucius D. Clay worked out a cooperative relationship with his Soviet counterparts and resisted demands to "get tough" with the Russians, even after they had become commonplace in Washington.[32]

Resistance to Stalin's imperialism also developed slowly because Marxism-Leninism at the time had such widespread appeal. It is difficult now to recapture the admiration revolutionaries outside the Soviet Union felt for that country before they came to know it well. "[Communism] was the most rational and most intoxicating, all-embracing ideology for me and for those in my disunited and desperate land who so desired to skip over centuries of slavery and backwardness and to bypass reality itself," Djilas recalled, in a comment that could have been echoed throughout much of what came to be called the "third world."[33] Because the Bolsheviks themselves had overcome one empire and had made a career of condemning others, it would take decades for people who were struggling to overthrow British, French, Dutch, or Portuguese colonialism to see that there could also be such a thing as Soviet imperialism. European communists—notably the Yugoslavs—saw this much earlier, but even to most of them it had not been apparent at the end of the war.

Still another explanation for the initial lack of resistance to Soviet expansionism was the fact that its repressive character did not become immediately apparent to all who were subjected to it. With regimes on the left taking power in Eastern and Central Europe, groups long denied advancement could now expect it. For many who remembered the 1930s, autarchy within a Soviet bloc could seem preferable to exposure once again to international capitalism, with its periodic cycles of boom and bust.[34] Nor did Moscow impose harsh controls everywhere at the same time.[35] Simple administrative incompetence may partially account for this: one Russian historian has pointed out that "[d]isorganization, mismanagement and rivalry among many branches of the gigantic Stalinist state in Eastern Europe were enormous."[36] But it is also possible, at least in some areas, that Stalin did not expect to *need* tight controls; that he anticipated no serious challenge and perhaps even spontaneous support. Why did he promise free elections after the war? Maybe he thought the communists would win them.

One has the impression that Stalin and the Eastern Europeans got to know one another only gradually. The Kremlin leader was slow to recognize that Soviet authority would not be welcomed everywhere beyond Soviet borders; but as he did come to see this he became all the more determined to impose it everywhere. The Eastern Europeans were slow to recognize how confining incorporation within a Soviet sphere was going to be; but as they did come to see this they became all the more determined to resist it, even if only by withholding, in a passive but sullen manner, the consent any regime needs to establish itself by means other than coercion. Stalin's efforts to consolidate his empire therefore made it at once more repressive and less secure.[37] Meanwhile, an alternative vision of postwar Europe was emerging from the other great empire that established itself in the wake of World War II, that of the United States, and this too gave Stalin grounds for concern.

III

The first point worth noting, when comparing the American empire to its Soviet counterpart, is a striking reversal in the sequence of events. Stalin's determination to create his empire preceded by some years the conditions that made it possible: he had first to consolidate power at home and then defeat Nazi Germany, while at the same time seeing to it that his allies in that enterprise did not thwart his long-term objectives. With the United States, it was the other way around: the conditions for establishing an empire were in place long before there was any clear intention on the part of its leaders to do so.[38] Even then, they required the support of a skeptical electorate, something that could never quite be taken for granted.

The United States had been poised for global hegemony at the end of World War I. Its military forces played a decisive role in bringing that conflict to an end. Its economic predominance was such that it could control both the manner and the rate of European recovery. Its ideology commanded enormous respect, as Woodrow Wilson found when he arrived on the Continent late in 1918 to a series of rapturous public receptions. The Versailles Treaty fell well short of Wilson's principles, to be sure, but the League of Nations followed closely his own design, providing an explicit legal basis for an international order that was to have drawn, as much as anything else, upon the example of the American constitution itself. If there was ever a point at which the world seemed receptive to an expansion of United States influence, this was it.

Americans themselves, however, were not receptive. The Senate's rejection of membership in the League reflected the public's distinct lack of enthusiasm for international peace-keeping responsibilities. Despite the interests certain business, labor, and agricultural groups had in seeking overseas markets and investment opportunities, most Americans saw few benefits to be derived from integrating their economy with that of the rest of the world. Efforts to rehabilitate Europe during the 1920s, therefore, could only take the form of private initiatives, quietly coordinated with the government. Protective tariffs hung on well into the 1930s—having actually increased with the onset of the Great Depression—and exports as a percentage of gross national product remained low in comparison to other nations, averaging only 4.2 per cent between 1921 and 1940.[39] Investments abroad had doubled between 1914 and 1919 while foreign investment in the United States had been cut in half;[40] but this shift was hardly sufficient to overcome old instincts within the majority of the public who held no investments at all that it was better to stand apart from, rather than to attempt to dominate, international politics outside of the Western hemisphere.[41]

This isolationist consensus broke down only as Americans began to realize that a potentially hostile power was once again threatening Europe: even their own hemisphere, it appeared, might not escape the consequences this time around.[42] After September 1939, the Roosevelt administration moved as quickly as public and Congressional opinion would allow to aid Great Britain and France by means short of war; it also chose to challenge the Japanese over their occupation of China and later French Indochina, thereby setting in motion a sequence of events that would lead to the attack on Pearl Harbor.[43] Historians ever since have puzzled over this: why, after two decades of relative inactivity on the world scene, did the United States suddenly become hyperactive? Might the administration have realized that it would never generate public support for the empire American elites had long desired without a clear and present danger to national security, and did it not then proceed to generate one?[44] Can one not understand the origins and evolution of the Cold War in similar terms?[45]

There are several problems with such interpretations, one of which is that they confuse contingency with conspiracy. Even if Roosevelt had hoped to maneuver the Japanese into "firing the first shot," he could not have known that Hitler would seize this opportunity to declare war and thereby make possible American military intervention in Europe. The Pacific, where the United States would have deployed most of its strength in the absence of Hitler's declaration, would hardly have been the platform from which to mount a bid for global hegemony. These explanations also allow little room for the autonomy of others: they assume that Hitler and the Japanese militarists acted *only* in response to what the United States did, and that other possible motives for their behavior—personal, bureaucratic, cultural, ideological, geopolitical—were insignificant. Finally, these arguments fail to meet the test of proximate versus distant causation. The historian Marc Bloch once pointed out that one could, in principle, account for a climber's fall from a precipice by invoking physics and geology: had it not been for the law of gravity and the existence of the mountain, the accident surely could not have occurred. But would it follow that all who ascend mountains must plummet from them?[46] Just because Roosevelt *wanted* the United States to enter the war and to become a world power afterwards does not mean that his actions alone made these things happen.

A better explanation for the collapse of isolationism is a simpler one: it had to do with a resurgence of authoritarianism. Americans had begun to suspect, late in the nineteenth century, that the internal behavior of states determined their external behavior;[47] certainly it is easy to see how the actions of Germany, Italy, and Japan during the 1930s could have caused this view to surface once again, much as it had in relations with tsarist Russia and imperial Germany during World War I. Once that happened, the Americans, not given to making subtle distinctions, began to oppose authoritarianism everywhere, and that could account for their sudden willingness to take on several authoritarians at once in 1941. But that interpretation, too, is not entirely adequate. It fails to explain how the United States could have coexisted as comfortably as it did with authoritarianism in the past—especially in Latin America—and as it would continue to do for some time to come. It certainly does not account for the American willingness during the war to embrace, as an ally, the greatest authoritarian of this century, Stalin himself.

The best explanation for the decline of isolationism and the rise of the American empire, I suspect, has to do with a distinction Americans tended to make—perhaps they were more subtle than one might think—between what we might call benign and malignant authoritarianism. Regimes like those of Somoza in Nicaragua or Trujillo in the Dominican Republic might be unsavory, but they fell into the benign category because they posed no serious threat to United States interests and in some cases even promoted them. Regimes like those of Nazi Germany and imperial Japan, because of their military capabilities, were quite another matter. Stalin's authoritarianism had appeared malignant when linked to that of Hitler, as it was between 1939 and 1941; but when directed against Hitler, it could come to appear quite benign. What it would look like once Germany had been defeated remained to be seen.

With all this, the possibility that even malignant authoritarianism might harm the United States remained hypothetical until 7 December 1941, when it suddenly became very real. Americans are only now, after more than half a century, getting over the shock: they became so accustomed to a Pearl Harbor mentality—to the idea that there really are deadly enemies out there—that they find it a strange new world, instead of an old familiar one, now that there are not. Pearl Harbor was, then, the defining event for the American empire, because it was only at this point that the most plausible potential justification for the United States becoming and remaining a global power as far as the American people were concerned—an endangered national security—became an actual one.[48] Isolationism had thrived right up to this moment; but once it became apparent that isolationism could leave the nation open to military attack, it suffered a blow from which it never recovered. The critical date was not 1945, or 1947, but 1941.

It did not automatically follow, though, that the Soviet Union would inherit the title of "first enemy" once Germany and Japan had been defeated. A sense of vulnerability preceded the identification of a source of threat in the thinking of American strategists: innovations in military technology—long-range bombers, the prospect of even longer-range missiles—created visions of future Pearl Harbors before it had become clear from where such an attack might come. Neither in the military nor the political-economic planning that went on in Washington during the war was there consistent concern with the USSR as a potential future adversary. The threat, rather, appeared to arise from war itself, whoever might cause it, and the most likely candidates were thought to be resurgent enemies from World War II.[49]

The preferred solution was to maintain preponderant power for the United States, which meant a substantial peacetime military establishment and a string of bases around the world from which to resist aggression if it should ever occur. But equally important, a revived international community would seek to remove the fundamental causes of war through the United Nations, a less ambitious version of Wilson's League, and through new economic institutions like the International Monetary Fund and the World Bank, whose task it would be to prevent another global depression and thereby ensure prosperity. The Americans and the British assumed that the Soviet Union would want to participate in these multilateral efforts to achieve military and economic security. The Cold War developed when it became clear that Stalin either could not or would not accept this framework.[50]

Did the Americans attempt to impose their vision of the postwar world upon the USSR? No doubt it looked that way from Moscow: both the Roosevelt and Truman administrations stressed political self-determination and economic integration with sufficient persistence to arouse Stalin's suspicions—easily aroused, in any event—as to their ultimate intentions. But what the Soviet leader saw as a challenge to his hegemony the Americans meant as an effort to salvage multilateralism. At no point prior to 1947 did the United States and its Western European allies abandon the hope that the Russians might eventually come around; and indeed negotiations aimed at bringing them around would continue at the foreign ministers' level, without much hope of success, through the end of that year. The American attitude was less that of expecting to impose a system than one of puzzlement as to why its merits were not universally self-evident. It differed significantly, therefore, from Stalin's point of view, which allowed for the possibility that socialists in other countries might come to see the advantages of Marxism-Leninism as practiced in the Soviet Union, but never capitalists.[51] They were there, in the end, to be overthrown, not convinced.

IV

The emergence of an opposing great power bloc posed serious difficulties for the principle of multilateralism, based as it had been on the expectation of cooperation with Moscow. But with a good deal of ingenuity the Americans managed to *merge* their original vision of a single international order built around common security with a second and more hastily improvised concept that sought to counter the expanding power and influence of the Soviet Union. That concept was, of course, containment, and its chief instrument was the Marshall Plan.

The idea of containment proceeded from the proposition that if there was not to be one world, then there must not be another world war either. It would be necessary to keep the peace while preserving the balance of power: the gap that had developed during the 1930s between the perceived requirements of peace and power was not to happen again. If geopolitical stability could be restored in Europe, time would work against the Soviet Union and in favor of the Western democracies. Authoritarianism need not be the "wave of the future"; sooner or later even Kremlin authoritarians would realize this fact and change their policies. "[T]he Soviet leaders are prepared to recognize *situations*, if not arguments," George F. Kennan wrote in 1948. "If, therefore, situations can be created in which it is clearly not to the advantage of their power to emphasize the elements of conflict in their relations with the outside world, then their actions, and even the tenor of their propaganda to their own people, *can* be modified."[52]

This idea of time being on the side of the West came—at least as far as Kennan was concerned—from studying the history of empires. Edward Gibbon had written in *The Decline and Fall of the Roman Empire* that "there is nothing more contrary to nature than the attempt to hold in obedience distant provinces," and few things Kennan ever read made a greater or more lasting impression on him. He had concluded during the early days of World War II that Hitler's empire could not last, and in the months after the war, he applied similar logic to the empire Stalin was setting out to construct in Eastern Europe.[53] The territorial acquisitions and spheres of influence the Soviet Union had obtained would ultimately become a source of *insecurity* for it, both because of the resistance to Moscow's control that was sure to grow within those regions and because of the outrage the nature of that control was certain to provoke in the rest of the world. "Soviet power, like the capitalist world of its own conception, bears within it the seeds of its own decay," Kennan insisted in the most famous of all Cold War texts, his anonymously published 1947 article on "The Sources of Soviet Conduct." He added, "the sprouting of those seeds is well advanced."[54]

All of this would do the Europeans little good, though, if the new and immediate Soviet presence in their midst should so intimidate them that their own morale collapsed. The danger here came not from the prospect that the Red Army would invade and occupy the rest of the continent, as Hitler had tried to do; rather, its demoralized and exhausted inhabitants might simply vote in communist parties who would then do Moscow's bidding. The initial steps in the strategy of containment—stopgap military and economic aid to Greece and Turkey, the more carefully designed and ambitious Marshall Plan—took place within this context: the idea was to produce instant intangible reassurance as well as eventual tangible reinforcement. Two things had to happen in order for intimidation to occur, Kennan liked to argue: the intimidator had to make the effort, but, equally important, the target of those efforts had to agree to be intimidated.[55] The initiatives of 1947 sought to generate sufficient self-confidence to prevent such acquiescence in intimidation from taking place.

Some historians have asserted that these fears of collapse were exaggerated: that economic recovery on the continent was already underway, and that the Europeans themselves were never as psychologically demoralized as the Americans made them out to be.[56] Others have added that the real crisis at the time was within an American economy that could hardly expect to function hegemonically if Europeans lacked the dollars to purchase its products.[57] Still others have suggested that the Marshall Plan was the means by which American officials sought to project overseas the mutually-beneficial relationship between business, labor, and government they had worked out at home: the point was not to make Wilsonian values a model for the rest of the world, but rather the politics of productivity that had grown out of American corporate capitalism.[58] All of these arguments have merit: at a minimum they have forced historians to place the Marshall Plan in a wider economic, social, and historical context; more broadly they suggest that the American empire had its own distinctive internal roots, and was not solely and simply a response to the Soviet external challenge.

At the same time, though, it is difficult to see how a strategy of containment could have developed—with the Marshall Plan as its centerpiece—had there been nothing to contain. One need only recall the early 1920s, when similar conditions of European demoralization, Anglo-French exhaustion, and American economic predominance had existed; yet no American empire arose as after World War II. The critical difference, of course, was national security: Pearl Harbor created an atmosphere of vulnerability Americans had not known since the earliest days of the republic, and the Soviet Union by 1947 had become the most plausible source of threat. The American empire arose *primarily*, therefore, not from internal causes, as had the Soviet empire, but from a perceived external danger powerful enough to overcome American isolationism.[59]

Washington's wartime vision of a postwar international order had been premised on the concepts of political self-determination and economic integration. It was intended to work by assuming a set of *common* interests that would cause other countries to *want* to be affiliated with it rather than to resist it. The Marshall Plan, to a considerable extent, met those criteria: although it operated on a regional rather than a global scale, it did seek to promote democracy through an economic recovery that would proceed along international and not nationalist lines. Its purpose was to create an American sphere of influence, to be sure, but one that would allow those within it considerable freedom. The principles of democracy and open markets required nothing less, but there were two additional and more practical reasons for encouraging such autonomy. First, the United States itself lacked the capability to administer a large empire: the difficulties of running occupied Germany and Japan were proving daunting enough.[60] Second, the idea of autonomy was implicit in the task of restoring European self-confidence; for who, if not Europeans themselves, was to say when the self-confidence of Europeans had been restored?

Finally, it is worth noting that even though Kennan and the other early architects of containment made use of imperial analogies, they did not see themselves as creating an empire, but rather a restored balance of power. Painfully—perhaps excessively—aware of limited American resources, fearful that the domestic political consensus in favor of internationalism might not hold, they set out to reconstitute *independent* centers of power in Europe and Asia.[61] These would be integrated into the world capitalist system, and as a result they would certainly fall under the influence of its new hegemonic manager, the United States. But there was no intention here of creating satellites in anything like the sense that Stalin understood that term; rather, the idea was that "third forces" would resist Soviet expansionism while preserving as much as possible of the multilateralist agenda American officials had framed during World War II. What the United States really wanted, State Department official John D. Hickerson commented in 1948, was "not merely an extension of US influence but a real European organization strong enough to say 'no' both to the Soviet Union and to the United States, if our actions should seem so to require."[62]

The American empire, therefore, reflected little imperial consciousness or design. An anti-imperial tradition dating back to the American Revolution partially accounted for this: departures from that tradition, as in the Spanish–American War of 1898 and the Philippine insurrection that followed, had only reinforced its relevance—outside the Western hemisphere. So too did a constitutional structure that forced even imperially minded leaders like Wilson and the two Roosevelts to accommodate domestic attitudes that discouraged imperial behavior long after national capabilities had made it possible. And even as those internal constraints diminished dramatically in World War II—they never entirely dropped away—Americans still found it difficult to think of themselves as an imperial power. The idea of remaking the international system in such a way as to transcend empires altogether still lingered, but so too did doubts as to whether the United States was up to the task.[63] In the end it was again external circumstances—the manner in which Stalin managed his own empire and the way in which this pushed Europeans into preferring its American alternative—that brought the self-confidence necessary to administer imperial responsibilities into line with Washington's awareness of their existence.

V

The test of any empire comes in administering it, for even the most repressive tyranny requires a certain amount of acquiescence among its subjects. Coercion and terror cannot everywhere and indefinitely prop up authority: sooner or later the social, economic, and psychological costs of such measures begin to outweigh the benefits. Empires that can accommodate dissent, defuse it, and perhaps even reorient themselves to reflect certain aspects of it, are more likely to survive than those that simply try to suppress it.[64] Resilience is as important as rigidity in designing buildings, bridges, and baseball bats: the world of politics is not all that different.

It is apparent now, even if it was not always at the time, that the Soviet Union did not manage its empire particularly well. Because of his personality and the structure of government he built around it, Stalin was—shall we say—less than receptive to the wishes of those nations that fell within the Soviet sphere. He viewed departures from his instructions with deep suspicion, but he also objected to manifestations of independent behavior where instructions had not yet been given. As a result, he put his European followers in an impossible position: they could satisfy him only by seeking his approval for whatever he had decided they should do—even, at times, before he had decided that they should do it.

An example occurred late in 1944 when the Yugoslavs—then the most powerful but also the most loyal of Stalin's East European allies—complained politely to Soviet commanders that their troops had been raping local women in the northern corner of the country through which they were passing. Stalin himself took note of this matter, accusing the Yugoslavs—at one point tearfully—of showing insufficient respect for Soviet military sacrifices and for failing to sympathize when "a soldier who has crossed thousands of kilometers through blood and fire and death has fun with a woman or takes some trifle." The issue was not an insignificant one: the Red Army's behavior was a problem throughout the territories it occupied, and did much to alienate those who lived there. Stalin's only concern, though, seems to have been that the Yugoslavs were failing to meet the standards of deference and obedience he expected from allies; for their part, the Yugoslavs began to wonder, apparently for the first time, just whose interests international communism as directed from Moscow was supposed to serve.[65]

Similar questions arose regarding Yugoslav plans for a postwar Balkan federation. Stalin had initially supported this idea, perhaps as an excuse for removing American and British military representatives from former enemy states like Romania, but he soon developed reservations. The Yugoslavs themselves might become too powerful; and their propensity for hot-headedness—evident in their claims to Trieste and their shooting down of two American Air Force planes in 1946—might provoke the West. Orders went out that the Yugoslavs were to proceed slowly in their plans to take over Albania, and were to stop assisting the Greek guerillas altogether.[66] Within the context of the Cold War, these actions reflected Stalin's caution about confronting the British and the Americans; to that extent, they defused tensions. But to the militant Yugoslavs, they suggested the arrogance of an imperial authority determined to subordinate their interests—which they had defined largely in ideological terms—to those of the Soviet state.

Stalin did little better managing Western European communists, despite the fact that they still regarded themselves as his loyal supporters. In May 1947, the French Communist Party voted no confidence in the government of Premier Paul Ramadier, only to have him expel their representatives from his cabinet. The Italians, with strong American encouragement, threw out their own communists later that month.[67] Andrei Zhdanov, who managed the Soviet Communist Party's relations with its foreign counterparts, sharply reprimanded the French comrades for acting without Moscow's authorization and therefore arousing concerns in the minds of "Soviet workers." He then passed on this communication to all other European communist parties.[68] The implication seemed to be that none of them should do anything without consulting Moscow first, a requirement that would obviously be difficult to meet for communists who had responsibilities within national governments and therefore some obligation to consider national interests.

The Americans' unexpected offer of Marshall Plan aid to the Soviet Union and Eastern Europe in June 1947, caused even greater difficulties for Stalin's management of empire—which is precisely what Kennan hoped for when he recommended making it.[69] In one of the stranger illusions arising from their ideology, Soviet leaders had always anticipated United States economic assistance in some form. Lenin himself expected American capitalists, ever in search of foreign markets, to invest eagerly in the newly formed USSR, despite its official antipathy toward them.[70] Stalin hoped for a massive American reconstruction loan after World War II, and even authorized Molotov early in 1945 to offer acceptance of such assistance in order to help the United States stave off the economic crisis that Marxist analysis showed must be approaching.[71] When the Marshall Plan was announced Stalin's first reaction was that the capitalists must be desperate. He concluded, therefore, that the Soviet Union and its East European allies should indeed participate in the plan, and quickly dispatched Molotov and a large delegation of economic experts to Paris to take part in the conference that was to determine the nature and extent of European needs.[72]

But then Stalin began to reconsider. His ambassador in Washington, Nikolai Novikov, warned that the American offer to the Soviet Union could not be sincere: "A careful analysis of the Marshall Plan shows that ultimately it comes down to forming a West European bloc as a tool of US policy. All the good wishes accompanying the plan are demagogic official propaganda serving as a smokescreen."[73] Soviet intelligence picked up reports—accurate enough—that American Under-Secretary of State William Clayton had been conspiring with British officials on using the Marshall Plan to reintegrate Germany into the West European economy and to deny further reparations shipments to the

Soviet Union.[74] This information, together with indications at Paris that the Americans would require a coordinated European response, caused Stalin to change his mind and order his own representatives to walk out. "The Soviet delegation saw those claims as a bid to interfere in the internal affairs of European countries," Molotov explained lamely, "thus making the economies of these countries dependent on US interests."[75]

Curiously, though, Stalin did not at first demand that the East Europeans follow the Soviet example. Instead he instructed their delegations to attend follow-up sessions of the Paris conference, but to "show . . . that the Anglo-French plan is unacceptable, prevent its unanimous approval and then . . . withdraw from the meeting, taking with them as many delegates of other countries as possible."[76] These orders stood for only three days, however, because Stalin then considered again: what if the East Europeans—especially the Czechs, whose communists did not yet completely control the government—chose not to follow the script and proceeded to accept Marshall Plan aid? Accordingly, a new message went out stating awkwardly that the Soviet Communist Party Central Committee "proposes refusing to participate in the meeting, that is, sending no delegations to it. Each country may give the reasons for its refusal as it sees fit."[77]

Unfortunately, the Czechs and the Poles, following the earlier instructions, had already announced their intention to attend. The Poles quickly changed their mind but the Czechs procrastinated, more because of confusion than determined resistance.[78] Stalin responded by peremptorily summoning their leaders to Moscow. He had been persuaded "on the basis of material reasons," he told them, that the Americans were using the Marshall Plan to consolidate a Western coalition hostile to the Soviet Union:

The Soviet government has therefore been surprised by your decision to accept this invitation. For us it is a matter of friendship. . . . If you go to Paris you shall demonstrate your will to cooperate in the action of isolating the Soviet Union. All the Slavonic states have refused, not even Albania feared to refuse, and therefore, we think you should reverse your decision.[79]

Stalin's intentions were now clear to all including himself: there would be no East European participation in the Marshall Plan, or in any other American scheme for the rehabilitation of Europe. "I went to Moscow as the Foreign Minister of an independent sovereign state," Czech Foreign Minister Jan Masaryk commented bitterly. "I returned as a lackey of the Soviet government."[80]

But the Kremlin boss too had shed some illusions. Marxist-Leninist analyses had long predicted, not just a postwar economic collapse in the West, but eventual conflict between the British and the Americans. In a September 1946 report from Washington which Molotov had carefully annotated, Ambassador Novikov had insisted that "the United States regards England as its greatest potential competitor." The Anglo-American relationship, "despite the temporary attainment of agreements on very important questions, [is] plagued with great internal contradictions and cannot be lasting."[81] By early 1947, Stalin was even offering the British a military alliance: as one report to Molotov put it, "Soviet diplomacy has in England practically unlimited possibilities."[82] What the Marshall Plan showed was how wrong these assessments were. Capitalists, it now appeared, could indeed reconcile their differences; they considered the Soviet Union a greater threat to all than each posed to the other; time was not on Moscow's side. Ideology again had led Stalin into romanticism and away from reality. Once he realized this—in Europe at least—he never quite recovered from the shock.

VI

The United States, in contrast, proved surprisingly adept at managing an empire. Having attained their authority through democratic processes, its leaders were experienced—as their counterparts in Moscow were not—in the arts of persuasion, negotiation and compromise. Applying domestic political insights to foreign policy could produce embarrassing results, as when President Truman likened Stalin to his old Kansas City political mentor, Tom Pendergast, or when Secretary of State James F. Byrnes compared the Russians to the US Senate: "You build a post office in their state, and they'll build a post office in our state."[83] But the habits of democracy had served the nation well during World War II: its strategists had assumed that their ideas would have to reflect the interests and capabilities of allies; it was also possible for allies to advance proposals of their own and have them taken seriously.[84] That same pattern of mutual accommodation persisted after the war, despite the fact that all sides acknowledged—as they had during most of the war itself—the disproportionate power the United States could ultimately bring to bear.

Americans so often deferred to the wishes of allies during the early Cold War that some historians have seen the Europeans—especially the British—as having managed *them*.[85] The new Labour government in London did encourage the Truman administration to toughen its policy toward the Soviet Union; Churchill—by then out of office—was only reinforcing these efforts with his March 1946 "Iron Curtain" speech. The British were ahead of the Americans in pressing for a consolidation of Western occupation zones in Germany, even if this jeopardized prospects for an overall settlement with the Russians. Foreign Secretary Ernest Bevin determined the timing of the February 1947 crisis over Greece and Turkey when he ended British military and economic assistance to those countries, leaving the United States little choice but to involve itself in the eastern Mediterranean and providing the occasion for the Truman Doctrine.[86] And it was the desperate economic plight of the West Europeans generally that persuaded newly appointed Secretary of State George C. Marshall, in June 1947, to announce the comprehensive program of American assistance that came to bear his name.

But one can easily make too much of this argument. Truman and his advisers were not babes in the woods. They knew what they were doing at each stage, and did it only because they were convinced their actions would advance American interests. They never left initiatives entirely up to the Europeans: they insisted on an integrated plan for economic recovery and quite forcefully reined in prospective recipients when it appeared that their requests would exceed what Congress would approve. "[I]n the end we would not *ask* them," Kennan noted, "we would just *tell* them, what they would get."[87] The Americans were flexible enough, though, to accept and build upon ideas that came from allies; they also frequently let allies determine the timing of actions taken. As a consequence, the British, French, and other West Europeans came to feel that they had a stake in what Washington was doing, despite the fact that it amounted to their own incorporation within an American sphere of influence.[88]

One might argue, to be sure, that European elites agreed to all of this for their own self-interested reasons; that the European "masses" were never consulted. It is worth remembering, however, that free elections ultimately ratified alignment with the United States in every country where that took place. The newly-formed Central Intelligence Agency, not always confident of such outcomes, did take it upon itself at times to manipulate democratic processes, most conspicuously in the Italian elections of April 1948.[89] But these covert efforts—together with clandestine CIA support for anti-communist labor unions and intellectual organizations—could hardly have succeeded had there not already existed in Europe a widespread predisposition to see the Americans as the lesser of two evils, and perhaps even as a force for good. "I am entirely convinced," the French political theorist Raymond Aron insisted, "that for an anti-Stalinist there is no escape from the acceptance of American leadership."[90] French peasants did not see it all that differently.

The habits of democracy were no less significant when it came to defeated adversaries. The Roosevelt administration had planned to treat Germany harshly after the war; and even after the President himself backed away from the punitive Morgenthau Plan in late 1944, its spirit lingered in the occupation directive for American forces, JCS 1067, which prohibited doing anything to advance economic rehabilitation beyond the minimum necessary to avoid disease or disorder.[91] The American design for a postwar world based on economic integration and political self-determination seemed not to apply, or so at first it appeared, to occupied Germany.

Uneasiness about this inconsistency soon developed, though; and in any event Americans far from Washington customarily maintained a certain irreverence toward orders emanating from it. General Clay concluded almost at once that his instructions were unworkable and that he would either get them changed, sabotage them, or ignore them. Here he followed the lead of his own troops who, having found prohibitions against fraternizing with the Germans to be ridiculous, quickly devised ways of circumventing them. Confronted with inappropriate directives in a difficult situation, the American occupiers—with a breezy audacity that seems remarkable in retrospect—fell back upon domestic instincts and set about transplanting democracy into the part of Germany they controlled.[92]

Soviet occupation authorities too, we now know, found themselves hampered by unclear directives ill-suited to the problems they faced; some of them managed to carve out a fair amount of autonomy, at times in defiance of Moscow's wishes.[93] But it was what was done with autonomy that made the difference. The Red Army, repeating its practices elsewhere in Eastern Europe, indulged in looting and physical assaults on so massive a scale that the full extent of it is only now becoming known: reparations extractions removed about a third of the Soviet zone's industrial capacity and Russian troops raped as many as *two million* German women in 1945 and 1946. As the historian Norman Naimark has emphasized,

women in the Eastern zone—both refugees from further east and inhabitants of the towns, villages, and cities of the Soviet zone—shared an experience for the most part unknown in the West, the ubiquitous threat and the reality of rape, over a prolonged period of time.[94]

Whereas the American occupation authorities at first forbade fraternization but quickly reversed that policy, their Soviet counterparts initially encouraged such contacts but eventually had to prohibit them altogether because of the hostility they generated.[95] Certainly the Russians did little to evolve practices or build institutions that promised Germans within their zone—apart from Communist Party functionaries—a stake in their success.

The United States could of course hold out the prospect of economic recovery and the Soviet Union could not: this certainly made the advantages of democracy more evident than they might otherwise have been. But democratization, under Clay's leadership, was well under way before there was any assurance that Germans would receive Marshall Plan aid or anything comparable. Authoritarianism, which was all Moscow would or could provide, was by far the less attractive alternative.[96] "Soviet officers bolshevized their zone," Naimark has concluded, "not because there was a plan to do so, but because that was the only way they knew to organize society. . . . By their own actions, the Soviet authorities created enemies out of potential friends."[97] Or, as General Clay recalled years afterwards: "We began to look like angels, not because we were angels, but we looked [like] that in comparison to what was going on in Eastern Europe."[98]

The Americans simply did not find it necessary, in building a sphere of influence, to impose unrepresentative governments or brutal treatment upon the peoples that fell within it. Where repressive regimes already existed, as in Greece, Turkey, and Spain, serious doubts arose in Washington as to whether the United States should be supporting them at all, however useful they might be in containing Soviet expansionism.[99] Nor, having constructed their empire, did Americans follow the ancient imperial practice of "divide and rule." Rather, they used economic leverage to overcome nationalist tendencies, thereby encouraging the Europeans' emergence as a "third force" whose obedience could not always be assumed. It was as if the Americans were projecting abroad a tradition they had long taken for granted at home: that civility made sense; that spontaneity, within a framework of minimal constraint, was the path to political and economic robustness; that to intimidate or to overmanage was to stifle. The contrast to Stalin's methods of imperial administration could hardly have been sharper.

VII

Stalin saw the need, after learning of the Marshall Plan, to improve his methods of imperial management. He therefore called a meeting of the Soviet and East European communist parties, as well as the French and the Italian communists, to be held in Poland in September 1947, ostensibly for the purpose of exchanging ideas on fraternal cooperation. Only after the delegations had assembled did he reveal his real objective, which was to organize a new coordinating agency for the international communist movement. Stalin had abolished the old Comintern as a wartime gesture of reassurance to the Soviet Union's allies in 1943, and the International Department of the Soviet Communist Party, headed by the veteran Comintern leader, the Bulgarian Georgii Dimitrov, had taken over its functions.[100] What had happened during the spring and summer of 1947 made it clear, though, that these arrangements provided insufficient coordination from Stalin's point of view.

Delegations arriving at Szklarska Poręba were greeted by a militant speech from Zhdanov, picturing the world as irrevocably divided into two hostile camps: "The frank expansionist program of the United States," he charged, was "highly reminiscent of the reckless program, which failed so ignominiously, of the fascist aggressors, who, as we know, also made a bid for world supremacy."[101] The attendees were then invited to consider—and after some reservations on the part of the Poles unanimously approved—a Soviet proposal for the creation of a "Cominform," its headquarters to be located in Belgrade, a pointed gesture in the light of Stalin's earlier concerns about independent tendencies among the Yugoslavs.[102] The French communist leader Jacques Duclos summed up the new procedures succinctly: "Paris and Rome will be able to submit their proposals, but they shall have to be content with the decisions to be adopted in Belgrade."[103]

Even with the Cominform in place, the momentary independence Czechoslovakia demonstrated must have continued to weigh on Stalin's mind. That country, more than any other in Eastern Europe, had sought to accommodate itself to Soviet hegemony. Embittered by how easily the British and French had betrayed Czech interests at the Munich conference in 1938, President Eduard Beneš welcomed the expansion of Soviet influence while reassuring Marxist-Leninists that they had nothing to fear from the democratic system the Czechs hoped to rebuild after the war. "If you play it well," he told Czech Communist Party leaders in Moscow in 1943, "you'll win."[104]

But Beneš meant "win" by democratic means. Although the Communists had indeed done well in the May 1946 parliamentary elections, their popularity began to drop sharply after Stalin forbade Czech participation in the Marshall Plan the following year. Convinced by intelligence reports that the West would not intervene, they therefore took advantage of a February 1948 government crisis to stage a *coup d'état*—presumably with Stalin's approval—that left them in complete control, with no further need to resort to the unpredictabilities of the ballot box.[105] This development came as no surprise in Washington: Kennan had predicted that the Soviet Union would sooner or later crack down on those East European states where communists did not fully dominate the government. Czechoslovakia had figured most prominently on that list.[106] But to an unprepared American and Western European public, the Prague takeover was the most appalling event yet in the emerging Cold War, occurring as it did in the country whose abandonment by the West only ten years earlier had led directly to World War II. There followed shortly thereafter the suicide, or murder, of Masaryk, son of the founder of the country and himself a symbol—now a martyr—to the fragility of Czech liberties.[107]

Because of its dramatic impact, the Czech coup had consequences Stalin could hardly have anticipated. It set off a momentary—and partially manufactured—war scare in Washington.[108] It removed the last Congressional objections to the Marshall Plan, resulting in the final approval of that initiative in April 1948. It accelerated plans by the Americans, the British, and the French to consolidate their occupation zones in Germany and to proceed toward the formation of an independent West German state. And it caused American officials to begin to consider, much more seriously than they had until this point, two ideas Bevin had begun to advance several months earlier: that economic assistance alone would not restore European self-confidence, and that the United States would have to take on direct military responsibilities for defending that portion of the Continent that remained outside Soviet control.[109]

Stalin then chose the late spring of 1948 to attempt a yet further consolidation of the Soviet empire, with even more disastrous results. Reacting to the proposed establishment of a separate West German state, as well as to growing evidence that the East German regime had failed to attract popular support, and to the introduction of a new currency in the American, British, and French sectors of Berlin over which the Russians would have no control, he ordered a progressively tightening blockade around that city, which lay within the Soviet zone. "Let's make a joint effort," he told the East German leaders in March. "Perhaps we can kick them out."[110] Initial indications were that the scheme was working. "Our control and restrictive measures have dealt a strong blow at the prestige of the Americans and British in Germany," Soviet occupation authorities reported the following month. The Germans believed that "the Anglo-Americans have retreated before the Russians," and that this testified to the latter's strength.[111] Suspend the new currency and the plans for a West German state, a self-confident Stalin told Western diplomats early in August, "and you shall no longer have any difficulties. That may be done even tomorrow. Think it over."[112]

But the Soviet leader's plans, by this time, had already begun to backfire. There was now a quite genuine war scare in the West, one that intensified pressures for an American–West European military alliance, accelerated planning for an independent West Germany, further diminished what little support the communists still had outside the Soviet zone, and significantly boosted President Truman's re-election prospects in a contest few at the time thought he could win.[113] Nor did the blockade turn out to be effective. "Clay's attempts to create 'an airlift' connecting Berlin with the western zones have proved futile," Soviet officials in that city prematurely reported to Moscow in April. "The Americans have admitted that the idea would be too expensive."[114] In fact, though, the United States and its allies astonished themselves as well as the Russians by improvising so successful a supply of Berlin by air that there was no need to make concessions. Stalin was left with the choice he had hoped to avoid—capitulation or war—and in May 1949, in one of the most humiliating of all setbacks for Soviet foreign policy, he selected the first alternative by lifting the blockade.[115]

The Berlin crisis demonstrated that Soviet expansionism in Europe had generated sufficient resistance from the United States and its allies to bring that process to a halt. Stalin had never been prepared to risk a military confrontation—at least not in the foreseeable future—and the West's response to the blockade, which included the deployment to British bases of apparently atomic-capable bombers, made it clear that further advances might indeed produce this result. The Soviet leadership, a Red Army general recalled many years later, had not been prepared to commit suicide over Berlin.[116]

There remained, though, the task of consolidating Soviet control over those territories where communists already ruled, and here too 1948 proved to be a turning point, because for the first time this process provoked open resistance. Despite appearances of solidarity, Soviet–Yugoslav relations had become increasingly strained following earlier disagreements over the Red Army's abuse of Yugoslav civilians, plans for a Balkan federation, and support for the Greek communists. The fiercely independent Yugoslavs were finding it difficult to defer to the Soviet Union, whose interests seemed increasingly at odds with those of international communism. Stalin himself alternated between cajoling and bullying their leaders, sometimes including them in lengthy late-night eating and drinking sessions at his dacha, at other times upbraiding them rudely for excessive ideological militance and insufficient attention to Moscow's wishes. Tensions came to a head early in 1948 when the Yugoslavs and the Albanians began considering the possibility of unification. Stalin let it be known that he would not object to Yugoslavia "swallowing" Albania, but this only aroused suspicions among the Yugoslavs, who remembered how the Soviet Union had "swallowed" the Baltic States in 1940 and feared that the precedent might someday apply to them. Their concerns grew when Stalin then reversed course and condemned Belgrade bitterly for sending troops into Albania without consulting Moscow.[117] By June of 1948, these disagreements had become public, and the communist world would never be the same again.

What had happened in Soviet–Yugoslav relations was, in one sense, only a continuation of the process by which Stalin came to recognize that East Europeans were not going to welcome the extension of Moscow's authority over them, while at the same time the East Europeans came to see just how coercive that authority was going to be. But the Yugoslavs alone had the capacity to resist: this communist government had not been installed by the Red Army and did not depend upon Soviet support to remain in power. Their experiences with Stalin had gradually transformed Tito and the other top Yugoslav communists from worshipful acolytes into schismatic heretics: the Soviet leader's personality proved no more "winning" for those who were in a position to make independent judgments than was the system he had created. The Soviet empire, it now appeared, would be able to maintain itself only by imposition; Tito's defection showed that whatever invitations might have been extended were likely to be withdrawn upon more intimate acquaintance.

Stalin responded to this insult in a wholly characteristic way: if he could not get at the Yugoslavs themselves, he would get at all other possible Yugoslav sympathizers elsewhere. There followed the East European purge trials, precise replicas of what Stalin had ordered within the Soviet Union a decade earlier when he detected heresy or the prospect of it.[118] By 1949–50, there were few overt Titoists left outside Yugoslavia. But there were also few people left—apart from the party and official bureaucracies who ran it—who believed that they had anything to gain from living within a Soviet sphere of influence: vast numbers of them now became closet Titoists, with results that would make themselves evident periodically over the years in places like East Berlin in 1953, Budapest and Warsaw in 1956, Prague in 1968, and everywhere all at once in 1989.

VIII

West Europeans were meanwhile convincing themselves that they had little to lose from living within an American sphere of influence. The idea of a European "third force" soon disappeared, not because Washington officials lost interest in it, but because the Europeans themselves rejected it.[119] The North Atlantic Treaty Organization, which came into existence in April 1949, had been a European initiative from the beginning: it was as explicit an invitation as has ever been extended from smaller powers to a great power to construct an empire and include them within it.[120] When Kennan, worried that NATO would divide Europe permanently, put forward a plan later that spring looking toward an eventual reunification and neutralization of Germany as a way of ending both the Soviet and American presence on the continent, British and French opposition quickly shot it down.[121] The self-confidence he and other American officials had set out to restore in Western Europe could now manifest itself, or so it appeared, only from within a framework of reassurance that only the United States could provide.

Since incorporation within the Soviet empire reassured no one, it is worth asking: why the difference? Why were allies of the United States willing to give up so much autonomy in order to enhance their own safety? How did the ideas of sovereignty and security, which historically have been difficult to separate, come to be so widely seen as divisible in this situation?

The answer would appear to be that despite a postwar polarization of authority quite at odds, in its stark bilateralism, from what wartime planners had expected, Americans managed to retain the multilateral conception of security they had developed during World War II. They were able to do this because Truman's foreign policy—like Roosevelt's military strategy—reflected the habits of domestic democratic politics. Negotiation, compromise, and consensus-building abroad came naturally to statesmen steeped in the uses of such practices at home: in this sense, the American political tradition served the country better than its realist critics—Kennan definitely among them—believed it did.[122]

Bargains of one kind or another were struck at every step along the way in constructing the American sphere of influence in Western Europe. The Truman administration extended a postwar loan to Great Britain to replace Lend-Lease, but only on the condition that the Labour government dismantle barriers to foreign trade and investment. When the effect proved to be disastrous for the British economy, the Americans moved quickly to relieve the strain by assuming responsibility for economic and military assistance to Greece and Turkey; but at the same time they took advantage of that situation, by way of the Truman Doctrine, to issue a far more sweeping call for containing Soviet expansionism than either Bevin or Attlee had expected. The United States then extended its offer of reconstruction aid to all of Europe under the Marshall Plan, but only on the condition that recipients submerge their old national rivalries and move toward economic and political integration, including Germany in this process.

The West Europeans, unlike the Soviet Union, agreed to this, but soon found a condition of their own to impose upon the Americans. This was the requirement of a formal military alliance with the United States, to which Washington acquiesced—but with the understanding that the British, the French, and their immediate neighbors would in turn agree to the formation of an independent West German state. Confronted with this unpalatable prospect, the French made the best of it by justifying NATO to themselves as an instrument of "double containment,"[123] directed against *both* the Soviet Union and the Germans. This made it possible for them to shift from an emphasis on punishing Germany to one directed toward economic cooperation with that country in the form of the Schuman Plan to create a European Coal and Steel Community, an initiative that surprised but gratified the Americans, who had been seeking the resolution of Franco–German rivalries by pushing integration in the first place.[124]

Meanwhile, a less obvious series of social compromises was going on within Western Europe. The Americans worried about the "tilt" toward the Left that had taken place as a result of the war; at the same time, though, they were cautious about pressuring the Europeans to move toward more centrist politics. A few officials in Washington understood that what they called the "non-communist Left" could itself become a center of resistance against the Soviet Union;[125] there was also a more widespread fear that excessively overt pressure might backfire. The West Europeans, though, also made compromises. The United States did not *have* to pressure the French and the Italians very much to move toward the center because the leftward "tilt" in those countries had never extended so far as a rejection of capitalism in the first place. Their people could easily see that the American assistance and protection they wanted would be more likely if they themselves took the initiative in building centrist political coalitions.[126]

What is significant, then, is not simply that the West Europeans invited the United States to construct a sphere of influence and include them within it; it is also that the Americans encouraged the Europeans to share the responsibility for determining how it would function, and that the Europeans were eager to do this. Washington officials were themselves often genuinely uncertain about what to do, and that provides part of the explanation for this pattern of mutual accommodation. But it also developed because the American vision of national security had become international in character: Franklin D. Roosevelt's most important foreign policy legacy may well have been to convince the nation that its security depended upon that of others elsewhere, not simply on whatever measures it might take on its own. Habits of compromise growing out of domestic politics made it easier than one might have thought for a formerly isolationist nation to adapt itself to this new situation; and those compromises, in turn, allowed West Europeans to define their interests in such a way as to find *common* ground with those of the United States.

IX

It would become fashionable to argue, in the wake of American military intervention in Vietnam, the Soviet invasions of Czechoslovakia and Afghanistan, and growing fears of nuclear confrontation that developed during the early 1980s, that there were no significant differences in the spheres of influence Washington and Moscow had constructed in Europe after World War II: these had been, it was claimed, "morally equivalent," denying autonomy quite impartially to all who lived under them.[127] Students of history must make their own judgments about morality, but even a cursory examination of the historical record will show that these imperial structures could hardly have been more different in their origins, their composition, their tolerance of diversity, and as it turned out their durability. It is important to specify just what these differences were.

First, and most important, the Soviet empire reflected the priorities and the practices of a single individual—a latter-day tsar, in every sense of the word. Just

as it would have been impossible to separate the Soviet Union's internal structure from the influence of the man who ran it, so too the Soviet sphere of influence in Eastern Europe took on the characteristics of Stalin himself. The process
was not immediate: Stalin did allow a certain amount of spontaneity in the
political, economic, and intellectual life of that region for a time after the war,
just as he had done inside the Soviet Union itself after he had consolidated his
position as Lenin's successor in 1929. But when confronted with even the
prospect of dissent, to say nothing of challenges to his authority, Stalin's
instinct was to smother spontaneity with a thoroughness unprecedented in the
modern age. This is what the purges had accomplished inside the USSR during
the mid-1930s, and Eastern Europe underwent a similar process after 1947.
There was thus a direct linkage from Stalin's earliest thinking on the nationalities question prior to the Bolshevik Revolution through to his management of
empire after World War II: the right of self-determination was fine as long as no
one sought to practice it.

The American empire was very different: one would have expected this from
a country with no tradition of authoritarian leadership whose constitutional
structure had long ago enshrined the practices of negotiation, compromise, and
the balancing of interests. What is striking about the sphere of influence the
United States established in Europe is that its existence and fundamental design
reflected as frequently pressures that came *from those incorporated within it* as
from the Americans themselves. Washington officials were not at all convinced,
at the end of World War II, that their interests would require protecting half the
European continent: instead they looked toward a revival of a balance among
the Europeans themselves to provide postwar geopolitical stability. Even the
Marshall Plan, an unprecedented extension of American assistance, had been
conceived with this "third force" principle in mind. It was the Europeans themselves who demanded more: who insisted that their security required a military
shield as well as an economic jump-start.

One empire arose, therefore, by invitation, the other by imposition. *Europeans*
made this distinction, very much as they had done during the war when they
welcomed armies liberating them from the west but feared those that came
from the east. They did so because they saw clearly at the time—even if a subsequent generation would not always see—how different American and Soviet
empires were likely to be. It is true that the *extent* of the American empire
quickly exceeded that of its Soviet counterpart, but this was because *resistance*
to expanding American influence was never as great.[128] The American empire
may well have become larger, paradoxically, because the American *appetite* for
empire was less that of the USSR. The United States had shown, throughout
most of its history, that it could survive and even prosper without extending its
domination as far as the eye could see. The logic of Lenin's ideological internationalism, as modified by Stalin's Great Russian nationalism and personal paranoia, was that the Soviet Union could not.

The early Cold War in Europe, therefore, cannot be understood by looking at
the policies of either the United States or the Soviet Union in isolation. What

evolved on the continent was an interactive system in which the actions of each side affected not only the other but also the Europeans; their responses, in turn, shaped further decisions in Washington and Moscow. It quickly became clear—largely because of differences in the domestic institutions of each superpower—that an American empire would accommodate far greater diversity than would one run by the Soviet Union: as a consequence most Europeans accepted and even invited American hegemony, fearing deeply what that of the Russians might entail.

Two paths diverged at the end of World War II. And that, to paraphrase an American poet, really did make all the difference.

THREE

Cold War Empires : Asia

If we imagine our country to be a family house, it is very dirty
inside. Firewood, trash, dust, fleas, bedbugs, and lice are everywhere. After the liberation, we have to clean our house carefully. . . .
[W]e need to get rid of all those dirty things and put our house in
order. Only when the house is cleaned up . . . will we invite our
guests to come in. True friends may come in earlier; they will also
help us in the cleaning.

Mao Zedong to Anastas Mikoyan, Xibaipo, February 1949[1]

I do not like to be flattered by others. But I am often flattered. This
annoys me. What I have said today, that is, that the Chinese
Marxists have become mature, and that the Soviets and the
Europeans should learn from you, is not flattering you. I am telling
the truth.

Josef Stalin to Liu Shaoqi, Moscow, July 1949[2]

DESPITE the unchallenged authority with which the United States and the
Soviet Union emerged from World War II, despite the precision with which
they demarcated spheres of influence, despite the universalist ideologies with
which they justified that process, the Cold War through the end of 1948 remained
primarily a European conflict. There was some sense in Moscow and Washington
that what was happening elsewhere might affect Soviet and American interests,
but little clarity as to how or even when this might happen. The imperial pres-
ences both sides had established in Europe functioned very differently, but they
had one thing in common: their Eurocentrism. As a consequence, the Cold War's
sudden expansion into Asia in 1949–50 caught everyone by surprise.

World War II left not just a single power vacuum in that part of the world, as
in Europe, but several. Japan's defeat destroyed an empire that had dominated
northeast Asia for decades. In China, the war had weakened the ruling
Nationalist government and strengthened its long-time Communist rivals,
preparing the way for renewed and intensified civil conflict. Elsewhere Japanese
victories undermined the authority of European colonial regimes, encouraging
independence movements on the Indian subcontinent and in southeast Asia.
How these developments would intersect with the emerging Soviet–American
Cold War, though, was not immediately apparent.

Each superpower had staked out certain positions in East Asia by the time the war ended, largely as a result of the *way* in which it had ended. The Americans, to whom it had fallen to do most of the fighting in the Pacific, made it clear that they and they alone would determine Japan's future. Unlike the situation in Germany, there would be no joint occupation of this defeated adversary, and only pro forma consultation with other wartime allies as to what occupation policies were to be. The Soviet Union, which declared war only days before Japan surrendered, insisted on retaining the *quid pro quo* Roosevelt had promised Stalin at the Yalta conference: port and railroad rights in Manchuria, together with the southern half of Sakhalin and all of the Kurile Islands. Soviet and American forces each occupied half of Korea, an improvisation made necessary by the unexpectedly abrupt Japanese military collapse. Officials in Washington and Moscow regarded each other's Asian intentions warily, it is true, but chiefly because of disagreements that had already developed over the future of Europe.

Prior to 1949, the Cold War had barely touched the Asian mainland. Despite the Chinese Communists' growing strength during the final years of World War II, the Soviet Union agreed at its end to recognize and cooperate with Chiang Kai-shek's Nationalist government: as Stalin himself would later admit, he failed to see that China was on the verge of the next great Marxist revolution. At the same time the Americans, frustrated by the Nationalists' military ineptitude, entrenched corruption, and declining popular support, were pressing them to include Mao Zedong's Communists in a new coalition government. When that failed to happen, the Truman administration began reconciling itself, with surprising equanimity, to something the Russians had hardly yet begun to think about: the prospect of a communist-controlled China.

Much as had been the case with the Europeans, it was left to Asians—and especially to the Chinese—to harden Cold War alignments through choices they themselves made. But whereas in Europe the pattern had been one of the Soviet Union imposing its authority and the United States being invited to reciprocate, in China the situation was reversed. The Chinese people chose to transfer their allegiance from the Nationalists to the Communists, hence Mao's great victory in 1949. Once in power his government, both for ideological reasons and because it feared an American attack, sought China's incorporation within a Soviet sphere of influence. By 1950, or so it seemed, a fundamental shift in the balance of power had taken place: nearly overnight the communist world appeared almost to have doubled its extent.

At the same time, and with very little notice beyond their borders, Koreans on both sides of the 38th parallel were setting in motion a series of events that would astonish everyone, themselves included, by starting the first major hot war of the Cold War era. That bloody three-year struggle would not only expand and intensify the contest in Asia; it would also reflect back upon Europe and ultimately upon the rest of the world as well.

I

The most significant difference between the situations in Asia and in Europe at the end of World War II was that the Soviet Union had played no significant role in defeating Japan. Relations between Moscow and Tokyo had been tense throughout the 1930s, and there had even been fighting along the border of Soviet-occupied Mongolia and Japanese-occupied Manchuria in 1939.[3] But once Germany invaded the Soviet Union in 1941, the Russians had their hands full, and neither the Americans nor the British were prepared to press them to enter the Pacific war.

That situation soon changed. The Americans had hoped to rely upon Chiang Kai-shek's immense manpower reserves to wear down Japanese forces before any invasion of Japan itself, much as the Red Army had weakened the *Wehrmacht* prior to the D-Day landings in Normandy. But the Nationalists' military performance had been so disappointing that by 1944 little more could be expected from them.[4] Persuading the Soviet Union to enter the Pacific war was the next best alternative, and it was in return for Stalin's promise to do so, following Germany's surrender, that Roosevelt agreed, at Yalta, to restore the Tsar's old sphere of influence in northeast Asia as it had been before Japan defeated Russia in 1905. Churchill resisted this arrangement, and the Chinese Nationalists, who still held sovereignty over Manchuria, were not even consulted. But most historians have concluded that Roosevelt granted Stalin nothing he could not have taken in any event.[5] And by the summer of 1945 Chiang had largely reconciled himself to these concessions, since in return Stalin was offering what seemed even more valuable: recognition of Nationalist authority and—by implication at least—a promise not to try to help the Chinese Communists seize power.[6]

Military requirements shifted again shortly after Roosevelt's death when the United States successfully tested its first atomic bomb. It quickly became clear to the few who knew this secret that Stalin's assistance in defeating Japan would not be needed after all. The Potsdam Conference, held during the last half of July 1945, saw a distinct cooling in Anglo-American enthusiasm for Soviet entry into the Pacific war. When that event finally took place on 8 August, two days after the destruction of Hiroshima, it came across as an undignified scramble on Stalin's part to salvage an unexpectedly unpromising situation. Such appearances did not deter Molotov from suggesting that the American supreme commander in Japan, General Douglas MacArthur, might like to share his administrative burdens with a Soviet marshal; nor did they discourage Stalin himself from requesting the entire island of Hokkaido as a Soviet occupation zone. The Russians could do little more than sulk, though, when the Americans—none too delicately—rejected these proposals.[7]

The unilateral American occupation of Japan contrasted strikingly, therefore, with the multilateral occupation to which Germany was subjected. Growing Soviet–American antagonism contributed to this outcome: the last thing the

Truman administration wanted in Japan was a replay of what it had already encountered in dealing with the Soviet Union in Europe. Stalin's unilateralism, in this sense, had already begun to exact a price. But even if things had gone smoothly in Europe, there is little reason to think that the Americans would have run the Japanese occupation much differently. The United States, after all, had played an even more decisive role in defeating Japan than the Soviet Union had in vanquishing Germany;[8] it had also installed in Tokyo one of the least consultative leaders in modern history. MacArthur paid little greater attention to the views of his British, Australian, and Chinese allies than he did to those of the Soviet representatives attached to his command. Washington officials deferred to him almost as completely as did the defeated—and now thoroughly intimidated—Japanese. It was no more in MacArthur's character to think multilaterally than it was in that of Stalin himself.

If MacArthur's methods were authoritarian, though, his results were remarkably democratic. He presided over Japan's transformation into a liberal, capitalist, and even pacifist society: the man who had driven unarmed veterans out of his own capital after the 1932 Bonus Army march now relished the role of radical social reformer. MacArthur would never have undertaken such sweeping measures, it has been suggested, had he not combined unlimited power and unprecedented arrogance with an abiding ignorance of the country for which he was responsible.[9] But where did MacArthur's democratic instincts come from? Would the Russians, if allowed to shape Japanese occupation policies, have produced a similar outcome? Did they in Germany, where they had such authority?

The victors, Stalin had accurately predicted, would impose their social systems on the territories they occupied: "it cannot be otherwise."[10] It is an indication of how deeply democratic values pervaded American culture that even an authoritarian like MacArthur could make transplanting them a major priority. There is no way to prove, had he handled things differently, that Japan would not still have emerged as an economic superpower, capable by the 1980s of challenging the Americans and demoralizing the Russians. Without MacArthur, though, it is much less likely that it would have done so as a democracy.[11] Indeed, the general so preoccupied himself with democratization that he neglected the Soviet–American rivalry preoccupying his superiors in Washington. His policies would remain insulated from theirs until well after the strategy of containment had begun to take shape.[12]

The Cold War more directly influenced developments in Korea, a former Japanese colony that did wind up under joint Soviet–American occupation. American war plans had not called for a landing on the Korean peninsula, but when Japan surrendered and an invasion became unnecessary, Truman authorized the diversion of troops to Korea to prevent the Red Army from completely controlling it. Developments in Europe influenced this decision much as they did the simultaneous one to deny a Soviet occupation zone in Japan. Nonetheless, Stalin seems not to have regarded the American deployment as a hostile gesture, and he accepted without protest Washington's suggestion of a hastily improvised demarcation line at the 38th parallel.[13] That frontier, in time, would become every bit as militarized as the one dividing Germany. For the first five years of the postwar era, though, Korea would remain a peripheral concern for both the United States and the Soviet Union.[14]

The emerging superpower contest indirectly affected one other power vacuum the Pacific war had left behind—the collapse of European colonial authority in south and southeast Asia. The United States had long cultivated, and congratulated itself upon, its anti-colonial tradition. Even the Philippines, whose seizure from Spain in 1898 had violated that principle, could now be cited in defense of it because Washington was going ahead with its promise to grant the Filipinos independence in 1946. Roosevelt had made no secret of his own hostility toward the British, French, and Dutch empires, but as one historian has commented, he "was anticolonial in everything he said and in little that he did."[15] It is unlikely, had FDR lived, that he would have tried to prevent allies from reasserting the authority they had lost at the hands of the Japanese, even though he might well have pushed them to begin preparing their colonies for eventual self-government. Order and stability would have been his first priority, with national liberation a more distant objective.

Truman's policy seemed similarly ambivalent at first glance, but Cold War logic was beginning to shape it. He continued Roosevelt's pressure on the British to quit India, seeing this as a way to relieve the military and economic burdens of an overstretched ally while preventing any possible communist appropriation of nationalist movements on the subcontinent.[16] He leaned even harder on the reluctant Dutch to grant independence to Indonesia, where there was no real prospect that communists might replace them.[17] But in French Indochina a communist, Ho Chi Minh, led the nationalist resistance, and Washington's enthusiasm for self-determination quickly evaporated. When Ho unilaterally declared Vietnamese independence in September 1945—pointedly quoting from the American Declaration of Independence as he did so—he received no encouragement at all from the country whose example he was emulating.[18] The Truman administration committed itself to restoring the pre-war position of the French in that part of the world, whatever text Ho had chosen to cite in seeking to eject them. One curious consequence was that American officials would find themselves, over the next several years, worrying more about Ho's Moscow connections than they did about those of Mao Zedong.[19]

II

The United States favored the Chinese Nationalists over the Chinese Communists during World War II, but this is hardly astonishing. The Nationalists were, after all, the internationally recognized government of China—even the Soviet Union acknowledged their legitimacy—and the Communists seemed little more than an obscure group of revolutionaries who engaged in long marches, lived in caves, and lectured one another on their own peculiar understanding of Marxism-Leninism. Washington did not begin to take them seriously until 1944, when it became apparent that their military assistance—like that of the Russians—might make up for the Nationalists' incompetence in fighting the Japanese. Even so, the relationship was a distant one, partly because of the continuing United States commitment to Chiang Kai-shek, but partly also because the Americans were already worrying that Moscow's influence might spread throughout China if Mao and his followers should ever win the civil war there. One reason Washington supported a strengthening of ties between Stalin and Chiang in 1945, paradoxically, was the hope the Soviet leader would use his influence to restrain Mao Zedong.[20]

Such thinking was not as wishful as it would later seem. To see why, it is worth tracing the evolution of Stalin's views on revolutionary prospects in China. There was no industrialized proletariat in that country: if revolution required mobilizing such a class, as Marxist theory suggested, it would never happen. But if the revolution expanded to accommodate peasants and bourgeoisie, it risked losing its Marxist character. Lenin had been willing to accept that possibility, ordering communists to be "particularly attentive to national feelings, anachronistic as these were, in countries and among peoples that have long been enslaved," and to ally themselves, but not amalgamate with, nationalist movements.[21]

That kind of balancing act could be dangerous, however, as Stalin discovered in 1927. The fledgling Chinese Communist Party, following orders from Moscow, had obediently aligned itself with the Chinese Nationalists under Sun Yat-sen and his successor, Chiang Kai-shek, in their efforts to unify that country. The Communists were then to supplant the Nationalists: as Stalin put it, "[t]hey have to be utilized to the end, squeezed out like a lemon, and then thrown away." As it happened, though, the Nationalists turned on the Communists, not only squeezing but almost annihilating them. Stalin rebounded quickly, ordering the Chinese Communists to defend themselves and moving against his own domestic critics—chief among them Trotsky—who had criticized his handling of the situation.[22] The experience cooled Stalin's enthusiasm for foreign revolutions linked to nationalism; it may also account for his pessimism about Mao's prospects in 1945.

The Kremlin boss liked to dismiss the Chinese Communists, in conversations with foreigners, as "margarine Marxists."[23] What he meant by this, though, remains unclear. As the Yugoslavs could have testified, Stalin considered all communists he could not control as having synthetic characteristics: his idea of a real revolution was that it should *not* be spontaneous, but rather instigated and directed from Moscow.[24] Chinese sources suggest that contrary to what Western scholars have long assumed, Mao came close to meeting that requirement. Contacts between the Comintern and the Chinese Communists were close throughout the 1930s and early 1940s, and it now appears that the latter took few initiatives, either in the diplomatic or military arena, that did not have Stalin's approval. Nor had Stalin written off the prospects for an *eventual*

Chinese Communist victory over the Nationalists. We know that he transferred captured Japanese weaponry to Mao's forces in Manchuria at the end of the war, and he quietly facilitated the consolidation of their positions there as the Red Army withdrew.[25]

Stalin nevertheless had several reasons for preferring to deal with Chiang Kai-shek. He was eager to avoid conflicts with the United States in East Asia, perhaps because American military capabilities there were more impressive than in eastern and central Europe. He saw the Nationalists as in a better position than the Communists to deliver the territorial concessions Roosevelt had promised at Yalta. He may even have anticipated the possibility of using a cooperative Nationalist China as a buffer against an American power base centered in Japan.[26] "You Chinese should be aware of this," Stalin told Chiang's son at the end of 1945: "[T]he Americans think they can use China as an instrument to satisfy their own interests, [and] when they do not need you anymore you are certain to be sacrificed."[27] It was for these reasons, then, that the Soviet leader encouraged Mao Zedong, once again, to cooperate with Chiang Kai-shek. Although disappointed, Mao dutifully obeyed.[28]

What is striking about Soviet and American policies regarding postwar China, therefore, is the extent to which they initially—if inadvertently—coincided. Both Washington and Moscow assumed that the Nationalists would reassert control over China in the wake of the Japanese surrender, and both sought to persuade the Chinese Communists to accept this outcome. Neither understood that the Communists and the Nationalists were not prepared to cooperate,[29] neither foresaw that the Communists would prove so much more successful than the Nationalists in winning support among the Chinese people. The significance of these surprises would only slowly dawn, first in Washington and then in Moscow, but even then only through perceptual lenses borrowed from the Cold War in Europe.

III

As a long series of examples ranging from Korea in the late 1940s to Bosnia in the early 1990s suggests, it is difficult for those outside a particular country, however powerful, to prevent those on the inside from trying to kill one another if they choose to do so. The problem is all the greater if the country is as large and as impervious to external influences as China has always been. The Nationalists and the Communists had seen World War II, not as a global conflict at all, but rather as a distraction from their own civil war that had been going on since the late 1920s. Each hoped that the struggle against Japan would enhance its own position at the expense of the other, and when the Japanese surrendered both moved quickly—with little regard for their allies' advice—to test each other's strength. This competition took the form, initially, of a race to see who could control northeastern China, especially Manchuria. At the end of

1945 the Chinese Communists—to the embarrassment of both Washington and Moscow—looked likely to win it.

The Truman administration at this point made two important decisions, each calculated to assist the Chinese Nationalists. First, it authorized the use of American air and naval forces to transport Chiang's troops from southern to northeastern China in an unacknowledged effort to forestall the Communists' advance there. Second, President Truman himself ordered General George C. Marshall to go to China to negotiate a political settlement between the Nationalists and the Communists. Justified at the time as support for a wartime ally, these decisions were also intended to minimize Soviet influence. The fear in Washington was that the Chinese Communists *might* be operating on orders from Moscow; the hope was that rushing Nationalist troops into Manchuria and incorporating the Chinese Communists into a Nationalist-led coalition government would stabilize the situation in such a way that the Soviet Union could not exploit it. Marshall's orders were categorical: he was to explore all opportunities for a settlement, except that under no circumstances was he to agree to any arrangement that might leave China under Moscow's control.[30]

By 1947 it had become clear that the Marshall mission had failed. Whether out of exasperation or rationalization, the Americans responded by taking a more relaxed view of the Chinese Communists and Mao Zedong. Whatever their public rhetoric, State Department officials had never regarded international communism as wholly monolithic: they understood all along that the Soviet Union was going to have difficulty controlling communism beyond its borders.[31] The Marshall Plan had been designed to exploit that prospect, and Tito's defection from the communist bloc would soon confirm its reality.[32] The possibility of an anti-Soviet variety of communism, therefore, seemed real enough in China, where Mao's movement owed little to Moscow but a great deal to a nationalist tradition contemptuous of foreign influences whatever their source. Truman and his advisers continued to worry, to be sure, that Stalin might use Chinese communism to his advantage; nor did they ever go so far as to welcome a communist victory in China. But such an outcome did not horrify them either. The fact that Marshall sought so persistently to *include* the Chinese Communists within a Nationalist-led coalition—precisely the kind of settlement he was opposing in Europe at the time—suggests that he had in mind the possibility of dealing in some way with Mao and his followers.

Chiang Kai-shek's supporters in the Congress and the media did not share this view, of course, and their pressure forced the administration to continue military and economic assistance to Chinese Nationalists, not least as a condition for supporting the Marshall Plan in Europe. But State Department strategists—Kennan chiefly among them—had quietly concluded that a communist China would not upset the overall balance of world power. Japan, the most important industrial-military center in East Asia, was under firm American control; meanwhile MacArthur, under pressure from Washington, had begun to shift his policies from an emphasis on punishing war criminals and reforming society to one that stressed rapid economic recovery. The idea here was to include Japan—like another defeated enemy, West Germany—within a chain of defensible strongpoints capable of containing Soviet expansionism. Whatever the China Lobby thought, the Truman administration had come to see China as more likely to be a swamp than a strongpoint for whoever controlled it.[33] Marshall, who had reason to know, warned the Senate Foreign Relations Committee early in 1948: "we cannot afford, economically or militarily, to take over the continued failures of the present Chinese Government to the dissipation of our strength in more vital regions."[34]

There followed a discreet but concerted effort to adapt European policies to the situation in East Asia. The United States would seek economic recovery and the geopolitical stability it seemed likely to bring, but only where it could control that process and count on quick results: hence the emphasis on rehabilitating Japan, together with securing whatever markets and raw materials it might need from Southeast Asia. Beyond this "great crescent," as Marshall's successor Dean Acheson referred to it, Washington would search for an "Asian Tito," and Mao Zedong might well be a plausible candidate. "The very basic objectives of Moscow are hostile to the very basic objectives of China," Acheson assured senators in an off-the-record comment early in 1950, and the Truman administration never wholly abandoned this view, even after the Korean War began.[35]

Confusion did exist, to be sure, as to whether the objective was to wean Mao and his followers away from Moscow, on the one hand, or to encourage the Chinese people to overthrow the Communists by portraying them as puppets of Moscow, on the other.[36] But as late as May 1951, well after the Chinese had intervened in Korea, the National Security Council could still list as the first objective of American policy in Asia the goal of "detach[ing] China as an effective ally of the USSR" by "stimulat[ing] differences between the Peiping and Moscow regimes" and by "creat[ing] cleavages within the Peiping regime itself by every possible means."[37] When Assistant Secretary of State Dean Rusk publicly condemned the People's Republic of China that same month as "a colonial Russian government—a Slavic Manchukuo in a larger scale," he was following precisely this strategy.[38]

IV

The conventional wisdom has been that the "wedge" strategy failed because the Truman administration failed to clarify its objectives, and because domestic politics—particularly the China Lobby's influence and the subsequent rise of McCarthyism—impeded its implementation. These explanations still make sense. Whatever the intentions that lay behind them, efforts to purge suspected subversives from government and other spheres of public life revealed that even Americans were not immune from at least a diluted form of Stalinist paranoia. The comparison is hardly exact: neither mass imprisonment nor mass murder resulted from such practices, and Truman himself courageously resisted many of them. But they did ruin lives and they certainly constrained policies; indeed given what was going on at home at the time, it is remarkable that the President and his administration were able to leave *any* possibility open for dealing with communists abroad.[39]

But these explanations focus exclusively on American perspectives: they fail to take into account how Mao Zedong himself assessed the feasibility—and the desirability—of cooperation with the United States. Recently released Chinese sources suggest strongly that, even with clearer purposes and a freer hand, the administration's attempts to lure the Chinese Communists away from the Soviet Union would not have succeeded. If Mao ever hoped for cooperation with the Americans, those expectations appear to have ended with the first phase of the Marshall mission early in 1946.[40] From then on he seems to have convinced himself that the United States was the chief adversary of the Chinese Communist revolution, and that he could ensure the success of that enterprise only by resisting the Americans, even if that meant inviting another "barbarian"—in this instance, the Soviet Union—to expand its influence in East Asia.[41] There were several reasons for this attitude on Mao's part.

First and foremost was ideology. The Chinese communist leader really did regard himself as a Marxist, even if he knew relatively little about Marxism itself and tended to look for guidance more to ancient Chinese manuals of statecraft.[42] "Only heroes could read *Das Kapital*," Molotov later acknowledged, with uncharacteristic sympathy.[43] The Soviet Union's achievement in industrializing itself had impressed Mao, and he was not inclined to worry excessively about its human costs. Despite the bad advice he had received from Stalin over the years—most recently when the Soviet leader had cautioned the Chinese Communists against crossing the Yangtze in their push for final victory against the Nationalists[44]—he saw in the Soviet system techniques which, adapted to Chinese conditions, could bring his country out of the decline into which it had fallen.[45] The Marxist-Leninist concept of "democratic centralism," moreover, provided a new and sophisticated justification for an old Chinese practice: the authoritarian rule of a single unchallengeable leader.[46] "No matter what divergences had existed between the CCP and the Soviet Union," a Chinese historian has concluded, "they were, in the final analysis, comrades fighting for the same cause and same ideals."[47]

Second, Mao felt rejected, and in some ways betrayed, by the United States. He had welcomed his first contacts with American military and diplomatic representatives during the war, and he cultivated close connections with a few individual Americans like the journalists Edgar Snow and Anna Louise Strong. But Mao tended to interpret American policy in crude ideological terms.[48] He resented Washington's continued support for Chiang Kai-shek. He distrusted—for good reason—the neutrality of Marshall's mediation efforts, especially when they coincided with American assistance in moving Chiang's troops into Manchuria. "It was the first time for us to deal with the U.S. imperialists," Mao later recalled. "We didn't have much experience. As a result we were taken in. With this experience, we won't be cheated again."[49]

There was a third and even more important reason why Mao was willing to invite in Soviet influence, and it is only recently that Chinese documents have revealed it. By the time the Communists had driven the Nationalists from the mainland and had begun to consolidate their own power—a process that went much faster than they themselves had anticipated—Mao had come to expect nothing less than American intervention inside China itself. He warned the Russians early in 1949 that the Americans were planning a military alliance with the Japanese and the Chinese Nationalists, that they would land some three million troops in northeast China, and that they would even launch nuclear attacks against targets in Manchuria, the Soviet Far East, and Siberia.[50] Since such an enterprise was about as far from what the Truman administration was actually contemplating as one can imagine, it is worth looking more carefully at how Mao got this peculiar idea into his head.

To begin with, he was Chinese, which is to say that he did not regard his country as occupying a marginal position in the universe.[51] The idea that China could be a peripheral and not a vital concern for anyone was difficult for him to grasp. And if China was important, as everything in Chinese culture and history suggested it must be, then it followed that the United States—the most powerful nation in the world—would never allow its puppet Chiang Kai-shek to be thrown out without doing everything possible to save him. Mao remembered the history of earlier American interventions in China, including not just the Boxer Rebellion of 1900 but also the Taiping uprising of 1850–64 which an obscure American adventurer, Frederick Townsend Ward, had helped to put down. He knew that the United States and its allies had intervened in Russia in 1918 in an effort to crush the Bolshevik revolution.[52] Since the Chinese revolution was, from Mao's point of view, the most significant development to have taken place since that time, it would be almost an insult if the Americans *did not* in some way again intervene. "[B]y seizing China, the United States would possess all of Asia," he warned in 1949. "With its Asian front consolidated, U.S. imperialism could concentrate its forces on attacking Europe."[53]

It was also the case that Mao had little understanding of how the American government worked; instead he simply projected his Marxist model of democratic centralism, as filtered through the tradition of Chinese authoritarianism, onto the American scene. This meant that he viewed all pronouncements by prominent Americans—whether generals in Tokyo, or right-wing political hacks on the floor of the Congress, or perfervid editorials in the China Lobby press—as reflecting the views of the current emperor in Washington, who happened to be that improbable Missouri mandarin Harry Truman. Mao had no way of distinguishing official policy from irresponsible rhetoric, of which there was plenty in Washington in those days. Had Chinese intelligence capabilities been better he might have avoided such oversimplifications, but these were largely limited at the time to reliance on the Soviet news agency TASS, to occasional reports from sympathetic Chinese-Americans, and to whatever American newspapers could be obtained in Warsaw or Hong Kong.[54]

Finally, we know that Stalin repeatedly sought to plant the possibility of

American intervention in Mao's mind. These warnings may have been deliberate exaggerations, intended to restrain the Chinese Communists from moving too quickly in driving out the Nationalists. But they may also have reflected genuine concern on Stalin's part: there is independent evidence documenting his fear that a war might break out with the United States for which the Soviet Union would be unprepared.[55] He made it clear early in 1949 that if the crossing of the Yangtze did provoke an American response, the USSR would not be able to come to China's assistance. Stalin also passed along to the Chinese Communists a Nationalist request that *he* mediate the Chinese civil war; and he sent Anastas Mikoyan secretly to meet with Mao—the first high Soviet official to make such a trip—to warn that a conflict with the Americans might break out.[56]

Mao ordered the crossing of the Yangtze anyway in April 1949, and his armies occupied Shanghai the following month. Neither event produced an American invasion, but Mao still regarded the prospect as serious and undertook several measures to deter it. He sought to instill self-confidence with public pronouncements stressing the difficulty any invader would have in occupying China, the extent to which Chinese numerical superiority would counter whatever technological advantages the Americans might be able to bring to bear, and the moral benefits to be derived from fighting in a "just war."[57] He reinforced military capabilities along the China coast, where he thought such an invasion likely to come.[58] And at the end of June 1949, he announced his famous "lean to one side" doctrine with respect to the Soviet Union, the first public confirmation that the still-to-be-proclaimed Peoples' Republic would seek to align itself with the USSR.

Because this event occurred just after the Truman administration had instructed Ambassador John Leighton Stuart to cut off informal discussions with the Chinese Communists, some Western historians have concluded that Washington in effect *pushed* Mao into the arms of the Russians, thereby missing an opportunity to build an amicable relationship a year before the Korean War broke out.[59] Chinese historians doubt this argument. From the sources available to them, it appears that Mao had long since written off any serious possibility of cooperation with the United States. He was prepared to tolerate occasional contacts with the Americans, but more for the purpose of attempting to discern when and where the attack he expected was likely to come than from any desire for friendly relations.[60]

Sensing that the United States was applying a "wedge" strategy, Mao went out of his way to assure Stalin that he was not about to become an "Asian Tito." The Chinese Communist Party bitterly condemned the Yugoslavs' defection, and it appears that the hitherto-puzzling incarceration of American Consul General Angus Ward in Shenyang (Mukden) late in 1948 was an effort to allay Soviet suspicions about the continuing presence of Western diplomats in Manchuria.[61] Mao's "lean to one side" speech, made on 30 June 1949, had the specific purpose, we now know, of smoothing the path for one of his chief lieutenants, Liu Shaoqi, who was secretly in Moscow at the time of the address.[62]

"Chairman Mao says that this leaning is on our initiative," another key subordinate, Deng Xiaoping, explained, "and is better than being forced to lean to one side in the future."[63]

V

Mao's strategy could hardly have worked, though, had Stalin spurned his advances. That had happened at the end of World War II, when the Soviet leader made clear his preference for dealing with the Chinese Nationalists. The fact that Mao so strongly sought to distance himself from Tito suggests how little self-confidence he had that his status as a fellow Marxist–Leninist—and now as victor in the Chinese civil war—would ensure Moscow's blessing. And yet, Mao badly wanted this: despite many discouragements over the years, his devotion to the distant Stalin still approached that of a fan for a superstar.[64]

Stalin's views, meanwhile, were changing, and for an interesting combination of geopolitical, ideological, and even emotional reasons. "If socialism is victorious in China and our countries follow a single path," he told his representative in that country, I. V. Kovalev, in 1948, "then the victory of socialism in the world will be virtually guaranteed. Nothing will threaten us. Therefore, we cannot withhold any effort or means in our support of the Chinese Communists." Kovalev recalls the old dictator reading aloud passages from Lenin's works "about the role of the Chinese revolution in the victory of socialism in the world."[65] With his usual caution, Stalin had put off a meeting with Mao himself until his victory was complete. But Liu Shaoqi's secret visit to Moscow in July 1949 provided an opportunity for testing the waters.

The Chinese record of these discussions reveals Stalin as at once humble, deferential, elegiac, sentimental, and militantly euphoric about a new dawn for the world revolutionary movement. He began by offering his Chinese visitors a most uncharacteristic apology for having misjudged their prospects, admitting that:

Our opinions are not always correct. . . . We know that we have made ourselves a hindrance to you. . . . You should certainly try to judge if our statements are correct or wrong, because we may give you erroneous advice as the result of lacking understanding of the true situation in your country. Whenever we have made a mistake, you should let us know, so that we may notice the mistake and correct it.

When a nervous Jiang Qing, Mao's wife and a member of the Chinese delegation, offered a carefully scripted toast "to the health of Comrade Stalin," her host responded emotionally:

Is it true that my health is also the source of everyone's happiness? I am afraid that is a flattery. . . . For me, what is most important is the friendship and unity between our two brothers, the Soviet and the Chinese parties. This unity is of tremendous significance to the world revolution. While Stalin is alive, our two peoples should unite with one another; when Stalin is no longer here, our two parties should still be united. . . . All the beautiful words and good wishes you have expressed to me make me happy. But we know that everyone will die.

Stalin then went on to offer a history lesson, tracing the course of revolutions over the past century: "Due to arrogance, socialists in Western Europe began to lag behind after the death of Marx and Engels. The center of the world revolution transferred from the West to the East. It is now transferring to China and East Asia." It followed, therefore, that

there should be some division of labor between us. . . . I hope that China will take more responsibility in helping the national and democratic revolutionary movements in colonial, semi-colonial, and subordinate countries. . . . The Soviet Union cannot play the same kind of role or have the same influence [in Asia] as China is in a position to do. . . . By the same token, China cannot have the same influence as the Soviet Union has in Europe. So, for the interests of the international revolution, . . . you may take more responsibility in working in the East, on those colonial and semi-colonial countries, so that you will play a more significant role there; and we will take more responsibility in the West, and work more on the West. In a word, this is our unshirkable duty.

Stalin concluded this monologue by noting that the Chinese had been referring to the Soviet Union as the "elder brother":

I sincerely hope that the younger brother will one day catch up with and surpass the elder brother. This is not only the hope of my colleagues and me; this is the historical rule: the latecomers will eventually surpass the advanced ones. Let's toast to the younger brother surpassing the elder.

The Chinese found this so astonishing that they froze in place and refused to drink. That offended the Russians, and the evening wound up in an uncomfortable stalemate. "Of course," Liu's interpreter, Shi Zhe, commented many years later, "I will never forget it."[66]

Several reasons for Stalin's new mood suggest themselves. He had never abandoned his commitment to world revolution; he was now acknowledging, though, that it might come not only through Soviet territorial expansion but also that of a second great communist state. His fear of war with the West suggested the need for an "indirect" strategy: hence the advantage of having the Chinese take the lead in the East.[67] Finally, Stalin may not have been averse to encouraging a certain amount of Chinese expansionism *away* from the Soviet Union as a way of embroiling Mao in peripheral conflicts and ensuring that his state did not become *too* powerful.

But these explanations assume crafty and unemotional calculation. What is striking about Stalin's conversations with his new Chinese allies is the emotion—even the sentimentality—they reflect. It is almost as if the aging dictator saw, in Mao's victory, a vicarious return to his own revolutionary youth; possibly also confirmation that he had been right all along in taking the position prior to 1927 that nationalism could be made to serve communist ends. Such a view would have complemented Mao's own assurances to Stalin that he was not going to follow Tito's model: that the Chinese comrades would not betray him. It would also help to explain the Kremlin leader's unexpected assurance to Liu Shaoqi that "the party of one state subordinating itself to the party of another state . . . is unacceptable and can never be." As Kovalev later recalled: "everything Stalin said here was true, but what he actually did was something else entirely. He tried to dominate not only Yugoslavia but the other parties of the socialist countries as well."[68] This does not necessarily mean, though, that the old despot wanted it to be that way. If people would only *agree* with him, as the polite Chinese seemed to be doing, there would be no *need* to dominate them.

Mao, however, was more prickly than Liu Shaoqi. Following the official proclamation of the People's Republic of China on 1 October 1949, he was eager to make the long-delayed pilgrimage to Moscow to meet Stalin himself, who was about to celebrate his 70th birthday. Mao worried, though, that gifts might suggest the payment of tribute. He finally settled on an assortment of Chinese cabbages, radishes, green onions and pears: what the Kremlin boss made of these—and how fresh they were upon arrival—is not clear.[69] The trip, which Mao insisted on making by rail, was long and uncomfortable; his mood did not improve when his train passed through Shenyang, in Manchuria, and he found more portraits of Stalin on display than of himself.[70] Western accounts of what happened after Mao's arrival in Moscow have explained the extraordinary duration of his visit—two full months—by assuming that tough negotiations must have been going on, that Mao and Stalin were already seriously at odds with one another. Certainly that was the impression the American State Department and Central Intelligence Agency sought to spread at the time, through a series of deliberate news leaks.[71]

Chinese and Soviet sources, however, suggest a more complex picture. It is one of a contrite but effusive Stalin apologizing—again—for not having anticipated Mao's success: "Now you are a winner, and a winner should not be criticized. This is a common law. . . . The victory of the Chinese revolution will change the balance of the whole world." It is one of an enigmatic Mao befuddling his Soviet hosts with untranslatable Chinese metaphors: "For this trip we hope to bring about something that not only looks nice but taste delicious."[72] It is one of Stalin receiving, from Kovalev, a highly critical report questioning Mao's loyalty—but then abruptly ending Kovalev's career as a China specialist and compromising an entire network of Soviet agents in that country by passing the document on to Mao himself, in an apparent effort to win his trust.[73] The visit saw cultural gaffes on both sides. The Chinese were treated to a ballet, "The Red Poppy," based inappropriately on Chiang's 1927 decimation of the Communists; the title made things worse by recalling China's long humiliation as a victim of the opium trade. Mao returned the slight by touring Leningrad without showing the least signs of interest as he went through the Winter Palace, Peterhof, the Smolny Institute, Kronstadt, or the World War II battlefields that surrounded the city. There were long periods of inactivity—at times even boredom—as if each side was waiting for the other to make a move. "I only had three tasks here," the Chinese leader later recalled complaining to his startled hosts: "the first was to eat, the second was to sleep, and the third was to shit."[74]

Finally, though, Mao let it be known that he had come to Moscow not just to celebrate Stalin's birthday, but to discuss substantive issues. The Russians responded by asking for suggestions. Mao proposed a range of options, extending from a joint communiqué emphasizing friendly relations to an outright military alliance. Stalin quickly chose the latter alternative, but Mao then further delayed matters by insisting that his prime minister, Zhou Enlai, come to Moscow—again by train—to negotiate it. After some difficulty in pinning the cautious Russians to a firm commitment, Zhou at last emerged with a formal treaty obligating the Soviet Union and People's Republic of China, in the event of an attack on either by a third party, to come to each other's assistance. The purpose of the alliance, Mao cabled the Central Committee in Beijing, was "to prevent Japan and its ally [presumably the United States] from invading China." The Chinese, in turn, would be able to use the Sino–Soviet pact "as a big political asset to deal with imperialist countries in the world."[75]

Mao thereby made explicit his invitation to a still wary Soviet Union to expand its influence in China for the purpose of deterring the Americans. This is not to suggest that he intended for China to become a Soviet satellite, or anything like that. Mao at no point was prepared to yield control of either his party or his country to anyone. Nor was the evolving relationship with the Soviet Union without difficulties: the atmosphere during his meetings with Stalin has been described as "both electric and indeterminate, with both leaders in a constant state of alert, searching out hidden meanings and potential traps in even the most innocent remarks of the other."[76] Nikolai Federenko, Stalin's exhausted interpreter, recalled "an almost physical sense [of] danger hanging over my head."[77]

It is clear now, though, that the Truman administration's assumptions—that Mao should logically fear the Russians more than he did the Americans, and would therefore welcome opportunities to improve relations with the United States—were incorrect. The Sino-Soviet Treaty of 1950 was what Mao wanted: it was in no way imposed on him, as the Soviet Union's alliances with its East European neighbors had been. It was a means of discouraging what Mao believed to be an immediately dangerous adversary by seeking the protection of another great power that might someday become a danger but was not now.[78]

In this sense, it had an analog in the North Atlantic Treaty of April 1949, in which the West Europeans had invited the Americans to guarantee their security against a feared Soviet invasion. Both commitments were a form of extended deterrence, put forward with some reluctance by the superpowers involved, and certainly with a good deal of worry about the expenditure of resources—and the danger of war—they might bring about. Both were provided, though, out of a concern that not to do so, and thereby to risk the collapse of allies, would be an even worse alternative. Both were directed against the threat of an attack that was in fact remote, if it ever existed at all. But statesmen operate on the basis of what they believe at the time, not what historians may conclude decades later. And it is not exactly unprecedented, in the history of empires, for them to act—whether by imposition or invitation— to relieve improbable or even wholly imaginary fears.[79]

VI

Nor is it unprecedented for small states situated along the periphery of empires, through their own self-centered behavior, to embroil great powers in unintended confrontations with one another. The sudden eruption of fighting on the Korean peninsula at the end of June 1950 is as clear a demonstration of that process as one can hope to find. It also illustrates how events can proceed for some time along parallel but separate tracks, only to converge all at once with unpredictable results. For what is striking about the Korean War is the extent to which its out- break, escalation, and ultimate resolution surprised everyone. Decisions made in Pyongyang, Moscow, Beijing, Seoul, Tokyo, and Washington determined what happened; and yet no one, in any of those capitals, anticipated it.

The early history of the Cold War had demonstrated, among many other things, that it was easier for the United States and the Soviet Union to occupy a country than to deoccupy it. By the end of 1945, the joint Soviet–American administration of Korea had come to resemble the situation in Germany, with neither side prepared to withdraw for fear that the other might not. But where Germany had obvious strategic importance for both superpowers, Korea did not appear to: American and Russian forces remained there more to restrain each other than from any strong conviction, in either Washington or Moscow, that the territory itself was significant.[80] Korea, in this sense, began a pattern that would become common during the Cold War—as it had been in past imperial rivalries[81]—in which the sheer presence of one side convinced the other that it had to be there too.

Korea also replicated another characteristic of empires, which was the ease with which peripheries can manipulate centers. Conditions on the peninsula had been anarchic following the Japanese surrender, and in the resulting con- fusion Soviet and American officials, distracted by concerns elsewhere, favored whichever factions seemed likely to restore order and promote their interests. Stalin settled quickly on Kim Il-sung, a young Russian-trained Korean commu- nist who had fought the Japanese alongside the Chinese Communists;[82] the Americans, less sure of themselves, eventually threw their support to Syngman Rhee, an elderly rebel against the Japanese who had spent much of his life in exile. Despite these differences Kim and Rhee had many things in common: both were ardent Korean nationalists, both claimed the right to lead the entire country, both were determined to end the occupation with its artificially imposed dividing line at the 38th parallel, both would prove to be unpre- dictable in their actions, and each utterly despised the other.

Remarkably enough for such an unpromising set of circumstances, the Soviet Union and the United States managed a mutual withdrawal of troops from Korea, although not by mutual agreement. The Truman administration had been looking for an excuse to pull out, and finally found one after the United Nations held elections in South Korea—the Russians refused to allow them in the North—in 1948. These brought Rhee to power, allowing him to form an undemocratic and strongly anti-communist government based in Seoul. Moscow stuck with the already installed and even less democratic government of Kim Il-sung in Pyongyang. Soviet forces left North Korea late in 1948, and the Americans had departed from South Korea by mid-1949. Despite the fact that the country itself remained divided, it appeared—briefly—as though Korea might become one territory over which the Cold War superpowers would choose *not* to compete.[83]

As it happened, though, Korea turned out to be the most bitterly contested of all Cold War battlegrounds. The reasons why are controversial, even today. Partly because we lacked access for years even to the most rudimentary North Korean, Soviet, and Chinese sources, but partly also because of the improbable juxtaposition of circumstances that produced the Korean War in the first place, its origins have been shrouded in an unusually bewildering array of officially sponsored myths and tortured historical interpretations. So simple a matter as whose troops crossed the 38th parallel first, on the morning of 25 June 1950, remained for years the subject of intense argument—let alone the question of for what purpose. The most prominent American historian of this conflict, having devoted well over a decade and some 1500 pages to studying its origins, could conclude as late as 1990 that "no one and everyone" was responsible: "Who started the Korean War? This question should not be asked."[84]

With the end of the Cold War, though, it has become possible not only to ask this question but to answer it. The best place to start is with the fact that in Korea the superpowers had superimposed their rivalry upon a civil war that would have existed in any event. Both Kim and Rhee were determined to unify the country on their respective terms, despite the fact that the 38th parallel—because of the 1948 United Nations-sanctioned elections in the south—now had a degree of international legitimacy going well beyond its original purpose as a military demarcation line. Both sides had been conducting raids across the parallel for some time prior to the outbreak of hostilities. Neither Korean leader could mount a full-scale invasion on his own, though: each would need to persuade his superpower sponsor to provide the necessary equipment and support.[85] The question boiled down, then, to whether the Soviet Union or the United States would sanction an attempt to reunify Korea by military means. The evidence now confirms that, after repeated attempts, Kim got a green light from Stalin early in 1950, while all Rhee received from Washington were yellow lights shading over into red.[86]

What, then, could have been going on in the mind of the normally cautious Soviet leader that led him to authorize an attack on South Korea? Stalin's new optimism about the prospects for international revolution provides a possible explanation. The Soviet push for influence in Western Europe had run up against its limits, what with the success of the Marshall Plan, the failure of the Berlin blockade, the formation of an independent West Germany, and the organization of NATO.[87] Asia looked more promising: the Chinese had shown that nationalism more easily aligned with communism there than in Europe; and as Stalin had none too subtly suggested to Liu Shaoqi the previous summer, there might well be other opportunities beyond Chinese borders. We now know that Stalin saw the situation in Indochina, where Ho Chi Minh was seeking Soviet and Chinese support in his war against the French, as one of them.[88]

The question remains, though, why Korea? Stalin certainly had reason to resent the Truman administration's continuing rejection of any Soviet role in the occupation of Japan, and he realized the extent to which the Americans were turning that country into a key military strongpoint: "Japan . . . will certainly lift itself up again," he told Mao in January 1950, "especially if the Americans continue their current policy."[89] With a Communist government now ruling China, he knew that the Soviet Union would eventually have to give up the ports and naval facilities it had secured in Manchuria at the end of World War II. The new Sino-Soviet Treaty provided for their transfer by 1952; we now know, though, that Stalin insisted on a secret protocol requiring that the Chinese prohibit economic involvement in Manchuria by the citizens of third countries, and that Mao agreed to this reluctantly and with considerable embarrassment.[90] It would have been characteristic of Stalin to wonder how long Beijing's willingness to protect Soviet interests in Manchuria would continue, and to think about alternative arrangements in northeast Asia in the event that it did not.

Then there was Stalin's opportunism, his tendency to advance in situations where he thought he could do so without provoking too strong a response. The Americans, after all, had made no secret of their relative lack of interest in Korea. Not only had they withdrawn their troops in 1949, but Secretary of State Acheson, in a well-intentioned but carelessly worded speech on 12 January 1950, had publicly excluded both South Korea and Taiwan from the American "defensive perimeter" in the Western Pacific. Acheson had not meant to write off either territory. But he was trying to explain American strategy at the time, which was—contrary to Mao's impressions—to avoid military conflicts on the Asian mainland and to stay out of the Chinese civil war. The South Koreans and the Chinese Nationalists, Acheson noted, would have to look to the United Nations for their defense, which so far had not proven to be a "weak reed" to lean upon.[91] Stalin and Mao, it appears, failed to grasp this perhaps excessively elegant circumlocution.

The Acheson speech, together with the top-secret National Security Council strategy review that preceded it—about which Stalin might have learned from such well-informed British spies as Guy Burgess—significantly reshaped Stalin's thinking on the risks of war with the United States in east Asia.[92] Prior to this point he had advised caution, repeatedly warning the Chinese about the risks of American intervention and, as late as 16 December 1949, disappointing Mao by defending the 1945 treaty he had signed with Chiang Kai-shek on the grounds that "a change in even one point could give America and England the legal grounds to raise questions about modifying also the treaty's provisions concerning the Kurile Islands, South Sakhalin, etc." But by 22 January 1950 Stalin's position had shifted radically. There would be a new Sino–Soviet treaty: the old arrangements were "not equitable." Would it not go "against the decisions of the Yalta Conference?" Mao asked. "True," Stalin replied:

it does—and to hell with it! Once we have taken up the position that the treaties must be changed, we must go all the way. It is true that for us this entails certain inconveniences, and we will have to struggle with the Americans. But we are already reconciled to that.[93]

This was an entirely new tone of aggressiveness on Stalin's part, and it surprised as much as it pleased Mao. The most plausible explanation is that the Kremlin boss saw a tempting opportunity, whether as a result of what Acheson said publicly or what the Truman administration had decided secretly, and he resolved, as Mao himself might have put it, to "seize the moment." It was within this context that Stalin received a suggestion from Kim Il-sung, who had also read Acheson's address, that the time had come to "liberate" South Korea.

Kim's proposal was by no means his first. A Soviet foreign ministry study done years afterwards discovered numerous earlier telegrams pressing for the forcible reunification of Korea, all of them rejected in Moscow.[94] But on 19 January 1950, Kim told the Soviet ambassador to North Korea, T. F. Shtykov, that with the liberation of China completed, it was time to take up the cause again:

The people of South Korea trust me and rely on our armed might. Partisans will not decide the question. . . . Lately I do not sleep at night, thinking about how to resolve the question of the unification of the whole country. If the matter of the liberation of the people of the southern portion of Korea is drawn out, then I can lose the trust of the people of Korea.

Stalin had earlier suggested, Kim went on, that it might not be necessary to invade the South because if Rhee attacked the North that would provide an excuse for counter-offensive operations. But Rhee was showing no signs of cooperating. As a consequence, Shtykov noted, Kim "thinks that he needs again to visit Comrade Stalin and receive . . . permission for offensive action. . . . Kim said that he himself cannot begin an attack, because he is a communist, a disciplined person, and for him the order of Comrade Stalin is law."[95] The South Koreans had "little hope of American assistance," Shtykov added on 28 January, since it appeared that "President Truman would leave Formosa as he had left China." Rhee himself had concluded that the Americans did not "intend to fight for the interests of South Korea."[96]

We now know that Stalin and Mao discussed the Korean situation while the Chinese leader was still in Moscow. Kim would "only listen to the voice for his ideas, not the voice against his ideas," Stalin commented, "he was really young and brave." What did the Chinese think? Would the Americans intervene? Mao replied, carefully, that "[t]he Americans might not come in because this is

Korea's internal affairs [sic], but the Korean comrades need to take America's intervention into account."[97] "I understand the dissatisfaction of Comrade Kim Il Sung," Stalin cabled Shtykov on 30 January, "but he must understand that such a large matter . . . needs large preparation. The matter must be organized so that there would not be too great a risk. If he wants to discuss this matter with me, then I will always be ready to receive him. . . . [T]ell him that I am ready to help him in this matter."[98]

According to North Korean participants in these events, Kim and his generals assured Stalin while visiting Moscow in April that "the Americans would never participate in the war. We were absolutely sure in this. . . . America was losing the giant, China, but still had not intervened. America would not participate in such a small war on the Korean Peninsula." Even if the United States did enter the conflict, it would be over in just a few days because the North Korean attack would spark guerilla uprisings from communist sympathizers in South Korea.[99] Still Stalin was cautious. He warned "the Korean friends" not to "expect great assistance and support from the Soviet Union, because it had more important challenges to meet than the Korean problem." He also made his final approval of the North Korean attack contingent upon Mao's consent, adding: "If you should get kicked in the teeth, I shall not lift a finger. You have to ask Mao for all the help."[100] Stalin informed Beijing in May that "owing to the changed international situation," he had agreed "with the Koreans' proposal to proceed toward reunification," but stipulated that "the question must be decided finally by the Chinese and Korean comrades together, and in case of a disagreement by the Chinese comrades, the resolution of the question must be put off until there is a new discussion."[101]

When Kim Il-sung visited him that same month, Mao was initially skeptical, warning once again of the possibility of American intervention, but in the end he gave his approval, apparently for two reasons. First, Kim pictured Stalin as more optimistic about the prospects for success than in fact he was. Second, and more important, Mao himself at the time was planning an invasion of Taiwan, and had requested Soviet military assistance.[102] Stalin had advised against this for fear of provoking the Americans, but during Mao's visit to Moscow—again almost certainly in response to Truman administration statements about not defending Taiwan—he had changed his mind and encouraged the Chinese to go ahead.[103] For Mao to have expressed reservations about an invasion of South Korea now might have revived Stalin's nervousness about supporting the projected attack on Taiwan. Mao asked Kim whether he would want the Chinese to station troops along the Korean border in the event that the Americans did intervene, but Kim assured him this would not be necessary. He then appears to have informed Stalin of Mao's enthusiasm, thereby achieving the feat of having exaggerated to both the Russians and the Chinese the degree to which each supported what he himself wanted to do.[104]

Stalin had already authorized a Soviet military buildup in North Korea, with representatives from the General Staff in Moscow handling detailed war planning. Approved by Stalin himself, even the most secret operational orders used the term "counterattack" to maintain the fiction that the South had moved against the North. "It was a fake," a North Korean general subsequently explained, "disinformation to cover ourselves."[105] Too visible a Soviet role in these operations, the cautious Kremlin boss warned Shtykov three days before the attack, "would provide justification for [American] intervention."[106]

How much Beijing knew of these plans remains in doubt: after Kim told him that Chinese help would not be required, Mao appears to have paid little attention to what was happening in Korea, even to the point of ordering a redeployment of several army corps to the Taiwan Strait only 48 hours before the North Korean attack took place.[107] The invasion, when it came, caught him as well as the South Koreans and the Americans off guard. The Central Intelligence Agency in one of its most egregious misjudgments—a "great big wart" on the organization's history, one official acknowledged years afterwards—had concluded as late as 19 June 1950 that a North Korean assault on South Korea had been contemplated but called off, and that Kim would confine his actions on the peninsula to propaganda and subversion.[108]

VII

But then it was the turn of the North Koreans, the Soviets, and much of the rest of the world to be surprised by the swiftness and decisiveness with which the United States came to the assistance of South Korea. To understand how this happened, one need only recall the Americans' memory of the Japanese takeover in Manchuria in 1931 and the 1938 Munich conference: had these outrages been resisted at the time, almost all Washington officials believed, World War II would never have occurred.[109] Only a full-fledged surprise attack, like the one at Pearl Harbor, could have convinced Truman and his advisers to reverse their carefully considered decision to disengage from the Asian mainland. Thanks to the ineptitude of Kim, Stalin, and Mao, that is exactly what took place.

Had Kim simply infiltrated guerillas into South Korea, as Ho Chi Minh would later do in South Vietnam, the American reaction would not have been nearly as dramatic. Had Kim contented himself with covert efforts to overthrow Rhee's government, it is not at all clear that the United States—which had little sympathy for so difficult an ally—would have done anything at all. But what actually occurred on 25 June 1950 was the first overt military assault across an internationally recognized boundary since the end of World War II. Given the risk of having it demonstrated again that aggression did pay; given the extent to which the United States feared a collapse of psychological self-confidence among allies if that should happen; given the Truman administration's sensitivity to the charge that it had done nothing to save Chiang Kai-shek's China; given Truman's own personal commitment to the United Nations and to the principle of collective security;[110] given all of this, nothing could have been better calculated to provoke a sharp American response than what Kim Il-sung persuaded Stalin and Mao to let him do.

Nor, it is important to note, did the United States alone react in this way. The decision to resist the North Korean invasion had strong initial support among many other states, several of whom sent their own troops to fight under the banner of the United Nations in the three-year war that followed. The world organization was able to play this role because the Soviet Union, since January, had been boycotting the Security Council over its failure to seat the People's Republic of China. Gromyko claims to have pleaded unsuccessfully with Stalin to send the Soviet representative, Jakob Malik, back to veto the American-sponsored resolution to defend South Korea; but "[o]n this occasion Stalin, guided for once by emotion, had not made the best decision."[111]

The Kremlin boss may have had a better reason for allowing the UN to proceed, however, than has previously been apparent. Shocked by the unexpected American response and by the possibility that the fighting in Korea might also involve the Chinese, Stalin may have reasoned that the Americans would be less likely to declare war—thereby, through the terms of the Sino–Soviet treaty, involving the Soviet Union as well—if military operations took place under United Nations auspices.[112] The obligation to keep allies on board did in fact restrain the Americans at several points from escalating the conflict,[113] so in this matter at least the old dictator in Moscow may have been shrewder than several of his own advisers realized.

There was such strong support in Washington for defending South Korea that some historians have found the conjunction of events too neat: the Truman administration, they have suggested, must have set the whole thing up.[114] What has given rise to these suspicions is the fact that the National Security Council, during the spring of 1950, had undertaken a fundamental policy reassessment in the wake of the "loss" of China and the Soviet atomic bomb. Completed in April, NSC-68 portrayed communism as a coordinated global movement, thereby abandoning the distinction between vital and peripheral interests that Kennan's containment strategy had emphasized. Its authors also called for a *tripling* of the American defense budget for the purpose of frustrating what they repeatedly characterized as "the Soviet design."[115] President Truman, a determined fiscal conservative if there ever was one, had not accepted the recommendations of NSC-68 at the time the fighting in Korea broke out; but he soon changed his mind and approved the document, which became the basis for foreign and military policy throughout the remainder of his administration. The dispatch of American troops to Korea, Acheson later acknowledged, "removed the recommendations of NSC 68 from the realm of theory and made them immediate budget issues."[116] But did anyone on the American side *plan* such an outcome? Were the North Koreans, the Soviets, and the Chinese somehow "maneuvered" into attacking South Korea, thereby providing the necessary excuse for a rearmament American officials had already decided upon?

Despite persistent efforts, no one has yet found convincing evidence to support such an argument. Although both sides had indeed been conducting raids along the 38th parallel, it is difficult to see how anyone in Seoul, Tokyo, or Washington could have been certain that one more such incursion from the south would provoke a massive invasion from the north. No documents have surfaced establishing that either Truman administration officials or General MacArthur were colluding with Rhee to get him to attack North Korea; indeed with the European situation still unsettled, it would have been a most unpropitious time to risk a land war in Asia. Nor is it easy to see why, if the whole affair was planned, United States and South Korean forces allowed themselves to suffer so humiliating a sequence of military defeats prior to MacArthur's brilliantly executed landing at Inchon in September 1950: set-ups are not supposed to be such closely run things. Finally, the new Soviet and Chinese sources pin down a chain of causation for the Korean War that requires neither speculation about "hidden" histories nor the insistence that there can never be unintended consequences.[117] As Stalin himself demonstrated more than once during the early Cold War, the blunders of an adversary can at times accomplish as much as one's own actions in resolving one's own dilemmas.

VIII

That gaps can develop between intentions and consequences becomes equally clear when one considers the way the Korean War expanded to involve the People's Republic of China. The Truman administration remained as determined as it had been prior to the North Korean attack to keep the United States out of what was left of the Chinese civil war. But the events of 25 June produced a reconsideration of the *methods* to be employed: the Seventh Fleet would henceforth patrol the Taiwan Strait, with orders to prevent *either* Chinese Communist *or* Chinese Nationalist military activity there while United Nations forces were fighting in Korea. The likelihood of such hostilities seemed high, since Chiang Kai-shek had been looking for an excuse to attack the mainland and Mao too had plans, at some point in 1950, to try to "liberate" Taiwan.[118] But as the Marshall mission had shown, external intervention in an internal conflict, whatever the form it takes or the motives that lie behind it, is rarely impartial in its effects.[119]

Secretary of State Acheson had not found it easy to sell his own State Department, to say nothing of the Pentagon, General MacArthur, and a vociferous set of pro-Nationalist critics inside and outside the Congress, on the wisdom of not defending Taiwan. The whole idea of a "defensive perimeter," after all, suggested the retention of offshore islands; excluding one of the largest for fear of alienating communists was not a popular position to take, especially after American intelligence during the spring of 1950 picked up evidence of Soviet air force deployments along the Chinese coastline.[120] Japanese planes had attacked the Philippines in December 1941 from bases on Taiwan: if Mao's forces should take the island and grant the Russians air facilities, they could easily threaten not only the Philippines but the entire western Pacific including Okinawa and Japan itself. For military as well as domestic political reasons, then, the Truman administration was already reconsidering its Taiwan policy at the time the fighting in Korea broke out.[121]

The decision to neutralize the Taiwan Strait, announced on 27 June, was not a difficult one for the President to make, but it had a profound effect in Beijing. Despite his role in helping to plan it, the North Korean attack and the swift United States response surprised Mao. Hypersensitive as always to indications that the Americans were about to invade China, he immediately interpreted the Seventh Fleet deployment, not as an effort to limit conflict, but as an initial step in expanding it. Noting that Washington had also taken the opportunity to increase economic and military assistance to the Filipinos and to the French in their struggle against the Viet Minh, Mao concluded that he now faced a coordinated American offensive, to be directed from Korea, Taiwan, the Philippines and Indochina. "The U.S. invasion of Asia," he told his State Council on 28 June, "can only touch off the broad and resolute opposition of the Asian people."[122]

Mao also appears to have decided, soon after this, that the Korean peninsula would be a good place for Chinese armies to confront the American aggressors. We know that he began building up troop strength in northeast China as early as July—after receiving advice from his military commanders that "one should open an umbrella before it starts to rain"[123]—and that he cancelled plans for his own invasion of Taiwan in August, weeks before MacArthur's landing at Inchon had created the possibility that the Americans might invade North Korea and approach the Manchurian border.[124] "If the U.S. imperialists win [in Korea]," Mao told his Politburo on 4 August, "they may get so dizzy with success that they may threaten us. We therefore must come to [North] Korea's aid and intervene in the name of a volunteer army, although we will select the best timing."[125]

As it happened, Mao anticipated MacArthur and explicitly warned Kim Il-sung to expect a landing at Inchon.[126] Kim took no precautions, though, and after it took place on 15 September, Zhou Enlai launched a series of diplomatic initiatives aimed at deterring United Nations forces from crossing the 38th parallel. These have been taken to mean that Mao was genuinely reluctant to get into the war, and that it was Washington's own neglect of Chinese warnings that brought about two and a half years of presumably unnecessary Sino-American conflict following China's intervention in late November.[127] More recent accounts, based on Chinese sources, suggest that Mao had intended to intervene all along, and that Zhou's maneuvers had more to do with establishing a plausible justification for entering the war—together with uncertainty over whether Soviet military assistance would be forthcoming—than with any reluctance on Mao's part to fight the Americans and their allies in Korea.[128] It now appears that neither interpretation is entirely correct.

On 29 September, a badly shaken Kim Il-sung warned Stalin that if United

Nations troops did indeed invade North Korea, his own forces would not be able to stop them, and his country could become "a military springboard of the US imperialists."

Therefore, dear Iosif Vissarionovich, we cannot help asking You to provide us with special assistance. In other words, at the moment when the enemy troops cross over the 38th parallel we will badly need direct military assistance from the Soviet Union. If for any reason this is impossible, please assist us by forming international volunteer units in China and other countries of people's democracy for rendering military assistance to our struggle.[129]

Stalin responded not to Kim but to Mao, requesting on 1 October that he send Chinese "volunteers" because "the situation of our Korean friends is getting desperate."[130] Mao acknowledged the next day that he had indeed *planned* to send troops to Korea, but "having thought this over thoroughly, we now consider that such actions may entail extremely serious consequences." Chinese forces were poorly equipped, there was no assurance that they would prevail against the Americans, and the resulting confrontation could easily "provoke an open conflict between the USA and China, as a consequence of which the Soviet Union can also be dragged into war." Such a conflict would completely disrupt "our entire plan for peaceful construction. . . we need peace." Not sending troops would be, of course, "very bad for the Korean comrades," who would now have to shift to partisan warfare. But there appeared to be no alternative.[131] "It *feels* sad," Mao told his colleagues that same day, "to stand by with folded hands and watch your neighbor [suffering from] a national crisis."[132]

Stalin reacted to this unexpected demonstration of doubts in Beijing by pulling out all the stops. He reminded Mao on 5 October that he had earlier talked of sending Chinese troops to Korea. Were he to do so, the Americans would not only have to accept a settlement on the peninsula favorable to the North Koreans; they would also have to abandon Taiwan and give up their plans for a separate peace with Japan and the revitalization of Japanese imperialism. China would get none of these benefits if it adopted a "passive wait-and-see policy." Of course Moscow had taken into account the possibility of a "big war" with the United States:

Should we fear this? In my opinion, we should not, because together we will be stronger than the USA and England, while the other European capitalist states (with the exception of Germany which is unable to provide any assistance to the United States now) do not present serious military forces. If a war is inevitable, then let it be waged now, and not in a few years when Japanese militarism will be restored as an ally of the USA and when the USA and Japan will have a ready-made bridgehead on the continent in a form of the entire Korea run by Syngman Rhee.[133]

Mao gave ground on 7 October, promising *eventually* to send up to nine divisions to Korea, but not at present.[134] That was not good enough for Stalin, given the North Koreans' increasingly desperate military situation.

"That you do not want to send troops to Korea is your decision," Stalin told Zhou Enlai and Lin Biao who, on Mao's instructions, had arrived on 9 October to explain the Chinese position. "[B]ut socialism in Korea [will] collapse within a very short period of time." The Russians and the Chinese should, accordingly, begin making plans to provide the North Koreans sanctuary. Shortly thereafter, on the 13th, Stalin ordered Kim Il-sung to evacuate North Korea altogether.[135] The Soviet Union would just have to get used to having the United States as its neighbor in east Asia, Khrushchev recalls his dejected superior as having concluded: "So what? If Kim Il Sung fails, we are not going to participate with our troops. Let it be."[136]

But the prospect of a North Korean collapse further shook the already shaken Chinese, who had not realized the seriousness of the military situation on the peninsula. Zhou asked Stalin whether the Chinese could count on Soviet air cover if they did in fact intervene. Stalin immediately replied that they could, as well as on other forms of Soviet military assistance.[137] Having digested this information, Mao sent word, also on 13 October, that "[p]ast hesitations by our comrades occurred because questions about the international situation, questions about Soviet assistance to us, and questions about air cover were not clear to them. At present, all these questions have been clarified." The Chinese would at once send nine divisions, however badly equipped, to defend North Korea. Soviet air support would be critical, though, and the Chinese hoped to see it in place within two months.[138] On receiving this message, Stalin quickly instructed Kim Il-sung to disregard the earlier order to evacuate his country. "I am glad," the relieved autocrat added, "that the final and favorable decision for Korea has been made at last."[139]

What this new information suggests is that although Mao had certainly inclined toward intervention since the summer of 1950 and had authorized preparations for it, when it came to the final order to proceed he got cold feet—presumably because of disagreements among his subordinates. There followed several days of indecision on his part and, as the Chinese record is careful to note, several sleepless nights. In the end he did decide, as he revealingly put it, to "order the Chinese People's Volunteers to march speedily to Korea and join the Korean comrades in fighting the aggressors and winning a glorious victory."[140] But it had taken intense pressure from Stalin to push him into this, and the Kremlin leader managed it in the end only by confronting the Chinese with the prospect of an immediate North Korean collapse.[141] Not to have intervened, Mao cabled a still skeptical Zhou, in his own version of a domino theory, would have meant that "the reactionaries at home and abroad would be swollen with arrogance when the enemy troops press on toward the Yalu River." He then added, in language whose circularity reflected the anxiety that lay behind it: "[W]e hold that we should enter the war. We must enter the war. Entering the war is greatly to our advantage; conversely, it is greatly to our disadvantage if we do not enter the war."[142]

Could alternative American policies have avoided the Sino–American war—for that is what it was—that lasted, at great cost to all sides, from late November 1950 through July 1953? Perhaps, but the new evidence narrows what the range of such actions might have been. Obviously if the United States had failed to respond to the North Korean attack in June 1950 it would not have found such a clear justification for interposing the Seventh Fleet in the Taiwan Strait and hence so irrevocably offending Mao Zedong. But Mao was already alienated from the Americans, and Acheson was finding it increasingly difficult to fend off critics of his position that Taiwan should remain outside the defensive perimeter he had proclaimed. It is entirely possible, therefore, that the naval deployment would have taken place in any event; and since Mao was planning his own invasion of Taiwan, any American action to protect Chiang Kai-shek would surely have incurred his wrath, quite apart from whatever was happening on the Korean peninsula.

Whether Mao would have intervened there if United Nations forces had stopped at the 38th parallel is more difficult to determine. He had preparations for intervention underway well before the Inchon landing; two weeks prior to that event, Chinese military commanders suggested that the best time to enter the war would be after the Americans and their allies had crossed into North Korea, but they did not make that a requirement for Chinese entry.[143] Given the parallel's impracticality as a military position, it was unlikely that MacArthur's forces could have returned, even if he had wanted them to, precisely to the pre-25 June 1950 dividing-line.[144] Disagreements within his own government as well as uncertainty about Soviet assistance complicated Mao's planning and may account for the ambiguous signals Beijing sent out during the first half of October. Stalin, conversely, was determined to have the *Chinese* confront the Americans but at the same time so determined *not* to have the Soviet Union do so that he would have sacrificed North Korea altogether had Mao refused to intervene.[145] It was a curious combination of *simultaneous* risk-taking and risk-avoidance, suggesting that Stalin was prepared *both* for a Sino-American war and an American occupation of the entire Korean peninsula. He left it to Mao to decide which it was to be.

Having made his choice, Mao did not look back. He lured MacArthur deeply into North Korea with a view to dividing his forces and overstretching his supply lines; there is little reason now to believe that, if United Nations forces had stopped at the narrow neck of the Korean peninsula just north of Pyongyang, the Chinese would not still have attacked them.[146] To "hook a big fish," Mao's top general Peng Dehuai explained, "you must let the fish taste your bait. MacArthur boasts that he has never been defeated. We'll see who is going to wipe out whom!"[147] By the end of 1950, the Chinese had reversed the tide of battle and driven the Americans and their allies back across the 38th parallel. Mao's ambitions expanded accordingly: he was now confident that he could push his enemies out of Korea altogether and achieve a decisive victory. The technological superiority of the United States, including the atomic bomb,[148] would count for little, he insisted, when set against his own massive manpower reserves and, even more important, the unshakeable *will and determination* of the Chinese people. Unexpected as it had been, the Korean War became, therefore, a challenge and an opportunity.[149] "[A]fter we have consumed hundreds of thousands of American lives in a few years," Mao cheerfully assured Stalin in

March 1951, "the Americans [will] be forced to retreat, and the Korean problem will be settled."[150] Or, as he would later put it: "they have many fewer people than we do."[151]

IX

The expansion of the Cold War into Asia could qualify as a comedy of errors if its consequences had not been so horrendously tragic. For although the Cold War in Europe had arisen over *issues*—the balance of power on the Continent and the clashing forms of government competing to determine it—the Cold War in Asia developed largely out of *inadvertence*. Neither the United States nor the Soviet Union had vital interests at stake on the mainland; both had been content to acknowledge Chiang Kai-shek and the Chinese Nationalists as the dominant power there at the end of World War II. Neither superpower played a significant role in bringing about the collapse of that regime, or the consequent victory of Mao Zedong and the Chinese Communists. Neither Washington nor Moscow paid much attention to what was happening on the Korean peninsula: indeed until the fighting broke out there in June 1950, Korea could have been cited as a promising example of Soviet–American *cooperation* to avoid conflicts arising from the untidy improvisations of 1945. The fact that the sharpest confrontations of the early Cold War came over what its principals regarded as peripheral concerns requires explanations.

One might be that it would have been *too* dangerous to fight over more important objects of contention like Germany, Eastern Europe, or Japan.[152] There is something to be said for this argument when one considers the precariousness with which Soviet conventional military superiority balanced the nuclear superiority of the United States during the early postwar era: both great powers worried about how easily they might slide into a devastating conflict neither could be certain of winning. War broke out, this logic would suggest, only where vital interests were *not* at stake, and where there could be some assurance of limiting the resulting violence.

But this explanation assumes control and calculation. What is immediately apparent, when one reviews what happened in east Asia between 1945 and 1950, is how little control over events officials in Washington and Moscow actually had, and how uncalculatingly—which is to say, how emotionally—they responded to the surprises they encountered in that part of the world.[153] In a pattern familiar from the history of empires, developments on the periphery of the Cold War unexpectedly affected its center. It is worth specifying more precisely just how this happened.

First, there was the tendency to assume that if one side withdrew, the other would seek to exploit the opening thereby created. The post-1945 division of Korea grew out of such reasoning; so too did the Americans' "tilt" toward Chiang Kai-shek at the time of the Marshall mission, the first in a series of decisions that embittered Mao Zedong. As the costs of maintaining a presence in Asia became apparent to both superpowers, fears of withdrawal gradually diminished: the United States began to reconcile itself to a Chinese Communist victory, and both sides managed disengagement from Korea. But by then other processes were at work that would be difficult to reverse.

One of these was the way ideology distorted reality. Mao, from 1946 on, was so convinced of the Americans' ill-will that he "tilted" toward Moscow to protect his revolution from a plot to throttle it that never existed. Stalin, surprised and pleased by the Chinese Communists' successes but still wary of their ultimate intentions, had little choice but to embrace such powerful allies, and to form a military and economic alliance with them. There was never an international communist monolith controlled from Moscow; but there was a common sense of ideological euphoria—a conviction that the forces of history were on their side—which very much influenced the actions, in late 1949 and early 1950, not only of Stalin and Mao, but also of Ho Chi Minh and Kim Il-sung.[154]

That ideological euphoria, in turn, diminished the caution that had shaped Stalin's previous behavior toward the United States. He thus allowed Kim Il-sung to talk him into something he had earlier refused to do: authorizing an effort to reunify the Korean peninsula by military means. Mao, more skeptical, went along because of his own designs on Taiwan; but when the North Koreans began to lose, he too threw caution to the winds and confronted the Americans, convinced that ideological zeal would ensure success.

The Americans themselves, through all of this, had acted ambiguously if not incautiously. They sent unclear signals in the way they handled the Marshall mission and the "defensive perimeter" strategy: these fed Mao's suspicions in the first instance and Stalin's opportunism in the second. Once the Truman administration made the decision to defend South Korea and to patrol the Taiwan Strait, though, a Sino-American military clash may have been unavoidable. One of the surprises that emerges from the new documents is Mao's eagerness to resist the Americans—apart from his momentary bout with bad days and sleepless nights during the first half of October 1950—if for no other reason than to demonstrate that the Chinese people had at last "stood up" against the imperialists.[155]

This was, on his part, a major miscalculation. For not only had Mao exaggerated the Truman administration's hostility to the revolution he had made; he also underestimated the threat to China's independence that would come, in time, from the country he had invited to expand its influence there, the Soviet Union. There is no little irony in the fact that by the end of his life Mao had found it necessary to invite the Americans back into China to counterbalance the Russians, even to the point of welcoming personally to Beijing, in 1972, Richard M. Nixon, the American politician whose career had most benefited, in in the 1950s, from condemning "Red China," and all its works.[156] The Chairman was not far-sighted in all things.

But the least far-sighted leader was Stalin. For it was he who gave the North Koreans the green light to invade South Korea, yet he cannot have intended the results that would flow from that single act. These would include the unanticipated American military intervention on the Korean peninsula, but also the first signs of disillusionment on Mao's part—resulting from Stalin's stinginess in providing promised military assistance to the Chinese—with his Soviet ally. Mao from this time on became considerably more cautious about relying on Moscow's help, and considerably less deferential to Moscow's authority.[157]

Nor were the effects of Stalin's imprudence confined to Asia. Fearing—incorrectly as it turned out—that the attack on South Korea was only the preliminary to a larger Soviet military offensive in Europe or the Middle East, the Truman administration, now implemented NSC 68's recommendation to triple the American defense budget. It also decided to station American troops permanently in Europe, as well as to take the action Stalin may have feared most of all, which was to rearm the West Germans. It is difficult to see what relationship there could possibly have been between the intentions Stalin had in mind when he told Kim Il-sung to go ahead, and the consequences this short-sighted action in time produced.[158]

Just as previous empires had often blundered into the defense of interests they would never have thought worthy of defense had those blunders not occurred, so the Cold War empires found themselves embroiled in a set of conflicts in East Asia far removed from the theater in which the Cold War had originated. Those conflicts would soon spread to involve much of what would come to be called the "third world." Even more ironic is the fact that they so often involved real fighting, while those over Europe, the most important object of Cold War contention, never did. There could hardly be clearer testimony to the ease with which nations can confuse vital with peripheral interests, and the extent to which the outcomes of actions can sometimes fail—quite miserably— to correspond with the objectives that lie behind them.

FOUR

Nuclear Weapons and the Early Cold War

I fear that machines are ahead of morals by some centuries, and when morals catch up perhaps there'll be no reason for any of it. . . . [W]e are only termites on a planet, and maybe when we bore too deeply into the planet there'll [be] a reckoning—who knows?

Harry S. Truman, 16 July 1945[1]

Atomic bombs are meant to frighten those with weak nerves.

Joseph Stalin, 17 September 1946[2]

IT is a rare thing to see practices that have persisted since the beginning of recorded time reverse themselves. And yet that is what began to happen, we can now see, on 6 August 1945, the date the world learned simultaneously of the existence and the lethality of nuclear weapons. Prior to that moment, improvements in weaponry had, with very few exceptions, increased the costs of fighting wars without reducing the propensity to do so. From the invention of axes and spears through bows and arrows, gunpowder and guns, warships, tanks, submarines, high explosives, and aerial bombardment, each advance in technology seemed only to widen the devastation and expand the toll of killed and injured: efficiency came to be measured in rubble and corpses.[3]

By the beginning of the twentieth century, weapons of war were themselves contributing to the outbreak of wars. Without the naval arms rivalry of the pre-1914 era—and particularly without *Dreadnought* and its successors—World War I might never have happened.[4] Without U-boats and their use by the Germans, the United States might never have entered that conflict. Without the mobility that made possible a *Blitzkrieg*, with its alluring promise of a quick and cheap victory, Hitler might never have carried World War II beyond its "phony" stage. Without a carrier-based air force, Japan could hardly have attacked Pearl Harbor in 1941.

It comes as something of a surprise, then, to realize that the most striking innovation in the history of military technology has turned out to be a cause of peace and not war. Over half a century has now passed since President Truman's second atomic bomb devastated Nagasaki, on 9 August 1945. In the wake of that event, the great powers turned out tens of thousands of nuclear weapons, most of which they aimed provocatively at one another. And yet at no point did those who controlled them see fit to use even a single such device against anyone for any reason, despite the fact that the Cold War provided any number of occasions that would earlier have justified resort to the most sophisticated armaments available. Even if this taboo on nuclear use should someday break down—a possibility the proliferation of nuclear technology will make more and more likely over the years—the end of the Cold War has made it most *unlikely* that a global conflagration, of the kind those who lived through the Cold War so greatly feared, would be the result. The ancient principle that if weapons are developed opportunities will be found to use them can, therefore, no longer be taken for granted, and that is a shift of major proportions in the long and lamentable history of warfare.

What caused the shift was the quantum jump in the level of violence nuclear weapons could produce. Their distance from conventional arms—to resort to a football metaphor—was roughly that between getting a new kind of shoe allowing better traction in tackling the other team's players, on the one hand, and, on the other, developing a device capable of instantly destroying not only the other team but also one's own, to say nothing of the playing field, the spectators, the stadium, the parking lot, and the television rights. It is no wonder nuclear weapons, from the very beginning, gave rational people pause.[5]

But history has been full of irrational people: indeed, given the profound differences historical, cultural, ideological and psychological backgrounds can make in human behavior, one has to wonder whether there is any single standard for "rationality" in the first place. What seems most striking now about nuclear weapons is not that they were developed or that people feared them. It is rather that they forced, slowly but steadily, the emergence of a new kind of rationality capable of transcending historical, cultural, ideological and psychological antagonisms of the kind that had always, in the past, given rise to great power wars.

That new rationality grew out of the simple realization that as weapons become *more* devastating they become *less* usable.[6] But that is a revolutionary idea in the history of warfare, implying as it does a severance of the link between advances in armaments and the purposes to which they are put. It helps to account for why the ultimate instrument of war became, during the Cold War at least, the ultimate inducement to peace.

I

Nuclear weapons were developed in a traditional way, but in an untraditional place. The way was traditional because scientific advances—particularly the discovery of atomic fission in the late 1930s—coincided with an opportunity to use them, which was the onset of World War II: it was not the first time the prospect of a war had stimulated the development of technologies with which to fight it. The place, though, was unexpected. Despite its impressive industrial capabilities and deeply-rooted military traditions, the United States through most of its history had hardly led the world in developing new war-fighting technologies. Americans had tended to imitate rather than to originate weaponry, and during the 1920s and 1930s they barely managed to maintain functional professional forces at any level.[7] The army he commanded was still training with horses and mules when in October 1941 the President of the United States authorized a crash program, in collaboration with British and Canadian allies, to produce an atomic bomb.[8]

Without Franklin D. Roosevelt's particular combination of audacity, imagination, and chilling realism, events might have taken a different course: it is not at all clear that a more conventional chief executive would have committed immense resources to so unproven a technology at such a critical time. But Roosevelt had decided, long before most of his countrymen, that Hitler's Germany threatened American security in the most fundamental way. To counter that danger he was prepared, while remaining officially neutral, to sanction a wide range of extraordinary measures, of which the decision to build the bomb was only one.[9] Economics and geography left allies little choice but to go along: the United States alone possessed underused industrial facilities allowing the necessary research, development, and production without significant risk of enemy attack.[10]

In a curious way, the strengths of democratic institutions contributed to this outcome. An innovative mix of public and private educational funding had made several American universities, by the 1930s, competitive with their European counterparts in the rapidly-evolving field of nuclear physics. Meanwhile the rise of anti-Semitism in Nazi Germany—a costly indulgence on Hitler's part—quickly lost him, by way of emigration to those institutions, many of Europe's best physicists.[11] The priorities of survival *and* ambition, of science *and* morality, coincided for these individuals in the most compelling manner, with an atomic bomb the ultimate result. Nor did the German scientists who stayed behind do all they might have to provide their *Führer* with an equivalent instrument, perhaps for fear of what the combination of absolute evil with absolute power might mean.[12]

Having acquired this awesome weapon, the United States used it against Japan for a simple and straightforward reason: to achieve victory as quickly, as decisively, and as economically as possible. Had the atomic bomb been ready in time, Germany might well have been the first target: neither the British nor the Americans had shown inhibitions about flattening that country's cities with conventional weaponry.[13] Hiroshima and Nagasaki were destroyed, the latter probably unnecessarily, to shock the Japanese into surrendering and thereby to avoid the casualties—on both sides and whatever their extent—that might occur in forcing Japan's defeat by more orthodox means.[14] "Let there be no mistake about it," Truman later recalled. "I regarded the bomb as a military weapon and never had any doubt that it should be used."[15]

Military decisions rarely take place in geopolitical vacuums, though, and this one was no exception. It did indeed occur to Truman and his advisers that demonstrating the atomic bomb's effectiveness would impress, perhaps even intimidate the Soviet Union: given their already strained relationship with Moscow, it would have been surprising if such thoughts had *not* surfaced.[16] A few of the scientists who developed the bomb went even further: they favored using it as a way of frightening their own government, the Russians, and the rest of the world into a collective abhorrence of future war.[17] But these justifications were of secondary, not determining, importance in the summer of 1945. It has never been easy to think calmly or systematically about *how* one is fighting a war *while* one is fighting it. Nuclear weapons would eventually force warriors and statesmen alike into such self-reflection; but World War II was the last great conflict to be settled within the ancient paradigm that saw no gap between the utility and destructiveness of weaponry.[18] It that context, the decision to use the atomic bomb made sense.

II

Postwar uses, though, were something else again: here the actions the United States took failed to fit traditional patterns of great power behavior. To see this point, assume counterfactually that a hypothetical Country X had gained exclusive control over what seemed, at first glance, to be an "absolute" weapon.[19] Would one not expect X, as a matter of the highest national priority and at all costs, to try to keep its rival Y and any other potential rivals from *ever* getting the device? Would one not anticipate that X would use its monopoly, while it existed, to pressure and if necessary coerce other nations into following its wishes? Would one not predict that X would undertake the immediate mass production of its new weapon, with a view to ensuring continuing superiority even if monopoly were no longer possible? And would one not regard X as very likely, if it should ever get into another military conflict at whatever level, to use its new instrument of warfare to ensure victory as long as there was no realistic prospect of retaliation by Y or anyone else? Abstraction suggests that all of these things *should* have happened during the period in which the United States enjoyed an effective nuclear monopoly. The fact that in reality *none* of them did requires explanation.

Why did the United States not resort to preventive war to keep the Soviet Union or anyone else from ever developing nuclear weapons? The Joint Chiefs of Staff did briefly consider, immediately after Hiroshima and Nagasaki, how military action might bring about a permanent atomic monopoly; but these ideas went nowhere. One reason had to do with the nation's image of itself: Americans did not start wars. "It might be desirable to strike the first blow," Pentagon planner General George A. Lincoln acknowledged in September 1945, but "it is not politically feasible under our system to do so or to state that we will do so."[20] Subsequently, there was occasional talk of initiating an attack on the USSR for the purpose of knocking out its nuclear facilities, but always in the context of what might happen *after* an effort at international control through the United Nations had failed, *or* in a situation in which the Soviet Union had already accumulated sufficient capabilities to allow an attack on the United States or its allies.[21] As late as 1948, President Truman could still wonder whether atomic weapons would be available for any kind of offensive military operations "because the people of the United States might not at the time permit their use for aggressive purposes."[22]

Then there was a more practical difficulty: American officials were at no point certain, prior to 1950, that they could actually win a preventive war against the Soviet Union if they were to start one. The production of atomic weapons had proceeded at what seems in retrospect a remarkably relaxed pace, so that at the time he proclaimed the Truman Doctrine in March 1947, the President understood there to be only fourteen bombs in the American arsenal.[23] When the Berlin blockade began in the spring of 1948 only fifty unwieldy and unassembled weapons were available, and just over thirty B-29s equipped to carry them.[24] It was not at all clear how many targets would have to be hit or where they all were: the best intelligence on the USSR came from German aerial photographs taken early in World War II, and in some instances from pre-war and even pre-1917 maps.[25] The Air Force itself concluded in 1949 that the destruction of some seventy Soviet cities would not, "per se, bring about the capitulation, destroy the roots of Communism, or critically weaken the power of the Soviet leadership to dominate the people." Meanwhile, "the capability of Soviet armed forces to advance rapidly into selected areas of Western Europe, the Middle East, and the Far East would not seriously be impaired."[26] And if one could achieve victory, what then? "Conquering the Russians is one thing," Secretary of Defense James Forrestal pointed out, "and finding what to do with them afterward is an entirely different problem."[27]

If preventive war was impossible, though, atomic diplomacy might not be. Could the United States use the fact of exclusive possession to *coerce* the Soviet Union and other potential adversaries into cooperation? During the summer of 1945 Secretary of War Henry L. Stimson had briefly advocated withholding information about the bomb until the USSR transformed itself into a constitutional democracy; and Secretary of State James F. Byrnes definitely expected the American monopoly to induce the Russians into making diplomatic concessions.[28] President Truman himself appeared to endorse such unilateralism when he warned, in his first radio address after Nagasaki, that "[t]he atomic bomb is too dangerous to be loose in a lawless world," hence the United States, Great Britain, and Canada, "who have the secret of its production, do not intend to reveal that secret until the means have been found to control the bomb so as to protect ourselves and the rest of the world from the danger of total destruction."[29]

What is remarkable about these attitudes is not that they existed but how quickly they were given up. Within weeks of Hiroshima American officials had abandoned the idea that an atomic monopoly could become a usable instrument of diplomacy, shifting instead to an immediate search for international control. This happened for several reasons. Molotov had proven *more* difficult to deal with, not less, at the first postwar foreign ministers' conference, held in London in September 1945, thereby shaking the self-confidence of those who had hoped the bomb would be a latter-day version of Theodore Roosevelt's "big stick."[30] "The joint development of this discovery with the UK and Canada must appear to the Soviet Union to be unanswerable evidence of an Anglo-American combination against them," Under-Secretary of State Dean Acheson warned later that month. "It is impossible that a government as powerful and power conscious as the Soviet Government could fail to react vigorously to this situation."[31]

There could be no assurance, moreover, that the Russians would not themselves build a bomb. Their scientists understood the principles well enough, and the Americans had obligingly confirmed many of them shortly after Hiroshima by publishing their own detailed account of how they had accomplished the feat.[32] The Manhattan Project had been a multinational effort, a fact that discouraged attempts to think about its product as a purely American problem—or opportunity. The President and his advisers therefore embarked, with support from the British and the Canadians, upon an ambitious effort to place all atomic weapons under the authority of the United Nations: the United States would deny the bomb to potential adversaries by ultimately—although under safeguards of its own design—denying it to itself.

The international control scheme the Americans put forward in the spring of 1946—first drafted by Acheson and future Atomic Energy Commission chairman David E. Lilienthal in cooperation with the atomic scientists, and then modified by the American spokesman at the United Nations, Bernard Baruch—reflected widely-held but transitory attitudes: awe at the new kind of warfare the United States had brought into existence together with a determination to find a new approach to world politics to go with it; faith in the United Nations and in the international legal procedures it would presumably rely upon; deference to the advice of the scientists who had built the bomb; the lingering hope of avoiding a hostile relationship with Moscow. These were cautious proposals, tilted toward maintaining the American monopoly as long as possible, a fact the Russians were quick to point out. But they were not simply gestures concealing a search for permanent nuclear hegemony. One ought not to minimize the guilt American leaders felt, if only subconsciously, over Hiroshima and Nagasaki, or the sense of responsibility—manifesting itself as a characteristic effort at reform and perhaps redemption—they drew from what they had done.[33]

What these officials did *not* feel was the need to undertake serious negotiations with the Soviet Union to determine its price for accepting international control. The Baruch Plan reflected a domestic compromise, not an international one. It balanced what the atomic scientists insisted on offering against what the military and a skeptical Congress were prepared to relinquish. The Americans presented it, as a consequence, on a "take it or leave it" basis, and by the beginning of 1947 Stalin had chosen the latter option.[34] He thus left the Truman administration few alternatives but to make whatever it could of its atomic monopoly before the Russians' own bomb development project, now assumed to be underway, brought it to an end.

Having given up on atomic diplomacy when they initiated the search for international control, the President and his advisers now found it difficult to return to it. Committed to the principle of civilian control over the military, Truman insisted on denying the Pentagon the most basic information about how many atomic bombs were available, or on what their effects would be if employed. He did not, as he put it, want to have "some dashing lieutenant colonel decide when would be the proper time to drop one."[35] There could be little coordination, then, between contingency plans for war with the Soviet Union and the weapons available with which to fight it; nor was there any assurance, if war came, that Truman would authorize use of these weapons in the first place.[36] It was almost as if the President—whose own attitude toward nuclear weapons was more ambivalent than he wanted it to appear to be[37]—considered it as important to keep his own military guessing as it was to have the Russians do the same. Devising strategies to impress Moscow, under such constraints, was no easy matter.

These difficulties became clear in April 1948, when Winston Churchill suggested giving Stalin the choice of either abandoning Berlin and eastern Germany, or having his cities razed. The former Prime Minister's thoughts on how to handle the Soviet Union had commanded great respect in Washington, if not universal assent, when put forward in his famous March 1946 "Iron Curtain" speech. But this new proposal gained no greater attention within the Truman administration than had a similar one from the eccentric British philosopher Bertrand Russell, who had advocated using "any degree of pressure that may be necessary . . . [to] secure Russian acquiescence." "You know better than I the practical infirmities in [Churchill's] suggestion," Ambassador Lewis Douglas cabled Under Secretary of State Robert Lovett, and that was the end of it.[38]

Truman did, to be sure, approve the ostentatious deployment of B-29s to British bases during the Berlin blockade later that summer.[39] But there was less to this initiative than met the eye, and certainly much less than what Churchill—or Russell—had in mind. No overt threats to use atomic bombs accompanied it, and the bombers sent carried no such weapons, a fact the Russians could easily have determined given the distinctive external appearance of atomic-capable B-29s, as well as the presence of the Soviet spy Donald Maclean on the joint Anglo-American committee within which information on atomic weapons was exchanged.[40] The B-29 maneuver was a hasty improvisation, a quick fix intended to compensate for another problem Truman's emphasis on civilian priorities had created: the weakness of American conventional forces, brought about by the extraordinarily tight budgets within which the President had forced the Pentagon to operate.[41]

The administration therefore left itself little choice but to rely upon its atomic monopoly as a means of deterring the Russians. That capability was by no means insignificant. It is possible that without it the Americans would never have run the risks involved in defending Berlin, encouraging the formation of an independent West German state, and creating the North Atlantic Treaty Organization.[42] But capability was not strategy. Dependence on nuclear weapons grew more out of desperation than deliberate preference. Truman and those around him had not yet sorted out the competing priorities of public opinion, the domestic economy, constitutionality, morality, and the national-security state. Their failure to do so, in turn, impeded efforts to think systematically about how one might exploit the American nuclear advantage.

Washington officials did not *feel* self-confident during the summer and fall of 1948. If they ran risks, it was because they thought it riskier not to do so. That was because the American atomic monopoly had not deterred Stalin from running risks of his own: indeed, it may even have *encouraged* him to do so.

III

The United States built its atomic bomb because it perceived, wrongly as it turned out, that Hitler might have a similar priority. The Soviet Union began work on its bomb because it perceived, quite rightly, that the United States was already constructing one. Roosevelt made his decision to go ahead in October 1941 with a potential but highly probable adversary, Nazi Germany, in mind. When Stalin authorized a research project—not yet a bomb—the following year, he too had a potential but probable adversary in mind: for the moment, though, it was an ally.

Soviet authorities first learned that atomic weapons might be possible, it now appears, from the *New York Times*. Hoping to alert the White House to the military potential of atomic fission, science correspondent William Laurence published a story on 5 May 1940, claiming—erroneously—that the Germans were extracting uranium-235 for use in bombs. Roosevelt, already aware of fission research, paid no attention; but as it happened Yale historian George Vernadsky sent the clipping to his father, the Russian mineralogist Vladimir Vernadsky, who passed it on to the Soviet Academy of Sciences. That organization, in turn, set up a Uranium Commission which quickly established the probable feasibility of a chain reaction and called for a systematic effort to locate uranium deposits throughout the USSR.[43]

The German invasion in June 1941 delayed this search; it also diverted Soviet physicists into work that seemed more likely to produce immediate military benefits.[44] But by this time the spies Soviet intelligence had recruited at Cambridge University during the 1930s had begun monitoring British nuclear research, and one of them—probably John Cairncross—reported that London and Washington were collaborating to build a uranium bomb. NKVD chief Lavrenti Beria duly informed his boss.[45] Stalin's initial reaction, by one account, was characteristically suspicious: "I do not believe this. And I advise you not to believe that it is possible to win a war using some kind of chemical element that no one has seen. Doesn't this seem like pure propaganda to you? Done deliberately to distract our scientists from work on new kinds of weapons for the army?"[46]

Further reports accumulated, though, not just from spies in Britain but from Soviet agents who had cultivated contacts with American physicists, among them J. Robert Oppenheimer, soon to become director of the Manhattan Project. How much substantive information these efforts yielded—if any at all—is still not clear, but the fact that they took place suggests continuing interest on Beria's part, whatever Stalin's attitude.[47] Meanwhile, more useful intelligence was beginning to flow from Klaus Fuchs, a German émigré scientist who had joined the British project and would subsequently move to Los Alamos.[48]

Stalin refused to take even these reports seriously, though, until another of those quirky events occurred—like Vernadsky's newspaper clipping—that sometimes alter the course of history. A young Soviet physicist, Georgii Flerov, looking for citations to his own work in British and American journals, noticed that references to nuclear physics were no longer appearing in them. Finding his supervisors uninterested in this pattern, he took the risky step of writing directly to Stalin in April 1942, suggesting that if the allies were going to such lengths to conceal such research, it *must* be important.[49] Invisible molecules may have been difficult to understand but invisible information was not: Stalin immediately got the point. Perversely, Anglo–American attempts to ensure the Manhattan Project's security were what alerted him to its significance.

"Reportedly the White House has decided to allocate a large sum to a secret atomic bomb development project," the NKVD cabled its agents in New York, London, and Berlin in June, 1942. "Relevant research and development is already in progress in Great Britain and Germany. . . . Please take whatever measures you think fit to obtain information on . . . the theoretical and practical aspects of the atomic bomb projects," and on "the likely changes in the future policies of the USA, Britain, and Germany in connection with the development of the atomic bomb."[50] What is interesting about this sequence of events is that it was primarily concern about the British and Americans, and only to a lesser extent the Germans, that led Stalin to authorize this intensification of espionage.[51] It appears to have made no difference to him that two of the nations against whom he acted were wartime allies, while only one was an adversary. "You are politically naive," he is said to have told a senior Soviet scientist who in October 1942 suggested simply *asking* Roosevelt and Churchill about the bomb, "if you think that they would share information about the weapons that will dominate the world in the future."[52]

Whether Stalin was right about that is an interesting question. Security was an obvious priority in the Manhattan Project, but it focused chiefly on the danger of *German* espionage; the possibility that Soviet penetration might be the more serious problem did not fully dawn on the Americans until after the war.[53] The atomic physicists had by no means abandoned their conviction that science should be an open, international, and elite enterprise, even as they accommodated themselves uneasily to the censorship, compartmentalization, and restrictions on movement the United States government required. The resulting tension produced prophetic insights into the need for the international control of atomic weapons, as well as alternative visions of a long and costly arms race, possibly even a cataclysmic future war.[54] From this point of view, telling the Russians about the bomb could seem the right thing to do. "I can see that there might be some arguments for doing that," Oppenheimer conceded in 1943; but he added—referring to Soviet espionage efforts—"I don't like the idea of having it moved out the back door."[55]

Roosevelt did not immediately rule out informing the Soviet Union. He took seriously the Danish physicist Niels Bohr's recommendations to this effect during the spring and summer of 1944, despite an earlier agreement with Churchill to withhold such information from "third parties except by mutual consent." We may never know why, in September, F.D.R. finally yielded to Churchill's objections and rejected Bohr's advice. The Warsaw uprising was fresh in the President's mind, though, and his own Soviet experts were now warning against trusting Moscow on far less consequential matters than the atomic bomb.[56] He had also known, for at least a year, that the Russians were attempting to steal its secrets.[57] What is surprising in retrospect is not that Roosevelt rejected cooperation with the USSR in developing this weapon, but rather that he responded as calmly as he did to evidence of Soviet espionage.

The reason is not likely to have been, as some Soviet sources have suggested, that key administration officials and atomic scientists were passing sensitive information to the Russians on their own.[58] The more plausible explanation is that war was still to be won, the USSR was still an invaluable ally, and as such it seemed entitled to every benefit of the doubt despite its leader's less than trustful attitude. The Manhattan Project was itself unknown to all but a tiny minority of Americans; in another perverse twist, more vigorous efforts to prevent Soviet agents from stealing its secrets might have compromised its secrecy. And, of course, no one in the United States at the time—neither the scientists nor the diplomats nor top officials of the Roosevelt administration—knew what we know now and what Stalin must have known then: that there was going to be a Cold War.

Espionage appears to have been of greater assistance to the Soviet bomb development project than we had once thought.[59] As early as March 1943, Igor V. Kurchatov, Oppenheimer's Russian counterpart, was assessing the information it yielded as having "huge, inestimable, significance for our state and science." Not only did spying confirm the importance of the work going on in the West; it also made it possible "to bypass many very labor-intensive phases of working out the problem and to learn about new scientific and technical ways of solving it."[60] "It was a very good intelligence operation by our Chekists," Molotov recalled years afterwards. "They neatly stole just what we needed."[61]

Even so, progress was slow while the war was going on. One problem was that there were few known sources of uranium within the USSR. Perhaps because

Leninist doctrine assumed the venality of capitalists as well as their enmity, the Soviet government even attempted, in 1943, to *purchase* sufficient uranium from the United States to construct an atomic pile similar to the one that had produced the first chain reaction at the University of Chicago a few months earlier—this even as efforts to crack the secrets of the Manhattan Project were continuing at full pace. The Americans, by this time dimly aware of Soviet espionage but worried that a refusal to sell might only confirm its findings, did provide some of the requested commodity, although in much smaller quantities than the Russians had requested.[62] The uranium shortage persisted until the Red Army moved into Czechoslovakia and eastern Germany, where known supplies were available.[63]

The more serious reason for the absence of an all-out Soviet effort was that Kremlin leaders were slow to understand what atomic weapons could actually do. Molotov, to whom Stalin had assigned the initial responsibility for nuclear research, appears to have had little sense of what it was all about. Beria, who took over early in 1945, saw the implications more clearly, but even he never fully trusted the intelligence reports his agents inside the Manhattan Project provided: "if this is disinformation," he threatened one of his subordinates, "I'll put you all in the cellar."[64]

When President Truman at last did tell Stalin about the atomic bomb at the Potsdam Conference on 24 July 1945, shortly after the first test in the New Mexico desert, it was hardly a surprise to the Soviet leader: he had known about the possibility of such a weapon long before Truman had.[65] He said only that he hoped the Americans would make good use of it against the Japanese. Stalin reacted more revealingly immediately afterwards: "Truman is trying to exert pressure, to dominate," he told Beria:

His attitude is particularly aggressive toward the Soviet Union. Of course, the factor of the atomic bomb [is] working for Truman. . . . But a policy of blackmail and intimidation is unacceptable to us. We therefore gave no grounds for thinking that anything could intimidate us. Lavrentiy, we should not allow any other country to have a decisive superiority over us. Tell Comrade Kurchatov that he has to hurry with his parcel. And ask him what our scientists need to accelerate work.[66]

When Stalin later berated Kurchatov for not having advanced bomb development faster, the scientist excused himself by invoking all that the Soviet Union had been through during the war: "So much has been destroyed, so many people have died. The country is on starvation rations, there is not enough of anything."

Stalin was unmoved. "If a child does not cry," he replied, "the mother does not understand what he needs. Ask for anything you like. You will not be turned down."[67] He then dangled material inducements before the astonished scientist: "we can always make it possible for several thousand persons to live well, and . . . better than very well, with their own dachas, so that they can relax, and with their own cars." It was "not worth spending time and effort on small-scale work, rather, it is necessary to conduct the work broadly, on a Russian scale, and . . . in this regard, utmost assistance will be provided."[68]

The American atomic bomb had elevated Soviet physics from invisible molecules to a matter of state security, and as a consequence Soviet physicists gained the freedom to follow the Western example espionage had given them. In contrast to his disastrous interference with Soviet genetics, Stalin imposed no ideological guidance: Kurchatov did not become Lysenko. The physicists, in turn, made the most of the opportunity; so much so, indeed, that they would need no espionage-supplied model when they turned their skills, as they soon did, to the construction of a hydrogen bomb.[69] Was it not dangerous to grant the atomic scientists so much physical and intellectual autonomy, Beria at one point asked. "Leave them in peace," his boss—now in a less nurturing mood—replied. "We can always shoot them later."[70]

IV

"Hiroshima has shaken the whole world," Stalin admitted to his physicists a few days after the event. "The balance has been broken. Build the bomb—it will remove the great danger from us."[71] The danger Stalin foresaw was not that of direct attack. Despite a sense of frustration, even shock, that the United States had forged so far ahead in this new category of weaponry, there was no immediate concern in Moscow that the Americans would actually use their atomic bombs against the USSR. Stalin appears to have derived this reassurance, however, more from spy reports that confirmed quite accurately the tiny number of bombs in the American arsenal than from charitable judgments about the American character.[72]

More significant was the threat of psychological intimidation. "The bombs dropped on Japan were not aimed at Japan but rather at the Soviet Union," Molotov recalled. "They said, bear in mind you don't have an atomic bomb and we do, and this is what the consequences will be like if you make a wrong move!"[73] Stalin himself, according to Andrei Gromyko, expected the Americans and the British to use their monopoly "to force us to accept their plans on questions affecting Europe and the world. Well, that's not going to happen."[74] Nor would Stalin wait for the Americans to try: he quickly embarked upon a strategy designed to counter the practice of atomic diplomacy before the Truman administration had even attempted it.[75]

The Soviet government took the official position that the atomic bomb had made no difference at all in the postwar balance of power. This was why Molotov had gone out of his way at the September 1945 London foreign ministers' conference to show his disdain for the new weapon, to the point of making heavy-handed jokes about it at the expense of Secretary of State Byrnes. "Here's to the Atom Bomb," he toasted at one point, in a sodden attempt to spook the Americans: "We've got it."[76] As the pugnacious Foreign Minister later acknowledged: "We had to set a tone, to reply in a way that would make our people feel more or less confident."[77] Stalin had no qualms about Molotov's performance. "The failure of the conference," he commented, "will be Byrnes's failure, and we should not grieve over this."[78] But when Molotov repeated his tactics at the Moscow foreign ministers' conference in December, even Stalin thought he had gone too far: "This is too serious a matter to joke about," he insisted in front of the visiting American and British delegations. "We must now work together to see that this great invention is used for peaceful ends."[79]

The Americans and British had come to Moscow to seek Soviet participation in a United Nations commission on the international control of atomic energy—the first stage in what would become the Acheson–Lilienthal and later the Baruch Plan. Some Soviet officials regarded the visit as evidence that their tough line on the bomb had already paid off;[80] perhaps for that reason the Soviet Union did agree to participate in the United Nations discussions. A consensus on international control was never close, though, because both American plans required establishing a powerful international agency that would control all facilities for producing atomic weapons before the United States would relinquish its monopoly. The Soviet position provided for the immediate destruction of existing weapons with no mechanisms to prevent other states from building them.[81] Dimitri Skobel'tsyn, a scientist on the Soviet delegation, summarized the situation for Beria and Molotov in October 1946:

If the Baruch plan is accepted, then every independent activity in the development of atomic production in countries which have signed the agreement has to be curtailed and handed over to an international (in reality, probably, an American) organization. This international organization would then . . . proceed to control our resources. We reject such help and are determined to carry out by our own efforts all the research and preparatory work necessary for setting up atomic production in our country, as America did in the years of the war.[82]

When Molotov subsequently told the United Nations that the Soviet Union would soon have an atomic bomb "and other things," even his boss was impressed. "Well, that was strong stuff," Stalin commented. "We still had nothing," Molotov acknowledged, "but I was up to date on the matter."[83]

Whatever his foreign minister said in public, Stalin now had a better sense of what atomic weapons could do. Soviet representatives toured Hiroshima two weeks after the atomic bombing, and sent back detailed reports of the devastation they had witnessed. At the invitation of the United States, Soviet scientists also attended the first postwar atomic bomb tests, conducted on Bikini Atoll in 1946.[84] Worried that the Americans might someday try to attack them, Stalin insisted that Soviet bomb production facilities be well hidden, often in underground bunkers and in one instance even under a lake.[85] "That is a powerful thing, pow-er-ful!" he admitted to Milovan Djilas in 1948, by which time the Soviet Union had already made considerable progress toward constructing its own bomb.[86] As late as July 1949, only weeks before the first Soviet test and with the weapon very much on his mind, Stalin was warning Liu Shaoqi's visiting delegation that "[i]f we, the leaders, undertake [war], the Russian people would not understand us. Moreover, they could chase us away. For underestimating all the wartime and postwar efforts and suffering. For taking it too lightly."[87]

As the time for the test approached, Stalin worried about not having an extra bomb in reserve: "What if [the Americans] press on with their atomic bombs and we have nothing to contain them?" Could the scientists not divide the first bomb into two, just in case? When they explained that smaller bombs would lack the critical mass to sustain a chain reaction, Stalin according to one account, tried to make sense of the science in ideological terms: "Critical mass . . . critical mass. It is also a dialectical notion!"[88] The Soviet leader's nervousness probably explains his otherwise puzzling decision not to announce the successful experiment, conducted on 29 August 1949, so that it was left to the Americans, whose air-sampling techniques quickly picked up evidence that an atomic explosion had occurred inside the USSR, to reveal the news three weeks later.[89] "Did it look like the American one?" Beria, who witnessed the test, demanded excitedly: "Very much alike? We didn't screw it up? Kurchatov isn't pulling our leg, is he?"[90]

Stalin had chosen to gamble—correctly as it turned out—that his scientists could provide him with his own atomic bomb, and therefore the basis for a deterrent capability, before the United States could accumulate enough weapons to be confident of defeating the Soviet Union by launching a preventive war.[91] A key aspect of this strategy was to show no fear, even though fears there surely were. Diplomacy therefore had to be conducted, and for the most part was, as if the American atomic bomb did not exist: this was the point of Stalin's best known pronouncement on such weapons, which was that they were "meant to frighten those with weak nerves."[92] He was in a position to know.

The only moments at which the Russians *may* have moderated their actions out of concern for American nuclear capabilities were the 1948 Berlin blockade crisis and Stalin's attempt to discourage Mao Zedong early in 1949 from crossing the Yangtze; but even in these instances the cause and effect relationship was hardly conclusive. "It is difficult to deduce any evidence that this monopoly on our part influenced Soviet policy . . . or abated its aggressiveness," the Soviet expert Charles E. Bohlen concluded the following year.[93] Decades later, historian David Holloway assessed the impact of the American atomic bomb in only slightly different terms: "It probably made the Soviet Union more restrained in its use of force, for fear of precipitating war. It also made the Soviet Union less cooperative and less willing to compromise, for fear of seeming weak."[94]

Why did Stalin's gamble succeed? Why was he so much more skillful in defusing American atomic diplomacy than he was in conducting his own foreign policy during this period? Espionage certainly had something to do with it: the spies apparently did detect, and convey to Moscow, the most sensitive secret of the early United States nuclear program, which was how unimpressive the nation's nuclear capabilities actually were. Stalin could take certain risks—the Czech coup, the Berlin blockade, the authorization to Kim Il-sung to attack South Korea—because he knew that the United States did not yet have the capacity to attack and be sure of vanquishing the Soviet Union, even in the unlikely event that it should choose to do so.[95] The American nuclear arsenal would soon expand exponentially; but this happened only after—and partly because—the American nuclear monopoly no longer existed. Timing means quite a great deal in strategy, and the spies allowed Stalin to calculate it with unusual precision.

It helped as well that Stalin had a clearer idea than the Americans of what might constitute atomic diplomacy. An old hand at intimidating others, he saw the danger of appearing to be intimidated himself well before Truman and his advisers—obviously less experienced in this area—had worked out ways to accomplish that objective. Washington officials never transformed their atomic monopoly into an effective instrument of peacetime coercion. Had the roles been reversed, it is unlikely that Stalin would have had such difficulties.

All of this raises, then, an interesting question: did the fact that the world's first nuclear state was also a democratic state make a difference? It obviously did when it came to espionage. The scale of Soviet operations in this area was remarkable, but so too was the trust the American, British, and Canadian governments extended to their own citizens—and to their wartime ally—on so secret a matter.[96] Pressures from allies, the atomic scientists, and public opinion pushed the Truman administration into seeking international control, leaving it unclear for over a year whether the United States could even count on retaining atomic bombs into the postwar era.[97] After that point had been resolved, Truman's staunchly literal commitment to the principle of civilian supremacy discouraged exploration of how atomic bombs might affect the relationship between force and diplomacy. So too did his insistence on so closely restricting information about the number and capabilities of these weapons that Soviet intelligence probably knew more about them than Pentagon planners did. Nor did self-images of appropriate behavior go away: if democracies did not start wars, neither did they find it easy, in the absence of blatant provocation, to threaten them.

We should not make too much of this argument, though, because one characteristic of nuclear weapons themselves, whether they exist within democracies or autocracies, was beginning to come into play at this point: it was easy to think of reasons why one might need such instruments when one did not yet have them, but it was difficult to know just what to do with them once one got them. Stalin, as well as Truman, would soon face this problem.

V

The Truman administration responded to the Soviet bomb test in much the same way that Stalin had absorbed the news from Alamogordo, Hiroshima and Nagasaki four years earlier. Although each side had known of the other's work on atomic weapons, confirmation of an actual capability, in each instance, came sooner than expected. Even if the timing could have been anticipated, the psychological impact could hardly have been. The Americans had guessed that it would take the Russians anywhere from five to twenty years to get the bomb, but they had fallen into the bad habit of pushing their range of estimates forward each year,[98] so that the revelation that the USSR had managed it in four could not but be a shock—very much like the one the Russians had felt, despite their excellent intelligence sources, in the summer of 1945. President Truman's initial reaction to the fact that there were now two nuclear powers also paralleled earlier Soviet behavior: he denied that anything significant had changed. "The eventual development of this new force by other nations was to be expected," he assured the nation. "This probability has always been taken into account by us."[99]

But Truman, unlike Stalin, did not—perhaps in a democracy could not—feign unconcern for very long. By early 1950, he had taken several steps to deal with the new situation, the combined effects of which were simultaneously to *increase and decrease* reliance on nuclear weapons. He thereby produced a muddle, not a strategy. The President and his advisers were as uncertain about what they could actually *do* with nuclear weapons when they left office in 1953 as they had been in 1949.

The first stage in the American adjustment to a bipolar nuclear world was to expand the production of atomic bombs, something that would have happened even if there had been no Soviet test in August 1949. Technical breakthroughs were making it possible to build more powerful weapons with smaller amounts of fissionable material, just as budget constraints were forcing the Pentagon to rely increasingly on its atomic capabilities. All that the Soviet atomic explosion did here was to accelerate that process: there had been only about 200 weapons in the American arsenal at the time it took place; there would soon be many more.[100]

The second American adjustment was more dramatic. Under pressure from some—but by no means all—of the atomic scientists, concerned about the consequences if he did not go ahead and the Soviet Union did, President Truman authorized research at the end of January 1950 on a new and far more powerful form of weapon based on nuclear fusion, not fission. American physicists had understood the theoretical possibility of such a "super-bomb" since 1942. Whether because they found the implications appalling, as some did, or because of uncertainty over how to proceed, as was the case with others, the scientists had maintained, as McGeorge Bundy has put it, a "benign conspiracy of silence on the subject." The President himself apparently knew nothing of it until October 1949.[101]

Despite serious disagreements among his advisers,[102] Truman had little difficulty deciding to build such a weapon once he understood that the Russians could also do so. International control, he believed, was no longer feasible. His suspicions of Stalin now equaled those the Kremlin leader had held of him four and a half years earlier, when Stalin had ordered his own all-out effort to construct an atomic bomb. There could be no assurance that the Russians would refrain from practicing thermonuclear diplomacy if they possessed thermonuclear weapons and the Americans did not. Everybody had predicted the end of the world when he decided to aid Greece and Turkey, Truman commented as he signed the announcement, on 31 January 1950, that the United States would build a hydrogen bomb. "[B]ut we did go ahead, and the world didn't come to an end. [It] would be the same case here."[103]

The final element in Truman's response to the Soviet atomic bomb was, however, an attempt to *de-emphasize* the utility of nuclear weapons altogether. NSC-68, drafted during the late winter and early spring of 1950, tacitly acknowledged how hard it would be to find military purposes for these new instruments of warfare by making the case for a massive buildup of *conventional* forces, whatever the budgetary implications. It was imperative, insisted the document's authors—Paul Nitze most influential among them—"to increase as rapidly as possible our general air, ground and sea strength and that of our allies to the point where we are militarily not so heavily dependent on atomic weapons."

NSC-68 questioned neither the increase in the production of fission weapons nor the decision to build the hydrogen bomb. But it did, for the first time, raise the issue of how believable nuclear threats would be in a world with more than one nuclear power. The danger was "piecemeal aggression against others, counting on our unwillingness to engage in atomic war unless we are directly attacked." The risk was "having no better choice than to capitulate or precipitate a global war."[104] What this argument implied, therefore, was a double paradox: as nuclear weapons became more numerous and more powerful, they also became less usable; but as nuclear weapons became less usable, one needed more of them to deter others who possessed them. Logic, in this field, was not what it was elsewhere.

There was at the time, and has been since, a good deal of agonizing over whether the American decisions of 1949–50 set off a new and even more lethal arms race, thus closing off any possibility of a renewed effort at international control.[105] Insofar as the hydrogen bomb is concerned, though, the evidence is now quite clear: the Russians began work on their own thermonuclear device *before* the Americans did. For whatever reason—whether the nature of an authoritarian society or differences in scientific culture or both—the distinction between fission and fusion weapons never carried the weight within the Soviet Union that it did in the United States.[106] Andrei Sakharov, who more than any other individual developed the Soviet "super," put the matter bluntly shortly before his death:

The Soviet government (or, more properly, those in power: Stalin, Beria, and company) already understood the potential of the new development, and nothing could have dissuaded them from going forward with its development. Any U.S. move toward abandoning or suspending work on a thermonuclear weapon would have been perceived either as a cunning, deceitful maneuver or as evidence of stupidity or weakness. In any case, the Soviet reaction would have been the same: to avoid a possible trap, and to exploit the adversary's folly at the earliest opportunity.[107]

"The decision to develop the hydrogen bomb was seen as a logical next step," the most careful scholar of Soviet nuclear history has concluded, "and occasioned none of the soul-searching that took place in the United States."[108]

VI

Despite the fact that two great powers now possessed atomic bombs, despite the projects both now had to develop thermonuclear weapons, the feasibility of war itself was not yet in question. Well into the 1950s, military planners in both Moscow and Washington clung to the reassuring notion—if reassurance could have meaning in such a context—that World War III, should it ever come about, need not differ all that much from World War II.

Old paradigms persist long after the conditions that gave rise to them have ceased to exist,[109] and it is clear now that Soviet and American war planning reflected this tendency. Holloway has documented striking parallels in the way strategists on both sides tried to adapt to the unfamiliarity of atomic bombs by imposing familiarity on them: when one confronts an abyss, it is perhaps natural to want to minimize its depth. Both assumed the use of such weapons in any new world war, but neither regarded them as likely to be decisive. Asymmetries in conventional capabilities—the Red Army's substantial, though not overwhelming, ground force superiority in Europe, the United States' naval and air predominance—would, the planners expected, lock a future war into the pattern of the last one. The Russians would occupy most of Europe, probably also parts of the Middle East and Northeast Asia. The United States and its surviving allies would rely, first, upon strategic bombing, and only much later on invasions to try to retake these territories. Still for the most part safe from attack because the Russians lacked an effective long-range bombing capability and possessed only a rudimentary navy, the American "arsenal" would provide the munitions and much of the manpower necessary to accomplish these tasks, as it had in 1917–18 and 1941–5. Traditional, not nuclear, capabilities would determine which side prevailed in the end.[110]

Given the decisiveness with which just two atomic bombs had forced Japan's surrender, these attitudes might seem antiquated, even ostrich-like. But it was not all that clear to either Russian or American military experts that the *physical* effects of atomic weapons were all that revolutionary. Soviet observers who inspected the ruins of Hiroshima and Nagasaki, as well as those who witnessed the 1946 Bikini tests, found the power of the new weapon awesome, but they did not regard it as *so* powerful as to render war itself, or the possibility of survival in war, obsolete.[111] Some Americans who saw the evidence first-hand came to similar conclusions. Nitze, for example, noted that earlier firebomb raids against Tokyo and other cities had been at least as devastating: the significance of atomic bombs lay in their efficiency, not their implications for the future of warfare.[112] Moreover, widely dispersed Soviet targets would hardly resemble those in Japan. Holloway has pointed out that during the *first four months* of the war with Germany in 1941, the Russians had sustained casualties and physical destruction exceeding the Americans' estimates of the damage *all* their approximately 200 atomic bombs in 1949 could have produced. Soviet intelligence at the time, it appears, made similar calculations.[113]

Psychological effects, though, required different measurements: these the military staffs left to their political superiors. Atomic bombs were terror weapons as well as strategic weapons, and it was precisely their efficiency that was so terrifying—as the Japanese, more than anyone else, had reason to know. The only individual ever to have ordered the military use of atomic bombs understood this from the start. Truman never thought it possible to separate physical and psychological considerations when it came to these new methods of conducting war, and insisted on treating them as revolutionary for that reason. No stranger to the uses of terror, Stalin too thought about the bomb in psychological terms: hence his own form of "atomic diplomacy," which deprecated the importance of the weapon even as he was making the most desperate efforts to obtain it; hence his own fears, once he had it, that he might be even *less* secure.

How one estimates the outcome of a Soviet–American war fought, say, in 1950 depends therefore upon how one balances physical versus psychological effects. In physical terms, the two superpowers were relatively evenly—if asymmetrically—matched. One can imagine a tiger versus shark standoff, rather like that between the French and the British during the Napoleonic Wars, in which dissimilar military capabilities could have kept each belligerent, for some time, from getting at and hence prevailing against the other. But that would have required steady nerves indeed on both sides. The psychological consequences of a Russian *Blitzkrieg* crashing through to the English Channel, or of just a few atomic bombs wiping out Moscow or Leningrad, are much more difficult to guess.

Time, though, was not on the Russians' side: the growing American atomic stockpile was gradually narrowing the gap between the physical and the psychological. It might indeed have been difficult to defeat the Soviet Union with only 200 atomic bombs, but we know now, and Stalin's spies may well have allowed him to know then, that the United States had 299 weapons by the end of 1950, 438 by 1951, and 841 by 1952. The Russians during the last year of Stalin's life had only about fifty atomic bombs, or an approximate 17–1 disadvantage.[114] The Soviet attainment of a *physical* atomic capability, therefore, can hardly have provided Stalin much *psychological* reassurance. Like Truman, he must have wondered, having got them, just what good such weapons actually were.

VII

The outbreak of fighting in Korea in June 1950 provided the first hard evidence. The Korean War demonstrated how awkward it would be to use atomic bombs even in the most desperate military circumstances: from this perspective, they proved to be irrelevant to the outcome of that conflict. But from another perspective they were of critical importance, for Korea determined how hot wars, during the Cold War, were to be fought. The rule quickly became that neither the United States nor the Soviet Union would confront the other directly or use all available force; each would seek instead to confine such confrontations within the theaters in which they had originated. This pattern of tacit cooperation among bitter antagonists could hardly have emerged had it not been for the existence, on both sides, of nuclear weapons.

The caution the Soviet Union showed during the Korean War is understandable. Stalin had indeed been imprudent in allowing Kim Il-sung to attack South Korea, but he was prudent to the point of hyper-cautiousness once it became clear that his actions had provoked an unexpected American military response. The Soviet Union had few if any atomic bombs available at the time the war broke out, and no feasible means of delivering them upon American targets.[115] Surely Stalin had this deficiency in mind when he warned the North Koreans, before their invasion, that they would have to look to the Chinese for help if the United States did intervene; surely it explains his statements to the Chinese, after the Inchon landing, that the Soviet Union was not yet ready to fight a third world war; surely it accounts for his willingness to tolerate a North Korean defeat and an American military presence within striking distance of Vladivostok;[116] surely it influenced the extraordinary lengths to which Stalin went to conceal what we now know to have been the Soviet air force's extensive involvement in Korea in support of Chinese and North Korean troops.[117] The Chinese, less knowledgeable than the Russians about atomic bombs, were more willing to fight the nation that had invented them. Their sacrifices in the end—not the Soviet attainment of a nuclear capability—prevented Stalin's worst fears of what might happen on the Korean peninsula from coming to pass.

Chinese thinking about nuclear weapons was strikingly inconsistent. On the one hand, Mao Zedong had long ago dismissed the atomic bomb as "a paper tiger which the US reactionaries use to scare people."[118] His concerns about Americans invading China had focused on the use of conventional forces, although he acknowledged that nuclear weapons might be employed. In either case, technological superiority would mean little because the Chinese could always fall back upon their enormous manpower reserves: "As long as the green mountains are there, one need not worry about firewood."[119] After the Korean War began Mao went out of his way to taunt the Americans—less than coherently—about their nuclear impotence:

We will not allow you to use the atomic bomb. But if you insist on using it, you may use it. You can follow the way you choose to go, and we will go our own way. You can use the atomic bomb. I will respond with my hand grenade. I will catch the weak point on your part, hold you, and finally defeat you.[120]

"[W]e cannot but allow them to use it because we do not have [the bomb] and thus we are in no position to stop them," Mao admitted to his Politburo on 4 August. But "we are not afraid, and we just have to get prepared."[121] Part of the preparation involved deprecation: American atomic weapons, the Chinese press claimed blithely two months later, only equaled "two to three thousand tons of TNT."[122] Chinese officers in Korea were told that such bombs were "not for actual combat use," and one journal confidently assured its readers that these weapons would annihilate anyone who tried to use them.[123]

Even as Mao minimized American atomic bombs, though, he expected the far more primitive Soviet nuclear arsenal to intimidate the United States. The Sino-Soviet alliance, in his mind, always had the purpose of deterring the Americans: now it would prevent them from employing their most powerful weapons in Korea. "It is the United States who should be afraid of using atomic bombs against us," a Chinese press editorial proclaimed shortly before Mao ordered intervention there, "because its densely concentrated industries are more vulnerable to serious damage by Soviet nuclear retaliation."[124] Whether the Chairman believed in this early form of "extended deterrence" or was simply seeking to reassure nervous subordinates is difficult to say. Significantly, though, Chinese leaders were assuring each other as late as the fall of 1952 that the Americans would not use anything more powerful than tactical nuclear weapons in Korea because "the United States is under great pressure of world opinion and is also deterred by possible Soviet nuclear retaliation."[125] It is also worth noting that Mao saw no need to begin his own bomb development project until after the Russians made it clear, during the first Quemoy–Matsu crisis two years later, that they would not risk war with the Americans to help the Chinese regain Taiwan.[126] Only when Mao realized how small and leaky the Soviet nuclear umbrella was did he became uncomfortable under it.

But it is American attitudes about nuclear weapons in Korea that are the most difficult to explain. Because Soviet capabilities were still so rudimentary, the United States retained an *effective* atomic monopoly at the time the war broke out.[127] The defeats American troops suffered in the wake of the initial North Korean attack and subsequent Chinese intervention were as humiliating as any in the nation's military history.[128] The taboo on the use of nuclear weapons in limited wars—indeed the very notion of a "limited" war itself—had not yet taken root: the Korean War defined these principles, but there was little reason to expect, when it broke out, that its conduct would reflect them.[129] That it did so stemmed from what the world's most experienced nuclear power learned about the kind of warfare its new weapons had now made possible.

The Truman administration tried to use its atomic superiority advantageously in Korea, but never succeeded. One problem was the absence of appropriate targets. Atomic bombs had originated, after all, within the context of World War II strategic bombing campaigns: they were meant for use against industrial facilities, transportation networks, and military strongpoints, not for interdicting peasant armies picking their way along mountain trails with little more than what men could carry on their backs. It was not at all clear that atomic bombing, in such a war, would produce decisive results: the enemy might keep coming, and so obvious a demonstration of the bomb's ineffectiveness could impair its credibility elsewhere.[130] As a remarkably well-informed Soviet intelligence report put it in January 1953:

[T]he U.S. military leaders are not convinced of the practicality of using the atomic bomb in Korea. They are afraid that, if the use of atomic weapons does not ensure the real preponderance of the United States, a final blow will be dealt to U.S. prestige. What's more, in this case they believe that the existing U.S. stockpile of atomic weapons would considerably lose its importance as a means of intimidation.[131]

Better not to use the atomic bomb at all, in short, than to run the risk that its use might fail to produce the intended result.

It was also the case that, despite their nuclear superiority, American officials still worried about war with the Soviet Union. The primary concern here was indeed the Sino-Soviet Treaty, which obligated the Russians to come to China's defense in case of attack. Use of the bomb against Mao's troops inside Korea or against their supply facilities in Manchuria might bring the USSR into the conflict: there was little awareness in Washington of how badly Stalin wanted to avoid such an outcome. If war did come, the Soviet air force would be able to bomb Japan or South Korea; even more dangerously, the fighting could spread to more vital—but still vulnerable—regions like Europe or the Middle East, a prospect that would turn the Korean struggle into a sideshow.[132] The treaty Mao and Stalin signed, then, achieved the deterrence they had hoped for. At the same time the advantage the United States held over the Soviet Union in nuclear weapons and delivery capabilities counted, in this instance, for very little.[133]

Yet another difficulty grew out of the features that distinguished atomic weapons from all others in the first place. Truman himself claimed not to have lost sleep over the destruction of Hiroshima and Nagasaki, but there is ample evidence to suggest that he hoped never again to have to make a comparable decision. As long as any other country—especially the Soviet Union—had nuclear capabilities the United States would have to have them, but that by no means implied automatic use in future wars. "We will never use [the bomb] again if we can possibly help it," the President had promised privately in 1949.[134] Military professionalism, paradoxically, may also have discouraged nuclear use: soldiers have often felt psychological resistance—at times even moral abhorrence—toward technologies that threaten to alter familiar ways of fighting.[135] Such instincts could have had something to do with why the Joint Chiefs of Staff found it so difficult to identify appropriate targets for atomic bombing in Korea.

But even if Truman and his generals had been comfortable with the idea of employing nuclear weapons there, allies would not have been. The military effort in Korea was, after all, a multinational enterprise fought under the United Nations flag, a fact which did—as Stalin may have anticipated[136]—inhibit American freedom of action. When the President let slip at a November 1950 press conference that the use of nuclear weapons in Korea had always been "under consideration," alarmed Europeans made it clear that the price the United States would pay if it took such action would include allied solidarity, not just on the Korean peninsula but elsewhere as well.[137] Thanks again to the involvement of his spy, Maclean, in top-secret Anglo–American discussions of this issue in Washington the following month, Stalin was almost certainly aware of its importance.[138]

So what did the Truman administration actually *do* with nuclear weapons during the Korean War? It used that conflict to justify a massive rearmament effort, following the guidelines of NSC-68, that significantly boosted American nuclear and conventional capabilities. It repeated the 1948 deployment of B-29s—atomic-capable this time, but without atomic bombs—to British bases, as well as to American facilities on Guam. Following the firing of General Douglas MacArthur in the spring of 1951 it even sent nuclear weapons to accompany this latter group of bombers, but then quickly moved them back to the United States. It spoke periodically of expanding the war into China, with the implication that it might use nuclear weapons there; at no point did it explicitly threaten such use, though, whether in Korea or elsewhere.[139] And that, as far as we now know, is it: the Truman administration took no further action, despite the fact that its superiority over its sole nuclear rival was greater than it would ever be again.

VIII

Dwight D. Eisenhower and his Secretary of State, John Foster Dulles, did not at first share Truman's uncertainty about what one might do with nuclear weapons. Dulles had called loudly during the 1952 campaign for a "policy of boldness" that would make American military power "a deterrent of war instead of a mere means of waging war after we got into it," and by the time of the election he had persuaded an initially skeptical Eisenhower that only reliance on nuclear weapons would make containment work over the long haul at a reasonable cost. The Korean War was dragging on inconclusively, both men believed, because Truman had failed to use all of the strength available to end it. The new administration was determined, as quickly as possible, to do better.[140]

Eisenhower and Dulles remembered having threatened the use of nuclear weapons in Korea if the fighting there continued; they convinced themselves that such threats had indeed induced the North Koreans and the Chinese Communists to sign the armistice of July 1953. "[W]e were prepared for a much more intensive scale of warfare," Dulles recalled several months later. "[We] had already sent the means to the theater for delivering atomic weapons. This became known to the Chinese through their good intelligence sources and in fact we were not unwilling that they should find out." When asked years later why the Chinese accepted an armistice in Korea, Eisenhower responded bluntly: "Danger of an atomic war."[141]

It is much less clear in retrospect, though, that cause and effect corresponded this closely. The National Security Council did discuss the *possibility* of using nuclear weapons in Korea during the first few months of the Eisenhower administration. The president himself is on record as having described such devices as "simply another weapon in our arsenal," while Dulles stressed the need to break down the "false distinction"—promoted, he darkly noted, by Moscow—that had set "atomic weapons apart from all other weapons as being in a special category." But the administration was no more precise than its predecessor in threatening actual use in Korea while the fighting was still going on. Its most explicit warnings came *after* the armistice, and in the context of how it would respond to a violation. Eisenhower did authorize the transfer of completed bombs to the military for overseas deployment; this happened only on the eve of the armistice and as part of a general shift in procedures for handling nuclear weapons, though, not—as Dulles later claimed—as part of a scheme to apply pressure on the Chinese. Plans for nuclear use during the final months of the Korean War were, as the historian Roger Dingman has written, "more discursive than decisive."[142]

Nor is there evidence that they impressed the Chinese Communists. The authorities in Beijing did carefully monitor Eisenhower's campaign statements calling for more aggressive strategies in Korea, but—still confident that the Soviet atomic bomb would deter the Americans—they interpreted these as presaging intensified amphibious operations, not a nuclear offensive.[143] When asked years later about their reaction to American nuclear threats in Korea, Chinese officials denied even having heard of them. If Dulles did intend the transfer of atomic weapons and their means of delivery as a signal to Beijing, it was one the intended recipients apparently missed.[144]

Why, then, did the Korean War end? Because Stalin died, or so it now appears. It is easy enough for us in retrospect to see how that conflict damaged Soviet interests;[145] but the aging Kremlin autocrat did not view the situation similarly. He had worried in the fall of 1950 that the war might expand to involve the Soviet Union. He played a major role in setting up cease-fire negotiations between the North Koreans, the Chinese, and the United Nations command in June 1951, presumably as a way of lessening that danger.[146] It may be that an increasingly inflexible United States negotiating position, especially with respect to the forced return of Chinese and North Korean prisoners-of-war, prolonged these negotiations and therefore the fighting.[147] But it does not follow from all of this that Stalin was eager to end the Korean War: indeed, new evidence strongly suggests that once the battlefront had stabilized, he was keen to keep the conflict going. "[T]he war in Korea should not be speeded up," he cabled Mao in June 1951. It could even be a useful learning experience for the Chinese,

since a drawn out war, in the first place, gives the possibility to the Chinese troops to study contemporary warfare on the field of battle and in the second place shakes up the Truman regime in America and harms the military prestige of the Anglo-American troops.[148]

The Chinese and the North Koreans, Stalin instructed Mao the following November, should continue "using flexible tactics in the negotiations" but at the same time "pursue a hard line, not showing haste and not displaying interest in a rapid end to the negotiations."[149]

Kim Il-sung was complaining, by July 1952, that "the enemy almost without suffering any kind of losses constantly inflicts on us huge losses in manpower and material values."[150] Even then, though, Stalin saw no reason to bring the war to an end. "The North Koreans," he told Zhou Enlai the following month, "have lost nothing, except for casualties that they suffered during the war." There had of course been "many" of these—Stalin said nothing of Chinese casualties—but the war had paid off because it had revealed the Americans' weakness:

Americans are merchants. Every American soldier is a speculator, occupied with buying and selling. Germans conquered France in 20 days. It's already been two years, and [the] USA has still not subdued little Korea. What kind of strength is that? America's primary weapons . . . are stockings, cigarettes, and other merchandise. They want to subjugate the world, yet they cannot subdue little Korea.

"No," Stalin insisted, "Americans don't know how to fight. . . . They are pinning their hopes on the atom bomb and air power. But one cannot win a war with that."[151]

Perhaps because they had a clearer sense of Soviet long-term interests, Stalin's successors took a less sanguine—and sanguinary—view. Eager to explore the possibilities for relaxing tensions with the West, they saw Korea as the obvious place to start.[152] Within two weeks of the old dictator's death in March 1953, the Soviet Council of Ministers informed both Mao and Kim of its view

that it would be incorrect to continue the line on this question which has been followed until now, without making alterations in that line which correspond to the present political situation and which ensue from the deepest interests of our peoples, the peoples of the USSR, China and Korea, who are interested in a firm peace and have always sought an acceptable path toward the soonest possible conclusion of the war in Korea.[153]

Or, in less convoluted language, whatever Stalin's interest in making war, they were ready to make peace.

The exhausted North Koreans did not object, nor did the Chinese: the Soviet Union all along had provided less military assistance than they had hoped for—and had insisted that they pay for it. Their economy was dangerously overstretched.[154] Stiff United Nations resistance had long since forced Mao to abandon his grandiose plans for driving the Americans off the Korean peninsula: a 1954 Pentagon estimate placed the ratio of Chinese to American casualties at ten to one—surely an exaggeration—but the Chinese themselves have acknowledged a three-to-one imbalance.[155] And the Eisenhower administration's public rhetoric may have given Beijing at least a vague sense that if it did not accept an armistice they might soon face a wider war, even if not a nuclear one.[156]

Mao had the option of treating a military stalemate as a victory: as an authoritarian leader, he could impart greater malleability to the meaning of words than could his democratic counterparts in the West. Even if his initial victories had given him delusions of grandeur—rather like MacArthur's under similar circumstances—his fundamental objective in Korea had been to demonstrate that the Chinese people had "stood up" to the Western imperialists. "This time we have really felt out the US armed forces," Mao boasted in September 1953. "If you do not come into contact with [them], you might be afraid of them. We fought with them for thirty-three months, and we have become thoroughly acquainted with them. US imperialism is not such an awesome thing, it is just what is, and that's all."[157]

So did nuclear weapons play any significant role in the Korean War? At one level, the answer has to be: not at all. It is difficult to show that the North and South Koreans, the Chinese, or the Americans and their allies fought the ground war in Korea any differently from the way they would have if nuclear weapons had not even existed. The gap between the power of such weapons and their practical applications was so great as to render them useless, which is why Mao could get away with treating them in exactly this way.

At another level, though, nuclear weapons were supremely significant, for the Korean War could hardly have remained what it was—a limited war—in their absence. Despite Stalin's posturing before Zhou Enlai, we can assume that he did not really share Mao's official view of American atomic bombs as paper tigers.[158] "How he quivered!" Khrushchev later recalled of Stalin. "He was afraid of war. He knew that we were weaker than the United States. We had only a handful of nuclear weapons, while America had a large arsenal of nuclear arms."[159] Eisenhower certainly saw this: "They must be scared as hell," he remarked of the new Soviet leaders just prior to the Korean armistice.[160]

But the Americans also behaved cautiously. Their awareness of a Sino-Soviet Treaty linked to a Soviet nuclear capability—primitive though it was—deterred them from expanding the war into China despite their nuclear superiority; it may also have kept them from making an issue of Soviet air involvement in Korea, despite what must have been abundant evidence of it.[161] Washington too feared what a wider war in a nuclear age might bring. "You must be prepared to use force in such a way as not to involve the use of ultimate force," Acheson later explained. "If you don't limit it, the world is gone."[162]

It was in this sense, then, that the new weapons proved their worth. They frightened both sides into thinking twice—indeed into thinking repeatedly—about the risks of escalation. Apart from common sense, never an entirely reliable mechanism, the pre-nuclear age had had few means to keep small conflicts from dragging great powers into big wars. Even as they multiplied potential levels of violence, nuclear weapons reinforced rationality, even prudence, even among antagonists with no other basis for mutual trust.[163]

IX

On 1 November 1952, the United States rearranged a small portion of the earth's surface by detonating the first thermonuclear device—not an operational weapon—on a Pacific atoll that proved too fragile to survive the blast. Little celebration accompanied this final technological accomplishment of the Truman administration, though, and the President himself, as if ashamed by it, would not even announce the test publicly for another two weeks.[164] Few of those who had favored building hydrogen bombs now expected them to provide any lasting advantage over the Soviet Union, a judgment quickly confirmed when the Russians detonated their own primitive version—also not an operational weapon—just nine months later, on 12 August 1953.[165] By the end of 1955, both sides would have fully functional thermonuclear bombs as well as long-range bombers from which to drop them; both were on the way to developing missiles capable of delivering such weapons on each other's territory almost instantaneously. The United States would retain quantitative and qualitative superiority in nuclear weapons for years to come, but the age of mutual vulnerability—the ability of each side to inflict catastrophic damage upon the other—had clearly arrived.

The American monopoly over nuclear weapons, while it lasted, yielded unimpressive results. Stalin and Mao quickly sensed that the way to defuse this danger was to deprecate it, to treat it as a "paper tiger" whose capacity to frighten people depended solely upon their willingness to be frightened. It was critically important, as Stalin insisted, never to *show* "weak nerves," even if—as he clearly did to the day he died—one suffered from them. Both dictators practiced a strategy Kennan had once recommended to the United States and its Western European allies for confronting Soviet conventional force superiority :

We are like a man who has let himself into a walled garden and finds himself alone there with a dog with very big teeth. The best thing for us to do is surely to try to establish, as between the two of us, the assumption that the teeth have nothing whatsoever to do with our mutual relationship—that they are neither here nor there. If the dog shows no disposition to assume that it is otherwise, why should we raise the subject and invite attention to the disparity?[166]

Why, though, did the American nuclear dog not bite? Or bark? Or at least derive some benefit from its expensively acquired teeth?

Democracy surely had something to do with it. We will never know for certain what Stalin or Mao might have done with a nuclear monopoly, but it seems reasonable to assume that they would have brushed aside the competing domestic priorities, the concerns about civil-military relations, the worries about what allies would say, and—most particularly—the moral qualms that afflicted the Truman administration and, in time, Eisenhower's as well. Authoritarians tend to wield power authoritatively.

As the only American president to enjoy a nuclear monopoly, one might have expected Harry S. Truman himself, of all people, to have been more assertive. That he was not has been taken as reflecting an inadequate understanding of nuclear strategy: "[M]aturity of strategic thinking had yet to arrive in Washington," two recent historians of this subject have concluded; for the Truman administration, nuclear weapons provided only "a convenient means to avoid tough decisions and painful choices."[167]

Perhaps so. But one might also argue that Truman was *more* mature than most others at the time because he saw, almost from the start, that nuclear weapons were going to change the meaning of "strategy" itself. That word implies the calculated relationship of means to ends; but Truman persistently maintained that in a nuclear age such calculations were no longer possible. When an adviser reminded him in October 1945 that he had an atomic bomb up his sleeve, the President acknowledged this but commented: "I am not sure that it can ever be used."[168] "[W]ar has undergone a technological change which makes it a very different thing from what it used to be," the President explained seven years later in his final State of the Union message:

The war of the future would be one in which man could extinguish millions of lives at one blow, demolish the great cities of the world, wipe out the cultural achievements of the past—and destroy the very structure of a civilization that has been slowly and painfully built up through hundreds of generations. Such a war is not a possible policy for rational men.

Truman concluded by revealing what he would say to Stalin—who retained his belief in the eventual inevitability of war through the final weird months of his life[169]—if the two should ever meet again, face to face:

You claim belief in Lenin's prophecy that one stage in the development of communist society would be war between your world and ours. But Lenin was a pre-atomic man, who viewed society and history with pre-atomic eyes. Something profound has happened since he wrote. War has changed its shape and dimension. It cannot now be a "stage" in the development of anything save ruin for your regime and your homeland.[170]

Little noticed at the time nor widely remembered since,[171] Truman's January 1953 valedictory anticipated the difficulties all of his successors would have—as would those elsewhere in the world who would come to possess them—translating the physical power of nuclear weapons into effective instruments of statecraft. The absence of coherent strategy in the Truman administration, therefore, may have demonstrated not so much lack of sophistication as an abundance of it. Truman's nuclear education simply preceded that of everyone else.

FIVE

The German Question

"Now, Mr. Molotov," Bevin demanded: "what is it that you want?
. . ."

"I want a unified Germany," said Molotov.

"Why do you want that? Do you really believe that a unified
Germany would go communist? They might pretend to. They
would say all the right things and repeat all the correct formulas.
But in their hearts they would be longing for the day when they
could revenge their defeat at Stalingrad. You know that as well as I
do."

"Yes," said Molotov, "I know that. But I want a unified
Germany."

Harold Nicholson[1]

"We were fortunate in our opponent."

Dean Acheson[2]

B Y the time Truman left office and Stalin died, early in 1953, the basic pat
terns of the Cold War were firmly established. Neither the United States nor
the Soviet Union would accept the other's vision of a postwar world, even as
neither would risk war—at least not intentionally—to achieve their own. Both
sought allies but did not always control them; both built nuclear weapons but
found it difficult to know what to do with them. Neither proved capable of separating foreign policy from domestic influences, but those influences differed
enormously, producing correspondingly dissimilar external behavior. Certain
that history was on their side, the first generation of Cold War statesmen proceeded from strikingly divergent views of history itself and where it was taking
them.

One common destination, they would have been surprised to learn, was to
be three and a half additional decades of confrontation. The issues over which
Soviet–American conflict had arisen at the end of World War II were still unre-
solved, for the most part, in the mid-1980s: indeed their very irresolution had
become, by then, so familiar a feature of international life as to seem to some
observers reassuringly normal.[3] Cold War history is, at least in part, the story of
how what was thought to be unendurable became endurable; how order and
stability, if rarely justice, evolved from bitter and sustained rivalry.

Surely the nuclear revolution provides one explanation. These new weapons raised the costs of challenging the status quo even as they lowered the burdens of defending it: once they were in place on both sides and in sufficient quantity, they created a kind of stalemate that neither thought it could safely change.[4] Surely Soviet and American military-industrial complexes found the "managed" competition of deterrence and counter-deterrence very much to their advantage: they could prepare for war without the mess of waging it. Surely domestic politics in both the democratic West and the authoritarian East continued to play a role: Stalin had no monopoly on the ancient practice of using external enemies to justify internal policies.[5] Surely the existence of allies encouraged continuity, for the trouble of constructing an alliance can make its perpetuation seem as vital as its purposes. And surely, too, the sheer passage of time slowly accustomed those who fought the Cold War to its omnipresence. It became, in a way, the geopolitical equivalent of a Skinner box, within which it was difficult to see that alternative patterns of stimulus and response might be possible.

One of these alternatives—a path not taken—was a negotiated settlement that might have ended the conflict before it became a habit. It is easy now to say that the Cold War could only have disappeared when the Soviet Union did; but we ought not to accept this proposition without testing it. Were there opportunities to resolve outstanding differences through diplomacy? Did the West do all it could to pursue them, if they existed? To what extent is it fair to conclude that the victors in the Cold War, by refusing to accept anything *short* of victory, themselves perpetuated it?

It is not as though no negotiations took place. The wartime allies agreed, in 1946, on peace treaties for former German satellites, and the Council of Foreign Ministers continued to meet regularly if unproductively through the end of 1947. The international control of atomic energy was thoroughly discussed at the United Nations, even if no agreement emerged. Soviet and Western diplomats attempted to resolve the Berlin blockade crisis through the summer and fall of 1948, and eventually succeeded in the spring of 1949. After the Korean War broke out, behind-the-scenes contacts involving all combatants eventually led to formal—if for another two years futile—armistice negotiations. Further talks would produce a fragile Indochina settlement in 1954, a mutual withdrawal of occupation forces from Austria in the spring of 1955, and the first of many Cold War summits: the meeting between the American, Soviet, British, and French heads of government that took place at Geneva in July of that year.

And yet there was a frustrating quality to all of these deliberations, because none of them addressed the issues that were keeping the Cold War going. They failed to dismantle Soviet and American spheres of influence in Europe, or to slow the intensifying nuclear arms race, or to restrain competition in what was coming to be called the "third world." Above all, they left Germany divided, thereby perpetuating a situation which, if it had not directly caused the Cold War, did more than anything else to delay its settlement. The German question provides a useful case, hence, through which to explore the possibility that opportunities existed, but were missed, to end the Cold War at an earlier stage in its history.

I

The most striking anomaly of the Cold War was the existence of a divided Europe, within which there resided a divided Germany, within which there lay a divided Berlin. No one in Washington, Moscow, or anywhere else had sought such an arrangement, so at odds with all previous standards of geopolitical logic. Few who witnessed how it came about prior to 1949 would have expected it still to be in place as late as 1989. Still the passage of time can make even the oddest situations seem ordinary. This one would become so in the years following construction of the Berlin Wall in 1961, to such an extent that the abrupt collapse of that structure and the system it symbolized twenty-eight years later came as an even greater surprise than its creation. Some strange mechanism seems to have been at work in Germany that allowed the bizarre over the years to become unexceptionable, only to reverse the procedure virtually overnight.

Germany was going to be divided at the end of World War II whatever else happened: invasion on several fronts by several enemies ensured different treatment from that accorded the Japanese. In this sense, Hitler himself—who collected enemies as avidly as he did bad art—was the architect of German disunity, as of so much else.[6] Presumably, though, the occupying powers could have reunited Germany quickly had they agreed on what its character was to be. There were two reasons why they were unable to do this.

The first had to do with lessons of the past. Would punishing the Germans more harshly than after the first world war provide the best protection against a third? Or had the Versailles Treaty failed precisely because of its harshness? Permanent partition would make sense if the punitive option were chosen; reunification if the goal was to be reconciliation. The problem here was not that the Americans, British, and Russians disagreed with one another, but rather that they were themselves unsure of what course to follow.[7] Only the French were clear on the need for punishment and partition; but they were hardly in a position to affect what their more powerful allies would eventually do.[8] Disarray within as much as among the victors, therefore, could have delayed a German settlement, even if there had been no Cold War.

But of course there was a Cold War, and it became the second and more significant reason for Germany's division. What each superpower most feared was that its wartime enemy might align itself with its Cold War adversary: if that were to happen, the resulting concentration of military, industrial, and economic power could be too great to overcome. "[T]he Soviets have abandoned the policy to weaken Germany but are relying instead on their belief that a reasonably strong Germany is more to their advantage," White House aide Clark M. Clifford warned President Truman in September 1946.[9] That same week Soviet Ambassador Nikolai Novikov reported to Moscow: "[T]he United States is considering the possibility of terminating the Allied occupation of German territory before the main tasks of the occupation—the demilitarization and democratization of Germany—have been implemented. This would create the prerequisites for the revival of an imperialist Germany, which the United States plans to use in a future war on its side."[10]

It was this convergence of concerns—how to avoid the danger of a resurgent Germany itself, on the one hand, *and* the threat of a Germany on the wrong side in the Cold War, on the other—that made its future so central an issue in the evolution, if not the actual origins, of that conflict. But that convergence did not occur simultaneously in Moscow and Washington. It is now clear that Stalin came to see Germany as a postwar *and* a Cold War problem well before the Americans did.

New evidence reveals that Stalin met with the leaders of the German Communist Party (KPD) as early as 4 June 1945, to lay out plans for incorporating a reunified Germany within Moscow's sphere of influence. Two principal instruments would accomplish this: the Red Army would control the Soviet occupation zone, while the KPD would seek popular support beyond the reach of Soviet military authority. Germany would at first be divided, with its eastern territories administered by the Russians, the remainder by the Western allies. Within the east the KPD would merge with the Social Democrats (SPD) to form the Socialist Unity Party (SED), thus following the example of other Eastern and Central European communist parties which were, under Soviet instructions, organizing "national fronts" with non-communist parties on the left. Having consolidated its position in the east, the SED, operating under KPD control, would then solicit the allegiance of Social Democrats and other sympathetic Germans in the west, and by these means bring about unification.[11] "[A]ll of Germany must be ours," Stalin assured the Yugoslavs in the spring of 1946, "that is, Soviet, Communist."[12]

Several things are worth noting about this plan. First, it shows that Stalin wanted *both* partition *and* reunification: the first would make the second possible on terms he could accept. Second, it reveals his assumption—a year *before* they decided to do it—that the Americans, British, and French would treat their zones as a single unit: that view was at odds with Moscow's official position at the time, which was to favor common economic and administrative structures for all of Germany. Third, it confirms that Stalin hoped to see Soviet influence spread throughout Germany without his having to impose it: the KPD–SPD merger is hard to explain except as an effort to increase the German communists' popularity in the west.[13]

But if that is true, then Stalin's plan also suggests a fourth point, which is that his strategy was out of line with his tactics. The Soviet Union was not winning friends among Germans anywhere by allowing its army to rape women, pillage property, indiscriminately extract reparations, or unilaterally transfer large portions of prewar territory to the Poles.[14] As one Soviet official admitted: "there are more Communists in the Western part of the country, which [has] not been in touch with the Red Army, than in Berlin."[15] Finally, Stalin appears to have given little thought to what his wartime allies might do, within their own occupation zones, that might interfere with his grand design. How did the Russians mean to bring it all about, the Yugoslavs asked one of the great man's subordinates. He answered: "I don't know myself!"[16]

The Americans, however, were at least as confused in the summer of 1945. Supporters of the defunct Morgenthau Plan in the War and Treasury Departments continued to call for punishment and possible partition without regard to how this might affect relations with the Soviet Union: their influence lingered, as we have seen, in the provisions of JCS 1067, the official directive for the occupation of Germany. General Lucius Clay, on the scene, had a very different view: he stressed the need for rehabilitation and quick reunification; but he carefully insulated his thinking from Cold War controversies elsewhere, assumed Moscow's cooperation, and saw the most likely resistance as coming from the French. Meanwhile a third group, centered in the State Department, supported Clay on rehabilitation but thought reunification unlikely, not so much because of what the Russians were doing inside Germany but because of what was happening elsewhere in Eastern Europe. George Kennan put this argument in its starkest form: "We have no choice but to lead our section of Germany—the section of which we and the British have accepted responsibility—to a form of independence so prosperous, so secure, so superior, that the East cannot threaten it."[17]

It was left to the British to push the Truman administration into choosing between these alternatives. More accustomed than the Americans to thinking about balances of power, more skeptical about Soviet intentions, more worried about the costs of administering separate zones, the British Foreign Office had been quicker to see Kennan's logic than his own government had been. During the summer of 1946, Foreign Secretary Ernest Bevin maneuvered Secretary of State James F. Byrnes into proposing that the American and British occupation zones become a single economic unit,[18] thereby beginning the process of zonal consolidation Stalin had foreseen a year earlier. General George C. Marshall, who replaced Byrnes early in 1947, still hoped to find an acceptable basis for reunification at a four-power foreign ministers' meeting in Moscow that would run from early March through late April. But forty-three unproductive sessions with Molotov made it clear that that was not likely to happen.

The Soviet foreign minister's reputation for repetitiously tedious obstinacy has misled historians into assuming that nothing much occurred at Moscow. Being stuck in the Soviet capital with little to do but listen to Molotov—particularly at a time when the President had just proclaimed the Truman Doctrine—must have seemed, to Marshall, Bevin, and French Foreign Minister Georges Bidault, like serving on a sequestered jury in a very long trial. But they put the experience to good use by holding informal conversations on the future of Germany. These produced the first consensus among *all* the Western allies, including the French, in support of Bevin's view that a truncated and rehabilitated Germany would be less dangerous than a unified state that might come under Soviet control.[19]

The discussions must have taken place within range of Stalin's eavesdropping devices.[20] But the Soviet leader, in this instance, failed to see what was happening under his nose and even inadvertently encouraged it. The failure to agree on Germany, he told Marshall as the conference drew to a close, was not so tragic:

[T]hese were only the first skirmishes and brushes of reconnaissance forces on this question. . . . [C]ompromises were possible on all the main questions including demilitarization, political structure of Germany, reparations and economic unity. It was necessary to have patience and not become depressed.[21]

These relaxed remarks profoundly alarmed Marshall—almost certainly because Stalin's reassurances in the past had provided so little basis for reassurance. If the Kremlin boss was optimistic about Germany then that was ample reason for the West not to be: he must have a plan, and he must think that it was succeeding. What it might be was not yet clear, but the status quo, as Charles E. Bohlen recalled, was bad enough: "All the way back to Washington, Marshall talked of the importance of finding some initiative to prevent the complete breakdown of Western Europe."[22]

   The product of these ruminations was, of course, the Marshall Plan, for which Marshall himself, quite properly, has received most of the credit. But Stalin too ought to be remembered as at least an unwitting architect, because it was his apparent confidence that time was on his side in Germany that drove the American Secretary of State to propose the initiative in the first place. The United States now set out to reverse that perception, not only in Stalin's mind but, more significantly, in the minds of the Europeans whose actions would ultimately determine what happened on the Continent. Washington's promise of economic assistance achieved that psychological effect long before the aid in question had actually arrived, with the result that the Americans soon had a sphere of influence in Europe that was at least as solid as its Soviet counterpart.[23] The Marshall Plan had an equally decisive effect, we can now see, on Stalin's hopes for a reunified Germany under Soviet control.

II

It was clear by this time that Europe could not revive without Germany: earlier ideas for rehabilitating Germany's neighbors while punishing the Germans themselves—particularly through such measures as an internationalization of the Ruhr—had come to seem increasingly unworkable.[24] But Stalin's rejection of the Marshall Plan excluded eastern Germany from it, along with the rest of Eastern Europe. The idea of a western Germany linked to a reviving Western Europe therefore gained support through the last half of 1947. After yet another foreign ministers' conference failed to produce progress toward reunification, the Americans, British, and French began openly planning the consolidation of their occupation zones and the establishment within them of a provisional German government.[25] By June 1948, the three allies plus the Benelux countries had agreed to allow the West Germans "those governmental responsibilities which are compatible with the minimum requirements of occupation . . . and which ultimately will enable them to assume full governmental responsibility."[26] This "London Conference program," as it came to be known, was not yet an irrevocable decision to divide Germany: the participants claimed to be acting primarily to promote economic recovery, and left open the possibility of subsequent reunification.[27] But there were stark geopolitical implications in what they had decided to do.

One of these was the abandonment of any further pretense at four-power cooperation. Stalin's intentions with respect to Germany were still not clear to western observers, but his behavior elsewhere in Europe left little reason to assume their benevolence. Clay, who had earlier resisted letting Cold War concerns shape his policies, now shifted to a completely opposite view: "we must have the courage to proceed quickly with the establishment of a government for western Germany. . . . 42 million Germans in the British and American zones represent today the strongest outpost against Communist penetration that exists anywhere."[28] The western occupying authorities were, in short, coming to think of the Germans more as future allies than as defeated adversaries.[29] And once they began to involve the Germans in local and regional administration, it was difficult to restrict them to that level; efforts to rebuild German self-confidence produced—not very surprisingly—German self-confidence.[30] By the summer of 1948, then, the idea of establishing of a separate West German state had gained considerable momentum.

Stalin's 1945 plan, conversely, was losing it. He had expected that economic distress in western Germany would cause class consciousness to merge with national consciousness, so that the inhabitants of that region would seek unification with the east by electing parties on the left under Moscow's control. This was not a completely implausible prospect: Germans had, in the past, demonstrated the capacity to produce authoritarian governments by constitutional means. But Hitler gained and retained power in 1933 by promising an economic *and* a national revival. Stalin was unable to do the same. The brutal behavior of Soviet troops in Germany, the forced merger of the SPD with the KPD, the territorial concessions to Poland, all took their toll. "Deviations from Marxist positions pose a substantial danger for the [SED]," a worried Colonel S. I. Tiul'panov, who handled propaganda for the Soviet occupation authorities, reported to Moscow in September 1946: "[W]e run the danger of allowing the party to revert to extreme nationalism."[31] Remarkably enough, Stalin allowed free municipal elections in the Soviet zone the following month, despite warnings—correct, as it turned out—that the SED would fare badly in them. One desperate apparatchik even suggested, shortly before this embarrassment, that Moscow might want to send in musical groups, symphonies, opera and theater troupes to demonstrate to the resentful Germans the superiority of Russian culture.[32]

The task Stalin faced in Germany was one for which he was ill-prepared: he had to win the support of people he could not entirely control. It would have been easy enough to impose his will inside the Soviet zone, but only by ruining prospects for incorporating the rest of Germany within Moscow's sphere of influence. To achieve that larger goal, he would have to make his policies in the east attractive in the west, no simple task given his reliance on such seedy and subservient characters as Pieck, Grotewohl, and Ulbricht.[33] Stalin was loath to abandon reunification: he appears to have clung, almost to the end of his life, to the illusion that ideology sooner or later would override nationalism and bring all Germans, by their own choice, into the socialist camp. But this was, yet again, an example of romanticism residing within authoritarianism.[34] In the light of what was happening in western Germany at the time, it was never a realistic strategy.

The Marshall Plan gave Germans outside the Soviet zone a choice: they could follow the Stalinist path toward national unity, knowing that the Soviet Union's capacity to bring about economic recovery was minimal and likely to remain so; or they could seek immediate economic assistance through alignment with the United States and its allies, knowing that the effect might be to postpone German reunification for years to come. When put that way, the dilemma was not too difficult to resolve: the material benefits of prosperity—especially when linked to the political advantages of democracy—outweighed, for most West Germans, whatever the psychological satisfactions of reunification might have been. "Unfortunately, at a certain stage," Nikita Khrushchev would later comment, "ideological issues are decided by the stomach, that is, by seeing who can provide the most for people's daily needs."[35]

Pieck acknowledged as much when he warned Soviet officials, late in March 1948, that support for the Marshall Plan was growing in western Germany while the SED had lost ground and was coming to be seen as the "so-called Russian official party."[36] Tiul'panov was even more pessimistic. He admitted to the East Germans that

the Soviet occupation force in Germany has made incredible . . . mistakes, which unfortunately can only be rectified with great difficulty. As the only excuse, I can only say that we never previously had to deal with a Socialist occupation. Perhaps I can give assurance that if in the future we should be compelled once again by our opponents to carry through another Socialist occupation then we will have learned from our experiences in Germany and will do it better.[37]

Increasingly worried about winning elections even within the east, the SED leaders, with Moscow's approval, now began planning their own separate regime.[38] "The West will make Western Germany their own," Stalin explained to the Yugoslavs, "and we shall turn Eastern Germany into our own state."[39]

It is not yet clear to what extent this shift in strategy influenced Stalin's decision to begin tightening restrictions on Western access to Berlin. But it has long been apparent—and such Soviet documents as are available now confirm—that the blockade was a reaction to the London Conference program in general, and to its plans for currency reform in particular. The idea, a Soviet foreign ministry official noted, was to "take steps which would not only restrict separate actions of the US, Britain, and France in Germany but also efficiently thwart their plans of knocking together a Western bloc, with Germany to be incorporated in it."[40]

Stalin's grudging acknowledgement that the blockade had failed, early in 1949, allowed the configuration of postwar Germany to fall into place. The Western allies hastened to proclaim the Federal Republic of Germany (FRG), whose "Basic Law," or provisional constitution, went into effect in May 1949. The German Democratic Republic (GDR) was established, under Soviet sponsorship, the following October, with Berlin remaining under four-power occupation deep within its territory. A set of arrangements hastily improvised at the end of the war had hardened into an improbable but indefinite status quo: the postwar German settlement, or so it seemed, was to be the postwar European settlement projected down to the level of a divided country and even a divided capital. How long this situation would last was not clear at the time. But one thing was: none of the parties concerned—neither the Berliners, nor the West or East Germans, nor the Americans and their allies, nor the Russians—saw it as a permanent solution.

III

Washington's role in all of this had been uncharacteristically passive: officials there gave relatively little thought to the German problem as a whole during the early postwar years, preoccupied as they were with containing Soviet expansionism, reviving the European economy, and demonstrating resolve in Berlin. The British had been more purposeful, nudging the Truman administration toward a consolidation of occupation zones which then complemented the Marshall Plan; having gone that far, it seemed to make sense to form a separate West German state. Policy emerged incrementally, though: no one sat down to determine whether Kennan's 1945 vision of an indefinitely divided Germany would provide the basis for a sustainable policy. Meanwhile another British initiative—Bevin's idea of a military alliance that would link the United States to Western Europe—was gaining support on both sides of the Atlantic without anyone having decided how the West Germans were going to fit into it. For a country whose geopolitical significance should have been obvious, Germany's future was being determined on a surprisingly *ad hoc* basis.

It was Kennan who first questioned this process: "We should not consent," he argued in August 1948, "to let the important decisions depend entirely on the action of others."[41] Although the Truman administration had accepted the substance of what he recommended in 1945, Kennan resisted this apparent vindication: he so strongly distrusted conventional wisdom that he could reject his own arguments when they seemed likely to attain that status.[42] As director of the State Department's Policy Planning Staff, it was his responsibility, in any event, to think ahead; and as he did so during the midst of the Berlin blockade, he came to the conclusion that the indefinite division of

Germany—the very thing he had advocated at the end of the war—would be a great mistake.

How could a stable settlement in Europe ever evolve if the spheres of influence the United States and the Soviet Union had constructed there extended so far as to divide a single nation—potentially the most powerful on the Continent—between them? This system would keep Germany down, to be sure, but it would also lock the Cold War in by complicating any mutually negotiated withdrawal of Soviet and American forces from the advanced positions they had occupied at the end of the war. Several things could then happen, none of them good. The American public might grow tired of sustaining such a military burden at a time when it was also financing European recovery; cuts in Congressional appropriations might then force a unilateral pull-back the Russians could exploit. The Soviet Union itself might promise such a pull-back, knowing that it could rapidly reintroduce its forces from neighboring Poland; the Americans would have no comparably convenient staging area. Even if these events did not occur, the Germans would not stand for having Soviet and American troops indefinitely on their soil. Sooner or later they would make their own settlement, not necessarily to the advantage of the United States. "[T]he development of life in Europe cannot await the composure of east–west differences," Kennan concluded. "Something must be done; and something will be done, whether we like it or not."[43]

The alternative, he argued, should be free elections throughout Germany, the formation of a central government, and the withdrawal of occupation forces into enclaves just inside the country's borders: this plan came to be known within the State Department as "Program A." The American, British, and Soviet positions would be supplied by sea, an important aspect of Kennan's proposal since it would remove Moscow's principal excuse for keeping the Red Army in Poland. A four-power high commission would initially monitor the actions of the new German government, but the Germans themselves would bear primary responsibility for their own affairs.[44] Kennan hoped that they would align with neither the Soviet nor the American side, but rather constitute a "third force" in Europe: this would fit his larger strategy of seeking to deny the Russians potential centers of industrial-military power without having the United States dominate them.[45] It was only on such a basis, he insisted, that one could begin to see how the Cold War might end.

Kennan gave the impression, in his memoirs, that Program A was never taken seriously in Washington,[46] but this is not correct. The plan was throughly discussed within the Policy Planning Staff and reviewed by outside consultants, all with the approval of Secretary of State Marshall. Shortly after Acheson took over the State Department in January 1949, he in turn read Program A and indicated his general agreement with it. He did not understand, he commented, "how we ever arrived at the decision to see established a Western German government or State."[47] Both approaches to the German question—continued division and eventual unification—received careful consideration prior to a May 1949, foreign ministers' meeting to which the Western allies had agreed in return for the Russians' lifting of the Berlin blockade. "Just as the unification of Germany is not an end in itself," Acheson observed, "so the division of Germany is not an end in itself."[48]

Program A generated resistance, though, from Pentagon planners, who found Kennan's idea of military enclaves questionable, and even more from those Americans whose energies had gone into developing the London Conference program. It would amount to "turning the show over to Russia and the Communists without a struggle," General Clay complained: "We have won the battle, but . . . [we] are writing an armistice as if we had lost the battle."[49] Moreover, as diplomat Robert Murphy pointed out, the choice need not be between reunification and continued division: a prosperous West Germany linked to Western Europe could serve as a "magnet" that would in time attract the East Germans, detaching *them* from Soviet control.[50] Acheson had made no effort, meanwhile, to persuade the British and the French of Program A's merits, or to prepare the West Germans for it; and shortly before the foreign ministers met, an oversimplified version leaked to the press. The resulting speculation that the United States might withdraw its forces sent shivers down European spines, and the Secretary of State immediately shelved Kennan's plan.[51]

The demise of Program A was not so much the abandonment of an objective as of a process. Kennan had hoped that policy on Germany could emerge as had the Marshall Plan: from a careful balancing of long-term interests against immediate capabilities that would allow the United States to seize the initiative and shape the outcome. Murphy's "magnet" strategy had evolved, however, from incremental adjustments and hasty improvisations. No one on the American side designed it; the British, the French, and increasingly the West Germans— from whom the idea of a "magnet" may have originated[52]—largely drove it. Reunification would remain the declared goal, but neither the United States nor its allies would risk security or prosperity to achieve it. As Paul Nitze, an expert on the distinction between declaratory and actual policies, would later remember: "Even those who feared the strength of a reunited Germany saw no prospect of its being accomplished and therefore no danger in supporting it as an objective."[53]

There were those, however, who feared the strength even of a divided Germany: this became clear when the issue of rearming the West Germans suddenly arose in the summer of 1950. British and French support for the London Conference program had been based on the expectation that the new government in Bonn would have no military forces of its own;[54] indeed, there had been so little disagreement over this point that it had hardly come up prior to the signing of the North Atlantic Treaty and the establishment of the German Federal Republic. But once there was a West German state *and* a NATO alliance, there would have to be a military relationship between them. The situation, from NATO's standpoint, was not encouraging: estimates were that the Soviet Union could draw on some 175 divisions in any future war while the alliance would be able to manage only 12. Experts knew better, but even so there was then and remains now no question of Soviet conventional-force superiority on the Continent.[55]

Whatever the military imbalance, resistance to rearming the West Germans remained strong in the United States, Western Europe, and even among many West Germans. The Truman administration had had to scramble to persuade Congress of the need to arm NATO *allies* in the summer of 1949,[56] and despite NSC-68's conclusion that American military capabilities, together with those of the new alliance, were "dangerously inadequate,"[57] few people in Washington and still fewer in London, Paris, or Bonn were ready to contemplate the prospect of a new German army so soon after the defeat of the old one. Chancellor Konrad Adenauer himself, who worried publicly and often about the inadequacy of West German defenses, would only go so far as to endorse the idea of a federal police force.[58]

From a purely military standpoint, rearming the Germans would make sense, just as it would to have accepted General Francisco Franco's invitation to construct American air bases in Spain or to have included the Chinese Nationalists on Taiwan within the self-proclaimed United States "defensive perimeter" in the western Pacific. All of these options were considered in the Pentagon during the spring of 1950.[59] But for the Truman administration the *political* costs of yielding to military expediency, in each of these instances, outweighed the advantages. "[D]ecidedly militaristic," President Truman snapped, when a Defense Department report in June imprudently coupled rearming the West Germans with support for Franco. "Both as wrong as can be."[60]

The outbreak of fighting in Korea later that month erased the gap between military desirability and political feasibility in the minds of American officials, though, and West German rearmament, like bases in Spain and the defense of Taiwan, now became realistic possibilities. Korea, it appeared, might be only a prelude to more substantial Soviet military offensives elsewhere: if that were to happen, fastidiousness in selecting allies would seem foolish. East German party leader Ulbricht helped advance this viewpoint by imprudently citing Kim Il-sung's example as a way to reunify Germany: "If the Americans in their imperialist arrogance believe that the Germans have less national consciousness than the Koreans, then they have fundamentally deceived themselves."[61] Moved by the obvious alarm the West Germans felt—but also by their equally obvious willingness to resist—American High Commissioner John J. McCloy cabled Washington on 18 July: "If no means are held out for the Germans to fight in an emergency my view is that we should probably lose Germany politically as well as militarily without hope of regain. We should also lose, incidentally, a reserve of manpower which may become of great value in event of a real war and could certainly be used by the Soviets against us."[62]

But even though the British and the French had pushed for the creation of an independent West German state, and even though the Korean crisis had badly shaken them, they did not find it easy to accept German rearmament. To reassure them, the Truman administration—confronting the unaccustomed prospect of budgetary plenty, Korea having so dramatically legitimized the arguments of NSC-68[63]—decided to send four army divisions to Western Europe to supplement its occupation forces inside Germany. The French at this point proposed another of their palliatives, like the idea of a European Coal and Steel Community earlier in the year,[64] designed to ease the pain of collaborating with the Germans. At the suggestion of Premier René Pleven, it was agreed that the FRG would have no army of its own, but rather that its military forces would be integrated into those of a multinational European Defense Community, coordinated with but apart from NATO. The Americans, in turn, enhanced the Pleven Plan's appeal by announcing that the universally respected General Dwight D. Eisenhower would come out of retirement to become NATO's first Supreme Commander.[65]

This intricate sequence of commitments and compromises transformed the NATO alliance from what it had been in 1949—a promise that the United States would assist the Europeans in case of a Soviet attack—into an arrangement that would place American troops squarely in the path of such an invasion if it should ever occur.[66] There they would fight, if necessary, alongside the West Germans, who would certainly be honorary if not actual NATO partners. What the Russians had most dreaded was about to come to pass: a West Germany rehabilitated, rearmed, and thoroughly incorporated within an American sphere of influence. What they could hardly have anticipated was the extent to which their own actions had brought this about.

The critical decisions that shaped the future of West Germany—zonal consolidation, the London Conference program, the European Coal and Steel Community, the Pleven Plan—were in each case improvisations suggested by allies and accepted by the Americans: Washington had no "grand design." Neither, though, was what happened an accident. Each of these initiatives was a response to what Stalin had done: his initial reluctance to reach a four-power agreement on Germany, his rejection of the Marshall Plan, his decision to blockade Berlin, his authorization to Kim Il-sung to invade South Korea.[67] To this extent, the Soviet leader inadvertently founded and rearmed West Germany. He was in this instance, as in so many others, the ultimate source of his own worst fears.

Stalin was not oblivious to all of this, though. The more we learn about his policy toward Germany during the last four years of his life, the more it makes sense to see it as an increasingly desperate series of maneuvers aimed at reversing the unfavorable trend he had set in motion and salvaging his own scheme for a reunified Germany under Soviet control. The final and most dramatic of these initiatives, launched early in 1952, would be the aging autocrat's own version of Kennan's Program A.

IV

Old men normally do not like surprises, but Stalin sprang more than his share in his declining years. The Korean War, of course, was the biggest; but he also took the time, while it was going on, to participate in an extended debate on linguistics (in which he predictably prevailed), to convene the first Soviet Communist Party Congress in thirteen years, to publish—or have published under his name—a monograph on *Economic Problems of Socialism in the USSR*, to declare the new American ambassador in the Soviet Union, George Kennan, *persona non grata*, and to begin a new round of purges involving several of his closest associates, ultimately even his own physicians.[68] Within this period of increasingly erratic behavior, though, Stalin suddenly launched what some observers have regarded as his most enlightened act of statesmanship: the proposal of 10 March 1952 for a four-power conference to arrange free elections throughout Germany, which would in turn establish an independent, reunified, rearmed, but neutral state.[69] It was as if he had somehow stumbled upon Kennan's rejected proposals from three years earlier, and had decided to make them his own.

There was little inclination in Western capitals to explore this offer. It arrived just after the NATO allies had agreed, at Lisbon, on an ambitious conventional force build-up—including West German forces operating through the European Defense Community—that would have gone some distance toward redressing the military imbalance in Europe. It preceded, by only a few weeks, the signing of treaties ending the occupation regime in West Germany and incorporating that state into the EDC. Intelligence reports had anticipated that the Russians would offer just such an exchange of reunification for neutralization,[70] and there was little doubt that it would attract support within an increasingly prosperous and self-confident FRG. Adenauer's preference for alignment with the United States and Western Europe was by no means universally popular among his countrymen, not least because it seemed to postpone reunification indefinitely, if not to abandon that objective altogether.[71] Nor was there confidence that a unified Germany would always remain neutral: few who remembered the Rapallo agreement of 1922 and the Molotov–Ribbentrop pact of 1939 could rule out the possibility that Germans and Russians might again be tempted into disastrous collaboration.[72]

As in earlier crises involving Germany, it was the British—not the Americans—who shaped the Western response. Foreign Secretary Anthony Eden acknowledged that the Soviet government might "now be prepared to pay [a] bigger price" to prevent West Germany's integration into Western Europe. But there would be too many risks involved in finding out: the safer choice would be to "strengthen support for West Ger[man] rearmament within [an] EDC framework."[73] Acheson himself was willing to consider negotiations with the Russians, if for no other reason than to "convince Ger[man]s we mean business and are not afraid to talk," to "expose Sov[iet] insincerity," and "if Sov[iet]s are really prepared to open Eastern Zone, [to] force their hand."[74] But the British and the French as well as Adenauer rejected this course, and there ensued what Eden called the "battle of the notes": a series of carefully-drafted public exchanges with Moscow that delayed any action on the Soviet initiative until the projected treaties had been signed ending the occupation and bringing West Germany into the EDC.[75] Stalin himself soon abandoned his proposal;

and his successors never revived it, committing themselves instead to ensuring East Germany's survival.

Ever since, though, the question has lingered: could Stalin have been serious? If he feared, above all else, the alignment of a former adversary with a current and future one—as there is every reason to think he did—would it have been so implausible to sacrifice an increasingly unpopular and ineffective East German regime in order to forestall such an outcome?[76] Should the United States and its Western European allies not at least have tested Stalin's sincerity? Did not their own preoccupation with building strength cause them to miss an opportunity to moderate, if not to end, the Cold War in Europe, and to achieve German reunification almost four decades earlier than it was in fact accomplished?[77]

It is clear now that Stalin never wanted a separate East German state. He repeatedly sought to restrain the German communists from taking measures within the Soviet zone that might alienate Germans elsewhere,[78] and he appears to have agreed only reluctantly—*after* it had become obvious that there was to be an independent West Germany—to the establishment of the German Democratic Republic in the fall of 1949. Even then, the SED received only associate membership in the Cominform. The GDR did not participate on an equal basis with other East European satellites in major diplomatic initiatives, and the Soviet Union did not establish full diplomatic relations with it until after Stalin's death. It is entirely possible, then, that the Soviet leader *did* see the East Germans as expendable: the question was under what circumstances he would be prepared to expend them.[79]

The idea for the March 1952 note came from the Soviet Foreign Ministry. Such an initiative, Deputy Foreign Minister Gromyko suggested, would strengthen "the struggle for peace and against remilitarization of West Germany," and would "help the advocates of Germany's unity and of peace to unmask the three Western powers' aggressive intentions." Prior Soviet and East German efforts to achieve this had not worked, the Poles and the Czechs were told. The new approach was intended "to develop a respective campaign in the press and among the German population against the aggressive policy of the three powers concerning West Germany."[80] The East Germans themselves were informed that West German membership in the EDC would be equivalent to membership in NATO itself, and that the purpose of the note was to prevent that development by bringing down the Adenauer government.[81] Soviet diplomat Vladimir Semyonov recalled Stalin asking: was it *certain* the Americans would turn the note down? Only when assured that it was did the Soviet leader give his approval, but with the warning that there would be grave consequences for Semyonov if this did not prove to be the case.[82]

The initial Western response, conveyed on 25 March, must have made Semyonov nervous, for it was not a flat rejection. It observed that the United Nations had already established a commission to investigate whether the facilities for free elections existed inside Germany, and invited the Soviet Government to say whether it would be allowed into East Germany and East

Berlin.[83] But this was enough for Stalin. "[I]rrespective of any proposals that we can make on the German question," he told East German leaders Ulbricht and Pieck on 7 April, "the Western powers will not agree with them and will not withdraw from Germany in any case."

They say that they have there their army [to defend] against us. But the real goal of this army is to control Europe. The Americans will draw West Germany into the Atlantic Pact. They will create West German troops. Adenauer is in the pocket of the Americans. All ex-fascists and generals also are there. In reality there is an independent state being formed in West Germany. And you must organize your own state.

Henceforth the line of demarcation between the two halves of Germany was to be seen "not as a simple border but as a dangerous one. One must strengthen the protection of this frontier."[84] It might still be too soon to construct socialism in the GDR, the Kremlin boss cautioned. But in July the SED Party Conference announced an all-out program to do just that. Stalin did not object.[85]

Although the "battle of the notes" continued through the summer, it had a decidedly perfunctory character. Kennan, now serving in Moscow, saw signs of a Soviet position "having been prepared by hacks supplied only with grudging, cryptic and guarded instr[uction]s and told to make [the] best of it."[86] But as he himself would later acknowledge, much the same could be said of his own government's attitude.[87] Acheson's expressions of interest in German reunification were abstract and fleeting.[88] The Secretary of State found it easier to go along with than to try to reverse the momentum that had built up within the Truman administration and among its European allies—now including the West Germans themselves—behind completing as quickly as possible the division and consolidation Kennan himself, ironically, had recommended in 1945.

That this process frightened Stalin is clear enough. He received an intelligence report in July 1952 warning that the EDC would not be able to control West Germany, which might once again attack France *and* seek to regain territories lost to the Soviet Union, Poland, and Czechoslovakia at the end of World War II.[89] "What guarantee is there," he asked in *Economic Problems of Socialism*, which appeared in October, "that Germany and Japan will not rise to their feet again, will not attempt to break out of American bondage and live their own independent lives? I think there is no such guarantee."[90] But it is not at all clear that Stalin would ever have negotiated seriously with the Americans, British, and French to keep this from happening: from 1945 on his consistent position had been that only a Germany under Moscow's control could, with any reliability, ensure the Soviet Union's safety. The March 1952 note may have represented a last fragile hope on Stalin's part that he could achieve this outcome by popular consent and without a war: had there been any possibility of this, the East German communists surely would have been expendable. A Soviet-dominated Germany, however, would not have been. Stalin, as Molotov later put it, "would never have abandoned the conquests of socialism."[91]

If such a Germany was not to be—and Stalin seems to have become convinced that his offer had failed *before* the West had formally rejected it—then a socialist East Germany firmly incorporated within the Soviet bloc would be the next best alternative. The Soviet leader finally settled on this option during the last months of his life. The battle of the historians over Stalin's note would continue for decades afterwards, but the battle in his own mind was over: there was, here, no "missed opportunity." Stalin was not about to implement Program A.

V

Stalin's death on 5 March 1953, however, opened up what may have been a more promising opportunity to reunify Germany; although only very briefly and through the actions of a distinctively odious historical agent, the long-time Soviet secret police chief Lavrentii Beria. From the day of the old dictator's demise his successors began trying to free themselves from his oppressive legacy. Part of this process was a strikingly more conciliatory approach to the outside world. As early as 1 April, a State Department official was noting that during the past several weeks there had been "more Soviet gestures toward the West than at any other similar period," and that the climate for negotiations looked sufficiently promising that the United States should begin to formulate the positions it might take.[92] In response to this new mood President Eisenhower, on 16 April, made a dramatic speech deploring the costs and risks of the nuclear arms race, welcoming the new initiatives emanating from the Kremlin, and calling on it to "help turn the tide of history." To the astonishment of almost everyone, *Pravda* on 25 April ran a full and accurate translation, an event the new American ambassador to the Soviet Union, Charles E. Bohlen, described as "unparalleled in the Soviet Union since the institution of the Stalinist dictatorship."[93]

Germany was an area where new approaches were urgently needed. Ulbricht's program of forced industrialization and collectivization, which he had rushed to implement after Stalin abandoned his own reunification proposal in the summer of 1952, had quickly proven disastrous. By the end of the year the Soviet Union was heavily subsidizing the East German regime, and the East Germans themselves were fleeing as rapidly as they could to West Germany—some 120,000 left in the first four months of 1953.[94] At Stalin's funeral, Ulbricht appealed for further economic assistance, but the new Soviet leaders turned him down, advising him instead to slow the pace of socialization. Ulbricht refused: he was, Molotov later admitted, "a politically conscious comrade, who was somewhat blunt and lacked flexibility."[95] Within weeks the new government in Moscow was facing a major crisis in its East German satellite. The Presidium of the Soviet Council of Ministers met to consider the problem on 27 May, and it was there that a remarkable new initiative on Germany surfaced, from none other than Beria.

Most of what we know about this plan comes from Beria's enemies, who used it as one of their excuses for arresting and subsequently executing him; but a rare surviving sympathizer has now confirmed its basic outlines.[96] The scheme appears to have assumed that continued efforts to force socialism on East Germany would only saddle the Soviet Union with a permanently unstable satellite, while facilitating West Germany's ever-closer alignment with the EDC, NATO, and the United States. Would the Soviet Union not benefit more from a unified and neutral Germany which, even if *capitalist*, could serve to *balance* both Soviet and American influence in Europe? Might the West Germans not be prepared to *pay* the USSR substantial reparations in order to have East Germany demoted to some kind of subordinate status within a single German state? If indeed these were the general outlines of Beria's program, they went well beyond Stalin's March 1952 note, which would have accepted reunification only in the form of a socialist state under Soviet control. "[A]ll we want is a peaceful Germany," Molotov recalls Beria as arguing, "and it makes no difference whether or not it is socialist."[97]

Beria had apparently chosen to use the German issue—and the prospect of improving relations with the West that such an approach might bring—to bolster his own position within the Kremlin leadership, and eventually to secure his position as successor to Stalin. This was only one of several dramatic measures he was contemplating at the time: the others included restricting Communist Party control over state institutions, dismantling the official terror apparatus he himself had helped to install during the late 1930s, and allowing greater cultural and political autonomy to the non-Russian nationalities.[98] It was neither the first nor the last time in Russian history that the very architects of authoritarianism had produced, from within, a perceptive self-diagnosis, coupled with the compulsion to reform.[99]

Worried as much by Beria's ambitions as by his ideas on Germany, however, his Presidium colleagues objected strongly, insisting instead on a reversion to Stalin's pre-1952 policy of restraint while at the same time leaving the way open for the eventual reunification of the entire country under Soviet control. The idea, as Molotov remembered it, was to be one of "pursu[ing] a path toward socialism, not forcibly but cautiously, and maneuvering skillfully until our position was stronger." [100] Orders went out that the East Germans were to abandon Ulbricht's program of rapid socialization in favor of a more modest approach, aimed at "the recovery of the political situation in the GDR and . . . a strengthening of our positions . . . in Germany itself" as well as bringing about "maximal division of the opponent's forces and the exploitation of every oppositional current against the tactics of the mercenary Adenauer clique."[101]

The East German government announced the new policy on 10 June, but Ulbricht immediately sabotaged it by failing to rescind an unpopular measure that had increased labor norms by 10 per cent. This combination of relaxation with continuing repression proved a volatile mix, and on 16–17 June workers in East Berlin and elsewhere in East Germany rose up in revolt, the first time such a thing had happened on such a scale anywhere within the postwar Soviet sphere of influence. Red Army troops quickly suppressed the uprising, with relatively few casualties.[102] But it soon became clear that there had been a very prominent casualty in Moscow.

On 26 June, at a tense Presidium meeting arranged by Khrushchev, Beria's colleagues confronted, arrested and charged him with treason: the scene could have graced "Godfather" movies of a subsequent generation. By the end of the year, he had been tried and executed, thereby earning the ironic—but well-deserved—distinction of being the last Soviet leader to suffer such a fate.[103] Beria's downfall meanwhile ensured Ulbricht's survival: he was now able to move against his own potential opponents with impunity. The East German leader may, or may not, have planned it all this way. But he certainly wrecked what little was left of Beria's German initiative; and the resulting disorders gave Beria's rivals in the Kremlin the excuse they needed to move against him. Having done so, it would have been difficult for any of them—at least as long as the succession struggle was under way—to oppose Ulbricht, since that would have suggested association with rebellion and treason.[104] The culture of distrust Stalin had left behind now linked his heirs to an East German leader Stalin himself had never trusted.

Had things turned out otherwise—had Beria succeeded Stalin and then revived his original proposals on the future of Germany—an interesting situation would have arisen. For if we understand his ideas correctly they came as close as the Soviet Union ever did, prior to the Cold War's end, to proposing a basis for German reunification the West might have accepted. It is even possible that Beria's program could have survived his demise: there were well-known precedents in Soviet history for the victors taking over the policies of the vanquished.[105] No such program could have succeeded, though, without some willingness on the part of the United States, Great Britain, France, and especially West Germany to consider reunification in the first place. It is worth asking, then, whether the West had become so accustomed to the reality of a divided Germany that it was no longer willing to examine alternatives.

VI

Kennan thought so. "Our people [are] unwilling to contemplate at any time within the foreseeable future, under any conceivable agreement with the Russians, the withdrawal of United States forces from Germany," he noted in September 1952, just before his expulsion from Moscow. "Our stand [means] in effect no agreement with Russia at all and the indefinite continuation of the split of Germany and Europe."[106] It is not so clear in retrospect that the Western position was in fact this rigid: certainly it is difficult to establish any specific point during the early 1950s at which the Americans categorically rejected the desirability, or even the eventual feasibility, of reunification.[107] But this was definitely a long-term goal. There were more immediate priorities—deterring the Russians, reassuring the Europeans, keeping the Americans involved in both tasks—and pursuing them did have the effect, whatever the intent, of keeping Germany divided.

"It is time America began sailing by the stars and not by the driftwood float-ing by," an uncharacteristically brash national security adviser Robert Cutler admonished President Eisenhower during a discussion on Germany in August, 1953. "Should we just wait for events and make policies to meet them, or should we have alternatives worked out in advance?"[108] Kennan had made the same point four years earlier; but Eisenhower and his advisers had no greater success than their predecessors in separating long-term interests with respect to Germany from the more pressing requirements of fighting the Cold War. Their first systematic review of this problem, completed by the National Security Council that same month, reflected the difficulty. The goal, it stated, was to be:

Firm association of a united Germany, or, at a minimum, the Federal Republic, with the West, preferably through an integrated European Community, to enable Germany to participate in the defense of the West and make the greatest possible contribution to the strength of the Free World, with the least danger of its becom-ing a threat thereto.[109]

But what if a divided Germany was itself perpetuating the Cold War? What if a united but neutral Germany might lessen the need to defend the West or to strengthen the Free World in the first place? Was the treatment, as Kennan had been insisting since 1949, only prolonging the illness?

One who worried about this, curiously enough, was the man who had forced Kennan into retirement early in 1953, the new Secretary of State, John Foster Dulles. The time had come, he suggested to Eisenhower on 6 September, for "a spectacular effort to relax world tensions" based upon the creation of a "broad zone of restricted armament in Europe, with Soviets withdrawn from satellites and U.S. from Europe." The current situation there was inherently unstable: sooner or later, American troops would have to leave, either because the Europeans would come to regard their bases "as lightning rods rather than umbrellas" for growing Soviet nuclear capabilities, or because they would sim-ply reject an increasingly irritating American military presence in their midst. Having a new and more conciliatory regime in the Kremlin could hasten this process. Why not make a major push now for liberalization in Eastern Europe, the international control of nuclear weapons and guided missiles, an end to the Soviet Communist Party's world revolutionary mission, and an opening up of East–West trade, all with a view to preparing the way for Europe to regain con-trol of its own affairs under the most favorable possible circumstances for the United States?[110]

This breathtaking proposal was not just speculative brainstorming: that was hardly Dulles's style. Rather, it responded to several concerns that were in the air at the time. One had to do with the new administration's determination to cut the defense budget: it was not at all clear, Eisenhower had complained in March during a discussion on overseas troop deployments, "whether national bankruptcy or national destruction would get us first."[111] There was also the danger of being *too* protective: would the West Europeans *ever* assume their full responsibilities for defense as long as the Americans were there to do it for them?[112] Meanwhile, pressures were intensifying to test the new Soviet leaders' sincerity by engaging them in negotiations: Eisenhower himself had encouraged these with his 16 April speech, and in May Winston Churchill, now back in power as British Prime Minister, had called publicly for a summit conference with Stalin's successors to take place "without delay."[113] Finally, Adenauer, whose Christian Democratic government won triumphant re-election on the day Dulles drafted his memorandum, had himself called during the campaign for new four-power talks, and was evolving a negotiating position based on creating a demilitarized zone that would remove Soviet forces from Poland and East Germany.[114]

Eisenhower responded to Dulles's memorandum by expressing "emphatic agreement that renewed efforts should be made to relax world tensions on a global basis," and that "mutual withdrawals of Red Army Forces and United States Forces could be suggested as a step toward relaxing these tensions." But the President saw at least one immediate difficulty with such a proposal: "any withdrawal that seemed to imply a change in *basic* intent would cause real turmoil abroad."[115] Other problems quickly surfaced. Could the United States afford to abandon its forward bases in Europe, from which it would deliver nuclear weapons if war came, in the absence of a comprehensive agreement with the Russians on nuclear arms control? But how far could such talks proceed without dismantling bases? Was Adenauer really seeking disengagement, or was his willingness to endorse negotiations just a tactic to undercut advocates of reunification? Would such discussions enhance or endanger prospects for the European Defense Community Treaty, the delicate structure, as yet unratified by the French, into which a rearmed Germany was to fit?

Had the Russians at this moment renewed Stalin's March 1952 offer, or put forward some version of Beria's May 1953 plan, it is not at all clear what the Western response would have been. Although the Americans and their allies had not written off the possibility of German reunification, neutralization—even within a capitalist framework—would have been much more difficult for them.[116] It is worth pointing out, however, that one reason Eisenhower and Dulles so strongly favored the EDC was that they so strongly opposed West German membership in NATO. German rearmament was necessary, they believed, but German ambitions were still to be feared, especially if Germany regained a military establishment of its own not under European control. "[T]he German government structure," James B. Conant, the new United States High Commissioner in Germany, warned, "is too new to trust the final command of a national army to the hands of the unknown German leaders of the future."[117] Adenauer himself, to the Americans' relief, shared this view. He would not have accepted neutralization, but neither was he eager to see Germany develop an independent military capability. For him, as for Eisenhower and Dulles, the EDC had become a way of reconciling these positions: they all worried, as four-power talks approached early in 1954, about what impact a new Soviet proposal on Germany might have on its prospects.[118]

They need not have. The Russians still saw the EDC as only a disguise for West German membership in NATO, and failed to explore the possibility of reunification within such a framework. Indeed, as Dulles cabled Eisenhower, "Molotov made [his] German proposal so extreme, calling in effect for complete Sovietization [of] all Germany and withdrawal [of] US, UK and French forces, that we believe Western position has been greatly strengthened by exhibition of his uncompromising approach."[119] The principal reason the Soviet government took such a rigid position, it now appears, is that in the wake of the June 1953 uprisings in East Germany it had committed itself to the survival of the Ulbricht regime.[120] Stalin's idea of reunification had been to proceed from a position of strength in the East to project Soviet influence over West Germany; but it was now painfully apparent that it would take longer than expected for the East Germans to reach such a position. "The German people have not yet had time to be educated in the great advantage of Communism," Khrushchev admitted to Eisenhower at the 1955 Geneva summit.[121] An East German collapse, in the meantime, would be a humiliating defeat for the USSR. "The GDR was our ally," Khrushchev later emphasized:

We had a strategic, economic, and political—as well as an ideological—stake in its independence. To allow [West] Germany to create a single capitalist German state allied with the West would have meant for us to retreat to the borders of Poland. That would have been a major political and military setback. It would have been the beginning of a chain reaction, and it would have encouraged aggressive forces in the West to put more and more pressure on us. Once you start retreating, it's difficult to stop.[122]

Ulbricht had thus maneuvered himself into a position of strength *by being weak*;[123] and much of what happened afterward in Germany grew out of this particular accomplishment.

Meanwhile, American allies were taking actions of their own that would further diminish prospects for German reunification. To the intense disgust of Eisenhower and Dulles, the French National Assembly in August 1954 refused to ratify the EDC treaty, despite the fact that the French themselves had proposed this option in 1950. Perceiving, correctly enough, that the Americans had no alternative, the British quickly stepped in with the suggestion that West Germany simply become a member of NATO.[124] With an equanimity that surprised everyone including themselves, the French accepted this idea, and the FRG joined the alliance in May, 1955. Four years of debate over the EDC had produced no EDC, but it did buy time—no insignificant commodity. For with an ingenuity at least equal to that of Ulbricht, Adenauer had skillfully used that interval to gain the confidence of his Western European neighbors, so that the idea of Germans in NATO seemed far less dangerous than when that possibility had first surfaced half a decade earlier.[125]

American leadership did not bring this about. What happened instead was that the United States allowed its allies—the French, the British, and especially the West Germans—to determine the conditions under which West Germany would again become a military power. Postponing reunification and joining NATO was hardly the only way in which Germany could have rearmed: indeed, as the historian Marc Trachtenberg has pointed out, "Adenauer was viewed by western statesmen, especially by those who remembered Weimar, as almost too good to be true, as much more committed to the West than they logically had any right to expect from a German statesman." Because of this, though, the West German chancellor gained "considerable leverage, amounting almost to veto power, over the policy the Western Powers could pursue on the German question."[126] The effect was to undercut whatever interest in reunification still existed in Washington, much as Ulbricht's actions had ruled out further efforts, in Moscow, to explore such options.

The Russians reacted surprisingly mildly to West Germany's incorporation within the NATO alliance, probably because they had never taken the EDC alternative seriously in the first place. They did immediately organize the Warsaw Treaty Organization, with East Germany as a prominent member; but they also accepted a long-delayed treaty providing for the mutual withdrawal of occupation forces from Austria and went ahead with plans for the July summit conference in Geneva. Two months later, Khrushchev welcomed Adenauer himself on an official visit to Moscow, applauding in particular the West German chancellor's warnings on the danger of nuclear war. "Not only were we keeping our number one enemy in line," he recalled, "but Adenauer was helping us to keep our other enemies in line, too."[127] Neither at this meeting, nor at a subsequent foreign ministers' conference later that year, did the Russians seek to revive the issue of reunification; instead they cheerfully established diplomatic relations with the FRG as well as the GDR. "The Germans are beginning to get 'uppish' again," Khrushchev explained to British officials early in 1956, "and it was probably a good thing for everybody that Germany was divided."[128]

"The German problem," another historian, Frank Ninkovich, has observed, "was analogous to the dual key system that the Americans use to control the launch of nuclear-tipped missiles—nothing happens unless both operators agree to turn their keys simultanously."[129] The metaphor captures the edginess with which the United States and the Soviet Union approached the German question, the ambivalence with which they sought simultaneously to rely upon and to contain German power, and the asynchronous character of their efforts to reach agreements on Germany's future. Kennan's Program A, Stalin's note, Beria's plan, and even Dulles's scheme for a "spectacular effort to relax world tensions" had been based on the premise that there could somehow, someday, be a simultaneous turning of the keys. But there were multiple hands on each of these, and it was allies on both sides—including German allies—who kept them from being turned.

VII

The continued division of Germany was, therefore, a *convenient*, perhaps even a comfortable option for the Americans, the Russians, and their respective allies; however illogical the post-1945 map of that country might be, the statesmen of

1955 had come to prefer it over other alternatives. It remained to be seen, though, whether this would serve as a *stable* long-term settlement of the German question, and hence as a basis for peace in Europe. If it had been possible to divide Germany and all of its potential forms of power with perfect symmetry, so that each side gained no more than the other from having its half of the country in its respective alliance; if it had then been possible to ensure the equality of the alliances themselves; and if the two superpowers who sponsored those alliances had in turn shared common objectives—if all of these things had happened, then stability might have emerged spontaneously from this situation. But it is no more feasible to divide a country equally and equitably than it is to divide a person or a family. Vital organs, functions, and responsibilities tend to be be asymmetrically distributed. King Solomon's dilemma is an ancient one: it was too much to expect that something like it would not, sooner or later, undo the tacit agreement that had evolved, among Germany's old adversaries and among many Germans themselves, to accept the status quo.

One important asymmetry had to do with material capabilities: as Eisenhower's National Security Council pointed out in 1953, West Germany had "nearly three times the population, about five times the industrial output, and almost twice the size" of East Germany.[130] This disparity in itself would give the FRG disproportionate weight in any calculation of the intra-German—or intra-European—balance of power. The East Germans had done remarkably well in rebuilding their own economy, considering the difficulties imposed by the need to shift its alignment from west to east, the absence of Marshall Plan aid, and Soviet reparations removals, which continued until 1953.[131] But the West German economic achievement was more than remarkable: the term "miracle" had now become commonplace in characterizing the success of Christian Democratic expansionist capitalism, presided over by economics minister Ludwig Erhardt. "West Germany had the support of the United States, a rich country that you could say had robbed the entire world and grown fat off the first and second world wars," Khrushchev later complained. "In this way, the competition was uneven from the very start."[132]

Another asymmetry was political in character. The West Germans had chosen and, on the whole, were satisfied with their government; neither was true in East Germany.[133] There had been no free elections in that territory since 1946, and although the GDR's constitution, adopted in 1949, closely resembled the FRG's "Basic Law," the actual practice of politics had diverged dramatically with the GDR having become, by the early 1950s, a rigidly Stalinist authoritarian state.[134] Economic progress took place under conditions that approximated forced labor, with improvements in living standards sacrificed in favor of "bootstrap industrialization."[135] The June 1953 riots revealed the extent of the discontent these policies produced. Although the Ulbricht regime, under pressure from Moscow, did afterwards relax some of its most oppressive policies, the overall reality of a command economy operating within a command political structure did not change. Beria's example had shown how easily reforms could lead to revolution; but Khrushchev learned his own painful lesson in this regard when his de-Stalinization campaign, set in motion at the 20th Soviet Party Congress, produced a near-rebellion in Poland and an actual one in Hungary late in 1956. East Germany's calm throughout these disruptions only appeared to confirm Ulbricht's wisdom in retaining tight controls.[136]

Finally, there was a military asymmetry. Despite the fact that West German rearmament was now proceeding within NATO alliance, the Soviet Union and its Warsaw Pact allies retained an overwhelming conventional force advantage, with all the risks of psychological intimidation—to say nothing of actual invasion—this entailed. Like its predecessor, the Eisenhower administration had hoped to compensate by extending an American security umbrella over Western Europe through the promise to use nuclear weapons in the event of an attack; but as Soviet nuclear and missile capabilities developed, this commitment seemed less and less credible. If, though, the Americans were to place those weapons directly in the path an invasion from the east would have to take, they would surely use them. That prospect would diminish the likelihood of such an invasion, or the threat of one, in the first place. Such was the logic behind the "nuclearization" of NATO: the effort, begun as early as 1953, to integrate the United States' nuclear capabilities, now extending down to the "tactical" level, with the conventional forces of its Western European allies. But this solution created the new problem of how much control those allies—especially the West Germans, who had voluntarily relinquished the right to develop nuclear weapons when they joined NATO—would have over these devices.[137] The reassurance that was supposed to come from deterrence was not, in this instance, particularly satisfying.

George Kennan had all of these asymmetries in mind when, in October 1957, he revived Program A, this time as a private citizen, and this time in public. If the deadlock over Germany was not removed, he insisted in the most controversial series of Reith Lectures ever delivered over the BBC, "the chances for peace are very slender indeed." A division of Germany of course had to occur after the war,

[b]ut there is danger in permitting it to harden into a permanent attitude. It expects too much, and for too long a time, of the United States, which is not a European power. It does less than justice to the strength and abilities of the Europeans themselves. It leaves unsolved the extremely precarious and unsound arrangements which now govern the status of Berlin—the least disturbance of which could easily produce a new world crisis. It takes no account of the present dangerous situation in the satellite area. It renders permanent what was meant to be temporary. It assigns half of Europe, by implication, to the Russians.[138]

Kennan's new call for disengagement accomplished the impressive feat of uniting Acheson, now in retirement and thoroughly committed to orthodoxy on the German question, with such vociferous former critics as Dulles and Vice President Richard Nixon. The former Secretary of State's public attack on his former adviser's "rather mystical attitude" toward power relationships, Nixon noted, had made it clear that there was no support for Kennan's ideas on the part of "any responsible or influential American political leader."[139] The reaction in Western Europe was not much more sympathetic: "Whoever says such things," the West German foreign minister Heinrich von Brentano complained, "is no friend of the German people."[140]

The Soviet response, at first glance, seemed warmer. In December 1957 Nikolai Bulganin, the Chairman of the Soviet Council of Ministers, publicly endorsed the Rapacki Plan, a proposal already put forward by Polish Foreign Minister Adam Rapacki calling for the creation of a nuclear-free zone in central Europe and the eventual withdrawal of Soviet and American forces from that region. But the Rapacki Plan had been under discussion in Warsaw and Moscow since 1956, and Soviet documents now suggest that it was primarily intended, as earlier Kremlin foreign policy initiatives had been, to undercut the position of the West German government, not as a serious move toward disengagement.[141]

There was, in short, little interest on either side in any comprehensive new attempt to reunite Germany, despite the fact that the asymmetries inherent in its division were obvious. Given the reality of the Cold War, attempting to remove these asymmetries—without any assurance of who might most benefit from doing so—seemed riskier than simply learning to live with them. This assumed, though, their *stability*: that they would not become any *more* asymmetrical than they now were. Kennan had not been willing to make that assumption, and his Reith lecture identified with considerable prescience the asymmetry most likely to get out of hand: "The future of Berlin is vital to the future of Germany as a whole: the needs of its people and the extreme insecurity of the Western position there would alone constitute reasons why no one in the West should view the present division of Germany as a satisfactory permanent solution, even if no other factors were involved at all."[142]

VIII

Stalin's 1948 blockade having failed, the former German capital still lay under joint American–British–French–Soviet occupation 110 miles inside what was now the German Democratic Republic. Although the East Germans had long since closed off their own border with West Germany, the Western powers retained access rights to the city, and it was still possible for Germans to travel freely from sector to sector within it. The contrast between West and East Berlin graphically displayed the economic and political disparities that had come to distinguish the FRG from the GDR; predictably, the city became the primary channel through which East Germans could flee their own state and settle in the West. The Western allies, together with the West Germans, actively encouraged this process, with the result that between 1945 and 1961, approximately one sixth of all East Germans departed for the West, most of them through Berlin.[143] There was no corresponding flow of people in the opposite direction.

On 27 November 1958, Khrushchev announced that if the West did not agree, within six months, to transform Berlin into a demilitarized "free city," the Soviet Union would give the East Germans control over all access routes to West Berlin.[144] Historians have long wondered what impelled the Kremlin leader to issue this ultimatum, thereby setting off the longest and one of the most dangerous of all Cold War crises. Soviet and East German documents now permit at least a provisional answer. The Berlin controversy of 1958–61 reflected the asymmetries that persisted in Germany, even as both sides had begun to reconcile themselves to that country's continued division. But it would hardly have happened in the way that it did had those underlying circumstances not intersected with the distinctive personalities of Nikita Khrushchev and Walter Ulbricht.

As early as February 1956, Khrushchev had passed the word to the East Germans that because "[t]his conflict between socialism and capitalism proceeds in the GDR as a country with open borders . . . particular attention by all forces in the peace camp must be directed toward GDR victory in the competition." Credibility was at stake: no less a notable than Mao Zedong had warned that a failure there "would be a failure of the entire peace camp," and the Soviet leader apparently agreed with this assessment.[145] But the East Germans were insisting that their state could not prosper as long as West Berlin existed in their midst, raising constant questions about their sovereignty and providing opportunities for their most skilled citizens to flee.[146] The Soviet ambassador to the GDR, Mikhail Pervukhin, was responding to their concerns when he suggested to Moscow in February 1958 that "the Berlin question can be resolved independently from resolving the entire German problem, by the gradual political and economic conquest of West Berlin."[147]

Complicating this situation was the fact that the United States and its allies, worried about the military balance in Europe following the Soviet Union's demonstration of an inter-continental ballistic missile capability, had decided late in 1957 to place American intermediate range missiles in Europe and to create a NATO nuclear weapons stockpile which presumably would be available to the West Germans.[148] The Russians knew that they could not prevent the Americans from ultimately sharing their nuclear weapons should they choose to do so. But as A. A. Smirnov, the Soviet ambassador in Bonn, pointed out: "Our general goal is to . . . exert a braking influence on the arming of the Bundeswehr. If all the countries of the socialist camp unite their efforts in that direction, then the arming of the Bundeswehr might be delayed for two to three years, which would be a serious victory for our general cause."[149]

Conditions within the GDR, meanwhile, were worsening. Yuri Andropov, head of the Soviet Communist Party Central Committee's department on relations with socialist countries, warned in August 1958 that "the flight of the intelligentsia from the GDR has reached a particularly critical phase." The numbers were up 50 per cent from 1957, and refugee reports indicated that people were now leaving as much for political as for economic reasons.[150] There were also vague fears, in both East Berlin and Moscow, that the West Germans and their American allies might be planning to exploit growing East German vulnerabilities. Developments in the Middle East and Asia had distracted the United States for several years, Ulbricht noted, but now that the last of these—the Quemoy-Matsu crisis of August–September 1958—appeared to have been resolved, "Germany would be next." The time had come to "speak to West Germany in a different language. We can't always be telling Adenauer that we propose negotiations, and he refuses them."[151]

Khrushchev's first reaction was cautious: it might well be possible to resolve the Berlin issue independently of the German question as a whole, he acknowledged, perhaps even through negotiations with the Western powers. But this would require a series of concerted actions on the part of the entire Eastern bloc. Ulbricht should take no unilateral action against West Berlin.[152] The Russians did encourage the East Germans to raise once again the possibility of a four-power settlement, which they did in September;[153] when there was no satisfactory Western response, though, Khrushchev appears to have become impatient. Acting against the advice of several of his own German experts, he decided to go ahead with a tough speech on 10 November calling for a German peace treaty, and then with the 27 November ultimatum. It was so striking a departure from the deliberate approach he had earlier advised that the Soviet foreign ministry would not even get around to drafting the proposed treaty with the East Germans for another month. Ulbricht and his colleagues certainly welcomed this new aggressive stance, but there is no clear evidence that they pushed Khrushchev into acting when he did.[154]

So why did he act? Khrushchev was, of course, a volatile personality, much more inclined than Stalin to do things on the spur of the moment.[155] But there appears to have been some element of calculation in Khrushchev's timing: the Soviet Union's new nuclear and missile capabilities, he believed, gave it an immunity from American retaliation that his predecessor had never enjoyed. "The leaders of the United States," he told one of his advisers in September, 1958, "are not such idiots [as] to fight over Berlin."[156] Intelligence derived from agents in Bonn and Paris as well as the interception of foreign embassy communications in Moscow appeared to confirm this assessment.[157] Accordingly, it should be possible now—as it had not been in 1948—to exploit the city's geographical vulnerability and extract western concessions by applying and relieving pressure on it, as Soviet interests seemed to require.[158] "Berlin is the testicles of the West," Khrushchev is said to have explained at one point. "Every time I want to make the West scream, I squeeze on Berlin."[159]

In response, he appears to have believed that the United States and its allies would either liquidate their position in West Berlin or, more likely, acknowledge the GDR as an independent state by dealing with it directly on access to that city. Either concession would be a major coup for Soviet and GDR policy which might also slow down or even reverse the nuclearization of NATO. Certainly Khrushchev was trying to push the West into negotiations. "What are your counter proposals?" he asked Senator Hubert Humphrey on December 3. "What do your Secretary of State and your President suggest?"[160]

Had it been left to the Americans alone, there might have been counter-proposals. Dulles had expressed doubts, even before Khrushchev issued his ulti-matum, as to whether the United States should sacrifice itself for West Berlin, and after that event he raised the possibility that the Western occupying powers might indeed deal with the East Germans as "agents" for the Soviet Union.[161] Eisenhower complained that this was "another instance in which our political posture requires us to assume military positions that are wholly illogical."[162] It would not be easy to explain to the man in the street "why we worry about the shape of the helmet of the official to whom we present credentials."[163] Vociferous West German objections, though, prevented the exploration of alternatives. Since 1955, Adenauer had insisted on enforcing the principle that no state—apart from the Soviet Union itself—could have diplomatic relations with *both* the FRG and the GDR. Despite the fact that his own country had just concluded a trade agreement with the East Germans, the German chancellor warned that if the Americans and their allies had *any* dealings with them, this might fatally derange the delicate compromise by which his countrymen had postponed reunification in favor of alignment with the West.[164]

At the same time, though, the West Germans could hardly be happy with the means by which the Eisenhower administration proposed to defend West Berlin. At the insistence of the Americans, NATO strategy had come increasingly to rely upon the first use of nuclear weapons in the event of war; but NATO esti-mates as early as 1955 had shown that they could kill as many as 1.7 million Germans and incapacitate another 3.5 million.[165] If the Russians did turn over the access routes to the East Germans, Pentagon plans called for sending a small convoy with a platoon-size combat escort through; if it was rebuffed or fired upon, a division-size unit would follow. The point would be to convince all con-cerned of Washington's willingness, in the words of the Joint Chiefs of Staff, "to use whatever degree of force may be necessary."[166] Should the Soviet Union still not back down, Dulles told Adenauer in February 1959, then a general war would result "in which we obviously would not forego the use of nuclear weapons."[167] The German Chancellor, whose fondness for that city was never overwhelming, is said to have responded: "For God's sake, not for Berlin!"[168]

Once again, it was left to the British to propose a way out. Why not fall back upon the familiar solution of a four-power foreign ministers' conference to be in session at the time Khrushchev's ultimatum expired in May? This might, Dulles acknowledged, "provide [the] Soviets with a way out of their extreme Berlin position if they wanted to find it."[169] Prime Minister Harold Macmillan then took it upon himself—over strong objections from Adenauer, Eisenhower, and a now terminally ill Dulles—to visit Khrushchev in Moscow. Little came of these talks, but the following month, in Washington, Macmillan reminded a skeptical Eisenhower that a greater willingness to negotiate in July 1914 might have avoided a catastrophic war in which Great Britain had lost two million young men. Any future war would probably result in the deaths of 20–30 mil-lion Englishmen. The President tried to top this argument, noting that minimal American casualties in an all-out thermonuclear war would be 67 million: "we don't escape war by surrendering on the installment plan."[170] But he had already begun to raise with his advisers the possibility of "startl[ing] Macmillan a little bit by saying that now that he has seen Khrushchev, [the] President is thinking of asking Khrushchev to come over here."[171] This dramatic proposal was supposed to have been contingent on progress being made at the foreign ministers' conference. Eisenhower's subordinates failed to convey that message, however, and the irate President was stuck, as he put it, with having "to pay the penalty and hold a meeting he despised."[172]

Khrushchev had, in the meantime, allowed his Berlin ultimatum deadline to pass—it had coincided, as it happened, with Dulles's funeral on 27 May—thereby disappointing the East Germans, who had been making detailed plans for how they would deal with the new "free city" of West Berlin.[173] But there were few signs of progress: indeed the Soviet leader was brutal in a conversation with W. Averell Harriman late in June:

[W]e are determined to liquidate your rights in Western Berlin. What good does it do you to have 11 thousand troops in Berlin? If it came to war, we would swallow them in one gulp. . . . You can start a war if you like, but remember it will be you who are starting it, not we. . . . West Germany knows that we could destroy it in ten minutes. . . . If you start a war, we may die but the rockets will fly automatically.[174]

The Eisenhower–Khrushchev talks, held at Camp David in September, were not quite so blunt, but they got no further than an agreement to disagree. "[T]here was nothing more inadvisable in this situation than to talk about ultimatums," the President emphasized, since "[b]oth sides knew very well what would happen if an ultimatum were to be implemented." Khrushchev responded that he could not understand "why a peace treaty was regarded by the American people as a threat to peace." If Eisenhower objected to the existence of two Germanies, why did he support the existence of two Chinas? The President admitted that "human affairs got very badly tangled at times and that we would simply have to try to straighten them out."[175]

Both leaders had expected to continue this conversation in the spring of 1960 at a summit conference in Paris and during an Eisenhower visit to the Soviet Union, but the U-2 incident in May prevented that from happening. Despite his violent rhetorical reaction to that event, Khrushchev did not seize the occasion, as he might well have done, to renew his ultimatum on Berlin. "We are realists and we will never pursue a gambling policy," he told the East Germans on his way back from the aborted summit:

Under present conditions, it is worthwhile to wait a little longer and try to find a solution for the long-since ripe question of a peace treaty with the two German states. This will not escape our hands. We had better wait, and the matter will get more mature.[176]

What this suggests is that Khrushchev himself, not the East Germans, determined the course and timing of events with respect to Berlin from the fall of 1958 through the summer of 1960. The Soviet leader "squeezed" when he thought he could get Western concessions, but he refrained from doing so when the results seemed likely to be more than he had bargained for. Despite his occasional hair-raising threats, he behaved quite carefully during this period. Berlin was a lever that could be adjusted as necessary;[177] it was not a button to push, after which there could be no turning back.

IX

The Berlin crisis of 1960–1 followed a different pattern: this time it was Ulbricht who drove the process, with Khrushchev scrambling to keep up. Requirements of alliance solidarity—much the same phenomenon that had caused Eisenhower and Dulles to allow Adenauer a near-veto over how they responded to the 1958 ultimatum—pushed a reluctant Soviet leader to confront the United States and its own allies in the summer of 1961. Both superpowers now had to face explicitly the question that had been implicit in 1958–9: would Berlin be worth a nuclear war? Fortunately, they managed to agree that it would not be and, despite grave misgivings on the part of each of their German clients, to devise a mutually tolerable if draconian solution.

The citizens of East Germany did not share Khrushchev's view of West Berlin as a device with which to squeeze the West. For them, it provided a chance to escape to the West, and as conditions in the GDR continued to worsen, more and more of them took advantage of this opportunity. Ambassador Pervukhin described the problem clearly in a report to Moscow in December, 1959:

> The presence in Berlin of an open and, to speak to the point, uncontrolled border between the socialist and capitalist worlds unwittingly prompts the population to make a comparison between both parts of the city, which, unfortunately, does not always turn out in favor of Democratic Berlin.[178]

This exodus of East Germans through West Berlin—many of them highly trained professionals—was depriving the GDR of precisely the people it needed to compete with the FRG: the numbers rose from 144,000 in 1959 to almost 200,000 in 1960. An additional 50,000 East Berliners did not flee but preferred taking even menial jobs in West Berlin to what the GDR was able to provide them. "Why don't we raise our salaries for this category of people?" Ulbricht asked rhetorically in a meeting with Khrushchev late in 1960: "First of all, we don't have the means. Secondly, even if we raised their salary, we could not satisfy their purchasing power with the goods that we have, and they would buy things with that money in West Berlin."[179]

As a result of these difficulties, Khrushchev and Ulbricht began to see the Berlin issue in different ways. The Soviet leader was content with the status quo, since his periodic threats to alter it provided such a convenient way of unsettling the Americans and their allies. "[W]e have not lost the two years which have passed since the time of the initiation of our proposal," he explained to Ulbricht, "but [we] have shaken up their position. . . . [L]uckily, our adversaries haven't gone crazy; they still think and their nerves still aren't bad." For

Ulbricht, though, perpetuating the status quo amounted to undermining his regime: if the GDR was going to survive, the question of Berlin would have to be settled, one way or another. "[A]mong our population there is already a mood taking shape where they say—you only *talk* about a peace treaty, but don't *do* anything about it."[180] Nor, as the unfortunate Beria had learned in 1953, was the East German leader above applying his own forms of leverage against his patrons in Moscow: Khrushchev would now discover this as well.

The first signs of independent action came in January 1960, when the East Germans casually passed the Russians a copy of a note to the Western occupying powers protesting Anglo-American–French behavior in Berlin. An astonished Soviet diplomat pointed out that Moscow had not been informed. The East Germans in this instance apologized: in the rush, they had not had time to consult, which "of course was not right and was a great omission."[181] But in the fall of that year, they began modifying carefully established procedures by which Western officials could enter East Berlin without having to provide identification to GDR border guards. This time, the Russians objected more vigorously, complaining that these unilateral actions could affect their own rights to enter West Berlin. The East Germans backed down, but Ulbricht warned Khrushchev that "[w]e cannot have a situation in which . . . the representatives of the states which do not want to recognize the GDR can come into the capital of the GDR without identifying themselves."[182] In January 1961 the East Germans went even further: they dispatched an official delegation to the People's Republic of China, whose differences with the Soviet Union had now become embarrassingly public. The Russians found out about it only when the East Germans stopped over at the Moscow airport.[183]

One purpose of this last maneuver may have been to apply pressure on Khrushchev during an important series of discussions with Ulbricht that had begun the previous November. The two leaders appeared to have agreed on a set of priorities, ranked in order of their preference: (1) Western acceptance of a four-power peace treaty recognizing both Germanies and making West Berlin a free-city; or (2) an interim four-power accord on Berlin pending the negotiation of a peace treaty; or (3) a separate peace treaty between the Soviet Union, its allies, and the GDR that would give the East Germans control over access rights to West Berlin.[184] There was little prospect of the first two, though, and East Germany's difficult economic situation was making the third less desirable: the West Germans would surely cut off all economic contacts, which would throw the GDR into a position of even greater dependence on the Soviet Union.

Khrushchev reluctantly promised aid, but criticized the East Germans for not having done more to build a self-sufficient economy: "you did not disentangle yourselves [from the West Germans]; you got used to thinking that Germany was one."[185] Ulbricht, some weeks later, responded equally bluntly: the Soviet Union had insisted on extracting reparations from East Germany, at a time when West Germany was receiving "large credits from the USA to save the monopoly capitalist system and German militarism. . . . This is the main reason that we have remained so far behind West Germany in work productivity and standard of living. . . . The booming economy in West Germany, which is visible to every citizen of the GDR, is the main reason that over ten years about two million people have left our Republic."[186]

One solution to the dilemma would be to try to pressure the new Kennedy administration into doing what Eisenhower had been unwilling to do: sign a four-power peace treaty on Germany that would acknowledge East German sovereignty and make West Berlin a free city. But Kennedy and his advisers, if anything, were *less* inclined to negotiate on Berlin. They felt a strong need to demonstrate toughness in dealing with the Russians,[187] and from Kennedy's perspective there was no great urgency about the matter. "[We will] just have to live with the situation," he told West Berlin Mayor Willy Brandt in March, 1961: "it [is] very hard to find grounds for agreement with the Soviets on anything beyond perhaps removing restrictions on crabmeat. . . ."[188] Ambassador Llewellyn Thompson was warning from Moscow, however, that "in [the] absence [of] negotiations Khrushchev will sign separate treaty with East Germany and precipitate [a] Berlin crisis this year." This "could involve [a] real possibility of world war, [and] we would almost certainly be led back to [an] intensified Cold War relationship."[189] Kennedy himself—despite his doubts that there was anything to negotiate about—had already proposed a summit meeting to Khrushchev, from which it would obviously be difficult to exclude Berlin.[190]

The Soviet leader did not respond to this proposal until May, by which time Kennedy's administration was reeling from the double humiliation of the CIA's failure to overthrow Fidel Castro's regime in Cuba with its ill-conceived landing at the Bay of Pigs and the Soviet Union's success in achieving the first manned orbital flight around the earth. These developments—together with his growing concern "that the West Berlin issue had been growing like a tumor on an otherwise healthy body"—appear to have persuaded Khrushchev that he could and should push Kennedy on Berlin.[191] The resulting encounter at Vienna on 3–4 June can only be characterized as a disaster. Both leaders had been led to expect that the other would offer concessions,[192] and when this did not happen, Khrushchev renewed his promise to sign a separate peace with the GDR if there was no agreement, within six months, to change the status of West Berlin. Should the United States insist on starting a war over this issue, "there was nothing the USSR could do about it. . . . History will be the judge of our actions."[193] "What I said," the Soviet leader later admitted, "might have sounded like a threat to Kennedy."[194]

Kennedy's first—and rather shaken—reaction was to revert to his interest in maintaining the status quo: "the situation there is not a satisfactory one," he observed, "but because conditions in many areas of the world are not satisfactory today it is not the right time now to change the situation in Berlin and the balance in general. . . . If we accepted Mr. Khrushchev's suggestion the world would lose confidence in the US and would not regard it as a serious country." He then added, somewhat superfluously: "It is an important strategic matter that the world believe the US is a serious country." The difficulty was that "either Mr. Khrushchev did not believe that the US was serious or the situation in that area was so unsatisfactory to the Soviet Union that it had to take this drastic action." Khrushchev failed to follow up on what may have been an invitation to talk candidly about his difficulties with the East Germans, insisting that "[t]he decision to sign a peace treaty is firm and irrevocable." It would be, Kennedy responded, "a cold winter."[195]

This conversation was quite enough to change Kennedy's mind about the status quo. "He just beat hell out of me," the president told James Reston. "I've got a terrible problem. If he thinks I'm inexperienced and have no guts, until we remove those ideas we won't get anywhere with him. So we have to act."[196] Former Secretary of State Acheson emphatically agreed, advising Kennedy in a long report submitted on 28 June that:

> The issue over Berlin . . . is far more than an issue over that city. It is broader and deeper than even the German question as a whole. It has become an issue of resolution between the U.S.A. and the U.S.S.R., the outcome of which will go far to determine the confidence of Europe—indeed of the world—in the United States. . . . Nothing could be more dangerous than to embark upon a course of action of the sort described in this paper in the absence of a decision to accept nuclear war rather than accede to the demands which Khrushchev is now making, or their substantial equivalent.[197]

Kennedy did not agree with all of Acheson's recommendations—to the latter's intense annoyance[198]—but he did announce, in a dramatic television address on 25 July, that "we cannot and will not permit the Communists to drive us out of Berlin, either gradually or by force."[199] In the meantime, the President had decided to ask Congress for up to six new Army and two new Marine divisions, an improved airlift capability, the authority to triple draft calls and call up the reserves, and a civil defense program that would support the construction of fallout shelters aimed at reducing the number of Americans killed in a nuclear attack to—50 million.[200]

It was rather more than Khrushchev had expected. "Only a mad man can declare war today," he told John McCloy the next day. Kennedy was a "reasonable, young man full of enthusiasm [who] wishes [to] display that energy. However, if war should occur he would be [the] last President because no one knows what would happen after war."[201] The new chief executive, Khrushchev worried, might not fully control the situation. "[W]hen our 'friend' Dulles was alive," he explained to a meeting of Warsaw Pact leaders early in August,

> they had more stability. . . . He would reach the brink, as he put it himself, but he would never leap over the brink, and [nevertheless] retained his credibility. . . . . If Kennedy says it, he will be called a coward. . . . [H]e is too much of a light-weight both for the Republicans as well as for the Democrats. And the state is too big, the state is powerful, and it poses certain dangers.[202]

But Khrushchev himself was not fully in control. We have known for some time that the Soviet military resented his cutbacks in conventional forces; he now found it necessary to appease them by announcing a substantial increase in their budget and a resumption of nuclear testing, suspended by informal agreement with the United States since 1958. Disagreements with the Chinese Communists and their stubborn supporters, the Albanians, were also an increasing concern throughout the summer of 1961.[203] It may well have been Ulbricht and his colleagues, though, who caused the Soviet leader the greatest unease.

Khrushchev had stressed the need for the East Germans to take no unilateral action until the prospects for a four-power agreement on Berlin had been fully explored.[204] But as Ambassador Pervukhin warned Foreign Minister Gromyko in May,

[o]ur friends have expressed their view more than once that they are absolutely not satisfied with the current situation of the GDR. . . [They] sometimes exercise impatience and a somewhat one-sided approach to this problem, not always studying the interests of the entire socialist camp or the international situation at the given moment.[205]

The warning was prophetic, for on 15 June, just after the Vienna summit, Ulbricht gave an unusually high-profile press conference in East Berlin at which he emphasized that the proposed separate peace would give the GDR control over all access routes to West Berlin. Did this mean closing off the Brandenburg Gate? He responded soothingly: "Nobody has the intention of building a wall."[206]

But Ulbricht's reassurances were like Stalin's: they tended not to reassure. By the next morning, refugee centers in West Berlin were jammed with East Germans seeking to get out before Ulbricht got around to doing what he said he would not do. The rate of those leaving soon rose to a thousand a day.[207] There is as yet no hard evidence that the GDR leader *intended* to produce this effect, any more than there is that he *intended* to provoke the June 1953 riots by failing to rescind the order raising labor norms. In both instances, though, the *consequences* of his actions extended all the way to Moscow: in 1953 by discrediting Beria, and in 1961 by pushing Khrushchev into a final—if humiliating—resolution of the Berlin crisis.[208]

The idea of building a wall was not new: the GDR had had contingency plans for this since at least 1952.[209] But Khrushchev had resisted this option because he hoped—by means of his "free city" proposal—to detach West Berlin from West Germany, not to isolate it from East Germany.[210] The massive increase in the refugee flow that followed Ulbricht's press conference, though, together with the escalating international crisis his own ultimatum to Kennedy had set off, appears to have convinced him that this was no longer a viable policy. Pervukhin had already conveyed Ulbricht's warning that "if the present situation of open borders continues, collapse is inevitable. . . . [H]e refuses all responsibility for what would then happen. He could not guarantee that he could keep the situation under control this time."[211] On 3 August, in Moscow, the East German leader proposed to his Warsaw Pact colleagues the euphemistic solution of imposing "control along the GDR borders, including the borders in Berlin, comparable to the control along the state borders of the Western powers." If the United States and its allies did not then agree to a comprehensive German treaty, the Soviet Union would sign a separate peace with the

GDR. Presumably Khrushchev, who introduced Ulbricht, had given his approval.[212]

Whether intended or not, signals emanating from Washington suggested that the United States would not interfere with the construction of a wall. The Chairman of the Senate Foreign Relations Committee, J. William Fulbright, said publicly that he did not understand why the East Germans did not simply close their borders, and the *New York Times* had echoed this point on 6 August.[213] Kennedy himself, in his speech of 25 July, had carefully referred to the American commitment to *West* Berlin, not to Berlin as a whole—a point not missed by either the Russians or the East Germans.[214] A few days later the President told Walt Rostow:

Khrushchev is losing East Germany. He cannot let that happen. If East Germany goes, so will Poland and all of eastern Europe. He will have to do something to stop the flow of refugees—perhaps a wall. And we won't be able to prevent it. I can hold the Alliance together to defend West Berlin but I cannot act to keep East Berlin open.[215]

"Our really vital interests," Secretary of State Dean Rusk told a group of American ambassadors in Europe on 9 August, were "(1) the Western presence in West Berlin and (2) our physical access to the city with a view to sustaining not only our military forces but also the life and liberty of the civilian population of the city."[216] And on 12 August Rusk warned the American embassy in Bonn that the "danger of [the] escape hatch being closed [and] rising tension between Moscow and [the] Free World" had created the possibility of an "explosion along 1953 lines" in East Germany. "It would be particularly unfortunate" if such an event should be "based on [the] expectation of immediate Western military assistance."[217]

The erection first of a barbed-wire barrier, and then of a wall, around West Berlin, which began early the next morning, did not at first appear to have settled the German question for the next three decades. What came across instead was the sheer brutality of the action—the literally Solomon-like sundering of a city and its people—together with the posturing both superpowers went through to show that the fact that a wall now stood in Berlin did not mean that they had lost their power or resolve. The Americans brought General Clay out of retirement and sent him back to West Berlin, where he occupied himself with having his troops tear down simulated walls—but not the real one. Khrushchev responded even more spectacularly by authorizing a series of huge thermonuclear bomb tests. And then, on 27 October, Soviet and American tanks confronted one another muzzle to muzzle at Checkpoint Charlie for several hours—the first and last time so dangerous a thing happened during the Cold War—before finally withdrawing.[218]

But much of this, it soon became clear, was the kind of redirected aggression certain animal species go through when they want to intimidate but not attack one another: they may kick up dirt, rattle branches, and make loud noises, but they rarely go much beyond that. Behind the scenes in Washington and Moscow, a different view was taking shape. Kennedy expressed it best when he told his aides: "It's not a very nice solution, but a wall is a hell of a lot better than a war."[219] The President reassured the unhappy West Germans and West Berliners, reined in General Clay, and took advantage of a secret channel provided by Khrushchev—KGB agent Georgi Bolshakov—to end the standoff at Checkpoint Charlie.[220] The Soviet leader reciprocated by conveniently forgetting his assurances to Ulbricht that a peace treaty would follow construction of the wall: "steps which could exacerbate the situation, especially in Berlin," he told the once again disappointed East German leader, "should be avoided."[221]

Both the Americans and the Russians now felt that they had gone about as far as they could go for their German friends. They were, after all, facing the prospect of seeing their own cities destroyed for the sake of a city they themselves had been trying to destroy only sixteen years earlier. Kennedy caught the absurdity of the situation when he complained, a few hours after his confrontation with Khrushchev at Vienna:

It seems silly for us to be facing an atomic war over a treaty preserving Berlin as the future capital of a reunited Germany when all of us know that Germany will probably never be reunited. . . . God knows I'm not an isolationist, but it seems particularly stupid to risk killing a million Americans over an argument about access rights on an *Autobahn* . . . or because the Germans want Germany reunified. If I'm going to threaten Russia with a nuclear war, it will have to be for much bigger and more important reasons than that.[222]

As Khrushchev recalled: "We didn't want a military conflict. There was no necessity for one. We only wanted to conduct a surgical operation." Besides, he added, if it had not been for the wall, the Soviet Union would have been obliged to send unskilled labor to support the sagging East German economy: "we didn't want our workers to clean their toilets."[223]

X

Even fraternal socialist solidarity, it seems, had its limits. To die for Berlin—or even to sacrifice greatly for it—was no more attractive an option in Moscow than in Washington. The wall in this sense liberated the Russians and the Americans, even as it confined the Germans and particularly the Berliners. Still, one cannot but wonder how the possibility of dying for Berlin could ever have arisen in the first place. How could the two most powerful nations in the world have come to behave over this issue like rival street gangs, investing minute pieces of territory, even the color and insignia of each side's uniforms, with such symbolic significance as to risk not only the other's destruction but their own as well?

One answer lies in the extent to which postwar Germany was both strong and weak at the same time. Because it had been the strongest nation in Europe prior to 1945, neither of the post-1945 superpowers would allow a reunified Germany to align with its adversary: the division of the country, in this sense, was imposed from without and became unavoidable once the Cold War was under way. But once their country was divided, the Germans' weakness *itself became a strength*: by being on the verge of collapse—and, as time went on, by simply *threatening* to collapse—West and East Germans could raise the specter of a former enemy falling under the control of a future enemy anytime they wanted.

It was the dire economic condition of western Germany that brought about zonal consolidation, Marshall Plan aid, and the London Conference program; having gone this far, the occupiers found establishing West Germany to be the sensible next step. From 1949 on, though, that state played an increasingly important role in determining the terms of its own rearmament and reintegration into the rest of Western Europe. By 1955 Adenauer had gained a virtual veto over whatever negotiating positions his other NATO allies might put forward. Who could know what foolish things other West Germans might do, he would warn, if he were not in charge? This argument was persuasive enough to discourage the Eisenhower administration from exploring a Berlin settlement in the wake of Khrushchev's first ultimatum; certainly the need to convince Adenauer of his own toughness influenced Kennedy's initial handling of the second one. Not until the new president and his advisers began to reconcile themselves—very discreetly—to the benefits of a Berlin wall did American policy on Germany break loose from what was, in effect, West Germany's domination of it.

A similar pattern developed on the other side. Ulbricht did not dominate Stalin; but when the Kremlin leader's plan for the peaceful absorption of all Germany from the Soviet-controlled east fell through, he had no better option than to allow the East German communists their own separate Stalinist state. The June 1953 uprising—set off at least in part by Beria's interest in a reunified, neutral, and even non-socialist Germany—had the unexpected effect of solidifying Ulbricht's position and binding Khrushchev to him, so that a single Germany was no longer a serious possibility for the Russians. Khrushchev himself determined the timing of the 1958 Berlin crisis, but he acted both to apply pressure on the West and to relieve pressure on East Germany. Ulbricht himself, it now appears, pushed Khrushchev into issuing the 1961 ultimatum, and then into building the wall. The Soviet Union's declaration of independence from its East German client came only when Khrushchev too saw the advantages of that edifice, and refused to honor his promise to Ulbricht to combine its construction with the long-awaited peace treaty giving the GDR control over access routes to West Berlin.

What allowed German weakness to become German strength was, of course, the superpowers' preoccupation with credibility. Having installed and then attached their own reputations to their respective clients, they found it difficult—at least until directly confronted with the prospect of nuclear war—to disengage from them. Washington and Moscow fell into the habit of letting their German allies determine their German interests, and hence their German policies. The purpose of an alliance, presumably, is to build sufficient strength either to prevent or conclude conflict: negotiations, as Kennan and even Dulles knew, are a vital part of that process. But in this situation alliances became ends in themselves. Preserving their solidarity took precedence over attempting to resolve the disputes that had required their creation in the first place. The pattern is particularly clear in the intellectual progression of Dean Acheson: from failing to understand, in 1949, how the United States could ever have gotten itself into supporting the creation of an independent West German state, he had come around, by 1961, to being willing to risk nuclear war rather than have East German border guards stamp American passports. Fortunately neither Eisenhower nor Kennedy nor Khrushchev took so rigid a view: even so, one cannot help but wonder whether there might not have been a better way of handling things.

Credibility is, after all, a state of mind, not an objective, independently measurable reality. It is what one makes it before others can make anything of it; credibility can hardly be on the line until one has chosen to put it there. For whatever reason, the Cold War encouraged a curious fecklessness on the part of the superpowers when it came to how and where they risked their reputations. Berlin was the most dramatic example, but hardly the only one.

This becomes even more puzzling when one recognizes that the Germans' own commitment to reunification—of which Berlin became a symbol—was asymmetrical. Their country and their capital were divided; but the majority of West Germans were willing to tolerate that reality in order to ensure that reunification under Soviet auspices did not occur. As their economic "miracle" took hold, their interest in reunification on more favorable terms diminished. Adenauer himself never abandoned the goal but he would never have sacrificed much to achieve it, however bitter he may have been about the wall and the Americans' willingness to tolerate it. East Germans also had to accept division—and later the wall—but we can now see that they did not, to the same degree as the West Germans, lose their interest in reunification. For as long as the wall stood, there were always a few of them who would risk their lives trying to get over, under, or around it: that many more wanted to "reunify" with West Germany became obvious in 1990, when the citizens of the GDR showed no hesitancy in abandoning their state altogether once the opportunity to choose was finally opened to them.

The wall itself was a moral obscenity, as anyone who ever saw it can never forget. But so too were the less visible nuclear weapons and other instruments of mass destruction that were justified at the time, and are widely regarded even now, as having kept the peace; similar judgments might be made, as well, of certain covert operations and other crafty maneuvers to which both sides in the Cold War resorted. Perhaps the wall, in its own blatant way, performed a similar function. For not the least of the ironies associated with that conflict was the frequency with which the act of compromising moral principles—at times, even corrupting them—became a kind of life-preserver. The costs were great; they might have been much greater. Foul means do occasionally produce fair results.

SIX

The Third World

[N]o one [can] open a bridge between the West and East as readily as
you. This is because for you are open the doors to Persia, India,
Afghanistan, and China.

> Stalin's remarks to the Congress of Muslim Communists, Moscow,
> November 1918[1]

You have to understand the importance of your position and that
you are fulfilling a historic mission of unprecedented significance. . . . Let's add to China's population of 475 million, the populations of India, Burma, Indonesia, [and] the Philippines. If the
people of these countries listen to you, the Japanese probably also
will listen to you. . . . The peoples of Asia are looking to you
with hope. There is no other Party in the world that has such far-
reaching prospects. You have numerous disciples.

> Stalin's remarks to a visiting Chinese delegation, Moscow, July 1949[2]

HAD it been possible to monitor the worst nightmares of Western statesmen during the early Cold War, among them would have been the
prospect that Stalin *might* be saying what we now know he *did* say to his new
Chinese comrades in the summer of 1949. Once it had become clear that
Western Europe and Japan were reasonably secure, what worried officials in
Washington, London, and Paris was indeed their fear that the Soviet Union—
now a global superpower—would revive the appeal Soviet Russia—then a weak
revolutionary state—had directed toward the dependent peoples of Asia, Africa,
and Latin America three decades earlier. Containment might not prevent
Moscow's advance in those parts of the world that had cause to remember—and
to resent—what Europe had done to them over several centuries of imperial
domination. The Cold War could yet be lost, so to speak, "by the back door."

Americans found this prospect all the more painful because democratic values seemed likely here to undermine rather than reinforce Western interests. In
Europe, Wilsonian principles of self-determination and market capitalism had
complemented the balancing of power: idealism and realism worked well
together because the alternative Soviet model had so little beyond oppression
to offer. But in much of the rest of the world the West itself had been the oppres-
sor, whether through formal or informal means of exploitation. Paths to libera-

tion and livelihood could quite plausibly appear to lie through Moscow and, after 1949, Beijing. The Kremlin was planning to use China, the newly formed Central Intelligence Agency warned, "as an advanced base to facilitate Soviet penetration of Southeast Asia, including Indonesia and the Philippines; the out-flanking of India-Pakistan and the strategically important areas of the Middle and Near East; and eventually control of the entire Asiatic continent and the Western Pacific."[3] The threat Americans thought they had warded off in Europe and Japan—Moscow's capacity to transform misery into power—seemed only to have shifted to a wider arena. And this time Washington's allies, as former and remaining colonialists, were facilitating that process.

Now that the "second world" no longer exists, it is easy to dismiss these "first world" concerns about the "third world" as having been excessive, perhaps even manufactured.[4] They were real enough at the time, though: on this issue there was little difference between what Western leaders said openly and behind the scenes.[5] Their pessimism, we can see today, was ill-founded: the Marxist-Leninist model ultimately proved to be as unattractive in these parts of the world as it did everywhere else. But there was nothing predetermined about this outcome. Things *could* have gone the other way, and at the mid-point of the 20th century there were plenty of people on both sides in the Cold War who thought they just might. It is worth considering, then, why neither the dreams of revolutionaries nor the nightmares of those who opposed them actually materialized.

Daunting interpretive difficulties immediately arise. The "third world," as everyone came to understand that term during the Cold War, contained coun-tries as dissimilar as Mexico, Saudi Arabia, India, Nigeria, and the Philippines. One has to wonder what, if anything, so diverse an array of nations could have had in common. These were not all colonies at the end of World War II: some had not been since the 19th century, a few had never been. They were not all "non-aligned": most of them did in time affiliate with either Washington or Moscow. They do not fit easily within the "center–periphery" relationship "world systems" theorists like to talk about:[6] that terminology implies a single "center", when what shaped events in the "third world" was the tension between competing poles of attraction. Even racism, inescapably important though it was in determining "first" and "second" world attitudes toward the "third world"—and vice versa—explains little about how the Cold War devel-oped there: alliances frequently crossed racial lines, antagonisms could easily arise within them.[7]

"Third world" countries did, however, share one characteristic: they were pre-dominantly pre-industrial. Like most of the European colonial powers, the United States and the Soviet Union had long since industrialized, although by radically different means; had they not done so they could hardly have aspired to global leadership in the first place. There was, thus, a sharp disparity in *mate-rial* capabilities between the "first" and "second" worlds, on the one hand, and the "third" world, on the other. The existence of this power gradient—with quarreling superpowers at one end of it—created the potential for an imperial rivalry on a global scale, extending well beyond what the Cold War in Europe and Northeast Asia had thus far produced.[8]

Washington and Moscow would at times use their power to impose their will on "third world" peoples, in ways not greatly different from the pre-World War II behavior of the British, French, Dutch, Germans, Italians, and Portuguese. Certainly a kind of dependency arose, as a result. But the history of these earlier empires—as well as older ones going back through the Ottomans, Russians, Spanish, Chinese, Romans, and Greeks—suggests that even in such situations influence can flow in both directions. The Cold War in the "third world" was no exception to the pattern.

Antagonists in that conflict tended to calculate victories in terms of failures, retreats, and humiliations inflicted upon their opposites. Symbolic triumphs often exceeded the value of the territories in which they occurred; in another pattern familiar from the history of empires, the game itself was what counted, rather than whatever it was the game was supposed to accomplish. Reputation emerged as a vital interest, with credibility the standard against which to measure it.[9] This situation gave power to those who were supposed to have been on the receiving end of power: the "third worlders" themselves, who learned to manipulate the Americans and the Russians by laying on flattery, pledging solidarity, feigning indifference, threatening defection, or even raising the specter of their own collapse and the disastrous results that might flow from it.[10]

Like the Europeans and the Chinese, therefore, the "third world" was in a position to choose during the Cold War. But the fact that so much of it was simultaneously rejecting colonial legacies created a handicap for the Americans, whose connections with colonialism were much more visible than those of their Soviet rivals. Moscow had one other advantage as well, which was that industrialization in the USSR had proceeded much more rapidly than in the capitalist west. For people suspicious of capitalism anyway because of its links to imperialism, this record of accelerated development—this lure of a short cut to economic prosperity and social justice—provided yet another incentive to look to Marxism-Leninism as a model.[11]

There were good reasons, therefore, why neither the Americans nor their allies could take the "third world" for granted as the Cold War expanded into it. The collapse of colonialism was creating new opportunities for Soviet and now Chinese expansionism; but propping up colonialism risked accelerating that tendency. Western authority seemed to be fragmenting even as the "Sino-Soviet bloc" was consolidating.[12] However diverse the "third world" might be, one other thing it had in common was the dilemma it posed for the foreign policy of the United States.

I

Given their history Americans had ample cause to dislike colonialism; even so, it is easy to forget how proudly *anti*-colonial they were at the end of World War II. They were about to give up their only major colony, the Philippines, which they had acquired almost as an afterthought during the Spanish–American War. They had convinced themselves, through the so-called Good Neighbor policy, that their sphere of influence in Latin America was not exploitative at all, but rather provided mutual benefits. And Franklin D. Roosevelt, who felt especially strongly about colonialism, had made a point of opposing it in the Atlantic Charter and in many pronouncements that followed. He was truly far-sighted in anticipating how quickly nationalism would take hold after the war, especially in Asia, and how difficult it was going to be for the Europeans to retain their empires there and elsewhere.[13]

F.D.R.'s anti-colonialism was hardly absolute. He cooperated with colonialists to defeat the Japanese; he doubted that subject peoples could prepare themselves quickly for self-government and feared the consequences of pushing them prematurely in that direction; he used United Nations trusteeships for former enemy colonies to advance American strategic interests with little regard to local consequences.[14] But these compromises should not obscure the direction Roosevelt set for United States policy. It was one that looked toward *eventually* implementing the Wilsonian idea of self-determination throughout the world. That in itself was enough to gain Washington widespread, if not always well-informed, admiration.

When Ho Chi Minh cited the American Declaration of Independence while prematurely proclaiming the end of French rule in Indochina, therefore, it was not an entirely cynical gesture.[15] Nor was Ho alone in his expectations. The Atlantic Charter set off waves of anti-authoritarian sentiment in Latin America; Arabs looked to the United States to remove British and French influence from the Middle East; and throughout South and Southeast Asia hopes grew that the Americans would not only liberate those regions from the Japanese, but also from the European colonial overlords the Japanese had so easily overthrown.[16]

The years 1945–8 dashed many of these expectations. The Truman administration had little to say about a "Good Neighbor" policy for Latin America. Arabs found the new President more interested in creating a Jewish "homeland" in Palestine than in supporting self-determination in the Middle East. Truman did endorse independence for India, and he used economic and political leverage to force the Dutch from the East Indies.[17] But he seemed equally determined to restore the prewar position of the French in Indochina. The emerging Cold War determined some—but not all—of these positions.

Neglecting Latin America was normal for the United States in peacetime; surely Washington's interest in that area would have diminished, even without a Soviet threat. Truman's Middle East policy ignored as much as it reflected Cold War concerns: strategic requirements (air bases within bombing range of the

Soviet Union) and economic interests (oil) provided strong arguments for align-ment with the Arabs; but the President placed humanitarian and domestic political considerations above such priorities when he recognized the new state of Israel.[18] With a Labour government in power, the British would have left the Indian subcontinent whatever Washington did; nor would the Dutch have found it easy to hang on in what was to become Indonesia, even if Americans had never heard of the place. In none of these situations was there any imme-diate prospect that what the United States did—or did not do—might bring communists to power.

Where that possibility existed, though, Cold War considerations quickly came into play. Indochina was the prime example: in no other region did national liberation appear as likely to bring social revolution. However Jeffersonian his rhetoric, Ho was the only avowed Marxist dominating an anti-colonial movement with any prospect of immediate success. His country there-fore became a kind of laboratory in which the Truman administration sought to design a strategy that would maintain support for nationalism without at the same time advancing the interests of communism. "We cannot shut our eyes to . . . [the] continuing existence [of] dangerous, outmoded colonial outlook and methods in [the] area," Secretary of State George C. Marshall cabled the American embassy in Paris in February 1947; but "it should be obvious that we are not interested in seeing colonial empires and administrations supplanted by philosophy and political organizations emanating from and controlled by [the] Kremlin."[19]

Setting nationalism against communism did not seem, at first, all that diffi-cult. Roosevelt's legacy of rhetorical opposition to empires had by no means dis-appeared; meanwhile the Soviet Union itself was carving out an empire in Eastern Europe and appeared likely to attempt the same thing elsewhere.[20] Kennan's containment strategy had sought to distinguish between popularly supported Marxist movements like those in Yugoslavia and China, and those imposed by Moscow:[21] the implication was that international communism car-ried within itself seeds of nationalist fragmentation. The Marshall Plan relied upon overt and covert cooperation with the non-communist left in Europe, and some State Department officials even argued for supporting communists in the "third world" where they had nationalist aspirations. Ho himself, after all, had cooperated with the Office of Strategic Services during the final months of the war.[22] "[I]f we put ourselves sympathetically on the side of . . . nationalism, which is the dominant spiritual force in [Asia]," Secretary of State Dean Acheson told the Senate Foreign Relations Committee in October 1949, "we have put ourselves on the side of the thing which more than anything else can oppose communism."[23]

But that was Acheson's *general* position. He took a very different view with respect to the *specific* problem of Indochina: "Question whether Ho as much nationalist as Commie is irrelevant," he cabled American officials in Hanoi: "all Stalinists in colonial areas are nationalists. With achievement natl aims (i.e., independence) their objective necessarily becomes subordination state to

Commie purposes."[24] The contradiction here was between theory and practice. Nationalism might well override communism in most instances, but how could one be certain, in *each* instance, that that would occur? How could one determine how long it might take? What about collateral effects? Mao's impending victory in China enhanced Indochina's importance as a source of raw materials and potential markets, especially for an emerging Japanese economy cut off from the Asian mainland.[25] Nor could events in Southeast Asia remain separate from those in Europe: a French collapse in Indochina would surely undermine morale in France and thereby weaken NATO. European security might yet require "third world" stability.[26]

It makes little sense to seek consistency in Acheson's thinking: it only reflected the ambivalence afflicting the Truman administration at the time. Was it better to help the French suppress the Viet Minh, thereby containing communism while outraging nationalism, an outcome sure to generate future resentment against the United States in Southeast Asia and future opportunities for the Soviet Union and China? Or was it preferable to give the French no help at all, thereby ensuring another victory for communism in Asia while at the same time humiliating a vital partner in the task of restoring stability to Europe?

The solution Acheson and his colleagues eventually settled on turned out to be paradigmatic: Washington would support the French in their efforts to defeat Ho's insurgency while at the same time pushing them to prepare Vietnam, Laos, and Cambodia for eventual independence. The idea was simultaneously to bolster *and* reform the colonial regimes there.[27] By encouraging a gradual transfer of power to nationalist but anti-communist leaders—the French proposed the feckless Vietnamese emperor Bao Dai—the United States would attempt the same integration of self-determination with containment that had succeeded in Western Europe. With no better alternative, the Truman administration recognized Bao Dai's government in February 1950, and in May began sending direct military assistance to his French guardians in Indochina.[28] This uneasy balancing of bolstering and reform would soon become a standard American response to the problem of communism and nationalism in the "third world" as a whole.

Had it not been for the shift from a wartime vision of "one world"[29] to a postwar perception of two, Americans might have managed a more comfortable alignment of principles and interests. They could have continued to insist that colonialism was an anachronism without worrying about the implications—for national security, for the international balance of power—of ending it. The disorder sure to result would not have seemed dangerous in a world without enemies. But as the Cold War expanded, instability, whatever its source, posed risks. It had moved the United States to revive and protect Western Europe and Japan: in neither instance had there been any prospect of outright military attack. When such an attack did come, unexpectedly in South Korea, fears of instability elsewhere made that country's defense a vital interest. It was not at all clear, therefore, that Americans could afford any longer to indulge their anti-colonial sentiments if the effect was to be destabilization and a consequent expansion of Soviet influence. They were becoming, to their intense embarrassment, accomplices in colonialism, if not direct practitioners of it.

II

Just what were the prospects that the Soviet Union might benefit from the resentments the "developing" world felt toward its "developed" counterpart? How realistic were the fears that kept Western leaders so on edge about the "third world"? It is useful to suggest, here, two possibilities: a "passive" model, in which the USSR would simply await revolutions in colonial and dependent areas whose leaders would seek Moscow's assistance; and an "active" model, in which the Kremlin would itself attempt to foment such revolutions, gaining control of them as it did so.

Lenin had favored the latter approach. Convinced that capitalism required the exploitation of colonies for their raw materials and markets, he launched an appeal, soon after the Bolshevik Revolution, for the "Peoples of the East" to overthrow their European masters. He even authorized a congress of such peoples, held in Baku in 1920 and attended by almost 2,000 Asian delegates, at which fellow Bolshevik Grigorii Zinoviev called for a *jihad* against imperialism and capitalism amidst a frenzied waving of swords, daggers, and revolvers.[30] There was no follow-up, though, probably because of a dilemma Soviet leaders would repeatedly face and never quite solve: what *kind* of revolution were they seeking to promote in these parts of the world?

Stalin's 1927 setback in China had shown how an alignment of communism with nationalism could backfire: nationalists might hijack the revolution and turn it against the communists; communists themselves might begin to behave as nationalists.[31] The Soviet Union therefore shifted to a "passive" model of revolutionary development: that is why it was slow to take up the opportunities created by World War II and its aftermath. We have already seen how Stalin went out of his way to support Chiang Kai-shek in 1945, failing to sense how close the Chinese Communists were to seizing power. He withheld any endorsement of Mohandas Gandhi in India, and after independence the Communist Party there persistently attacked Prime Minister Jawaharlal Nehru.[32] Ho Chi Minh found no immediate encouragement in Moscow either, partly because of Stalin's distrust of nationalism, partly because the Soviet leader, like the Americans, tended to view Indochina from a European perspective: support for Ho might undermine the French Communist Party. "Moscow was no more responsive than Washington," the historian George Kahin has noted, "to the hopes of Vietnamese nationalists."[33]

The Soviet Union did not give up on "third world" revolutions. Stalin withdrew Soviet troops from China and Iran, he explained in May 1946, to expose the British and the Americans as imperialists and thus "unleash a movement of liberation in [the] colonies," but this appears to have been a long-term objective, not any plan for immediate action.³⁴ Andrei Zhdanov took note, at the organizational meeting of the Cominform in September 1947, of a "sharpening of the crisis of the colonial system," and made a point of including within the emerging "socialist camp" such states as Vietnam, Indonesia, India, Egypt, and Syria. When insurrections broke out in Burma, Malaya, the Philippines, and Indonesia after a conference of communist-controlled youth organizations at Calcutta in February 1948, some American officials saw a sinister pattern developing. But the Cominform granted membership to no Asian communist party; the Calcutta gathering was a large, public, and unwieldy affair that produced no clear instructions on anything; and the uprisings appear to have arisen spontaneously against newly independent national governments rather than surviving colonial regimes.³⁵ All of this was, at best, only shaky evidence for the CIA's claim, made later that year, that "[t]he USSR is effectively exploiting the colonial issue . . . . giving active support through agitators, propaganda, and local Communist parties to the nationalist movements throughout the colonial world."³⁶

A great deal changed, though, with the victory of communism in China. Stalin's conversations with Liu Shaoqi during the latter's secret visit to Moscow in July, 1949, make it clear that the Kremlin boss had shifted his thinking about the prospects for revolution in Asia. Under his new "division of labor" strategy, the "younger brother" would seek to exploit Western vulnerabilities in colonial and dependent areas; the "elder brother" would provide guidance and material assistance.³⁷ The Chinese, a participant in these discussions recalled, "were inspired by Stalin's support and his statement that the center of the revolutionary movement had shifted from the West to the East. . . . As a result, Mao Zedong and Liu Shaoqi soon began work on original strategy and tactics for the revolutionary movement in the Asian countries."³⁸

Liu announced the new strategy at a November 1949 conference of Asian trade unions held in Beijing, in a speech cleared ahead of time with Stalin. The Chinese model for revolution, Liu proclaimed, might "become the main path toward the liberation of other people in the colonial and semicolonial countries where similar conditions exist."³⁹ Early in January 1950, during Mao's visit to Moscow, *Pravda* published Liu's speech, confirming Stalin's approval. Two weeks later Mao, while still in the Soviet capital, authorized the new Chinese government to recognize Ho's Democratic Republic of Vietnam. The Soviet Union quickly followed suit. And in February, Ho himself turned up in Moscow on a secret visit to discuss revolutionary strategy with Stalin and Mao.⁴⁰

Encouraged by meetings with Chinese officials in Beijing, Ho proposed an alliance comparable to the one Stalin was about to sign with Mao. When the Soviet leader pointed out that his presence in Moscow was supposed to be a secret, Ho is said to have responded: "That is easy. You can simply have me flying in the air for a while, then organize a welcoming reception at the airport and release news of my visit to the public. After that we can work on a Soviet–Vietnamese alliance." Stalin rejected this ingenious idea: "only you Orientals could have this kind of imagination." He later explained his "division of labor" strategy, noting that although the Soviet Union strongly supported the Vietnamese revolution, he preferred to have "the Chinese comrades take over the principal responsibility of supporting and supplying the Vietnamese people."[41]

The Chinese themselves needed little encouragement, for despite its unique characteristics, Mao's revolution followed French and Russian precedents from 1789 and 1917 in its determination to set an example for the rest of the world. Ambitious visions are probably necessary if revolutions of any kind are to occur: those who would overturn old orders require some basis for suspending belief in the existence of practical difficulties. "Without such inspiration," the historian John Garver has noted, "too few people are willing to assume the risks and pay the sacrifices associated with rebellion against established authority. With ideological inspiration, adequate numbers of people are inspired to storm the heights for the sake of creating a new heaven on earth."[42]

But as earlier developments in France and Russia suggest, it is not easy to extinguish such revolutionary zeal once revolutions have come to power. Exporting the movement abroad can be a means of securing and legitimizing it at home—hence Lenin's conviction that without revolutions in Germany and the rest of Europe, the one he had made in Russia would not survive. International revolution can also serve national interests—hence Stalin's tendency to link the spread of Marxism-Leninism with an expanding Soviet sphere of influence. Which motive most influenced Mao in 1950 would be difficult to say: Garver probably has it right when he concludes that "[t]he new Chinese state was inspired by a powerful sense of mission *at once* nationalist *and* ideological."[43] Soviet encouragement, in the form of Stalin's flattering "division of labor" strategy, could only make the case for revolutionary expansion that much more compelling.

We have already seen how Mao justified Chinese entry into the Korean War by fusing national and ideological concerns. He feared having the military forces of a perceived adversary—the United States—approach Chinese borders; Stalin, seeing Soviet borders also at risk, worried about the same thing. But Mao, unlike Stalin, viewed this challenge as an opportunity. By killing "hundreds of thousands" of Americans, the Chinese army would demonstrate that the Chinese people had "stood up," thereby consolidating the revolution at home, advancing it abroad, and—not least in Mao's mind—impressing a Soviet leader who had shown himself to be intimidated by the prospect of war.[44] Intervention in Korea was, thus, an investment in geopolitical, ideological, and personal credibility.

Mao could hardly refrain, under these circumstances, from supporting Ho Chi Minh's revolution in neighboring French Indochina. He had included that territory, along with South Korea and Taiwan, on his list of locations from which the Americans and their allies might launch the expected effort to crush Chinese Communism. The fact that some of Chiang Kai-shek's forces had fled from China into Indochina could only strengthen Mao's sense of the territory's importance.[45] These geopolitical considerations fed back into ideological ones.

Was not Stalin himself encouraging Chinese assistance? Would not the Chinese revolution itself suffer a humiliating defeat if the imperialists suppressed Ho's insurgency?

III

Viet Minh contacts with the Chinese Communists had always been more extensive than with the Soviet Union. Ho himself had spent years in China and spoke Chinese easily; after Mao's victory, the Vietnamese and the Chinese quickly exchanged emissaries. Liu Shaoqi made a point of including Vietnam in his November 1949 speech announcing Beijing's support for revolutionary movements elsewhere, and in January 1950 he told the Chinese representative to Ho Chi Minh: "It is the duty of those countries which have achieved the victory of their own revolution to support peoples who are still conducting the just struggle for liberation . . . . it is our international obligation to support the anti-French struggle of the Vietnamese people."[46]

We now know that the Chinese decided to provide military assistance to the Viet Minh just as the United States was deciding to supply the French: both initiatives grew out of the Communists' victory in China; both *preceded* the outbreak of the Korean War. Ho formally asked for Chinese help in April 1950, and that same month Mao authorized the dispatch of military advisers to Vietnam. He reaffirmed his decision two days after the North Koreans invaded South Korea, explaining that the Chinese task in Indochina was of worldwide significance. If it failed, Liu added, this would cause difficulties for the Chinese revolution itself.[47] Mao's determination to aid Ho is all the more striking given the fact that the fighting in Korea forced him to defer his own plans to invade Taiwan.[48]

Drawing on their experience against Chiang Kai-shek, Chinese advisers helped Ho and his chief strategist, Vo Nguyen Giap, plan a successful fall offensive against the French which forced them away from the China–Vietnam border and allowed future military assistance to flow unimpeded. A French counter-offensive regained the initiative temporarily early in 1951, but the Chinese and the Vietnamese worked out a defensive strategy of holding on until they would be strong enough again to confront the French.[49] "By relying on the Chinese revolutionary lessons, and relying on Mao Zedong Thought," Ho told a visiting Chinese delegation in February, "we have further understood the thoughts of Marx, Engels, Lenin, and Stalin so that we have won a great deal of victories in the past year. *This we shall never forget.*"[50]

The end of the Korean War affected the Indochina situation in several ways. It allowed the Chinese to increase their military assistance to the Viet Minh; but the Americans did the same for the French. Cautious about provoking direct United States military intervention, Mao nonetheless encouraged Ho to take the offensive in northwest Vietnam along the Laotian border. The French commander, General Henri Navarre, attempted to block this move by seizing the strategically located village of Dien Bien Phu in November 1953; the Chinese moved quickly, however, to turn this new threat into yet another opportunity. Convinced that wiping out a large number of French would have "not only military but great political significance, and . . . a great impact upon the international situation," Mao urged Ho to besiege Dien Bien Phu, promising all necessary military support.[51]

Plans were already under way for an international conference on both Korea and Indochina. Well aware of disagreements in Washington, London, and Paris over what to do about the latter territory, the Chinese calculated that a humiliating French defeat there would significantly weaken the West's negotiating position. Zhou Enlai cabled Chinese advisers in Vietnam in March 1954 that "[in] order to achieve a victory in the diplomatic field, you may need to consider if you could follow our experiences on the eve of the Korean armistice to win several battles in Vietnam." Mao himself provided tactical advice to the Viet Minh during the battle for Dien Bien Phu, stressing—no doubt with the upcoming Geneva Conference in mind—that "the final attack should start ahead of the previous schedule."[52] In line with Mao's suggestions and with promises of whatever military assistance they needed, the Viet Minh launched the final offensive on 5 May. Two days later the French surrendered.

The Viet Minh prevailed, therefore, with a great deal of help from their Chinese friends. Beijing played a major role in formulating strategy, training troops, and keeping them supplied: to that extent, this was a highly successful application of Stalin's "division of labor" strategy. The Chinese and their Vietnamese allies did not, however, see eye to eye on everything. Cultural differences together with the long legacy of Chinese imperialism had caused some tensions before the victory at Dien Bien Phu;[53] and once the contest shifted from the battlefield to the conference table, geopolitics began to override ideology in the thinking of Mao and Zhou. This made it necessary for Ho to settle for much less at Geneva than he and his fellow Viet Minh thought they had earned.[54]

The Chinese had several reasons for wanting a compromise in Indochina. Like their Soviet mentors in the 1920s, they hoped for recognition within the world community as a normal state, even as they would continue to be a revolutionary one. The Geneva conference would be their first "appearance" in international diplomacy, and they were eager to make a good impression.[55] The new French government of Pierre Mendes-France was keen to cut its losses in Indochina; a Viet Minh push for additional territory might undercut his position, something neither the Chinese nor their Soviet allies wanted.[56] Mao and his close advisers also took seriously warnings Eisenhower and Dulles had made, prior to Dien Bien Phu's fall, that the United States might yet intervene in Indochina. The Chinese repeatedly stressed the danger that too stubborn a Viet Minh position could bring the Americans in:[57] here their cautions echoed those Stalin had made to them prior to the Korean War.

With these considerations in mind, Zhou and the Soviets persuaded the reluctant Viet Minh to agree to the withdrawal of all foreign troops from

Indochina—including their own from Laos and Cambodia—as well as the "temporary" partition of Vietnam at the 17th parallel. "It is possible to gain all Vietnam through peace," Zhou explained to Ho Chi Minh:

It is possible to unite Vietnam through elections when [the] time is ripe. This requires good relations with south-east Asian countries as well as among the Indochinese countries. . . . The answer is to unite them through peaceful efforts. Military means can only drive them to the American side. . . . Peace can increase the rift between France and the USA. . . . Peace can drive Great Britain and the USA apart. . . . All in all, peace has all the advantages. It can isolate the USA.

If the Americans should block peace, Zhou added, "we cannot but fight on. . . . We will be morally in the right. Every one will sympathize with us. Peace will come eventually after a period of fighting. By that time, the USA will be more isolated."[58]

In Southeast Asia, then, there was some basis for Western fears of an orchestrated campaign, directed from Moscow and Beijing, aimed at exploiting anti-colonial grievances. Stalin specifically encouraged the Chinese to aid Ho Chi Minh, and the assistance they provided the Viet Minh may well have been decisive in defeating the French. The Soviet and Chinese governments cooperated closely prior to and during the Geneva Conference of 1954, and their combined pressure induced a reluctant Ho to accept the uneasy compromise that ended the first stage of the long struggle for Indochina. Geopolitical *and* ideological concerns determined the nature of this joint enterprise: it would be difficult to sort out which was more important when and for whom; nor is it necessary, since in this situation geopolitical and ideological interests complemented one another. Since it was the Viet Minh who were at odds with their Soviet and Chinese comrades at Geneva, there was little doubt as to who would have to yield. What would happen when Moscow and Beijing reached dissimilar conclusions about geopolitics and ideology remained to be seen.

IV

The pattern differed in the Middle East. Resistance to colonialism certainly was growing in that part of the world, as in Southeast Asia; but there was no systematic Soviet effort to take advantage of this situation while Stalin was alive. Moscow's quest for influence in the huge strip of territory that stretched from Morocco to India and Pakistan began only under Khrushchev, and even then it is not always clear who was using whom: the leaders of these countries appear to have manipulated the Russians as often as the Russians manipulated them. The situation *looked* serious from the perspective of Washington, London, and Paris, though, partly because of Europe's dependence on Middle Eastern oil, partly because colonialism was obviously on the way out, partly because the Soviet Union and China had effectively exploited anti-colonial sentiment in East and Southeast Asia.[59] As a result, the Americans and their British and

French allies began a campaign to contain Soviet influence in the Middle East *before* that influence had begun to manifest itself. Their intrusiveness, we can now see, opened more doors for Moscow in that region than it closed.

The Iranian and Turkish crises of 1946 first brought the Cold War to the Middle East, but these were hardly successful efforts on Moscow's part to exploit anti-colonial sentiment: their effect, instead, was to raise fears of *Soviet* colonialism. Stalin's plans to separate Iranian Azerbaijan from the rest of the country backfired badly, undercutting the position of the pro-Soviet Tudeh Party and easing the way for an expansion of British and American influence at the invitation of the Iranians themselves.[60] Simultaneous Soviet demands for territorial concessions and naval bases from Turkey fared no better: even Molotov admitted, in retrospect, that Stalin had gone too far in trying to control the Dardanelles.[61] Soviet behavior in these two instances reflected much the same combination of defensive and offensive impulses exhibited in Eastern Europe and Northeast Asia. Stalin wanted secure boundaries but also subservient spheres of influence beyond them. Sensitivity to nationalism was not high on his list of priorities.[62]

Despite their favorable outcome, the Iranian and Turkish crises did raise Western concerns about the Middle East. As these mounted they exposed the same dilemma that was worrying the Americans in Southeast Asia. Because of its limited military capabilities the United States would have to cooperate with the British and French in that part of the world; but their colonialism was making the region vulnerable in the first place. Continuing British control over the Suez Canal, the veteran American diplomat Loy Henderson complained in 1947, was "poisoning the atmosphere of the whole Near and Middle East so rapidly and to such an extent that . . . the relations of the Arab world with the Western world may be seriously impaired for many years to come."[63] No one within the American government was more determined than Henderson—an old and embittered Russian hand—to contain Soviet expansionism. His warnings about discreditable allies, therefore, suggest how seriously the dangers of collaborating with colonialists were taken in Washington at the time.

Further complicating the American position was the peculiar mix of humanitarian compassion, domestic political expediency and personal stubbornness that had led President Truman—against strong advice from his diplomatic and military advisers—to support a Jewish homeland in Palestine. This course of action, the State Department Policy Planning Staff insisted, "would be construed by the Arabs as a virtual declaration of war against the Arab world."[64] When Truman went ahead and recognized the new state of Israel anyway in May 1948, many Washington officials feared that the decision would hand the Russians an enormous advantage. Not only would it threaten "some of our most vital interests in the Middle East and the Mediterranean," Kennan argued; it could also "disrupt the unity of the western world and . . . undermine our entire policy toward the Soviet Union."[65] The United States now carried the burden of association with Zionism as well as colonialism.

Economic and strategic concerns made these liabilities seem all the more dangerous. The reconstruction of Western Europe required access to Middle Eastern oil: estimates indicated that by 1951 the Europeans would be importing 80 per cent of their petroleum from that region. Nor was the United States confident about the long-term adequacy of its own reserves.[66] The British-run Suez Canal was a vital link for world trade as well as Western military transport, and British air bases nearby would bring some 94 per cent of the Soviet Union's oil refineries within range of American B-29s if war should break out.[67] When war did come in Korea, the effect was to intensify anxieties about the Middle East. Truman himself saw the North Korean attack as a diversion for Soviet military ambitions in Iran; even if these did not materialize, growing nationalist pressures in Egypt and elsewhere could still undermine the West's position in the region.[68]

The United States found itself, therefore, in the awkward position of having to balance its anti-colonialism against its alliances. Tilting too far in either direction—by alienating new friends in the Middle East or old friends in Western Europe—could create openings for a Soviet threat that would endanger them both. Washington needed a way to ease the British and the French out of their remaining possessions without leaving a power vacuum the Russians might exploit. It wanted to encourage peaceful relations among the successor states— no easy task given the hostility that existed between the Israelis and their Arab neighbors, on the one hand, and the Indians and the Pakistanis, on the other. And it hoped to ensure that nationalism—whatever forms it took in the Middle East—remained resistant to whatever lures Moscow might dangle before it.

The Soviet Union under Stalin, though, was a remarkably inefficient angler. Communist parties had indeed been active across the entire region from French North Africa to India, but unlike the situation in China and Vietnam they had gained only minimal influence. Sheer ignorance was part of the explanation: precisely *because* the Soviet Union was not a colonial power, the Russians knew little about what was happening in the Middle East. Caution, too, was involved. Khrushchev recalls Stalin as having regarded the area as a British preserve: "Not that Stalin wouldn't have liked to move into the Near East—he would have liked to very much—but he realistically recognized that the balance of power wasn't in our favor and that Britain wouldn't have stood for our interference."[69]

Compounding the problem was Stalin's tendency to insist that all communists follow guidelines determined in Moscow. This made it difficult to apply Marxism-Leninism within particular countries and to build a popular base of support for it: local party interests were not always compatible with Soviet national interests.[70] Stalin's demands on Turkey and Iran did little to enhance the prospects of communists inside those countries; nor did Moscow protest when authorities in Egypt regularly arrested and imprisoned local communists.[71] Soviet ineffectiveness in the Middle East becomes clear when one considers how Moscow handled three particular episodes: the creation of the state of Israel, the Egyptian coup of 1952, and the CIA-sponsored coup against the government of Mohammed Mossadeq in Iran in 1953.

It is often forgotten today that the Soviet Union *supported* the formation of a Jewish state in Palestine. There seem to have been several reasons for this position: it was a way of exploiting American differences with the British, who still held a United Nations mandate over that territory; it ensured continuing turmoil, raising the possibility that Soviet troops might enter the region as part of an international peace-keeping force; and the Russians apparently hoped, through the Israeli Communist Party, to gain some influence within the new state itself.[72] Moscow's unusual alignment with White House policy was one of the reasons the State Department so strongly opposed it. If the Russians were *for* an independent Israel, Under-Secretary of State Robert Lovett warned, inappropriately, perhaps the Americans were "buying a pig in a poke. How did we know what kind of Jewish State would be set up?"[73] But in the end it was the Russians who missed a considerable opportunity for winning friends among Israel's enemies in the Arab world. "The USSR delegation cannot but express surprise," a disappointed Andrei Gromyko told the United Nations late in May 1948, that "the Arab states . . . [are] carrying out military operations aimed at the suppression of the national liberation movement in Palestine."[74]

The Russians acted equally short-sightedly in their relations with Egypt. They negotiated a deal to barter Egyptian cotton for Soviet grain in 1948, but then irritated Cairo by selling the cotton on the world market at prices below what the Egyptians were charging. They abstained when the United Nations Security Council, in 1951, condemned Egypt for denying Israel the use of the Suez Canal. And when a military coup overthrew the unpopular King Farouk in July 1952, setting in motion the events that would bring Gamal Abdul Nasser to power, the Kremlin's initial response, Khrushchev later admitted, was that it was "just another of those military take-overs which we had become so accustomed to in South America."[75] A disaffected Czech diplomat recalled that Egyptian communists had first tried to "capture the revolution and use it for our own purposes;" but when the new government discovered this, they switched to attempting either "to overthrow the revolution or to discredit it by calling the revolutionary government a pawn of the West."[76] The idea that it might be worth working *with* rather than against Egyptian nationalism seems not to have occurred.

The most egregious example of Soviet misjudgment with regard to nationalism in the Middle East, though, came shortly after Stalin's death, when the United States and Great Britain orchestrated a successful coup against the government of Mohammed Mossadeq in Iran, which had nationalized British-owned oil facilities and driven the pro-Western Shah out of the country. Contrary to fears in Washington and London, Moscow's relationship with Mossadeq was distant and distrustful. One Soviet intelligence report described the Iranian leader, in May 1953, as determined "to smash the national liberation movement and suppress opposition elements around the Shah in order to create the conditions for further collusion with American monopolies." The Russians did pick up information on the planned CIA coup, which took place in August, but they failed to share it with Mossadeq because they perceived him as a "bourgeois nationalist." Not until November did the Foreign Ministry reassess the situation, conclude that the Soviet Union and the Tudeh Party had suffered a major defeat, and acknowledge that the Shah's restoration was likely to keep Iran firmly within the Western camp for years to come.[77]

V

It seems clear in retrospect that Western anxieties about Soviet advances in the Middle East were, at least while Stalin was alive, quite exaggerated. Anti-colonialism endangered British and French interests, to be sure, but it did not ensure gains for the Soviet Union: Moscow's ineptitude prevented that. The United States, no friend to colonialism, retained considerable influence in the region, despite its ties to the colonialists and its support for Israel. The Americans quickly established close connections with the Egyptian military officers who replaced King Farouk; the coup against Mossadeq could hardly have succeeded had the Americans not been seen, in Iran, as a welcome alternative to the British.[78] Given other parts of the world where the trends were less favorable, one wonders whether Washington might have gotten by in the Middle East with a policy of "wise and masterly inactivity."[79] We will never know, though, for hyperactivity is what developed.

The principal reason for this was what one might call the "hydraulic" theory of geopolitics: that dams built or dikes bolstered in some locations diverted the Soviet expansionist impulse toward others. As a 1952 Policy Planning Staff review warned, the very efforts the United States had made to stabilize situations elsewhere—the creation of NATO, intervention in Korea, protection for Japan and Taiwan, assistance to the French in Indochina—could make the Middle East *more* vulnerable: "the general picture appears to be one of such continuing weakness as to constitute an invitation to a shift in the theater of primary pressure if further Communist progress were to be successfully blocked in other areas."[80]

Having deployed its resources so widely in Western Europe, the Mediterranean, and Northeast Asia, though, the United States could not even contemplate defending the Middle East on its own. "Where will the stuff come from?" General Omar Bradley, the Chairman of the Joint Chiefs of Staff, wanted to know: "It will take a lot of stuff to do a job there."[81] That left Great Britain and France, still dominant military powers in the region, but their capabilities were rapidly declining, not least because resistance to colonialism was so rapidly growing. The question for the Americans, then, was how to reinforce their allies without taking on their baggage.[82]

Confronted with difficulties, policy-makers tend to fall back upon what has worked in the past. NATO had been remarkably successful in overcoming national differences: not only had the Germans and the French submerged old animosities in order to confront a new Soviet adversary, but so too had the

Greeks and the Turks, as of 1951 the newest members of the alliance. For want of any better idea, the possibility of extending NATO or something like it into the Middle East seemed worth exploring. The Truman administration therefore responded positively when the British proposed setting up a Middle East Command (MEC), to be based at the Suez Canal and run by them, linking NATO with the British Commonwealth and the countries of the region itself for the purpose of deterring and if necessary defeating any future Soviet attack.[83]

Similar methods do not always succeed, though, in dissimilar situations. A clear and present Soviet danger had made it easy to win support for NATO in Europe; in the Middle East, the Russians were a much more distant concern. Arabs regarded the British, the French, and now the Israelis as their principal oppressors; the MEC came across to them—fairly enough—as a lifeline for enfeebled imperialists, not for prospective victims of Soviet aggression.[84] The Egyptians, whose cooperation was vital if the plan was to proceed, refused to have anything to do with it. A youthful but assertive Nasser explained to John Foster Dulles in May, 1953, that the Soviets "have never occupied our territory . . . but the British have been here for seventy years. How can I go to my people and tell them I am disregarding a killer with a pistol sixty miles from me at the Suez Canal to worry about somebody who is holding a knife a thousand miles away?"[85]

Dulles needed no instruction on the evils of colonialism. His opposition to it mixed elements of American exceptionalism, Wilsonian internationalism, Christian moralism, geopolitical opportunism, and historical determinism, all of this "occasionally welling up inside Foster," as an awed British diplomat would later recall, "like lava in a dormant volcano."[86] The Secretary of State was sincere when he assured the Egyptians that United States "does not believe that certain peoples and races have the right to determine the fate of other peoples." But Dulles was also a Cold War hydraulicist, convinced that dangers contained in one region could spill over easily into others: "The Communists already rule one-third of the world," he warned, and what was happening in Indo-China provided "evidence that Communists seek further expansion." Too vigorous an assertion of Egyptian nationalism—especially if it forced a premature British withdrawal from Suez—would leave power vacuums the Russians might exploit. *"Don't create a moment of danger."*[87]

The Egyptians, to Dulles's disappointment, responded regionally rather than globally.[88] "British influence must *entirely disappear*," Nasser insisted. Could the British not retain "technical control" of their bases, Dulles asked, somewhat in the way that the Ford Motor Company provided parts, supplies, and training to its Egyptian dealers? Unmoved by this analogy from the world of corporate capitalism, Nasser was adamant: the Egyptians must know "when all the British will be gone." "How can we get the talks going again?" Dulles asked. "By getting the British to agree to the Egyptian point of view."[89]

This 1953 conversation foreshadowed much that would follow. It shows the Secretary of State juggling the competing priorities of anti-colonialism and anti-communism. It reveals his tone-deafness with respect to nationalism: suggesting that the Egyptians treat their interests in Suez like an automobile dealership was not helpful. It also illuminates contrasting world views. Dulles tried to lecture the Egyptians on Cold War hydraulics; they reacted by badgering him about local politics. Dulles drew a characteristically sweeping conclusion: "We must abandon our preconceived notions of making Egypt the key country in building the foundations for a military defense of the Middle East," he told the National Security Council upon his return. "[T]he so-called northern tier of nations, stretching from Pakistan to Turkey, were feeling the hot breath of the Soviet Union on their necks, and were accordingly less preoccupied with strictly internal problems or with British and French imperialism."[90]

Dulles therefore shifted to a new blueprint that would bind Turkey, Iran, Iraq, and Pakistan firmly to the West. There was architectural ingenuity in this "northern tier" scheme, for since Turkey had now joined NATO and since Pakistan would become a founding member of the Southeast Asian Treaty Organization (SEATO)—another Dulles edifice constructed after the Geneva settlement on Indochina in 1954—the effect would be to surround the Soviet Union and China with an interlocking network of alliances. These would serve, the Secretary of State apparently hoped, as a kind of geostrategic Great Wall to keep Moscow and Beijing from projecting their influence into areas where the locals—like Nasser—were insufficiently sensitive to its dangers.

The Egyptian strongman was no ideologue in the pattern of Stalin and Mao. He had no vision of a historically determined revolution sweeping the world; but he did see his mission as one of eliminating colonialism throughout the Middle East and Africa. From that perspective, his interests paralleled Dulles's; he certainly did not rule out working with the Americans to achieve them.[91] How to proceed was at issue, though. Nasser would move immediately without regard to how this might affect the Cold War; Dulles would do so only if assured there would be no effect. Arab unity was also a problem. Nasser saw it as vital in eradicating colonialism; Dulles's "northern tier" enterprise at best would distract other Arabs from this task, at worst could cloak colonialism in Cold War trappings, like the earlier and now-aborted MEC.[92] Slow to grasp these differences with the Egyptian leader, the Americans offered him economic and military assistance; the CIA even came forward with a $3 million personal bribe. Nasser accepted the cash, but used it to build a functionlessly conspicuous tower in the middle of Cairo, allowing it to become known locally, in honor of CIA agent Kermit Roosevelt, as *el wa'ef rusfel*, or "Roosevelt's erection."[93]

This was not an auspicious symbol for American policy in the Middle East. By the time Turkey and Iraq signed the Baghdad Pact, in February 1955, Dulles's "northern tier" wall-building had so alienated Nasser that the Secretary of State decided the United States should not become a member. Was this not "practically disowning our own child?" the American embassy in Ankara wanted to know. It was all "tactics and timing," Under Secretary of State Herbert Hoover, Jr., explained lamely on his boss's behalf. Noting that Nasser was about to attend a conference of Asian and African leaders in Bandung, Dulles suggested to the Egyptian ambassador that the Indonesian trip would offer his superior a "great opportunity [to] broaden his horizon and consider matters reaching beyond [the] area upon which he has concentrated in the past."[94] As often happened with the Secretary of State, his prophecy came true, but not quite as he intended.

Washington had welcomed the movement toward non-alignment when it began with Yugoslavia's defection from the Soviet bloc in 1948: no one had expected Tito to affiliate openly with the West. Nehru's insistence on keeping India neutral caused the Americans greater concern, but they could attribute much of this to the Indian leader's formidably prickly personality. The nation remained a democracy within the British Commonwealth; moreover Pakistan, seeking to counterbalance India, seemed eager to join whatever alliances the Americans might propose.[95] Egypt's movement toward non-alignment was more unsettling—not least because Dulles's "northern tier" project had so obviously brought it about. Tito and Nehru had encouraged Nasser to join the non-aligned camp, but he did not actually do so until he arrived in Bandung in April 1955. There he broadened his horizons indeed by meeting the always-impressive Zhou Enlai. Tito, Nehru, and Zhou, in turn, deferred respectfully to Nasser, pointedly treating him—as Dulles pointedly had not—as the leading figure in the Arab world.[96]

Egyptian sources have insisted that it was only then—and in reaction to a devastating Israeli raid against Gaza two months earlier—that Nasser raised the possibility of obtaining Soviet arms. "I think they would be prepared to give a positive answer," Zhou allowed, proceeding to pave the way. "It is impossible for the socialist camp to adopt the role of spectator in the inevitable battle in the Middle East," he reported back to Mao Zedong, who passed his assessment on to Moscow:

As I see it, our position obliges us to assist the nationalist forces in this battle for two reasons—because their victory would be in the interest of the socialist camp and because it would thwart all attempts of the western imperialists to complete the encirclement of the eastern camp. My conclusion is that the logic of history points to the nationalist movement as the coming force in the Middle East, and that we should make our approach to it as friendly as we can.[97]

It seems clear now, though, that the Russians did not need the Chinese to alert them to these opportunities. Nasser himself had broached the subject of arms sales at least a year earlier, and discussions had been going on sporadically ever since.[98] Bandung was significant because the Egyptian leader for the first time acknowledged openly his ties to "the other side," and began to use them as leverage in his dealings with the Americans and the British. It was Nasser's own version of Cold War hydraulics.

VI

The Soviet Union, following Stalin's death, had been moving toward a more sophisticated understanding of nationalism in the Middle East, and

Khrushchev's victory over Malenkov in the succession struggle—clear by early 1955—accelerated the trend.[99] Tito, now reconciling with Moscow, assured the new Soviet leader that "Nasser was a young man without much political experience," but "if we gave [him] the benefit of the doubt, we might later be able to exert a beneficial influence on him, both for the sake of the Communist movement and . . . the Egyptian people."[100] Khrushchev's reaction to Zhou's similar advice is not on record, but he was fully prepared to jettison the old Stalinist notion that nationalism was a bourgeois phenomenon likely to work against Moscow's interests.[101] There followed a vigorous Soviet campaign to woo the "third world," with the volatile but gregarious Khrushchev and his vacuous head of government, Nikolai Bulganin, showing up in exotic locales like Afghanistan and India which Stalin would never have dreamed of visiting. An invitation to Cairo seemed not so implausible a prospect.[102]

"We should make a concerted effort to 'woo' Nasser," a worried Eisenhower told his advisers just before he met Khrushchev and Bulganin at the 1955 Geneva summit conference.[103] Dulles, however, would only go so far. Despite ample warning that a Soviet arms deal was in the works, he refused to match it: this provoked Nasser—who still would have preferred American weapons—into announcing publicly, in September, a massive purchase of military equipment from Czechoslovakia. Dulles understood clearly enough how a strategically placed "neutral" like Nasser could play both superpowers off against one another, but competing with Moscow in the Middle East was likely to be "an expensive process" and he was reluctant to play the game. He admitted, though, that "we will not be able to put a good face on the matter. It will be regarded as a major defeat."[104]

There was, however, one card left. The Egyptians assigned vast symbolic as well as economic importance to the construction of a high dam at Aswan on the Nile, a gigantic project that would protect the country from floods and provide a reliable source of water for irrigation. American officials knew from the start that the Russians might fund the project if they and the British did not.[105] But by the spring of 1956, Eisenhower and Dulles had reached the limits of their patience with Nasser: he was undermining the Baghdad Pact, he had impeded an Arab–Israeli settlement, he had invited Soviet influence into the Middle East, and in May he even recognized the People's Republic of China. Prime Minister Anthony Eden and his ministers were talking—surprisingly openly—about deposing or even assassinating the Egyptian leader.[106] The last straw came when members of Congress objected that funding the dam might increase Egypt's cotton production, thereby lowering American prices for that commodity. Dulles called in Nasser's ambassador on 19 July, informed him that his government would have to look elsewhere for financing, and suggested—summoning all his customary tact—that Cairo might want to scrap the project altogether since its costs could generate "resentment and a feeling by the Egyptians that the limitations imposed tended to interfere with the independence which they so cherished."[107]

Nasser retaliated on 26 July by nationalizing the Suez Canal, setting off the most dangerous Middle Eastern crisis of the early Cold War. The question is worth asking, therefore: what were Eisenhower and Dulles thinking when they cut off funding for the dam? Resistance to being manipulated was certainly part of it: they had tried to get along with Nasser since 1953; he had reciprocated by playing them off against the Russians. An increasingly hard-line British attitude was also part of the explanation: Dulles's move came as no surprise to Eden and his colleagues, who welcomed it.[108] But there is another explanation for the Aswan decision that has received surprisingly little attention, and it has to do with the Secretary of State's warning to the Egyptian ambassador about the project's costs.

These would require great sacrifices from the Soviet Union and its satellites as well as the Egyptians; so much so, Eisenhower and Dulles thought, that they might undermine Khrushchev's authority at home while causing the Egyptians themselves to tire of the Soviet embrace. "If Egypt finds herself thus isolated from the rest of the Arab world, and with no ally in sight except Soviet Russia," the President had noted in March, "she would very quickly get sick of that prospect and would join us in the search for a just and decent peace in that region."[109] Just before delivering the bad news to the Egyptian ambassador, the Secretary of State told his brother, CIA director Allen Dulles: "if they [the Russians] do make this offer we can make a lot of use of it in propaganda within the satellite bloc. You don't get bread because you are being squeezed to build a dam."[110]

A kind of Middle Eastern "wedge" strategy, thus, was at work here.[111] Finding that Nasser was playing them off against the Russians, Eisenhower and Dulles in effect *encouraged* the Egyptians to go ahead and align with the Soviet camp, in the expectation that each ally would make life miserable for the other. The idea echoed an approach Dulles had devised for straining the Sino-Soviet relationship;[112] but here it reflected exasperation more than careful consideration. Nor did it work, for with his seizure of the Suez Canal, Nasser found a way to turn the tables and drive his own wedge, directly into the heart of the NATO alliance.

VII

There is no need here to review the uninspiring story of how the French, the Israelis, and ultimately the British conspired, in response to Nasser's surprise, to set up an Israeli invasion of the Sinai, thus *appearing* to put the now Egyptian-run Suez Canal at risk. As intended, these maneuvers triggered provisions of the 1954 Anglo-Egyptian treaty by which the British had withdrawn their forces from the canal zone, on the condition that they could reintroduce them if any other country should threaten it. The authors of that document had not contemplated that the British, in what one historian has called "an almost incomprehensibly foolish manner," would themselves *arrange* for an attack. [113] Compared to this astonishing performance, Dulles's policies were clear-headed and competent. Nor has evidence surfaced that the Americans knew in advance about the plot, despite their use of newly developed U-2 reconnaissance airplanes to monitor the military deployments associated with it.[114]

When the British–French–Israeli invasion forced them to choose, Eisenhower and Dulles came down, with instant decisiveness, on the side of the Egyptians. They preferred alignment with Arab nationalism, even if it meant alienating pro-Israeli constituencies on the eve of a presidential election in the United States, even if it meant throwing the NATO alliance into its most divisive crisis yet, even if it meant risking whatever was left of the Anglo-American "special relationship," even if it meant voting *with* the Soviet Union in the United Nations Security Council at a time when the Russians were themselves invading Hungary and crushing—far more brutally than anything that happened in Egypt—a rebellion against their own authority there.[115] The fact that the Eisenhower administration itself applied crushing economic pressure to get the British and French to disengage from Suez, and that it subsequently forced an Israeli pull-back from the Sinai as well—all of this, one might have thought, would have won the United States the lasting gratitude of Nasser, the Egyptians, and the Arab world.[116] Instead, the Americans lost influence in the Middle East as a result of Suez, while the Russians gained it.

Cleverness in Moscow was one reason why. After several days of hesitation, Khrushchev startled the world on 5 November by publicly threatening rocket attacks, presumably with nuclear warheads, on Great Britain, France, and Israel if they did not at once accept a cease-fire. Given what we know now—and what was suspected then—this was an empty gesture: it was a cheap way of rattling the West while winning favor with the Arabs.[117] Nasser himself acknowledged privately that it had been the Americans, not the Russians, who defeated Anglo-French–Israeli aggression.[118] But the actual cease-fire followed Khrushchev's fulminations closely enough to suggest a cause and effect relationship, and many people at the time—especially in Europe and the Middle East—saw it that way. Khrushchev was not shy about taking credit: "Our use of international influence to halt England, France, and Israel's aggression against Egypt in 1956 was a historic turning point. . . . Previously they had apparently thought that we were bluffing when we openly said that the Soviet Union possessed powerful rockets. But then they saw that we really had rockets. And this had its effect."[119]

Still, the Eisenhower administration might have turned the Suez crisis to its advantage had it had the good sense, at this point, to leave well enough alone. The President had just won triumphant re-election; his leverage over discredited allies had never been greater; his reputation in the Arab world—even to a lesser extent that of his Secretary of State—had never been higher. The Russians, for all their blustering, could not match these assets: not, that is, until Dulles, never one for "wise and masterly inactivity," proceeded to squander them.

The Secretary of State had not yet relinquished his conviction that it was up to the *United States* to keep Soviet influence from flowing into the Middle East. It was not enough to rely on Arab nationalism, however much Washington might have supported it during the Suez crisis; moreover, Nasser personally was not to be trusted.[120] These were curiously imperial attitudes for someone as sensitive as Dulles was about obsolescent colonialism; but as Diane Kunz has pointed out, he was fully capable, "if the situation demanded . . . [of violating] the same principles he had recently labeled sacred."[121] The situation Dulles saw, at the end of 1956, was one in which a British–French defeat had left a large power vacuum in the Middle East. The United States, he thought, *precisely because* it had earned the goodwill of the region's inhabitants, should now move to fill it.

Even though he was recovering from cancer surgery, Dulles took on this task with all of his usual hyperactivity, ingenuity, and absence of irony. The "northern tier" idea was still a good one in principle, he noted at one point: perhaps having *Iran* join *SEATO* might strengthen it?[122] Yes, he had originally suggested the Baghdad Pact, he explained to the ambassadors of its member states, but the United States could not now sign it because the alliance had "unfortunately become involved in area politics and was not universally viewed as an instrument solely to oppose communism and Soviet aggression."[123] There might, however, be another way.

Dulles recalled what had happened in an adjacent part of the world a decade earlier when President Truman had responded to an unexpected power vacuum—also the result of British weakness—by proclaiming a doctrine.[124] A comparably dramatic *unilateral* commitment to defend the Middle East might now deter the Russians, reassure the Arabs, and at the same time maintain an appropriate distance from the British and the French. Eisenhower, who rarely questioned Dulles's advice with respect to that part of the world, agreed to go along.[125] Hence it was that on 5 January 1957 the President found himself standing where his predecessor had stood almost ten years before, asking the Congress of the United States to provide economic and military assistance to the countries of the Middle East, as well as the authority to use American armed forces "to secure and protect the territorial integrity and political independence of nations requesting such aid against overt armed aggression from any nation controlled by international communism."[126]

No sooner had Eisenhower finished his speech, though, than it became apparent that it was not 1947 all over again. Key members of Congress who usually supported administration initiatives expressed open skepticism about this one, approving it with considerable misgivings.[127] Reaction in the Arab states and Israel, Allen Dulles carefully informed the NSC a few days later, had "thus far been reserved," and in Syria and Jordan "cool."[128] Subsequent CIA assessments were blunter: both the Baghdad Pact and the Eisenhower Doctrine, it reported in October, "are probably believed by almost all Arabs to indicate American preoccupation with Communism to the exclusion of what they consider to be the more pressing problems of the area."[129] The State Department itself, by this time, had come to the same conclusion: Eisenhower's pronouncement, "with its 'stand up and be counted' character with respect to international Communism, [had been] incompatible with the Arab brand of 'neutralism', and traditional Arab reluctance to be committed."[130] "Where's the vacuum?"

Khrushchev is said to have asked. As was his habit, he provided his own answer: "It's all in their heads."[131]

The Eisenhower Doctrine reached its logical conclusion on 15 July 1958, when United States marines, backed by naval and air support with nuclear capabilities, stormed ashore at Beirut in support of a Lebanese government that had been one of two in the entire region to endorse that pronouncement—only to be greeted by astonished sunbathers, ecstatic soda-pop vendors, and cynical reporters.[132] President Camille Chamoun had sought the Americans' protection as a means of undercutting his own domestic rivals; recognizing what would get attention, he pictured the crisis as one sparked by external communism. To their credit, Eisenhower and Dulles saw the dangers of yielding to this invitation and initially resisted it. But when rebels suddenly and violently overthrew the pro-Western government of Nuri al-Said in Iraq on 14 July, Washington and London panicked. British troops went into Jordan, and the marines landed at Beirut the next day. Quickly realizing that they had been had, the Americans withdrew their support from Chamoun, mediated a settlement with his rivals, and in October quietly moved the marines out.[133] "I found it hard to believe that we'd accomplished anything at all," a CIA agent involved in these events later recalled. Although the governments of Lebanon and Jordan were still in place, "[n]o Arab state east of Suez could any longer be called pro-Western in the sense we'd once intended."[134]

Arab nationalism was "like an overflowing stream," Secretary of State Dulles gravely informed the NSC two weeks after the landing in Beirut. "[Y]ou cannot stand in front of it or oppose it frontally, but you must try to keep it in bounds. . . . Although Nasser is not as dangerous as Hitler was, he relies on the same hero myth, and we must try to deflate that myth." This time, though, Eisenhower rejected Dulles's hydraulics—which now seemed to focus as much on the threat from Nasser himself as from the Russians. "[A]cceptance of the right of the Arab peoples to determine their form of government," the President observed mildly, might give the State Department "flexibility in the area. We could support Nasser when this was not contrary to our interests." But then he added, more brutally: "Since we are about to get thrown out of the area, we might as well believe in Arab nationalism."[135]

It was as sharp an acknowledgement of a Dulles foreign policy fiasco as Eisenhower ever made. There followed a full and hotly debated NSC review of Middle Eastern policy, with the President in the end approving the following statement:

It has become increasingly apparent that the prevention of further Soviet penetration of the Near East and progress in solving Near East problems depends on the degree to which the United States is able to work more closely with Arab nationalism and associate itself more closely with such aims and aspirations of the Arab people as are not contrary to the basic interests of the United States. In the eyes of the great mass of Arabs, considerable significance will be attached to the position which the United States adopts regarding the foremost current spokesman of radical pan-Arab nationalism, Gamal Abdel Nasser.[136]

So the crafty Egyptian won the recognition he had always wanted, after all. Looking back on these years, Mohamed Heikal, a Cairo journalist and close Nasser associate, pointed out that the Russians "had been, so to speak, sucked into the Middle East by events. It was not they who started the great offensive but Egypt who had forced it upon them."[137] Had Dulles in 1953 embraced the policy Eisenhower finally imposed in 1958, Nasser might never have invited the Russians in: his fundamental sympathies, we can now see, always lay with the West.[138]

But because the Secretary of State believed in filling all power vacuums—even those left, in the Middle East, by the despised British and French—he allowed the United States to inherit the enmities imperial powers normally attract when they seek too heavy-handedly to project their influence.[139] Determined to force a Cold War frame of reference on a region more concerned with resisting imperialism than containing communism, Dulles deadened his own sensitivities to nationalism, thereby opening opportunities for the Soviet Union, which would retain a significant presence in Egypt for the next decade and a half and elsewhere in the Middle East for another decade and a half after that. Because of his tendency to *fret, hover, and meddle*—his inability to see when things were going well and need not be re-engineered—Dulles transformed his own country into the new imperial power in the Middle East in what he knew to be a post-imperial age.

VIII

In 1957, Heikal visited Moscow, interviewed Khrushchev, and while doing so lit up a cigar. "Are you a capitalist?" the Soviet leader demanded: "Why are you smoking a cigar?" "Because I like cigars," Heikal replied. But Khrushchev seized the offending weed and extinguished it in an ashtray, muttering: "A cigar is a capitalist object. You're not a capitalist because you're a friend of Nasser." Six years later, Heikal saw Khrushchev again, who this time presented him with a whole box of cigars—good ones, too. "Mr. Chairman, I'm shocked," Heikal responded. "Don't you remember what you did to my cigar? Why have you changed?" "I haven't changed," Khrushchev chuckled. "It's these cigars that have changed. Since the revolution in Cuba these cigars have become Marxist-Leninist cigars."[140]

And so they had. If this conversation suggests paternal pride on Khrushchev's part the impression is not misplaced, for in Fidel Castro he found a worthy heir to the Bolshevik revolutionary tradition and an example for the rest of the "third world." Mao had never shown Khrushchev the deference he had accorded Stalin, and was now well on the way to becoming an annoying—even dangerous—critic.[141] Ho Chi Minh had an uncompleted civil war on his hands because of the settlement the Chinese and the Russians had forced on him in 1954, and was in no position to export revolution outside of Indochina. Nasser had never seriously considered becoming a Marxist-Leninist: to Khrushchev's irritation, he preferred keeping Egyptian communists locked up.[142] But Castro's victory and subsequent turn toward Moscow presented an unexpected opportunity, not unlike the one Mao had offered Stalin a decade earlier. Khrushchev's hopes for Latin America quickly swelled to match those of his predecessor for China.

Prior to that point, such prospects had seemed remote. The United States had long dominated Latin America economically and militarily: it understood the advantages of hemispheric hegemony long before it began to think about global hegemony. Communist parties existed throughout the region, but they were mostly mouthpieces for disaffected intellectuals. There was hardly any industrial proletariat, and the Catholic church retained the peasantry's overwhelming allegiance. Comintern efforts had fallen victim to the same ignorance of local conditions that defeated them elsewhere. Because of the distances involved attempts to promote trade, even to arrange diplomatic contacts with the USSR, had languished. When they thought about Latin America at all, one specialist on the subject has suggested, Soviet leaders did so with a kind of "geographical fatalism" that in effect surrendered it to Washington's influence.[143]

Communism to the south concerned officials in Washington, to be sure, but less than one might have expected. The Federal Bureau of Investigation had handled intelligence operations in Latin America during World War II and continued to report regularly on communist activities there; its director, J. Edgar Hoover, diminished the impact, though, by detecting Marxist-Leninists *everywhere*. Truman's White House for the most part filed and forgot his periodic alarms.[144] Secretary of State Marshall found himself literally besieged in Bogotá because of riots—widely blamed on communists—during the April 1948 founding meeting of the Organization of American States; however, surprisingly few repercussions followed. The most important consequence of the *Bogotázo*, as it came to be known, was probably the impression it made on the young Fidel Castro, who was one of the rioters.[145] George Kennan toured Latin America on behalf of the State Department early in 1950, returning with the pessimistic conclusion that "harsh governmental methods of repression may be the only answer."[146] But Acheson suppressed the Kennan report and it had no influence on US policy in the region—Washington hardly needed to be reminded that cooperation with authoritarians was an available option.[147]

This became particularly clear in June 1954, when the Eisenhower administration allowed the Central Intelligence Agency to repeat its performance in Iran by overthrowing the government of President Jacobo Arbenz in Guatemala. Several points about this much-debated episode are now clear. First, Washington did *not* act chiefly to protect the interests of the United Fruit Company, substantial though those were: that corporation had greater influence over the Truman administration than over Eisenhower's. Second, although Arbenz himself was not then a communist, he did rely heavily on support from the Guatemalan Communist Party and was very much under its influence. Third, Arbenz and his supporters together instituted the most successful land reform program seen in Latin America up to that time—a record the Americans would come to envy as the Alliance for Progress began to falter a decade later. Fourth, despite dark warnings from Dulles that Russian ambitions in the western hemisphere dated back to Tsar Alexander I and had given rise to the Monroe Doctrine in the first place, the Soviet Union did little to encourage Arbenz, a point that bears further elaboration.[148]

Arbenz's attraction to Moscow resembled that of a moth for a distant star. Like many Latin American intellectuals, he found in the sweeping totality of Marxist theory a substitute for *caudillismo* and Catholicism.[149] He read extensively on the Soviet Union and learned a few simple things: that an exploited class had come to power there, that it had eliminated illiteracy and raised standards of living, that it had defeated Nazi Germany, and that, as a friend recalled him saying, "it had never harmed Guatemala." "[T]hrough all this reading," Arbenz's wife remembered, "Jacobo was convinced that the triumph of communism in the world was inevitable and desirable. . . . Capitalism was doomed."[150] The Guatemalan president, in short, was Don Quixote, with Moscow the alluring and incorruptible Dulcinea.

The Kremlin's response, like Dulcinea's, was not all that it might have been. "We were knocking on the Soviets' door," one Guatemalan communist later acknowledged, "but they didn't answer." *Pravda* and *Kommunist* did run a few optimistic articles about the prospects for revolution in Latin America; and the Czechs were authorized to sell the Guatemalans—for cash—obsolete and largely inoperable German military equipment left over from World War II.[151] Direct Soviet–Guatemalan contacts, though, appear to have been limited to a visit by a Soviet diplomat interested in bartering agricultural equipment for bananas: the deal fell through when each side realized that the other had no refrigerated ships, and that the bananas could only travel under the auspices of the United Fruit Company. When historian Piero Gleijeses searched Guatemalan archives seized by the CIA for evidence of Soviet financial support, all he found were peremptory demands from the Moscow bookstore *Mezhdunarodnya Kniga* that the local Communist Party settle outstanding balances of $12.35 and $10.60— which it immediately did. "You people are crazy," a Mexican communist commented: "we haven't paid them a cent for at least 10 years."[152]

The CIA's intervention was a massive overreaction to a minor irritant. It did little to alter the course of events inside Guatemala, where Arbenz's regime had made so many enemies among the landowners and the military that it probably would not have lasted in any event.[153] It did nothing to contain Soviet ambitions in Latin America—those hardly existed at the time. It did, however, in several ways, affect what happened later in Cuba. It produced over-confidence in Washington about covert operations. It generated resentment throughout the hemisphere, where knowledge of American complicity quickly became overt. And it influenced certain individuals in a way no one could have anticipated. Castro himself did not observe the events in Guatemala City, but an unemployed Argentine physician named Ernesto "Che" Guevara did and the memory never left him. He went on from there to Mexico City, where for the first time he met Castro, then in exile after a bungled attack on the Moncada army bar-racks in Santiago, Cuba. Together they plotted Castro's December 1956 return to the island on the leaky yacht *Granma*, no doubt inspired by the ease with which the CIA's ragtag rebels had overthrown Arbenz. Two years of fighting in the Sierra Maestra followed, and on 1 January 1959, President Fulgencio Batista and his government fled Havana. The youthful rioter in the *Bogotázo*—along with the traumatized witness from Guatemala City—was now running Cuba.[154]

The Eisenhower administration responded remarkably calmly to Castro's vic-tory. Batista's corrupt, inefficient, but conspicuously pro-American regime had long been an embarrassment;[155] moreover, Vice President Richard M. Nixon had almost been lynched in Caracas several months earlier when an enraged mob attacked his motorcade.[156] It had been the tenth anniversary of the *Bogotázo*, and this time Washington took the message seriously: Nixon told the Cabinet, on his return, that it was time to recognize "the advent of the lower classes into the political scene and the ensuing requirement that American ambassadors . . . broaden their contacts beyond the traditional elite."[157] The tri-umph in Havana of a popularly supported guerrilla movement promising land reform and social justice was not, therefore, an entirely unwelcome develop-ment. "The Provisional Government appears free from Communist taint," Secretary of State Dulles informed Eisenhower, "and there are indications that it intends to pursue friendly relations with the United States."[158]

Once again Dulles was a bad prophet, although because he was soon to resign and die, he had little to do, this time, with falsifying his own prophecy. That responsibility rests, about equally, with others in the Eisenhower administra-tion, and with Castro himself. Nixon's 1958 trip had indeed led to a keener awareness of the need to support political and economic reform in Latin America; but this did not extend to the same acceptance of nationalism and non-alignment—even anti-Americanism—that Eisenhower had come around to after many hard lessons in the Middle East. The United States was not prepared to treat Castro as Nasser, a fact that became evident when the Cuban leader accepted an invitation from the American Society of Newspaper Editors—point-edly *not* seconded by the White House—to visit the United States in April 1959.

Castro made the usual rounds, even appearing, speaking hesitant English, on "Meet the Press," where the formidable May Craig, fearsome in flowered hat, extracted nervous assurances that he had no communists in his government.[159] Eisenhower avoided a meeting, assigning that task instead to Nixon and Dulles's successor, Christian A. Herter. The new Secretary of State found Castro interesting, immature, confused, and somewhat "wild" when conversing in Spanish. It sounded like what Nehru had said about the Arabs, the President commented: "When they begin to speak, a kind of accumulated emotional frenzy develops, with the speaker exciting the mob and the mob exciting the speaker."[160] Nixon's observations were weightier:

The one fact we can be sure of is that [Castro] has those indefinable qualities which make him a leader of men. Whatever we may think of him he is going to be a great factor in the development of Cuba and very possibly in Latin American affairs generally. He seems to be sincere. He is either incredibly naive about Communism or under Communist discipline—my guess is the former. . . . [H]is ideas as to how to run a government or an economy are less developed than those of almost any world figure I have met in fifty countries. But because he has the power to lead . . . , we have no choice but at least to try to orient him in the right direction.[161]

That, in retrospect, was just the point. Eisenhower had finally understood, with respect to Nasser, that efforts to manage—or "orient"—would only backfire: one had to take the Egyptian leader on his own terms and then see what was possible. With Castro, he never got that far.

One explanation, surely, was geography. It was easier to recognize the limits of power when required to wield it halfway around the world. Ninety miles offshore was quite a different matter. Had the United States not always, in the past, controlled the Caribbean? Had it not demonstrated, in dispatching Arbenz, newly acquired professional skills in such operations? Interests also were dissimilar: Nasser had nationalized the Suez Canal but nothing else—American-owned facilities in the Middle East had remained untouched. Cuba, though, was full of American property ranging from ranches and sugar mills to nightclubs and baseball franchises; Castro had not concealed his plans to take over many of these assets. Timing too was a problem: Eisenhower had had six years to experiment with approaches to Nasser; only two remained to him now for dealing with Castro, and the distractions of a presidential campaign—even though he himself would not be running—were sure to dominate one of them. The Cuban situation simply left less room for maneuver, for trial and error, than had been the case with Egypt.

But there was another equally important reason for the breakdown in Cuban–American relations: Castro himself. We can now see that he was much closer, in temperament, priorities, and style of leadership, to Mao Zedong and Ho Chi Minh than to Tito, Nehru, and Nasser. The latter group were balancers: the ideologies they proclaimed only occasionally dictated their actions; nonalignment allowed them to tilt this way or that, thereby playing both sides in the Cold War off against one another. Mao and Ho, conversely, were bandwagoners: ideology told them the direction in which history was moving, and they were determined to climb aboard—or even, in Mao's case after Stalin's death, to take the driver's seat.[162]

Castro began his career as a revolutionary with no ideology at all: he was a student politician turned street fighter turned guerrilla, a voracious reader, an interminable speaker, and a pretty good baseball player. The only ideas that appear to have driven him were a lust for power, a willingness to use violent means to get it, and an unwillingness to share it once he had it. If he followed any example, it was that of Napoleon, not Marx.[163] Despite the influence of his own brother Raúl and Guevara, both avowed Marxists,[164] Castro did not start thinking of himself in those terms until well after he had deposed Batista and assumed the title—his choice—of Maximum Leader. Washington's hypersensitivity may have pushed him in that direction: he had always been anti-American, and could rarely resist the temptation to needle Uncle Sam. But it seems more likely that Marxism-Leninism appealed to Castro for domestic and personal reasons. As an authoritarian and historically determined ideology, it provided the best possible excuse for not holding elections, which might allow future rivals to emerge. And if taking this path should attract support from the Soviet Union, then so much the better.[165]

IX

For the Russians, all of this came as an enormous surprise; one of them remembered it as "a completely unexpected miracle."[166] Castro's insurgency had attracted little attention and no support from Moscow. His relations with the Cuban Communist Party—unlike those of Arbenz with the Guatemalan communists—had been distant and uneasy. "At the time that Fidel Castro led his revolution to victory," Khrushchev later admitted, "we had no idea what political course his regime would follow."[167] Over the summer and fall of 1959, though, Castro repaired relations with the Cuban communists as his relations with Washington deteriorated; he also put out feelers to Moscow regarding trade and possible arms sales. The Russians responded warily, not knowing what to make of a revolutionary so at odds with their own experience who seemed to be espousing their ideology. They did, however, send a KGB representative to Havana—there were, as yet, no diplomatic relations—and in February 1960, at Castro's invitation, Anastas Mikoyan, Deputy Chairman of the Soviet Council of Ministers, arrived to assess the situation for himself.[168]

One of Castro's biographers describes the Cubans "watch[ing] eagerly, like expectant children on Three Kings' Day, as the Soviet delegation descended from the sleek Aeroflot jet."[169] Certainly they were delighted to receive sympathy and promises of support from an alternative superpower; the Russians, in turn, relished the opportunity to upstage the United States in its own backyard. The socialist system, Mikoyan confidently assured the Cubans, had proven its superiority over capitalism: "It is obvious that the owners, whatever their administrative abilities, cannot manage their economy, because of forces beyond their control."[170] But the Soviet visitor found much more in Cuba than the satisfaction of unsettling the Americans: the place had the invigorating effect on him of an ideological Fountain of Youth. "I have been told," Eisenhower noted several months later, "that Mikoyan on returning to Moscow from Cuba, was exuberantly rejuvenated, finding that what was going on in the youthful and disorganized Cuban revolution brought him back to the early days of the Russian Revolution."[171] Mikoyan himself subsequently confirmed this in a conversation with Dean Rusk: "You Americans must realize what Cuba means to us old Bolsheviks. We have been waiting all our lives for a country to go Communist without the Red Army. It has happened in Cuba, and it makes us feel like boys again!"[172]

The Mikoyan visit, Secretary of State Herter concluded, "was a long step toward the breaking of the remaining links between the Government of Cuba and the American family of nations and presages the establishment of close working relations between Cuba and the Soviet Union."[173] Eisenhower must have agreed, because in March 1960 he authorized the CIA to begin planning Castro's removal.[174] The Cuban leader was not like other neutralists, the President later explained to his old friend, British Prime Minister Harold Macmillan:

Castro fully incorporates the Communists in his regime, carries out a precipitate revolution against the existing social order, and is far more internationalist in his pretensions to spread his revolution to surrounding countries than the usual type of nationalist whom the Communists court. If the Communists could find other leaders who met Khrushchev's standards of "peaceful coexistence" and Mao's of a Communist revolutionary we would be in very serious trouble indeed.[175]

"Castro is really the very Devil," Macmillan sympathized, but then proceeded to miss the point. "He is your Nasser, and of course with Cuba sitting right at your doorstep the strategic implications are even more important than the economic. . . . I feel sure Castro has to be got rid of, but it is a tricky operation for you to contrive and I only hope you will succeed."[176] Given Macmillan's eagerness to exterminate Nasser in 1955–6,[177] Eisenhower might have taken this as a warning. But then Macmillan alone among Eden's ministers had escaped Suez with his reputation intact. That fact, too, would not have escaped Eisenhower.

Meanwhile, Khrushchev's pronouncements on Cuba had progressed, with characteristic momentum, from cautiousness through encouragement to belligerency and bristling militancy. By July he was openly threatening the United States with a Soviet missile attack if it should try to invade Cuba, while declaring the Monroe Doctrine dead and in need of burial, "so as not to foul the air with its putrefaction."[178] Soviet theorists of international relations quickly adapted to the new line, confirming that revolutions in the "third world" could indeed arise from the actions of enlightened "bourgeois nationalists" like Castro: neither working classes nor communist parties were required.[179] And in September 1960 the Soviet and Cuban leaders finally met—having arrived in New York for a meeting of the United Nations General Assembly—in the improbably seedy surroundings of the Hotel Theresa in Harlem. Castro had moved his delegation there to irk the State Department and establish solidarity with the oppressed African-American proletariat, an act that obliged not only Khrushchev but Nasser, Nehru, and an array of other world leaders, as well as an assortment of American left-wing intellectuals, to make the pilgrimage to 125th Street. It was the biggest thing that had happened, one local commented, since the death of W. C. Handy.[180]

Certainly it was the most memorable General Assembly session ever. The disheveled Cubans, decked out in combat fatigues, punctuated a long Khrushchev speech with raucous cheers at each mention of their revolution. The Soviet leader himself enlivened the proceedings by attempting to shout down Macmillan; when this did not succeed he took off his shoe and banged it at the unflappable prime minister. "A pity," Gromyko later sighed, "but it does happen." Castro made his own unforgettable impression when he took the podium: "We will do our best to be brief," he assured the delegates, and then proceeded to harangue them on the evils of American imperialism for some four and a half hours, the longest oration ever given at the United Nations. The assembled representatives of the first, second, and third worlds reacted, for once, in harmony: they listened attentively for a while, but then began to fidget, and then to slumber, and then—as discreetly as possible—to steal away.[181] None could ignore Cuba any longer, though; none could confidently assume, whatever his platform manner, that Castro's revolutionary example would not catch on and spread throughout dependent and deprived parts of the world.

X

"Indeed, comrades, life has greatly surpassed even the boldest and most optimistic predictions and expectations." It was an exuberant, even triumphant Khrushchev, speaking to the Higher Party School of the Institute of Marxism-Leninism in Moscow on 6 January 1961:

Our era . . . [is] an era of Socialist revolutions and national liberation revolutions; an era of the collapse of capitalism and of liquidation of the colonial system; an era of the change to the road of socialism by more and more nations; and of the triumph of socialism and communism on a world scale.

For the first time in history, the socialist camp's military strength could compel the imperialists, "under the threat of the downfall of their system, not to unleash a world war." But "national liberation wars" would continue "as long as imperialism exists, as long as colonialism exists. . . . Such wars are not only admissible but inevitable." Khrushchev then turned to the example of Cuba:

A war took place there too. [I]t . . . started as an uprising against the internal tyrannical regime supported by U.S. imperialism . . . However, the United States did not interfere in that war directly with its armed forces. The Cuban people, under the leadership of Fidel Castro, have won. Can such wars flare up in the future? They can. Can there be such uprisings? There can. . . . The Communists fully support such just wars and march in the front rank with the peoples waging liberation struggles.[182]

When these pronouncements became public a few days later, Eisenhower, who had taken a lot of Khrushchev rhetoric over the years, dismissed them as nothing new; but after 20 January, his view would no longer matter. John F. Kennedy's reaction was quite the opposite: "Read, mark, learn, and inwardly digest," the president-elect instructed his advisers on the eve of taking office. "This is our clue to the Soviet Union."[183]

It might seem odd that the youngest man ever elected to the White House should have worried so much about stagnation, decline, and obsolescence, but worry he surely did. The carefully contrived cadences of Kennedy's inaugural address, delivered with Khrushchev's "wars of national liberation" speech very much in mind, rang with the urgency of regaining momentum in the Cold War. And on 30 January, in his first State of the Union address, the new president warned explicitly that "the tide of events has been running out, and time has not been our friend."[184]

Kennedy's pessimism was partly political: having viewed Eisenhower's policies with alarm during the campaign, it would not do now to see no cause for alarm.[185] But there was much more to it than that. J.F.K. *believed* what Khrushchev had only recently begun to assert: that underlying historical forces gave Marxism-Leninism the advantage in the "third world." Fears that this *might* be true had circulated in Washington since the late 1940s, and Kennedy during his congressional and senatorial career had certainly shared them. During the 1950s, though, social scientists began to find a theoretical justification for these concerns: the development process itself, they insisted, created periods of vulnerability at which communists could seize power.

As Walt Rostow put it in his influential 1960 book *The Stages of Economic Growth*, Marxism-Leninism was "a kind of disease which can befall a transitional society if it fails to organize effectively those elements within it which are prepared to get on with the job of modernization."[186] Cuba's revolution came just in time to confirm Rostow's conclusions, or so it appeared: if communists could take over there, where could they not take over? Kennedy's ties to the academic world had always been closer than Eisenhower's, and he made a point of bringing Rostow onto the NSC staff. Development theory now had an indefatigable, if interminable, spokesman at the top, a fact that did nothing to lessen the new president's sense that history itself had turned against the United States.

Eisenhower's plan to overthrow Castro offered a tempting quick fix. Having called publicly for such an operation during the campaign, having few means apart from faith in Allen Dulles to assess its feasibility, there was never a real chance that Kennedy would not go through with it. Whether Eisenhower would have handled the project differently, or whether, had Kennedy himself done so, it would have produced the intended result, is difficult to say. What actually happened at the Bay of Pigs in April 1961 was a monumental disaster for the United States and the Cuban exiles the CIA had recruited, comparable only to the humiliation the British and the French had suffered at Suez five years earlier. Eisenhower, like Macmillan, emerged unscathed: however unfairly, it was Kennedy's reputation—none too strong to begin with—that took the damage.[187] Castro, it seemed, was more firmly in place than ever.

When Khrushchev met Kennedy at Vienna in June, he could not resist rubbing it in. The botched invasion had "only strengthened the revolutionary forces and Castro's own position, because the people of Cuba were afraid they would get another Batista and lose the achievements of the revolution. Castro is not a Communist but U.S. policy can make him one." Kennedy acknowledged that the whole thing had been a mistake, but pointed out that if Castro were to use Cuba as a base from which to subvert other countries in the western hemisphere, that would endanger the United States. Khrushchev scoffed: "Can six million people really be a threat to the mighty U.S.?" Then he really rubbed it in:

The U.S. has no colonies but it supports colonial countries, that is why the people are against it. There was a time when the United States was a leader in the fight for freedom. As a matter of fact, the Russian Czar refused to recognize the United States for twenty-six years because he regarded the United States as an illegitimate creature. Now the United States refuses to recognize New China—things have changed, haven't they?

Khrushchev followed this by restating the premises of his 6 January speech: nuclear war was out because nobody could win it; communists would prevail in any conventional conflict; wars of national liberation were "holy wars" which nobody could stop and which the Soviet Union would support. The United States was on the wrong side of history.[188] No wonder Kennedy felt battered after this experience.[189]

But Khrushchev, we can now see, was posturing: in fact, the Bay of Pigs had caused *him* to begin to *lose* confidence about Castro and the Cuban Revolution. His memoirs explain why: "We welcomed Castro's victory, of course, but at the same time we were quite certain that the invasion was only the beginning and that the Americans would not let Cuba alone." The country was vulnerable to attack, lying only a few miles off the American coastline "stretched out like a sausage, a shape that makes it easy for attackers and incredibly difficult for the island's defenders. There are infinite opportunities for invasion, especially if the invader has naval artillery and air support." The problem of how to defend Cuba "was constantly on my mind . . . . one thought kept hammering away at my brain: what would happen if we lost Cuba?"

I knew it would have been a terrible blow to Marxism-Leninism. It would gravely diminish our stature throughout the world, but especially in Latin America. If Cuba fell, other Latin American countries would reject us, claiming that for all our might the Soviet Union hadn't been able to do anything for Cuba but make empty protests to the United Nations. We had to think up some way of confronting America with more than words. We had to establish a tangible and effective deterrent to American interference in the Caribbean. But what, exactly?[190]

It is perhaps best, for the moment, to leave Khrushchev to ponder this problem, noting only the irony that what Kennedy regarded as his most embarrassing failure had the unexpected effect of deflating Khrushchev's euphoria over one of his greatest successes—rather in the way American intervention in South Korea abruptly diminished Stalin's hopes in East Asia. If Washington felt seriously enough about such matters as to undertake military action, then that took them beyond little boys' games. Reputations were on the line. Humiliation could result. Stagnation, decline, and obsolescence would surely follow. Desperate remedies might be required.

XI

Thirty-three years after these events, the Clinton administration asked the small South American republic of Guyana to accept William C. Doherty, Jr., executive director of the American Institute for Free Labor Development, as its next United States ambassador. Guyana's president, Cheddi Jagan, surprised Washington with the polite reminder that Doherty had once participated in a CIA plot to overthrow him. The State Department quickly withdrew the nomination and began a quiet review of Caribbean history. It turned up the fact that Jagan had led the country once before, as prime minister while it was still British Guiana, that he had been an admirer of Karl Marx, and that the Kennedy administration had regarded him as a major threat to the stability of the region, second only to Fidel Castro.

Kennedy had met Jagan in Washington in October 1961, and "Meet the Press" had interrogated him on his communist connections. He made no better impression than Castro, and Kennedy ordered the CIA to get rid of him. The Agency worked through Doherty's institute to bribe local labor unions and instigate riots for that purpose. When those measures failed, the British deferred granting independence until Jagan eventually fell from power and into obscurity, only to emerge again as Guyana's president after the country's first free elections in 1992. Having reacquired this history in the summer of 1994, the State Department and the CIA dealt with it by withholding the relevant documents from the normal 30-year declassification process, despite the fact, as an amused Jagan observed, that "everybody in Guyana knows what happened."[191]

Bill Clinton had been a precocious teenager when Kennedy was in the White House and could not have been expected to know. But the fact that none of his senior advisers remembered the crisis in British Guiana either suggests how much has changed since the days when Americans saw dominoes lined up, ready for toppling, all over the "third world." Was it *all* a false alarm? Was there *ever* the prospect that Moscow might spread its influence—as Lenin, Stalin, and Khrushchev had hoped—by means of revolutionary uprisings in colonial and dependent regions? To try to answer by generalizing about the "third world" as a whole would only demonstrate the vacuousness of that artificial—though still irreplaceable—term. Distinctions, of several kinds, are called for.

First, regional distinctions. In Southeast Asia, what Washington feared did indeed happen—for a time. Stalin encouraged the Chinese Communists to support Marxist revolutions beyond their borders, and they did so with impressive success in Indochina. There is every reason now to credit Chinese military assistance as a major reason—maybe even the critical reason—for the Viet Minh victory over the French in 1954. Paradoxically, though, Soviet and Chinese pressure restrained Ho Chi Minh from extending his triumph south of the 17th parallel, and Sino-Soviet cooperation to support other revolutions in Asia never materialized.[192] In the Middle East, Soviet influence expanded because of John Foster Dulles's bungling. Nasser invited it in to counter the intrusive and over-protective Americans, who came only belatedly to appreciate his independent role in that part of the world. In Latin America, Moscow expected nothing and gained a lot, but Washington was only partly to blame. Like Stalin and Mao but unlike Nasser, Castro was a true revolutionary authoritarian: it seems clear enough now that the United States could have gotten along with him *only* if it had been prepared to endorse, without question, his dictatorial rule.

Second, distinctions with respect to the foreign policy of the United States. The argument that it systematically used its "central" position to exploit "peripheries" during the Cold War seems much too simple. For one thing, the Americans were always ambivalent about colonialism: their record in opposing it was by no means consistent, but neither did they consistently defend it, as the Suez crisis strikingly demonstrated. Nor did economic interests determine American policy: they were always present and occasionally dominant; but they were embedded within a complicated network of other concerns—military credibility, alliance solidarity, humanitarianism, fear of communism, irritation at anti-Americanism, Congressional and interest group pressures, Cold War hydraulics. Nor were the Americans even in charge much of the time: the existence of a rival superpower "center" placed "peripheries" in a position to manipulate Washington about as often as the other way around.

Third, distinctions with respect to Soviet foreign policy. We have tended to think of it as cold, calculating, even Clausewitzian in its precise alignment of interests with ideology. What we have not understood is that the very nature of authoritarianism discouraged realism and exaggerated emotion: if Stalin, Mao, or Khrushchev felt strongly about something, who was to challenge them? Why did Stalin respond so warmly to Mao when logic should have told him a new rival was emerging? Why did Mao abandon his own plans to take Taiwan to assist beleaguered comrades in North Korea and northern Indochina? Why were Mikoyan and Khrushchev so moved by what had happened in Cuba? Why, for that matter, would Mao later launch the Great Cultural Revolution? Why would Leonid Brezhnev, in his declining years, go adventuring in places like Angola, Mozambique, Somalia, Ethiopia, and Afghanistan? What links these episodes is a pattern of geriatric over-exertion: the efforts of old revolutionaries, for reasons more sentimental than rational, to rediscover their roots, to convince themselves that the purposes for which they had sacrificed so much in seizing power had not been totally overwhelmed by the compromises they had had to make in actually wielding power.

Finally, distinctions with respect to history. It is easy now to sit back and say that the United States and its allies never had much to worry about in the "third world"—that there was *no* prospect that Marxism-Leninism would catch on there. But the failure of fears to materialize does not establish their immateriality. Revolutionary ideologies have indeed, in the past, spread widely: none more so than the American example of 1776. Apart from the chroniclers of such revolutions, who is to say what precise mix of long-term and short-term forces, of principles and personalities, of circumstances and contingencies, causes their ideas to take root? It would be the height of arrogance for historians to condemn those who made history for not having availed themselves of histories yet to be written. Nightmares always *seem* real at the time—even if, in the clear light of dawn, a little ridiculous.

SEVEN

Ideology, Economics, and Alliance Solidarity

Some comrades . . . consider that the contradictions between the socialist camp and the capitalist camp are more acute than the contradictions among the capitalist countries; that the USA has brought the other capitalist countries sufficiently under its sway to be able to prevent them from going to war with one another. . . . These comrades are mistaken. They see the outward phenomena that come and go on the surface, but they do not see those profound forces which, although they are so far operating imperceptibly, will nevertheless determine the course of developments. . . . Would it not be truer to say that capitalist Britain, and, after her, capitalist France, will be compelled in the end to break from the embrace of the U.S.A. and enter into conflict with it in order to secure an independent position and, of course, high profits? Let us pass to the major vanquished countries, Germany (Western) and Japan. . . . To think that these countries will not try to get on their feet again, will not try to smash the U.S. 'regime,' and force their way to independent development, is to believe in miracles.

Joseph Stalin[1]

After all, our friends may say to us, "Listen dear comrades, you are trying to teach us to build socialism, but you don't know how to raise potatoes in your own country, you cannot provide for the people, there is no cabbage in your capital."

Nikita Khrushchev[2]

THE victory of communism in Cuba—and the prospect that that triumph might repeat itself elsewhere in the "third world"—raised a specter of Western vulnerabilities so powerful that it would push the United States, during the early 1960s, into an ambitiously ill-conceived campaign somehow to "immunize" the modernization process in Asia, Africa, and Latin America against the possibility that Marxism-Leninism might infect it. The most visible result—at once foolish and tragic (but all the more tragic for being foolish)—was a protracted and costly military effort to save South Vietnam, the single greatest error the United States made in fighting the Cold War. Robert S.

McNamara, one of those chiefly responsible, has now admitted: "we were wrong, terribly wrong."[3]

What the Americans were wrong about was that as Vietnam went, so the rest of the "third world" would go. The idea that any single state could dominate so vast a region, or that its diverse inhabitants might embrace a single ideology, now seems one of the strangest artifacts of Cold War thinking.[4] The post-Cold War era has revealed how durable national, cultural, ethnic, religious, and linguistic particularities really are; but that is only to acknowledge that they must have been present throughout the Cold War itself as they had been for decades, even centuries, preceding it. They ensured that the "third world" would find its own way whatever cold warriors in Washington or Moscow did.

When after years of devastating warfare South Vietnam finally did go communist, in 1975, it set an example only for its immediate neighbors, Laos and Cambodia. A much larger neighbor, China, had by then aligned itself with the United States against the Soviet Union: whatever their ideological differences, Richard Nixon and Mao Zedong found much in common in the realm of geopolitics. During the next few years Mao's successor Deng Xiaoping would revive capitalism within what remained only symbolically a Marxist-Leninist state; meanwhile the USSR, having stuck more faithfully to Marxist-Leninist principles, would sink slowly into economic stagnation and political fragmentation. By the mid-1990s market economies had taken root, not just in China, but also in a unified Vietnam and even a disunited former Soviet Union. Communism clung to power only in Cuba and North Korea.

This outcome was hardly predetermined, though; indeed, in 1945 it would have seemed highly unlikely. Capitalism had, after all, crashed badly during the 1930s and a great war quickly followed: had not Lenin predicted just such a result?[5] Even Franklin D. Roosevelt and his advisers attributed the rise of fascism in Europe and of militarism in Japan to the breakdown in international economic cooperation that had accompanied the Great Depression.[6] Americans and Russians could agree, at the end of World War II, that capitalism as practiced in the past was an unstable system, ill-suited to organizing the future. The Cold War had to do, at least in part, with the different solutions they devised to deal with this problem.[7]

The Americans, drawing on their domestic experiences, hoped to reform capitalism without ruining it. Progressivism under Theodore Roosevelt and Woodrow Wilson, Republican corporatist associationalism during the 1920s, and F.D.R.'s New Deal all had sought to balance the competing claims of private property, open markets, and government regulation, albeit in distinctive ways and with divergent results. Meanwhile, in England, John Maynard Keynes was working out a theoretical basis for avoiding future depressions, and his ideas too found their way into Washington's wartime planning for the postwar era. As victory approached, though, there was no assurance that any of these approaches would restore and then sustain prosperity. It had taken Pearl Harbor to force Keynesian levels of spending on an administration as yet unprepared to accept Keynesian logic; and although the result was spectacular—a near-doubling of gross national product within five years[8]—a highly abnormal situation had produced it. Even approximating such a performance in peacetime, much less extending it to a world devastated by war, would be a daunting task indeed.

The Soviet Union had constructed a radically different domestic system, based on the abolition of private property with the state controlling markets and commanding means of production: in 1945 its accomplishments seemed substantial. We tend today to remember the *costs* of forced industrialization in the USSR, both in lives lost and inefficiencies tolerated. But for anyone who lived through the depression and the war, there had to be much that was impressive about a government that had achieved full employment *before* it had gone on to defeat the most powerful state in Europe. Not even the United States had managed that. No wonder Stalin's methods, and the ideology that had inspired them, seemed to many around the world at least as applicable to the postwar era as did those of the United States.[9]

When, then, did the tide turn? At what point did the shift take place from the situation that existed at the end of World War II, when the future of capitalism itself seemed problematic, to the one that existed at the end of the Cold War, when Marxist-Leninists could look only to the enfeebled examples of Kim Il-sung and Fidel Castro? The process was of course a gradual one, but if there was a critical decade—there was never a single critical moment—it would have been the 1950s. For despite Khrushchev's noisy claims about capitalism's grandchildren living under communism it was during those years that conditions began to favor the western democracies over their Marxist-Leninist rivals. These not only ensured the survival of capitalism and the weakening of communism; they also eased American efforts to maintain formal alliances and project informal influence, with the result that even as Washington was worrying that it might someday lose the "third world," Moscow was well on the way to losing the "second."

What happened during the 1950s, to put it in Lenin's terms, was that the "internal contradictions" within his own ideology exceeded those of the one he had sought to overthrow. It became clear for the first time that the Soviet Union and its allies could maintain authoritarian leadership—a fundamental requirement in Marxist-Leninist states—only by means that ensured economic obsolescence. Reforms intended to restore competitiveness shattered authority, both internally and within the international communist movement. This was, it turned out, rather more than a contradiction: it was a fatal flaw.

I

Neither American nor Soviet leaders appear to have foreseen, during World War II, how incompatible their economic systems were going to be. The Russians, fighting literally for survival, lacked the time or the resources to focus on such issues: all Soviet planning for postwar institutions seems improvised when contrasted with Stalin's precision in specifying postwar territorial requirements. The Americans, for their part, *preferred* thinking about structures instead of settlements. To do otherwise, they feared, might disrupt both the wartime alliance and domestic political bipartisanship.[10] The international organizations the Americans designed were intended, without exception, to involve the Soviet Union as well as surviving capitalist states.[11] Among these was the so-called Bretton Woods system, the proposed mechanism for managing the peacetime international economy. One of that plan's chief architects, Assistant Treasury Secretary Harry Dexter White, explained the reasoning clearly enough: "You can't have a cannon on board ship that isn't tied down because [the Russians] can do a lot of damage if they are not in."[12]

Soviet representatives dutifully attended the July 1944 conference that established the World Bank and the International Monetary Fund but also—more important—set the principles that were to encourage postwar recovery. These included price stability through fixed exchange rates, reductions in barriers to international trade, and an integration of markets with government planning.[13] The Russians may not have grasped the purpose of these guidelines—which was to salvage capitalism—nor do they appear to have given much thought to how their own command economy might relate to them. Their chief interest seems to have been the reconstruction loan the Americans were dangling before them as an inducement to participate, and perhaps also securing further acknowledgement of their country's status as a great power.[14]

From Moscow's perspective, anxiety over the future of capitalism had caused the Americans to raise the loan possibility in the first place: hence Molotov's curious offer on behalf of his government, some months later, to help the Americans ease *their* transition from war to peace by accepting a $6 billion loan, to be used to purchase capital goods in the United States. "As a banker," Ambassador W. Averell Harriman later commented, "I've had many requests for loans but Molotov's was the strangest request I have ever received."[15] Harriman was willing to "disregard the unconventional character of [Molotov's proposal] and . . . chalk it up to ignorance of normal business procedures and the strange ideas of the Russians on how to get the best trade."[16] But the incident exposed a major gap in expectations.

The Americans, thinking as was their habit in multilateral terms, had sought to incorporate the Soviet Union within their plans for restructuring the postwar global economy. Isolating any part of it, they believed, would risk a return to the rivalries of the 1930s. Integration was the objective, not yet containment: common economic interests were supposed to overcome whatever geopolitical and ideological differences might arise. The Russians, thinking as was their habit in Marxist-Leninist terms, interpreted American behavior as reflecting self-doubt, not self-confidence; as an indication of how worried the Americans were about a postwar depression. Why else would they offer credits to rebuild a non-capitalist state? Both sides expected economics to shape politics, but they had very different ideas of how this was to happen.

What actually took place in 1945, of course, was the opposite: politics shaped economics. Accumulating Soviet–American disagreements over Eastern Europe diminished prospects for getting a Russian loan through Congress and, once the war ended, resurgent isolationism—manifested in a reluctance to make postwar financial commitments to anyone—meant that even a proposed loan to Great Britain was an uphill battle. Angered by the Truman administration's unnecessarily ungraceful termination of Lend-Lease, the Soviet government turned to the extraction of reparations from Germany and its former satellites as a primary source of reconstruction assistance.[17] There remained, though, the Bretton Woods agreements, which prospective participants had to ratify by the end of the year.

We now know that as late as the final week of December 1945, Soviet trade and foreign ministry officials were recommending ratification on the grounds that this might yet yield reconstruction credits: "In the case of our non-participation . . . the USSR may become isolated . . . , which will affect the conditions of international credit in the postwar period."[18] At the last minute, Stalin himself vetoed Soviet membership. A hurriedly revised foreign ministry memorandum noted that "as the government of the U.S.A. did not offer the USSR a credit, our membership in these organizations could be read as our weakness, as a forced step taken under the pressure of the U.S.A. Our negative attitude . . . would show our independent position in this matter." The Soviet Union might later join the Bretton Woods system "at the most convenient moment." But it could afford to wait until the Americans and their allies "take measures towards [an] additional invitation [to] the USSR to participate in these organizations."[19]

Casual though it was, Stalin's decision caused a strong reaction in Washington, where it seemed wholly inexplicable to those who had counted on a multilateral approach to postwar problems. Why should the Soviet Union flatly reject membership in such praiseworthy organizations as the International Monetary Fund and the World Bank, especially since their designers had gone out of their way to accommodate Soviet interests?[20] Kennan, then serving as *chargé d'affaires* in Moscow, recalls the State Department passing on to him, "in tones of bland innocence, the anguished cry of bewilderment that had floated over the roof of the White House from the Treasury Department to the other side. How did one explain such behavior on the part of the Soviet government? What lay behind it?"[21]

Seizing the occasion—"They had asked for it. Now, by God, they would have it."[22]—Kennan fired back his famous 8,000-word "long telegram" of 22 February 1946. In it, he predicted that, whatever the official line, "Soviet policy will really be dominated by [the] pursuit of autarchy for [the] Soviet Union and Soviet-dominated adjacent areas taken together." The Russians were likely to turn "a cold official shoulder . . . to the principle of general economic collaboration among nations."[23] That conclusion was almost as shocking, in Washington at the time, as Kennan's larger argument that the Soviet Union could not be reasoned with, only contained. For Stalin's unexpected action forced American officials to abandon their vision of a postwar world organized according to economic logic. It brought them face to face with the ideological and strategic realities of the Cold War.[24]

The result was not an abandonment of Bretton Woods, only of its universalism. The Marshall Plan incorporated the ideas of unrestricted trade and open markets within the framework of containment, so that what had been a scheme for integrating the Soviet Union became a device for isolating it. The invitation to join the World Bank and the International Monetary Fund had been sincere; the one to participate in the Marshall Plan was only symbolic. The Soviet response was similar in both instances: initial interest when it looked as though reconstruction assistance might result, but then rejection when it became clear that involvement in the world economy would be the price.[25]

It probably would not have made much difference if the Russians had joined one or both of these organizations. They surely would have pulled out as the incompatibility of Stalinist autarchy with Western multilateralism—to say nothing of the clash in political values that lay behind them—gradually emerged. "There was simply no middle ground between the two," Martin Malia has noted: "One mode required a multiparty system and a market, whereas the other required a single Party and a command economy."[26] Soviet participation could have delayed Washington's efforts to get European reconstruction under way, though, and in this sense Stalin's decision was short-sighted. So too was his failure to understand the long-term significance of what he had rejected.

For the Bretton Woods–Marshall Plan synthesis did more than anything else to ensure that the global economy did not again crash as it had in the 1930s; by the 1960s it was prospering as never before. To take a single example, world steel production increased from 106 million metric tons in 1947 to 265 in 1955 to 505 in 1965; but the American share of it *decreased* from 54% to 39% to 26% in those same years.[27] This is as good an indication of *world* economic recovery as any other and it was not Stalin's autarchy that brought it about. Rather, as Henry R. Nau has explained:

The premise of freer trade ensured competition, especially for smaller countries; the premise of price stability ensured a stable environment for domestic investment and stable exchange rates for expanding trade; and the premise of flexible domestic economies ensured prompt adjustment to changing market conditions and comparative advantage.[28]

What the Americans had devised, in short, was a lubrication system for global capitalism.[29]

It would not last forever: during the late 1960s the United States would find its responsibilities as chief lubricator increasingly burdensome, and in 1971 the Nixon administration would allow a central feature of Bretton Woods—fixed exchange rates based on the dollar's convertibility into gold—to collapse altogether.[30] By then, though, capitalism was largely lubricating itself, a fact made clear ironically enough by its resiliency in absorbing the "oil shocks" of 1973 and 1979. The main effect of Bretton Woods was to buy time and minimize friction, thereby allowing the emergence of a thriving international economy closely linked to one, but not both, of the Cold War superpowers.[31]

II

What did Stalin and those who advised him *think* was going to happen within the capitalist world? Why was he so confident that the Soviet system could remain apart from it and still prevail? What were capitalism's "internal contradictions" supposed to be, and what benefits did the Russians expect to derive from them?

Stalin's starting-point was the assumption that capitalist economies were mutually repulsive, not attractive. This was an old Leninist idea, based on the belief that capitalists by their nature sought above all else to gratify immediate economic interests. It followed that they could not cooperate for very long, and that the states they ran would sooner or later get into wars with one another. Imperial rivalries would be the most likely cause; these, Lenin insisted, had already produced World War I. "Thus, out of the universal ruin caused by the war a world-wide revolutionary crisis is arising which, however prolonged and arduous its stages may be, cannot end otherwise than in a proletarian revolution and its victory."[32]

From this, it was no great leap to Stalin's belief in the inevitability of future wars. Capitalists would at first fight them but the Soviet Union would eventually be drawn in, overthrowing an old order fatally weakened by the capitalists' own greedy belligerency. That had been the context for Stalin's February 1946 "election" speech, in which he claimed that World War II had been no "casual occurrence," rather "the inevitable result of the development of world economic and political forces on the basis of modern monopoly capitalism."[33] Stalin's thinking must also have influenced Soviet diplomatic reporting from London and Washington during and immediately after the war, which persistently stressed the likelihood of *Anglo-American* conflict.[34]

These views, interestingly, did not go unchallenged in Moscow. The well-known—and, in retrospect, brave—Soviet economist Eugen Varga had been arguing since the 1930s that capitalist states were more capable of cooperating than Lenin's model had allowed. As the USSR increased its influence in the postwar world, the United States and Great Britain would align their policies with one another, if only for self-preservation. American hegemony—the subordination of British interests to those of Washington—would probably result. But although Varga's views circulated openly, Stalin never endorsed them and eventually forced their repudiation.[35]

The Soviet leader's final pronouncement on this subject, made in his 1952 book, *Economic Problems of Socialism in the USSR*, showed no evidence of reconsideration, either in the light of Varga's work or the actual course of events since the end of World War II. That cataclysm had occurred, Stalin reiterated, because "the struggle of the capitalist countries for markets and their desire to crush their competitors proved in practice to be stronger than the contradictions between the capitalist camp and the socialist camp." It followed from this "that the inevitability of wars between capitalist countries remains in force."[36]

These ideas are remarkable for what they reveal of how ideology can obscure reality in authoritarian systems. They certainly confirm the doubts Kennan had raised in 1946 about the Soviet government's capacity for objective judgment: "who, if anyone, in this great land actually receives accurate and unbiased information about the outside world[?]"[37] But an even more interesting issue is why Stalin's diagnosis of the postwar situation did *not* turn out to be accurate. His understanding of what had caused World War II, after all, was not so far from that of top American officials at the time. What was different about the late 1940s that so confounded Soviet expectations?

First, it would seem, there was precisely the fact that World War II *had* occurred, and that American and British planners were determined to keep such a thing from ever happening again. The opportunity to redesign the international system was, in their minds, a "second chance," and both the United Nations and Bretton Woods reflected their determination to seize it.[38] Varga himself had noted the possibility that capitalists might learn from experience and evolve accordingly.[39] Stalin, conversely, fell into one of the most dangerous traps of theoretical analysis: the pretension to universalism across space and time. Like Marx, Lenin, and some American social scientists, he appears to have believed that theories can freeze history just as amber freezes flies. He ignored the possibilities of adaptation, whether inspired by intelligence, fear, or both at once.[40]

Second, the situation at the end of World War II was no longer one in which capitalist powers balanced each other. Stalin had anticipated at least tripolarity: like many in the West, he failed to understand the extent of British decline, or of American ascendancy.[41] Contradictions among capitalists might well have arisen if multipolarity had returned, but bipolarity was what developed: Stalin got his models wrong. Washington encountered less resistance from capitalists elsewhere than if there had been capitalists of roughly equal strength. The postwar era more closely resembled the *early* stages of imperialism, when a powerful center can control weak peripheries with little opposition, than the late imperialism of clashing centers and rebellious peripheries about which Lenin had written.[42]

Third, the Americans surprised the Soviets—and probably themselves—by the way they used their disproportionate power. Their policies were, to be sure, self-serving: those of great states always are. Certainly they expected to benefit, as the British had before them, from leading the world toward an economic order its leading economy had designed.[43] What was unanticipated was Washington's willingness to subordinate economic to geopolitical objectives. In a pattern quite different from what Lenin had predicted, the United States sacrificed immediate economic gains to invest in long-term geopolitical stabilization.[44] The Marshall Plan reflected this approach: it was the peacetime extension of a wartime innovation, Lend-Lease, in which Washington had broadened traditional criteria for calculating profit and loss to include—or so it seemed at the time—the fate of western civilization. Analogous bookkeeping explains American efforts to promote European integration and Japanese rehabilitation:

the idea was to reconstitute independent centers of power that would balance the Soviet Union; but the price—willingly if not always wisely paid—was to create future economic competitors. It is too simple to say, then, that the United States consistently used its predominance to exploit other states. For it also *allowed its own exploitation* by opening its markets to the products of countries it considered geopolitically vital, even as it tolerated discrimination from them against its own.[45]

Fourth, in seeking to reconstruct the postwar international economic order, the Americans proved remarkably adaptable. Apart from the most general principles of market capitalism they imposed no uniform blueprint; they were flexible as to both the format and the timing of economic integration. The Bretton Woods rules had accommodated Marxist command economies: the Soviet Union excluded itself from that system. Despite the fact that several of its European allies—notably Great Britain—had social democratic governments, the United States encouraged them to take the lead in planning European recovery. "Many of those Americans responsible for the Marshall Plan would actually have preferred socialist governments in the area," Tony Smith has pointed out, "thinking them particularly amenable to a fresh start in regional affairs and able to commit their governments more easily to planned schemes of integration."[46] General Douglas MacArthur was similarly ecumenical in occupied Japan, where he carefully preserved imperial prerogatives—Hirohito's and his own—even as he pushed vigorously for decartelization, labor unions, and land reform.[47] The result, in Western Europe and Japan, was a series of experiments that stretched the limits of capitalism beyond what Americans would have been prepared to accept at home.[48]

Finally, in seeking to explain why capitalist contradictions failed to develop, it is important to remember that economics alone did not determine all that happened. The stark *geopolitical* reality of a Soviet presence in the middle of Europe and in Northeast Asia—a clear and present danger to the capitalist order that had existed only in *ideological* terms at the end of World War I—itself lubricated the efforts of capitalists to save themselves. It made the Americans more willing than in the 1920s to manage the world economy, and it made the West Europeans and the Japanese more receptive to American management. Once again, Varga had anticipated that the growth of Soviet power might provoke just such a response,[49] but Stalin never saw this. He was singularly insensitive to the possibility that he himself—objectively speaking—was capitalism's greatest ally.[50]

There is no way to specify, with any precision, how critical the American role was in the rehabilitation of capitalism after World War II. Left to themselves, the Europeans and the Japanese might well have recovered on their own;[51] had they done so, they would surely have reasserted their own authority within the global economy. Washington's postwar hegemony arose as much from their self-destructive prewar behavior as from anything the United States did to bring that preeminence about; it could not have been expected to last indefinitely.[52] What worried the Europeans and the Japanese, though, was the prospect that they might *not* be left to themselves: that in the absence of an American alternative, a Marxist-Leninist model of economic development might be forced upon them, either by the Soviet Union or—more likely—by their own desperation if there seemed to be no other way to overcome the effects of depression and war. That the Americans played no necessary role in securing the roots of postwar capitalism is, therefore, at best an unproven proposition.[53] Certainly this was not the view of those the Americans aided at the time.

It is possible to conceive of another alternative: a capitalist revival that might still have fulfilled Lenin's prophecy by giving rise to imperialist wars. Stalin had this prospect in mind when he warned that Germany and Japan might rise to their feet again, breaking out of "American bondage."[54] Capitalism's recovery without such conflicts was what really refuted Marxist-Leninist theory, and the American role here may have been more critical than in the salvaging of capitalism itself. To account for it, we will have to consider another lubricant the United States devised for the postwar international system: the diffusion of democratic culture.

III

Political scientists now regularly insist, not just as theory but almost as a law, that democracies do not fight one another.[55] If this view is correct, then as the number of democracies increases the likelihood of war should diminish. Historians, as is their habit, are more skeptical; but even they must acknowledge that the number of democracies more than doubled during the Cold War. By one count, there were twenty with a population over a million when it began and forty-eight at the time it ended—before the Soviet Union's collapse caused the number to rise well beyond that point. All of these were capitalist states in the sense that they allowed private property and market economies. None fought wars with one another while democratic institutions were functioning.[56] Did democracy itself, therefore, help to stabilize capitalism?

For all their wartime rhetoric about self-determination, the Americans had no plans to promote that objective comparable to their blueprints for collective security and economic recovery: the National Endowment for Democracy was a creation of Reagan's administration, not Truman's.[57] There were repeated instances in which the United States compromised and even corrupted democratic principles: the Yalta settlement on Eastern Europe and Northeast Asia; the covert manipulation of other countries' internal affairs; association with right-wing authoritarian regimes in much of Asia, Africa, Latin America, and parts of Europe; susceptibility to McCarthyism at home, with all its lingering after-effects. The ultimate violation of democracy may have been to rely so heavily on nuclear weapons as an instrument of deterrence, for this strategy came close to placing everyone in the world at the mercy of those few whose fingers—and minds—were on the trigger.[58]

And yet—future historians will probably find it *more* difficult to disassociate the United States from the postwar expansion of democracy than from the revival of capitalism, which might have happened on its own. Resolving this paradox requires focusing not so much on the Americans' policies as on their practices: on how they behaved when given authority beyond their borders, and on the lessons those subjected to that authority drew from the experience. The clearest examples have to do with the German and Japanese military occupations, the management of NATO, and the movement toward European integration.

The strategy of containment, as Kennan and its other architects understood it, sought to prevent the Soviet Union from controlling defeated but still potentially dangerous enemies.[59] How this was to happen, though, was much less apparent. Destroying German and Japanese power altogether risked leaving vacuums Stalin would surely try to fill. Restoring it without removing authoritarian tendencies would avoid that prospect, but raise questions as to why the United States had fought the war in the first place. In the end, the Americans settled on a third course: reviving Germany and Japan while transforming those countries into democracies along the way.

This may have been the most successful of all United States initiatives during the Cold War, in that *democratization* proved to be such an effective method of *stabilization*.[60] But nobody in Washington planned it that way. No one ordered Clay, for example, to allow German press criticism of his policies, or to encourage their review by the American Civil Liberties Union: "I thought it was part and parcel of teaching the Germans the meaning of democracy."[61] No one demanded that MacArthur push as vigorously as he did in Japan for universal suffrage, parliamentary democracy, and women's rights.[62] Both generals promoted these and other democratic practices to set examples; both had the faith of missionaries that democracy, if introduced from the ground up, would root itself even in inhospitable terrain. All previous modern military occupations, MacArthur liked to argue, had generated as much resentment as they had alleviated.[63] It is revealing that he in particular—arguably one of the most authoritarian Americans of this century—should have seen in the construction of representative institutions a way to shatter that precedent.

Little in the history of either Germany or Japan suggested that this would be easy.[64] But Clay and MacArthur could see that what the Germans called a *Stunde Null* ("zero hour") mentality gripped both societies. Defeat had left a psychological vacuum from which there had emerged a social frontier. And one characteristic of frontiers is that new cultures injected into them can take hold in ways that replicate, with remarkable fidelity, even distant and alien origins.[65] The view from Germany and Japan in the summer of 1945 was not so different from what the Aztecs saw when Cortéz's ships appeared on the horizon in 1519: old institutions seemed suddenly useless, and conquerors took on the attributes of gods.[66]

But the Aztecs in the end resisted. So too, although with equal lack of success, did those Germans who fell under Soviet occupation. Why did the West

Germans and the Japanese—for whom democratization was as sweeping a cultural transformation—not do so? Part of the answer, of course, was precisely the existence of a Soviet alternative: the fear of getting something worse. Part of it was surely the attraction of American wealth and the consumerism it generated.[67] Part of it was that the Americans found it difficult to treat their enemies brutally once they had surrendered: the pattern on the Soviet side was very different, and may well have reflected dissimilarities in domestic cultures as well as wartime experiences.[68] But part of the answer, too, has to do with why democracy is such a subversive ideology in the first place: it works, as does capitalism, by sharing stakes in its own success.

Obviously what happened in Germany and Japan does not fully explain why democracy spread so widely elsewhere after 1945. Decolonization—a quite separate process—also rooted democratic processes in new territories, especially in regions like India where the British had prepared the way. But the balance of world power was unlikely to tilt in one direction or another according to what took place in former colonial dependencies. Germany and Japan, because of their industrial-military potential, were pivotal: Kennan had recognized this when he made them the hinge-points of his strategy. What Clay and MacArthur discovered was that democratizing those countries could not only contain Soviet power but also undermine its justification. They opened up, for the Germans and the Japanese, a path to rapid economic development that did *not* require authoritarian politics. A great deal indeed hinged on the making of that point.

Washington's management of the North Atlantic Treaty Organization—and NATO's management of Washington—confirmed another proposition, which was that capitalist states could indeed cooperate. Leninist theory suggested the opposite, and even Kennan had worried that a permanent peacetime military alliance might tempt American leaders into an imperial pattern of behavior against which the Europeans and the American public would eventually rebel.[69] Had the United States tried to build NATO by bribing or bullying its members, something like this could well have happened. As Marc Trachtenberg has observed, though, "the politics of the alliance never really became a politics of mutual resentment."[70] Just as the Germans and the Japanese chose not to overthrow the institutions their American occupiers had imposed upon them, so the NATO allies clung to their military relationship with the United States, even after the adversary that had inspired it had ceased to exist.

It is hard to see evidence of American *design* in all of this, for had it been left to Washington alone there might never have been such an alliance. Once European initiatives led to NATO's establishment, however, American *habits* became conspicuous within it. The Truman and Eisenhower administrations ran the alliance much as Clay and MacArthur had run occupied Germany and Japan: in ways that reflected democratic culture.

NATO was by no means a relationship of equals, any more than the individual states within the United States are equivalent in territory, population, or resources. But in both systems *power alone did not define relationships*. American officials saw nothing strange in combining executive leadership with a careful acknowledgement of individual sovereignties; familiarity with federalism discouraged the view that strength could override the need for negotiation and compromise. Without stopping to consider that it might have been otherwise, Truman and Eisenhower handled NATO much as they did the Congress of the United States: by cutting deals instead of imposing wills.[71]

It was not that the Americans lacked the capacity to force their allies into line. They had it and sometimes used it, most obviously against Great Britain in the wake of the 1956 Suez debacle.[72] What is surprising is how rarely this happened; how much effort the United States put into persuading—quite often even deferring to—its NATO partners. Coercion clashed with what the Americans understood the alliance to be about: they thought of it as a *voluntary* form of association, like the Articles of Confederation and the Constitution of 1787.[73]

Democracies also allow multiple constituencies to interact at multiple levels. Such systems are open, not just to the appeals their leaders make to one another, but to a wider and more cacophonous range of voices emanating from the public, the media, interest groups, even transnational organizations. These complicate the lives of policy-makers, to be sure. But they can also encourage new institutions—and new methods of consultation—to supplement traditional diplomacy. They enhance the possibility of sharing principles, not just balancing power. They create a buffer against bullying, smoothing out disparities of raw strength and providing recourse against the arrogance these can bring. They even parallel, in a way, the working of markets under capitalism: if the free exchange of commodities stabilizes economies, then surely the free exchange of ideas stabilizes democracies and the alliances they form with one another.[74]

It follows that influence, in democratic alliances, flows in multiple directions: it does not simply reflect who has predominant power and who does not. To see this, we need only look at the extent to which the NATO allies shaped the alliance. In addition to having originated it, they certainly had a hand in determining which countries would enjoy American protection and what form it would take. Geographical logic would hardly have designated Italy an "Atlantic" power while Franco's Spain was not; nor would strategic logic have justified deploying large numbers of United States troops in highly exposed positions across central Europe.[75] Washington did, to be sure, insist on rearming the West Germans. But the French were able to sidetrack that process for four years by first proposing and then rejecting the European Defense Community; the British in the end came up with the formula that completed it.[76] Nor was NATO's "nuclearization" entirely imposed from Washington: the Europeans themselves chose this path when they rejected more conventional but costlier means for defending themselves.[77] The logic linking all of these decisions was that of politics: the *balancing* of competing interests within a system all had an interest in sustaining.

The Americans even allowed NATO's concerns to shape their policies outside that system. Objections from allies, as much as anything else, kept the United

States from escalating the Korean War after Chinese intervention.[78] Fears of a backlash within NATO discouraged Washington from pressing the French to end their debilitating colonial wars in Indochina and Algeria. Eisenhower gave Adenauer a veto over negotiations with Moscow on German reunification, even as he gave in to pressures from other NATO allies to meet the new Soviet leaders at the 1955 Geneva summit.[79] And surely Eisenhower's and Kennedy's responses to the alleged strategic missile "gap" of the late 1950s and early 1960s would make little sense without taking into account their hypersensitivity to NATO's interests.[80]

The history of NATO, therefore, is largely one of compromise despite the predominant position of the United States. But what impelled a superpower to allow smaller powers so much authority? Realist theory is no more useful than Leninist theory in answering this question, because it assumes that all states always to want to accumulate power. Democratic theory, however, provides a rationale for *diffusing* power to strengthen a shared purpose. The NATO treaty was widely viewed in 1949 as a departure from the old American principle of non-entanglement in European affairs: whether appropriately or not, the text most often cited was Washington's Farewell Address of 1796.[81] But it may be that NATO functioned as well as it did because it drew on an even older set of American principles: the proper text here would have been the *Federalist Papers* of 1788.

The ultimate test for any system is its capacity for self-organization: it must sooner or later adapt, without external assistance, to the environment surrounding it.[82] The United States led the way in democratizing Germany and Japan; and in NATO the West Europeans together with the Americans constructed a democratic alliance. European integration, though, resulted primarily from actions Europeans themselves took, building on these earlier initiatives. There had been talk since the end of the war of a "United States of Europe"—a favorite phrase of Churchill's that suggested more emulation than innovation—and certainly the Americans encouraged integration by making joint planning a prerequisite for Marshall Plan aid and by providing NATO's security guarantee. But there was no consensus in Washington on proceeding further, toward either a European federation or some form of European union with the United States.[83]

It was at this point that the Europeans seized and never really relinquished the initiative. With the French and West German decision to establish the European Coal and Steel Community in 1950, a process of self-organization began that led directly to the founding of the European Economic Community, its subsequent emergence as the European Community, and now the European Union—with all of its shortcomings an acknowledged major power in the post-Cold War world.[84] At the same time and also with American protection, the Japanese were organizing their own quietly efficient emergence as an economic superpower. Together, these developments would create difficulties for the United States in the last three decades of the 20th century, although by no means as grave as those that afflicted the Marxist-Leninist world. The question arises once again, then: is this what the Americans intended at the time the Cold War began?

They certainly did seek the emergence of *independent* centers of power in the postwar world: that was how containment was supposed to work. They certainly sought, at the same time, to *integrate* those centers economically, politically, and culturally: only that would prevent a return to the anarchy of the prewar era. "It may well be," John Foster Dulles wrote Harold Macmillan late in 1955,

that a six-nation [European] community will evolve protectionist tendencies. It may be that it will show a trend toward greater independence. In the long run, however, I cannot but feel that the resultant increased unity would bring in its wake greater responsibility and devotion to the common welfare of Western Europe.[85]

Americans saw little contradiction in pursuing independence and integration simultaneously, because their own domestic system had long since achieved the most sustainable balance between these tendencies that the world had yet seen. To the extent that the Americans were imperialists, it was with a view to exporting that balancing act elsewhere in the world. If they lacked foresight, it was with respect to just how successful that enterprise would be. For Lenin, concerned as always with who exploited whom, such activities would surely have justified use of the term "imperial." But because not everyone else saw them that way, they did not produce the results Lenin had expected. Meanwhile, his own system was struggling with what turned out to be far more serious internal contradictions.

IV

We have already seen how Stalin replaced Lenin's vision of spontaneous proletarian uprisings taking place in the most advanced industrial countries with one that linked the progress of world revolution to the expanding territorial and geopolitical influence of the Soviet Union.[86] It involved imposing authoritarian politics and command economics on countries whose citizens were in no better position to question the process than were those of the USSR itself. This did not happen all at once, though, for we have also seen that until 1947 a fair amount of flexibility existed within Eastern Europe. It is therefore possible to say that Soviet power adapted itself, for a time, to local circumstances.

What distinguished Stalin's behavior from that of the Americans was this: when resistance began to arise within his sphere, he sought to smother it, not compromise with it. Tito's complaints about the Soviet–Yugoslav relationship were no more serious than those that arose routinely between London, Paris, and Washington: the British and the French frequently challenged American priorities with respect to the treatment of Germany, the terms of economic assistance, and the need for military protection. The Truman administration responded by sticking to its position in some instances, but in others it permitted its European allies to reshape its policies.

Stalin was more consistent, which is to say less accommodating. Instead of negotiating with Tito, he declared him a heretic and did all he could—short of war—to overthrow him. At the same time he clamped down on whatever remnants of independent thought remained in Eastern Europe. Government and party leaders in that part of the world quickly learned what had long been clear inside the Soviet Union itself: that Stalin's idea of a dialogue with the "opposition," loyal or not, was a purge trial, followed by a quickly executed sentence. The last thing he wanted was *independent* centers of power in Europe or elsewhere; rather he sought to make them *dependent*. As he aged, the Soviet leader grew less and less prepared to wait for the inexorable forces of history to bring the workers of the world, by their own choice, into the Soviet camp.

This insistence on dependency shows up clearly in Stalin's attitude toward German reunification: he was for it *only* if Moscow could run the resulting state. His proposals for unity through neutrality, as in March 1952, do not appear to have been sincere; certainly Stalin was never as committed to this idea as Kennan and several of his State Department colleagues were to Program A.[87] Even more significant, the Soviet Union had no plans to ensure a peaceful Germany by enmeshing it, as the Americans and West Europeans ultimately chose to do, within a web of economic and military ties to its neighbors. Perhaps Stalin feared the Germans too much; perhaps he thought the East Europeans too weak; and in any event the need to control Germany provided a convenient excuse for continuing to dominate Eastern Europe. But for the Americans, the need to control Germany was an excellent reason for promoting an *independent*—albeit integrated—Western Europe.

Stalin believed in integration too, but of a different sort. He wanted the economies of Eastern Europe connected closely to the USSR, not to each another. Just as he ensured that communist parties there could communicate only through Moscow and not among themselves,[88] so he sought to extract benefits unilaterally from the countries within his sphere of influence without encouraging their economic cooperation. The result was to retard and perhaps even reverse modernization: one estimate suggests that the Soviets *took from* Eastern Europe—in the form of reparations and other removals for use in reconstruction—about as much as the Americans *put into* Western Europe through the Marshall Plan.[89] Stalin handled the communist regime in China in much the same way, demanding economic concessions while celebrating Mao Zedong's revolutionary credentials.[90] New evidence suggests that he even tried to make shipments of lead from North Korea the price for authorizing its attack on South Korea: "I hope that Kim Il Sung will not refuse us in this."[91]

What all of this suggests is that Stalin's plans for expanding the Soviet Union's influence beyond its borders contained a major contradiction. On the one hand, he clung to the notion, growing out of his belief in the instability of capitalism, that proletarians in other countries would eventually choose the socialist model: hence, his illusions with respect to Germany and Eastern

Europe at the end of the war as well as his euphoria when the Chinese unexpectedly did move in that direction. But on the other hand, Stalin's economic policies caused the Soviet presence in those regions to come across as exploitative, and this generated resentment among the very people whose loyalty he had hoped to win. The old dictator expected capitalists to forego long-term economic advantages for immediate and selfish gains; but he anticipated that communists would focus only on the long-term advantages that were to come from building a socialist order, overlooking the immediate sacrifices this involved. The reverse, we can now see, is what actually happened.

The Soviet Union, for this reason, never came close to building relationships based on a sense of *mutual* interest extending across all levels of society. Communist parties and government bureaucracies might see advantages in alignment with Moscow, but the people under them rarely did. This pattern contrasts strongly with the one in Western Europe and Japan, where the democratic process regularly returned governments that had supported association with Washington. Stalin's legacy, then, was to leave in place the structures for building a socialist order, but with no foundation of popular support.

His eventual successor, Nikita Khrushchev, worried a great deal about this. He understood clearly that unless socialism began to provide greater benefits, whatever support it had would disappear and its appeal where it did not yet exist would quickly fade. Proud of what the Soviet Union had accomplished within his lifetime, its new leader nonetheless lacked Stalin's confidence that the laws of history alone would secure its future. Khrushchev's single greatest priority was to humanize Marxism-Leninism, so that people would *want* to be associated with it. "If one does not show concern for the growth of material and spiritual wealth," he was still warning on the eve of his overthrow in 1964, "then people will listen today, they will listen tomorrow, and then they will say: 'Why do you always promise us everything in the future, talking, so to speak, about life beyond the grave? The priest has already talked to us about that.'"[92]

There was reason for concern, at the time of Stalin's death, that a command economy might never provide sufficient benefits to win widespread support. In Western Europe, and particularly in West Germany, the Bretton Woods–Marshall Plan model had shown that market economies could not only prosper but sustain themselves by democratic means. Nothing like this had happened in Eastern Europe: indeed the June 1953 riots in East Berlin, where contrasts between the two systems had been so clear, suggested how easily unrest could spread elsewhere in Eastern Europe, perhaps even to the Soviet Union itself.[93] Khrushchev was determined to ward off that danger, to find some middle ground between the repression that was sure to generate further discontent, on one hand, and reforms that might create excessive expectations, on the other. The paths he chose, though, were no freer from contradictions than Stalin's had been.

Consider first the problem of authority, without which Khrushchev could do nothing at all. The post-Stalinist system provided no easy way to elicit agreement among government and party officials on what to do. Reform got entangled with the struggle over succession, so that it was often necessary to eliminate rivals—as Khrushchev did Beria and Malenkov—before assessing the feasibility of their policies.[94] Stalin had used this technique to consolidate his own power after Lenin's death; but even then it had been a lengthy and cumbersome process. Because Khrushchev refrained from killing those who lost out—apart, of course, from Beria and later the Hungarian rebel Imre Nagy—he never evoked the fear that Stalin did.[95] His emergence as preeminent Soviet leader, then, failed to carry with it the automatic obedience of his subordinates; nor could he count on soliciting their advice without simultaneously encouraging their ambitions.

Then there was the task of managing reform. Khrushchev appears to have considered only a top-down method: he insisted that all improvements—even those in literature and the arts—result from central planning. In practice this often meant his own enthusiasms (or lack thereof). Some areas, such as housing and consumer goods, showed modest improvements. There was for a time an intellectual "thaw." But in the all-important agricultural sector Khrushchev's policies failed miserably. The reason was his resistance to local experimentation; instead he insisted on experimenting with the entire country by imposing—and then frequently altering—uniform requirements with respect to crops, fertilizers, and the use of agricultural machinery.[96] In a state as large and diverse as the USSR this could hardly work, but as one of his biographers notes, "the failure of each successive scheme to achieve the promised miracles led Khrushchev merely to intensify his frantic search for a new cure-all."[97] Only in retirement does he appear to have lost faith—and even then, not much—in the virtues of central planning.[98]

To his credit, Khrushchev did seek to civilize Soviet society by eliminating Stalin's worst abuses. His reforms ranged from so small a matter as restoring normal working hours for top officials, who for years had had to adapt their schedules to that of their nocturnal boss, to abolishing indiscriminate arrests and releasing most of the surviving prisoners Stalin had dispatched to the GULAG.[99] Khrushchev even initiated the first investigations of Stalin's crimes: "It's inevitable that people will find out what happened," he remembers arguing, "if they start asking us about it after we've kept silent, they'll already be sitting in judgment over us. . . . I'd rather we raised the matter ourselves."[100] The obvious difficulty here, though, was how to disassociate himself and his colleagues—all of them products of Stalin's regime—from the discredited tyrant himself; or, to put it another way, how to preserve central direction of the party, the economy, and the state while scrapping the methods by which that direction had hitherto been accomplished. Self-criticism was not as easy for the Russians as for the Chinese, Khrushchev admitted to Zhou Enlai; were they to go too far, Zhou reported to Mao Zedong, "their current leadership would be in trouble."[101]

Solidifying the international communist movement was yet another priority. Khrushchev acknowledged that Stalin had unnecessarily alienated the Yugoslavs, and he embarked on the delicate task of rebuilding relations with them without angering the Chinese, who still respected—even if they no longer worshipped—his predecessor. The new Kremlin leader made his first trip to Beijing in October 1954, and followed it with one to Belgrade in May 1955. Neither went easily: the Chinese were inscrutable and Tito was smug. "[S]ome of the things Mao said put me on my guard," Khrushchev recalls, while "the Yugoslav comrades smiled scornfully and made sarcastic remarks."[102] There were two larger problems here. Khrushchev could hardly repudiate Stalin's legacy without relinquishing the Soviet Communist Party's long-standing claim to infallibility. But that, in turn, left little justification for his own continued authority over communist parties elsewhere, a point upon which Mao and Tito—for all their other differences—could certainly agree. Khrushchev could not have both reform and revolutionary unity, and this too was a contradiction of some substance.

Finally, Khrushchev hoped to improve relations with the United States. Reform at home required cutting military expenditures, hence the need to relax tensions abroad. He therefore overrode objections from his inherited foreign minister, Molotov, and made the concessions necessary to conclude a long-stalled treaty ending the four-power occupation of Austria.[103] This gesture in turn paved the way for the first postwar summit—and Khrushchev's debut as a world statesman—at Geneva in July 1955.[104] But even this strategy contained contradictions. The Americans remained wary, seeing in Khrushchev's very flexibility a tactic that might lull the West into complacency, delaying German rearmament and the consolidation of NATO.[105] Even more significantly, Khrushchev's determination to reduce military spending led him to follow Eisenhower's example and rely increasingly on nuclear weapons—but with a difference. The American "new look" was a strategy of deterrence aimed at *maintaining* the status quo. Khrushchev found it all too tempting to try to use his nuclear capabilities to *alter* the status quo.[106] The result would be not to relax tensions, but to drive them to new heights.

Stalin's demise, therefore, did not remove the contradictions afflicting the Marxist-Leninist world; if anything, it multiplied them. The old dictator had been prepared to live with such strains: like Marx, Lenin, and Mao, he understood that contradictions within a structure can counter one another, providing those outside of it—or on top of it—a harsh means of control.[107] Khrushchev, more humane by temperament, hoped to *resolve* contradictions: the idea of continuing to live under conditions of permanent crisis was thoroughly repugnant to him.[108] As James Richter has noted, "he was brimming with confidence that the moral appeal of the Soviet Union's socialist system and its efforts for peace would soon turn the tide in the ideological struggle."[109] The risk in Khrushchev's effort to remove contradictions, though—perhaps this was the greatest contradiction of all—was that of losing control.

V

The 20th Congress of the Communist Party of the Soviet Union, which convened in Moscow in February 1956, was the first since Stalin's death, and hence a crucial opportunity for Khrushchev: "we would have to prove that we were able to assume full responsibility for governing the Party and the country." It was his style, when confronting multiple problems, to try to solve as many of them as possible with a single dramatic stroke:[110] on this occasion he would do so by exorcising the great ghost himself. "We arranged for a special closed session of the Congress, and I delivered my speech. The delegates listened in absolute silence. It was so quiet in the huge hall you could hear a fly buzzing."[111] "[T]he old patterns of thought [had] formed such a thick layer," Georgi Arbatov recalled years later, that when Khrushchev attacked Stalin it "came like a bolt out of the blue, shaking the Party and our whole society to its roots."[112]

Khrushchev made three points in his "secret" speech and in his other pronouncements at the Congress, each of them explosive. First, he acknowledged not just the fallibility of a system that had claimed infallibility, but its inhumanity as well: his condemnation of Stalin was an unprecedented admission by a regime still in power that it had committed massive crimes. Second, he repudiated the doctrine of inevitable conflict: contrary to what Stalin had taught (and Lenin had believed), the contradictions of capitalism need not produce a war, which meant that communism could prevail through "peaceful coexistence." Third, there was more than one way to achieve this victory: the Soviet Union would no longer tell communist parties elsewhere how to proceed, but would rather encourage their adaptations to local conditions.[113] Khrushchev's objective in all of this was to liberate Marxism-Leninism from Stalin, its hijacker. Only then, he was convinced, could it thrive.

But what if the two could not be separated? What if Stalinism *was* the highest form of Marxism-Leninism? What if the latter could not function without at least elements of the former? What if, as Henry Kissinger has suggested, "[a]pprenticeship to Stalin had guaranteed psychological malformation," so that his heirs "made their nightmarish existence . . . tolerable [only] by a passionate belief in the system to which they owed their careers"?[114] Like Mikhail Gorbachev three decades later, Khrushchev knew that years of stagnation had left grave difficulties, and he set about removing them in ways that would be at once forceful and humane.[115] But because both men were incorrigible optimists, neither found it easy to accept what their predecessors had taken for granted: that the system survived only by *balancing* contradictions, and that resolving these might wreck it. Gorbachev would discover this about the Soviet Union itself. Khrushchev was spared that revelation, but not its implications for the unity of the Marxist-Leninist world.

De-Stalinization did for a time secure Khrushchev's position at home, but it severely weakened his authority over communism elsewhere. With the glaring exception of Tito, Stalin had always managed to elicit the loyalty of communists outside the Soviet Union, whether through his prestige or his threats or both.[116] No one could credibly challenge him as the world's preeminent Marxist-Leninist; he had repeatedly shown what could happen to whoever he suspected of harboring such aspirations. Stalin relied on terror but never the large-scale use of force—certainly not the Red Army—to bring recalcitrant comrades into line. It was generally enough to lift a finger, or raise an eyebrow, or sign a death warrant.

Khrushchev, in contrast, got much less respect. Always garrulous, often obsequious, at times bibulous, he never mastered those economies of gesture, speech, and presence that made Stalin seem so formidable.[117] Having relinquished the instruments of terror by which his predecessor had built such a fearsome reputation, he then tried at the 20th Party Congress to disassociate himself from Stalin altogether. It was a brutal irony that these *departures* from Stalinism so quickly got Khrushchev into a position in which he felt he had to use force, at a level Stalin had never found necessary, to keep the communist world from coming apart.

Authoritarian states that attempt reform risk revolution: it is harder than in a constitutional system to find footing in between.[118] Beria had discovered this, disastrously for himself, in East Germany in June 1953; Khrushchev at that time had thrown his support to Ulbricht and the forces of reaction.[119] But three years later, having come out not only for reform but for multiple paths in achieving it, the new Kremlin leader confronted a similar situation in Poland.

The long-time Communist Party leader there, Boleslaw Bierut, had died shortly after the 20th Party Congress, and the Poles took advantage of those two events to begin releasing political prisoners and removing other Stalinists from the government. As if to justify these moves, they also saw to it that Khrushchev's "secret" speech did not remain so: with further help from Israeli and American intelligence, it appeared in the *New York Times* on 4 June.[120] A workers' strike, followed by riots, broke out later that month in Poznan, and by October pressures were building within the Polish Communist Party to bring to power an old and, in Moscow's view, unreliable victim of Stalin's anti-Titoist purges, Wladyslaw Gomulka.

Khrushchev now found himself in an awkward dilemma. His own endorsement of diversity among Marxist-Leninists would make it difficult to prevent the Poles from going ahead; but if they did, Gomulka's resentment against the Russians—sure to be shared by many of his countrymen—might leave the Soviet Union with a hostile power between it and an equally alarmed East Germany. Khrushchev's first instinct was to bully the Poles: in an act Stalin would never have considered, he flew uninvited to Warsaw on 19 October, the day the Polish party plenum was to elect Gomulka, and demanded admission to the meeting. "The treacherous activity . . . has become evident, this number won't pass here!" he bellowed at the airport—so loudly, the Polish record notes, that even the chauffeurs could hear. But then an astonishing thing happened. Gomulka talked back:

[I]f you talk with a revolver on the table you don't have an even-handed discussion. I cannot continue the discussion under these conditions. I am ill and I cannot fill such a function in my condition. We can listen to the complaints of the Soviet comrades, but if decisions are to be made under the threat of physical force I am not up to it. My first step in Party work, which I am taking after a long break, must be interrupted.[121]

The Poles refused Khrushchev admission to the plenum, elected Gomulka as planned, and made it clear that if the Russians interfered—ominous troop movements were taking place—they would arm their own workers and resist. At the same time, Gomulka offered reassurances that he had no intention of taking Poland out of the Warsaw Pact. Khrushchev quickly calmed down: "Here was a man," he later recalled,

who had come to power on the crest of an anti-Soviet wave, yet who could now speak forcefully about the need to preserve Poland's friendly relations with Soviet Russia and with the Soviet Communist Party. Perhaps I didn't appreciate this fact right at that moment, but I came to appreciate it afterwards.[122]

It looked as though Poland had "adopted a course that will eliminate the unpleasant state of affairs," Khrushchev reported back to the Soviet party presidium on 24 October: "Finding a reason for an armed conflict now would be very easy, but finding a way to put an end to such a conflict would be very hard."[123] However graceless the process may have been, a Kremlin leader had for the first time *compromised* with another communist state on who its leader was to be.

If this was progress, though—and surely it was—it did not last. Even as Khrushchev spoke, disturbing reports were coming in from Budapest: "the situation in Hungary," he warned the presidium, "is extremely serious."[124] The Russians had authorized the removal of an unpopular party boss, Mathias Rakosi, in July; but unrest had continued to build there and news of the Polish compromise turned it into an outright rebellion. "[T]he leaders of the party and members of the government did not adopt the measures called for by the urgency of the situation," a Soviet analysis later noted. "Many of them were simply incapable of evaluating the state of things realistically."[125]

After some confusion, Khrushchev reluctantly ordered the Red Army into Budapest to restore order, but to everyone's surprise it failed to do so: "the arrival of Soviet troops into the city has had a negative effect on the mood of the residents," one Hungarian party official reported cautiously to Moscow.[126] The residents had in fact responded with stones, grenades, and Molotov cocktails; local army and internal security forces looked likely to join them; and the government and party structure throughout much of the country seemed on the verge of collapse. Shifting his allegiance to the side of the rebels, the new Hungarian party leader, Imre Nagy, negotiated the withdrawal of Soviet forces from Budapest on 28 October. Shortly thereafter he announced that Hungary would leave the Warsaw Pact to become a neutral state.[127] Khrushchev's Polish settlement, it appeared, had produced a Hungarian debacle.

But this time he did act decisively. Worried that events might get out of hand elsewhere in Eastern Europe—but also aware that the simultaneous Suez crisis had preoccupied the United States and its allies—Khrushchev on 31 October secured the Soviet presidium's approval for all-out military intervention in Hungary. He spent the next several days rallying support from the Chinese, the Yugoslavs, the Poles, and the other East Europeans, each of whom—with varying degrees of enthusiasm—went along. On 4 November the Red Army moved in, and after three days of fighting in which some 20,000 Hungarians and 3,000 Soviet troops were killed, Hungary was safely back in the Soviet camp. The Yugoslavs granted Nagy asylum in their embassy but eventually released him under a promise of safe conduct from his successor, Janos Kadar—only to have the Russians seize the unfortunate rebel for trial and subsequent execution.[128] Khrushchev proved that he could be ruthless when he had to be.

That, though, was the painful point: Khrushchev *had* to be ruthless to hold his alliance together. He had hoped to make Marxism-Leninism attractive enough that Stalinist methods would not be needed to ensure its unity; but even the briefest experiment with de-Stalinization had set off centrifugal tendencies in Eastern Europe that ended in a bloodbath. "He was a kind man in normal human relationships," Fedor Burlatsky, one of his advisers, later recalled,

but in politics he did not recognize kindness, especially when it seemed to him that "class interests" had been infringed. Still smouldering in his heart were the ashes of the Stalin he himself had cast down. He executed Nagy as a lesson to all other leaders in socialist countries, thinking as he did so of Gomulka and Kadar, and perhaps also of Tito and Mao. In his eyes political expediency was superior to morality. Humanity came second to security.[129]

"You need to give your people the right orientation," Khrushchev lectured demoralized Hungarian communists after it was all over. "You need to tell them that this [Nagy's movement] was a counterrevolution. If it was not, then how could we have used weapons?"[130] It was indeed Khrushchev's voice but Stalin's logic: "if they had *not* been enemies of the people, how could we have shot them?"

The Warsaw Pact survived, as did Khrushchev, although narrowly.[131] But after 1956 no one could maintain the illusion that it was an Eastern European NATO: an alliance based on voluntary participation and democratic methods of operation. Despite Khrushchev's reforms, the asymmetry of imposition versus invitation remained. As a consequence, the Soviet Union could never count upon the loyalty of its European "allies:" it would have to watch *them* just as carefully as it did those of the United States. Little had really changed, then, since Stalin's day: the great ghost was not so easily exorcised after all.

VI

Stalin's ghost also haunted Khrushchev's relationship with his Chinese "allies," for here too exorcism produced an unexpected result. It was not a compromise, as in Poland, or a rebellion, as in Hungary; instead it was a schism, in which true believers fell into a long and debilitating quarrel over what within their common faith was true and therefore to be believed. Tito's heresy had never reached that level because Yugoslavia never claimed the right to lead Marxist-Leninists throughout the world. But Mao Zedong's dissent was, for international communism, what the Protestant Reformation had been for the Roman Catholic Church. Only this time the reformers were within the established institution. The schismatics wanted to keep things as they had been.

Khrushchev failed to get the consent of his Chinese comrades before denouncing his predecessor at the 20th Party Congress—probably because he decided to go ahead only at the last moment.[132] They were therefore as unprepared as all the other delegations present; unlike most of them, though, they protested. Stalin had "belonged not only to the CPSU [Communist Party of the Soviet Union] but also to other countries' communist parties," Marshal Zhu De, who attended on Mao's behalf, reminded his hosts. "[Y]ou have criticized him without consulting the other parties. . . ." When apprised of this complaint, Khrushchev dismissed it more curtly than he should have: "Stalin was the leader of our party and we Soviet communists have the right to treat him as we deem fit."[133] But surely it was asking a lot to continue to claim leadership over the world communist movement, on the one hand, while unilaterally disposing of its central icon, on the other. Mao soon found ways to point this out.

The Chairman's respect for Stalin had diminished considerably with the passage of time. The old dictator had done less than he might have to assist the Chinese military effort in Korea: fearing American nuclear retaliation, he had behaved, to Mao's disgust, more like a paper tiger than a real one. At the same time, as Khrushchev later admitted, "in many areas of our economic relations we had thrust ourselves into China like colonizers. . . . Stalin's demands for concessions from China were intolerable."[134] Mao put up with all of this patiently, and on Stalin's death could still hail him as "the greatest genius of the present age."[135] The tribute "was not for Stalin," he later admitted, but "for the Soviet Communist Party. . . . [Y]our emotion tells you not to write these pieces, but your rationality compels you to do so."[136] By the mid-1950s, he was complaining that Stalin had at no point adequately supported China's revolution: the Kremlin boss had even regarded him as a "Chinese Tito."[137] Li Zhisui, Mao's physician, remembered being shocked "to hear that he and Stalin had in fact never gotten along."[138]

As a symbol, though, Stalin was still extremely useful to Mao. The reason had to do with his belief that the Chinese revolution had to replicate the stages the Russian revolution had gone through. There was no other example of a successful socialist uprising, so it was natural for the Chinese to want to follow the Soviet Union's path: hence their frequent references to that country as the "elder brother," from whom the "younger brother" must learn.[139] Mao, though, was surprisingly literal about this. We have seen how he expected an American invasion of China in 1949 because the United States and its allies had sent troops to Siberia and North Russia in 1918:[140] the Korean and Indochinese conflicts, as he perceived it, were the functional equivalent of such foreign inter-vention. He had allowed a brief period of experimentation with state-sponsored capitalism, analogous to Lenin's New Economic Policy. He had then collect-ivized agriculture and launched a Five-Year Plan for rapid industrialization, both based carefully on the Soviet model.[141] He was even willing to wait "eight-een or even more years" for diplomatic recognition from the United States, because it had taken seventeen to recognize the Soviet Union.[142] And he was certainly developing, as Khrushchev noted, a "cult of personality": "I believe Mao suffered from the same megalomania Stalin had all his life."[143] Dr. Li would later confirm that Mao was "China's Stalin, and everyone knew it."[144]

It is true that Mao *adapted* the Soviet experience to the peculiar circumstances of China—often with peculiar results. He hoped also to *compress* the stages of revolutionary development, so that the transition to communism would take place more rapidly than in the USSR. But he appears never to have considered departing from the *sequence* Lenin and Stalin had pioneered: "The victory of socialist construction in the Soviet Union," he had insisted at the time of Stalin's death, "proved in the most real-life terms the infinite correctness of Marxism-Leninism and concretely educated working people throughout the world on how they should advance toward a good life."[145] This was not just the politeness of an obituary, because five years later in a candid private conversa-tion Mao could still assure the Soviet ambassador that "nine out of ten fingers of yours and ours are quite the same with only one finger differing. . . . We trust your people, because you are from a socialist country, and you are sons and daughters of Lenin."[146]

Khrushchev, Mao understood correctly enough, was neither a Lenin nor a Stalin. It was of no little consequence that he had come to Beijing, in 1954, instead of waiting for Mao to come to Moscow: the point would hardly have been lost on any Chinese ruler with imperial aspirations.[147] The new Kremlin boss posed no threat, though, until he took it upon himself to try to de-Stalinize Marxism-Leninism just as Mao was entering into his Stalinist phase. Khrushchev was "handing the sword to others, helping the tigers harm us," Mao fumed privately. "If they don't want the sword, we do. We can make the best use of it. The Soviet Union may attack Stalin, but we will not. Not only that, we will continue to support him."[148]

As was his habit when confronting resistance, Mao did not immediately take the offensive. He acknowledged that although Stalin had been "a great Marxist" and "a good and honest revolutionary, ... in the course of a long period of time he made a number of great and serious mistakes, the primary ones of which were listed in Khrushchev's speech."[149] He endorsed Moscow's handling of the Polish and Hungarian crises: they could be read, after all, as an indication either of the need for de-Stalinization or as an acknowledgement of its dan-gers.[150] Zhou Enlai, who visited Moscow and Warsaw early in 1957, explained to the Poles that "relations between our countries ought to be like the relations between brothers and not like the relations between a father and a son, like the past . . . relations between the USSR and Poland." The Chinese had told the

Russians that "their position regarding the relations with fraternal parties is not always correct. But we do not believe this ought to be spoken of in public, so [that] we do not weaken the USSR."[151]

Mao himself revisited Moscow in November, on the 40th anniversary of the Bolshevik Revolution. When Khrushchev revived Stalin's old suggestion of a "division of labor" between the Russians and the Chinese in promoting world revolution, he respectfully declined on the grounds that "the CPSU should be the one and only center of the international Communist movement, and the rest of us should be united around that center." But Khrushchev, who had never trusted Mao, was uneasy: "we couldn't help suspecting that his thoughts were probably very different from his words."[152] This was, we now know, true enough. Relations between the two parties, Mao later complained, had not been "brotherly" at all but more like those "between father and son or between cats and mice."[153] Moreover, the Soviets and their European allies lacked revolutionary self-confidence.[154] "Khrushchev lost the support of the people when he started the campaign against Stalin," Mao explained to his advisers, noting the perfunctory reception Muscovites had accorded the two leaders on their ride in from the airport. "No wonder they have lost their enthusiasm."[155]

Enthusiasm, for Mao, was the essence of revolution. He never got over his fear that bureaucracies—party, government, or otherwise—might stifle it. It was bizarre, though, to attribute the loss of Soviet revolutionary élan to the hapless Khrushchev, and to hint that a return to Stalinism might revive it. Unless, of course, what Mao meant by "enthusiasm" was an *enforcement* of ardor coupled with a *smothering* of spontaneity on a mass scale, a condition Stalin would surely have understood. This was, indeed, the direction Mao had settled on by the time he made his Moscow visit.

Khrushchev's de-Stalinization campaign had initially weakened Mao's authority by encouraging warnings from within his own party about autocratic leadership: these surfaced at the 8th Party Congress, held in Beijing in September 1956. Mao himself appeared to confirm them the following February, when he made his famous call to let "one hundred flowers bloom and one hundred schools of thought contend."[156] There followed a remarkable outpouring of criticism from all sides, much of it directed against the party generally, some against Mao personally. Then, in June, he abruptly changed course, encouraging a counterattack on "rightists" who, he claimed, were attempting to wreck the revolution. "We want to coax the snakes out of their holes," Mao explained. "Then we will strike. My strategy is to let the poisonous weeds grow first and then destroy them one by one. Let them become fertilizer."[157]

"[T]he slogan was intended as a provocation," Khrushchev remembered. "It was proclaimed in order to encourage people to express themselves more openly so that any flowers whose blossom had the wrong color or scent could be cut down and trampled in the dirt."[158] This may exaggerate Mao's foresight; but it is not unreasonable to see his "anti-rightist" campaign, once he decided to launch it, as echoing Stalin's purges. The Soviet leader too had enjoyed luring real and imagined enemies into the open, then lopping off their heads. The results in China were not as bloody: "we won't kill anyone," Mao promised, pragmatically enough, "because if we were to kill anyone we would have to kill them all."[159] But the repressions were extremely thorough. Whatever enthusiasm was to develop would do so only under the tightest controls.

Mao then chose to follow Stalin in yet another sense—except that this time he wound up killing many more people than the Kremlin autocrat had ever dreamed of doing. The Great Leap Forward had complex roots and multiple objectives;[160] but it was fundamentally a rejection of planning in favor of enforced mass energy and enthusiasm. Although earlier efforts to emulate Soviet collectivization and industrialization had not worked out, Mao was not totally repudiating Stalin's example: the great "genius" too, at times, had become impatient with planning and had glorified the sheer force of will. The most famous instance was his promotion, in 1935, of the Stakhanovite movement, inspired by the feat of the miner Alexei Stakhanov, who in a single night was supposed to have mined 102 tons of coal, some fourteen times his norm.[161] What Mao did in 1958, though, was to abandon planning altogether and substitute will on a national scale: all of China would be organized into people's communes, which would in turn—through the use of backyard furnaces—double the nation's steel production within a year. Mao would make Stakhanovites by the hundreds of millions.

"It was obvious what Mao was up to," Khrushchev recalled: "he thought that if he could match England and then catch the US by the tail in five years, he would be able to outdistance the Party of Lenin and surpass the strides the Soviet people had made since the October Revolution."[162] To their credit, the Russians appear to have foreseen at least some of the consequences that lay ahead: the Chinese ambassador in Moscow reported, in October 1958, that the Soviet leadership "lacked sage understanding of the . . . new thoughts and new practices that have emerged in our [economic] development." The idea of "obtaining food without paying for it," in particular, was "incomprehensible" to them.[163] "It was perfectly clear to us," Khrushchev added,

that Mao Zedong had started down a wrong path that would lead to the collapse of his economy and, consequently, the failure of his policies. We did all we could to influence the Chinese and stop them before it was too late, but Mao thought he was God. Karl Marx and Lenin were both in their graves, and Mao thought he had no equal on earth.[164]

His own physician has pictured Mao as "a frog looking at the sky from the bottom of a well, thinking he was seeing the world. He had no basis for asserting that the communist world would overtake the capitalist one . . . , no knowledge of what the capitalist world was like."[165]

For a while, it all seemed to work. The communes were organized, the crops did come in, the steel was turned out.[166] But then it became obvious that the steel was unusable, having been forged by throwing whatever would melt into home-made furnaces with no quality controls. Even worse, the peasants had largely abandoned their crops and were cutting down their forests—often also cutting up their furniture—to keep the fires going. In their eagerness to comply with Mao's directives, party officials inflated their reports as production dropped off.[167] The Chairman proudly toured the country, relishing the statistics his subordinates were feeding him, reassured by the fires lighting the landscape as far as one could see on either side of his private train as it sped through the night. But Li Zhisui, travelling with Mao, wondered "how the furnaces had appeared so suddenly and how the production figures could be so high." It turned out that

[w]hat we were seeing from our windows . . . was staged, a huge multi-act nationwide Chinese opera performed especially for Mao. The party secretaries had ordered furnaces constructed everywhere along the rail route, stretching out for ten *li* on either side. . . . In Hubei, [the] party secretary . . . had ordered the peasants to remove rice plants from faraway fields and transplant them along Mao's route, to give the impression of a wildly abundant crop. . . . All of China was a stage, all the people performers in an extravaganza for Mao.

The Chairman, it seems, had imported, and vastly improved upon, yet another Russian product: the Potemkin village. But even after discovering the deception, Mao "gave no order to halt the backyard steel furnaces. . . . [He] still did not want to do anything to dampen the enthusiasm of the masses."[168]

Mao's experiment in economics did surpass the record of everyone else in the world, although not in the manner he had intended: the Great Leap Forward, it is now clear, produced the most devastating famine in modern history. We will never know how many people died, but estimates of the toll range from 16 to 27 million, with the higher figure probably the more accurate one. Earlier Chinese famines had come nowhere near this appalling total, nor had the one Stalin's collectivization of agriculture set off inside the Soviet Union.[169] It is possible, indeed, that the combined deaths from the famine *and* the purges in the USSR, *together with* those Hitler caused in the Holocaust, would still not match the number this single Maoist initiative, between 1958 and 1961, is thought to have brought about.[170] The Chairman, whose visage once adorned the t-shirts and dormitory walls of his Western admirers, therefore probably holds the record as the greatest mass murderer of all time.

But was the Great Leap Forward an experiment in *Marxist-Leninist* economics? Khrushchev, for obvious reasons, was desperate to deny that. Aware that the Chinese were starving by the millions—how many millions would not become clear for years to come—at least as worried by Mao's apparent willingness to expend millions more in a nuclear war,[171] he warned in June 1960 that ideology could be taken *too* literally: "We live in a time when we have neither Marx, nor Engels, nor Lenin with us. If we act like children who, studying the alphabet, compile words from letters, we shall not go very far." The Chinese, now on the defensive, shot back that Khrushchev was being "arbitrary, and tyrannical." He had "treated the relationship between the great Communist Party of the Soviet Union and our Party not as one between brothers, but as one between patriarchal father and son."[172]

That response, in turn, was enough to make Khrushchev, on 16 July, abruptly announce the withdrawal of all forms of economic and technical assistance to

China, just as the Beijing government was focusing on the scale of the disaster it confronted and beginning to think about how to recover from it.[173] The effects were devastating: "Your withdrawal of experts has inflicted damages upon us, thus causing us a great deal of difficulties," Deng Xiaoping admitted to a Soviet delegation two months later. But "[t]he Chinese people are . . . determined to make up for the losses with our own hands and build our own nation."[174]

The implications, from Moscow's perspective, were that the Chinese had perverted—even caricatured—the planning process that was at the center of the Marxist-Leninist model. We now know, though, that Khrushchev's own methods were closer to those of Mao—if far less costly in human lives—than he was prepared to acknowledge. At the 22nd Party Congress, held in the fall of 1961, the Kremlin leader predicted, on the basis of what he claimed was a carefully designed program, that in per capita production the Soviet Union would, by 1970, surpass the United States. Communism itself would be in place by 1980. Marxism–Leninism would prevail, not by military force, but by demonstrating its unquestionable economic superiority.[175] Khrushchev's speech-writer Fedor Burlatsky recalls, though, that the statistics supporting these claims "were complete fabrications—pure wishful thinking." The Soviet economy by then was in serious trouble; Khrushchev had made his projections against the advice of his own planners.[176] Simply proclaiming lofty goals, he *and* Mao appear to have believed, would overcome all difficulties: the will of the people was what counted; professional expertise was not required. Both leaders, in this sense, were like frogs at the bottom of wells, aspiring to reach the sky but with no idea of how to get there.

And what of John F. Kennedy, who had just committed the United States to place a man on the moon by 1970 without any clear idea as to how this was to be accomplished?[177] The difference, it would appear, was that Kennedy did not insist upon an ideologically correct method of making his great leap: he would get there by whatever method worked. Neither Khrushchev nor Mao would accept that kind of pragmatism in their economic planning. They imposed strict ideological constraints, and they took it upon themselves, personally, to determine how these would be applied. It was as if Kennedy had insisted that only Democrats, or Roman Catholics, or citizens of Massachusetts could work in the space program, that the science involved required legitimation in the writings of Woodrow Wilson and Franklin D. Roosevelt, and that failures would be fixed only when he personally recognized them as such. Khrushchev had the good sense not to run his own space program that way: the absurdity would have been obvious. But the economy was far more important to him and to his country in the long run than launching Sputniks, and such absurdities afflicted it—as was the case in Mao's China—at almost every step of the way.

The reason was that neither could bear to share authority. Khrushchev *had* to be the boss; Mao *had* to be the emperor. Both came out of cultures—ideological and national—that distrusted spontaneity: despite their revolutionary origins, they feared it deeply. What this meant was that originality, innovation, insight, wisdom—and moral compassion—could only with great difficulty reach the top. For Marxist-Leninist systems to draw upon these qualities, they had to be present already in the leader, who really did have to be, as Mao said of Stalin, "the greatest genius of the present age." That was setting high standards indeed, and perhaps it explains why the more democratic statesmen of the West—who saw no threat to their authority in seeking the advice of others—generally came closer to landing where they had planned to when they began to leap.

VII

By the time Khrushchev was forced from office in October 1964, wars among capitalists, of the kind Lenin and Stalin had anticipated, were nowhere in sight. Wars between communists and capitalists looked likely to be confined—after the shock of the Cuban missile crisis[178]—to "third world" conflicts like the one escalating in Vietnam. Wars among communists, though, were all too real a possibility: the ideological schism between the Soviet Union and the People's Republic of China had become so intense during the Khrushchev years that as they ended his representatives were secretly discussing *with the Americans* plans for *joint preventive military action* against Chinese nuclear facilities in the Gobi desert.[179] It is difficult to know what to make of these contacts, which ended with the first Chinese nuclear test and Khrushchev's virtually simultaneous overthrow. But they do reflect a situation few Marxist-Leninist theorists had foreseen:[180] that the greatest risk of great power war could be between the greatest Marxist-Leninist states.

One might explain this unexpected development by the fact that Khrushchev and Mao, from the time they first met in Beijing in 1954, appear to have loathed one another as well as their respective surroundings.[181] The new Kremlin leader found the atmosphere in the Chinese capital "typically Oriental"—it is not clear what else he expected—"sickeningly sweet", and "nauseating." He discovered that he did not like green tea. He claims to have told his colleagues, upon his return, that conflict with China was inevitable.[182] "We took great care never to offend China until the Chinese actually started to crucify us," he later recalled, but "when they did start to crucify us—well, I'm no Jesus Christ, and I didn't have to turn the other cheek."[183] Mao thought little better of Moscow in 1957, or of his Soviet host. "It's not to our liking," he complained about the food. "Why did they dance that way, prancing around on their toes?" he demanded of Khrushchev, before walking out on a performance of *Swan Lake*. And when Khrushchev made a return visit to Beijing in 1958, Mao was deliberately rude to him, to the point of receiving his guest in swimming trunks: it was a way, he cheerfully admitted, of "sticking a needle up his ass."[184]

Western leaders, too, did not always get along: John Foster Dulles and Anthony Eden seem to have taken a particular pleasure in tormenting one another; and Charles de Gaulle chose to torment everyone—thereby transmuting the French strategic doctrine of *"défense tous azimuts"* into one of "offense in all directions." Such animosities could certainly sour relations within NATO, but they never shaped them to the extent that the Khrushchev–Mao rivalry affected the Sino-Soviet alliance. The reason was simple enough: apart from de Gaulle, no Western leader thought of himself as personifying a state.[185] There were always multiple channels of communication, and even if leaders at the top did despise one another, subordinates could always smooth things over. The revolutionaries who ruled in Moscow and Beijing, however, could not allow this. History, culture, and ideology combined to lock them into authoritarian methods of governing, which meant that their own emotions became state policy. The effect, paradoxically, was to throw diplomacy back to the days of absolute monarchs, when questions of war and peace could hinge upon their ability to avoid personally insulting one another.

If clashes of personality were one of the "contradictions" that undermined Marxist-Leninist solidarity, so too was a contrast in structures: the Western alliance proved to be far more flexible than its Eastern counterparts. To see this point, one need only contrast Hungary's *attempted* departure from the Warsaw Pact in 1956 with France's *actual* departure from its military role in NATO a decade later. The French, arguably, were the more important ally: their country was larger, wealthier, and more powerful than Hungary, and NATO's own headquarters lay within its territory. Certainly the Americans and their other allies worried about the precedent de Gaulle's withdrawal might set, and a few diehard Atlanticists responded bitterly to it. The overall reaction, though, was surprisingly mild: despite its abrupt expulsion, NATO's response was limited to expressions of regret, followed by quick action to remove its forces and facilities.[186] If it occurred to anyone in Washington or elsewhere even to think of treating de Gaulle as Khrushchev had dealt with Imre Nagy, they kept such thoughts to themselves. No one denounced the French president as a heretic, no one proposed overt or covert action to overthrow him, and France soon settled into a pattern of practical cooperation with NATO, even as in principle it remained aloof.[187]

Sometimes the things that *do not* happen in history—the things, indeed, that everyone assumes *could not* have happened—are nonetheless revealing. The fact that NATO could absorb and adapt to as easily as it did the challenge from Paris, while the Warsaw Pact felt obliged to resist and ultimately crush the one from Budapest; the fact that it is so difficult in retrospect to imagine these roles being reversed; the fact that neither side at the time gave serious thought to behaving otherwise—all of this suggests an important difference between the two great Cold War coalitions, which is that one was resilient and the other brittle. NATO, we can now see, was an *organic* alliance: it proved to be deeply rooted, in tune with its environment, capable even of shedding branches and limbs when necessary without serious damage. But both the Warsaw Pact and the Sino-Soviet alliance seem today to have been *inorganic*, even *crystalline* in character: they were impressive to look at and hard when touched, but under strain they shattered easily.[188]

What, though, might account for this difference? Here we come to a third "contradiction" in the Marxist-Leninist coalition, which has to do with its leaders' concept of democracy. They often chose to describe their regimes as "peoples' democracies," but there was always an ambivalence in the meaning of that term. One can see it best in Khrushchev. He was surely right when he insisted that however progressive a regime might be, it would sooner or later have to improve the lot of those who lived under it, otherwise they would overthrow it. In this crude sense, he understood the principle of representative government and even sought to explain it in his memoirs:

[I]n a democracy it is difficult for a leader to stay in power if he doesn't make a point of consulting with his followers. A democratic leader must have a good mind and be able to take advice. He must realize that his position of leadership depends on the people's will to have him as their leader, not on his own will to lead the people.

But Khrushchev immediately went on to reveal the limits of his understanding:

And the people will accept a leader only if he shows himself to be of the same flesh and blood as the Party. . . . [H]e holds his position of leadership by the will of the Party. In other words, he is not above the Party, but the servant of the Party, and he can keep his position only as long as he enjoys the Party's satisfaction and support.[189]

The circular reasoning here was striking: leaders must respond to the people, but the people will respond only to the Party—which of course, in a Marxist-Leninist society, can respond only to leaders *not* chosen by the people.

Western democratic leaders also worried, in the wake of World War II, about delivering on their promises and the loss of legitimacy that might accompany their failure to do so. But they never saw a single hierarchically organized Party, regulating everthing from the top, as the way out. Instead they relied upon two laterally organized and largely self-regulating mechanisms—market economics and democratic politics—which made a point of *not* assuming total wisdom and absolute competence at the top. These systems were *more* willing than their Marxist-Leninist counterparts to trust "the masses," *less* prepared to defer obediently to those who ruled them. For all its inefficiencies and occasional injustices, democratic capitalism proved during the critical decade of the 1950s that it could build societies based on sustained popular support as well as alliances capable of coordinated military action. Marxism-Leninism, in stark contrast, had shattered one alliance and held together another only by force; its economic achievements had been reduced, by 1960, to Khrushchev's hollow promises of overtaking the West in yet another decade—and to the great deaths that resulted from Mao's Great Leap.[190]

EIGHT

Nuclear Weapons and the Escalation of the Cold War

Even if the U.S. atom bombs were so powerful that, when dropped on China, they would make a hole right through the earth, or even blow it up, that would hardly mean anything to the universe as a whole, though it might be a major event for the solar system.

Mao Zedong, January 1955[1]

[T]he United States is piling up armaments which it well knows will never provide for its ultimate safety. We are piling up these armaments because we do not know what else to do to provide for our security.

Dwight D. Eisenhower, January 1956[2]

GIVEN the failure of the Marxist-Leninist model to deliver on its promises of economic prosperity and social justice; given the fact that the Sino-Soviet alliance was falling apart and that only the use of force had held the Warsaw Pact together; given the success with which the Western democracies had managed to organize their own economies and alliances—given all that had become clear by the beginning of the 1960s, why did the Cold War not end at that point? A *multi-dimensional* measurement of power might have concluded that the Soviet Union's cause, by that time, was already lost: that because its capabilities were becoming so *mono-dimensional*, narrowing as they had from the political, economic, ideological and military strengths of 1945 to little beyond the latter in 1961, there was no way in which it could hope to prevail over the United States, the coalition it had assembled, and the increasingly robust international economy the western democracies were building. Khrushchev's hyperbolic pronouncements, from that perspective, would have sounded like whistles in a graveyard.

They did not seem so at the time, though, because the Soviet Union's achievements in military technology overshadowed its failures in politics, economics, and ideology. Khrushchev's dilemmas with respect to de-Stalinization, agricultural and industrial modernization, and international communist solidarity were certainly known in the west,[3] but their significance was not.

Conventional wisdom still held that armaments chiefly determined influence; and the Kremlin was accumulating weaponry in forms and quantities that seemed to put at risk whatever advantage the Americans' nuclear superiority had given them since the end of World War II. Other kinds of strength looked much less important.

Neither the United States nor the Soviet Union had found it easy to know what to *do* with their nuclear arsenals once they had them: this had caused their leaders, by 1953, to *begin* rethinking the relationship between destructiveness and usability.[4] But the possibility that an absolute weapon could be absolutely useless was as yet far too revolutionary to comprehend. No one in Washington or Moscow then—or for decades to come—would have dreamed that the Cold War could end as decisively as World War II without the use of *any* military force whatever.[5] The conviction persisted that there must be *some* advantage in possessing nuclear weapons, if only statesmen and strategists could figure out what it was. That is what Eisenhower and Khrushchev set out to do: indeed, it became their central preoccupation.

This respect accorded nuclear capabilities greatly benefited, we can now see, the USSR. It focused competition within the only arena in which the Soviet Union's strength was increasing, thereby ensuring a kind of "home court advantage" that offset Moscow's weaknesses elsewhere. It created an impressive carapace, concealing from the west and perhaps from the Kremlin leaders themselves Marxism-Leninism's increasing internal contradictions. Kennan had anticipated the effect as early as 1947 when he compared the Soviet Union to the Buddenbrook family in Thomas Mann's great novel: it was like "one of those stars whose light shines most brightly on this world when in reality it has long ceased to exist."[6] John Foster Dulles did not always agree with Kennan, but on this point they thought alike: "Dictatorships usually present a formidable exterior," he wrote in 1950. Within, though, "they are full of rottenness."[7]

Dulles drew from this the principle that the United States should challenge Soviet authority aggressively: hence the "liberation" strategy which became so prominent a feature of the 1952 Republican presidential campaign.[8] But his practices—like those of the President he served—were much more circumspect: the Eisenhower administration came to see that even a few Soviet nuclear bombs could produce such devastation as to render any American nuclear advantage meaningless. The United States therefore refrained, for the most part, from exploiting Soviet weaknesses. Far from shifting the status quo, as he had promised to do while seeking office, Eisenhower used nuclear weapons to shore up and stabilize it. In an interesting inversion of military tradition, he saw *superior* capabilities as allowing only *defensive* responses.

Khrushchev, curiously, retained but inverted the logic: for him, nuclear *inferiority* required taking the *offensive*. Buoyed by Soviet achievements in building thermonuclear weapons and long-range rockets, aware nonetheless of how difficult it would be to match the strategic bombing capabilities of the United States, he managed to convince himself by the end of 1956 that if he *threatened* long and loudly enough to use his own small nuclear arsenal, he could counterbalance the much larger one the Americans had accumulated. In one sense, he was only updating Stalin's pre-1949 strategy, which sought to neutralize Truman's atomic monopoly by trivializing it. In another sense, Khrushchev was following the example of Eisenhower and Dulles, whose "New Look" relied on nuclear weapons to sustain Cold War competition at more reasonable costs than a full-scale conventional force arms race would have involved.[9] In no sense did Khrushchev want, or think the Soviet Union could survive, a nuclear war.

He was, however, more prepared than Truman or Eisenhower—or Stalin—had ever been to *risk* war: to threaten nuclear escalation in the belief that the West would prefer altering over maintaining the status quo. With all the flamboyance of a high-stakes poker player, Khrushchev raised the ante, confident that he could bluff his opponents into backing down. There were, however, three problems with this strategy: it depended on keeping Moscow's actual nuclear and missile capabilities secret, so that his adversaries would not know he was bluffing; it required controlling allies like Ulbricht and Mao, who confused the Soviet Union's real strengths with Khrushchev's rhetoric; and it assumed that the United States and its allies would take no countervailing measures. None of these propositions held. The early 1960s, as a consequence, would see the Cold War come as close to a nuclear war as it ever did.

I

Sometimes small things make big impressions on people's minds. After the first United States thermonuclear test, at the Pacific atoll of Eniwetok on 1 November 1952, investigators found it striking that the blast had incinerated birds in flight for miles around. Survivors "were sick, some grounded and reluctant to fly, and some [had] singed feathers, particularly the noddy terns and the sooty terns, whose feathers are dark in color. . . ."[10] The effect was much the same at the Semipalatinsk test site in Kazhakstan, where the Soviet Union's first hydrogen bomb exploded on 12 August 1953. Andrei Sakhahrov recalled driving

past buildings destroyed by the blast, braking to a stop beside an eagle whose wings had been badly singed. It was trying to fly, but it couldn't get off the ground. One of the officers killed the eagle with a well-aimed kick, putting it out of its misery. I have been told that thousands of birds are destroyed in every test; they take wing at the flash, but then fall to earth, burned and blinded.[11]

It might seem strange that the fate of birds should so stick in the minds of those who witnessed the first H-bomb tests. But there were few other ways of comprehending, on anything close to a human scale, calculations that placed the size of the Soviet blast at 400 kilotons—twenty times the size of the bomb that devastated Hiroshima—or its ten-megaton American counterpart, which produced an explosion twenty-five times more powerful than the one the Russians achieved.[12] This time there were no human victims. Birds would have to do.

From the time the world first learned of atomic weapons—and for the atomic scientists even before that—there had been hopes that these new and unprecedentedly cataclysmic means of destruction would keep the postwar era from becoming another prewar era. Beyond the undeniably important fact that neither the United States nor the Soviet Union had found occasion to use their bombs, though, little evidence of cooperation had as yet emerged. The "two atomic colossi" seemed doomed, as Eisenhower warned the United Nations late in 1953, "malevolently to eye each other indefinitely across a trembling world."[13] Reactions to burned birds at Eniwetok and Semipalatinsk provided one of the first hints that an awareness of common nuclear danger might be possible.

In contrast to atomic bomb tests, which impressed most but not all observers,[14] no one who actually witnessed a thermonuclear explosion appears to have come away without elemental feelings of awe mixed with dread. "I was stunned," the American scientist George Cowan recalled of Eniwetok. "I mean, it was big. . . . As soon as I dared, I whipped off my dark glasses and the thing was enormous, bigger than I'd ever imagined that it would be. It looked as though it blotted out the whole horizon."[15] N. A. Vlasov, who saw the first Soviet test, had "the general impression of a terrible and huge destructive force. . . . [T]he explosion had indeed been far more powerful than the explosion of the atomic bomb. The impact of it apparently transcended some kind of psychological barrier."[16] Sakharov, in particular, sensed this:

[W]hen you see all of this yourself, something in you changes. When you see the burned birds who are writhing on the scorched steppe, when you see how the shock wave blows away buildings like houses of cards, when you feel the reek of splintered bricks, when you sense melted glass, you immediately think of times of war. . . . The very moment of the explosion, the shock wave which moves along the field and which crushes the grass and flings itself at the earth. . . . All of this triggers an irrational and yet very strong emotional impact. How not to start thinking of one's responsibility at this point?[17]

I. V. Kurchatov, who had so effectively used the fruits of espionage to build Stalin's atomic bomb, went so far as to abandon further work on nuclear weapons after seeing the effects of the first air-dropped Soviet hydrogen bomb in November, 1955: "That was such a terrible, monstrous sight! That weapon must not be allowed ever to be used."[18]

But the leaders who would determine such uses did not normally don dark glasses or crouch in bunkers to view such tests.[19] As scientists on both sides began to understand the physical effects of the weapons they had created, another parallel emerged: they found themselves appalled by the apparent ignorance and irresponsibility of their bosses. J. Robert Oppenheimer had felt this as early as 1946 when he made the mistake of telling Harry S. Truman that he and the other atomic scientists "have blood on our hands." "Never mind," the shocked physicist remembered the president as having joked. "It'll all come out in the wash."[20] Sakharov had an eerily similar experience. On the evening of the 1955 Soviet test he gave a banquet toast: "May all our devices explode as successfully as today's, but always over test sites and never over cities." As he recalls it, "the table fell silent, as if I had said something indecent." Then Marshall Mitrofan Nedelin, Deputy Minister of Defense, arose to tell a parable:

An old man wearing only a shirt was praying before an icon. "Guide me, harden me. Guide me, harden me." His wife, who was lying on the stove, said: "Just pray to be hard, old man, I can guide it in myself." Let's drink to getting hard.

The implications, for Sakharov, were clear enough: "We, the inventors, scientists, engineers, and craftsmen, had created a terrible weapon; but its use would lie entirely outside our control. . . . Of course, I knew this already—I wasn't *that* naïve. But understanding something in an abstract way is different from feeling it with your whole being, like the reality of life and death."[21]

By that time Oppenheimer had learned the limits of his influence in the most painful way. Angered by his opposition, in 1949, to building the hydrogen bomb, several of his fellow scientists, including Edward Teller, its principal sponsor, sought to remove him from further work on nuclear weapons. Oppenheimer was vulnerable because of his leftist tendencies during the 1930s and his lack of candor in reporting approaches Soviet agents had made to him during the early 1940s. Revelations that the Manhattan Project had harbored real spies, coupled with the overall climate of McCarthyism, made his defense even more difficult. Swayed by Atomic Energy Commission chairman Lewis Strauss, Eisenhower refused to intervene, and after lengthy proceedings the Commission revoked Oppenheimer's security clearances, thereby eliminating him from government-sponsored nuclear research of any kind. "Charles, can you give me a number?" the newly uninformed physicist plaintively asked a friend a few days after the United States detonated its largest thermonuclear device ever at Bikini on 1 March 1954. "I said fifteen. He knew what it meant, of course. I knew I was breaking the law but Robert was an old friend of mine and I wasn't about to tell him, 'I can't tell you.' "[22]

The BRAVO test did indeed yield fifteen megatons—but it had been expected to produce only five. The crater was 250 feet deep and more than a mile across. The fireball extended two miles out from the test site, and the blast was felt for almost 200 miles in all directions. Most significantly, dangerously radioactive fallout spread hundreds of miles downwind, producing the first human casualties of the H-bomb era. Twenty-eight Americans and 236 Marshall Islanders were exposed, as was the crew of a Japanese fishing boat, the *Fukuryū Maru*, or *Lucky Dragon*. By the time they returned to Japan, on 14 March, most were ill and one subsequently died. Meanwhile elevated levels of radiation were detected around the world, setting off shock and some panic as people realized that even the *testing* of a *single* bomb could have environmental consequences for everyone.[23]

"[S]omething must have happened that we have never experienced before, and must have surprised and astonished the scientists," an uneasy Eisenhower admitted to uneasy reporters on 24 March.[24] A week later, at another presidential press conference called to reassure the public, AEC Chairman Strauss was asked how large a hydrogen bomb could be. "[A]s large as you wish," he too casually replied, "large enough to take out a city." A chorus of "Whats?" came from the members of the press, one of whom persisted: "Any city, New York?" "The metropolitan area, yes," Strauss admitted.[25] "Lewis," the President commented as they exited, "I wouldn't have answered that one that way." But by that time the administration had already committed itself to releasing film footage of the November 1952 test, and on the next day, as presidential press secretary James Hagerty noted: "All hell broke loose."[26] Imaginative editors quickly devised maps and photographs showing how little would have been left of New York if the BRAVO bomb had exploded there, confirming all too graphically what Strauss had said.[27]

Thoughts of thermonuclear conflagration shifted, as a result, from the realm of abstraction to what Sakharov called "the reality of life and death." There could no longer be any illusions that a war fought with such weapons—and the new long-range missiles being developed to carry them—would resemble World War II or any other previous human experience. "War up to now has been a contest," Eisenhower would later acknowledge, "but with nuclear missiles, it is no longer a contest, it is complete destruction."[28] His Secretary of Defense, Charles E. Wilson, put it in terms Sakharov might have used: "developments on both sides . . . are such that in time both will be able to destroy the world, including the birds."[29]

II

"Human minds recoil from the realization of such facts," Winston Churchill wrote Eisenhower on 9 March 1954, even before BRAVO's full effects had become known. Then in his final year as Prime Minister, the old statesman had dramatically altered his views on nuclear weapons. He had welcomed the atomic bomb in 1945 as a bulwark against the Russians, and in 1948 had even advised the Truman administration to threaten its use if Stalin refused to make concessions in Eastern Europe. But now the Soviet Union too had such bombs, and the bombs were becoming much bigger—to the point, as BRAVO demonstrated, of transforming small islands into clouds of radioactive debris: "You can imagine what my thoughts are about London," Churchill confided to Eisenhower. Devices meant to contain the Russians now posed greater risks than the Russians themselves:

The people, including the well-informed, can only gape and console themselves with the reflection that death comes to all anyhow, sometime. This merciful numbness cannot be enjoyed by the few men upon whom the supreme responsibility falls. They have to drive their minds forward into these hideous and deadly spheres of thought. All the things that are happening now put together, added to all the material things that ever happened, are scarcely more important to the human race.[30]

"[T]he prospects are truly appalling," Eisenhower replied, with what the author of such eloquence must have regarded as disappointing brevity. "Ways of lessening or, if possible, of eliminating the danger must be found."[31]

Doubts about the proposed solution, not complacency about the problem, caused the President to respond as he did. Churchill desperately wanted to cap his long career with one more trip to Moscow to negotiate personally with the Soviet leadership, as he had twice done with Stalin during World War II. But Eisenhower thought such contacts premature, nor was he prepared to entrust them to an increasingly feeble and emotional near-octogenarian.[32] Moreover, the Prime Minister had told him nothing he did not already know about nuclear war.

The President had found on his desk, when he took office in January 1953, a report from a panel of experts, Oppenheimer among them, claiming that with "careful planning and preparation," the United States might "survive" the detonation of as many as 2,500 atomic bombs on its territory. Survival would have "a rather specialized meaning," though: based on existing Soviet designs, that number of weapons would yield "an explosive energy equal to that of 100 million tons of high explosive—or 400 times the total load dropped on Germany by allied bombers in World War II."[33] Stunned by such figures, Eisenhower had warned the world, in his December 1953 speech to the United Nations, that a nuclear war would mean

the probability of civilization destroyed—the annihilation of the irreplacable heritage of mankind handed down to us generation from generation—and the condemnation of mankind to begin all over again the age-old struggle upward from savagery toward decency, and right, and justice.[34]

He sharpened the point several months after the BRAVO test, when South Korean President Syngman Rhee tried to convince him to launch a global crusade against communism. The rhetoric was all Churchill could have wished for:

[W]hen you say that we should deliberately plunge into war, let me tell you that if war comes, it will be horrible. . . . There will be millions of people dead. War today is unthinkable with the weapons which we have at our command. If the Kremlin and Washington ever lock up in a war, the results are too horrible to contemplate. I can't even imagine them.[35]

It was beginning to look as though "modern warfare imposes its own limitations," Eisenhower later told his advisers: "what do you do with the world after you have won a victory in such a catastrophic nuclear war?"[36] Missiles would make the situation even worse: if the point ever came at which "the Russians can fire 1000 a day at us and we can fire 1000 a day at them," then he personally "would want to take off for the Argentine."[37]

Dulles might well have accompanied him. Despite having persuaded Eisenhower, during the 1952 campaign, that "massive retaliation" made sense, despite having announced publicly in January 1954 that the United States would henceforth chiefly depend "upon a great capacity to retaliate, instantly, by means and at places of our own choosing,"[38] the Secretary of State found BRAVO to be more than he had bargained for. It was important, he admonished Strauss, to remember "the tremendous repercussions these things have." A "wave of hysteria" was driving our Allies away from us. They think we are getting ready for a war of this kind. We could survive, but some of them would be obliterated in a few minutes. It could lead to a policy of neutrality or appeasement.[39]

A few weeks later Dulles warned the National Security Council that "we could not sit here in Washington and develop bigger bombs without any regard for the impact of these developments on world opinion."[40] By November, he had concluded that "the increased destructiveness of nuclear weapons and the approach of an effective atomic parity are creating a situation in which general war would threaten the destruction of Western civilization and of the Soviet regime, and in which national objectives could not be attained through a general war, even if a military victory were won."[41]

In Moscow, too, visions of apocalypse were beginning to form. Georgi Malenkov, Chairman of the Council of Ministers, had shown sufficient self-confidence in August 1953 to announce the first Soviet H-bomb test four days before it occurred; he emphasized, though, that there were "no objective grounds for a collision between the United States and the USSR." Malenkov became more explicit on 12 March 1954, three days after Churchill wrote Eisenhower and while BRAVO's fallout was still circling the earth. The choice facing humanity, he announced, was no longer that between "cold" and "hot" war: the Cold War itself involved "preparing a new world war, which with modern weapons means the end of world civilization."[42] It was the first public acknowledgement by a Soviet official of what Truman and Eisenhower had already admitted: that nuclear weapons were making war itself obsolete. The implications for Stalin's doctrine of inevitable conflict were striking, for if war could indeed end world civilization, how could it possibly advance the Marxist-Leninist cause?

Malenkov's insight had little impact at the time because Khrushchev and Molotov forced him to repudiate it and return to the traditional view that any future conflict—even if fought with nuclear weapons—could only cause the collapse of capitalism. "A Communist should not speak about the 'destruction of world civilization' or about the 'destruction of the human race,'" Molotov complained, "but about the need to prepare and mobilize all forces for the destruction of the bourgeoisie." If people should come to believe that "in the event of war all must perish . . . [t]hen why should we build socialism, why worry about tomorrow? It would be better to supply everyone with coffins now."[43]

But there had been more to Malenkov's address than met the eye. He made it after having learned the preliminary results of a study by Kurchatov and three other Soviet physicists, hastily revised after the BRAVO test, which concluded that if a war should break out fought with *existing* stockpiles of *atomic* weapons, "dosages of radioactive emissions and concentrations of radioactive substances which are biologically harmful for human life and vegetation will be created on a significant part of the Earth's surface." There would soon be enough atomic bombs "to create conditions under which the existence of life over the whole globe will be impossible." It would only take the explosion of approximately 100 *hydrogen* bombs—presumably in the BRAVO range—to produce the same effect. "So, we cannot but admit that mankind faces an enormous threat of the termination of all life on Earth."[44]

Molotov, never much impressed by scientists, could shrug off such findings, but Khrushchev took them seriously. He claims to have been briefed on the physical effects of nuclear weapons as early as September 1953, and not to have been able to sleep for several days afterwards. "Then I became convinced that we could never possibly use these weapons, and . . . I was able to sleep again."[45] He took the other side to discredit Malenkov, whose resignation he ultimately orchestrated in February 1955. Having thereby established himself—for the moment—as Stalin's undisputed successor, Khrushchev played an old Stalinist trick and embraced his deposed rival's position.[46] Malenkov's heresy thus became Khrushchev's orthodoxy: that the common experience of a thermonuclear revolution had left the United States and the Soviet Union no choice but to seek common ground.

The July 1955 Geneva summit provided an excellent opportunity: it was the first face-to-face meeting between Soviet and American leaders since the end of World War II. Khrushchev maintained an uncharacteristically low profile, leaving it to his figurehead partner Nikolai Bulganin—Malenkov's successor as Soviet premier—to hear Eisenhower's warning that modern weapons had progressed to the point at which, because of prevailing wind patterns, any massive use of nuclear weapons could "destroy the Northern Hemisphere." The President went on to explain to his old wartime friend Marshal Georgi Zhukov that "[n]ot even scientists could say what would happen if two hundred H-bombs were exploded in a short period of time, but if the atmospheric conditions were right, the fall-out might destroy entire nations . . . ." Zhukov agreed, acknowledging that "if on the first day of the war the United States dropped three or four hundred bombs on the Soviet Union and they would do the same, it would be impossible to say what would happen to the atmosphere under those conditions."[47] Khrushchev saw the point readily enough, admitting to Eisenhower: "We get your dust, you get our dust, the winds blow, and nobody's safe."[48] The summit produced no specific agreements, but the new Kremlin boss found these exchanges encouraging: they showed "that our enemies probably feared us as much as we feared them."[49]

That was true enough, and it had been for some time. In a little-noted passage of his December 1953 United Nations address, Eisenhower had warned that "even a vast superiority in numbers of weapons, and a consequent capability of devastating retaliation, is no preventive, of itself, against the fearful material damage and toll of human lives that would be inflicted by surprise aggression."[50] If only a few Soviet nuclear weapons were to reach the United States, he reminded his advisers a year later, the results would be catastrophic: "Can you imagine what would happen in New York or Detroit or Washington or Pittsburgh or any one of our big cities, if they got hit by an atomic bomb?"[51] By February 1955 his own experts were raising the possibility of

death and destruction on a scale almost beyond knowing, and certainly beyond any sensibility to shock and horror that men have so far experienced. . . . [F]or the first time in history, a striking force could have such power that the first battle could be the final battle, the first punch a knockout.[52]

And in January, 1956, having reviewed the results of a Pentagon war game, a shaken President recorded in his diary that the entire federal government had been wiped out, that "something on the order of 65% of the population would require some kind of medical care, and in most instances, no opportunity whatsoever to get it," and that, "while these things were going on, the damage inflicted by us against the Soviets was roughly three times greater."[53]

As this last comment suggests, Eisenhower understood that the Russians too must be worried. It was reasonable to assume that they had conducted similar studies, "that they had some appreciation of the implications for destruction of their regime and their country as a result of the use of thermonuclear weapons on a strategic scale." They could not be "wholly out of their minds."[54] These were shrewd observations, for only a month after Eisenhower made them Khrushchev used the 20th Party Congress to jettison, once and for all, the doctrine of inevitable war. Lenin had put it forward, he pointed out, at a time when there were no socialist systems; but their creation had now greatly strengthened the forces of peace, creating the possibility of progress toward communism without the need to confront the world's remaining capitalist states. "[E]ither peaceful coexistence or the most destructive war in history," Khrushchev insisted, echoing Malenkov in 1954. "There is no third way."[55]

There had emerged, then, by early 1956, an impressive international consensus on the *ecological* consequences of a nuclear war: the entire northern hemisphere might well become unliveable. Contrary to what the scientists sometimes believed, their bosses were not oblivious to their findings: indeed, the science made its way to the top with remarkable speed. The next step, one might think, would have been cooperation, as the highest priority, to remove the danger. But this did not occur: the weapons continued to pile up; the crises became more, not less, frequent; and the Cold War now passed into its most frightening phase. There was a parallel ecological consciousness, but it occupied, as yet, only a portion of policy-makers' minds.

III

Also present was the curious belief—or so it seems now—that despite the incredible nature of these weapons each side's safety required projecting the most credible possible determination to use them. Given the utter disproportion between the effects thermonuclear bombs would have produced and any conceivable purpose that might have inspired a war fought with them, it is a wonder anyone took this argument seriously. The instinctive response today is to ridicule so gross a disparity between means and ends, rather in the spirit of that visionary Cold War cultural icon, the film *Dr. Strangelove*. But technological implications are often less obvious than technological innovations. Learning the uses—and the limitations—of any new technology can take a long time; and as a consequence subsequent generations are apt to regard those who go through this process as having held antiquated, even weird, notions. A prime example is the belief, tenaciously adhered to in both Washington and Moscow during the 1950s, that despite their destructiveness H-bombs had to be good for something.

The origins of this idea—"Strangelovian" is perhaps not too strong an adjective—go back, on the American side, to the debate that took place during 1949–50 over whether to construct such weapons in the first place. It was clear even then that each "super" bomb could have 1,000 times the power of the atomic bombs that destroyed Hiroshima and Nagasaki. For James B. Conant, the President of Harvard, a Manhattan Project veteran, and a member of the Atomic Energy Commission's General Advisory Committee, that was reason enough not to build them: their only conceivable purpose would be to kill civilians on a massive scale, and that amounted to genocide. The United States would soon have more than enough atomic bombs to destroy whatever Soviet military targets might exist in any future war. Moral *and* military logic rejected building anything bigger, *even if the Russians should themselves do so.*[56] Conant's argument convinced an initially ambivalent Oppenheimer, as well as Kennan, who saw in these new weapons a very old way of thinking: they reached "beyond the frontiers of western civilization, to the concepts of warfare which were once familiar to the Asiatic hordes." It was important to avoid "hypnotizing ourselves into the belief that they may ultimately serve some positive national purpose."[57]

Compelling as it was, this position came up short against another, influenced by Teller and Strauss, but most effectively advanced by General Omar Bradley, Chairman of the Joint Chiefs of Staff. Bradley took the view, unusual for a military officer, that the "super" should be built even if it had no military purpose. It was justification enough that such a device was possible, and that the Russians might get it. Hydrogen bombs were needed, not as an instrument of rationality but as insurance against irrationality: against the danger that Americans and their allies might panic if the USSR should develop this capability and the United States should not; against the prospect that such an asymmetry might tempt Soviet leaders to behave imprudently. The new weapon's uses were, therefore, chiefly *psychological*; to make them credible, though, real weapons together with means of delivering them would be required. The shift here was significant: the purpose of weaponry in the past had been to fight wars. Its new role would be to make wars sufficiently horrible that no one would want to start them.[58]

Both arguments proceeded from the assumption that thermonuclear weapons were indeed revolutionary; but they came to opposite conclusions about the desirability of developing them. To put it in terms from a later era, Conant was arguing for a "war-fighting" strategy that relied on conventional and if necessary atomic weapons: morality resided in keeping the war as discriminate as possible. Bradley was arguing for a "war-avoidance" strategy that ruled out no weapon however indiscriminate: morality demanded deterring war itself by making it as terrible as possible. Truman, as we have seen, fudged the choice. His decision to build the hydrogen bomb reflected Bradley's thinking, while his acceleration of atomic bomb production and his subsequent approval of NSC-68 responded to Conant's reasoning.[59] Eisenhower was more decisive.

Consider his response, shortly after the 1954 BRAVO test, when Admiral Arthur W. Radford, Bradley's successor as JCS chairman, reported what he thought the President would want to hear: that Pentagon planners feared "full exploitation of our nuclear capability might inflict such chaos and suffering in the Soviet Union as had not been known in Europe since the end of the Thirty Years War." Echoing a theme Eisenhower had often stressed, Radford wondered how the United States would cope with such a victory, and "how it might hope to establish a workable occupational regime." The Commander-in-Chief responded, according to the record, "with considerable vehemence and conviction," but in an unexpected way:

[I]n view of the development of the new weapons of mass destruction, with the terrible significance which these involved, everything in any future war with the Soviet bloc would have to be subordinated to winning that war. This was the one thing which must constantly be borne in mind, and there was little else with respect to war objectives that needed to worry anyone very much.

Ten years earlier, Eisenhower added, he might have agreed with Radford, but it was now "impossible and impractical even to consider these suggestions." This "might seem brutal," but because "we would never enter the war except in retaliation against a heavy Soviet atomic attack," there could be no other course than to "hit the Russians where and how it would hurt most."[60]

Only six days earlier Eisenhower had assured Churchill that he understood the "appalling" prospects of a thermonuclear conflagration. Only the day before he had acknowledged, in his press conference, that the BRAVO test had almost gotten out of hand. So what was going on here? How could the President be as concerned as we know he was about the consequences of a nuclear war, and at the same time as determined as he appeared to be—even in top secret discussions with his closest aides—to wage it?

The traditional explanation is economic: that Eisenhower thought the country could afford no other option. Convinced that Truman's conventional-force build-up was bankrupting the country, he shifted to "massive retaliation" to make the costs of containment bearable.[61] Certainly several of Eisenhower's advisers—notably his tight-fisted Treasury Secretary, George Humphrey—thought in just these terms; the President himself was keenly sensitive to the dangers of national insolvency. But the "economy" argument, if not wrong, is narrow, for we now know that Eisenhower was equally sensitive to the environmental consequences of a nuclear war. Hence the paradox: did it really make sense to risk the northern hemisphere just to balance the budget?

The President was even more paradoxical at the 203rd and 204th meetings of the National Security Council, which took place successively on 23 and 24 June 1954. At the first one, Eisenhower came out in favor of *abolishing* nuclear weapons altogether if there could be foolproof methods of verifying such a ban: "Let no one make the mistake . . . of imagining that if such a system were devised the President would not go along with it."[62] But the very next day, before the very same body, he was talking of *initiating* a war before the American nuclear advantage disappeared: "Should the United States now get ready to fight the Soviet Union?" He had "brought up this question more than once," and "had never done so facetiously."[63] How, though, could one be in favor *both* of starting a war to preserve nuclear superiority *and* of eliminating its central component?

There were other contradictions as well. Eisenhower knew that NATO could hardly defend itself without nuclear weapons, but that their use on European battlefields would probably kill more Europeans than would a Russian invasion.[64] He understood that nuclear capabilities were of little value in deterring or resolving "third world" conflicts;[65] but he adamantly opposed building the conventional forces that could play this role. He railed repeatedly against the numbers of nuclear weapons piling up on the American side, knowing that these more than matched what the Russians had;[66] but he did little to stop that process. Nothing, he warned, would be worse than war; but he insisted that the United States would go to war rather than yield even insignificant positions: witness his public threats against Beijing early in 1955, in defense of the two tiny Nationalist-held islands of Quemoy and Matsu, just off the China coast.[67] The Eisenhower record on nuclear weapons is, in short, riddled with *apparent* inconsistencies, and as a result historians have had great difficulty deciding what his strategy really was. He himself, despite the remarkably full record he left behind, did remarkably little to clarify the matter.[68]

But perhaps the consistency resides in the contradictions. In his classic work *On War*, that most subtle of strategists, Carl von Clausewitz, had coupled a vision of total and hence irrational violence with a demonstration of how difficult—and how foolish—it would be to attempt it. Clausewitz of course knew nothing of nuclear weapons: his "absolute war" was an abstraction, set up as a contrast to what military force, in reality, could feasibly accomplish.[69] Eisenhower knew both nuclear weapons and Clausewitz, though, having studied *On War* carefully as a junior officer serving in Panama during the 1920s.[70] And "absolute war" in the 1950s was entirely feasible: far from refuting Clausewitz, this made his method, for the President, all the more urgent. The point was not to design a strategy, which implies getting from here to there. It was rather to hold out a horror, in the interests of *not* getting there. Eisenhower sympathized, therefore, with the position Bradley had taken in 1949: that the best way to avoid a war was to make preparation for it credible while making the prospect of it appalling. Apprised early in 1957 that the United States might suffer 50 million casualties in a nuclear war, Eisenhower's response was unequivocal: "the only sensible thing for us to do was to put all our resources into our SAC [Strategic Air Command] capability and into hydrogen bombs."[71]

Those among the President's advisers who were thinking in terms of *strategy* recoiled from this reasoning. Dulles, we now know, objected strenuously and persistently, on the grounds that such inflexibility would frighten the allies and leave little choice beyond capitulation and all-out war when crises arose.[72] The military services, sensing few opportunities for increasing appropriations or professional advancement, made clear their opposition. So too did a diverse array of outside critics, among them Dean Acheson, Adlai Stevenson, George Kennan, Paul Nitze, John F. Kennedy, and Henry Kissinger.[73] Even Eisenhower's own National Security Council Staff repeatedly turned out studies challenging his position.[74] But the President remained unmoved: he never modified his conviction that *any* war was bound to escalate to the use of nuclear weapons. Not only was there no purpose in preparing for anything else, it would be *dangerous* to prepare for anything else.

Today we can see more clearly than was apparent then what was in Eisenhower's mind: his aim was to avoid all wars, not simply to deter nuclear war.[75] Military superiority, he understood better than anyone, guaranteed neither national nor international security. When bombs got to be the size of BRAVO or bigger, the fact that the Soviet Union had inferior capabilities meant very little: if even a few such weapons got through the effects would be as if thousands had.[76] The only protection was to compel Soviet leaders to see that there could be no advantage in ordering the use of even one. The way to do that was to make the Clausewitzian abstraction of "absolute war" seem as real as it could be. As Bradley had suggested, that required actual operational weapons, together with so credible an *appearance* of a determination to use them that even Eisenhower's closest advisers would not doubt his resolve.

The "flexible response" alternative Conant had recommended—and that so many of the President's critics, including Dulles, had come to support—was for Eisenhower no alternative at all because he saw it as likely to lead toward wars, not away from them. Its worst-case scenario would substitute the use of many atomic for fewer hydrogen bombs, but this would hardly improve matters from an ecological or a humanitarian standpoint. It would increase conventional forces, running up great costs and also great temptations to demonstrate the value of such forces—if only to justify their costs. It would provide few safeguards should the Soviets or the Chinese seek to strain American alliances and drain American resources through Korea-like entanglements: "We must now plan to fight peripheral wars on the same basis as we would fight a general war," Eisenhower insisted early in 1956.[77] The logic of "massive retaliation," in short, was to convince *all* adversaries that *any* such conflict *might* escalate to a level at which *none* could hope to prevail. The term had been "scoffed at," the President acknowledged. But it was "likely to be the key to survival."[78]

IV

Khrushchev, too, was sure that nuclear weapons had their uses; he could even have agreed with Eisenhower on what some of them were. He certainly did not

want a nuclear war, but believed that the best way to prevent one was to accumulate—or at least to appear to accumulate—the means of fighting one. He
understood the importance of credibility, of giving the other side no reason to
doubt his resolve. He saw that nuclear armaments could save money and
imposed even more radical cutbacks in Soviet conventional forces than
Eisenhower did within the United States.[79] He shared the President's sense that
psychology would do more than precise balances to shape world politics: numbers and capabilities of weapons were important, but not nearly as important as
the fears and hopes that existed in people's minds. Beyond that, though, the
similarities did not extend. The greatest difference was that Eisenhower drew
upon a lifetime of experience in dealing with issues of war and peace, while
Khrushchev appears to have relied upon the lessons of two dramatic days.

Early on the morning of 4 November 1956, Soviet forces invaded Hungary,
brutally suppressing the rebellion that had broken out there while blasting
hopes the Eisenhower administration had built up that Eastern Europe might
someday free itself from Moscow's domination. It was "a bitter pill for us to
swallow," the President acknowledged, "but what can we do that is really con-
structive?" The whole business was "shocking to the point of being unbeliev-
able."[80] What made it even more so was the fact that American nuclear
superiority had been useless in this crisis: indeed, fear of the Soviet Union's
wholly *inferior* nuclear capability had convinced Eisenhower of the need to *reassure* the Russians, rather than to *deter* them.

"In view of the serious deterioration of their position in the satellites, might
they not be tempted to resort to very extreme measures and even to precipitate
global war?" the President had asked the National Security Council on 26
October. After all, Hitler had known that "he was licked," but he had nonetheless "carried on to the very last and pulled down Europe with him in his
defeat."[81] With that depressing precedent in mind, Eisenhower arranged for
Dulles to say publicly, the next day, that the United States had "no ulterior purpose in desiring the independence of the satellite countries," and would not
"look upon these nations as potential military allies." He then instructed the
Secretary of State to call his own speech to the attention of Kremlin leaders, a
task Ambassador Charles E. Bohlen performed with Zhukov and Molotov in
Moscow on 30 October. To make certain the message got through Eisenhower
himself reiterated it in a nationally-televised address on 31 October, the same
day the Soviet Presidium gave its approval for military intervention in
Hungary.[82] Khrushchev still had to persuade the other Eastern Europeans and
the Chinese of the need to act—not a difficult task as it turned out—but he
could do so without concern that the United States or NATO might interfere.[83]

Eisenhower's caution on this occasion—critics would call it cowardice—illus-
trated very clearly the limits of nuclear superiority. He and Dulles had concluded soon after taking office that the United States could do little to reduce
the Soviet Union's sphere of influence, or alter its behavior. "The possibility of
war involving large numbers of atomic bombs has become so appalling," one
administration study concluded as early as June 1953, "that the importance of

avoiding it imposes drastic limitations on the policies by which the United States seeks to make progress toward these objectives."[84] The President put it more succinctly shortly thereafter: the question was "how much we should poke the animal through the bars of the cage."[85]

But on that same 4 November, 1956—as the Red Army was entering Budapest—Khrushchev used his nuclear *inferiority* to rattle cages throughout the Western world. Late that evening, he had Bulganin send notes to the British, the French, and the Israelis, asking what position they would find themselves in were they to be

attacked by stronger states, possessing all types of modern destructive weapons? . . . Were rocket weapons used against Britain and France, you would, most probably, call this a barbarous action. But how does the inhuman attack launched by the armed forces of Britain and France against a practically defenceless Egypt differ from this? . . . We are fully determined to crush the aggressors by the use of force and to restore peace in the [Middle] East.[86]

The occasion of course was the simultaneous Suez crisis, which Eisenhower was about to resolve by ordering the British and the French to accept a cease-fire. The Soviet warning, received on 5 November had no comparable impact on their decision to comply.[87] Because Eisenhower's ultimatum had been secret and Bulganin's public, however, there *appeared* to have been a cause-and-effect relationship. Khrushchev was certain of it: "The governments of England and France knew perfectly well that Eisenhower's speech condemning their aggression was just a gesture for the sake of public appearances. But when we delivered our own stern warning to the three aggressors, they knew we weren't playing games with public opinion. They took us very seriously."[88]

Surely there was something strange in all of this. The United States, at that time, had unquestioned military superiority over the Soviet Union. It was ahead in the development of thermonuclear weapons, as Khrushchev later admitted.[89] It now had so many atomic bombs that it had begun deploying them at the "tactical" level within NATO. Its Navy vastly outclassed any potential opponent. Its Strategic Air Command possessed such devastating capabilities—and such sophisticated means of jamming Soviet air defenses—that its commander could boast, if a war were to come,

[b]etween sunset tonight and sunrise tomorrow morning the Soviet Union would likely cease to be a major military power or even a major nation. . . . Dawn might break over a nation infinitely poorer than China—less populated than the United States, and condemned to an agrarian existence perhaps for generations to come.[90]

His own losses in such an all-out nuclear strike, General Curtis LeMay estimated, would not greatly exceed normal accident rates.[91] And yet—on 4–5 November 1956, it had been the *militarily weaker* Soviet Union, not the United States, that took the offensive. Nor would Khrushchev relinquish it for the next six years.

No one can be sure what would have happened if Eisenhower had issued a Khrushchev-like ultimatum warning the Soviet Union not to invade Hungary.

The idea was apparently discussed within the government,[92] but there is no evidence that the President ever seriously considered it. Despite assurances from Bohlen and the intelligence community that the Russians were not about to start World War III, Eisenhower continued to worry that with "their policy failing so badly in the satellites," the Kremlin leaders might be "ready to take any wild adventure. . . . [T]he Soviets are scared and furious, and there is nothing more dangerous than a dictatorship in this state of mind."[93]

There were other reasons for caution as well. Eisenhower had learned, from the public response to Dulles's "massive retaliation" speech and the BRAVO test in 1954, how careful one had to be, in a democratic country and within a democratic alliance, with what might even *appear* to be a threat to go nuclear: "our allies are absolutely scared to death that we will use such weapons."[94] Then there was the problem of where to stop: what would he do, Dulles had asked at one point, if after a nuclear warning the Vietminh went ahead and attacked South Vietnam: "Would we proceed to drop atomic bombs on Peking?" Eisenhower for once had no firm answer.[95] Finally, knowing that American capabilities were superior, Eisenhower had come to feel that he should not *have* to rely upon explicit threats to use them. Putting credibility on the line in small crises—even in large ones—might cheapen it: "Of course, in the defense of the United States itself we will certainly use nuclear weapons, but to use them in other situations will prove very difficult."[96]

For Khrushchev, though, even a few nuclear weapons could be very useful indeed. Public opinion did not constrain him from making threats. Since he had no plans actually to bomb Britain and France, he had no need to worry about how to implement them. And precisely because Soviet capabilities *were* inferior to those of the United States, it was vital not to appear to be intimidated *by* the United States: being behind required being belligerent.[97] Khrushchev here was repeating, not repudiating, Stalin's example; but he had an even better reason for respecting it. With all his faults, the old tyrant had foreseen, much more clearly than the Americans, how important long-range missiles were going to be.

"Stalin had a great instinct for technical things," Molotov recalled. He was "a fast learner and was quick to grasp anything new."[98] His ideas did not always work out: we now know that he pushed, in 1947, for something called the "antipodal bomber," a manned supersonic aircraft that was supposed to reach the United States from Soviet bases by hurling itself beyond the earth's atmosphere, and in 1949 for a huge "super-torpedo," armed with an atomic warhead, which when launched from a submarine was to penetrate an American harbor and blow the whole place up.[99] But with help from a few of Hitler's rocket scientists the missiles did take off, and Stalin was quick to exploit the breakthrough. The Americans, who had more German assistance, did less with it: they continued to rely chiefly on manned bombers, allowing the Soviet Union for the first time to lead the world in a potentially lethal form of weaponry.[100]

Stalin's successors, from whom he had withheld information on most of these developments, therefore inherited an unexpected legacy. Khrushchev has vividly described the Politburo's first briefing from Sergei Korolev, who played much the same role in developing the Soviet Union's missiles as Igor Kurchatov had with its atomic bomb:

[W]e gawked at what he showed us as if we were a bunch of sheep seeing a new gate for the first time. When he showed us one of his rockets, we thought it looked like nothing but a huge cigar-shaped tube, and we didn't believe it could fly. . . . We were like peasants in a marketplace. We walked around and around the rocket, touching it, tapping it to see if it was sturdy enough—we did everything but lick it to see how it tasted.[101]

The implications soon sank in, though, and by April of 1956, on his first and only visit to London, Khrushchev was finding it difficult to contain his excitement. When Mrs. Anthony Eden politely asked, over dinner, about the capabilities of Soviet missiles, he blurted out: "[T]hey have a very long range. They could easily reach your island and quite a bit further." It was "a little rude of me to have answered her as I did," Khrushchev later admitted. "We didn't mean to threaten anyone. We were simply trying to remind other countries that we were powerful and deserved respect, and that we wouldn't tolerate being talked to in the language of ultimatums."[102]

His reminders became more credible on 21 August 1957, when the Soviet Union successfully tested the world's first intercontinental ballistic missile: launched from Kazakhstan, its dummy warhead splashed down in the Pacific Ocean, some 4,000 miles away. Khrushchev himself witnessed a second launch on 7 September and was sufficiently impressed to authorize the use of a third ICBM on 4 October to send a simple satellite into orbit around the earth.[103] *Sputnik*, even more than BRAVO, brought the Cold War, quite literally, close to home. One needed no Geiger counter to measure this new manifestation of potential nuclear danger. All that was necessary was to look up, on a clear night, to see the sunlight reflecting off the spent rocket casing as it tumbled slowly in orbit, right over one's own house.[104]

People seemed to think, Eisenhower had warned the National Security Council, that "the country which first achieved an intercontinental ballistic missile would rule the world." He was "somewhat skeptical" of this, but he did not doubt "the profound and overriding political and psychological importance of the U.S. achieving such a weapon."[105] The President remained calmer than most Americans when the Russians got there first, although he could not resist reminding a group of scientists that he had "given top priority to the development of operational ballistic missiles at the earliest possible date." Would it not be useful, one of them responded, to have a presidential science advisor, who "could help the President not to forget such policy decisions?" Here even Eisenhower snapped: "The President interjected with vehemence that *he* had not forgotten this view but that those charged with the program had."[106]

Having managed to upset Mrs. Eden on his visit to London, and then the British and the French at the time of Suez, and now Eisenhower, the Americans, and much of the rest of the world with *Sputnik*, Khrushchev could see the outlines of a strategy emerging:

Of course, we tried to derive maximum political advantage from the fact that we were the first to launch our rockets into space. We wanted to exert pressure on American militarists—and also influence the minds of more reasonable politicians—so that the United States would start treating us better.

To be sure, the military balance still favored the West: "Our missiles were still imperfect in performance and insignificant in number. Taken by themselves, they didn't represent much of a threat to the United States."[107] But in a nuclear age, the uses of military force were as much psychological as actual—and the psychological effects of Soviet space achievements were too tempting to pass up: "I made speeches to bolster the morale of my people. I wanted to give our enemy pause . . . . I exaggerated a little. I said that we had the capability of shooting a fly out of space with our missiles."[108] "It always sounded good to say in public speeches that we could hit a fly at any distance with our missiles."[109]

As Khrushchev knew very well, there was a long history in Russia of what one might call "Potemkinism": building just enough of a capability to create the illusion that much more lay behind it.[110] The trick had sometimes even succeeded. He himself had witnessed an example as recently as the July 1955 Moscow air show, when the Soviet Air Force painted over the identifying numbers on the few "Bison" bombers it had and then flew them over the reviewing stand several times, alarming Western military observers and setting off a brief but intense "bomber gap" controversy in the United States.[111] "They really made an impression," Khrushchev later recalled.[112] He had not really been "thinking of going to war" on 5 November 1956, he admitted. But "the Soviet Union's latest threats of war had been correct and necessary."[113] Their results may well have convinced him that he could get away with a similar deception on a larger and more ambitious scale.[114]

For had he not, in two days' work, reasserted Soviet authority in Hungary, halted the British–French–Israeli invasion of Egypt, and humiliated the Americans, who despite their overwhelming military superiority had done nothing to stop him? Had he not balanced the embarrassment of having to use force in Eastern Europe with the prestige that came from thwarting imperialism in the Middle East? Had he not confounded his domestic critics, who would otherwise have seen his leadership as inept, even disastrous? And had he not accomplished all of this from a militarily inferior position for which he had compensated with loud talk? It was just the sort of brilliant improvisation Khrushchev loved; he would have been less than human not to have seen in it a pattern for the future. And Khrushchev was very human indeed.

V

John Foster Dulles had warned, even before the Hungarian and Suez crises, that despite his reforms Khrushchev was "the most dangerous person to lead the Soviet Union since the October Revolution." Previous Soviet leaders had behaved like chess players: Stalin "always calculated the results of a proposed action. Bad as he was, you at least knew what you were up against in dealing with him." Khrushchev, however, was "not a coldly calculating person, but rather one who reacted emotionally. He was obviously intoxicated much of the time and could be expected to commit irrational acts."[115] Dulles was wrong about Khrushchev's drinking habits, for despite several colorful episodes these do not appear to have caused him major difficulties.[116] But if one switches the intoxicant from alcohol to missiles, then the diagnosis becomes quite accurate.

Probably as a result of what he had accomplished on 4–5 November 1956— certainly as a consequence of what Soviet rocket scientists would achieve over the next year—Khrushchev went on a binge that would last through the end of the decade. It was, a close contemporary observer noted, as if "the sputnik is in itself sufficient to make up for all the weaknesses of the Soviet Union, as though it could provide the answer to everybody who has criticized the Soviet Union in any field."[117] As his missile-dependency deepened, Khrushchev began to act much as alcoholics tend to: his moods swung wildly between expansive amia- bility and boorish belligerence, he often acted on impulse, he became increas- ingly desperate as time went on. And he definitely failed the test of any good chess player, which is to think ahead.

Symptoms of Khrushchev's addiction began to appear in the wake of the first successful Soviet ICBM test. On 8 September 1957, *Pravda* ran an interview with Air Marshal Konstantin Vershinin implying that the USSR could now hit distant targets precisely and with little warning; only later did his commander-in-chief acknowledge that he had told Vershinin what to say.[118] Once *Sputnik* went up the following month, Khrushchev could no longer resist rubbing it in himself, assuring James Reston of the *New York Times* that "[w]e now have all the rockets we need: long-range rockets, intermediate-range rockets, and short- range rockets." After a second *Sputnik* orbited in November, he boasted to pub- lisher William Randolph Hearst, Jr., that "[i]f necessary, tomorrow we can launch 10, 20 satellites. All that is required for this is to replace the warhead of an intercontinental ballistic rocket with the necessary instruments. There is a satellite for you." Those same rockets Khrushchev added, just in case Hearst had missed the point, "now make it possible to hit a target in any area of the globe."[119]

These were gross exaggerations, for although the Soviet Union was deploying intermediate-range missiles that could reach some parts of Europe, it had no capability for multiple ICBM or satellite launches, and it was years away from precision targeting. The huge size and unreliable character of the Semyorka, the Russians' first ICBM, made it so unsuitable as an operational weapon that Khrushchev decided to skip putting it into production to concentrate instead on developing more sophisticated models. As a result, throughout the entire Eisenhower administration the Soviet Union's *total* arsenal of functional ICBMs would consist of *four* unprotected and highly visible Semyorkas based at a single, swampy site south of Archangel.[120] All the rest were imaginary.

It would take a while for the Americans to discover that, though, and in the meantime Khrushchev's rhetorical rockets produced an enormous impact in the United States. The editors of *Life* set the tone, claiming that the Soviets had "burst upon the world as the infinitely sinister front runners in the sophisticated and perilous science of space."[121] A presidential commission assigned to review the nation's defenses turned in such a pessimistic report, in the wake of *Sputnik*, that Eisenhower promptly classified it.[122] To little avail, though, because the well-informed columnist Joseph Alsop was soon predicting that the Russians within three years would have 1,000 ICBMs and the Americans only 70. This dangerous "missile gap" would give Moscow "unchallengeable superiority in the nuclear striking power that was once our specialty."[123]

How Khrushchev expected Western leaders to respond to his post-Sputnik braggadocio is not clear; but if he anticipated a replay of his Suez crisis triumph, he did not get it. Instead Eisenhower rattled a few weapons of his own, ticking off with grim specificity on national television the overwhelming retaliatory capability manned bombers, overseas bases, and a blue-water navy gave the United States: "as of today the over-all military strength of the Free World is distinctly greater than that of the Communist countries."[124] He also accelerated efforts already under way to create a NATO atomic stockpile and added a new initiative: an offer to station Thor and Jupiter intermediate-range ballistic missiles, equipped with thermonuclear warheads, at European bases.

Eisenhower regarded these IRBMs—still under development—as likely to be of little military significance when set against the multiple means of war-fighting already available to the United States. The point, though, was not to have a war, and from that perspective asymmetries in any category of weaponry if allowed to persist could create the basis for one, whether through a collapse of morale on one's own side or overconfidence on the other. The Thor and Jupiter deployments were to be a stop-gap measure, a "quick fix" designed to balance the Soviet IRBMs, to shield NATO until American ICBMs were ready, and to reassure the Europeans that even then they would retain, on their territory, means of defending themselves.[125] The first tangible result of Khrushchev's missile bluff, therefore, was a United States commitment to place actual missiles at points in Europe from which they could reach Soviet targets, an outcome he clearly did not anticipate.[126]

Eisenhower and Dulles, for their part, failed to foresee that this decision would reactivate long-standing Soviet suspicions that the Americans were about to arm the West Germans with nuclear weapons. There were no such plans, but the Americans refused to say so clearly because they thought it important to give their NATO partners some *sense* of control over the weapons deployed on their soil, even as the Americans were determined to retain actual control.[127] Ambiguities intended to reassure allies hence unsettled adversaries, and the Thor-Jupiter offer intensified the unease.

Like several of his other initiatives, Khrushchev's 1958 November ultimatum on Berlin was a single stone aimed at several birds:[128] anxiety over the stability of Ulbricht's East German regime, Chinese pressure to get tough with the imperialists, the possibility of exploiting the city's exposed position as "the testicles of the West." But at the center of his decision, made by all accounts on the spur of the moment, was an odd combination of nuclear fear mixed with nuclear arrogance. The fear was that unless he did something to stop the process, some Germans might soon gain some access to some nuclear weapons, as well as missiles capable of delivering them.[129] The arrogance arose from Khrushchev's sense that, despite his earlier failure to intimidate the Americans with his claims that a "missile gap" had left them far behind, he could now remove the German danger by turning up the volume of these assertions and increasing their frequency.[130]

Many exhibitions of Khrushchevian blustering followed. The most revealing of these, for what it showed of his ideological as well as his geostrategic thinking, was an extraordinary nine-hour conversation with former ambassador W. Averell Harriman in Moscow on 23 June 1959. Communism, Khrushchev instructed his guest, was "a new and higher form of social organization [which was] bound to replace capitalism," but that did not mean that Communism "would physically bury the capitalist world." Making revolution was up to proletarians in each country, and Harriman could take comfort in the fact that "the US is so rich and its standard of living so high that for the time being it can postpone revolution because it is able to buy off or bribe the workers." History was on the side of the Soviet Union, though, and so too was the military balance: "We developed the hydrogen bomb before the US. We have an intercontinental bomb which you have not. Perhaps this is the crucial symbol of our position."

It would take only a few Soviet missiles to destroy Europe: "One bomb was sufficient for Bonn and three to five would knock out France, England, Spain, and Italy." The United States would be in no position to retaliate because its missiles "could carry a warhead of only ten kilograms whereas Russian missiles could carry 1300 kilograms." But Khrushchev hastily added: "We are not aggressive. . . . We don't need West Berlin. . . . If we took West Berlin, we would simply have to feed it. We would rather let you feed it." Nevertheless, "[y]our generals talk of tanks and guns defending your Berlin position. They would burn." Still, "we don't want war over Berlin."

Having failed, with these gyrations, to shake Harriman, Khrushchev then shifted to another angle of attack: "You may have millions, but I have grandsons." The dispossessed of the world would inevitably prevail: after all, he himself had been a miner. As if on cue, Mikoyan added that he had been a plumber, Gromyko that he had been the son of a beggar, and First Deputy Premier Frol Kozlov that he had been a "homeless waif." Unmoved, Harriman responded that he too had "many contacts among the working class." This sent Khrushchev back to threats, but in terms he thought a "great capitalist" would understand:

If we spend 30 billion rubles on ballistic missiles in the next 5–6 years, we can destroy every great industrial center in the US and Europe. Thirty billion rubles is no great sum for us. In the Seven Year Plan, we are spending on power, gas, etc., no less than 125 billion rubles. Yet to destroy all of Europe and the US would cost us only

30 billion. We have this possibility. . . . I am frank because I like you as a frank capitalist. You charm us as a snake charms rabbits.

But then he flip-flopped again: "Or course, we will make some missiles but we won't use them. We know if you use yours, it would be silly. Who would lose more? Let us keep our rockets loaded and if attacked we will launch them."[131]

Most people would have found so schizophrenic a conversation with so powerful a leader alarming in the extreme, and surely that was what Khrushchev intended. Not Harriman, though: he knew inferiority complexes when he saw them; he was not about to be bullied by the kind of person who could say, in effect: "I'm going to destroy your country. Now let's have a nice lunch." His response—quite effective as it turned out—was simply to laugh.

[Khrushchev] asked, "What are you laughing about?" I said, "What you're talking about would lead to war and I know you're too sensible a man to want to have a war." He stopped a minute and looked at me and he said, "You're right."[132]

The "performance," Harriman reported succinctly, had been "all bluff." It suggested: "(1) Khrushchev's present lack of confidence in his missiles; (2) his desire to bolster the East German regime; (3) the possibility of progress in disarmament." Eisenhower should "keep the conversations going with the Soviets" but avoid pressing them, as Khrushchev was "an impetuous man whose reactions to ultimatums might be unpredictable."[133]

The President's response was much the same as Harriman's: anyone who behaved *that* oddly was only betraying insecurity. "[W]hat we have to do is to 'thaw out' the Russian defenses," he noted on 1 July. Several weeks later, advising Vice President Richard Nixon on what tone to take during his upcoming trip to the USSR, he recommended "a cordial, almost light, atmosphere, on the basis that once the Soviets get us worried they act tough."[134] Eisenhower was himself worried: "we are getting to the point where we must decide if we are trying to prepare to fight a war, or to prevent one."[135] But he was careful not to show this beyond his most immediate advisers. "About Berlin," he told them,

we say we will never have our rights there diminished. The Russians say this is an illogical position. We admit it is illogical, but we will not abandon our rights and responsibilities—unless there is a way made for us to do so.[136]

The comment was quintessential Eisenhower: hold out the prospect of an ultimate irrationality—all-out war—as a means of maintaining a more immediate irrationality—the West's outpost in the middle of East Germany—"unless there is a way made for us" to do otherwise. But what might that "way" be? An overwhelming application of Soviet military force? A negotiated settlement? Eisenhower never said, and probably he did not know.

Clarification, as it turned out, was unnecessary, because Khrushchev responded instantly when Eisenhower sought to "thaw" him out: all it took was an invitation to visit the United States.[137] Having threatened repeatedly to incinerate the place, the Kremlin leader was now thrilled to be invited to tour it. By the time he arrived in September, Khrushchev was on what was, for him, his best behavior, lifting the ultimatum on Berlin, stressing the need for "peaceful coexistence," and inviting Eisenhower to visit the Soviet Union the following year. He threatened to use his missiles only once, against the Mayor of Los Angeles, who had tried to score political points by being obnoxious.[138] He turned down an opportunity to witness an American missile launch, no doubt for fear he would have to reciprocate;[139] although in what may have been a sly gesture of self-confidence, the administration arranged for Khrushchev to take a special train up the California coast which passed through the middle of Vandenberg Air Force Base, where the first highly secret reconnaissance satellites were already being test-launched.[140]

The "thaw" produced no moderation in Khrushchev's claims about Soviet missile capabilities: "We now have stockpiled so many rockets, so many atomic and hydrogen warheads," he announced in November 1959, "that, if we were attacked, we could wipe from the face of the earth all of our probable opponents."[141] But by this time the United States was, quite obviously, catching up: its first ICBM, the Atlas, had become operational in 1958, second- and third-generation Titan and Minuteman ICBMs were under development as were hardened underground silos for them, and the Navy would soon deploy its remarkably efficient Polaris submarine-launched ballistic missile, a system that far surpassed Soviet experiments with such weapons.[142] These realities must have begun to sink in, for when United Nations Ambassador Henry Cabot Lodge, who had escorted Khrushchev around the United States, paid a return visit to Moscow in February 1960 and commented that the Russians were still ahead in strategic missiles, Khrushchev in an unguarded moment responded honestly, for once: "no we're not; not really."[143]

VI

Eisenhower already knew that. Well before Khrushchev came up with his "Potemkin" strategy, the Americans and their allies had begun to penetrate the secrecy upon which it depended. Traditional forms of espionage had produced few benefits: the West, by all accounts, placed no spies comparable to those the Russians recruited from the Manhattan Project or the British intelligence establishment. The CIA lacked even a low-ranking "mole" within the Soviet government until just before Stalin's death. "For all the money we spent on espionage," one of its officials later recalled, "nobody knew a helluva lot about what was happening in Moscow."[144] But technology was making possible an alternative approach, and here the Americans would in time excel.

We now know that Truman's administration, not Eisenhower's, began aerial reconnaissance over the Soviet Union. It took two forms: quick dashes into Soviet airspace by aircraft fitted out with cameras and electronic sensors; and the launching of hundreds of similarly equipped balloons designed to float over the territory of the USSR for subsequent recovery. Most of the complaints the

Russians made about such "provocations" hence had some basis; although spotty coverage and sporadic frequency meant that few of these operations produced useful information.[145] What Eisenhower did was to devise new and ultimately much more effective methods.

One of these was a far-sighted attempt to shift reconnaissance out of the realm of espionage altogether. Arms control could not rely upon ground inspections alone, the President told the British and French delegations at the July 1955 Geneva summit, because with thermonuclear weapons it was possible "to conceal enough explosive material to defeat a nation in a relatively small space." But, he added cryptically,

other things could be observed, among these was the means of delivery of these weapons. We might start off by devising a method of inspection that would be mutually acceptable, picking out items to be inspected. . . . A large item, such as 4-engine bombers could be checked on as it required large fields and factories to produce it. The same was true for atomic cannon, warships, and there might be other things that could be added to this. If this were done, what would be left to a potential aggressor[?] His capability for surprise would be severely limited.[146]

These comments foreshadowed Eisenhower's ostensibly "spontaneous" proposal to the Russians, a few days later, that each side allow aerial photography by the other.[147] He had carefully planned the "Open Skies" initiative, however, and it was not just a propaganda maneuver. Eisenhower was already anticipating reconnaissance satellites: he saw his idea as an important step toward legitimizing their use.[148]

Khrushchev turned it down as a ploy to gather intelligence, if not a joke. "Sometimes," he told Eisenhower, "someone would make a very far-reaching proposition expecting that the other person would not accept it; then if the other person were to accept it, the individual who proposed it would hardly know what to do." The President, unamused, reacted coldly: "Do you want to try me?"[149] Khrushchev did not, and the chances of his responding otherwise were remote. With few arms control experts and fewer means of evaluating new arms control proposals, Soviet leaders could take years—sometimes a decade or more—to accustom themselves to such innovative thinking.[150] Eisenhower, who had an alternative almost ready, was not prepared to wait: "I'll give it one shot. Then if they don't accept it, we'll fly the U-2."[151]

He had ordered development of this revolutionary aircraft in November, 1954, and by the time he went to Geneva eight months later Lockheed had it almost ready for flight-testing.[152] The U-2 flew its first operational missions, directly over Leningrad and Moscow, on 4 and 5 July 1956. Radar immediately detected it, but because the plane was well above the range of Soviet fighters and missiles, all the Russians could do was protest.[153] A pattern thus formed, whereby U-2s would fly carefully selected routes over the USSR, Khrushchev would immediately learn of the intrusion and sometimes file a complaint, and Washington would ignore it.[154] Embarrassment, on both sides, kept each from acknowledging what was happening: the Russians found it humiliating to have lost control of their airspace; the Americans were loath to admit that they were violating it. The U-2, then, was one of the first of many Cold War secrets Washington and Moscow shared, but kept—or tried to keep—from the rest of the world.[155]

The overflights quickly established that there was no "bomber gap," for as Eisenhower had anticipated aircraft facilities were highly visible and the numbers did not add up.[156] Counting missiles took longer, partly because Soviet IRBMs were based in remote areas and harder to see, but also for the very good reason that the ICBMs Khrushchev had claimed to have did not exist: the U-2s were searching for phantoms. Not until 1959, therefore, did sufficient evidence accumulate to suggest strategic "Potemkinism." The U-2s had discovered *no* ICBM launch platforms, Secretary of Defense Neil McElroy reported to Eisenhower on 12 February, which led him to ask for more overflights to try to find the ones that must surely exist. But the President had begun to suspect the truth, noting that as the bomber experience had shown, "we generally overestimate the capability of the USSR to outperform us." Any extensive new round of U-2 missions would be an "undue provocation," and "most unwise": after all, nothing would more quickly cause *him* to "request authority to declare war . . . than violation of our air space by Soviet aircraft."[157]

Eisenhower pointed out, on that occasion, that "the satellite, since it does not violate air space, . . . represents the greatest future in the reconnaissance area."[158] But it proved much more difficult to develop than had the U-2. The requirement was for an orbiting camera to eject a film capsule, which after re-entering the atmosphere would be snagged in mid-air by a specially equipped C-119 "flying boxcar." The first test took place within two weeks of Eisenhower's talk with McElroy, but after a year of frustrating failures the system still had not worked.[159] Had there been better luck, there would have been no need for the two U-2 flights the President reluctantly did authorize prior to the May 1960 Paris summit; even as things stood, he was tolerating intelligence overkill for there was little basis left to suspect a missile gap. There was, however, an increasingly potent Soviet anti-aircraft capability, and that was what brought down Francis Gary Powers over Sverdlovsk on May Day, as well as one of the Russians' own fighters that had scrambled to intercept him.[160] The flights both sides had tacitly agreed to conceal suddenly became very public.

The U-2 crisis exposed the impulsiveness and erratic improvisation that had already begun to show up in Khrushchev's behavior behind the scenes: as in his conversation with Harriman a year earlier, it is difficult to determine what he was trying to accomplish. He first sought to embarrass Eisenhower by gleefully withholding details until after the administration had issued a string of increasingly implausible cover stories. Having achieved this humiliation, Khrushchev then tried to rehabilitate the President's reputation by claiming that he could not possibly have known what his subordinates were doing—thereby goading the infuriated Eisenhower into acknowledging that he had personally approved each overflight. Despite this rebuff, Khrushchev gave every indication that he wanted the Paris summit to proceed, allowing his staff to prepare detailed position papers and even selecting a suitably impressive airplane in which to arrive.

Literally in mid-flight, though, he began to rethink his position: "I became more and more convinced that our pride and dignity would be damaged if we went ahead with the meeting as though nothing had happened."[161] So he redrafted his opening statement to demand a public apology from Eisenhower, and on arriving in Paris, as one of his own aides recalls it, "Khrushchev began play-acting." It was, Anatoly Dobrynin remembers, an "emotional attempt to bluff an apology out of Eisenhower by threatening to ruin the summit. He failed."[162]

Years later, when dictating his memoirs, Khrushchev seemed proud of the fact that "we had left Moscow with a set of documents pointing in one direction, and we landed in Paris with documents pointing in the opposite direction."[163] There was a perverse symmetry in the fact that a summit imperiled by the downing of one airplane was wrecked altogether by what happened on another. But the Soviet leader had little sense of what seems, in retrospect, most important about the U-2: that it had given Eisenhower the assurance he needed to *restrain* American military spending, and hence—indirectly—to ease the Soviet Union's own military burden.[164] It was also a very strange way to make policy: Moscow's position in world affairs was coming to depend, once again, upon the moods, whims, and impulses of a single dominant figure.[165] This one, however, was a good deal more volatile than Stalin had ever been—and he had a good many more weapons than Stalin had ever possessed.

"I'm still convinced that we handled the matter correctly," Khrushchev insisted: "if we hadn't stood up to the Americans, they would have continued to send spies into our territory."[166] This, too, is a curious remark, because on 18 August 1960, only three and a half months after the U-2 was shot down, the first successful Discoverer satellite went up from the California launchpad he himself had passed within sight of eleven months earlier. The next day, after this new "uninvited guest" had passed over the Soviet Union seventeen times, it ejected a film capsule and a waiting C-119 managed to hook it on the third attempt. The first fuzzy image was that of a Soviet airfield on a remote peninsula. Resolution was not as sharp as in the U-2's photographs, but it was impressive enough: objects as small as 20–30 feet across were visible. More impressive was the fact that this single roll of film from a single day's orbit yielded more coverage of Soviet territory than had *four years* of U-2 overflights.[167]

It would take many months and several more satellite launches to evaluate this flood of information, but by 21 September 1961 the CIA had seen enough to produce a national intelligence estimate reporting "a sharp downward revision in our estimate of present Soviet ICBM strength." Although the Russians now had between 250 and 300 operational IRBMs, the number of ICBMs capable of reaching the United States was between 10 and 25, and "this force level will not increase markedly during the months immediately ahead."[168] Joe Alsop, well-connected as always, published the story within four days: far from there being 1000 ICBMs, as he had predicted there would be three years earlier, it now looked as though the correct figure was "well under 50 . . . and, therefore, not nearly enough to allow the Soviets to consider a surprise attack on this country."[169]

Eisenhower's accomplishment in perfecting espionage from above, first with the U-2 and then through satellites, reversed a great geopolitical asymmetry: the Soviet Union's ability to keep its capabilities concealed, for the most part, from its adversaries. Still haunted by Pearl Harbor and the fears of surprise attack that memory inspired, the Americans had felt that they had little choice, throughout the first decade and a half of the Cold War, but to assume the worst and act accordingly. The new technologies of reconnaissance allowed first a glimpse, and then an impression, and then an unobstructed view of what lay behind the facade, and as a consequence a great many anxieties—at least for those cleared to receive this information—began to dissipate.

VII

Why, though, did Khrushchev keep up the facade for as long as he did? He must have realized from the day the first U-2 flew over the Soviet Union how difficult it was going to be to sustain strategic claims based on so little substance. He seems to have understood that the first-generation Semyorka ICBMs would be visible to aerial surveillance and hence vulnerable to attack: that may be one of the reasons he built so few of them.[170] He could see, from the film Powers exposed on his ill-fated mission, how sharp U-2 photographs were.[171] He knew about reconnaissance satellites: "Let them take as many pictures as they want," he retorted, at the Paris summit, when President Charles de Gaulle pointed out that they would soon be passing overhead.[172] And yet Khrushchev could still tell the United Nations General Assembly, in September 1960 that the Soviet Union was turning out missiles "like sausages from an automatic machine, rocket after rocket."[173]

"How can you say that," Sergei Khrushchev, himself a rocket engineer, recalls demanding of his father, "since we only have two or three?" Khrushchev responded by evading the issue: "The important thing is to make the Americans believe that. And that way we prevent an attack."[174] Addiction provides a possible explanation for why he thought he could get away with this even after the United States had perfected its reconnaissance capabilities. Alcoholics and smokers can know perfectly well that their habits are hurting and may even be killing them, and yet find it extraordinarily hard to give them up. Khrushchev had staked ideological ambitions, national prestige, and personal reputation on his missile claims. It would not have been easy to abandon them even under great pressure to do so. There was no such pressure, moreover, because Eisenhower never called his bluff. Why he did not is still a puzzle: perhaps sensitivity about revealing intelligence "sources and methods," possibly a reluctance to act without conclusive confirmation from reconnaissance satellites, very likely his own immense self-confidence, his conviction that it was quite enough to assure Americans they were safe without specifying the reasons.[175] But Khrushchev's greatest problem in abandoning strategic "Potemkinism" would have been with his allies: for even as technology was causing his adversaries to doubt his claims, ideology was leading his fellow Marxist-Leninists to take them all too seriously.

When Mao Zedong came to Moscow in November 1957 to celebrate the 40th anniversary of the Bolshevik Revolution, Khrushchev's euphoria was at its highest point. The first ICBMs and *Sputniks* had just been launched; the difficulties that would slow such accomplishments in the future were not yet evident. Despite his dislike for the new Kremlin boss and his objections to de-Stalinization, Mao jumped to the conclusion that these impressive technological feats had "objectively" advanced the cause of Marxism-Leninism: hence his famous announcement on that occasion that "the East wind" was now "prevailing over the West wind." When combined with China's inexhaustible manpower reserves and the rising revolutionary tide in the "third world," these new manifestations of Soviet military might made "the socialist forces . . . overwhelmingly superior to the imperialist forces."[176] "We shouldn't fear war," Khrushchev recalls Mao as having told the assembled comrades:

We shouldn't be afraid of atomic bombs and missiles. No matter what kind of war breaks out—conventional or thermonuclear—we'll win. As for China, if the imperialists unleash war on us, we may lose more than three hundred million people. So what? War is war. The years will pass, and we'll get to work producing more babies than ever before.

"What about us?" Czechoslovak leader Antonin Novotny wanted to know. "We have only twelve million people. . . . We'd lose every last soul in a war. There wouldn't be anyone left to start over." Khrushchev shared the sentiment, and found Mao's attitude profoundly unsettling: "I couldn't tell from his face whether he was joking or not."[177]

It was indeed, at times, hard to tell. Mao had long deprecated nuclear weapons as "paper tigers." He ignored Eisenhower's threats to use them during the Korean War, and paid only slightly greater attention during the Indochina crisis the following year. These episodes are misleading, though, because Mao still seems to have expected the Sino-Soviet Treaty to provide "extended deterrence" against American retaliation.[178] When the Russians made it clear, after he began shelling Quemoy and Matsu in September 1954, that they would not in fact shield him, Mao quickly ordered a crash program to build his own atomic bomb.[179] The date was 15 January 1955, two months *before* Eisenhower and Dulles got around to making a new round of even more explicit nuclear threats in defense of the Nationalist-held offshore islands.[180]

Although he assured his scientists that materialist dialectics made nuclear physics easy,[181] Mao assumed from the outset that they would need help and that Moscow would provide it. The Russians, eager to smooth things over, came through generously (if nervously), especially after the Chinese supported Khrushchev's crushing of the Hungarian uprising in the fall of 1956.[182] They worried, though, that Mao had not yet grasped what a nuclear war would mean. Mikoyan tried to explain these matters on a visit to Beijing, but with little success: "The Soviet Union is . . . . afraid we might provoke the United States," Mao concluded. "But we're not afraid of getting into trouble with other countries. I will definitely develop the atom bomb."[183]

One can interpret Mao's November 1957 Moscow performance, therefore, in several ways. The simplest is that he believed what he said: that China really could withstand a nuclear war better than anyone else, because there were more Chinese than anyone else. But he may also have been seeking to stiffen ideological resolve among the Russians and their East European allies who, as he saw it, had yet to recognize their own strength.[184] He could have been trying to embarrass Khrushchev by taking his missile claims more literally than even their maker had intended. And—being Mao—he could have had all of these purposes in mind at the same time: as his host noted, it was hard to tell.

When Khrushchev himself visited Beijing at the beginning of August 1958, Mao tried to persuade him—in one of his swimming-pool conversations—that "we obviously have the advantage over our enemies." The Soviets need only "provoke the Americans into military action, and I'll give you as many divisions as you need to crush them—a hundred, two hundred, one thousand divisions." Trying desperately to remain afloat, Khrushchev reminded Mao "that one or two missiles could turn all the divisions in China to dust. But he wouldn't even listen to my arguments and obviously regarded me as a coward."[185] That was true enough: "He wants to improve relations with the United States?" Mao exploded afterwards:

Good, we'll congratulate him with our guns. Our cannon shells have been in storage for so long they're becoming useless. So why don't we just use them for a celebration? Let's get the United States involved, too. Maybe we can get the United States to drop an atom bomb on Fujian. Maybe ten or twenty million people will be killed. Chiang Kai-shek wants the United States to use the bomb against us. Let them use it. Let's see what Khrushchev says then.[186]

Such a "celebration" was already in the works. Two days after United States forces landed in Lebanon on 15 July—and two weeks before Khrushchev's arrival in Beijing—Mao had authorized preparations for a new confrontation in the Taiwan Strait, one that would "pin down the U.S. imperialist [and] prove that China supports the national liberation movements in the Middle East with not only words but also deeds."[187] The shelling of Quemoy began on 23 August—with no warning whatever to Moscow.[188] "[O]ur Chinese friends, basing their position on the assumption that the solution of the Taiwan issue was solely the domestic affair of China, had not informed the Soviet government beforehand about their plans," the Soviet embassy in Beijing reported to Moscow. "It would not be entirely correct to regard the solution of the Taiwan issue . . . as purely a domestic affair of China."[189]

Concerned that things were getting out of hand, Khrushchev sent Gromyko to Beijing, where he arrived on 6 September. What he heard there shook even the unshakeable Soviet foreign minister. The purpose of the attack, Zhou Enlai informed him, had not been to take Taiwan or even the offshore islands, but to "prove to the Americans that the People's Republic of China is strong and bold enough and is not afraid of America." The Chinese knew that their actions might provoke a "local war" with the United States, and were "ready to take all the hard blows, including atomic bombs and the destruction of [their] cities." The Soviet Union need not get involved, unless of course the Americans went beyond the use of tactical nuclear weapons, in which case Moscow would obviously want to respond with a full-scale nuclear counterstrike.[190] Gromyko recalls Mao himself laying out a strategy that would lure United States forces deep into China, after which the Russians would "give them everything you've got." This left Gromyko utterly "flabbergasted," although he recovered quickly enough to warn that "such a proposal would not meet with a positive response by us. I can say that definitely."[191]

Chinese records suggest that most of this was Maoist bravado. Having decided to provoke a new Taiwan Straits crisis, the Chairman in fact became highly nervous about it, first losing sleep, then delaying the onset of shelling for almost a month, then asking his commanders to guarantee that it would kill no Americans when it finally began.[192] He appears to have seen the offshore islands much as Khrushchev saw Berlin: as a place where he could *apply and relax* pressure on the United States at will. "The noose was made by America itself," he explained, "and [yet] it throws the other end . . . to mainland China, letting us grasp it."[193] He found Washington's sharp response surprising: "Look, we have fired a few shells," he told the Supreme State Council on 5 September, a day *before* Gromyko arrived—the actual number, Mao acknowledged elsewhere, had been 30–50,000 in the first two days. "I did not expect that the entire world would be so deeply shocked."[194] He then went on to clarify his views about nuclear weapons:

First, we . . . oppose any war. So does the Soviet Union. . . . Second, however, we do not fear fighting a war. . . . We have only grenades and potatoes in our hands right now. A war of atomic and hydrogen bombs is of course terrible since many people will die. . . . Unfortunately, the decision will not be made by us. If the imperialists decide to fight a war, we have to be prepared for everything.

Mao insisted, as he had on other occasions, that "it is not so terrifying if half our population perishes. . . . Thinking about the history of the entire universe, I do not see any reason to be pessimistic about the future." But he acknowledged that "this is certainly talk in extreme terms." Its purpose was psychological: "if you fail to think about things in such extreme terms, how can you ever sleep?"

[I]f the imperialists . . . attack us first, using atomic bombs, it does not matter whether you fear fighting a war or not. . . . It is extremely dangerous to fear this and fear that every day, which will make our cadres and people feel discouraged. So I believe that [we] should be case-hardened toward fighting a war. We will fight if we have to.[195]

It is easy to see how such remarks, filtered through translation, could have alarmed Gromyko: they sound like lines from *Dr. Strangelove*. But if one absorbs the context while stripping out the references to grenades, potatoes, and imperialists, they could just as easily have been spoken—this would have frightened Gromyko even more—by Dwight D. Eisenhower.

Khrushchev's response was wholly in character. He waited until Zhou, with Mao's approval, had loosened the "noose" by calling for a resumption of talks with the United States; then he issued a blunt warning to the Americans that "[a]n attack on the Chinese People's Republic, which is a great friend, ally and neighbour of our country, is an attack on the Soviet Union."[196] It was his Suez ploy all over again: an attempt to look tough by claiming credit for an outcome already determined—in this case, if one can take Gromyko's nervousness as having contributed to it, by the Russians' own *absence* of toughness.[197] If the Soviet Union, "possessing terrible weapons which could not only stop but could devastate our common enemy, would allow itself not to come to your assistance," Khrushchev had his own Central Committee assure its Chinese counterpart three weeks later, it would be nothing less than "a crime before the world working class, . . . a retreat from the holy of holies of the Communists—from the teaching of Marxism-Leninism." The People's Republic had demonstrated its "nobility" by being willing to absorb a nuclear strike without involving the Soviet Union, but it was necessary now to show "that the unity of all brother Communist parties is unshakeable."[198]

As Khrushchev later admitted, though, "[i]t was getting harder and harder to view China through the eager and innocent eyes of a child. . . . China was China, and the Chinese were acting in increasingly strange ways." His chief concern now was a promise he had made, a year earlier, to provide Mao with a sample atomic bomb. It was ready for shipment, but the Taiwan Strait crisis had shown how hard it would be to predict what the Chairman might do with it. "In the end, we decided to postpone sending them the prototype."[199] Told to expect the device in November, the Chinese claim to have met trains arriving from Moscow for many months—none of which contained the long-overdue weapon. Only in June 1959 did the Russians confirm what must have been obvious: the bomb was not on its way, and there would be no further Soviet assistance to the Chinese nuclear program.[200]

Khrushchev made his final visit to Beijing the following September, immediately after his trip to the United States. "On the surface everyone was extremely polite, but I could sense that they were seething with resentment against the Soviet Union and against me personally."[201] Attempts to reason with the Chinese had not succeeded, so he tried lecturing instead: just because the socialist countries were strong did not mean that "we must test by force the stability of the capitalist system." *Soviet* Communists, he added pointedly, "consider it our sacred duty, our primary task . . . to utilize all possibilities in order to liquidate the Cold War." Implicit in the modifier was the admission that communists elsewhere might not agree.[202]

That they did not Mao would soon make clear enough. In a series of polemics published in connection with the 90th anniversary of Lenin's birth, in April 1960, the Chinese accused Khrushchev of "revising, emasculating, and betraying" the Founder's heritage by endorsing such principles as peaceful coexistence, the non-inevitability of war, and the possibility that communists could come to power by non-violent means.[203] It was as thorough a rejection of everything Stalin's successor stood for as one could imagine: "No longer could we rejoice," Khrushchev lamented, "about the solidarity of our socialist camp."[204]

The Sino-Soviet split had several causes, not the least of which were differences over the appropriate path to internal economic development.[205] But the single sharpest issue was a quarrel over the running of risks: Mao thought it feasible to challenge the United States on Quemoy and Matsu—and to push, more generally, for revolutions in the "third world"—because whatever his feelings about Khrushchev *he assumed the military superiority of the Soviet Union*: how else could the "east wind" hope to prevail against the "west wind"?[206] He had no way of knowing that such superiority did not exist, and Khrushchev had no easy way of breaking that bad news to him. The Kremlin boss had become, as one of his biographers has put it, "the victim of his own missile deception: Chinese leaders believed in the Soviet strategic advantage no less than the rest of the world, and they could not understand why Khrushchev . . . was so timid in dealing with the West."[207] The only explanation that made sense, in Beijing, was that he had abandoned Marxism-Leninism altogether—which gave Mao an excellent reason for abandoning allegiance to Moscow altogether.

VIII

Walter Ulbricht, too, found Khrushchev's timidity puzzling. The Soviet leader had not made good on his November 1958 threat to sign a separate peace with the German Democratic Republic that would have given it control over American, British, and French access to West Berlin. In the meantime, the East Germans' economic situation had gone from bad to much worse. "We cannot repeat the campaign in favor of a peace treaty as we did it before the Paris summit," Ulbricht admonished Khrushchev two years later. "We can do that only if something genuinely comes out of it."[208] The East Germans created their own Berlin crisis in the spring of 1961, dragging the reluctant Russians into it.[209] Although the evidence is less clear than in Mao's case, Ulbricht's reasoning was probably much the same: if the Soviet Union was as far ahead of the United States as Khrushchev claimed, why should it hesitate to use its military strength to solve the problem of Berlin?[210]

For a time, Khrushchev himself appears to have bought this argument. Concerned about the deteriorating economic situation in East Germany—and Ulbricht's increasing propensity to act unilaterally—he chose the occasion of his June 1961 Vienna summit with John F. Kennedy to issue a new ultimatum, very likely in the belief that having blinked over the Bay of Pigs, the new administration would hardly stand firm on Berlin. Kennedy unintentionally encouraged this view by acknowledging that "the ratios of power today are equal." It was like saying to an alcoholic: "Have another drink!" Khrushchev jumped at the opportunity, threatened war if he did not get his way, and contemptuously reminded Kennedy that "[t]he USSR lost 20 million people in the last war while the US lost 350 thousand."[211] Mao had horrified Khrushchev with a similar argument in 1957: the Soviet Union, he responded, had not *chosen* to fight the war that way.[212] But now Khrushchev was trying to horrify Kennedy. If Mao's methods worked, so much the better.

It is not clear even today why the President allowed himself to be so badly bullied. He was obviously ill-briefed on what to expect. He was under heavy medication for his chronic bad back, and this may have blurred his responses. But he may also have really believed that the "ratios of power" *were* approximately "equal." He had repeatedly claimed, while campaigning for the White House, that the United States had fallen behind the Soviet Union in both military strength and economic growth: it would hardly have been the first time a candidate came to believe his own rhetoric. When his Secretary of Defense, Robert McNamara, casually told reporters in February that a missile gap might not exist, Kennedy promptly disavowed him. Eisenhower recorded his successor as commenting, in April, that the two sides had "neutralized each other in atomic weapons and inventories."[213] And the CIA's authoritative estimate of Soviet ICBM strength, based on satellite reconnaissance, would not be ready until three months after the Vienna summit.[214]

Whatever the reason for Kennedy's acknowledgement of parity, Khrushchev's eagerness to exploit it backfired: the new President wound up standing *more* firmly than Eisenhower had on Berlin. Precisely because he thought he had appeared too weak Kennedy refused to compromise, with the result that several of his key advisers spent a strange summer trying to figure out how one might defend Western outposts there with nuclear weapons.[215] The results were inconclusive, but the fact that such planning took place at all was a departure from Eisenhower's practice, which had been to substitute the fear of war for war-fighting strategies, thereby obviating the need for them. Hoping to make nuclear weapons seem usable, Kennedy sought to portray their effects as manageable: hence his claim, in his 25 July television address, that with adequate civil defense measures the nation could survive a Soviet first strike.[216]

Khrushchev's first reaction was to do what came naturally, which was to beat up a convenient capitalist. The victim this time was John J. McCloy, a visitor at his Black Sea dacha. His host, McCloy reported, was "really mad," and "[k]ept emphasizing his rocket commands . . . implying his great superiority in this field." The United States might indeed make it through a nuclear exchange, but Europe would not and McCloy should understand that "there would be no Wall Street any longer because people would not tolerate [the] system unleashing wars." If such a conflict should break out, infantry would not decide it; what would were "rockets and nuclear bombs."[217] And, Khrushchev added, he had an especially big one in the works: a 100-megaton monster his scientists were eager to test. "Don't piss in your pants," he claimed to have told them: "You'll have your chance soon enough."[218]

Concern about atmospheric effects had finally brought the Americans, the Russians and the British around to an informal moratorium on testing in November 1958: only the French, since then, had exploded a nuclear bomb.[219]

But negotiations on a formal test ban had stalled; meanwhile pressures to resume testing were building in Washington and Moscow, both for technological reasons and as a reflection of an increasingly tense international situation. Kennedy had been on the verge of ending the moratorium at the time the Berlin Wall went up, but Khrushchev beat him to it: on 31 August 1961, Moscow announced a new round of explosions that would indeed include a 100-megaton bomb.[220]

The effort to build such a device had been under way for some time, and a key figure behind it, ironically, was Andrei Sakharov. Former colleagues have suggested that he saw the "Big Bomb" as a way to demonstrate "the absolute destructiveness and inhumanity of this weapon of mass annihilation, to impress on mankind and the politicians the fact that, in the event of a tragic showdown, there would be no winners."[221] Sakharov himself recalled only that he was still torn between "the conviction that our work was crucial in preserving the parity necessary for mutual deterrence," on the one hand, and his "bitterness, shame, and humiliation" over the biological and environmental consequences of testing, on the other.[222] He had been bold enough to ask Khrushchev whether a resumption might not jeopardize prospects for a test-ban treaty, only to receive, as he later remembered it, a harsh rebuke—and an explanation:

Leave politics to us—we're the specialists. . . . [w]e have to conduct our policies from a position of strength. . . . Our opponents don't understand any other language. . . . I'd be a jellyfish and not Chairman of the Council of Ministers if I listened to people like Sakharov!

"My opinion hasn't changed, but I do my work and carry out my orders," the scientist later told Khrushchev.[223] Sakharov worked on the "Big Bomb," as his colleagues put it, "intensely, seriously, and without reservation," although he did persuade Khrushchev to let him reduce its size, so that the model finally dropped over the Novaia Zemlya test-site on 30 October produced an explosion of slightly over 50 megatons, not the 100 originally promised. Otherwise, Khrushchev acknowledged, "we might knock out all our windows."[224]

Even so, it was big enough: the single largest blast human beings had ever detonated—or have since—on the planet. The flash was visible 600 miles away. The fireball "was powerful and arrogant like Jupiter. . . It seemed to suck the whole earth into it." The mushroom cloud rose 40 miles into the stratosphere. The island over which the explosion took place was literally levelled, not only of snow but also of rocks, so that it looked to one observer like an immense skating rink. The entire spectacle was "fantastic, unreal, supernatural." One estimate calculated, on the basis of this test, that if Khrushchev's full 100 megaton bomb had been used instead, the resulting firestorm would have engulfed an area the size of the state of Maryland.[225]

Khrushchev said nothing to his scientists about the Vienna summit or the Berlin Wall, but it was "perfectly clear" to Sakharov "that the decision to resume testing had been politically motivated."[226] The reasons were not difficult to discern: the 22nd Party Congress was meeting in Moscow and Khrushchev had opened it by postponing, once again, his pledge to sign a separate peace with the East Germans. He had coupled this announcement, though, with another on the impending fifty–megaton bomb test.[227] It was useful, he explained to Sakharov, to "[l]et this device hang over the heads of the capitalists, like a sword of Damocles."[228]

It did not, however: instead the "Big Bomb" made Khrushchev look more ridiculous than awesome. One reason was its obvious military impracticality: even those who had insisted over the years that there had to be uses for atomic and hydrogen bombs could find none whatever for one of this size. This and other Soviet tests did cause concern in the West, but more for their environmental pollution than for their war-fighting potential: there was no panic comparable to what the Americans inadvertently provoked with their fifteen-megaton BRAVO test in 1954. The most important reason the "Big Bomb" fizzled, though, was that Khrushchev had at last exhausted Kennedy's patience: nine days before the test, the administration had exposed Soviet strategic "Potemkinism" for what it really was.

The task had fallen to Deputy Secretary of Defense Roswell Gilpatric, who quietly informed the Business Council in Hot Springs, Virginia, on 21 October that the Iron Curtain was "not so impenetrable as to force us to accept at face value the Kremlin's boasts." It was now clear that:

The destructive power which the United States could bring to bear even after a Soviet surprise attack upon our forces would be as great as—perhaps greater than—the total undamaged force which the enemy can threaten to launch against the United States in a first strike. In short, we have a second strike capability which is at least as extensive as what the Soviets can deliver by striking first. Therefore, we are confident that the Soviets will not provoke a major nuclear conflict.[229]

The speech resulted more from circumstance than from careful planning. Administration officials had noted with interest the Soviets' reaction to McNamara's missile gap *faux pas* earlier in the year: they had immediately scaled back their claims to superiority and for several weeks did not return to them.[230] At the same time, a young Defense Department consultant named Daniel Ellsberg had been monitoring reconnaissance satellite photographs. Frustrated by the Air Force's reluctance to take them as seriously as he thought it should, Ellsberg began pushing for a quiet warning to Khrushchev that the United States knew there was no missile gap, then for a presidential speech saying much the same thing. Kennedy rejected both of these options.

But when Khrushchev announced the resumption of nuclear testing and began brandishing his 100-megaton bomb, the President decided he would have to do something to reassure the NATO allies: it would not be enough to announce that the United States too would soon start testing, or to leak the results of the CIA's definitive 21 September estimate on Soviet missile strength. It was in this context that Ellsberg's idea resurfaced. Gilpatric got the assignment as the highest-level official who could expose Khrushchev's bluff without having the act seem excessively provocative; his superiors would then quietly confirm what he had said. And so the speech was made, chiefly with a view to blunting the impact of Khrushchev's "Big Bomb."[231] Its effect, though—not clearly foreseen in Washington—went much further: what Gilpatric wound up doing was toppling all the facades, leaving the leader of the rival superpower looking like a latter-day Wizard of Oz, who for all his pompous posturing and belligerent bellowing had turned out to be "a little old man, with a bald head and a wrinkled face," in short, "a humbug."[232]

The reaction in Moscow was as if an extremely sore toe had been trodden upon: "Brandishing the might of the United States, [Gilpatric] threatened us with force," a shocked Defense Minister Rodion Malinovsky complained on 23 October. He then claimed—falsely but revealingly—that the Soviet Union had already put in place a functioning anti-missile defense system. Finally, he took it out on the unfortunate West Europeans, some of whom *were* within range of real Soviet missiles: "You must understand, madmen, that it would take really very few multimegaton nuclear bombs to wipe out your small and densely pop-ulated countries and kill you instantly in your lairs!"[233] Radio Moscow soon detected "a clearly organized campaign whose aim . . . is to intimidate the Soviet Union and exacerbate still further the international situation."[234] Khrushchev, who knew more than he might have wanted to admit about threats of force and organized campaigns, was unusually subdued for the next several weeks, revert-ing to old habits only in a December speech in which he bragged that the Americans "do not have fifty- and one-hundred-megaton bombs . . . we have them already and even more."[235] It was a blustery but transparent outburst, with its hot air showing. It hardly impressed anyone at all.

That same month there arrived in East Berlin a report from two East German diplomats in Beijing, based in turn on conversations with a Polish colleague, summarizing what the Chinese had been saying about Khrushchev. Like many Soviet-era documents it took an Aesopian tone, expressing its authors' views through those of others. It was a devastating assessment of what a half decade of strategic "Potemkinism" had actually achieved:

The Chinese . . . believe that when one makes a deadline, this absolutely must be observed. When one rescinds a deadline which has been set in such a way, one raises not only doubt and a lack of a credibility among his own people, but must give the impression to the adversary that he has bluffed. . . . [T]his will then only induce the adversary to even firmer policies, to greater demands, and to stronger provoca-tions. . . . In the case of the Suez aggression, the Soviet ultimatum, which was taken seriously, scared the imperialists and forced them to stop their aggression. The rescinding of the deadline for the conclusion of a [German] peace treaty, however, has only encouraged the enemy.[236]

Or, to put it another way, part of the problem with being a Wizard is that one's *own* acts become increasingly hard to follow.

IX

Nuclear weapons, it is now clear, had a remarkably *theatrical* effect upon the course of the high Cold War. They created the mood of dark foreboding that transfixed the world as the late 1950s became the early 1960s. They required statesmen to become actors: success or failure depended, or so it seemed, not on what one was really doing, but on what one *appeared* to be doing. They obscured long-term trends that were already determining how the Cold War was going to end, keeping that outcome very much in suspense. It was no accident that *Dr. Strangelove* reached the screen in 1964: the play upon which Stanley Kubrick based his film had been running for quite some time.

Mao managed the most memorable lines: the world might blow up, but the universe would hardly notice; the solar system would probably survive; these thoughts made it easier for him to sleep nights. "Strangelovian" they certainly were, but was their substance all that different from the willingness of Eisenhower and Khrushchev—both of whom understood the ecological consequences of any mass use of thermonuclear weapons—to put the world at risk rather than their own reputations for toughness?

Which of them risked more is not as obvious as it might seem. Khrushchev's strategic "Potemkinism" depended heavily upon his ability to bluff, to bully, in short to unsettle the international status quo—even if his objective was only to rearrange it. Eisenhower used superior capabilities more soberly: faced with Khrushchev's missile bluff he showed commendable restraint, and he exhibited genuine foresight in preparing the way for the overhead reconnaissance revolution that would in time allow the arms control agreements he failed to achieve.

And yet—Eisenhower did nothing to control the *numbers* of nuclear weapons accumulating in the American arsenal, or to prevent his subordinates from devising a "single integrated operations plan," or SIOP, that would have provided, if a Soviet attack had appeared imminent, for the *simultaneous* use of *all* 3,267 available nuclear weapons against *all* Marxist-Leninists: not just the USSR but also the People's Republic of China, Eastern Europe, North Korea, North Vietnam, and presumably Albania as well.[237] Perhaps the SIOP was just an oversight; but Eisenhower did not normally neglect war planning. Perhaps, more disturbingly, it reflected his Clausewitzian design of avoiding all war by making the prospect of fighting any war as horrible as possible. It worked—but who is to say that it was any less risky, in its own way, than Khrushchev's strategic "Potemkinism"?

Kennedy tried to lower these risks, without much help, one has to say, from his Kremlin counterpart. His solution was to rely *less* than Eisenhower had on nuclear weapons, while making his willingness to use them seem even *more* real than that of his predecessor. It was, itself, a theatrical performance—like Khrushchev's, a tough act—and it carried its own share of risks. Not the least was Kennedy's shift from Eisenhower's emphasis on avoiding wars to his own on how one might actually fight them. And in the middle of it the new

President decided, without carefully weighing consequences, to do what
Eisenhower had never done, which was to declare his adversary a strategic
humbug.

"Now, that'd be goddamn dangerous, I would think," Kennedy blurted out at
one point during the Cuban missile crisis, when he tried to imagine how
Khrushchev might respond to the placement of American missiles in Turkey—
before any of his advisers could remind him that the United States *had already*
placed missiles in Turkey.[238] Was it any less dangerous to expose Moscow's
Maximum Leader, onstage and in full view of the audience, as the Wizard of Oz?

NINE

The Cuban Missile Crisis

[H]umans have been doing mad things with technology, which is
more highly developed than their abilities to organize and make
policy.

Fidel Castro, 11 January 1992

Would I have been ready to use nuclear weapons? Yes, I would have
agreed to the use of nuclear weapons. Because, in any case, we took
it for granted that it would become a nuclear war anyway, and that
we were going to disappear. Before having the country occupied—
totally occupied—we were ready to die in defense of our country.

Fidel Castro, 11 January 1992[1]

WHAT is there *new* to say about the Cuban missile crisis? No episode in
the history of international relations has received such microscopic
scrutiny from so many historians. Theorists have generalized exuberantly from
this single specific event. Surviving participants have spent much of their lives
reliving what they did during those critical thirteen days.[2] And whether alive at
the time or not yet born, almost everyone who knows anything about the last
half of October 1962, regards it as the moment at which the world came closer
than ever before, or since, to a nuclear conflagration.

So surely we know what happened. Was it not Nikita Khrushchev's contempt
for John F. Kennedy's weakness—revealed at the Bay of Pigs, the Vienna summit, and the Berlin Wall—that led him to place medium- and intermediate-
range ballistic missiles in Cuba? Was he not seeking, through this bold stroke,
to redress a strategic balance upset by Washington's belated acknowledgement
that there was no missile gap? Did not Kennedy's courageously hawkish but
coolly crafted response thwart this scheme, producing a triumph for the
Americans and abject humiliation for the Russians? Did not both sides conclude
from the experience that neither should ever again run such risks?

Historians still answer "yes" to that last question—but *only* to that one. New
American, Soviet and Cuban sources are revealing most other conventional wisdom about the crisis to be highly questionable. Khrushchev placed missiles in
Cuba, these materials suggest, because he saw Kennedy as aggressive, not passive. He acted at least as much from an emotional compulsion to save Fidel

Castro's revolution as from any calculated determination to correct a strategic imbalance. Kennedy may well have been the most *dovish* member of his admin-istration—not a hawk at all—but he comes across as even *more* courageous for having taken that stance. Lessons about decision-making that long ago made their way into the crisis-management textbooks turn out to have been largely irrelevant to the outcome of this one. That settlement was itself a *compromise*, not a clear-cut victory for either side; and a third side, the Cubans, did more than previously suspected to bring it about. Finally, the long-term effect was not so much to humiliate the Soviet Union as to bolster its image as an equal to the United States in a Cold War that would continue for another three decades.[3]

What has *not* changed, in all of these revisions and reconsiderations, is the central place the Cuban missile crisis occupies in Cold War history: if anything, it appears to have been a *more* important turning-point than we had earlier believed it to be. It was the only episode after World War II in which *each* of the major arenas of Soviet–American competition intersected: the nuclear arms race to be sure, but also conflicting ideological aspirations, "third-world" rivalries, relations with allies, the domestic political implications of foreign policy, the personalities of individual leaders. The crisis was a kind of funnel—a historical singularity, if you like—into which everything suddenly tumbled and got mixed together. Fortunately no black hole lurked at the other end, although new evi-dence confirms how easily one might have. Instead a different kind of Cold War emerged that would evolve into a "long peace": a contest by no means free of tension and even crises on a smaller scale, but one conducted within an inter-national system to which the superpowers slowly accustomed themselves. Soviet and American leaders would find fewer and fewer incentives over the years to try to alter that system—until 1989, when circumstances converged once again, very abruptly and to everyone's astonishment, to alter it for them.

I

The Cuban missile crisis arose, it now appears, because Khrushchev understood more clearly than Kennedy that the West was winning the Cold War. Kennan had predicted that its outcome would depend upon whether Western Europe and Japan—key centers of industrial–military power left adrift at the end of World War II—wound up within a Soviet or an American sphere of influence.[4] By 1961 that issue had been resolved: democratic politics and market econom-ics had prevailed in the countries that counted. The Marxist-Leninist alternative retained its appeal in much of the "third world," to be sure, but it lacked any capacity for coordinated action. Moscow might occasionally benefit from what happened there, as with Castro's revolution, but it could hardly create or con-trol such opportunities.

Meanwhile, Marxism-Leninism was delivering less than promised where already in place. It had yet to meet Khrushchev's requirement that it surpass capitalism in raising the living standards of ordinary people: by June 1962, conditions inside the Soviet Union had so deteriorated that he had to order the Red Army to fire on strikers in Novocherkassk who were protesting rising food prices.[5] It had produced national rivalries more often than international solidarity: although Washington's alliances remained reasonably solid, Moscow's functioned only through coercion in Eastern Europe and in the case of China had collapsed altogether. Nor could the Soviet Union claim a favorable military balance: at the time of the missile crisis the American advantage in strategic weaponry was 17–1, about what it had been a decade earlier.[6]

Whatever his claims about having history on his side, Khrushchev had long recognized the need to help it along. Each of his major international initiatives—strategic "Potemkinism," attempts to repair relations with Tito and Mao Zedong, applying and then relaxing pressure on Berlin, conciliatory gestures toward the United States and its allies, the multi-megaton nuclear tests—had been designed to reverse alarming trends. Their failure left the Soviet leader with a *general* sense of desperation: this was not, however, the *immediate* reason for the great gamble he took in Cuba. Here he was responding to American provocations—one so calculated that it qualifies as a plot, the other so lacking in calculation that it seems almost inadvertent. Both came as legacies from Eisenhower; both reflected Kennedy's fear that the *United States* might still lose the Cold War.

The plot was the effort to eliminate Castro, which did not end with the fiasco at the Bay of Pigs. Instead, Kennedy authorized—or at least acquiesced in—an elaborate series of CIA-sponsored sabotage and assassination attempts directed against Cuba and its Maximum Leader. The motive remained that of the botched invasion; only the means were different.[7] Nor did the White House rule out another military assault. Kennedy gave no explicit go-ahead; but maneuvers in the Caribbean during the spring and summer of 1962 went well beyond the ordinary, perhaps with a view to being prepared if Castro should indeed be deposed or killed.[8] He wanted "no military action within the next three months," the President told the Joint Chiefs of Staff on 15 October, the day before he learned that Soviet missiles were in Cuba. But as the note-taker recorded, "he can't be sure as he does not control events."[9] Robert S. McNamara, J.F.K.'s Secretary of Defense, has adamantly denied that the administration intended military action; he has acknowledged, though, that "if I had been a Cuban leader, I think I might have expected a U.S. invasion."[10]

Castro certainly anticipated one; so too, it is now clear, did Khrushchev. He had seen the Bay of Pigs as a sign not of Kennedy's weakness, but rather of the President's determination to crush the only socialist revolution that had succeeded in the Western hemisphere. It had been "foolish" of the Americans to attempt the invasion, Mikoyan explained to Castro, "[b]ut that fact indicated that they would try again to organize an aggression against Cuba."[11] Khrushchev recalls being "haunted by the knowledge that the Americans could not stomach having Castro's Cuba right next to them. They would do something."[12] His ally's anxieties, Castro remembers, were both personal and ideological:

Nikita loved Cuba very much. . . . He had a weakness for Cuba, you might say—emotionally, and so on—because he was a man of political conviction, a man with a political doctrine, a political theory, and he was consistent with that doctrine. He thought in terms of capitalism versus socialism. He had very firm convictions.[13]

The Cuban revolution had been "a great success" for Marxism-Leninism, Mikoyan assured Castro shortly after the crisis. Its suppression would have meant

a two or three times larger defeat of the whole socialist camp. Such a defeat would throw back the revolutionary movement in many countries. Such a defeat would bear witness to the supremacy of imperialist forces in the entire world. That would be an incredible blow which would change the correlation of forces between the two systems. . . . We were and are considering to be our duty, a duty of communists, to do everything necessary to defend the Cuban revolution, to frustrate the imperialist plans.[14]

Khrushchev's decision "sprang from both his heart and his head," one of his generals has concluded. "It was both an old Bolshevik's romantic response to Castro and to the Cuban revolution and an old soldier's strategem for deploying Soviet force to defend an endangered outpost and ally."[15] It had been necessary, Khrushchev himself told his ambassador in Havana, "because there is no other way to protect Cuba's revolution."[16]

The very unexpectedness—even irrationality—of Moscow's commitment would make it work, Foreign Minister Andrei Gromyko prematurely assured Khrushchev following a meeting with Kennedy on 18 October —two days *after* the President had learned of the missiles' presence in Cuba, but four days *before* he revealed this fact to the Russians and to the rest of the world: "the Administration and the overall American ruling circles are amazed by the Soviet Union's courage in assisting Cuba." Their reasoning, as Gromyko understood it, was as follows:

The Soviet government recognizes the great importance which the Americans place on Cuba and its situation, and how painful that issue is to the USA. But the fact that the USSR, even knowing all that, still provides such aid to Cuba, means that it is fully committed to repulsing any American intervention in Cuba. There is no single opinion as to how and where that rebuff will be given, but that it will be given—they do not doubt.

Going out on a very long limb, Gromyko concluded that "in these conditions a USA military adventure against Cuba is almost impossible to imagine."[17]

Where, though, did Khrushchev get the idea of using *missiles* to defend the Cuban revolution? This is where inadvertence comes in, for it appears that the Americans gave it to him. Eisenhower and Dulles, after all, had first placed medium- and intermediate-range missiles in exposed locations when they responded to Khrushchev's post-*Sputnik* threats by offering NATO American Thors and Jupiters. Liquid-fueled, surface-deployed, and of questionable accuracy, these first-generation MRBMs and IRBMs had little military value—but that was not their purpose. It was rather to reassure the countries hosting them while unsettling the country at which they were aimed: this "quick fix" would span the brief period of vulnerability that would exist until American ICBMs were ready. *Time* magazine reduced the policy to its bare essentials: "IRBM + NATO = ICBM."[18]

In the end, though, only the British, the Italians and the Turks agreed to receive the American missiles and even they felt little sense of urgency. Negotiations took so long that the weapons were obsolete by the time they arrived in Great Britain and Italy. Kennedy came close to cancelling the Turkish deployment—15 Jupiters—altogether in the summer of 1961. He allowed it to proceed only after the Turks vehemently protested and Khrushchev renewed his Berlin ultimatum, thereby discouraging concessions of any kind. The Jupiters went to Turkey later that year and became operational under American command early in 1962.

Not until 22 October—the day Kennedy revealed that Soviet missiles were in Cuba—did the first Turkish crews man a launch site under "dual-key" procedures sharing control of these now antiquated rockets with the Americans.[19] But by that time J.F.K. appeared to have forgotten about them altogether. Khrushchev's placing missiles in Cuba, he mused on the first day of the crisis, was "just as if we suddenly began to put a major number of MRBMs in Turkey." "Well, we *did*, Mr. President," someone had to remind him.[20]

Khrushchev, unlike Kennedy, never lost track of the Turkish Jupiters. Long before they were sent he had made it clear that he would regard American missiles in a state bordering the Soviet Union as a threat—even a personal affront. He harangued Richard Nixon about them during the Vice President's visit to Moscow in 1959.[21] After the Bay of Pigs, he linked them implicitly to the situation in Cuba, and at the Vienna summit the connection became explicit. Turkey and Iran were at least as threatening to the Soviet Union as Cuba was to the United States, he warned Kennedy. "They march in its wake, and they have US bases and rockets." Washington had "set a precedent for intervention in [the] internal affairs of other countries. . . . This situation may cause miscalculation."[22]

The Kremlin leader was not just posturing: his associates remember his complaints to them as having been equally vehement. They tended especially to surface when he vacationed, as he often did, on the Black Sea. "What do you see?" he would ask visitors after handing them binoculars. "Nothing," they would reply, puzzled. Their host would then seize the binoculars, survey the horizon, and make his point: "*I* see U.S. missiles in Turkey, aimed at *my dacha*."[23] It was on a subsequent visit to the Black Sea, this time in Bulgaria, that Khrushchev apparently hit on the idea of reciprocating by sending Soviet MRBMs and IRBMs—of which he had plenty—to Cuba:

The Americans had surrounded our country with military bases and threatened us with nuclear weapons, and now they would learn just what it feels like to have enemy missiles pointing at you; we'd be doing nothing but giving them a little of their own medicine.

Khrushchev acknowledged that he had the Soviet Union's strategic inferiority in mind—no doubt also Kennedy's public exposure of it by way of the Gilpatric speech—when he made this decision: "our missiles would have equalized what the West likes to call 'the balance of power.'" But this was, he claimed, a secondary consideration: "The main thing was that the installation of our missiles in Cuba would, I thought, restrain the United States from precipitous military action against Castro's government."[24] The Jupiters in Turkey not only suggested a means of protecting the Cuban revolution; they also provided, at least in Khrushchev's mind, an emotional, moral, and even a *legal* justification for doing so.[25]

Castro was at first skeptical, but not because "we were afraid of the dangers that might follow the deployment of the missiles here." Rather, "the presence of the missiles would in fact turn us into a Soviet military base," with damage to his revolution's image elsewhere in Latin America.

So if it had been just for our own defense, I think that, in full honesty . . . we would not have accepted the deployment of the missiles. But, indeed, we regarded the deployment of the missiles as something that would strengthen the socialist camp—something that, to a certain extent, would help to improve the so-called balance of power.

What Castro had in mind was the *strategic* balance. He assumed that "the fighting capacity of each of the two big powers in the nuclear sphere was quite similar." Like Mao and Ulbricht, he had taken Khrushchev's rhetoric about rockets at face value:

You've got to go back to those times. . . . Don't you remember the great Soviet might, when they first put a man in space with colossal rockets? Don't you remember when Nikita said that the Soviet Union had missiles that could hit a fly in the air? I'll never forget that statement.

The Soviet MRBM-IRBM deployment, Castro seems to have thought, might just break the strategic stalemate. At a minimum, it would bolster "the socialist countries—the ones we regarded as our allies, our friends, our brothers, as sharing a common ideology."[26] Marshall Sergei Biryuzov, who negotiated the initial arrangements with Castro, came back "with the impression that Cuba's leaders saw themselves much more as benefactors of the Soviet Union and its socialist cause than as our dependants."[27]

Castro's reasoning therefore inverted Khrushchev's. The Soviet leader gave first priority to defending Cuba; the strategic balance was, for him, an important but secondary consideration. If missiles in the Caribbean shifted it, so much the better; he understood, though, that they could not reverse it. For Castro, it was the other way around: the strategic balance was primary, with Soviet military protection a useful bonus. "I thought the Soviets had several hundred intercontinental missiles," he has admitted. "We imagined thousands, even more, because that was the impression that was created." Had he known the truth, "I would have counseled prudence, since for us there was no anxiety, no fear, in the thought that we were going to be invaded, and that they were going to crush us. . . . We were not afraid of fighting."[28]

The truth, in the summer of 1962, should not have been difficult to get. But Castro appears not to have read—or at least not to have believed—Gilpatric's speech.[29] Nor was Khrushchev eager to confirm its contents: he found it as difficult to tell the Cubans what the actual strategic balance was as he had the East Germans and the Chinese. Castro accepted Soviet rockets almost as easily as he accepted Khrushchev's claims to be turning them out like sausages: if the Russians needed a new retail outlet, he would oblige. And if these weapons should indeed tilt the strategic balance in favor of the socialist camp, then they would be worth the risk, however irrelevent they might be in warding off the United States Marines.

Soviet missiles went to Cuba, therefore, because Khrushchev and Castro were too solicitous of what each *believed* to be the other's interests—and too polite to probe deeply enough to make sure. Both *wanted* to find common cause: here as elsewhere, though, Marxism-Leninism produced more romanticism than realism. It convinced Khrushchev that he should risk the security of the Soviet state to rescue an unruly gang of youthful revolutionaries in Havana, of all places: one wonders what Lenin or Stalin would have made of such sentimentality.[30] It kept Castro from seeing the difference—after almost everyone else had come to see it—between Khrushchev's "Potemkin village" and the Soviet Union's actual strategic capabilities: "perhaps you should have told us the number of missiles the Soviets had," the Cuban leader admitted to an old CIA hand years later. "We didn't know any better."[31] Nor had either Khrushchev or Castro thought very carefully about what the American response to their highly secret joint venture might be.

II

Castro claims to have opposed secrecy on the grounds that Cuba had nothing to be ashamed of in accepting Soviet missiles. Kennedy administration veterans have acknowledged that had the deployment been handled openly it would have been more difficult to oppose, given the precedent the Americans had set by placing their own IRBMs and MRBMs in Great Britain, Italy, and Turkey.[32] Despite Khrushchev's plans to use that precedent as a *public justification* once his missiles were in place and he had announced their presence,[33] he appears never to have considered the possibility of a *public deployment*. Mikoyan later explained the reasons to Castro:

If the strategic armaments were deployed under conditions of secrecy and if the Americans were not aware of their presence in Cuba, then it would have been a powerful means of deterrence. We proceeded from that assumption. Our military specialists informed us that strategic missiles can be reliably concealed in the palm forests of Cuba.[34]

Without even raising the issue of Russian familiarity with palm trees, this argument makes no sense: how could the Americans have been deterred by a deterrent of whose existence they were to remain unaware?[35] Stalin and Mao had understood that deterrents have to be visible: hence their *open* announcement of a Sino-Soviet treaty in 1950.[36] Khrushchev and Castro negotiated a similar Soviet–Cuban accord in August, 1962, but the Russians refused to make it public, and in the rush of events surrounding the crisis that fall it was never formally signed.[37]

In a narrow sense, secrecy paid off. The deployment was a remarkable logistical feat, involving not only MRBMs and IRBMs but also IL-28 medium-range bombers, MIG-21 fighter-interceptors, anti-aircraft missile batteries, short-range battlefield rockets, and some 42,000 Soviet troops together with the necessary support facilities. It was the largest amphibious operation the Soviet Union had ever mounted,[38] and even though it took place just off their own coastline, the Americans seemed hardly to notice. They could see that a military build-up was under way, but until the first U-2 photographs confirmed the missile emplacements on 15 October, Kennedy and his advisers had no idea of its scope—or of the fact that strategic weapons were involved.[39] Even then, their estimates of Soviet manpower in Cuba ranged from *four to ten times* too low.[40]

But secrecy also caused problems, not the least of which was the difficulty the Russians had gathering and then sharing information with one another and with their Cuban allies. For months military planners in Moscow were not allowed to use typists: all documents had to be handwritten. To enhance the deception, troops went to the Caribbean encumbered with skis, parkas, and heavy winter uniforms. The missiles, when they reached their destinations, looked disappointingly unlike palm trees.[41] Khrushchev himself, according to Mikoyan, "gave the order to place the missiles into vertical position only at night, but to maintain them in a lying-down position in the daytime"[42]—if so, this certainly helped American photo-interpreters. Apparently no one in Moscow had anticipated U-2 overflights, which increased dramatically after they detected large, *horizontal* canvas-covered cylinders.[43] The Cubans themselves had little sense of what kind of weapons they were getting or how they might be used.[44] And of course Castro had agreed to the whole deployment under the mistaken impression—which Khrushchev failed to correct—that the Soviet Union and the United States possessed approximately the same number of ICBMs: "Had we known then what we know now about the balance of power, we'd have realized the practical importance—the military importance—of these forty-two missiles, because, by being deployed in Cuba, they were transformed from medium-range missiles into strategic missiles."[45]

The greatest disadvantage of secrecy, however, was that it required lying at the top. Khrushchev deceived Kennedy about the existence of offensive weapons in Cuba, both through official channels and through KGB agent Georgi Bolshakov, upon whom the two leaders had come to rely for highly sensitive communications.[46] Gromyko even lied to the President face to face on 18 October, by which time J.F.K. knew what was happening. "From the start, the undertaking held the seeds of its own failure," General Anatoli Gribkov, who organized the logistics, has since acknowledged, in that it "ensured Kennedy's angry feeling of personal betrayal and blocked the path to any superpower relationship built on mutual trust."[47] And yet, trust was what Khrushchev hoped for: as one recent assessment of the crisis has concluded, "he believed that Soviet-American relations would *improve* after Kennedy was informed of the missiles."[48]

But deception, for Khrushchev, was nothing new: he had been lying outrageously for years about his ICBM capabilities. Why did Kennedy react so slowly to those claims, waiting for months before exposing their fraudulence, and so quickly to the prospect of MRBMs and IRBMs in Cuba? One obvious reason is that the Cuban missiles were real, not rhetorical; it is also the case that they did, in a way, alter the strategic balance. *Precisely because* Khrushchev had so few inter-continental missiles, the formula "IRBM + *Cuba* = ICBM" yielded a much larger result than had its American equivalent when applied to NATO. Given the United States' vast strategic bombing capabilities, missile deployments in Europe added only slightly to the number of nuclear warheads the Americans could deliver on Soviet targets. Khrushchev's Cuban missiles, however, would have doubled, perhaps even tripled, the number of Soviet warheads capable of reaching the United States.[49]

There was, to be sure, some logic in McNamara's insistence at the time that numbers did not matter: that because of the damage only a few nuclear explosions could do, the Russians did not need equivalence to achieve deterrence. Soviet missiles in Cuba changed the strategic balance "not at all," he told Kennedy on the first day of the crisis; and three decades later McNamara was still insisting that nuclear *parity* had existed in 1962, even with a 17–1 imbalance in deliverable warheads.[50] Significantly, though, neither McNamara nor anyone else in the Kennedy administration stuck to that view then. They quickly realized that whatever the military effects of an abrupt doubling or tripling of Soviet strategic capabilities, the *political* effects could be devastating. The reason had to do with the difference between authoritarian and democratic forms of government.

However much he personally resented American missiles in Turkey, Khrushchev did not have to worry about their domestic political implications. He could, for the most part, control the information the Soviet public received, and hence its response. He had long since beaten back potential rivals within the Kremlin: none was in a position to use the Turkish Jupiters as an excuse to challenge his leadership. Kennedy enjoyed no such advantages. Since Castro's revolution, Cuba had dominated political debates in the United States, including J.F.K.'s own memorably televised exchange with Richard Nixon during the 1960 campaign. As rumors of Soviet military activity increased in the summer and early fall of 1962, pressures from Congress, the press, and the Cuban exile community became intense. Republican Senator Kenneth Keating charged specifically—and as it turned out remarkably accurately—that the Russians were putting IRBMs and MRBMs into Cuba, and that the President was doing nothing about it.[51] Kennedy himself acknowledged publicly on 4 September that if

Keating's claims should turn out to be correct, "the gravest issues would arise."[52]

Unaccustomed to having his own leadership questioned, Khrushchev failed to see how seriously his deception, had it succeeded, would have undermined Kennedy's. If anyone in Moscow had bothered to ask, the newly appointed Soviet ambassador in Washington, Anatoly Dobrynin, has recalled, "we could have predicted the violent American reaction to [Khrushchev's] adventure once it became known." Even Castro understood this: it had been one of the reasons he favored an open deployment. But Dobrynin learned of missiles in Cuba not from Khrushchev or Gromyko but from Secretary of State Dean Rusk, only an hour before Kennedy announced their presence to the world. "Khrushchev wanted to spring a surprise on Washington; it was he who got the surprise in the end when his secret plan was uncovered."[53]

There was, therefore, a *political* asymmetry that distinguised Cuban from Turkish missiles. Whatever the difference between a secret and an open deployment—and it is worth noting that the Turkish deployment, while no secret, was not widely publicized[54]—it is always dangerous to try to deceive a democracy. Dictators can, to a point, control the degree of their own embarrassment: if reasons of state suggest the need to proceed as if nothing had happened, they can usually manage to do that. Democratic leaders cannot: however they may persuade themselves that being tricked has changed nothing, their political opponents will quickly convince them otherwise. The problem is not simply an American one: it applies, to one degree or another, within any democratic state, and certainly within a democratic coalition.[55] Once again, then, the Russians' ignorance of democracy served them badly. But this time, the *consequences* were democratic: the danger of nuclear war would affect everyone quite impartially, democrats, authoritarians, and all those in between.

III

Of the many "dogs that did not bark" during the Cold War, surely the nuclear war that did not result from the Cuban missile crisis is the most significant. With all their new evidence, historians have yet to alter their view that this was the point at which the world came closest to that appalling prospect. *Just how close*, though, remains at issue. Kennedy himself rated the danger of war—not necessarily nuclear war—as about one in three, but the tendency afterwards was to lower the odds. Hawks found it inconceivable that Khrushchev would have used nuclear weapons to defend Cuba in the face of such overwhelming American superiority. Doves insisted that whatever the numerical balance Kennedy would never have authorized an invasion of the island.[56] By 1988, McGeorge Bundy, J.F.K.'s national security adviser, was acknowledging that "the objective risk of escalation to the nuclear level may have been as large as 1 in 100." Even so, he was careful to add, "in this apocalyptic matter the risk can be very small indeed and still much too large for comfort."[57]

Calculating risks retrospectively is almost as difficult as trying to anticipate them: in any complex system so many things *can* go wrong that it is difficult to know what might—or might have.[58] A reasonable place to start, though, is with those in command. How much were Kennedy and Khrushchev prepared to concede before ordering the use of nuclear weapons? Who depended upon whom to back down?

Khrushchev risked much by sending MRBMs and IRBMs to Cuba, but he conceded much once Kennedy made it clear that he would not tolerate their presence. Rather like a cat that has ventured beyond its own territory and then, when discovered, scampers nervously—and a bit guiltily—back to safety, the Soviet leader agreed not only to withdraw his missiles but also the IL-28 bombers as well as most of the troops and equipment that had accompanied them. He did so in the face of vociferous objections from the Cubans, who felt both bypassed and betrayed: while the missiles were in place, Castro told Mikoyan, "we did not even arrest anyone, because the unity of the people was so staggering." But now Cubans were "consumed by a sense of disappointment, confusion, and bitterness." An even angrier Che Guevara claimed to be speaking for Castro when he fumed that while "the USA wanted to destroy us physically," Khrushchev's concessions "destroyed us legally." "We see your readiness to die beautifully," Mikoyan snapped back, "but we believe that it isn't worth dying beautifully."[59]

There were those on the American side who thought Khrushchev might have accepted much more: that if the United States had chosen this moment to attack and depose Castro, the Russians would have swallowed that, too. "We should invade today!" General Curtis LeMay is said to have demanded of Kennedy.[60] Whether that view was correct or not, Khrushchev had clearly demonstrated his willingness to back down—and to accept a remarkable amount of humiliation along the way—rather than risk a nuclear war.

It has not been as clear that Kennedy would have done the same. Because he was a democratic leader who had to worry about domestic political consequences—but *particularly* because he was a Democratic president vulnerable to Republican charges of appeasement—the consensus has long been that backing down would have been extraordinarily difficult for him. Early critics went so far as to suggest that he would have risked a nuclear war rather than trade even worthless missiles in Turkey.[61] Several of Kennedy's own advisers, worried about the implications for NATO if it should ever become known that he had sacrificed the Turkish Jupiters under pressure, went so far as to rewrite history by claiming that J.F.K. had ordered the weapons out earlier and that the State Department had failed to comply.[62] His management of the crisis, they maintained, had been consistently firm and uncompromising: courage, as they profiled it, was inflexibility. For many of their readers, though, what came across not was courage at all, but a dangerously "Strangelovian" stubbornness. There is reason now to suspect that J.F.K. might have seen it that way too.

The evidence comes from Kennedy himself, by way of two tricks he played on his own subordinates. One was his decision—known only, apparently, to his brother Robert—to tape the meetings of his principal advisory group during the crisis, the Executive Committee (or ExComm) of the National Security Council.[63] These recordings reveal a very different J.F.K. from the one ExComm participants depicted in their retrospective accounts. They show him repeatedly pushing for a compromise: "We can't very well invade Cuba," he insisted at one point, "when we could have gotten [the Soviet missiles] out by making a deal on the same missiles in Turkey." If it should come out that such an option had not been explored, then "I don't see how we'll have a very good war."[64] Despite the well-meaning custodians of his historical legacy, J.F.K. managed to get the last word.

The President's other deception was to conceal from all but his closest advisers his most important attempts to resolve the crisis. One of these was the *explicit* assurance his brother Robert Kennedy gave Ambassador Dobrynin that the administration would soon remove the Turkish Jupiters, even though it could not be seen to have done so in exchange for a Soviet withdrawal of missiles from Cuba. Dobrynin relayed R.F.K.'s comments to Moscow:

The greatest difficulty for the president is the public discussion of the issue of Turkey. Formally the deployment of missile bases in Turkey was done by a special decision of the NATO Council. To announce now a unilateral decision . . . to withdraw missile bases from Turkey—this would damage the entire structure of NATO and the US position as the leader of NATO. . . . . [I]f such a decision were announced now it would seriously tear apart NATO.

Nevertheless, Dobrynin has R.F.K. adding, "President Kennedy is willing to come to agree on that question with N. S. Khrushchev, too. I think that in order to withdraw these bases from Turkey, we need 4–5 months."[65] Although long suspected, this is the first confirmation from a contemporary source of something neither the President nor his brother wanted known at the time: that a private promise to pull out the Jupiters accompanied J.F.K.'s public pledge not to invade Cuba. *That*, then, was the deal Khrushchev accepted.[66]

But what if he had he not? We now know that Kennedy left himself at least one other non-military alternative. It would have come in the form of a *public* appeal from United Nations Secretary General U Thant, arranged ahead of time by Rusk through former UN official Andrew Cordier, for a Cuba–Turkey missile trade. Kennedy would then *publicly* have accepted. Only the President, his brother, and Rusk knew of this unexecuted plan, which astonished Kennedy's other advisers when the former Secretary of State revealed it in 1987.[67] There is no way to know for sure that J.F.K. would have used it, but the fact that it was ready to go—together with evidence from the ExComm tapes that the President was pushing hard for such an exchange—suggests strongly that he would have.[68]

And what if the Cordier initiative had failed, there had been an American landing in Cuba, and Khrushchev had responded as Kennedy expected him to do by attacking the Turkish Jupiters? The evidence here is less than conclusive, but the President did issue explicit orders that the Jupiters were not to be launched without his permission, "even in the event of a selective nuclear or non-nuclear attack on these units by the Soviet Union in response to actions we may be taking elsewhere."[69] The ExComm tapes hint strongly that there was a plan to absorb such a strike—that is, *a direct Soviet nuclear assault on a NATO ally*—without retaliating. The idea, historian Philip Nash writes, would have been to "liquidate one's least valuable military assets in order to eliminate one of the most glaring drawbacks of the airstrike option [in Cuba]—the possibility that it would trigger an escalatory spiral culminating in World War III."[70]

What all of this suggests, then, is that with everything that has been published over the years about John F. Kennedy and the Cuban missile crisis, we are only now coming to understand the role he played in it. Far from neglecting the dangers of nuclear war, he had a keen sense of what they were. Far from opposing a compromise, he pushed for one more strongly than anyone else in his administration. Far from relying on the ExComm he bypassed it at the most critical moments, and may have seen it as more useful for consensus-building than for decision-making.[71] Far from placing the nation and the world at risk to protect his own reputation for toughness, he probably would have backed down, in public if necessary, whatever the domestic political damage might have been.[72] There may be, in short, room here for a new profile in courage—but it would be courage of a different kind from what many people presumed that term to mean throughout much of the Cold War.

IV

All of this assumes, though, as Kennedy apparently did, that he himself would determine whether American nuclear weapons would be used. New and unsettling evidence calls that proposition into question. The problem was not so much that some rogue military commander would try to start a nuclear war, as in *Dr. Strangelove*. It lay, rather, in the mundane but potentially risky set of conditions that can arise when any large military organization goes on heightened alert.

The attack on Pearl Harbor succeeded because military intelligence failed to distinguish a few sinister signals from many that were benign.[73] By the late 1950s the Soviet Union could reach American targets with nuclear weapons, which meant that the consequences of any equivalent error would be grave indeed. With this in mind, the Pentagon established the Defense Condition (Defcon) alert system in 1959. Even under normal conditions it kept the Strategic Air Command at a higher level of readiness than other military forces, and with the discovery of Soviet missiles in Cuba—a Pearl Harbor in the making, or so it seemed—the Joint Chiefs of Staff ordered an alert status shift from Defcon 5 to 3, with SAC going on Defcon 2, the highest possible level short of war itself.[74]

But alerts require departures from standard procedures. Two things then tend to happen. First, systems become more tightly interconnected, or "coupled":

units unaccustomed to working closely with one another must now do so. Second, unexpected events take on alarming implications: memories of Pearl Harbor become more vivid. Both patterns appeared as American forces went on alert during the Cuban missile crisis—with results that could themselves have produced dangerous surprises.[75]

The Strategic Air Command immediately dispersed long-range bombers and fighter-interceptors from their normal bases, but it failed to inform air defense units—also on high alert—about these flight plans. It more than quintupled the number of B-52s kept airborne, but in order to do so may have flown some with nuclear weapons whose arming circuitry had not yet been certified as safe. Minuteman missile crews, under pressure to bring these new silo-based ICBMs on line as quickly as possible, bypassed normal safety procedures, in effect "hot-wiring" their weapons in ways that risked unauthorized launches. Cape Canaveral continued missile tests during the crisis: one of them caused a New Jersey radar unit to conclude—fortunately only briefly—that a Soviet missile was on its way from Cuba. Reports of saboteurs attempting to penetrate an air force facility near Duluth set off an aircraft launch alarm at another base in Minnesota where nuclear-equipped F-106s scrambled, only to be stopped from taking off at the last minute when the Duluth infiltrators turned out to have been a lone inquisitive bear.

What made these situations dangerous was that if an accidental nuclear detonation had occurred on United States territory or elsewhere, such an event might have looked like a deliberate Soviet attack. SAC regional commanders had the authority to respond with nuclear weapons—even without orders from Washington—if they had "unambiguous" evidence that war had begun. Under conditions of high alert, any explosion of a nuclear weapon, whatever the reason for it, could have seemed "unambiguous." Nor, in the resulting confusion, would it have been easy to check to see if other detonations had occurred: the only detection system in place at the time was mounted on top of *telephone poles* at strategic locations around the country. It is not too difficult, therefore, to see how the United States could have convinced itself that a nuclear attack was taking place, even if one was not.

We know less about Soviet alert procedures, so it is harder to say what might have persuaded Moscow that the USSR was under attack. It came out at the time, though, that an American U-2 had strayed into Siberian airspace on the most critical day of the crisis, 27 October: what had not been known until recently was that when Soviet MIGs scrambled to intercept it, F-102A interceptors in turn took off from Alaska to intercept them. Because they were on alert status, these planes carried nuclear-tipped air-to-air missiles which their pilots were authorized to use if they thought it necessary. We also know now that even as ICBMs at Vandenberg Air Force base were being fitted with their own nuclear warheads for a possible attack on the Soviet Union, no one stopped missile *testing* from that base either, so that an Atlas ICBM took off from there on 26 October, presumably monitored by the Soviet ships nearby that routinely performed that function. And although the Pentagon ordered that no Jupiters be launched from Turkey without explicit presidential permission, it failed to extend that requirement to sixteen American F-100s on fifteen-minute alert at Incirlik air base, also armed with nuclear weapons and Soviet target lists. Khrushchev's Black Sea dacha, therefore, was still at risk.

Screw-ups can happen in any large organization. Most are resilient enough—which is to say, loosely "coupled" enough—to survive them. But military alerts during the Cuban missile crisis required "coupling": units that had rarely, if ever, had to coordinate their procedures now found themselves forced to do so. They managed it largely by improvisation; but in that highly charged atmosphere, there were numerous "close calls" as unexpected results created, or could have created, the impression that a Soviet attack was under way. Apart from the Siberian U-2 incident, it is unlikely that Kennedy himself, or the Defense Department, or the Joint Chiefs of Staff knew about these: most were never reported up the chain of command. Those in command, therefore, *thought* they had more control over the nuclear weapons at their disposal than they actually did. However many fall-back positions Kennedy had, things still could have fallen out very differently from what he intended.

V

What about "close calls" on the other side? Here departures from standard procedures began, not with a military alert, but rather with Khrushchev's decision to send missiles—and, we now know, a large number of nuclear weapons—to an exposed location thousands of miles beyond effective Soviet military control.[76] The Americans often deployed their nuclear warheads abroad during the Cold War, but always with *non-nuclear* means of protection: air and naval superiority, together with a globe-circling network of bases, made this possible. Lacking such means, the Soviet Union had always kept its nuclear weapons confined to its own territory, or to the ships and submarines of the Soviet Navy.[77] Khrushchev saw in Cuba an opportunity to shatter these constraints—but only by extending strategic assets well beyond his conventional military capabilities.

On 4 October 1962, the Soviet freighter *Indigirka* docked at Mariel with a lethal cargo: 36 warheads in the 200–700 kiloton range for MRBMs that had already arrived separately; 80 cruise missile warheads, each in the 5–12 kiloton range; 12 charges for short-range Luna rockets at 2 kilotons each; and 6 atomic bombs for IL-28 medium-bombers. Another 24 warheads in the 200–800 kiloton range, for IRBMs, reached the port of La Isabela on another freighter, the *Alexandrovsk*, but were never unloaded because the missiles for which they were intended never arrived.[78] Assuming these figures—which come from Soviet sources—to be accurate, there were at the time the crisis broke at least 158 strategic and tactical nuclear weapons in Cuba, 42 of which (the MRBM warheads plus the IL-28 bombs) could have reached some part of the United States.[79]

Ironically, Khrushchev's *defensive* intentions—his determination to save

Castro's revolution from another American invasion—provide the most plausible explanation for this unprecedented deployment. While visiting Moscow in August 1962, Che Guevara had asked his host what would happen when the Americans discovered that there were missiles in Cuba. "You don't have to worry," Khrushchev is said to have replied. "[I]f there is a problem, we will send the Baltic fleet."[80] This was no joke: he had already authorized the dispatch of 11 submarines, 2 cruisers, 4 destroyers, 16 torpedo boats, and an array of other support vessels, but it would obviously take time to organize such a flotilla. Until it arrived, *tactical* nuclear weapons would protect Soviet troops and the *strategic* missile emplacements they were constructing: they were intended, according to Gribkov, as "back-up defenses for Soviet forces in the Caribbean which were too far away to reinforce quickly by conventional means." The assumption was "that using the low-yield, short-range nuclear weapons in combat limited to Cuba would not provoke massive nuclear retaliation against the Soviet Union."[81]

But this was a shaky proposition, for several reasons. Even after the Americans discovered missiles in Cuba, they did not know for sure that nuclear weapons were also there. They *assumed* so with respect to warheads for the MRBMs and IRBMs, although they never actually confirmed their presence. Reconnaissance flights revealed that Luna short-range rockets were on the island, but these could operate with either conventional or nuclear warheads and the likelihood of the latter being sent seemed low. Troops preparing for a possible invasion, therefore, were relieved of the tactical nuclear weapons that would normally have accompanied them. They "did not need such arms to succeed," General William Y. Smith has recalled, "and given U.S. estimates of the small number of Soviet forces on Cuba, planners saw no sense in the island's defenders employing battlefield atomic weapons and thereby risking escalation."[82] Had there been an American landing, then, it would have encountered a Soviet force at least four times larger than intelligence estimates had indicated, *and* one unexpectedly equipped with nuclear firepower. The Russians might well have fought desperately, because as Gribkov has pointed out, morale was high and "we had no way of leaving Cuba, no avenue for withdrawal."[83]

This is not to say that had there been an invasion, nuclear weapons would have been used. Perhaps Soviet troops would have melted into the mountains to fight a Castro-like guerrilla war, leaving their missiles and warheads behind them. Perhaps the Americans would have refrained from pressing the attack, thereby allowing the Russians a graceful exit. Perhaps Khrushchev would have tolerated Castro's overthrow and the Red Army's humiliation. Perhaps Kennedy still would have cut a deal. Perhaps—but all sides are fortunate, in retrospect, not to have had to rely upon these counterfactuals becoming fact.[84] For each of them would have required preserving *control* while avoiding *emotionalism*. And yet the Americans' experience of managing nuclear weapons under conditions of high alert suggests how easily control might have been lost. The Russians were deploying theirs in totally unfamiliar terrain, under the probability of imminent military attack, on behalf of allies whose emotions were running about as high as they ever do. As Castro later explained to Mikoyan: "Our people are very impulsive."[85]

Khrushchev, to some extent, anticipated these dangers. He had initially authorized General Issa Pliyev, who commanded Soviet forces in Cuba, to use tactical nuclear weapons only *if* an attack was under way and *if* he could not reach Moscow to confirm permission. But Khrushchev rescinded that oral order in writing on 22 October, upon learning that the Americans had discovered the Soviet missile emplacements. He thereby strengthened control from the top as alert levels rose, something Kennedy did not immediately do. At no point did Khrushchev give anyone else the authority to launch MRBMs or IRBMs; nor were strategic or tactical warheads apparently ever placed on the rockets that were to carry them. Pliyev did ask for permission to move the warheads closer to their delivery vehicles on the night of 26 October, but he was not allowed to do so and received an even stronger warning against using *any* nuclear weapons without Moscow's *explicit* approval. There were no permissive action links or other comparable safeguards against unauthorized use, though, so Khrushchev had to depend totally upon Pliyev and his subordinates to keep that from happening.[86]

Soviet air defense units were under equally explicit orders not to fire on American reconnaissance planes, despite the detailed information they were collecting on the missile deployment.[87] And yet, on 27 October, at almost the same moment the wayward U-2 was violating Siberian airspace, another one piloted by Major Rudolph Anderson was indeed shot down over Cuba. Castro took public responsibility, but when Khrushchev complained to him about this risky act the Cuban leader suggested pointedly that "[t]he Soviet command can furnish you with additional reports of what happened."[88] It soon came out that although the Cubans had indeed opened fire on low-flying American planes that day, Anderson's high-altitude U-2 had been shot down by a *Soviet* anti-aircraft unit acting on orders from Lieutenant General Stepan Grechko, commander of Soviet air defenses in Cuba.

Pliyev had earlier asked for authorization to fire on American planes if they attacked Soviet facilities; but Moscow had not responded and certainly had not given permission to shoot down an unarmed U-2. Unable to reach Pliyev but with his forces on high alert, Grechko apparently jumped to the conclusion that because the Cubans were firing war had begun and all restrictions were off: "These officers did not so much disobey orders as react, in a reasoned military manner, as they understood the situation required," Gribkov later recalled.[89] Castro himself explained the incident differently: "These soldiers were all together. They had a common enemy. The firing started, and in a basic spirit of solidarity, the Soviets decided to fire as well."[90]

Either way, Pliyev had lost control, which meant that Khrushchev had also. And who *was* Pliyev? Could Khrushchev really count on him to re-establish Moscow's authority over air defenses and—much more important—to maintain it over nuclear weapons? He was, as it happened, best known for having led the world's last great *cavalry* charge, against the Japanese in Manchuria during

World War II—and for having commanded the troops that only months earlier had shot down rioters in the streets of Novocherkassk. Khrushchev had, to be sure, given that order and Pliyev had obeyed it. But the Kremlin commander-in-chief might well have wondered, at this point in the missile crisis, whether rewarding Pliyev with the Cuban appointment had been the wisest thing to do.[91]

Khrushchev had all the more cause to worry about emotionalism in Cuba because of a cable Castro had sent him shortly before Anderson's plane was shot down. Insisting that an American invasion was imminent, it warned that the danger such an attack would pose for humanity "is so great that the Soviet Union must never allow the circumstances in which the imperialists could launch the first strike against it." If the imperialists

actually carry out the brutal act of invading Cuba in violation of international law and morality, that would be the moment to eliminate such danger forever through an act of clear and legitimate defense, however harsh and terrible the solution would be, for there is no other.[92]

Khrushchev replied that this amounted to asking "that we be the first to launch a nuclear strike against the territory of the enemy," which in turn "would have been the start of a thermonuclear world war. Dear Comrade Fidel Castro, I consider this proposal of yours incorrect, although I understand your motivation." If such a conflict had broken out,

the United States would have sustained huge losses, but the Soviet Union and the whole socialist camp would have also suffered greatly. As far as Cuba is concerned, it would be difficult to say even in general terms what this would have meant for them. . . . There's no doubt that the Cuban people would have fought courageously or that they would have died heroically. But we are not struggling against imperialism in order to die . . . .[93]

Firmness was indeed desirable, the shaken Kremlin leader reminded the increasingly unstable Maximum Leader just after word had come of the U-2 shootdown. But it was important "not to be carried away by sentiment."[94]

Castro "was a very hot-tempered person," Khrushchev later acknowledged. "We understood that he failed to think through the obvious consequences of a proposal that placed the planet on the brink of extinction."[95] How, though, had Castro come to think this way? Was it just a coincidence that just four years earlier Khrushchev had found himself trying to convince another revolutionary romantic—who had also seemed to expect Moscow to respond with nuclear weapons if the Americans attacked his territory—that survival had much to recommend it?[96]

Perhaps the casualness with which both Mao Zedong and Fidel Castro regarded the prospect of nuclear war reflected their militancy as founding revolutionaries: their glorification of sheer will, their disdain for practicalities. But they also shared, along with Walter Ulbricht, a certain perplexity: why did Khrushchev's strategic behavior not more closely match his strategic claims? Had they known more about the strategic balance, as Castro has since suggested with respect to himself, they too might have tempered romanticism with realism. But Khrushchev never informed his allies and they did not restrain themselves—with the interesting result that they wound up frightening *him* as much as anyone else.

VI

So who prevailed in the Cuban missile crisis? Kennedy certainly thought the United States had: hence his famous warning to subordinates—and to reporters who still in those days accepted such guidance—not to humiliate Khrushchev by boasting too openly. It really had been "a great victory" though, the President could not refrain from telling Congressional leaders: "We have resolved one of the great crises of mankind."[97] Most historians have seen the outcome much as he did: one of them could write confidently as late as 1990 that there was "little doubt as to who the real winners and losers were." After all, Khrushchev himself had admitted, in a quote prominently cited by that historian, "that we were obliged to make some big concessions in the interests of peace."[98]

But Khrushchev added, in a comment *not* cited: "It was a great victory for us, though, that we had been able to extract from Kennedy a promise that neither America nor any of her allies would invade Cuba."[99] He elaborated in a passage withheld from the original edition of his memoirs:

The aim of the American aggressors was to destroy Cuba. Our aim was to preserve Cuba. Today Cuba exists. So who won? It cost us nothing more than the round-trip expenses for transporting the rockets to Cuba and back.[100]

Rationalizations these may have been, but they were not just retrospective ones. "We feel that the aggressor came out the loser," Khrushchev cabled Castro immediately after the crisis. "He made preparations to attack Cuba but we stopped him. . . . We view this as a great victory."[101] Mikoyan, following this lead, insisted that by putting the missiles in *and* then taking them out, "the main objective—salvation of Cuba—had been achieved."[102]

Some skepticism is surely in order here: Khrushchev had not *intended* a quick round-trip Caribbean cruise for Soviet troops, missiles, and nuclear warheads. Veterans of the operation still smart from the humiliation of having to pull their weapons out under American supervision; and although Khrushchev's handling of the crisis was not the main reason his colleagues overthrew him two years later, it did play a role.[103] The fact that the Soviet Union concentrated so heavily on building real ICBMs over the next two decades was hardly a vote of confidence in Khrushchev's rhetorical ICBMs, or their MRBM surrogates in Cuba.[104]

But what if—as now seems likely—Khrushchev's chief purpose had not been to shift the strategic balance but rather to save the Cuban revolution? Would the United States, in the absence of a missile deployment, have attempted a bigger and better-planned Bay of Pigs? There has long been ample evidence that the Kennedy administration was trying to get rid of Castro *by all means short of an invasion.* Given the unprecedented level of American military activity in the Caribbean in the months and particularly the weeks before the crisis broke, it seems foolish to claim that the next step would never have been taken—especially if one of the CIA's many assassination plots against Castro had actually succeeded.[105]

From that perspective then, Khrushchev could claim victory: whatever the prospect of an American attack on Cuba before the missile crisis, there was never a serious one after it.[106] Sabotage efforts and assassination attempts continued on a reduced scale through most of 1963, but by the time of his own assassination Kennedy was quietly exploring a *modus vivendi* with Castro.[107] The Maximum Leader was still in charge in Havana when Khrushchev was deposed the following year, as he was when the ex-Soviet leader dictated his memoirs, as he was when the Soviet Union itself finally collapsed, as he still is today. Whatever else one might say about it, the missile crisis settlement provided extraordinarily effective life insurance for a regime whose life expectancy no one, initially, would have rated as very high.

Nor did the Soviet Union suffer as much as one might have anticipated from its "humiliation" in Cuba: it would survive as a Cold War superpower, after all, for another three decades. It did so, to be sure, on an increasingly narrow power base. Moscow's economic, ideological, cultural, and moral example had largely lost its appeal by 1962, leaving only military strength as an effective means of projecting influence. But the missile crisis shocked the United States and its allies into realizing the precariousness of their own security, for all the diversity upon which it rested. If only a few inaccurately aimed Soviet nuclear warheads could wreak more havoc than in all previous wars combined, did it really mean all that much to have prevailed economically, ideologically, culturally, and even morally? The west therefore began narrowing its *criteria* for calculating power even as the Soviet Union's *capabilities* for projecting power were also narrowing.

Both sides as a consequence came to see military credibility as more important than its non-military counterparts. Both agreed tacitly to compete within the single arena in which the Soviet Union was still capable of putting up a respectable fight. Just as the six-shooter compensated for disparities in physical strength on the American frontier—or at least in movies about it—so the capacity for nuclear destruction offset gross deficiencies in the Soviet Union's ability to feed, clothe, and house its own people, or to manage its alliances, or to influence those beyond the reach of its own military control. The result was an *apparent* stalemate: a "long peace," to quote the same historian who characterized the Cuban missile crisis as a victory for the United States.[108]

Viewing the Cold War as a "long peace" was not so much wrong as shortsighted. The Soviet–American competition did take on a certain stability, even predictability, after 1962. Neither side would ever again initiate direct challenges to the other's sphere of influence. Anomalies like a divided Germany and Korea—even absurdities like a walled capitalist West Berlin in the middle of a communist East Germany, or an American naval base on the territory of a Soviet ally just off the coast of Florida—came to seem quite normal. The strategic arms race intensified in the wake of the missile crisis, but it was conducted within an increasingly precise set of rules, codified in formal agreements like the Limited Nuclear Test Ban Treaty of 1963, the Non-Proliferation Treaty of 1968, and the Strategic Arms Limitation Treaty of 1972, as well as the equally important informal understanding that both sides would tolerate satellite reconnaissance. By the late 1970s the Cold War had evolved, or so it seemed, into a robust, sustainable, and at least at the superpower level, *peaceful* international system.[109]

We now know, though, that the "long peace" was not a *permanent* peace. The Soviet Union's military strength failed in the end to save it; its non-military weaknesses eventually destroyed it. But it took a very long time for that to happen. By discouraging external challenges, by continuing to convey an Oz-like image long after the original Wizard's forced retirement, nuclear weapons and the fear they generated may well have stretched out the process of decay inside the USSR—in effect slowing down time—although they could not reverse it. Not the least of the Cold War's oddities is that its outcome was largely determined before two-thirds of it had even been fought.

TEN

The New Cold War History: First Impressions

And despite the many failings of the United States, there was no doubt that the world, for all its misery, was a better place than it would have been without American resistance to Joseph Stalin's vision.

Warren I. Cohen[1]

Readers should not be misled by the confident tone of the literature (including my own observations) into confusing opinion with established truth.

Eric Hobsbawm[2]

HISTORY does not end, but historians sooner or later must. The patience of readers, the constraints imposed by publishers, the limits of our own energy and insight—all of these require that we find convenient points at which to conclude our books. When writing about war, this is usually not difficult. Most wars begin and end at specific points; and although historians may debate their origins, conduct, and consequences, they rarely disagree about their dates. Nor is there apt to be much doubt about who won, although there may be about why. Such certainties are possible because historians generally wait until wars are over to begin writing about them. Beginnings, endings, and consequences tend to be, by then, self-evident.

Consider what the history of any great war might look like if accounts of it began to appear before the fighting had ceased. Historians would hardly be able to draw equally and dispassionately upon the archives of each belligerent, with a view to determining who started it. Available sources would be biased and incomplete. Winners and losers would remain unclear, as would the circumstances of victory or defeat. A history of World War I composed as late as the winter of 1918, or of World War II completed in 1942, would differ dramatically from those familiar to us; for these would be histories written from *within* a great event, not after it. It is precisely that quality of coming *after* that causes us—most of the time—to regard a narrative as "historical" in the first place.

World War I took four years to fight; World War II required six. The Cold

War, however, dragged on for four and a half decades: more than *ten times* the length of the 1914–18 war, *seven times* that of 1939–45. Historians chose, reasonably enough, not to await the Cold War's end before beginning to write about it. This meant, though, that until recently their real histories resembled our imaginary histories of the two world wars: they lacked equivalent access to archives on each side, and they were written without knowing how it would all come out.[3] Despite divergent and often discordant interpretations, all Cold War historians—whether of orthodox, revisionist, post-revisionist, corporatist, international, cultural, or post-modernist persuasions—fell into the unusual habit of working within their chosen period rather than after it.[4]

What seems most striking now about this "old" Cold War history are not the disagreements that took place among its practitioners but rather its common characteristics. It showed little of the detachment that comes from following, not reflecting, a historical epoch.[5] It gave one side disproportionate attention: whether critical or complementary, most of this scholarship focused on the United States, its allies, or its clients. It neglected the fact that *two* superpowers dominated the post-1945 world; that each often acted in response to what the other had done; and that third parties responded to—but sometimes manipulated—each of them. It emphasized *interests*, which it mostly defined in material terms—what people possessed, or wanted to possess. It tended to overlook *ideas*—what people believed, or wanted to believe.

There were various reasons for these deficiencies. The Cold War went on for so long that toward its end few experts on it had experienced any other international system: comparisons across time and space faded as a result. Marxist-Leninist states got slighted because they kept so much of their history so carefully hidden: until the late 1980s none had even begun to open the kind of archives routinely available in the west. "Realist" and "neorealist" theorists of international relations regarded what went on inside people's heads as hard to measure, and therefore easy to dismiss.[6]

The "new" Cold War history is likely to depart from these patterns in several ways. It will treat its subject as a discrete episode with a known beginning and end, not as a continuing or even permanent condition. It will place the Cold War within the stream of time; it will not confuse the Cold War *with* the stream of time. It will acknowledge that there have been, and will assuredly be, other ways of organizing international relations than those practiced after World War II. It will therefore place its subject within a broader comparative framework than the "old" Cold War history managed to do.

The "new" Cold War history will be multi-archival, in that it will at least *attempt* to draw upon the records of *all* major participants in that conflict. It will abandon the asymmetry that provided clinical detail on the public *and* behind-the-scenes behavior of western leaders, but little beyond speculation when it came to backstage maneuvering within the Marxist-Leninist world. It will thus be a truly international history, affirmative action for the "second" as well as the "first" and "third" worlds.[7]

The "new" Cold War history will take ideas seriously: here the way that con-flict ended is bound to reshape our view of how it began and evolved. For the events of 1989–91 make sense only in terms of ideas. There was no military defeat or economic crash; but there was a collapse of legitimacy. The people of one Cold War empire suddenly realized that its emperors had no clothes on. As in the classic tale, though, that insight resulted from a shift in how people thought, not from any change in what they saw.

All of these practices—knowing the outcome, having multiple sources, pay-ing attention to ideas—are decidedly old-fashioned. They are the way history is written most of the time. They suggest not only that the "old" Cold War history is out of date; it was also *an abnormal way of writing history itself*. It was the prod-uct of an abnormal age, which was the Cold War itself. Like the post-Cold War world in which it exists, the "new" Cold War history is only getting us back to normal.

But what does it all amount to? How might this view of the Cold War from the outside—and from the "other side"—change our understanding of it? What follows are first impressions, gleaned from writing this book, stated as a series of hypotheses. They are, most emphatically, subject to refinement, revision, and even subsequent rejection in the light of additional evidence. They represent what I think we know *now* but did not know, at least not as clearly, while the Cold War was going on. We will surely know *more*, though, as time passes and the Cold War completes its lengthy progression from that most frightening of contemporary anxieties to just another distant, dusty, historical memory.

I

The first of these hypotheses is that *the diversification of power did more to shape the course of the Cold War than did the balancing of power*.

A key assumption of the "old" Cold War history was that with the defeat of Germany and Japan, the international system shifted from a multipolar to a bipolar configuration.[8] The great powers of Europe appeared to have commit-ted a kind of collective suicide, leaving the United States and the Soviet Union as even greater superpowers. Whereas earlier history had seen several large states competing within the global arena, the future now lay, or so it seemed, in the hands of only two. Alexis de Tocqueville had predicted in 1835 that Russians and Americans would one day dominate the destinies of half the earth, and in 1945 it certainly looked as though their time had come.

This switch from multipolarity to bipolarity also impressed theorists. "Realists" interpreted it to mean that only the balancing of power would ensure peace.[9] By the 1970s, "neo-realists" saw bipolarity as so deeply rooted that sta-bility was sure to result from it. Their most influential spokesman, Kenneth Waltz, foresaw the possibility that the Cold War might someday end—but only because bipolarity would make that possible. The Soviet Union and the United

States would dominate the post-Cold War world, he predicted in 1979, for as far into the future as one could foresee.[10]

Obviously both the historians and the theorists got it wrong. The error arose, I think, from the way we calculated power during the Cold War years. We did so almost entirely in monodimensional terms, focusing particularly on military indices, when a multidimensional perspective might have told us more. The end of the Cold War made it blindingly clear that military strength does not always determine the course of great events: the Soviet Union collapsed, after all, with its arms and armed forces fully intact. Deficiencies in other kinds of power—economic, ideological, cultural, moral—caused the USSR to lose its superpower status, and we can now see that a slow but steady erosion in those non-military capabilities had been going on for some time.

To visualize what happened, imagine a troubled triceratops.[11] From the outside, as rivals contemplated its sheer size, tough skin, bristling armament, and aggressive posturing, the beast looked sufficiently formidable that none dared tangle with it. Appearances deceived, though, for within its digestive, circulatory, and respiratory systems were slowly clogging up, and then shutting down. There were few external signs of this until the day the creature was found with all four feet in the air, still awesome but now bloated, stiff, and quite dead. The moral of the fable is that armaments make impressive exoskeletons, but a shell alone ensures the survival of no animal and no state.

Had we understood better that power exists in multiple forms; had we perceived that some kinds of power can exist in a bipolar configuration while others are distributed more widely; had we allowed for the possibility that power, whether within a state or a system of states, can evolve either toward or away from diversity; had we grasped these subtleties, we might have seen sooner than we did that bipolarity was an artifact of the way World War II ended and therefore also of the improbable series of events that had caused World War II. It was *not* a fundamental change in the nature of the international system. That system remained *multidimensional* throughout the Cold War, and the Soviet Union's slow descent into monodimensionality is what eventually killed it. Multidimensionality may be multipolarity more accurately conceived.

II

Another hypothesis that emerges from the "new" Cold War history is that *the United States and the Soviet Union built empires after World War II, although not of the same kind.*

Most "old" Cold War historians acknowledged that despite its anti-imperial traditions the United States constructed an empire after 1945: what they debated was whether this happened intentionally or by inadvertence. Was the American empire the result of a domestically rooted drive for markets and investment opportunities abroad? Or was it an accidental by-product of having rushed to fill a power vacuum in Europe, a reflex that would cause Americans to meddle wherever else in the world they thought there *might* be a Soviet threat? Either way, credibility became the currency in which the United States, like most empires in the past, counted its assets.

Much the same was true, it now appears, of the Soviet Union. Partly driven by ideological and geostrategic ambitions, partly responding to the opportunities that lay before him, Stalin too built a postwar European empire. With Mao's victory, he hoped—not quite trusting his own good fortune—to extend it to China; Khrushchev sought similar objectives in the "third world." But as problems developed, whether in Korea or later in Cuba, fears of falling dominoes surfaced about as often in Moscow as in Washington: hence Stalin's extraordinary pressure on the Chinese to save Kim Il-sung; hence Khrushchev's remarkable risk-taking in defense of Fidel Castro.

From an imperial perspective there was little new here. All empires fear losing credibility; one might conclude, therefore, that the Soviet and American empires did not differ all that much from one another. But other findings from the "new" Cold War history suggest that such an "equivalency" argument, at least as far as Europe and Japan are concerned, would be quite wrong. To see why, consider another issue all empires have had to face: will their subjects collaborate or resist? The difficulty of managing any empire is bound to vary accordingly; but it is the *occupied*, not the occupiers, who make this choice. Even the apparently powerless have that much power.

More than a decade ago, the historian Geir Lundestad revealed distinctive patterns of collaboration and resistance when he pointed out that the West Europeans "invited" the United States to construct an empire and include them within it, in the hope of containing the empire the Russians were imposing on eastern Europe.[12] This argument still makes sense, but with certain refinements.

One is that Stalin appears also to have *hoped* for an "invitation," especially in Germany, perhaps elsewhere in Eastern Europe, possibly even in Japan. The disarray now evident in his policies toward these regions may reflect the fact that it never came. If so, the Europeans and the Japanese become critical players, for while it was hardly within their power to prevent Soviet or American domination, they were free to welcome or fear that process. Their responses were not always overt, especially in countries the Red Army occupied. Resistance is no less significant, however, for taking sullen or subtle forms: officials in Moscow soon lost whatever illusions they might have had that they could count, in a crunch, upon their East European and German "allies." The Americans, if anything, *underestimated* the loyalty of their NATO partners and the Japanese. In Europe and Northeast Asia, then, these were hardly equivalent empires.[13] The American presence had a strong base of popular support, confirmed repeatedly as free elections kept the governments in power that had invited it. The Soviet presence never won such acceptance: that, no doubt, is why free elections within Moscow's sphere of influence ceased to be held.

Patterns blur, to be sure, when one looks elsewhere. It is clear now that the

Chinese—or at least their new communist leaders—initially extended an invitation to the *Russians* and resisted what they saw as threats from the Americans. In Southeast Asia as well as the Middle East, Africa, and Latin America, invitations to both superpowers were periodically advanced and withdrawn. Whether the Russians or the Americans responded more brutally—or more humanely—is difficult to say: as always, the "third world" defies easy generalizations. Decisions to collaborate or resist depended upon time, place, and circumstances.

But the "third world" did not, in the end, determine the Cold War's outcome. What took place in Europe and Japan largely did, and there the results were decisive: where possible, the inhabitants resisted the Soviet Union and collaborated with the United States; where impossible, most wished passionately that they could have done so. That raises the question of why Washington's empire, in those pivotal regions, generated so much less friction than Moscow's.

III

One answer may be that *many people then saw the Cold War as a contest of good versus evil, even if historians since have rarely done so.*

Let me focus here on a single significant case: it has to do with what happened in Germany immediately after the war as its citizens confronted their respective occupiers. What Stalin sought there, it now seems clear, was a communist regime in the east that would attract Germans in the west without requiring the use of force, something the Russians could ill afford given their own exhaustion and the Americans' monopoly over the atomic bomb.[14]

Obviously, this is not what he got. Germans first voted with their feet—fleeing to the west in huge numbers to avoid the Red Army—and then at the ballot box in ways that frustrated all of Stalin's hopes. But this outcome was not foreordained. There were large numbers of communist party members throughout Germany at the end of the war, and their prestige—because of their opposition to the Nazis—had never been higher. Why did the Germans so overwhelmingly welcome the Americans and their allies, and fear the Russians?

It has long been known that the Red Army behaved brutally toward German civilians in those parts of the country it occupied, and that this treatment contrasted strikingly with that accorded the Germans in the American, British, and French zones. What we had not known, until recently, is how pervasive the problem of rape was: Red Army soldiers may have assaulted as many as *two million* German women in 1945–6. There were few efforts for many months to stop this behavior, or to discipline those who indulged in it. To this day, some Soviet officers recall the experience much as Stalin saw it at the time: troops that had risked their lives and survived deserved a little fun.[15]

Now, obviously rape in particular, and brutality in general, is always a problem when armies occupy the territory of defeated adversaries. Certainly Russian troops had good reason to hate the Germans, given what they had done inside the Soviet Union. But these semi-sanctioned mass rapes took place precisely as Stalin was trying to *win the support* of the German people, not just in the east but throughout the country. He even allowed elections to be held inside the Soviet zone in the fall of 1946, only to have the Germans—women in particular—vote overwhelmingly against the Soviet-supported candidates.[16]

The incidence of rape and other forms of brutality was so much greater on the Soviet than on the western side that it played a major role in determining which way Germans would tilt in the Cold War that was to come. It ensured a pro-western orientation from the very beginning of that conflict, which surely helps to account for why the West German regime was able to establish itself as a legitimate government while its East German counterpart never did.

What happened here was not a reflection of high policy; it was rather a matter of occupying armies, in the absence of clear orders, falling back upon their own domestic standards of acceptable behavior. The rules of civil society implicit in democratic politics made the humanitarian treatment of defeated enemies seem natural to the Western allies. Their troops did not have to be ordered to do this—they just did it, and it did not occur to them to do otherwise. Much the same thing happened, with equally important results, in occupied Japan. But thanks to Stalin and Hitler, Russian troops came out of a culture of brutality with few parallels in modern history. Having been brutalized themselves, it did not occur to many of them that there was anything wrong with brutalizing others. And it did not occur to their leaders to put a stop to this process until after it had lost them Germany.

In this instance, then, civility on one side and its absence on the other played an enormous role in shaping the course of events. The rapes dramatized differences between Soviet authoritarianism and American democracy in ways that could hardly have been more direct. Social history, even gender history, intersected with inhumanity to make diplomatic history. What this suggests, then, is that historians of the Cold War need to look quite carefully at what those who *saw* distinctions between good and evil *thought and did* about them. For when people vote with their feet, it generally means they have ideas in their minds. But to understand these, we have to take seriously what *they at the time believed*.

No historian looking at the religious practices of late antiquity, or at the medieval peasantry, or even at revolutions in America, France, or Russia, would doubt the importance of seeking out the voices and viewpoints of everyday life. And yet, when looking at the origins, the evolution, and the end of the Cold War—or for that matter at the gap between popular and academic perceptions of the past today—historians seem to want to tell the public what its memories ought to be.[17] A little self-scrutiny might be in order here, to see whether we are treating the distant past and the recent past in exactly the same way.

IV

If the American empire generated less resistance than did its Soviet counterpart, another reason may be that *democracy proved superior to autocracy in maintaining coalitions.*

Democratic principles seemed ill-suited to foreign policy as the Cold War began. The founding fathers of "realism"—Morgenthau, Kennan, Lippmann, E. H. Carr—tended to blame Wilsonian "legalism-moralism" for having led to the League of Nations, the Washington Naval Treaties, the Kellogg–Briand Pact, and all the other well-meaning gestures that had failed so conspicuously to prevent World War II.[18] None of these initiatives, they insisted, had taken into account the actual power relationships that determined the course of international relations. If the western democracies were to survive in the postwar world—which was likely to be as cold and cruel as the prewar world—they would have to abandon the illusion that they could conduct diplomacy as they ran their domestic affairs. It would be necessary to learn about balances of power, covert operations, and the permanent peacetime uses of military force— idealists, in short, would have to master the cynical art of *Realpolitik.*

As always with Kennan, there was a certain ambivalence. On the one hand, he stressed how little use he had for democratic procedures in the making of foreign policy: witness his memorable comparison of democracy to "one of those prehistoric monsters with a body as long as this room and a brain the size of a pin."[19] On the other hand, he expected containment to work by having the United States remain true to its principles, which presumably included those of democratic politics: "The greatest danger that can befall us in coping with this problem of Soviet communism, is that we shall allow ourselves to become like those with whom we are coping."[20]

This danger, it is now clear, never materialized. Despite frequent departures from them, the United States on the whole retained its traditional values; it also allowed these, from time to time, to shape its Cold War policies. It did so, to be sure, less from intention than instinct: when otherwise unsure what to do, Americans tended to revert to their democratic habits and encourage others to adopt them as well.[21] Far from being the impractical idealism the "realists" feared, though, such behavior turned out to be eminently realistic. Consider three key episodes, all of which illustrate the extension of American domestic practices into the foreign policy realm: the democratizations (by way of military occupation) of Germany and Japan, the management of the NATO alliance, and the encouragement of European integration.

What each of these had in common was the stake in the success of the enterprise the Americans gave their allies by involving them in design, organization, and administration. German and Japanese occupations provided the fewest opportunities, yet even here it is striking to what extent Generals Clay and MacArthur adapted their reforms to local conditions while still, for the most part, making them stick. NATO was very much a joint venture: Europeans proposed it, and the United States permitted them a surprising amount of influence over its structure and strategies. European integration for years has flourished independently of the Americans, but it could hardly have arisen had not Washington insisted upon European cooperation in return for economic and military assistance during the late 1940s. Only then did the process become self-organizing, with a character very much its own.

It is difficult to imagine the Soviet Union acting similarly. Its occupation policies in Germany backfired, failing to generate popular support. The Warsaw Pact never operated as NATO did: there was little sense of mutual interest, especially after the events of 1956. Once the Korean War was over, the Sino-Soviet alliance functioned no better. Nor was there spontaneous economic or political integration within the Soviet sphere: instead, everything had to be routed through and managed from Moscow, in the classic manner of old-fashioned empires.

The Americans constructed a new kind of empire—a democratic empire—for the simple reason that they were, by habit and history, democratic in their politics. They were used to the bargaining and deal-making, the coercion and conciliation, that routinely takes place within such a system. They did not automatically regard resistance as treason. Their example, as a consequence, spread easily; it also coexisted comfortably with other democracies where they were already in place.

The Russians, coming out of an authoritarian tradition, knew of no way to deal with independent thinking other than to smother it. The slightest signs of autonomy, for Stalin, were heresy, to be rooted out with all the thoroughness of the Spanish Inquisition. The result was surely subservience, but it was never self-organization. To the extent that it gave others a stake in the enterprise, that stake may have been as much in welcoming failure as success.

In this sense, then, preserving democratic ideals turned out to be a very realistic thing for the west to have done. The Kennan of the X article was a lot more prescient than the Kennan haunted by visions of democratic dinosaurs.

V

A related hypothesis is that, in contrast to democratic realism, *Marxism-Leninism during the Cold War fostered authoritarian romanticism.*

In his recent book, *Diplomacy*, Henry Kissinger faults Hitler for having fallen prey to visions based more on emotion than on rational calculation. Stalin, he claims, was brutally realistic, prepared to take as long as necessary to achieve his goals, willing to adapt ideology as needed to justify them. For Hitler, Kissinger seems to be saying, ideology determined objectives, and practical difficulties were not allowed to stand in the way. For Stalin, it was the other way around: the objectives determined the ideology, which was adjusted as necessary to shifting circumstances.[22] That certainly has been the standard view of how

Marxist-Leninist states functioned, and as a consequence the "old" Cold War history failed to take ideology very seriously.

The new sources suggest the need to reconsider, for they seem to suggest that ideology often *determined* the behavior of Marxist-Leninist regimes: it was not simply a justification for actions already decided upon. In one sense, this should hardly surprise us. The Soviet Union, the People's Republic of China, and other such states based their very legitimacy upon an ideology which, with its premium on orthodoxy and its deep distrust of heresy, permeated all aspects of daily life. Why, except for ideology, would Kremlin leaders retain a system of collectivized agriculture that had repeatedly shown itself not to work? Why, for that matter, insist on a command economy in the first place, since the evidence of its failures was almost as compelling? Foreign policy too reflected ideology, in ways that resist alternative explanations.

Take, for example, what we now know to have been Stalin's persistent belief, after 1945, that the next war would take place within the *capitalist* world. It came, of course, from a literal reading of Lenin: capitalists were so greedy, the great man had insisted, so preoccupied with finding ways to cheat or exploit one another, that they would never be able to cooperate on anything for very long. But these Leninist expectations kept Stalin from seeing what was really happening during the early postwar years: Soviet behavior in Eastern Europe and Germany was causing the West Europeans and the Americans to combine in a coalition directed against *him*. Stalin imagined one Europe while ensuring, through his actions, that a totally different one would actually evolve.

Then there is Mao Zedong, who now appears to have been a much more committed Marxist-Leninist than previously suspected. Chinese and Soviet sources show him consistently subordinating national to ideological interests: this led him, quite short-sightedly, to suspect the Americans and trust the Russians. It is difficult otherwise to account for Mao's extraordinary deference to his "elder brother" in the Kremlin, his willingness to accept an "unequal treaty" with Moscow, and the massive sacrifices China made in the Korean War. Not until after Stalin's death did an independent Chinese foreign policy emerge; but even that had an ideological basis. It was just that Mao now considered himself to be chief ideologist.

Ideology also helps to explain Stalin's uncharacteristic aggressiveness in the months preceding the Korean War. He interpreted Mao's victory as evidence that the revolutionary tide, contained in Europe, had shifted to Asia. He fell, as a consequence, into a kind of geriatric romanticism, encouraging the Chinese to support insurgencies elsewhere and authorizing Kim Il-sung to attack South Korea. It was as if Stalin chose to celebrate his seventieth year by trying to recapture his revolutionary youth: his ideological vision made him a naive and sentimental as well as a brutal old man.

And lest that pattern seem unique, consider what we now know of Khrushchev, who responded to Castro's revolution in Cuba in much the same way. There could have been little strategic logic in *creating* a Caribbean outpost at least as indefensible as the one the Americans and their allies had *inherited* in

West Berlin. From an ideological perspective, though, Cuba was all-important: it might provide the spark that would set off Marxist uprisings throughout Latin America. There was little hard evidence of such a prospect, but even the possibility—however remote—had an intense *emotional* hold in Moscow. One has the image here, not so much of a Bismarck or even a Lenin, but of aging Ponce de Leons in search of an ideological Fountain of Youth.

The new materials suggest, then, that Kissinger was right about Hitler, and would have been right about Stalin and his successors as well as Mao had he applied to them a similar model of emotionally based ideological romanticism. For there seems to have been something about authoritarians that caused them to lose touch with reality. Being a communist provided no greater safeguard against tilting at windmills than being a fascist. The explanation is not difficult to discern: autocratic systems reinforce, while discouraging attempts to puncture, whatever quixotic illusions may exist at the top.

VI

Why, though, if the Americans had multidimensionality, collaboration, morality, and realism all going for them, did the Cold War last as long as it did? Here the "new" history suggests yet another hypothesis, which is that *nuclear weapons exchanged destructiveness for duration.*

The proposition that nuclear weapons kept the Cold War from getting hot is an old and familiar one, although still not universally accepted.[23] The new technology of warfare is supposed to have created constraints against escalation not previously present, and as a result crises that in other periods would have caused great wars during the Cold War did not. There seems little doubt now that the nuclear revolution indeed had this restraining effect. But there was a price to be paid—even though it was surely worth paying.

If, as suggested above, retaining a diversified power base helped the west win the Cold War—if one triceratops remained healthy while the other slowly sickened—then it would be worth specifying *when* the Soviet Union completed the transition from multi- to monodimensionality. One might have expected this to happen shortly before the struggle ended. But the new evidence indicates—on this point old evidence more carefully analyzed might also have suggested—that the process was virtually complete by the early 1960s. The Cold War went on for another three decades. How come?

This is where nuclear weapons come in, for they encouraged the monodimensional measurement of power. McNamara insisted that a 17–1 advantage for the United States in 1962 still translated into *effective* nuclear parity because the prospect of only a few nuclear explosions on American soil would deter Washington from doing anything that might provoke them. Unconvinced, Soviet leaders used the years that followed to seek actual parity with the United States, and by 1970 they had largely succeeded. But look what was happening here: both sides had tacitly agreed to calculate their strengths in the particular category of power—if one agrees that the "third world" offered little, the *only* category—in which the Soviet Union could still match the United States. It was as if the ailing triceratops somehow convinced its adversary to focus only on its external appearance, disregarding its reflexes, blood pressure, X-rays, and stool samples.

There developed, as a result, a fixation on the nuclear arms race as the focus of Soviet–American relations. Future generations are sure to wonder at this. Why was so much time spent worrying about intricate numerical balances in categories of weapons no one could use? Or on the negotiation of arms control treaties that reduced no arms? How did the idea ever take hold that security could lie in the deliberate cultivation of mutual vulnerability? That defense was a bad thing?

Not until the Reagan administration would anyone seriously question these orthodoxies—whether it did so out of ignorance or craft is still not clear. What is apparent is that the United States began to challenge the Soviet Union during the first half of the 1980s in a manner unprecedented since the early Cold War. That state soon exhausted itself and expired—whether from unaccustomed over-exertion or Gorbachev's heroic efforts at resuscitation is also still not completely clear.

Nuclear weapons preserved the image of a formidable Soviet Union long after it had entered into its terminal decline. We will never know whether the USSR could have been successfully—but also safely—confronted at an earlier date; for the Cuban missile crisis convinced western leaders, perhaps correctly, that their own nations' survival depended upon that of their adversary. Efforts to shake the other side seemed far too dangerous to undertake. There was, therefore, a trade-off: we avoided *destruction*, but at the price of *duration*; the Cold War went on much longer than it might have had nuclear weapons never been invented. Given the fact that they did exist, the Cold War could have ended with a bang at just about any point. It took decades to arrange a whimper.

VII

What is there new to say about the old question of responsibility for the Cold War? Who actually started it? Could it have been averted? Here I think the "new" history is bringing us back to an old answer: that *as long as Stalin was running the Soviet Union a cold war was unavoidable.*

History is always the product of determined *and* contingent events: it is up to historians to find the proper balance between them. The Cold War could hardly have happened if there had not been a United States and a Soviet Union, if both had not emerged victorious from World War II, if they had not had conflicting visions of how to organize the postwar world. But these long-term trends did not in themselves *ensure* such a contest, because there is always room for the unexpected to undo what might appear to be inevitable. *Nothing* is ever completely predetermined, as real triceratops and other dinosaurs discovered 65 million years ago when the most recent large asteroid or comet or whatever it was hit the earth and wiped them out.

Individuals, not asteroids, more often personify contingency in history. Who can specify in advance—or unravel afterwards—the particular intersection of genetics, environment, and culture that makes each person unique? Who can foresee what weird conjunctions of design and circumstance may cause a very few individuals to rise so high as to shape great events, and so come to the attention of historians? Such people may set their sights on getting to the top, but an assassin, or a bacillus, or even a carelessly driven taxicab can always be lurking along the way. How entire countries fall into the hands of malevolent geniuses like Hitler and Stalin remains as unfathomable in the "new" Cold War history as in the "old."

Once leaders like these do gain power, however, certain things become highly probable. It is only to be expected that in an authoritarian state the chief authoritarian's personality will weigh much more heavily than those of democratic leaders, who have to share power. And whether because of social alienation, technological innovation, or economic desperation, the first half of the twentieth century was particularly susceptible to great authoritarians and all that resulted from their ascendancy. It is hardly possible to imagine Nazi Germany or the world war it caused without Hitler. I find it increasingly difficult, given what we know now, to imagine the Soviet Union or the Cold War without Stalin.

For the more we learn, the less sense it makes to distinguish Stalin's foreign policies from his domestic practices or even his personal behavior. Scientists have shown the natural world to be filled with examples of what they call "self-similarity across scale": patterns that persist whether one views them microscopically, macroscopically, or anywhere in between.[24] Stalin was like that: he functioned in much the same manner whether operating within the international system, within his alliances, within his country, within his party, within his personal entourage, or even within his family. The Soviet leader waged cold wars on all of these fronts. The Cold War *we* came to know was only one of many from *his* point of view.

Nor did Stalin's influence diminish as quickly as that of most dictators after their deaths. He built a *system* sufficiently durable to survive not only his own demise but his successors' fitful and half-hearted efforts at "de-Stalinization." They were themselves its creatures, and they continued to work within it because they knew no other method of governing. Not until Gorbachev was a Soviet leader fully prepared to dismantle Stalin's structural legacy. It tells us a lot that as it disappeared, so too did the Cold War and ultimately the Soviet Union itself.

This argument by no means absolves the United States and its allies of a considerable responsibility for how the Cold War was fought—hardly a surprising conclusion since they in fact won it. Nor is it to deny the feckless stupidity with which the Americans fell into peripheral conflicts like Vietnam, or their exorbitant expenditures on unusable weaponry: these certainly caused the Cold War to cost much more in money and lives than it otherwise might have. Nor is it to claim moral superiority for western statesmen.[25] None was as bad as Stalin—or Mao—but the Cold War left no leader uncorrupted: the wielding of great power, even in the best of times, rarely does.

It is the case, though, that if one applies the always useful test of counterfactual history—drop a key variable and speculate as to what difference this might have made—Stalin's centrality to the origins of the Cold War becomes quite clear. For all of their importance, one could have removed Roosevelt, Churchill, Truman, Bevin, Marshall, or Acheson, and a cold war would still have probably followed the world war. If one could have eliminated Stalin, alternative paths become quite conceivable. For with the possible exception of Mao, no twentieth-century leader imprinted himself upon his country as thoroughly and with such lasting effect as Stalin did. And given his personal propensity for cold wars—a tendency firmly rooted long before he had even heard of Harry Truman—once Stalin wound up at the top in Moscow and once it was clear his state would survive the war, then it looks equally clear that there was going to be a Cold War whatever the west did. Who then was responsible? The answer, I think, is authoritarianism in general, and Stalin in particular.

VIII

Finally, how will the Cold War look a hundred years hence? Not as it does today, it seems safe enough to say, just as the Cold War we now know looks different from the one we knew, or thought we knew, while it was going on. It ought to humble historians to recognize how much their views of the past—any past, no matter how distant—reflect the particular present in which they find themselves. We are all, in this sense, *temporal* parochials. There follows, then, one last hypothesis: *"new" Cold War historians should retain the capacity to be surprised.*

It would be foolish for this book or any other to claim definitive conclusions on the basis of the fresh but very incomplete evidence the Cold War's end has placed at our disposal. Surprises are bound to lie ahead, whether from new documents or new perspectives or their interconnections. Revisionism is a healthy historiographical process, and no one, not even revisionists, should be exempt from it.

It would be equally short-sighted to dismiss new evidence solely because it fits—or does not fit—existing interpretations. The temptation, among established Cold War historians, is certainly there.[26] Surely we will produce better history, though, if we alter our perspectives to accommodate our sources than if we select from those sources only what sustains our preconceptions. Pre-Darwinian paleontologists insisted for years on the immutability of species despite the fossil evidence that lay before their eyes. Historians who fail to take new sources seriously risk a similarly antiquated commitment to the immutability of theses.

"Triumphalism" too can mislead.[27] To the extent that it reviews what the west did right during the Cold War—as well as what it did wrong—it is a valid historical method, since otherwise one would be hard-pressed to explain why the Cold War ended as decisively as it did. But when "triumphalism" fosters complacency, it goes too far. It obscures the fact that victories, more often than not, carry within themselves the seeds of their own undoing. Enemies may disappear but historical processes rarely do: self-congratulation can get in the way of seeing what these are, where they are going, and what they may portend.

Just because market capitalism and democratic politics triumphed during the Cold War is no guarantee that they will continue to do so. Capitalism still distributes wealth and status unevenly, as Marx said it did. Democracy still gives voice to the alienation that results: people do not necessarily vote the way economists think. Where did communism and fascism come from in the late nineteenth and early twentieth centuries—to say nothing of the great reform movements in the United States and Western Europe—if not from a clash of unregulated markets with an expanding political franchise? And yet the post-Cold War world has seen an unprecedented push for economic integration *and* political self-determination, with almost no thought given to how each might relate to the other.[28]

It is, therefore, too soon to write authoritarianism's obituary. Despite the setbacks it suffered during the Cold War, that form of government has a much longer history than does democracy. It would be temporally parochial in the extreme to conclude that its day is done. If Marxism-Leninism generated so many internal contradictions that it ultimately collapsed, why should we regard democratic capitalism as exempt from similar tendencies? How do we know we are not living within a long historical cycle, one that may sweep us back to a world of authoritarians—although almost certainly not of the Marxist-Leninist variety—all over again?

And yet—surprises happen. There are instances in which historical ecology itself shifts, in which behavior that has flourished for as far back as we can detect suddenly ceases to do so. Bad habits, like ill-adapted life-forms, do sometimes become extinct. This happened to slavery and dueling during the eighteenth and nineteenth centuries, and it may be happening to great-power war as the twentieth century draws to a close.[29] Stephen Jay Gould, a post-Darwinian paleontologist who takes a *very* long view, likes to tell of a particular species of fish which flourished for millions upon millions of years, all of that time superbly in tune with its environment—until the pond dried up.[30]

It may be that the west prevailed during the Cold War not so much because of the success of its institutions or the wisdom of its leaders—although surely there was some of both—as because that conflict just happened to take place at the moment in history when the conditions that had for thousands of years favored authoritarianism suddenly ceased to do so. Perhaps (let us hope so) the pond simply dried up.

NOTES

CHAPTER I

1. Alexis de Tocqueville, *Democracy in America*, ed. J. P. Mayer, trans. George Lawrence (Garden City, NY: Doubleday, 1969), pp. 412–13.
2. François Genoud, ed., *The Testament of Adolf Hitler: The Hitler-Bormann Documents, February–April 1945*, trans. R. H. Stevens (London: Icon Books, 1961), p. 107.
3. Tocqueville, *Democracy in America*, p. 413.
4. Norman E. Saul, *Distant Friends: The United States and Russia, 1763–1867* (Lawrence: University Press of Kansas, 1991) is the most comprehensive history of the early Russian–American relationship; but see also Nikolai N. Bolkhovitinov, *The Beginnings of Russian–American Relations, 1775–1815*, trans. Elena Levin (Cambridge, Mass.: Harvard University Press, 1975).
5. John Lewis Gaddis, *Russia, the Soviet Union, and the United States: An Interpretive History*, 2nd edn. (New York: McGraw Hill, 1990), pp. 11–16.
6. Ibid. 31–41. See also Geoffrey Barraclough, *An Introduction to Contemporary History* (London: C. A. Watts, 1964), pp. 102–5.
7. US Bureau of the Census and the Social Science Research Council, *The Statistical History of the United States from Colonial Times to the Present* (Stamford, Conn.: Fairfield, 1965), pp. 57–8.
8. Frederick F. Travis, *George Kennan and the American–Russian Relationship, 1865–1924* (Athens: Ohio University Press, 1990). This George Kennan was a cousin of a grandfather of the better-known George F. Kennan, the principal architect of "containment" during the Cold War.
9. For the statistics, see Michael W. Doyle, "Kant, Liberal Legacies, and Foreign Affairs, Part I," *Philosophy and Public Affairs* 12 (Summer 1983), 209–10. Norman E. Saul, *Conflict and Concord: The United States and Russia, 1867–1914* (Lawrence: University Press of Kansas, 1996) now provides the fullest account of the pre-World War I deterioration in Russian–American relations.
10. The terms "February" and "October Revolutions", of course, reflect the old pre-revolutionary Russian calendar. The Tsar was overthrown, by the Western calendar that the Bolsheviks soon adopted, on 15 Mar. 1917, and the Provisional Government in turn was deposed on 7 Nov. 1917.
11. Gaddis, *Russia, the Soviet Union, and the United States*, pp. 51–5; Christopher Lasch, *The American Liberals and the Russian Revolution* (New York: Columbia University Press, 1962), pp. 1–30.
12. Richard Pipes, *The Russian Revolution* (New York: Knopf, 1990), provides the best recent account of these developments; see esp. pp. 121–52.
13. Richard Pipes, *Russia Under the Bolshevik Regime* (New York: Knopf, 1994), p. 166.
14. Thomas Knock, *To End All Wars: Woodrow Wilson and the Quest for a New World Order* (New York: Oxford University Press, 1992) provides the best recent overview. But see also Tony Smith, *America's Mission: The United States and the Worldwide Struggle for Democracy in the Twentieth Century* (Princeton:

Princeton University Press, 1994), esp. pp. 84–109; Frank Ninkovich, *Modernity and Power: A History of the Domino Theory in the Twentieth Century* (Chicago: University of Chicago Press, 1994), esp. pp. 37–68; and Henry Kissinger, *Diplomacy* (New York: Simon & Schuster, 1994), pp. 43–55. Betty Miller Unterberger, *The United States, Revolutionary Russia, and the Rise of Czechoslovakia* (Chapel Hill: University of North Carolina Press, 1989) discusses the Wilsonian principle of self-determination in practice.

15. A point made long ago by Arno Mayer, *Political Origins of the New Diplomacy, 1917–1918* (New Haven: Yale University Press, 1959). See also Barraclough, *An Introduction to Contemporary History*, pp. 113–14; and N. Gordon Levin, Jr., *Woodrow Wilson and World Politics: America's Response to War and Revolution* (New York: Oxford University Press, 1968).
16. Pipes, *The Russian Revolution*, p. 525. For the American liberal-capitalist heritage, see Robert W. Tucker and David C. Hendrickson, *Empire of Liberty: The Statecraft of Thomas Jefferson* (New York: Oxford University Press, 1990).
17. See Barbara Tuchman, *The Zimmermann Telegram* (New York: Viking, 1958).
18. For a valiant attempt to downplay Lenin's influence—which the author admits does not entirely succeed—see Alexander Rabinowitch, *The Bolsheviks Come to Power: The Revolution of 1917 in Petrograd* (New York: Norton, 1978), esp. p. xxi.
19. See James Gleick, *Chaos: Making a New Science* (New York: Viking, 1987), pp. 11–31.
20. Best explained in George F. Kennan, *The Decision to Intervene* (Princeton: Princeton University Press, 1958). For a review of subsequent literature, see Eugene P. Trani, "Woodrow Wilson and the Decision to Intervene in Russia: A Reconsideration," *Journal of Modern History* 48 (Sept. 1976), 440–61.
21. I follow here the conclusions of George F. Kennan, *Russia and the West under Lenin and Stalin* (Boston: Little, Brown, 1961), esp. p. 119; but see also Pipes, *Russia Under the Bolshevik Regime*, pp. 6–8.
22. There is now an extensive literature on this issue. The major works include Charles S. Maier, *Recasting Bourgeois Europe: Stabilization in France, Germany, and Italy in the Decade after World War I* (Princeton: Princeton University Press, 1975); Michael J. Hogan, *Informal Entente: The Private Structure of Cooperation in Anglo-American Economic Diplomacy, 1918–1928* (Columbia: University of Missouri Press, 1977); Melvyn P. Leffler, *The Elusive Quest: The American Pursuit of European Stability and French Security, 1919–1933* (Chapel Hill: University of North Carolina Press, 1979); and Frank Costigliola, *Awkward Dominion: American Political, Economic, and Cultural Relations with Europe, 1919–1933* (Ithaca: Cornell University Press, 1984).
23. The point is well made in Paul Kennedy, *The Rise and Fall of the Great Powers: Economic Change and Military Conflict from 1500 to 2000* (New York: Random House, 1987), pp. 327–9.
24. The best recent analysis is Lloyd E. Ambrosius, *Woodrow Wilson and the American Democratic Tradition: The Treaty Fight in Perspective* (New York: Cambridge University Press, 1987).
25. Russell F. Weigley, *The American Way of War: A History of United States Military Strategy and Policy* (New York: Macmillan, 1973), pp. 245–8. See also Thomas H. Buckley, *The United States and the Washington Conference, 1921–22* (Knoxville: University of Tennessee Press, 1970); and Roger Dingman, *Power in the Pacific: The Origins of Naval Arms Limitation, 1914–1922* (Chicago: University of Chicago Press, 1976).
26. Charles P. Kindleberger, *The World in Depression: 1929–1939* (Berkeley: University of California Press, 1973), esp. p. 28.

27. The argument is made in Arnold A. Offner, *American Appeasement: United States Foreign Policy and Germany, 1933–1939* (Cambridge, Mass.: Harvard University Press, 1969); and in Robert A. Divine, *The Reluctant Belligerent: American Entry into World War II*, 2nd edn. (New York: Knopf, 1979).

28. See Pipes, *Russia Under the Bolshevik Regime*, pp. 215–17; also Joan Hoff Wilson, *Ideology and Economics: U.S. Relations with the Soviet Union, 1918–1933* (Columbia: University of Missouri Press, 1974). For domestic anti-communism, see Robert K. Murray, *Red Scare: A Study in National Hysteria, 1919–1920* (Minneapolis: University of Minnesota Press, 1955); also Peter G. Filene, *Americans and the Soviet Experiment, 1917–1933* (Cambridge, Mass.: Harvard University Press, 1967).

29. Pipes, *Russia Under the Bolshevik Regime*, pp. 236–9.

30. See Robert C. Tucker, *Stalin in Power: The Revolution from Above, 1928–1941* (New York: Norton, 1990) pp. 70–1, 128; also Eric Hobsbawm, *The Age of Extremes: A History of the World, 1914–1991* (New York: Pantheon, 1994), p. 380.

31. Tucker, *Stalin in Power*, 455. See also, on the functional ability of paranoids, Alan Bullock, *Hitler and Stalin: Parallel Lives* (New York: Knopf, 1992), pp. 360–1; and Raymond Birt, "Personality and Foreign Policy: The Case of Stalin," *Political Psychology* 14 (1993), 607–25.

32. Robert Conquest, *The Harvest of Sorrow: Soviet Collectivization and the Terror-Famine* (New York: Oxford University Press, 1986), p. 306, and *The Great Terror: A Reassessment* (New York: Oxford University Press, 1990), pp. 484–7; Dimitri Volkogonov, *Stalin: Triumph and Tragedy*, ed. and trans. Harold Shukman (New York: Grove Weidenfeld, 1991), p. 524; T. R. Ravindranathan, "The Legacy of Stalin and Stalinism: A Historiographical Survey of the Literature, 1930–1960," *Canadian Journal of History* 29 (Apr. 1994), 131–2. For comparisons with the Holocaust, see Charles Maier, *The Unmasterable Past: History, Holocaust, and German National Identity* (Cambridge, Mass.: Harvard University Press, 1988), pp. 73–5; also Paul Hollander, "Soviet Terror, American Amnesia," *National Review* 46 (2 May 1994), 28–39. New information on the number of Stalin's purge victims appears in V. P. Popov, "State Terror in Soviet Russia, 1923–1953: Sources and Their Interpretation," *Russian Social Science Review* 35 (Sept., 1994), 48–70.

33. Tucker, *Stalin in Power*, pp. 276–82. For Lenin's terror, see Pipes, *The Russian Revolution*, pp. 789–840; also Dimitri Volkogonov, *Lenin: A New Biography*, trans. and ed. Harold Shukman (New York: Free Press, 1994), esp. pp. 233–45.

34. *Khrushchev Remembers: The Glasnost Tapes*, trans. and ed. Jerrold L. Schecter with Vyacheslav V. Luchkov (Boston: Little, Brown, 1990), p. 37.

35. Tucker, *Stalin in Power* makes the most compelling overall case for this argument; but see also Richard Crockatt, *The Fifty Years War: The United States and the Soviet Union in World Politics, 1941–1991* (New York: Routledge, 1995), p. 31; Vladislav Zubok and Constantine Pleshakov, *Inside the Kremlin's Cold War: From Stalin to Khrushchev* (Cambridge, Mass.: Harvard University Press, 1996), pp. 10, 20; and, for some chilling examples of how the Stalinist mentality could affect those who worked within the Soviet system, Pavel Sudoplatov and Anatoli Sudoplatov, with Jerrold L. Schecter and Leona P. Schecter, *Special Tasks: The Memoirs of an Unwanted Witness—A Soviet Spymaster* (Boston: Little, Brown, 1994), esp. pp. 50–86, 278–84.

36. Tucker, *Stalin in Power*, pp. 228–32. For a fine fictional portrayal of this moment, see Nicholas Mosley, *Hopeful Monsters* (New York: Vintage, 1993), pp. 197–243.

37. Bullock, *Hitler and Stalin*, p. 537. See also Donald Cameron Watt, *How War Came: The Immediate Origins of the Second World War, 1938–1939* (New York: Pantheon,

1989) pp. 610–12; and Hugh D. Phillips, *Between the Revolution and the West: A Political Biography of Maxim M. Litvinov* (Boulder: Westview Press, 1992), pp. 161–2. Two general but contrasting accounts of this period are Jonathan Haslam, *The Soviet Union and the Struggle for Collective Security in Europe, 1933–39* (New York: St. Martin's Press, 1984); and Jiri Hochman, *The Soviet Union and the Failure of Collective Security, 1934–1938* (Ithaca: Cornell University Press, 1984).

38. Tucker, *Stalin in Power*, pp. 233–7.

39. These comparisons are based primarily upon Bullock, *Hitler and Stalin, passim*; but see also Tucker, *Stalin in Power*, pp. 591–2; and Norman Rich, *Hitler's War Aims: Ideology, the Nazi State, and the Course of Expansion* (New York: Norton, 1973). On Hitler's personal responsibility for World War II, see John Mueller, *Retreat from Doomsday: The Obsolescence of Major War* (New York: Basic Books, 1989), pp. 64–8. R. C. Raack, *Stalin's Drive to the West, 1938–1945: The Origins of the Cold War* (Stanford: Stanford University Press, 1995) makes the important point, though, that Stalin did see a war between Nazi Germany and the Western democracies as likely to advance Soviet interests.

40. Gaddis, *Russia, the Soviet Union, and the United States*, pp. 132–43.

41. See e.g. Martin Gilbert, *Winston S. Churchill: Finest Hour, 1939–1941* (Boston: Houghton Mifflin, 1983), pp. 101–2.

42. A favor he chose not to reciprocate later in the year when he received information from his spy, Richard Sorge, in Tokyo, that the Japanese were planning to attack Pearl Harbor. See Valentin M. Berezhkov, *At Stalin's Side: His Interpreter's Memoirs from the October Revolution to the Fall of the Dictator's Empire*, trans. Sergei V. Mikheyev (New York: Birch Lane Press, 1994), p. 261.

43. Volkogonov, *Stalin*, pp. 394–6.

44. Quoted in Amy Knight, *Beria: Stalin's First Lieutenant* (Princeton: Princeton University Press, 1993), p. 109.

45. See Bullock, *Hitler and Stalin*, pp. 766–7; also Hobsbawm, *The Age of Extremes*, p. 392, and Rich, *Hitler's War Aims*, pp. 224–46.

46. A point George Orwell made in 1946, noted in Michael Shelden, *Orwell: The Authorized Biography* (New York: HarperCollins, 1991), pp. 435–6. Richard Pipes has recently re-emphasized the common authoritarian roots of communism and fascism in *Russia Under the Bolshevik Regime*, pp. 240–81; but see also the classics on this subject, Hannah Arendt, *The Origins of Totalitarianism* (New York: Harcourt, 1951), and Carl J. Friedrich and Zbigniew Brzezinski, *Totalitarian Dictatorship and Autocracy* (Cambridge, Mass.: Harvard University Press, 1956), as well as Abbott Gleason, *Totalitarianism: The Inner History of the Cold War* (New York: Oxford University Press, 1995).

47. See, on the importance of Lend-Lease, *Khrushchev Remembers: The Glasnost Tapes*, p. 84; also Robert Conquest, *Stalin: Breaker of Nations* (New York: Viking Penguin, 1991), p. 247.

48. Randall Bennett Woods, *A Changing of the Guard: Anglo-American Relations, 1941–1946* (Chapel Hill: University of North Carolina Press, 1990) provides the most recent account of Anglo-American disagreements over the nature of the postwar world.

49. John Lewis Gaddis, *The Long Peace: Inquiries into the History of the Cold War* (New York: Oxford University Press, 1987), pp. 21–9.

50. Melvyn P. Leffler, *A Preponderance of Power: National Security, the Truman Administration, and the Cold War* (Stanford: Stanford University Press, 1992), pp. 19–24. See also Robert A. Divine, *Second Chance: The Triumph of Internationalism in America During World War II* (New York: Atheneum, 1967); and John Lewis

Gaddis, *The United States and the Origins of the Cold War, 1941–1947* (New York: Columbia University Press, 1972), pp. 1–31.

51. Divine, *Second Chance*, pp. 168–74. See also Akira Iriye, *The Globalizing of America, 1913–1945* (New York: Cambridge University Press, 1993), pp. 199–200.
52. Theodore A. Wilson, *The First Summit: Roosevelt and Churchill at Placentia Bay 1941* (Boston: Houghton Mifflin, 1969).
53. See e.g. Mikhail Gorbachev, *Perestroika: New Thinking for Our Country and the World* (New York: Harper & Row, 1987), p. 142.
54. Warren F. Kimball, *The Juggler: Franklin Roosevelt as Wartime Statesman* (Princeton: Princeton University Press, 1991), pp. 95–9.
55. See Lloyd C. Gardner, *Spheres of Influence: The Great Powers Partition Europe, from Munich to Yalta* (Chicago: Ivan R. Dee, 1993), pp. 149–50.
56. Divine, *Second Chance* provides the most thorough account.
57. Volkogonov, *Stalin: Triumph and Tragedy*, p. 505. See also Viacheslav Chubarov, "The War After the War," *Soviet Studies in History* 30 (Summer 1991), 44–6.
58. For the centrality of Stalin to all aspects of Soviet policy during this period, see Vladislav Zubok and Constantine Pleshakov, "The Soviet Union," in David Reynolds, ed., *The Origins of the Cold War in Europe: International Perspectives* (New Haven: Yale University Press, 1994), esp. pp. 57, 63, 68; David Holloway, *Stalin and the Bomb: The Soviet Union and Atomic Energy, 1939–1954* (New Haven: Yale University Press, 1994), p. 370; and Lydia V. Pozdeeva, "The Soviet Union: Territorial Diplomacy," in David Reynolds, Warren F. Kimball, and A. O. Chubarian, eds., *Allies at War: the Soviet, American, and British Experience, 1939–1945* (New York: St. Martin's Press, 1994), pp. 378–9.
59. My analysis here follows Tucker, *Stalin in Power*, pp. 45–50. But see also Raack, *Stalin's Drive to the West*, pp. 12–15, 20, 103; Zubok and Pleshakov, *Inside the Kremlin's Cold War*, p. 13; William Taubman, *Stalin's American Policy: From Entente to Detente to Cold War* (New York: Norton, 1982), pp. 10–30; Bernard S. Morris, *Communism, Revolution, and American Policy* (Durham: Duke University Press, 1987), pp. 7–10, 30–1; Gabriel Gorodetsky, "The Formulation of Soviet Foreign Policy: Ideology and *Realpolitik*," in Gorodetsky, ed., *Soviet Foreign Policy 1917–1991: A Retrospective* (London: Frank Cass, 1994), pp. 30–44; and Lars H. Lih's "Introduction" in Lih, Oleg V. Naumov, and Oleg V. Khlevniuk, eds., *Stalin's Letters to Molotov, 1925–1936* (New Haven: Yale University Press, 1995), pp. 5–6.
60. Sudoplatov, *Special Tasks*, p. 102.
61. Milovan Djilas, *Conversations with Stalin*, trans. Michael B. Petrovich (New York: Harcourt, Brace & World, 1962), p. 114.
62. Hugh Thomas, *The Spanish Civil War* (New York: Harper, 1961), pp. 214–17, 452–5. See also George Orwell's classic account, *Homage to Catalonia* (New York: Harcourt, 1952); and, for new information on Stalin's purges within the Comintern, Kevin McDermott, "Stalinist Terror in the Comintern: New Perspectives," *Journal of Contemporary History* 30 (1995), 111–30.
63. Christopher Andrew and Oleg Gordievsky, *KGB: The Inside Story of its Foreign Operations from Lenin to Gorbachev* (New York: HarperCollins, 1990), pp. 184–232; Genrikh Borovik, *The Philby Files: The Secret Life of Master Spy Kim Philby*, ed. Philip Knightley (Boston: Little, Brown, 1994), pp. 23–168; Allen Weinstein, *Perjury: The Hiss–Chambers Case* (New York: Knopf, 1978), pp. 112–57. See also, for the activities of the American Communist Party, Harvey Klehr, John Earl Haynes, and Fridrikh Igorevich Firsov, *The Secret World of American Communism* (New Haven: Yale University Press, 1995).

64. Raack, *Stalin's Drive to the West*, pp. 11–36; also Zubok and Pleshakov, *Inside the Kremlin's Cold War*, p. 37. For a more general discussion of Stalin's views on the relationship between war and revolution, see William Curti Wohlforth, *The Elusive Balance: Power and Perceptions during the Cold War* (Ithaca: Cornell University Press, 1993), pp. 40–6.

65. *Molotov Remembers: Inside Kremlin Politics: Conversations with Felix Chuev*, ed. Albert Resis (Chicago: Ivan R. Dee, 1993), p. 63. See also Wohlforth, *The Elusive Balance*, pp. 43–4, 76; and Holloway, *Stalin and the Bomb*, pp. 151–2.

66. Tucker, *Stalin in Power*, pp. 551–77; Volkogonov, *Stalin*, pp. 501, 550–1.

67. Wohlforth, *The Elusive Balance*, p. 61. For the relative looseness with which Nazi Germany was run, see Bullock, *Hitler and Stalin*, pp. 424–8, 434–5.

68. For a scientific analogue, see Gleick, *Chaos*, pp. 83–118.

69. Tucker, *Stalin in Power*, p. 469.

70. Bullock, *Hitler and Stalin*, pp. 464–5.

71. Taubman, *Stalin's American Policy*, p. 16.

72. Zubok and Pleshakov, *Inside the Kremlin's Cold War*, p. 25; Berezhkov, *At Stalin's Side*, pp. 236–8.

73. Litvinov to Molotov, 2 June 1943, and Gromyko dispatch, 14 July 1944, both printed in Amos Perlmutter, *FDR & Stalin: A Not So Grand Alliance, 1943–1945* (Columbia: University of Missouri Press, 1993), pp. 243, 268. See also Zubok and Pleshakov, *Inside the Kremlin's Cold War*, pp. 28–31; and Vladimir O. Pechatnov, "The Big Three After World War II: New Documents on Soviet Thinking about Post War Relations with the United States and Great Britain," Cold War International History Project [hereafter CWIHP] Working Paper 13 (July 1995).

74. Steven Merritt Miner, *Between Churchill and Stalin: The Soviet Union, Great Britain, and the Origins of the Grand Alliance* (Chapel Hill: University of North Carolina Press, 1988), pp. 252–7.

75. *Molotov Remembers*, p. 45.

76. David Reynolds, et al., "Legacies: Allies, Enemies, and Posterity," in Reynolds et al., *Allies at War*, pp. 422–3.

77. Quoted in Gardner, *Spheres of Influence*, p. 103.

78. Ibid. 215–25; Gaddis, *The United States and the Origins of the Cold War*, pp. 133–73. See also Warren I. Cohen, *America in the Age of Soviet Power, 1945–91* (New York: Cambridge University Press, 1993), pp. 9, 249; and William Larsh, "W. Averell Harriman and the Polish Question, December, 1943–August 1944," *East European Politics and Societies* 7 (Fall 1993), 513–54.

79. Bohlen notes, Roosevelt–Stalin conversation, 1 Dec. 1943, *Foreign Relations of the United States* [hereafter *FRUS*]: *The Conferences at Cairo and Tehran, 1943* (Washington: Government Printing Office, 1961), pp. 594–5.

80. Berezhkov, *At Stalin's Side*, p. 240.

81. Bohlen notes, 6th plenary meeting, 9 Feb. 1945, *FRUS: The Conferences at Malta and Yalta, 1945* (Washington: Government Printing Office, 1955), p. 854.

82. *Molotov Remembers*, p. 51. See also Pozdeeva, "The Soviet Union: Territorial Diplomacy," p. 362.

83. Larsh, "W. Averell Harriman and the Polish Question," pp. 514–16. See also Vojtech Mastny, *Russia's Road to the Cold War: Diplomacy, Warfare, and the Politics of Communism, 1941–1945* (New York: Columbia University Press, 1979), pp. 58–9, 133–44; and Karel Kaplan, *The Short March: The Communist Takeover in Czechoslovakia: 1945–1948* (New York: St. Martin's Press, 1987), pp. 3–5.

84. Zubok and Pleshakov, *Inside the Kremlin's Cold War*, pp. 117–19. See also Tuomo Polvinen, *Between East and West: Finland in International Politics, 1944–1947*, ed. and trans. D. G. Kirby and Peter Herring (Minneapolis: University of Minnesota Press, 1986), esp. pp. 280–1; and Jussi Hanhimäki, " 'Containment' in a Borderland: The United States and Finland, 1948–49," *Diplomatic History* 18 (Summer 1994), 353–74.

85. W. Averell Harriman and Elie Abel, *Special Envoy to Churchill and Stalin, 1941–1946* (New York: Random House, 1975), p. 405. See also Zubok and Pleshakov, "The Soviet Union," pp. 64–9; and Wohlforth, *The Elusive Balance*, pp. 51–3. An implicit confirmation of the view that Polish Communists expected to be welcomed in Poland occurs in an interview with Jakub Berman in Teresa Toranska, *"Them:" Stalin's Polish Puppets*, trans. Agnieska Kolakowska (New York: Harper & Row, 1987), p. 257.

86. *Khrushchev Remembers: The Glasnost Tapes*, p. 100. See also Kaplan, *The Short March*, pp. 1–2; and Djilas, *Conversations with Stalin*, p. 154.

87. For more on this, see Chapter II.

88. The Carpatho-Ukraine, formerly part of Czechoslovakia, had been annexed by Hungary with Hitler's approval in 1939; in 1943 Stalin demanded and received agreement from the Czech government-in-exile to its postwar incorporation into the Soviet Union.

89. Zubok and Pleshakov, "The Soviet Union," p. 60.

90. See, on this important point, Raack, *Stalin's Drive to the West*, pp. 67–71.

91. The point is best confirmed by reading George Orwell's classic novels *Animal Farm* (New York: Harcourt, 1946) and *1984* (New York: Harcourt, 1949); but see also Shelden, *Orwell: The Authorized Biography*, pp. 369–70.

92. I have borrowed this example from Conquest, *Stalin*, pp. 229–30, 256–8. But see also, for new information, Raack, *Stalin's Drive to the West*, pp. 73–101; and Knight, *Beria*, pp. 103–4.

93. Amy Knight provides chilling examples of the casualness with which Stalin could authorize the punishment of whole classes of individuals. See ibid. 126–7.

94. George F. Kennan, *Memoirs: 1925–1950* (Boston: Atlantic Little, Brown, 1967), pp. 199–215, describes the reaction in Washington; but see also Larsh, "Harriman and the Polish Question," pp. 550–1, which emphasizes how the events in Warsaw eroded Harriman's earlier sympathy for the Soviet position on Poland.

95. Krystyna Kersten, *The Establishment of Communist Rule in Poland, 1943–1948*, trans. John Micgiel and Michael H. Bernhard (Berkeley: University of California Press, 1991), provides a fine account, based on Polish sources, of how Soviet authority was imposed against the wishes of the majority of Poles.

96. See Timothy Garton Ash, *The Polish Revolution: Solidarity* (London: Penguin Books, 1983).

97. David Remnick, *Lenin's Tomb: The Last Days of the Soviet Empire* (New York: Random House, 1993), pp. 3–9. Sudoplatov, *Special Tasks*, pp. 276–8, provides an interesting account of the Katyn cover-up.

98. Deborah Welch Larson, *Origins of Containment: A Psychological Explanation* (Princeton: Princeton University Press, 1985), p. 37. See also Alexander L. George, "Ideology and International Relations: A Conceptual Analysis," *Jerusalem Journal of International Relations* 9 (1987), 6.

99. Among those who have suggested that such a thing can happen are Michael J. Hogan, "The Vice Men of Foreign Affairs," *Reviews in American History* 21 (1993),

esp. p. 327; and Bruce Cumings, " 'Revising Postrevisionism,' or, The Poverty of Theory in Diplomatic History," *Diplomatic History* 17 (Fall 1993), especially 549–56.

100. Kenneth M. Jensen, ed., *Origins of the Cold War: The Novikov, Kennan, and Roberts "Long Telegrams" of 1946* (Washington: United States Institute of Peace, 1991) conveniently reprints the Kennan and Roberts dispatches. See also Kennan, *Memoirs: 1925–1950*, pp. 290–7; and Frank Roberts, *Dealing with Dictators: The Destruction and Revival of Europe, 1930–70* (London: Weidenfeld & Nicolson, 1991), pp. 107–10. For Churchill's speech and its background, see Fraser Harbutt, *The Iron Curtain: Churchill, America, and the Origins of the Cold War* (New York: Oxford University Press, 1986).

101. Kennan to James F. Byrnes, 20 Mar. 1946, *FRUS: 1946*, vi. 723.

102. See Chapters II and III.

103. Stalin to Molotov, 9 Sept. 1929, in Lih et al., *Stalin's Letters to Molotov*, p. 178.

104. Volkogonov, *Stalin*, p. 391.

105. Knight, *Beria*, p. 133. See also Robert Chadwell Williams, *Klaus Fuchs: Atom Spy* (Cambridge, Mass.: Harvard University Press, 1987); and Chapter IV.

106. Gaddis, *The United States and the Origins of the Cold War*, pp. 80–92.

107. Knight, *Beria*, pp. 130–1.

108. Djilas, *Conversations with Stalin*, pp. 66, 73.

109. Andrei Gromyko, *Memoirs*, trans. Harold Shukman (New York: Doubleday, 1989), p. 98.

110. Peter Grose, *Gentleman Spy: The Life of Allen Dulles* (Boston: Houghton Mifflin, 1994), pp. 224–45, provides the most recent assessment of this once-controversial episode.

111. *Molotov Remembers*, p. 51.

112. See Steven Merritt Miner, "His Master's Voice: Viacheslav Mikhailovich Molotov as Stalin's Foreign Commissar," in Gordon A. Craig and Francis L. Loewenheim, eds., *The Diplomats: 1939–1979* (Princeton: Princeton University Press, 1994), pp. 65–100.

113. *Molotov Remembers*, pp. 45–6, 51.

114. David Reynolds, "Great Britain," in Reynolds, ed., *The Origins of the Cold War in Europe*, p. 80.

115. See e.g. Gaddis, *Strategies of Containment*, pp. 3–13.

116. Kennan, *Memoirs: 1925–1950*, pp. 224–34.

117. The details are well documented in Tucker, *Stalin in Power*, Bullock, *Hitler and Stalin*, Volkogonov, *Stalin*, Conquest, *The Great Terror*, and of course in Alexander Solzhenitsyn's influential trilogy, *The Gulag Archipelago* (New York: Harper & Row, 1974–8). But see also Molotov's simultaneously poignant and chilling account of Stalin's ordering the arrest of his own wife, in *Molotov Remembers*, pp. 322–5. James M. Goldgeier has recently argued that Stalin's approach to diplomatic bargaining drew upon his methods for consolidating power internally—not a reassuring conclusion (*Leadership Style and Soviet Foreign Policy: Stalin, Khrushchev, Brezhnev, Gorbachev* (Baltimore: Johns Hopkins University Press, 1994), pp. 17–21, 34–51).

118. Djilas, *Conversations with Stalin*, pp. 132–3.

119. *Khrushchev Remembers: The Glasnost Tapes*, p. 132.

120. See Holloway, *Stalin and the Bomb*, p. 247; also Zubok and Pleshakov, *Inside the Kremlin's Cold War*, pp. 39–40. For an excellent description of Stalin's first meeting with the new American president, see David McCullough, *Truman* (New York: Simon & Schuster, 1992), pp. 416–20.

121. *Khrushchev Remembers: The Glasnost Tapes*, p. 67. The text refers to Aneurin Bevan, but this is obviously an error.

122. The phrase was that of Justice William O. Douglas, carefully noted in Secretary of the Navy James V. Forrestal's diary. See Walter Millis, ed., *The Forrestal Diaries* (New York: Viking, 1951), p. 134.

123. Stalin speech of 9 Feb. 1946, in Robert V. Daniels, ed., *A Documentary History of Communism*, rev. edn. (Hanover, NH: University Press of New England, 1984), p. 138 (emphases added). For more on the circumstances and implications of this speech, see Hugh Thomas, *Armed Truce: The Beginnings of the Cold War, 1945–46* (London: Hamish Hamilton, 1986), pp. 3–17; and Albert Resis, "Stalin, the Politburo, and the Onset of the Cold War, 1945–1946," *The Carl Beck Papers in Russian and East European Studies* #701 (Apr. 1988), pp. 13–17.

124. Robert C. Tucker, *The Soviet Political Mind: Stalinism and Post-Stalinist Change*, rev. edn. (New York: Norton, 1971), p. 91 (emphasis in original). See also Wohlforth, *The Elusive Balance*, pp. 62–5.

125. Hottelet's account of this conversation is summarized in *FRUS: 1946*, vi, 763–5, and was first published in the *Washington Post*, 21–5 Jan. 1952, shortly after Litvinov's death. See also Phillips, *Between the Revolution and the West*, pp. 172–3; and Jonathan Haslam, "Litvinov, Stalin, and the Road Not Taken," in Gorodetsky, ed., *Soviet Foreign Policy 1917–1991*, pp. 59–60.

126. Remnick, *Lenin's Tomb*, p. 15; also Zinovy Sheinis, *Maxim Litvinov* (Moscow: Progress Publishers, 1990), p. 350; and Haslam, "Litvinov, Stalin, and the Road Not Taken," p. 61. On the basis of a conversation with Anastas Mikoyan, though, Valentin Berezhkov claims that Stalin had Litvinov killed in an automobile accident (*At Stalin's Side*, pp. 316–19).

127. *Molotov Remembers*, p. 69. See also Berezhkov, *At Stalin's Side*, p. 319.

128. Volkogonov, *Stalin*, pp. 567–76.

129. "The Eighteenth Brumaire of Louis Bonaparte," originally published in 1852, quoted in Robert C. Tucker, ed., *The Marx–Engels Reader*, 2nd edn. (New York: Norton, 1978), p. 595.

130. See, for another example of this technique, Stephen Jay Gould, *Wonderful Life: The Burgess Shale and the Nature of History* (New York: Norton, 1989).

131. Wilfried Loth, *The Division of the World: 1941–1945* (New York: St. Martin's Press, 1988), pp. 304–11, makes a good case for the Cold War not having been predetermined; but I think he underestimates Stalin's role in bringing it about.

132. Taubman, *Stalin's America Policy*, p. 9; see also p. 74.

CHAPTER II

1. US Department of State, *FRUS: The Conferences at Cairo and Tehran, 1943* (Washington: Government Printing Office, 1961), p. 568.

2. *Molotov Remembers: Inside Kremlin Politics: Conversations with Felix Chuev*, ed. Albert Resis (Chicago: Ivan R. Dee, 1993), p. 8.

3. Kenneth N. Waltz, *Theory of International Politics* (New York: Random House, 1979) has been the most influential statement of this "neo-realist" point of view. For a further analysis of the strengths and weaknesses of "neo-realism," see Robert O. Keohane, ed., *Neorealism and Its Critics* (New York: Columbia University Press, 1986).

4. I have adapted this definition from one in Michael W. Doyle, *Empires* (Ithaca: Cornell University Press, 1986), p. 45. My thinking on the relationship

between imperial and Cold War history has been considerably influenced by the writings of Geir Lundestad, especially his "Empire by Invitation? The United States and Western Europe, 1945–1952," *Journal of Peace Research* 23 (Sept. 1986), 263–77; and *The American "Empire" and Other Studies of US Foreign Policy in a Comparative Perspective* (New York: Oxford University Press, 1990). For further justifications of this "imperial" framework of analysis in Cold War history, see John Lewis Gaddis, "The Emerging Post-Revisionist Synthesis on the Origins of the Cold War," *Diplomatic History* 7 (Summer 1983), 181–3; and Donald J. Puchala, "The History of the Future of International Relations," *Ethics and International Affairs* 8 (1994), 183.

5. For the distinction between "formal" and "informal" empire, see Doyle, *Empires*, pp. 37–8; also Tony Smith, *The Pattern of Imperialism: The United States, Great Britain, and the Late-Industrializing World since 1815* (Cambridge: Cambridge University Press, 1981), pp. 51–68.

6. Doyle, *Empires*, pp. 25–6; also Edward Said, *Culture and Imperialism* (New York: Knopf, 1993), pp. 191–281.

7. Robert C. Tucker, *Stalin as Revolutionary, 1879–1929: A Study in History and Personality* (New York: Norton, 1973), pp. 168–70. Lenin had made a similar argument in 1913. See Richard Pipes, *Russia under the Bolshevik Regime* (New York: Knopf, 1994), p. 150.

8. The classic account is still Richard Pipes, *The Formation of the Soviet Union: Communism and Nationalism, 1917–23* (Cambridge, Mass.: Harvard University Press, 1954); but see also his more recent *Russia Under the Bolshevik Regime*, pp. 471–5.

9. See Lenin, "On the Question of the Nationalities or of 'Autonomization'," 30–1 Dec. 1922, in Robert V. Daniels, ed., *A Documentary History of Communism* (Hanover, NH: University Press of New England, 1984), i. 151–2. For Lenin's record on terror, see Richard Pipes, *The Russian Revolution* (New York: Knopf, 1990), pp. 789–840.

10. Witness the careers of Napoleon, a Corsican, and Hitler, an Austrian.

11. Quoted in Robert C. Tucker, *Stalin in Power: The Revolution from Above, 1928–1941* (New York: Norton, 1990), p. 43.

12. Ibid. 358–9. See also, on Stalin's Russian nationalism, Pipes, *Russia under the Bolshevik Regime*, p. 280; and Milovan Djilas, *Conversations with Stalin*, trans. Michael B. Petrovich (New York: Harcourt, Brace, 1962), p. 62.

13. This argument follows that of Tucker, *Stalin in Power*; but see also Vladislav Zubok and Constantine Pleshakov on Stalin's "revolutionary-imperial paradigm" in *Inside the Kremlin's Cold War: From Stalin to Khrushchev* (Cambridge, Mass.: Harvard University Press, 1996), p. 4.

14. See Chapter I.

15. See Chapter III.

16. *Molotov Remembers*, p. 8.

17. See Chapter I.

18. Ivo Banac, *With Stalin Against Tito: Cominformist Splits in Yugoslav Communism* (Ithaca: Cornell University Press, 1988), p. 17.

19. Sergei N. Goncharov, John W. Lewis, and Xue Litai, *Uncertain Partners: Stalin, Mao, and the Korean War* (Stanford: Stanford University Press, 1993), p. 189. See also *Khrushchev Remembers: The Glasnost Tapes*, trans. and ed. Jerrold L. Schecter with Vyacheslav V. Luchkov (Boston: Little, Brown, 1990), pp. 100–1.

20. *Molotov Remembers*, p. 59.

21. R. C. Raack, "Stalin Plans his Post-War Germany," *Journal of Contemporary*

History 28 (1993), 58–62; also Dietrich Staritz, "The SED, Stalin, and the German Question: Interests and Decision-Making in the Light of New Sources," *German History* 10 (Oct. 1992), 277. For more on this, see Chapter V.

22. Pavel Sudoplatov and Anatoli Sudoplatov, with Jerrold L. Schecter and Leona P. Schecter, *Special Tasks: The Memoirs of an Unwanted Witness—A Soviet Spymaster* (Boston: Little, Brown, 1994), p. 102.

23. Winston S. Churchill, *The Second World War: Triumph and Tragedy* (New York: Bantam, 1962), p. 252; Djilas, *Conversations with Stalin*, p. 182. See also, on Greece, Zubok and Pleshakov, *Inside the Kremlin's Cold War*, p. 127; and John O. Iatrides and Linda Wrigley, eds., *Greece at the Crossroads: The Civil War and Its Legacy* (University Park, PA: Pennsylvania State University Press, 1995).

24. For the Iranian crisis, see Louise Fawcett, *Iran and the Cold War: The Azerbaijan Crisis of 1946* (New York: Cambridge University Press, 1992); also N. I. Yegorova, "'The Iran Crisis' of 1944–46: A View from the Russian Archives," CWIHP Working Paper, #15 (May 1996), which on the basis of Soviet documents argues that the crisis grew out of a Soviet overreaction to growing British influence in postwar Iranian affairs. Amy Knight, *Beria: Stalin's First Lieutenant* (Princeton: Princeton University Press, 1993), pp. 141–2, suggests that Beria was behind both of these initiatives.

25. *Molotov Remembers*, p. 29.

26. Vojtech Mastny, *Russia's Road to the Cold War: Diplomacy, Warfare, and the Politics of Communism, 1941–1945* (New York: Columbia University Press, 1979), esp. pp. 306–13.

27. See, on this concept of political, economic, and social "fusion," Valerie Bunce, "The Empire Strikes Back: The Evolution of the Eastern Bloc from a Soviet Asset to a Soviet Liability," *International Organization* 39 (Winter 1985), 5; also George Schöpfin, "The Stalinist Experience in Eastern Europe," *Survey: A Journal of East and West Studies* 30 (Oct. 1988), 124–47. Norman N. Naimark, *The Russians in Germany: A History of the Soviet Zone of Occupation, 1945–1949* (Cambridge, Mass.: Harvard University Press, 1995), provides an excellent discussion of how this happened in Soviet-occupied Germany.

28. *Khrushchev Remembers: The Glasnost Tapes*, p. 102.

29. Karel Kaplan, *The Short March: The Communist Takeover in Czechoslovakia, 1945–1948* (New York: St. Martin's Press, 1987), p. 2.

30. See William Larsh, "W. Averell Harriman and the Polish Question, December 1943–August 1944," *East European Politics and Societies* 7 (Fall 1993), 513–54; also John Lewis Gaddis, *The United States and the Origins of the Cold War, 1941–1947* (New York: Columbia University Press, 1972), pp. 32–3.

31. Deborah Larson, *Origins of Containment: A Psychological Explanation* (Princeton: Princeton University Press, 1985), pp. 325–6.

32. Jean Edward Smith, *Lucius D. Clay: An American Life* (New York: Henry Holt, 1990) pp. 410–6.

33. Djilas, *Conversations with Stalin*, p. 59. See also, on the importance of ideology, David Reynolds, "Introduction," in Reynolds, ed., *The Origins of the Cold War in Europe: International Perspectives* (New Haven: Yale University Press, 1994), pp. 14–15.

34. Bunce, "The Empire Strikes Back," pp. 7–8; Jörg Roesler, "The Rise and Fall of the Planned Economy in the German Democratic Republic," *German History* 9 (Feb. 1991), 46–7; Igor Lukes, "A Road to Communism, 1938–1948," Norwegian Nobel Institute conference paper, Moscow, Mar. 1993, p. 15.

35. See Geir Lundestad, *The American Non-Policy towards Eastern Europe, 1943–1947*

(New York: Columbia University Press, 1978), p. 30; also the individual personal accounts in Thomas T. Hammond, ed., *Witnesses to the Origins of the Cold War* (Seattle: University of Washington Press, 1982).

36. Vladislav Zubok, "Eastern Europe's Place in the Priorities of Soviet Foreign Policy, 1945–1947," Norwegian Nobel Institute working paper, Jan. 1994, p. 13. See also Raack, "Stalin Plans His Post-War Germany," p. 56; and Naimark, *The Russians in Germany*, pp. 9–68.

37. The process is well described in Hammond, ed., *Witnesses to the Origins of the Cold War*, as well as in Adam B. Ulam, *The Communists: The Story of Power and Lost Illusions, 1948–1991* (New York: Scribner's, 1992), pp. 1–35. But see also the succinct statement of the problem in Pipes, *Russia Under the Bolshevik Regime*, p. 153.

38. Paul Kennedy, *The Rise and Fall of the Great Powers: Economic Change and Military Conflict from 1500 to 2000* (New York: Random House, 1987), pp. 327–33.

39. US Bureau of the Census, *The Statistical History of the United States from Colonial Times to the Present* (Stamford, Conn.: Fairfield,1965), p. 542. See also Lundestad, *The American "Empire"*, p. 53.

40. *Statistical History of the United States*, pp. 139, 565.

41. Thomas J. McCormick, *America's Half-Century: United States Foreign Policy in the Cold War* (Baltimore: Johns Hopkins University Press, 1989), pp. 23–4.

42. Melvyn P. Leffler, *The Specter of Communism: The United States and the Origins of the Cold War, 1917–1953* (New York: Hill & Wang, 1994), pp. 26–7; also David G. Haglund, *Latin America and the Transformation of U.S. Strategic Thought, 1936–1940* (Albuquerque: University of New Mexico Press, 1984).

43. Waldo Heinrichs, *Threshold of War: Franklin D. Roosevelt and American Entry into World War II* (New York: Oxford University Press, 1988) provides the best recent account.

44. See e.g. Charles A. Beard, *President Roosevelt and the Coming of the War, 1941* (New Haven: Yale University Press, 1948); and Charles C. Tansill, *Back Door to War: The Roosevelt Foreign Policy, 1933–1941* (Chicago: Regnery, 1952).

45. For a recent application of this thesis to the onset of the Korean War, see Bruce Cumings, *The Origins of the Korean War*, ii: *The Roaring of the Cataract, 1947–1950* (Princeton: Princeton University Press, 1990), esp. p. 433. See also, for a defense of this methodology, Cumings, " 'Revising Postrevisionism,' or, The Poverty of Theory in Diplomatic History," *Diplomatic History* 17 (Fall 1993), esp. pp. 539–46.

46. Marc Bloch, *The Historian's Craft*, trans. Peter Putnam (New York: Vintage, 1953), pp. 190–1. For a similar example, see E. H. Carr, *What Is History?* (New York: Vintage, 1961), pp. 136–41.

47. See John Lewis Gaddis, *Russia, the Soviet Union, and the United States: An Interpretive History*, 2nd edn. (New York: McGraw Hill, 1990), pp. 27–31.

48. Michael Howard has pointed out that insecurity has more often given rise to imperial behavior than have the perceived requirements of capitalism. See his *The Lessons of History* (New Haven: Yale University Press, 1991), pp. 22–5.

49. For more on these points, see John Lewis Gaddis, *The Long Peace: Inquiries into the History of the Cold War* (New York: Oxford University Press, 1987), pp. 20–9.

50. Robert A. Pollard, *Economic Security and the Origins of the Cold War, 1945–1950* (New York: Columbia University Press, 1985), pp. 1–32. See also Chapter VII.

51. See Georgi Arbatov, *The System: An Insider's Life in Soviet Politics* (New York: Times Books, 1992), pp. 72–3.

52. NSC-20/1, "U.S. Objectives with Respect to Russia," 18 Aug. 1948, in Thomas H.

Etzold and John Lewis Gaddis, eds., *Containment: Documents on American Policy and Strategy, 1945–1950* (New York: Columbia University Press, 1978), p. 187. I have discussed Kennan's understanding of containment at some length in *Strategies of Containment: A Critical Appraisal of Postwar American National Security Policy* (New York: Oxford University Press, 1982), pp. 25–88; but this should be supplemented by the more sophisticated analyses in Anders Stephanson, *Kennan and the Art of Foreign Policy* (Cambridge, Mass.: Harvard University Press, 1989), and Wilson D. Miscamble, *George F. Kennan and the Making of American Foreign Policy, 1947–1950* (Princeton: Princeton University Press, 1992).

53. George F. Kennan, *Memoirs: 1925–1950* (Boston: Atlantic–Little, Brown, 1967), pp. 129–30. See also, for Gibbon's influence, Stephanson, *Kennan and the Art of Foreign Policy*, pp. 93, 102; and Walter Hixson, *George F. Kennan: Cold War Iconoclast* (New York: Columbia University Press, 1989), p. 5. Kennan has told me that he read Gibbon on long transatlantic airplane flights during the war, thereby illustrating one of the few virtues of air travel in the pre-jet era.

54. *Foreign Affairs* 25 (July 1947), 566–82.

55. See Kennan, *Memoirs: 1925–1950*, pp. 407–8.

56. See e.g. Alan S. Milward, *The Reconstruction of Western Europe, 1945–51* (Berkeley: University of California Press, 1984); also Milward, "Was the Marshall Plan Necessary?" *Diplomatic History* 13 (Spring 1989), 231–53.

57. McCormick, *America's Half Century*, pp. 73–5.

58. Michael J. Hogan, *The Marshall Plan: America, Britain, and the Reconstruction of Western Europe, 1947–1952* (New York: Cambridge University Press, 1987). See also Charles S. Maier, *In Search of Stability: Explorations in Historical Political Economy* (Cambridge: Cambridge University Press, 1987), pp. 121–52.

59. Pollard, *Economic Security and the Origins of the Cold War*, pp. 246–7; also Melvyn P. Leffler, *A Preponderance of Power: National Security, the Truman Administration, and the Cold War* (Stanford: Stanford University Press, 1992), pp. 10–24.

60. See, for a related argument, Hadley Arkes, *Bureaucracy, the Marshall Plan, and the National Interest* (Princeton: Princeton University Press, 1972), p. 51.

61. See Gaddis, *Strategies of Containment*, pp. 55–65. I have also benefited here from reading a paper by Geir Lundestad, "The United States and European Integration, 1945–1995," presented at the European Association of American Studies meeting, Warsaw, Mar. 1996.

62. Hickerson memorandum, conversation with Lord Inverchapel, 21 Jan. 1948, *FRUS: 1948*, iii. 11. For more on the "third force" concept, see Gaddis, *The Long Peace*, pp. 57–61; Hogan, *The Marshall Plan*, pp. 187–8; Thomas Alan Schwartz, *America's Germany: John J. McCloy and the Federal Republic of Germany* (Cambridge, Mass.: Harvard University Press, 1991), pp. 18–19, 44–5; and, for the European roots of this idea, John W. Young, *Cold War Europe, 1945–1989: A Political History* (London: Edward Arnold, 1991), pp. 29–30.

63. Kennan particularly had doubts on this score, but so too did a much wider and diverse community. For examples, see Thomas G. Paterson, ed., *Cold War Critics: Alternatives to American Foreign Policy in the Truman Years* (Chicago: Quadrangle Books, 1971); but also, interestingly, Paul H. Nitze, *From Hiroshima to Glasnost: At the Center of Decision—A Memoir* (New York: Grove Weidenfeld, 1989), pp. 119–20.

64. See Ulam, *The Communists*, p. 21.

65. The story is told in Djilas, *Conversations with Stalin*, pp. 87–97, 110–11, with the quote from Stalin on p. 95. See also Naimark, *The Russians in Germany*, pp. 70–1; and Raack, "Stalin Plans His Post-War Germany," p. 61.

66. Banac, *With Stalin Against Tito*, pp. 28–34. See also Djilas, *Conversations with Stalin*, pp. 179–82; Zubok and Pleshakov, *Inside the Kremlin's Cold War*, pp. 125–8; and Leonid Gibiansky, "The 1948 Soviet–Yugoslav Conflict and the Formation of the 'Socialist Camp' Model," in Odd Arne Westad, Sven Holtsmark, and Iver B. Neumann, eds., *The Soviet Union in Eastern Europe, 1945–89* (New York: St. Martin's Press, 1994), pp. 26–46.

67. John W. Young, *France, the Cold War, and the Western Alliance, 1944–49: French Foreign Policy and Post-War Europe* (Leicester: Leicester University Press, 1990), pp. 146–7; James Edward Miller, *The United States and Italy, 1940–1950: The Politics of Diplomacy and Stabilization* (Chapel Hill: University of North Carolina Press, 1986), pp. 228–9.

68. Natalya I. Yegorova, "From the Comintern to the Cominform: Ideological Dimensions of Cold War Origins (1945–1948)," CWIHP conference paper, Moscow, Jan. 1993, pp. 22–3. See also Zubok and Pleshakov, *Inside the Kremlin's Cold War*, p. 129; and Leonid Gibiansky, "Problems of East European International-Political Structuring in the Formation of the Soviet Bloc in the 1940s," CWIHP conference paper, Moscow, Jan. 1993, p. 51.

69. Gaddis, *The Long Peace*, pp. 155–6.

70. Gaddis, *Russia, the Soviet Union, and the United States*, pp. 87–93.

71. Harriman, *Special Envoy to Churchill and Stalin*, pp. 384–5. For more on this, see Chapter VII.

72. My analysis here and in the next two paragraphs follows Mikhail M. Narinsky, "The Soviet Union and the Marshall Plan," and Scott D. Parish, "The Turn Towards Confrontation: The Soviet Reaction to the Marshall Plan, June 1947," both CWIHP conference papers, Moscow, Jan. 1993; also Geoffrey Roberts, "Moscow and the Marshall Plan: Politics, Ideology, and the Onset of the Cold War, 1947," *Europe–Asia Studies* 46 (1994), 1371–86; and Mikhail Narinsky, "Soviet Foreign Policy and the Origins of the Marshall Plan," in Gabriel Gorodetsky, ed., *Soviet Foreign Policy 1917–1991: A Retrospective* (London: Frank Cass, 1994), pp. 105–10. Galina Takhnenko, "Anatomy of a Political Decision: Notes on the Marshall Plan," *International Affairs* (Moscow) (July 1992), 111–27, reprints several key documents from the Soviet foreign ministry archives.

73. Novikov to Molotov, 24 June 1947, ibid., pp. 118–20. See also Novikov's dispatch of 9 June ibid., p. 116, as well as his analytical dispatch, "U.S. Foreign Policy in the Postwar Period," 27 Sept. 1946, in Kenneth M. Jensen, ed., *Origins of the Cold War: The Novikov, Kennan, and Roberts "Long Telegrams" of 1946* (Washington: United States Institute of Peace, 1991), p. 14.

74. Vyshinsky to Molotov, 30 June 1947, cited in Narinsky, "The Soviet Union and the Marshall Plan," pp. 6–7. Sudoplatov, *Special Tasks*, pp. 230–2, claims that the source was the spy Donald Maclean.

75. Molotov to Soviet embassies in Eastern Europe, 5 July 1947, 6.40 a.m., Takhnenko, "Anatomy of a Political Decision," p. 122. See also Karel Krátky, "Czechoslovakia, the Soviet Union, and the Marshall Plan," in Westad et al., *The Soviet Union in Eastern Europe*, p. 15. Roberts, "Moscow and the Marshall Plan," pp. 1378–9, suggests that opposition from the Yugoslavs may have influenced Stalin's decision that the Soviet Union should not participate.

76. Molotov to Soviet embassies in Eastern Europe, 5 July 1947, 8.15 a.m., Takhnenko, "Anatomy of a Political Decision," p. 123.

77. Molotov to Soviet embassies in Eastern Europe, 8 July 1947, ibid. 124. See also Narinsky, "The Soviet Union and the Marshall Plan," p. 12, for speculation as to the reasons for this policy reversal.

78. Kaplan, *The Short March*, pp. 73–4.
79. Quoted in Krátky, "Czechoslovakia, the Soviet Union, and the Marshall Plan," p. 18.
80. Ibid. 22. For Moscow's handling of the Finns' desire to participate in the Marshall Plan, see Zubok and Pleshakov, *Inside the Kremlin's Cold War*, pp. 131–2.
81. Novikov to Molotov, 27 Sept. 1946, in Jensen, ed., *Origins of the Cold War*, pp. 11, 13. See also Albert Resis, "Stalin, the Politburo, and the Onset of the Cold War, 1945–1946," *The Carl Beck Papers in Russian and East European Studies* #701 (Apr. 1988), 6–8, 13–16; and William Curti Wohlforth, *The Elusive Balance: Power and Perceptions during the Cold War* (Ithaca: Cornell University Press, 1993), pp. 66–8.
82. Ibid. 70–1.
83. Larson, *Origins of Containment*, pp. 178, 194.
84. One of the best discussions is still Kent Roberts Greenfield, *American Strategy in World War II: A Reconsideration* (Baltimore: Johns Hopkins University Press, 1963).
85. For an overview of this literature, see David Reynolds, "Great Britain," in Reynolds, ed., *The Origins of the Cold War in Europe*, pp. 80–3.
86. Alan Bullock, *Ernest Bevin: Foreign Secretary, 1945–1951* (New York: Norton, 1983); Fraser J. Harbutt, *The Iron Curtain: Churchill, America, and the Origins of the Cold War* (New York: Oxford University Press, 1986); and Anne Deighton, *The Impossible Peace: Britain, the Division of Germany, and the Origins of the Cold War* (New York: Oxford University Press, 1990) all provide good discussions of this British "management" of the Americans.
87. "Situation with Respect to European Recovery Program," 4 Sept. 1947, *FRUS: 1947*, iii. 402.
88. Essays on France and Italy by Georges-Henri Soutou and Ilaria Poggiolini, in Reynolds, ed., *The Origins of the Cold War in Europe* make this point clearly.
89. See Miller, *The United States and Italy*, pp. 243–9.
90. Quoted in Peter Coleman, *The Liberal Conspiracy: The Congress for Cultural Freedom and the Struggle for the Mind of Postwar Europe* (New York: Free Press, 1989), pp. 49–50.
91. Gaddis, *The United States and the Origins of the Cold War*, pp. 114–31.
92. Smith, *Lucius D. Clay*, pp. 331–52. See also Frank Ninkovich, *Germany and the United States: The Transformation of the German Question since 1945*, updated edn. (Boston: Twayne, 1995), pp. 26–47; and Tony Smith, *America's Mission: The United States and the Worldwide Struggle for Democracy in the Twentieth Century* (Princeton: Princeton University Press, 1994), pp. 146–76, which sees interesting analogies between Clay's policies and those of MacArthur in occupied Japan. For more on this, see Chapter VII.
93. Naimark, *The Russians in Germany*, pp. 24–5; also Zubok, "Eastern Europe's Place in the Priorities of Soviet Foreign Policy," pp. 18–19.
94. Naimark, *The Russians in Germany*, p. 107. See also, for the estimates on the scale of rapes and reparations removals, ibid. 132–3, 169; as well as Atina Grossmann, "A Question of Silence: The Rape of German Women by Occupation Soldiers," *October 72* (Spring 1995), 43–63.
95. Naimark, *The Russians in Germany*, pp. 92–7.
96. I have followed here the arguments of the Russian historian Alexei M. Filitov, "The Soviet Administrators and Their German 'Friends'," Norwegian Nobel Institute conference paper, Moscow, Mar. 1993, pp. 15–17.
97. Naimark, *The Russians in Germany*, pp. 467, 469.

98. Smith, *Lucius D. Clay*, p. 244.
99. The existence of authoritarianism in Greece and Turkey generated considerable opposition to the Truman Doctrine early in 1947, and the admission of these two countries to the North Atlantic Treaty Organization was delayed until 1952. Spain received no Marshall Plan aid, and was not admitted to NATO until 1982.
100. Zubok and Pleshakov, *Inside the Kremlin's Cold War*, pp. 119–21.
101. Daniels, ed., *A Documentary History of Communism*, ii. p. 148. The "two camps" formulation may have been inserted by Stalin himself. See Zubok and Pleshakov, *Inside the Kremlin's Cold War*, p. 133; also Gavriel Ra'anan, *International Policy Formation in the USSR: Factional "Debates" during the Zhdanovschina* (Hamden, Conn.: Archon Books, 1983), pp. 101–10; and Werner G. Hahn, *Postwar Soviet Politics: The Fall of Zhdanov and the Defeat of Moderation, 1946–53* (Ithaca: Cornell University Press, 1982), pp. 24–5, which suggests that Zhdanov personally had favored a more conciliatory policy toward the West.
102. This account is based on the detailed discussion in Gibiansky, "Problems of Eastern European International-Political Structuring," pp. 36–65. There is some evidence that Tito misinterpreted the location of the Cominform in Belgrade as a belated endorsement on Stalin's part of his more militant policies. See Banac, *With Stalin Against Tito*, pp. 25–6; also Geoffrey Swain, "The Cominform: Tito's International?" *Historical Journal* 35 (1992), 641–63.
103. Quoted in Yegorova, "From the Comintern to the Cominform," p. 24. This was, of course, no innovation, since the old Comintern had functioned in much the same way. See Pipes, *Russia Under the Bolshevik Regime*, pp. 177, 184–7, 420–1.
104. Igor Lukes, "A Road to Communism: Czechoslovakia, 1938–1948," Norwegian Nobel Institute conference paper, Moscow, Mar. 1993, pp. 1–11. See also Kaplan, *The Short March*, pp. 3–5.
105. Ibid. 55–188, and esp. the analysis in pp. 189–94.
106. PPS-13, "Resumé of World Situation," 6 Nov. 1947, *The State Department Policy Planning Staff Papers, 1947* (New York: Garland, 1983), i. 132. Lukes, "A Road to Communism," pp. 24–7, suggests that a less resigned stance on the part of the Americans and the British might have discouraged the coup.
107. John A. Armitage, "The View from Czechoslovakia," in Hammond, ed., *Witnesses to the Origins of the Cold War*, pp. 223–6. See also Leffler, *A Preponderance of Power*, pp. 203–6.
108. For more on this, see Smith, *Lucius D. Clay*, pp. 466–8; also Frank Kofsky, *Harry S. Truman and the War Scare of 1948: A Successful Campaign to Deceive the Nation* (New York: St. Martin's Press, 1993).
109. Lawrence S. Kaplan, *The United States and NATO: The Formative Years* (Lexington: University Press of Kentucky, 1984), pp. 49–51. For Bevin's attitude and the impact of the Czech coup, see Bullock, *Ernest Bevin: Foreign Secretary*, pp. 529–30. Bevin was by no means alone in this view. See Soutou, "France," in Reynolds, ed., *The Origins of the Cold War in Europe*, p. 105.
110. Mikhail Narinsky, "The USSR and the Berlin Crisis, 1948–1949," unpublished paper quoted in Zubok and Pleshakov, *Inside the Kremlin's Cold War*, p. 52. See also Charles F. Pennacchio, "The East German Communists and the Origins of the Berlin Blockade Crisis," *East European Quarterly* 24 (Sept. 1995), 294–314.
111. M. Dratvin and V. Semyonov to Molotov and Bulganin, 17 Apr. 1948, both quoted in Mikhail Narinsky, "Soviet Policy and the Berlin Blockade, 1948," CWIHP conference paper, Essen, June 1994, pp. 6–7, 9.

112. Soviet memorandum of Stalin's conversation with American, British, and French ambassadors, Moscow, 2 Aug. 1948, quoted ibid. 16.
113. Robert A. Divine, *Foreign Policy and U.S. Presidential Elections, 1940–1948* (New York: New Viewpoints, 1974), pp. 225–6; Warren I. Cohen, *America in the Age of Soviet Power, 1945–1991* (New York: Cambridge University Press, 1993), p. 48.
114. Dratvin and Semyonov to Molotov and Bulganin, 17 Apr. 1948, quoted in Narinsky, "Soviet Policy and the Berlin Blockade," p. 9.
115. Smith, *Lucius D. Clay*, pp. 497–530. The best overall account is Avi Shlaim, *The United States and the Berlin Blockade, 1948–1949: A Study in Crisis Decision-Making* (Berkeley: University of California Press, 1983); but see also Hannes Adomeit, *Soviet Risk-Taking and Crisis Behavior: A Theoretical and Empirical Analysis* (London: Allen & Unwin 1982), pp. 67–182; and, for the blockade as a reflection of Stalin's bargaining practices, James M. Goldgeier, *Leadership Style and Soviet Foreign Policy: Stalin, Khrushchev, Brezhnev, Gorbachev* (Baltimore: Johns Hopkins University Press, 1994), pp. 34–51.
116. Victor M. Gobarev, "Soviet Military Plans and Activities During the Berlin Crisis, 1948–1949," CWIHP conference paper, Essen, June 1994), pp. 5–6. See also Samuel R. Williamson, Jr., and Steven L. Rearden, *The Origins of U.S. Nuclear Strategy, 1945–1953* (New York: St. Martin's Press, 1993), p. 88. We now know that the bombers deployed did not actually have an atomic capability. For more on this, see Chapter IV.
117. Djilas, *Conversations with Stalin*, pp. 142–7, 179–80; Banac, *With Stalin Against Tito*, pp. 38–44.
118. Ibid. 132–4. There has long been speculation that Stalin also planned an actual military attack on Yugoslavia, coupled with a preventive strike against Western Europe as a whole. Beatrice Heuser, *Western "Containment" Policies in the Cold War* (New York: Routledge 1989), pp. 127–30, assesses this evidence, concluding that if such plans existed, they did so on nothing more than a contingency basis. David Holloway, *Stalin and the Bomb: The Soviet Union and Atomic Energy, 1939–1956* (New Haven: Yale University Press, 1994), pp. 285–7, interprets this evidence in terms of a Stalin effort to deter the Americans from expanding the Korean War by calling attention to Western European military vulnerabilities.
119. Gaddis, *The Long Peace*, pp. 67–71.
120. See, on this whole subject, Lundestad's classic 1986 article, "Empire by Invitation," now republished in a considerably expanded form in Lundestad, *The American "Empire"*, pp. 31–115.
121. See Chapter V.
122. See e.g. George F. Kennan, *American Diplomacy: 1900–1950* (Chicago: University of Chicago Press, 1951).
123. Ninkovich, *Germany and the United States*, pp. 82–3.
124. Schwartz, *America's Germany*, pp. 110–12.
125. Gaddis, *The Long Peace*, pp. 149–50.
126. I have based this argument on articles by Soutou and Poggiolini on France and Italy in Reynolds, ed., *The Origins of the Cold War in Europe*, pp. 96–143.
127. See Abbott Gleason, *Totalitarianism: The Inner History of the Cold War* (New York: Oxford University Press, 1995), p. 7; also John Lewis Gaddis, "On Moral Equivalency and Cold War History," *Ethics and International Affairs* 10 (1996), 131–48.
128. See Lundestad, *The American "Empire"*, pp. 55–6.

CHAPTER III

1. Shi Zhe, "With Mao and Stalin: The Reminiscences of a Chinese Interpreter," trans. Chen Jian, *Chinese Historians* 5 (Spring 1992), 40.
2. Shi Zhe, "With Mao and Stalin: The Reminiscences of Mao's Interpreter; Part II: Liu Shaoqi in Moscow," trans. Chen Jian, ibid. 6 (Spring 1993), 84.
3. Donald Cameron Watt, *How War Came: The Immediate Origins of the Second World War, 1938–1939* (New York: Pantheon, 1989), pp. 339–44.
4. Eric Larrabee, *Commander-in-Chief: Franklin Delano Roosevelt, His Lieutenants, and Their War* (New York: Harper & Row, 1987), pp. 543, 552–4.
5. The most recent account is Russell D. Buhite, *Decisions at Yalta: An Appraisal of Summit Diplomacy* (Wilmington, Del.: Scholarly Resources, 1986), pp. 85–104.
6. Odd Arne Westad, *Cold War and Revolution: Soviet–American Rivalry and the Origins of the Chinese Civil War, 1944–1946* (New York: Columbia University Press, 1993), pp. 32–6, 173.
7. W. Averell Harriman and Elie Abel, *Special Envoy to Churchill and Stalin, 1941–1946* (New York: Random House, 1975), pp. 500–1; Russell D. Buhite, *Soviet–American Relations in Asia, 1945–1954* (Norman: University of Oklahoma Press, 1981), pp. 107–8. Stalin apparently ordered Soviet forces to occupy Hokkaido despite Truman's rejection, but then changed his mind (see David Holloway, *Stalin and the Bomb: The Soviet Union and Atomic Energy, 1939–1956* (New Haven: Yale University Press, 1994), p. 131).
8. A point acknowledged, many years later, by Nikita Khrushchev. See *Khrushchev Remembers: The Glasnost Tapes*, trans. and ed. Jerrold L. Schecter and Vyacheslav V. Luchkov (Boston: Little, Brown, 1990), p. 84.
9. Tony Smith, *America's Mission: The United States and the Worldwide Struggle for Democracy in the Twentieth Century* (Princeton: Princeton University Press, 1994), pp. 170–1. For a critical assessment of MacArthur's role in Japan, see Michael Schaller, *Douglas MacArthur: The Far Eastern General* (New York: Oxford University Press, 1989), pp. 120–57.
10. Milovan Djilas, *Conversations with Stalin*, trans. Michael B. Petrovich (New York: Harcourt, Brace & World, 1962), p. 114.
11. I have followed here the argument in Smith, *America's Mission*, ch. 6. For the impact of the Japanese record on Mikhail Gorbachev, see Don Oberdorfer, *The Turn: From the Cold War to a New Era: The United States and the Soviet Union, 1983–1990* (New York: Poseidon Press, 1991), pp. 223–4.
12. Michael Schaller, *The American Occupation of Japan: The Origins of the Cold War in Asia* (New York: Oxford University Press, 1985) documents this shift. But see also George F. Kennan, *Memoirs: 1925–1950* (Boston: Atlantic, Little Brown, 1967), pp. 368–96.
13. William Stueck, *The Korean War: An International History* (Princeton: Princeton University Press, 1995), p. 19; Kathryn Weathersby, "Soviet Aims in Korea and the Origins of the Korean War, 1945–1950: New Evidence from the Russian Archives," CWIHP Working Paper 8, Nov., 1993, p. 8.
14. Charles M. Dobbs, *The Unwanted Symbol: American Foreign Policy, the Cold War, and Korea, 1945–1950* (Kent, OH: Kent State University Press, 1981), provides a good survey of this period.
15. Scott L. Bills, *Empire and Cold War: The Roots of US–Third World Antagonism, 1945–47* (New York: St. Martin's Press, 1990), p. 204.
16. H. W. Brands, *The Specter of Neutralism: The United States and the Emergence of the Third World, 1947–1950* (New York: Columbia University Press, 1989),

pp. 17–20; also Robert J. McMahon, *The Cold War on the Periphery: The United States, India, and Pakistan* (New York: Columbia University Press, 1993), pp. 14–17.

17. Robert J. McMahon, *Colonialism and the Cold War: The United States and the Struggle for Indonesian Independence, 1945–49* (Ithaca: Cornell University Press, 1981).
18. Lloyd C. Gardner, *Approaching Vietnam: From World War II through Dienbienphu* (New York: Norton, 1988), pp. 62–6.
19. John Lewis Gaddis, *The Long Peace: Inquiries into the History of the Cold War* (New York: Oxford University Press, 1987), p. 90.
20. Buhite, *Soviet–American Relations in Asia*, pp. 5–36. For the origins of this policy, see Michael Schaller, *The U.S. Crusade in China, 1938–1945* (New York: Columbia University Press, 1979), pp. 166–7.
21. Richard Pipes, *Russia Under the Bolshevik Regime* (New York: Harper & Row, 1994), p. 199. See also Nicola Miller, *Soviet Relations with Latin America, 1959–1987* (Cambridge: Cambridge University Press, 1990), pp. 36–8.
22. Adam Ulam, *Stalin: The Man and His Era* (New York: Viking, 1973), pp. 274–80. The quote from Stalin is on p. 276. For the Chinese perspective on these events, see Michael H. Hunt, *The Genesis of Chinese Communist Foreign Policy* (New York: Columbia University Press, 1996), pp. 86–7, 111–12.
23. *Khrushchev Remembers*, trans. and ed. Strobe Talbott (Boston: Little, Brown, 1971), p. 462.
24. Djilas, *Conversations with Stalin*, p. 132.
25. I have based these conclusions on reading Michael M. Sheng's as yet unpublished manuscript, "Ideology and Chinese Communist Foreign Policy: Mao Deals with Superpowers, 1935–50." See also his articles, cited below. Hunt, *The Genesis of Chinese Communist Foreign Policy* takes the more traditional view of a strained Soviet–Chinese Communist relationship.
26. Buhite, *Soviet–American Relations in Asia*, pp. 46–7; Westad, *Cold War and Revolution*, pp. 9–10.
27. Quoted ibid. 141.
28. Ibid. 80–1.
29. Brian Joseph Murray, "Western Versus Chinese Realism: Soviet–American Diplomacy and the Chinese Civil War, 1945–1950" (Ph.D. Dissertation, Columbia University, 1995) focuses on this pattern of mutual non-cooperation.
30. See Westad, *Cold War and Revolution*, pp. 79–139, for a good summary of the Marshall mission.
31. Gaddis, *The Long Peace*, pp. 149–64; also Gordon H. Chang, *Friends and Enemies: The United States, China, and the Soviet Union, 1948–1972* (Stanford: Stanford University Press, 1990), p. 3.
32. Beatrice Heuser, *Western "Containment" Policies in the Cold War: The Yugoslav Case, 1948–53* (New York: Routledge, 1989), provides the fullest discussion of the western response to Tito.
33. William Whitney Stueck, Jr., *The Road to Confrontation: American Policy toward China and Korea, 1947–1950* (Chapel Hill: University of North Carolina Press, 1981), pp. 56–7; Warren I. Cohen, *America in the Age of Soviet Power, 1945–1991* (New York: Cambridge University Press, 1993), pp. 51, 62.
34. Marshall executive session statement to Senate Foreign Relations and House Foreign Affairs Committees, 20 Feb. 1948, US Department of State, *United States Relations with China, with Special Reference to the Period 1944–1949* (Washington: Government Printing Office, 1949), p. 381.

35. Acheson executive session testimony, 29 Mar. 1950, US Congress, Senate Committee on Foreign Relations, *Historical Series: Reviews of the World Situation, 1949–1950* (Washington: Government Printing Office, 1974), p. 273. See also Ronald McGlothen, *Controlling the Waves: Dean Acheson and U.S. Foreign Policy in Asia* (New York: Norton, 1993). For more on the "wedge" strategy, see Chang, *Friends and Enemies*, *passim*; also Gaddis, *The Long Peace*, pp. 164–94; Heuser, *Western "Containment" Policies in the Cold War*, pp. 70–5; and David Allan Mayers, *Cracking the Monolith: U.S. Policy Against the Sino-Soviet Alliance, 1949–1955* (Baton Rouge: Louisiana State University Press, 1986).

36. Gaddis, *The Long Peace*, p. 173.

37. NSC-48/5, "United States Objectives, Policies and Courses of Action in Asia," *FRUS: 1951*, vi. 35, 37.

38. Mayers, *Cracking the Monolith*, pp. 103–4; Gaddis, *The Long Peace*, p. 172. Rusk's speech, delivered on 18 May 1951, is in the *Department of State Bulletin* 24 (28 May 1951), 843–8.

39. The best recent overview is Richard M. Fried, *Nightmare in Red: The McCarthy Era in Perspective* (New York: Oxford University Press, 1990). But see also, for some of the effects on individuals, Ellen W. Schrecker, *No Ivory Tower: McCarthyism and the Universities* (New York: Oxford University Press, 1986); and two books by Robert P. Newman, *The Cold War Romance of Lillian Hellman and John Melby* (Chapel Hill: University of North Carolina Press, 1989) and *Owen Lattimore and the "Loss" of China* (Berkeley : University of California Press, 1992).

40. Qiang Zhai, "The Making of Chinese Communist Foreign Relations, 1935–1949: A New Study from China," *Journal of American–East Asian Relations* 1 (Winter 1992), 471–7; He Di, "The Most Respected Enemy: Mao Zedong's Perception of the United States," *China Quarterly* #137 (Mar. 1994), 146–8; Odd Arne Westad, "Losses, Chances, and Myths: The United States and the Creation of the Sino-Soviet Alliance, 1945–1950," forthcoming in *Diplomatic History*. Hunt, *The Genesis of Chinese Communist Foreign Policy*, p. 171, places the date of Mao's disillusionment with the Americans somewhat later; but Michael M. Sheng, "America's Lost Chance in China? A Reappraisal of Chinese Communist Policy toward the United States before 1945," *Australian Journal of Chinese Affairs* 29 (Jan. 1993), 135–57, argues that there was never any chance for amicable relations between Mao and Washington.

41. Chen Jian, *China's Road to the Korean War: The Making of the Sino-American Confrontation* (New York: Columbia University Press, 1994), pp. 17–20, 40–2. For Mao's thinking on the traditional Chinese strategy of using barbarians to fight other barbarians, see Sergei N. Goncharov, John W. Lewis, and Xue Litai, *Uncertain Partners: Stalin, Mao, and the Korean War* (Stanford, Calif.: Stanford University Press, 1993), p. 204.

42. Harrison Salisbury, *The New Emperors: China in the Era of Mao and Deng* (Boston: Little, Brown, 1992), pp. 8–9, 51–3; Li Zhisui, *The Private Life of Chairman Mao*, trans. Tai Hung-chao (New York: Random House, 1994), p. 122.

43. Albert Resis, ed., *Molotov Remembers: Inside Kremlin Politics: Conversations with Felix Chuev* (Chicago: Ivan R. Dee, 1993), p. 81.

44. Chen, *China's Road to the Korean War*, p. 67. For a different interpretation of this episode, see Goncharov et al., *Uncertain Partners*, pp. 42–3.

45. Ibid. 20, 44–5; Chen, *China's Road to the Korean War*, p. 68; Hunt, *The Genesis of Chinese Communist Foreign Policy*, pp. 102, 218. But see also pp. 247–8, for a useful caution against making *too* much of the Soviet model.

46. Salisbury, *The New Emperors*, pp. 143–5.

47. Yang Kuisong, "The Soviet Factor and the CCP's Policy toward the United States in the 1940s," *Chinese Historians* 5 (1992), 18. See also Chen, China's Road to the Korean War, pp. 67, 90–1; and Steven M. Goldstein, "Nationalism and Internationalism: Sino-Soviet Relations," in Thomas W. Robinson and David Shambaugh, eds., *Chinese Foreign Policy: Theory and Practice* (New York: Oxford University Press, 1994), pp. 228–30.

48. Hunt, *The Genesis of Chinese Communist Foreign Policy*, pp. 148–51, provides useful examples.

49. Quoted in He Di, "The Evolution of the Chinese Communist Party's Policy toward the United States, 1944–1949," in Harry Harding and Yuan Ming, eds., *Sino-American Relations, 1945–1955: A Joint Reassessment of a Critical Decade* (Wilmington, Del.: Scholarly Resources, 1989), p. 40. See also, on the importance of the Marshall mission in shaping Mao's attitude toward the United States, Westad, *Cold War and Revolution*, pp. 169–70; Yang, "The Soviet Factor and the CCP's Policy toward the United States," p. 27; and Shu Guang Zhang, *Deterrence and Strategic Culture: Chinese–American Confrontations, 1949–1958* (Ithaca: Cornell University Press, 1992), p. 18.

50. I. V. Kovalev interview with S. N. Goncharov, "Stalin's Dialogue with Mao Zedong," *Journal of Northeast Asian Studies* 10 (Winter 1991), 51–2. See also Zhang, *Deterrence and Strategic Culture*, pp. 14–15; Chen, *China's Road to the Korean War*, p. 15; Salisbury, *The New Emperors*, p. 13; Hunt, *The Genesis of Chinese Communist Foreign Policy*, pp. 172–3; He Di, " 'The Last Campaign to Unify China': The CCP's Unmaterialized Plan to Liberate Taiwan, 1949–1950," *Chinese Historians* 5 (Spring 1992), 2–3.

51. Chen, *China's Road to the Korean War*, p. 22; Goncharov et al., *Uncertain Partners*, p. 204.

52. Zhang, *Deterrence and Strategic Culture*, pp. 16–18. For the Taiping uprising and the Boxer rebellion, see two books by Jonathan D. Spence, *The Search for Modern China* (New York: Norton, 1990), esp. pp. 170–8, 231–5, and *God's Chinese Son: The Taiping Heavenly Kingdom of Hong Xuiquan* (New York: Norton, 1996).

53. Quoted in Zhang, *Deterrence and Strategic Culture*, p. 21.

54. Ibid. 44; also He, "The Evolution of the Chinese Communist Party's Policy toward the United States," pp. 46–7; and Michael H. Hunt, "Mao and the Issue of Accommodation with the United States, 1948–1950," in Dorothy Borg and Waldo Heinrichs, eds., *Uncertain Years: Chinese–American Relations, 1947–1950* (New York: Columbia University Press, 1980), pp. 228–30. Odd Arne Westad has pointed out to me the role of the Chinese-Americans. Nancy Bernkopf Tucker, *Patterns in the Dust: Chinese–American Relations and the Recognition Controversy, 1949–1950* (New York: Columbia University Press, 1983) conveys clearly the diversity of American views on China at this time.

55. See e.g. Djilas, *Conversations with Stalin*, pp. 74, 153; Chen, *China's Road to the Korean War*, pp. 155–6; Goncharov et al., *Uncertain Partners*, p. 69; *Khrushchev Remembers: The Last Testament*, trans. and ed. Strobe Talbott (Boston: Little, Brown, 1974), p. 375.

56. Ibid. 238–9; Chen, *China's Road to the Korean War*, pp. 69–70; Zhang, *Deterrence and Strategic Culture*, pp. 19–20; Salisbury, *The New Emperors*, pp. 15–16. A detailed account of the Mikoyan visit appears in Shi, "With Mao and Stalin: The Reminiscences of a Chinese Interpreter," pp. 35–46.

57. Zhang, *Deterrence and Strategic Culture*, pp. 22–3; Goncharov et al., *Uncertain Partners*, p. 50.

58. Zhang, *Deterrence and Strategic Culture*, pp. 24–5.

59. See e.g. Hunt, "Mao and the Issue Accommodation with the United States," p. 232; also Warren I. Cohen, "Acheson, His Advisers, and China, 1949–1950," in Borg and Heinrichs, eds., *Uncertain Years*, pp. 36–7. For the debate over this issue, see Steven M. Goldstein, "Sino-American Relations, 1948–1950: Lost Chance or No Chance?" in Harding and Ming, eds., *Sino-American Relations, 1945–1955*, pp. 119–42.
60. Chen, *China's Road to the Korean War*, pp. 50–5; Zhang, *Deterrence and Strategic Culture*, p. 26. He, "The Evolution of the Chinese Communist Party's Policy toward the United States," *passim*; Yang, "The Soviet Factor and the CCP's Policy Toward the United States in the 1940s," *passim*.
61. Ibid. 30–1; Goncharov et al., *Uncertain Partners*, pp. 33–4; Chen Jian, "The Ward Case and the Emergence of Sino-American Confrontation, 1948–1950," *Australian Journal of Chinese Affairs* 30 (July 1993), 149–70. See also P. F. Yudin's report of a conversation with Mao on 31 Mar. 1956, published as "Mao Zedong on the Comintern's and Stalin's China Policy," *Far Eastern Affairs* #4–5 (1994), 138.
62. Goncharov et al., *Uncertain Partners*, pp. 27–8; Chen, *China's Road to the Korean War*, p. 72; Yang, "The Soviet Factor and the CCP's Policy toward the United States," pp. 33–4.
63. Bo Yibo, "The Making of the 'Leaning to One Side' Decision," trans. Zhai Qiang, *Chinese Historians* 5 (Spring 1992), 60.
64. See Goldstein, "Nationalism and Internationalism," p. 233.
65. Kovalev, "Stalin's Dialogue with Mao Zedong," p. 58. See also, for an intriguing Mar. 1948 document from the Taiwan archives that *purports* to be a Stalin speech calling for revolutionary uprisings throughout the "third world," Brian Murray, "Stalin, the Cold War, and the Division of China: A Multi-Archival Mystery," CWIHP Working Paper 12, June 1995.
66. Shi, "With Mao and Stalin: Liu Shaoqi in Moscow," pp. 82–6. For Kovalev's notes on this meeting, which generally confirm the Chinese account, see "Stalin's Dialogue with Mao Zedong," pp. 58–9.
67. See Goncharov et al., *Uncertain Partners*, p. 107.
68. Kovalev, "Stalin's Dialogue with Mao Zedong," pp. 59–60.
69. CCP Central Committee to Shandong Branch re Gifts for Stalin's Birthday, 1 Dec. 1949, in Goncharov et al., *Uncertain Partners*, p. 237. See also Salisbury, *The New Emperors*, pp. 94–5. Zhou Enlai later acknowledged to Stalin that the Chinese had been embarrassed by the splendor of the gifts other nations had sent (Soviet transcript, Stalin–Zhou Enlai conversation, 19 Sept. 1952, CWIHP *Bulletin* 6 and 7 (Winter 1995/6), 19).
70. Goncharov et al., *Uncertain Partners*, p. 84.
71. Gaddis, *The Long Peace*, pp. 165–6.
72. Chen, *China's Road to the Korean War*, pp. 79–80. A valiant attempt to explain this metaphor appears in Goncharov et al., *Uncertain Partners*, p. 86. For more on the difficulties of translation, see Nikolai T. Fedorenko, "Stalin and Mao Zedong (Part 1)," *Russian Politics and Law* 32 (July–Aug. 1994), 74–5, 79–83.
73. Goncharov et al., *Uncertain Partners*, pp. 94, 97; also *Khrushchev Remembers: The Last Testament*, pp. 243–4.
74. Chinese memorandum, Mao conversation with Soviet ambassador P. F. Yudin, 22 July 1958, CWIHP *Bulletin* 6 and 7 (Winter 1996), 156. See also Salisbury, *The New Emperors*, pp. 96–8; Goncharov et al., *Uncertain Partners*, p. 92; and Nikolai T. Fedorenko, "Stalin and Mao Zedong (Conclusion)," *Russian Politics and Law* 33 (Jan.–Feb. 1995), 82–4.

75. Zhang, *Deterrence and Strategic Culture*, pp. 30–1; *Khrushchev Remembers: The Last Testament*, p. 240. See also Shu Guang Zhang, "In the Shadow of Mao: Zhou Enlai and New China's Diplomacy," in Gordon A. Craig and Francis L. Loewenheim, eds., *The Diplomats: 1939–1979* (Princeton, NJ: Princeton University Press, 1994), pp. 348–9; Chen, *China's Road to the Korean War*, pp. 81–3; and, for the most detailed account, Goncharov et al., *Uncertain Partners*, pp. 92–129.
76. Ibid. 221. See also Salisbury, *The New Emperors*, pp. 100–2.
77. Federenko, "Stalin and Mao Zedong," p. 82.
78. Chen, *China's Road to the Korean War*, pp. 85, 90–1; Zhang, *Deterrence and Strategic Culture*, pp. 32–3; Goldstein, "Nationalism and Internationalism," pp. 231–2. See also Rosemary Foot, "New Light on the Sino-Soviet Alliance: Chinese and American Perspectives," *Journal of Northeast Asian Studies* 10 (Fall 1991), 17.
79. The classic account is Ronald Robinson and John Gallagher, with Alice Denny, *Africa and the Victorians: The Climax of Imperialism* (New York: St. Martin's Press, 1961). For a more recent interpretation, see Jack Snyder, *Myths of Empire: Domestic Politics and International Ambition* (Ithaca: Cornell University Press, 1991).
80. Stueck, *The Korean War*, pp. 19–23, provides a succinct overview of these events.
81. See e.g. Peter Hopkirk, *The Great Game: The Struggle for Empire in Central Asia* (New York: Kodansha International, 1992), which documents a similar tendency in the nineteenth century Anglo-Russian rivalry over Central Asia.
82. For new information from Chinese and Russian sources on Kim's background, see Gavan McCormack, "Kim Country: Hard Times in North Korea," *New Left Review* #198 (Mar.–Apr. 1993), 22–4; and Georgy Tumanov, "How the Great Leader was Made," *New Times* 17 (Apr. 1993), 24–6.
83. The most thorough history of developments in Korea prior to 1950 is Bruce Cumings, *The Origins of the Korean War: Liberation and the Emergence of Separate Regimes, 1945–1947* (Princeton: Princeton University Press, 1981), and *The Origins of the Korean War: The Roaring of the Cataract, 1947–1950* (Princeton: Princeton University Press, 1990). Shorter accounts include Dobbs, *The Unwanted Symbol*; and James Irving Matray, *The Reluctant Crusade: American Foreign Policy in Korea, 1941–1950* (Honolulu: University of Hawaii Press, 1985).
84. Cumings, *The Roaring of the Cataract*, p. 621.
85. Alexandre Y. Mansourov, "Did Conventional Deterrence Work? Why the Korean War Did Not Erupt in the Summer of 1949," paper prepared for the CWIHP–University of Hong Kong conference, "The Cold War in Asia," Jan. 1996, pp. 22–3.
86. The fullest discussions are now Goncharov et al., *Uncertain Partners*, pp. 130–54; and Chen, *China's Road to the Korean War*, pp. 85–90. See also *Khrushchev Remembers: The Glasnost Tapes*, pp. 144–6; and several important articles by Kathryn Weathersby, "Soviet Aims in Korea and the Origins of the Korean War," *passim*; "New Findings on the Korean War," CWIHP *Bulletin* 3 (Fall 1993), 1, 14–18; "The Soviet Role in the Early Phase of the Korean War: New Documentary Evidence," *Journal of American–East Asian Relations* 2 (Winter 1993), 425–58; "To Attack or Not to Attack? Stalin, Kim Il-sung and the Prelude to War," CWIHP *Bulletin* 5 (Spring 1995), 1–9; and "New Russian Documents on the Korean War," ibid. 6 and 7 (Winter 1995/6), 30–5. See also the exchange between Weathersby and Bruce Cumings, ibid. 120–2. My account generally follows these new treatments of the subject.
87. See the analysis in Goncharov et al., *Uncertain Partners*, pp. 60–1.

88. See ibid. 71–2; also Chapter VI.
89. Soviet transcript, Stalin–Mao meeting, 22 Jan. 1950, CWIHP *Bulletin* 6 and 7 (Winter 1995/6), p. 7.
90. Goncharov et al., *Uncertain Partners*, pp. 111–13, 119–27.
91. The famous speech was given at the National Press Club on 12 Jan. 1950, and appears in the *Department of State Bulletin* 22 (23 Jan. 1950), 111–18. For background, see Gaddis, *The Long Peace*, pp. 72–103.
92. For the impact of Acheson's speech on Stalin, Mao, and Kim, see Goncharov et al., *Uncertain Partners*, pp. 101–2, 142; also Chen, *China's Road to the Korean War*, p. 102. Vladislav Zubok, " 'To Hell with Yalta!' Stalin Opts for a New Status Quo," CWIHP *Bulletin* 6 and 7 (Winter 1995/6) 25, speculates on the espionage possibilities. We have long known that Burgess, in particular, carefully monitored Washington's East Asian policies. See Gaddis, *The Long Peace*, p. 166 n.
93. Soviet transcripts, Mao–Stalin meetings of 16 Dec. 1949, and 22 Jan. 1950, CWIHP *Bulletin* 6 and 7 (Winter 1995/6), 5–8. See also Odd Arne Westad, "Unwrapping the Stalin–Mao Talks: Setting the Record Straight," ibid. 23; and Zubok, " 'To Hell with Yalta!'," ibid. 24–7.
94. "Background Report on the Korean War," 9 Aug. 1966, printed in Weathersby, "The Soviet Role in the Early Phase of the Korean War," p. 441. See also Weathersby, "Korea, 1949–50: To Attack, or Not to Attack?", pp. 1–9.
95. Shtykov to Vyshinsky, 19 Jan. 1950, ibid. 8.
96. Shtykov to Vyshinsky, 28 Jan. 1950, quoted in Vladislav Zubok and Constantine Pleshakov, *Inside the Kremlin's Cold War: From Stalin to Khrushchev* (Cambridge, Mass.: Harvard University Press, 1996), p. 63.
97. Chen Jian interview with Mao's interpreter, Shi Zhe, quoted in Chen, *China's Road to the Korean War*, pp. 87–8. Nikita Khrushchev's taped memoirs confirm this account, but suggest that the exchange took place by cable after Mao's departure from Moscow (See Goncharev et al., *Uncertain Partners*, p. 143).
98. Stalin to Shtykov, 30 Jan. 1950, CWIHP *Bulletin* 5 (Spring 1995), 9. Russian historian Dimitri Volkogonov claims that Stalin authorized military preparations for supporting a North Korean attack on 9 Feb. 1950. (Volkogonov, "Should We Be Frightened by This? Behind the Scenes of the Korean War," in Petrov, "Soviet Role in the Korean War Confirmed," p. 52).
99. Quoted in Goncharov et al., *Uncertain Partners*, pp. 141–2. See also Weathersby, "The Soviet Role in the Early Phase of the Korean War," p. 433.
100. Quoted in Goncharov et al., *Uncertain Partners*, pp. 144–5. See also Volkogonov, "Should We Be Frightened by This?" in Petrov, "Soviet Role in the Korean War Confirmed," p. 52.
101. "Filippov" (Stalin's pseudonym) to Mao, May 1950, quoted in Weathersby, "The Soviet Role in the Early Phase of the Korean War," p. 430.
102. For Mao's plans to invade Taiwan, see He, " 'The Last Campaign to Unify China'," pp. 1–12; also Chen, *China's Road to the Korean War*, pp. 96–102.
103. Goncharov et al., *Uncertain Partners*, pp. 98–9.
104. Ibid. 145–7; Chen, *China's Road to the Korean War*, 112–13; Weathersby, "New Russian Documents on the Korean War," p. 30.
105. General Yoo Sung Chul, quoted in Goncharov et al., *Uncertain Partners*, p. 150. See also "Yu Song-Chol Reminiscences," in Petrov, "Soviet Role in the Korean War Confirmed," pp. 62–4. Gromyko informed Stalin on 20 June 1950 that the North Koreans had intercepted a South Korean military order to begin an

immediate attack on the north. "Comrade Shtykov reported that the order was transmitted so openly that the whole affair, in his opinion, is suspicious." (Printed in Weathersby, "The Soviet Role in the Early Phase of the Korean War, p. 447).

106. Volkogonov, "Should We Be Frightened by This?" in Petrov, "Soviet Role in the Korean War Confirmed," p. 53.
107. Goncharov et al., *Uncertain Partners*, pp. 152–4; Chen, *China's Road to the Korean War*, p. 134.
108. Douglas Jehl, "C.I.A. Opens Files on Cold War Era," *New York Times*, 1 Oct. 1993. See also Michael Warner, ed., *The CIA under Harry Truman* (Washington: CIA, 1994), pp. xxiii–xxiv.
109. See Ernest R. May, *"Lessons" of the Past: The Use and Misuse of History in American Foreign Policy* (New York: Oxford University Press, 1973), pp. 32–86; also for a more general discussion of how historical analogies influence policy decisions, Yuen Foong Khong, *Analogies at War: Korea, Munich, Dien Bien Phu, and the Vietnam Decisions of 1965* (Princeton: Princeton University Press, 1992).
110. Alonzo L. Hamby, *Man of the People: A Life of Harry S. Truman* (New York: Oxford University Press, 1995), pp. 265, 392, 537.
111. Andrei Gromyko, *Memoirs*, trans. Harold Shukman (New York: Doubleday, 1989), p. 102.
112. Goncharov et al., *Uncertain Partners*, pp. 161–2.
113. See Stueck, *The Korean War*, pp. 130–42.
114. This line of argument began with I. F. Stone, *The Hidden History of the Korean War* (New York: Monthly Review Press, 1952), and has been revived periodically since. See e.g. Joyce and Gabriel Kolko, *The Limits of Power: The World and United States Foreign Policy, 1945–1954* (New York: Harper & Row, 1972), pp. 565–99; and, most recently, extendedly, and at the same time elusively, Cumings, *The Roaring of the Cataract*, pp. 379–567. The argument is most clearly suggested on pp. 410–13.
115. NSC-68 is printed in full in *FRUS: 1950*, i. 235–92. For assessments of the significance of this document, see Ernest R. May, ed., *American Cold War Strategy: Interpreting NSC 68* (Boston: St. Martin's Press, 1993).
116. Dean Acheson, *Present at the Creation: My Years in the State Department* (New York: Norton, 1969), p. 420. See also Stueck, *The Korean War*, pp. 40–1.
117. For an interesting discussion of such methods, see the exchange between Bruce Cumings and Gideon Rose in *The National Interest* 39 (Spring 1995), 108–9.
118. Zhang, *Deterrence and Strategic Culture*, pp. 64–73; Goncharov et al., *Uncertain Partners*, pp. 148–9; Chen, *China's Road to the Korean War*, pp. 100–2.
119. See Douglas J. Macdonald, *Adventures in Chaos: American Intervention for Reform in the Third World* (Cambridge, Mass.: Harvard University Press, 1992), pp. 18, 50–1, 83.
120. This deployment is discussed in Zhang, *Deterrence and Strategic Culture*, pp. 72–3; and in He, "The Last Campaign to Unify China," pp. 8–9.
121. See Gaddis, *The Long Peace*, pp. 80–6; Chang, *Friends and Enemies*, pp. 72–5; Hamby, *Man of the People*, pp. 535–6.
122. Quoted in Goncharov et al., *Uncertain Partners*, p. 157. See also ibid. 181; also Zhang, *Deterrence and Strategic Culture*, pp. 73–4, 89–90; Chen, *China's Road to the Korean War*, pp. 126–30, 149–50; and Michael H. Hunt, "Beijing and the Korean Crisis, June, 1950–June, 1951," *Political Science Quarterly* 107 (1992), 458–9.
123. Quoted in Zhang, *Deterrence and Strategic Culture*, p. 91. The Chinese leaders frequently employed such maxims in discussing critical issues. Mao's military

commander in Korea, Peng Dehuai, justified entry into the war on the grounds that: "The tiger [presumably the United States] wanted to eat human beings; when it would do so would depend on its appetite. No concession could stop it." Politburo member Zhu De argued in favor of coming to the assistance of North Korea because "when the lips are destroyed, the teeth feel cold" (Quoted in Goncharov et al., *Uncertain Partners*, pp. 180, 182).

124. He, "The Last Campaign to Unify China," p. 15; Chen, *China's Road to the Korean War*, pp. 130–2.

125. Quoted in Shu Guang Zhang, *Mao's Military Romanticism: China and the Korean War, 1950–1953* (Lawrence: University Press of Kansas, 1995), p. 63.

126. Zhang, *Deterrence and Strategic Culture*, pp. 91–3; Chen, *China's Road to the Korean War*, pp. 137–48.

127. See e.g. Alexander L. George and Richard Smoke, *Deterrence in American Foreign Policy: Theory and Practice* (New York: Columbia University Press, 1974), pp. 184–234; Robert R. Simmons, *The Strained Alliance: Peking, P'yongyang, Moscow, and the Politics of the Korean Civil War* (New York: Macmillan, 1975), pp. 149–51; Rosemary Foot, *The Wrong War: American Policy and the Dimensions of the Korean Conflict, 1950–1953* (Ithaca: Cornell University Press, 1985), pp. 67–74.

128. See Chen, *China's Road to the Korean War*, pp. 179–81; Zhang, "In the Shadow of Mao," pp. 354–5; Zhang, *Mao's Military Romanticism*, p. 85.

129. Kim Il-sung to Stalin, 29 Sept. 1950, CWIHP *Bulletin* 6 and 7 (Winter 1995/6), 112.

130. Stalin to Mao, 1 Oct. 1950, ibid. 114.

131. Mao to Stalin, 2 Oct. 1950, ibid. 114–15. Another 2 Oct. telegram from Mao to Stalin has been published in China announcing the opposite: that the Chinese *had* decided to intervene. There are a few common elements in the two documents, notably a passage in the Chinese version indicating a worst-case scenario in which "the United States publicly declares war on China, undermines our plans for China's economic reconstruction, which has already begun, and sparks the dissatisfaction of [China's] national bourgeosie and other segments of the people (they are very afraid of war)." An English-language version appears in Goncharov et al., *Uncertain Partners*, pp. 275–6. Chinese sources indicate that although Mao did indeed draft such a telegram, it apparently was never sent. (Information provided by Shen Zhihua, of the Center for Oriental History, Beijing, at the CWIHP–University of Hong Kong conference on "The Cold War in Asia," 9 Jan. 1996.)

132. Quoted in Zhang, *Mao's Military Romanticism*, p. 81.

133. Stalin to Mao, 5 Oct. 1950, copy enclosed in Stalin to Kim Il-sung, 7 Oct. 1950, CWIHP *Bulletin* 6 and 7 (Winter 1995/6), 116–17.

134. Mao to Stalin, 7 Oct.1950, cited ibid. 116.

135. I have followed the account, here, of Alexandre Y. Mansourov, "Stalin, Mao, Kim, and China's Decision to Enter the Korean War, September 16–October 15, 1950: New Evidence from the Russian Archives," ibid. 102–3, which in turn is based on Mansourov's interview with a Soviet participant, Nikolai Federenko.

136. *Khrushchev Remembers: The Glasnost Tapes*, p. 147. For the suggestion of a North Korean government in exile, see Goncharov et al., *Uncertain Partners*, p. 189

137. Mansourov, "Stalin, Mao, Kim, and China's Decision to Enter the Korean War," ibid. 103.

138. Roschin [Soviet ambassador in Beijing] to Stalin, 13 Oct. 1950, ibid. pp. 118–19.

139. Stalin to Kim Il-sung, 14 Oct. 1950, ibid. p. 119.

140. Mao's directive of 8 Oct. 1950, in Goncharov et al., *Uncertain Partners*, p. 278. This directive is probably in response to Mao's 7 Oct. commitment to Stalin to intervene without specifying a date.

141. Chinese accounts tell this story quite differently. Drawing on Mao's presumably unsent telegram of 2 Oct. they insist that the Chinese were eager to enter the war, and that hesitation arose only when Stalin, at the last moment, *withdrew* his promise of air cover. According to these accounts, the Chinese decided to intervene anyway, impressing Stalin with their bravery, and in effect shaming him into providing the promised air cover after all. See Goncharov et al., *Uncertain Partners*, pp. 188–91; Chen, *China's Road to the Korean War*, pp. 196–200; and Zhang, *Mao's Romanticism*, pp. 82–4, all of which rely upon Chinese published documents. As Alexandre Mansourov has shown, though, original documents in the Soviet archives do not bear out these accounts, raising the possibility that at some point the Chinese materials were altered to conceal evidence of Mao's hesitancy. It is also possible that Zhou or someone in his entourage concocted the story of Stalin's withholding air support to account for their own reluctance to intervene (Mansourov, "Stalin, Mao, Kim, and China's Decision to Enter the Korean War," p. 103). The entire episode requires further research, but it is an interesting illustration of the problems that are increasingly likely to arise as it becomes possible to compare Soviet and Chinese primary sources on critical issues in Cold War history.

142. Mao to Zhou Enlai, 13 Oct. 1950, in Goncharov et al., *Uncertain Partners*, pp. 281–2. See also Chen, "China's Changing Aims during the Korean War," pp. 21–2; and, on Mao's proclivity for "domino" thinking, Hunt, "Beijing and the Korean Crisis," p. 464; as well as Thomas J. Christensen, "Threats, Assurances, and the Last Chance for Peace: The Lessons of Mao's Korean War Telegrams," *International Security* 17 (Summer 1992), 135. Maurice Meisner, *Mao's China and After: A History of the People's Republic* (New York: Free Press, 1986), pp. 107–8, points out that the Korean War broke out just as Mao was launching his agrarian reform program, so fears that "reactionaries at home" might strike back were not ill-founded.

143. Chen, *China's Road to the Korean War*, pp. 152, 218.

144. Christensen, "Threats, Assurances, and the Last Chance for Peace," pp. 130–1; Chen, *China's Road to the Korean War*, pp. 168–9.

145. Mansourov, "Stalin, Mao, Kim, and China's Decision to Enter the Korean War," p. 105, especially stresses this point.

146. Christensen, "Threats, Assurances, and the Last Chance for Peace," p. 139. Henry Kissinger, *Diplomacy* (New York: Simon & Schuster, 1994), pp. 480–2, makes the case for the "narrow neck" strategy.

147. Quoted in Zhang, *Mao's Military Romanticism*, p. 110.

148. To be discussed in the next chapter.

149. Chen, *China's Road to the Korean War*, p. 219.

150. Quoted in Jian Chen, "China's Changing Aims during the Korean War," *Journal of American–East Asian Relations* 1 (Spring 1992), 35. See also Hunt, "Beijing and the Korean Crisis," p. 467; Christensen, "Threats, Assurances, and the Last Chance for Peace," pp. 142–4.

151. Quoted in Zhang, *Mao's Military Romanticism*, pp. 221.

152. See Stueck's interpretation of the Korean War as a "substitute for World War III," in *The Korean War*, pp. 348–53.

153. Hunt, "Beijing and the Korean Crisis," pp. 477–8, warns against the tendency

to assume greater rationality on the part of all major actors in this situation than was actually present.

154. See Chen, *China's Road to the Korean War*, 77–8, 104, 112–13, 213–16; also Chen, "China's Changing Aims during the Korean War," pp. 40–1; Chen, "China and the First Indo-China War, 1950–54," pp. 89–94; and Philip West, "Confronting the West: China as David and Goliath in the Korean War," *Journal of American–East Asian Relations* 1 (Spring 1993), 5–28.
155. Zhang, *Deterrence and Strategic Culture*, pp. 116, 282.
156. He, "The Most Respected Enemy," pp. 144–8.
157. Chen, *China's Road to the Korean War*, p. 204.
158. See Kissinger, *Diplomacy*, pp. 491–2.

CHAPTER IV

1. Harry S. Truman Diary, 16 July 1945, in Robert H. Ferrell, ed., *Off the Record: The Private Papers of Harry S. Truman* (New York: Harper & Row, 1980), pp. 52–3.
2. Quoted in David Holloway, *Stalin and the Bomb: The Soviet Union and Atomic Energy, 1939–1956* (New Haven: Yale University Press, 1994), p. 171.
3. William H. McNeill, *The Pursuit of Power: Technology, Armed Force, and Society since A.D. 1000* (Chicago: University of Chicago Press, 1982); Martin Van Creveld, *Technology and War: From 2000 B.C. to the Present* (New York: Free Press, 1989); Donald Kagan, *On the Origins of War* (New York: Doubleday, 1995), esp. pp. 3–4. For an exception to this pattern, see John Keegan, *A History of Warfare* (New York: Knopf, 1993), pp. 43–6, on gun control in Tokugawa Japan.
4. The argument is vividly made in Robert K. Massie, *Dreadnought: Britain, Germany, and the Coming of the Great War* (New York: Random House, 1991). For dissenting views, see Michael Howard, *The Lessons of History* (New Haven: Yale University Press, 1991), p. 96; and Patrick Glynn, *Closing Pandora's Box: Arms Races, Arms Control, and the History of the Cold War* (New York: Basic Books, 1992), esp. pp. 1–44.
5. Michael S. Sherry, *The Rise of American Air Power: The Creation of Armageddon* (New Haven: Yale University Press, 1987), pp. 320–5, provides a good discussion of the differences between atomic and conventional weapons in the context of 1945. For a somewhat similar metaphor used by Franklin D. Roosevelt in 1939 to convey a sense of escalating danger, see Frank Ninkovich, *Modernity and Power: A History of the Domino Theory in the Twentieth Century* (Chicago: University of Chicago Press, 1994), p. 115.
6. Michael S. Sherry, *Preparing for the Next War: American Plans for Postwar Defense, 1941–1947* (New Haven: Yale University Press, 1977), p. 211, shows that this paradox affected American planners at the earliest stages of the nuclear era. John Mueller, *Retreat from Doomsday: The Obsolescence of Major War* (New York: Basic Books, 1989) makes an eloquent but ultimately unpersuasive argument that this realization would have taken hold after World War II even in the absence of nuclear weapons.
7. Thomas H. Buckley and Edwin B. Strong, Jr., *American Foreign and National Security Policies, 1914–1945* (Knoxville: University of Tennessee Press, 1987), pp. 111, 120–1.
8. Russell F. Weigley, *Eisenhower's Lieutenants: The Campaigns of France and Germany, 1944–1945* (Bloomington: Indiana University Press, 1981), pp. 1–2;

McGeorge Bundy, *Danger and Survival: Choices About the Bomb in the First Fifty Years* (New York: Random House, 1988), pp. 44–53.

9. Ninkovich, *Modernity and Power*, pp. 112–22; also Robert Dallek, *Franklin D. Roosevelt and American Foreign Policy, 1932–1945* (New York: Oxford University Press, 1979), pp. 199–232.

10. For American industrial under-utilization, see Paul Kennedy, *The Rise and Fall of the Great Powers: Economic Change and Military Conflict from 1500 to 2000* (New York: Random House, 1987), pp. 331–3.

11. Bundy, *Danger and Survival*, pp. 30–1.

12. The issue is discussed in Thomas Powers, *Heisenberg's War: The Secret History of the German Bomb* (New York: Knopf, 1993). See also David C. Cassidy, *Uncertainty: The Life and Science of Werner Heisenberg* (New York: W. H. Freeman, 1992).

13. Bundy, *Danger and Survival*, pp. 58, 64–5. See also Gregg Herken, *The Winning Weapon: The Atomic Bomb in the Cold War, 1945–1960* (New York: Knopf, 1980), p. 13 n.; James Hershberg, *James B. Conant: Harvard to Hiroshima and the Making of the Nuclear Age* (New York: Knopf, 1993), p. 211; and, for the non-nuclear strategic bombing campaigns of World War II, Sherry, *The Rise of American Air Power, passim*.

14. Ibid. 338–41. For Nagasaki, see Bundy, *Danger and Survival*, p. 94. Barton J. Bernstein, "A Postwar Myth: 500,000 U.S. Lives Saved," *Bulletin of the Atomic Scientists* 42 (June–July 1986), 38–40, points out that the actual American casualty estimates were much lower than the figure of half a million frequently cited in the memoirs of participants in this decision. But in the context of 1945, it would have been difficult to justify taking *any* more casualties than absolutely necessary. The best overall discussion of the decision to drop the bomb is Bundy, *Danger and Survival*, pp. 54–97; but see also two reviews of recent literature by J. Samuel Walker, "The Decision to Use the Bomb: A Historiographical Update," *Diplomatic History* 14 (Winter 1990), 97–114, and "History, Collective Memory, and the Decision to Use the Bomb," ibid. 19 (Spring 1995), 319–28; as well as Bernstein's balanced summary, "The Atomic Bombings Reconsidered," *Foreign Affairs* 176 (Jan./Feb. 1995), 135–52. I have also benefited from reading an as yet unpublished paper by Sadao Asada based on Japanese sources, "The Shock of the Atomic Bomb and Japan's Decision to Surrender," presented at the Society for Historians of American Foreign Relations annual convention, June 1995.

15. Harry S. Truman, *Memoirs: Year of Decisions* (Garden City, NY: Doubleday, 1955), p. 419. The National Air and Space Museum's aborted effort to mount a 50th anniversary exhibit on the atomic bombings of Japan provoked a raucous controversy among historians, veterans, and politicians early in 1995, but in the end it shed little new light on the actual decision to drop the bombs. Various dimensions of the debate appear in Michael J. Hogan, ed., *Hiroshima in History and Memory* (New York: Cambridge University Press, 1996).

16. The classic argument about intimidating the Russians is Gar Alperovitz, *Atomic Diplomacy: Hiroshima and Potsdam*, expanded and rev. edn. (New York: Penguin, 1985), originally published in 1965. See also Alperovitz's recent update of his argument, *The Decision to Use the Atomic Bomb and the Architecture of an American Myth* (New York: Knopf, 1995).

17. Martin J. Sherwin, *A World Destroyed: Hiroshima and the Origins of the Nuclear Arms Race* (New York: Vintage Books, 1987), pp. 200, 213; Richard Rhodes, *The Making of the Atomic Bomb* (New York: Simon & Schuster, 1986), pp. 508–9; Richard Rhodes, *Dark Sun: The Making of the Hydrogen Bomb* (New York: Simon & Schuster, 1995), pp. 203–4.

18. The non-use of poison gas is, of course, the obvious exception to this generalization; but what discouraged its employment was not so much its lethality as its unpredictability, a painful lesson learned in World War I. See ibid. 90–5, 100–1.
19. This was the title of the first serious collection of essays on nuclear strategy, Bernard Brodie, ed., *The Absolute Weapon: Atomic Power and World Order* (New York: Harcourt, Brace, & World, 1946). My use of counterfactuals here is very much influenced by the insightful way in which Bundy used them in *Danger and Survival*; but see also Philip Nash, "The Use of Counterfactuals in History: A Look at the Literature," *Society for Historians of American Foreign Relations Newsletter* 22 (Mar. 1991), 2–12.
20. Sherry, *Preparing for the Next War*, pp. 198–205. See also Rhodes, *Dark Sun*, pp. 225–6; Russell D. Buhite and Wm. Christopher Hamel, "War for Peace: The Question of an American Preventive War against the Soviet Union," *Diplomatic History* 14 (Summer 1990), 382; and Scott D. Sagan, "The Perils of Proliferation: Organization Theory, Deterrence Theory, and the Spread of Nuclear Weapons," *International Security* 18 (Spring 1994), 77–8.
21. Herken, *The Winning Weapon*, pp. 112, 223, 270–1; also Marc Trachtenberg, *History and Strategy* (Princeton: Princeton University Press, 1991), p. 22, 140; and Samuel R. Williamson, Jr., and Steven L. Rearden, *The Origins of U.S. Nuclear Strategy, 1945–1953* (New York: St. Martin's Press, 1993), p. 140.
22. Ibid. 85.
23. Alonzo L. Hamby, *Man of the People: A Life of Harry S. Truman* (New York: Oxford University Press, 1995), p. 400. Bundy, *Danger and Survival*, p. 202, points out that in Apr. 1947 there were *no usable* bombs in the American arsenal.
24. Michael D. Yaffe, " 'A Higher Priority than the Korean War!': The Crash Programmes to Modify the Bombers for the Bomb," *Diplomacy and Statecraft* 5 (July 1994), 362–3.
25. David Alan Rosenberg, "The Origins of Overkill: Nuclear Weapons and American Strategy," in Norman Graebner, ed., *The National Security: Theory and Practice, 1945–1960* (New York: Oxford University Press, 1986), p. 131.
26. "Evaluation of Effect on Soviet War Effort Resulting from the Strategic Air Offensive," 11 May 1949, in Thomas H. Etzold and John Lewis Gaddis, eds., *Containment: Documents on American Policy and Strategy, 1945–1950* (New York: Columbia University Press, 1978), p. 362. See also David Alan Rosenberg, "American Atomic Strategy and the Hydrogen Bomb Decision," *Journal of American History* 66 (June 1979), 64–7, 72–3; also Williamson and Rearden, *The Origins of U.S. Nuclear Strategy*, pp. 140–1; and Paul H. Nitze, with Ann M. Smith and Steven L. Rearden, *From Hiroshima to Glasnost: At the Center of Decision-Making—A Memoir* (New York: Grove Weidenfeld, 1989), pp. 109–10.
27. Quoted in Williamson and Rearden, *The Origins of U.S. Nuclear Strategy*, p. 70. See also, for Kennan's thoughts on this matter, PPS/38, "U.S. Objectives With Respect to Russia," 18 Aug. 1948, *The State Department Policy Planning Staff Papers: 1948* (New York: Garland, 1983), esp. pp. 396–411.
28. Godfrey Hodgson, *The Colonel: The Life and Wars of Henry Stimson, 1867–1950* (New York: Knopf, 1990), pp. 347–50; Robert L. Messer, *The End of an Alliance: James F. Byrnes, Roosevelt, Truman, and the Origins of the Cold War* (Chapel Hill: University of North Carolina Press, 1982), pp. 87–8, 113–14.
29. Radio address of 9 Aug. 1945, *Public Papers of the Presidents of the United States: Harry S. Truman, 1945* (Washington: Government Printing Office, 1961), pp. 212–13.

30. Messer, *The End of an Alliance*, pp. 115–39. See also John Lewis Gaddis, *The United States and the Origins of the Cold War, 1941–1947* (New York: Columbia University Press, 1972), pp. 263–7.
31. Acheson to Truman, 25 Sept. 1945, *FRUS: 1945*, ii. 49–50.
32. Bundy, *Danger and Survival*, pp. 134–6. For Soviet use of the official American report, Henry D. Smyth's *Atomic Energy for Military Purposes*, released on 12 Aug. 1945, see Holloway, *Stalin and the Bomb*, p. 173; also Rhodes, *Dark Sun*, pp. 182, 215–17.
33. See Messer, *The End of an Alliance*, p. 116; Walker, "The Decision to Use the Bomb," p. 106.
34. Bundy, *Danger and Survival*, pp. 166–76. See also Larry G. Gerber, "The Baruch Plan and the Origins of the Cold War," *Diplomatic History* 6 (Winter 1982), 69–95.
35. Quoted in Walter Millis, ed., *The Forrestal Diaries* (New York: Viking, 1951), p. 458.
36. Rosenberg, "American Atomic Strategy and the Hydrogen Bomb Decision," pp. 63–9.
37. See Hamby, *Man of the People*, pp. 335, 400, 444–5, 552; Williamson and Rearden, *The Origins of U.S. Nuclear Strategy*, p. 191; Rhodes, *Dark Sun*, p. 205; and John Lewis Gaddis, *The Long Peace: Inquiries into the History of the Cold War* (New York: Oxford University Press, 1987), pp. 106–7.
38. Douglas to Lovett, 17 Apr. 1948, *FRUS: 1948*, iii. 90. Russell's proposal appeared as "The Atomic Bomb and the Prevention of War," *Bulletin of the Atomic Scientists* 2 (1 Oct. 1946), 21. For the reception of Churchill's "Iron Curtain" speech, see Fraser J. Harbutt, *The Iron Curtain: Churchill, America, and the Origins of the Cold War* (New York: Oxford University Press, 1986), pp. 183–285.
39. Alexander George and Richard Smoke, *Deterrence in American Foreign Policy: Theory and Practice* (New York: Columbia University Press, 1974), pp. 107–39.
40. Harry R. Borowski, *A Hollow Threat: Strategic Air Power and Containment before Korea* (Westport, Conn.: Greenwood Press, 1982), pp. 125–8; Christopher Andrew and Oleg Gordievsky, *KGB: The Inside Story of Its Foreign Operations from Lenin to Gorbachev* (New York: HarperCollins, 1990), p. 377.
41. The classic account is still Warner R. Schilling, "The Politics of National Defense: Fiscal 1950," in Warner R. Schilling, Paul Y. Hammond, and Glenn H. Snyder, *Strategy, Politics, and Defense Budgets* (New York: Columbia University Press, 1962), pp. 1–266. But see also Townsend Hoopes and Douglas Brinkley, *Driven Patriot: The Life and Times of James Forrestal* (New York: Knopf, 1992), pp. 405–21; and, for the impact of budgetary considerations in encouraging reliance on a nuclear deterrent, Williamson and Rearden, *The Origins of U.S. Nuclear Strategy*, pp. 60, 86–7, 191.
42. See, for this argument, Melvyn P. Leffler, *A Preponderance of Power: National Security, the Truman Administration, and the Cold War* (Stanford: Stanford University Press, 1992), p. 308; also, in an unexpected alignment, James Schlesinger, "The Impact of Nuclear Weapons on History," *Washington Quarterly* 16 (Autumn 1993), 5–12, and Gar Alperovitz and Kai Bird, "The Centrality of the Bomb," *Foreign Policy* #94 (Spring 1994), 3–20.
43. Holloway, *Stalin and the Bomb*, pp. 59–63.
44. Ibid. 74–6.
45. Ibid. 82–3; Rhodes, *Dark Sun*, pp. 51–4; Andrew and Gordievsky, *KGB*, pp. 311–12; Pavel Sudoplatov and Anatoli Sudoplatov, with Jerrold L. Schecter and Leona P. Schecter, *Special Tasks: The Memoirs of an Unwanted Witness—A Soviet Spymaster*

(Boston: Little, Brown, 1994), pp. 173–4. Cairncross at the time was private secretary to Lord Hankey, chair of the British Scientific Advisory Committee, which had access to information on the British atomic bomb project, soon to be shifted to the US.

46. Quoted from an account by Vladimir Chikov in Stephen J. Zaloga, *Target America: The Soviet Union and the Strategic Arms Race, 1945–1964* (Novato, Calif.: Presidio Press, 1993), p. 11.

47. Ibid. p. 18; Sudoplatov, *Special Tasks*, pp. 174–5. See also Rhodes, *The Making of the Atomic Bomb*, pp. 446–8; and Rhodes, *Dark Sun*, pp. 121–6.

48. Robert Chadwell Williams, *Klaus Fuchs: Atom Spy* (Cambridge, Mass.: Harvard University Press,1987), pp. 60–1.

49. Holloway, *Stalin and the Bomb*, pp. 76–9, 86; Rhodes, *Dark Sun*, pp. 59–61.

50. Pavel Fitin to NKVD offices in New York, London, and Berlin, 14 June 1942, quoted in Vladimir Chikov, "How the Soviet Intelligence Service 'Split' the American Atom," *New Times* #16 (1991), 39.

51. See Holloway, *Stalin and the Bomb*, pp. 90, 364. The Anglo-Americans were, of course, considerably further along with their program than were the Germans.

52. Sudoplatov, *Special Tasks*, p. 181. See also Zaloga, *Target America*, p. 19, who emphasizes the Soviet government's unwillingness to share technology of any kind with its Western allies.

53. Bundy, *Danger and Survival*, p. 124. This point is also made with a certain amount of professional sympathy by Sudoplatov, *Special Tasks*, pp. 219–20. One exception to this pattern was General Leslie R. Groves, commander of the Manhattan Project, who does appear all along to have seen the Soviet Union as the ultimate threat (See Rhodes, *Dark Sun*, pp. 100, 155–6, 225).

54. Rhodes, *The Making of the Atomic Bomb*, pp. 525–8; Hershberg, *James B. Conant*, pp. 196–207.

55. Quoted in Rhodes, *Dark Sun*, p. 124.

56. The best discussion of the 1943 Quebec agreement, Bohr's subsequent initiative, and the probable reasons for its rejection is in Bundy, *Danger and Survival*, pp. 98–129. See also Gaddis, *The United States and the Origins of the Cold War*, pp. 86–8.

57. Ibid. 102–3; also Holloway, *Stalin and the Bomb*, p. 103.

58. Such allegations appear, with respect to Harry Hopkins, in Andrew and Gordievsky, *KGB*, pp. 287–9, 350; and with reference to Oppenheimer, Bohr, Enrico Fermi and Leo Szilard, in Sudoplatov, *Special Tasks*, pp. 181–202. Much of the resulting controversy revolves around what one makes of the fact that these men were sympathetic to the Soviet Union, and what legends old KGB hands may have spun out of this. If being a Soviet sympathizer in the middle of World War II was tantamount to spying, then most Americans would have qualified. Such claims will require much clearer confirmation before they can be taken seriously.

59. Rhodes, *Dark Sun* is particularly good at matching up what the spies were reporting with how the Soviet atomic scientists used this information. The argument about the importance of espionage has been made so frequently during the past several years that several surviving scientists have felt obliged to redress the balance, pointing out that not *everything* they knew about nuclear physics came from espionage. See David Holloway, "Soviet Scientists Speak Out," *Bulletin of the Atomic Scientists* 49 (May 1993), 18–19, along with an accompanying article by Yuli Khariton and Yuri Smirnov.

60. Kurchatov to M. G. Pervukhin, 7 Mar. 1943, quoted in Holloway, *Stalin and the Bomb*, p. 91. This document also appears in Sudoplatov, *Special Tasks*, pp. 446–51.

61. Albert Resis, ed., *Molotov Remembers: Inside Kremlin Politics: Conversations with Felix Chuev* (Chicago: Ivan R. Dee, 1993), p. 56.
62. Holloway, *Stalin and the Bomb*, p. 101. This episode is discussed briefly in Herken, *The Winning Weapon*, pp. 106–7, but pictured as an American effort to "smoke out" or perhaps even sabotage the Soviet bomb development project.
63. Zaloga, *Target America*, pp. 20–5; Rhodes, *Dark Sun*, pp. 213–14; Sudoplatov, *Special Tasks*, pp. 198–9.
64. Holloway, *Stalin and the Bomb*, p. 115. For Beria's role, see Zaloga, *Target America*, pp. 21–6; Knight, *Beria* pp. 132–5; and Yuli Khariton and Yuri Smirnov, "The Khariton Version," *Bulletin of the Atomic Scientists* 49 (May 1993), 26–7. For the impact of Hiroshima, see ibid. 129–33.
65. See Roald Sagdeev, "Russian Scientists Save American Secrets," ibid. 34.
66. Quoted from an account by Chikov in Zaloga, *Target America*, p. 27. See also Holloway, *Stalin and the Bomb*, pp. 116–18.
67. Zaloga, *Target America*, p. 27; also Holloway, *Stalin and the Bomb*, p. 132; Rhodes, *Dark Sun*, pp. 222–3.
68. Kurchatov's notes of a conversation on 25 Jan. 1946, CWIHP *Bulletin* 4 (Fall 1994), 5. Stalin is on record, in 1934, as having held out similar material inducements to top secret police officials prior to launching the purges. See Robert C. Tucker, *Stalin in Power: The Revolution from Above, 1928–1941* (New York: Norton, 1990), p. 273.
69. I have adapted these points from Holloway, *Stalin and the Bomb*, pp. 147, 206–13, 303, 317.
70. Ibid. 211.
71. Quoted in Zaloga, *Target America*, p. 29.
72. Holloway, *Stalin and the Bomb*, pp. 127–30, 153; see also *Molotov Remembers*, p. 56, and Sudoplatov, *Special Tasks*, pp. 209–10.
73. *Molotov Remembers*, p. 58. See also Holloway, *Stalin and the Bomb*, pp. 154–5, 253.
74. Andrei Gromyko, *Memoirs*, trans. Harold Shukman (New York: Doubleday, 1989), p. 110. Vladislav Zubok and Constantine Pleshakov suggest that Stalin backed down in the Aug. 1946 Turkish Straits crisis because Soviet espionage picked up evidence of American war planning for the possible use of atomic weapons. See *Inside the Kremlin's Cold War: From Stalin to Khrushchev* (Cambridge, Mass.: Harvard University Press, 1996), p. 93.
75. Sherwin, *A World Destroyed*, p. 238, has aptly termed this "reverse atomic diplomacy."
76. Holloway, *Stalin and the Bomb*, p. 156.
77. *Molotov Remembers*, p. 58. See also Holloway, *Stalin and the Bomb*, pp. 156–7.
78. Quoted in Zubok and Pleshakov, *Inside the Kremlin's Cold War*, p. 97.
79. Holloway, *Stalin and the Bomb*, p. 158.
80. Ibid. 159.
81. Ibid. 161–3.
82. Quoted in ibid. 164.
83. *Molotov Remembers*, p. 58. See also Holloway, *Stalin and the Bomb*, p. 258.
84. Ibid. 129, 163.
85. Zaloga, *Target America*, pp. 50, 52, 68. See also Rhodes, *Dark Sun*, p. 287.
86. Djilas, *Conversations with Stalin*, p. 153.
87. Quoted in Sergei N. Goncharov, John W. Lewis, and Xue Litai, *Uncertain Partners: Stalin, Mao, and the Korean War* (Stanford: Stanford University Press, 1993), p. 69. Holloway, *Stalin and the Bomb*, p. 265, provides an interesting analysis of this statement, linking it to Stalin's better-known toast to the Russian

people in May 1945: "Another people could have said to the government: you have not justified our expectations, go away, and we will install another government which will conclude peace with Germany and guarantee us a quiet life." Curiously, Stalin also made a point of showing the Chinese a film that *purported* to record a Soviet atomic bomb test—a month and a half before the actual first test took place (Ibid. 264).

88. Quoted in Zaloga, *Target America*, p. 59, which irritatingly cites no source. See also Khariton and Smirnov, "The Khariton Version," p. 28, and Holloway, *Stalin and the Bomb*, pp. 200–1, which questions the part of the story that has Stalin discussing dialectics. But see Tucker, *Stalin in Power*, p. 560, which documents a 1937 incident in which Stalin tried to make sense of a new kind of tank armor in terms of dialectics. And John Wilson Lewis and Xue Litai, *China Builds the Bomb* (Stanford: Stanford University Press, 1988), pp. 38–9, has evidence of Mao Zedong's lecturing *his* nuclear physicists on dialectics.

89. Rhodes, *Dark Sun*, pp. 368–74, provides a good discussion of the American long-range detection program and how it developed. Sudoplatov, *Special Tasks*, p. 211, recalls the surprise the American announcement created in Moscow, together with momentary fears that the security of the Soviet bomb project had been compromised.

90. Zaloga, *Target America*, p. 62. See also Rhodes, *Dark Sun*, pp. 364–8.

91. See Holloway, *Stalin and the Bomb*, p. 153.

92. Ibid. 171.

93. Bohlen to Paul Nitze, 5 Apr. 1950, *FRUS: 1950*, i. 223.

94. Holloway, *Stalin and the Bomb*, p. 272.

95. Ibid. 240. This information may have reinforced the signal sent by Acheson's defensive perimeter speech that led Stalin to assume an aggressive posture with respect to East Asia early in 1950. See, on this matter, Chapter III.

96. Rhodes, *Dark Sun*, pp. 39, 94–102, 120, 132. See esp., Rhodes's account of the difficulty defecting Soviet embassy code clerk Igor Gouzenko had in turning himself in to Canadian authorities in Sept. 1945 (ibid. 183–7). The US government would, of course, swing to an extreme of excessive *distrust* during the late 1940s and early 1950s.

97. Williamson and Rearden, *The Origins of U.S. Nuclear Strategy*, p. 85.

98. Bundy, *Danger and Survival*, p. 199. See also CIA Intelligence Memorandum 225, "Estimate of Status of Atomic Warfare," which concluded as late as 20 Sept. 1949, three weeks *after* the first Soviet test, that "the earliest possible date by which the USSR might be expected to produce an atomic bomb is mid-1950 and the most probable date is mid-1953" (Michael Warner, ed., *CIA Cold War Records: The CIA under Harry Truman* (Washington: CIA, 1994), p. 319).

99. *Truman Public Papers, 1949*, p. 485. See also David E. Lilienthal's notes on Truman's initial reaction, in *The Journals of David E. Lilienthal: The Atomic Energy Years, 1945–1950* (New York: Harper & Row, 1964), pp. 570–1.

100. Williamson and Rearden, *The Origins of U.S. Nuclear Strategy*, pp. 107–11; Bundy, *Danger and Survival*, p. 203.

101. Ibid. 202, 205.

102. To be discussed in Chapter VIII.

103. *Lilienthal Journals: The Atomic Energy Years*, p. 633. See also Gaddis, *The Long Peace*, p. 113.

104. NSC-68, United States Objectives and Programs for National Security," 14 Apr. 1950, in Etzold and Gaddis, eds., *Containment: Documents on American Policy and Strategy, 1945–1950* (New York: Columbia University Press, 1978), pp. 414,

417. For more on NSC-68, see Ernest R. May, ed., *American Cold War Strategy: Interpreting NSC-68* (Boston: St. Martin's Press, 1993).

105. See e.g. George F. Kennan, *Memoirs: 1925–1950* (Boston: Little, Brown, 1967), pp. 471–6; also Bundy, *Danger and Survival*, pp. 222–9.

106. Holloway, *Stalin and the Bomb*, pp. 295–9. Bundy, *Danger and Survival*, pp. 197–8, acknowledges this point, despite his suggestion, noted above, that a renewed effort at international control might have headed off Soviet H-bomb development.

107. Sakharov, *Memoirs*, p. 99.

108. Holloway, *Stalin and the Bomb*, p. 299.

109. The classic work, of course, is Thomas S. Kuhn, *The Structure of Scientific Revolutions*, 2nd edn., enlarged (Chicago: University of Chicago Press, 1970).

110. Holloway, *Stalin and the Bomb*, esp. pp. 239–40.

111. Ibid. 225–7; Rhodes, *Dark Sun*, pp. 261–3. The civilian Joint Chiefs of Staff Evaluation Board, in a highly classified 1947 report on the Bikini tests, did stress the social, economic, and even environmental damage any large-scale use of atomic weapons in war would probably cause, but it by no means ruled out the possibility of war itself. Instead it contented itself with recommending that the United States stay ahead of the Soviet Union in its atomic capabilities, and that the Congress pass legislation bypassing its constitutionally sanctioned responsibility to declare war in the event of a nuclear suprise attack. Needless to say, the report—and its proposed legislation—were never made public (Hershberg, *James B. Conant*, pp. 375–6).

112. Nitze, *From Hiroshima to Glasnost*, pp. 42–3.

113. Holloway, *Stalin and the Bomb*, p. 240.

114. Robert S. Norris and William M. Arkin, "Nuclear Notebook: Estimated U.S. and Soviet/Russian Nuclear Stockpiles, 1945–94," *Bulletin of the Atomic Scientists* 40 (Nov./Dec. 1994), 58–9.

115. Zaloga, *Target America*, pp. 63–79.

116. Goncharov et al., *Uncertain Partners*, pp. 145, 189, 191. These matters are discussed more fully in Chapter III.

117. Weathersby, "New Russian Documents on the Korean War," p. 32; Zhang, *Mao's Military Romanticism*, pp. 83–4, 176–81; Zubok and Pleshakov, *Inside the Kremlin's Cold War*, p. 66.

118. Lewis and Xue, *China Builds the Bomb*, p. 6.

119. Shu Guang Zhang, *Deterrence and Strategic Culture: Sino-American Confrontations, 1949–1958* (Ithaca: Cornell University Press, 1992), pp. 22–3. See also ibid., pp. 56–7; and I. V. Kovalev's interview with S. N. Goncharov, "Stalin's Dialogue with Mao Zedong," *Journal of Northeast Asian Studies* 10 (Winter 1991), 51–2.

120. Quoted in Jian Chen, "China's Changing Aims during the Korean War, 1950–1951," *Journal of American–East Asian Relations* 1 (Spring 1992), 20.

121. Quoted in Shu Guang Zhang, *Mao's Military Romanticism: China and the Korean War, 1950–1953* (Lawrence: University Press of Kansas, 1995), p. 63.

122. Zhang, *Deterrence and Strategic Culture*, p. 108.

123. Rosemary Foot, *A Substitute for Victory: The Politics of Peacemaking at the Korean Armistice Talks* (Ithaca: Cornell University Press, 1990), p. 179. See also Chen Jian, *China's Road to the Korean War: The Making of the Sino-American Confrontation* (New York: Columbia University Press, 1994), pp. 178, 192–3.

124. Foot, *A Substitute for Victory*, p. 179. See also Goncharov et al., *Uncertain Partners*, pp. 165–6, 182; also Lewis and Xue, *China Builds the Bomb*, p. 12.

125. Zhang, *Mao's Military Romanticism*, pp. 233–4.

126. Ibid. 26; Zhang, *Deterrence and Strategic Culture*, pp. 221–2. See also Chapter VIII.

127. Roger Dingman, "Atomic Diplomacy During the Korean War," *International Security* 13 (Winter 1988/9), 52.

128. This point is made by Jonathan D. Pollack, "The Korean War and Sino-American Relations," in Harry Harding and Yuan Ming, eds., *Sino-American Relations, 1945–1955: A Joint Reassessment of a Critical Decade* (Wilmington, Del.: Scholarly Resources, 1989), p. 224.

129. See Peter J. Roman, "Curtis LeMay and the Origins of NATO Atomic Targeting," *Journal of Strategic Studies* 16 (Mar., 1993), 55–6, which documents LeMay's surprise that atomic weapons were not immediately used in Korea.

130. Dingman, "Atomic Diplomacy During the Korean War," pp. 55, 90; Gaddis, *The Long Peace*, pp. 116, 125; Rhodes, *Dark Sun*, pp. 446.

131. Quoted in Zubok and Pleshkov, *Inside the Kremlin's Cold War*, p. 76.

132. Ibid. 117–18. For evidence that Stalin deliberately sought to exacerbate tensions in Europe at this time as a means of deterring American escalation in Korea, see Holloway, *Stalin and the Bomb*, pp. 285–6.

133. See Henry Kissinger, *Diplomacy* (New York: Simon & Schuster, 1994), p. 487; also Steven M. Goldstein, "Nationalism and Internationalism: Sino-Soviet Relations," in Thomas W. Robinson and David Shambaugh, *Chinese Foreign Policy: Theory and Practice* (New York: Oxford University Press, 1994), pp. 232–5.

134. *Lilienthal Journals: The Atomic Energy Years*, p. 474. My thinking here has been influenced by S. David Broscious, "Longing for an International Police Force, Banking on American Superiority: Harry S. Truman's Approach to Nuclear Energy," a paper prepared for a Nuclear History Program–Contemporary History Institute conference at Ohio University, Sept., 1991.

135. The point is made in Keegan, *A History of Warfare*, pp. 38, 48; and in Walter A. McDougall, *The Heavens and the Earth: A Political History of the Space Age* (New York: Basic Books, 1985), p. 266. See also Sherry, *The Rise of American Air Power*, pp. 328–9. For evidence that Eisenhower shared this view in 1945, see Stephen E. Ambrose, *Eisenhower: Soldier, General of the Army, President-Elect, 1890–1952* (New York: Simon & Schuster, 1983), pp. 425–6, 430.

136. See Chapter III.

137. Burton I. Kaufman, *The Korean War: Challenges in Crisis, Credibility, and Command* (New York: Knopf, 1986), pp. 111–14; Qiang Zhai, *The Dragon, the Lion, and the Eagle: Chinese–British–American Relations, 1949–1958* (Kent: Kent State University Press, 1994), pp. 84–5.

138. Holloway, *Stalin and the Bomb*, p. 285.

139. Dingman, "Atomic Diplomacy During the Korean War," pp. 55–79. See also Leffler, *A Preponderance of Power*, pp. 406, 452–3.

140. Gaddis, *The Long Peace*, pp. 123–4. See also, for the evolution of Eisenhower's and Dulles's thinking on this matter, Gaddis, *Strategies of Containment*, pp. 127–63; and John Foster Dulles, "A Policy of Boldness," *Life* 32 (19 May 1952), 146–60.

141. Sherman Adams, *Firsthand Report: The Story of the Eisenhower Administration* (New York: Harper, 1961), pp. 48–9. For Dulles's claim, see *FRUS: 1952–4*, v. 1811.

142. Dingman, "Atomic Diplomacy during the Korean War," pp. 81–7. See also Gaddis, *The Long Peace*, pp. 125–8; and Lewis and Xue, *China Builds the Bomb*, p. 14.

143. Zhang, *Deterrence and Strategic Culture*, pp. 132–7; Zhai, *The Dragon, the Lion, and the Eagle*, pp. 126–8; Zhang, *Mao's Military Romanticism*, pp. 233–4.
144. Zhang, *Deterrence and Strategic Culture*, pp. 133, 150; Foot, *A Substitute for Victory*, pp. 178–80; Holloway, *Stalin and the Bomb*, p. 335.
145. The major ones are discussed in the conclusion to the preceding chapter.
146. Stueck, *The Korean War*, pp. 204–10.
147. Ibid. 264–72; also Foot, *A Substitute for Victory*, pp. 210–12.
148. Stalin to Mao, 5 June 1951, CWIHP *Bulletin* 6 and 7 (Winter 1995/6), 59. See also Kathryn Weathersby, "New Russian Documents on the Korean War," CWIHP *Bulletin* 6 and 7 (Winter 1995/6), 34.
149. Stalin to Mao, 19 Nov. 1951, ibid. 72.
150. Kim Il-sung to Stalin, 16 July 1952, ibid. 77.
151. Soviet transcript, Stalin–Zhou Enlai conversation, 20 Aug. 1952, ibid. 12–13. See also Zubok and Pleshakov, *Inside the Kremlin's Cold War*, p. 75.
152. Holloway, *Stalin and the Bomb*, pp. 334–5; Foot, *A Substitute for Victory*, pp. 182–3; Knight, *Beria*, p. 186. See also *Khrushchev Remembers: The Glasnost Tapes*, trans. and ed. Jerrold L. Schecter and Vyacheslav V. Luchkov (Boston: Little, Brown, 1990), p. 147.
153. Malenkov to Mao and Kim, 19 Mar. 1953, CWIHP *Bulletin* 6 and 7 (Winter 1995/6) 80.
154. Zhang, *Deterrence and Strategic Culture*, pp. 130–1; Zhai, *The Dragon, the Lion, and the Eagle*, p. 131; Weathersby, "New Russian Documents on the Korean War," pp. 31–2.
155. Doris M. Condit, *History of the Office of the Secretary of Defense*, ii: *The Test of War, 1950–1953* (Washington: Government Printing Office, 1988), pp. 171–2. This study placed Chinese casualties—with no distinction made between killed and wounded—at between 1 and 1.5 million. United States battle deaths were 33,629, with an additional 92,134 wounded. Current Chinese sources claim a much smaller number of casualties—one estimate cites 152,000 killed, 230,000 wounded, 21,300 captured (Xu Yan, "The Chinese Forces and Their Casualties in the Korean War: Facts and Statistics," *Chinese Historians* 6 (Fall 1993), pp. 56–7). See also Zhang, *Mao's Military Romanticism*, p. 247, for a slightly different set of figures.
156. See ibid. 233; also Bundy, *Danger and Survival*, pp. 241–2.
157. Quoted in Zhang, *Deterrence and Strategic Culture*, p. 146. See also Philip West, "Confronting the West: China as David and Goliath in the Korean War," *Journal of American–East Asian Relations* 1 (Spring 1993), 18–19.
158. Neither did Mao, for that matter: "the United States is a real tiger and capable of eating human flesh," he warned the North Koreans shortly before the Inchon landing (Zhang, *Mao's Military Romanticism*, p. 73).
159. *Khrushchev Remembers: The Glasnost Tapes*, pp. 100–1.
160. Minutes, NSC meeting, 4 June 1953, *FRUS: 1952–4*, ii. 369.
161. See Martin Walker, *The Cold War: A History* (New York: Henry Holt, 1993), pp. 76–7.
162. Quoted in Ninkovich, *Modernity and Power*, p. 195.
163. For more on this, see Gaddis, *The Long Peace*, pp. 237–43.
164. Rhodes, *Dark Sun*, pp. 482–512; Williamson and Rearden, *The Origins of U.S. Nuclear Strategy*, pp. 180–1.
165. Zaloga, *Target America*, pp. 100–1. Sakharov, *Memoirs*, pp. 170–5, gives a vivid account of this test.
166. Kennan, *Memoirs: 1925–1950*, p. 408.

167. Williamson and Rearden, *The Origins of U.S. Nuclear Strategy*, p. 193. See also Rosenberg, "The Origins of Overkill," pp. 140–1.
168. Quoted in Hamby, *Man of the People*, p. 339.
169. Holloway, *Stalin and the Bomb*, pp. 291–2, 333.
170. *Truman Public Papers, 1952–3*, pp. 1124–6.
171. One exception is Bundy, *Danger and Survival*, pp. 233–5.

CHAPTER V

1. Harold Nicolson account of a Bevin–Molotov conversation, 2 Dec. 1947, in Nigel Nicolson, ed., *Harold Nicolson: Diaries and Letters, The Later Years: 1945–62* (New York: Atheneum, 1968), p. 116. I am indebted to Anne Deighton for this quotation.
2. Dean Acheson, *Present at the Creation: My Years in the State Department* (New York: Norton, 1969), p. 646.
3. See e.g. A. W. DePorte, *Europe Between the Super-Powers: The Enduring Balance* (New Haven: Yale University Press, 1979); also, for its assumption that bipolarity, if not the Cold War, would continue, Kenneth Waltz, *Theory of International Politics* (New York: Random House, 1979). Nor would I exempt from this pattern of thinking John Lewis Gaddis, "The Long Peace: Elements of Stability in the Postwar International System," *International Security* 10 (Spring 1986), 99–142.
4. See Chapters IV and VIII; also John Lewis Gaddis, *The United States and the End of the Cold War: Implications, Reconsiderations, Provocations* (New York: Oxford University Press, 1992), pp. 105–18; and Godfried van Bentham van den Bergh, *The Nuclear Revolution and the End of the Cold War: Forced Restraint* (London: Macmillan, 1992). An alternative argument appears in John Mueller, *Retreat From Doomsday: The Obsolescence of Major War* (New York: Basic Books, 1989).
5. Lenin's use of this idea is amply documented in Richard Pipes, *The Russian Revolution* (New York: Knopf, 1990), and *Russia Under the Bolshevik Regime* (New York: Knopf, 1994). For Mao Zedong's use of external adversaries, see Chen Jian, *China's Road to the Korean War: The Making of the Sino-American Confrontation* (New York: Columbia University Press, 1994), esp. pp. 215–20. H. W. Brands, *The Devil We Knew: Americans and the Cold War* (New York: Oxford University Press, 1993) is the best overall account of how much the same process could work within a democratic framework.
6. Henry Ashby Turner, Jr., *The Two Germanies since 1945* (New Haven: Yale University Press, 1987), pp. 31–2.
7. For British and American ambivalence, see Warren F. Kimball, *Swords or Ploughshares? The Morgenthau Plan for Defeated Germany* (Philadelphia: J. B. Lippincott, 1976). The contradictions in Stalin's thinking are discussed in R. C. Raack, "Stalin Plans His Post-War Germany," *Journal of Contemporary History* 28 (1993), 58–9.
8. Heike Bungert, "A New Perspective on French–American Relations during the Occupation of Germany, 1945–1948: Behind-the-Scenes Diplomatic Bargaining and the Zonal Merger," *Diplomatic History* 18 (Summer 1994),

333–52, suggests that even the French position was more flexible than it publicly appeared to be.

9. "American Relations with the Soviet Union," Sept. 1946, in Arthur Krock, *Memoirs: Sixty Years on the Firing Line* (New York: Funk & Wagnalls, 1968), p. 467.

10. Novikov to Molotov, 27 Sept. 1946, in Kenneth M. Jensen, ed., *Origins of the Cold War: The Novikov, Kennan, and Roberts "Long Telegrams" of 1946* (Washington: United States Institute of Peace, 1991), p. 15.

11. The principal source for this meeting is a recently discovered set of notes by Wilhelm Pieck on the German Communist Party leadership's meetings with Stalin, now published in Rolf Badstübner and Wilfried Loth, eds., *Wilhelm Pieck: Aufzeichungen zur Deutschlandpolitik 1945–1953* (Berlin: Akademie, 1993). See also, for evaluations, Raack, "Stalin Plans His Post-War Germany," pp. 62–8; David Pike, *The Politics of Culture in Soviet-Occupied Germany, 1945–1949* (Stanford: Stanford University Press, 1992), pp. 3–10; and, for a somewhat different interpretation from my own, Norman M. Naimark, *The Russians in Germany: A History of the Soviet Zone of Occupation, 1945–1949* (Cambridge, Mass.: Harvard University Press, 1995), pp. 258–9.

12. Milovan Djilas, *Conversations with Stalin*, trans. Michael B. Petrovich (New York: Harcourt, Brace & World, 1962), p. 153.

13. See Gavriel D. Ra'anan, *International Policy Formation in the USSR: Factional "Debates" during the Zhdanovschina* (Hamden, Conn.: Archon Books, 1983), pp. 89–90.

14. Naimark, *The Russians in Germany*, pp. 69–140; Raack, "Stalin Plans His Post-War Germany," pp. 61, 64; Turner, *The Two Germanies*, pp. 10, 18–20; Atina Grossmann, "A Question of Silence: The Rape of German Women by Occupation Soldiers," *October* 72 (Spring 1995), 43–63; and Charles F. Pennacchio, "The East German Communists and the Origins of the Berlin Blockade Crisis," *East European Quarterly* 24 (Sept. 1995), 295–314.

15. Ivan Smirnov to Arthur Werner, 30 Oct. 1945, quoted in ibid. 304. See also Raack, "Stalin Plans His Post-War Germany," pp. 61–3.

16. Djilas, *Conversations with Stalin*, pp. 153–4.

17. George F. Kennan, *Memoirs: 1925–1950* (Boston: Atlantic, Little Brown, 1967), p. 258. See also Charles E. Bohlen, *Witness to History: 1929–1969* (New York: Norton, 1973), pp. 174–7; and Jean Edward Smith, *Lucius D. Clay: An American Life* (New York: Henry Holt, 1990), pp. 277–95, 328–55.

18. Anne Deighton, *The Impossible Peace: Britain, the Division of Germany, and the Origins of the Cold War* (New York: Oxford University Press, 1993), esp. pp. 93–102, 224–6; also John Farquharson, " 'The Essential Division': Britain and the Partition of Germany, 1945–9," *German History* 9 (Feb. 1991), 22–8; Josef Foschepoth, "British Interest in the Division of Germany after the Second World War," *Journal of Contemporary History* 21 (1986), 391–411; and Sean Greenwood, "Bevin, the Ruhr and the Division of Germany: August 1945–December 1946," *Historical Journal* 29 (1986), 203–12.

19. Deighton, *The Impossible Peace*, pp. 135–67. See also Bungert, "A New Perspective on Franco-American Relations during the Occupation of Germany," *passim*; Forrest C. Pogue, *George C. Marshall: Statesman* (New York: Viking, 1987), pp. 168–96; John Gimbel, *The Origins of the Marshall Plan* (Stanford: Stanford University Press, 1976), pp. 186–93; and John W. Young, *France, the Cold War and the Western Alliance, 1944–49: French Foreign Policy and Post-War Europe* (Leicester: Leicester University Press, 1990), pp. 134–49.

20. I am indebted to one of my students, Steven Remy, for pointing out how much the Russians could have learned about future Western policies in Europe by surreptitiously monitoring — as they almost certainly did — the foreign ministers' conversations. See also Vladislav Zubok and Constantine Pleshakov, *Inside the Kremlin's Cold War: From Stalin to Khrushchev* (Cambridge, Mass.: Harvard University Press, 1996), p. 101.

21. Bohlen memorandum, Marshall–Stalin conversation, 15 Apr. 1947, *FRUS 1947*, ii. 343–4.

22. Charles E. Bohlen, *Witness to History: 1929–1969* (New York: Norton, 1973) p. 263. See also Robert Murphy, *Diplomat Among Warriors* (Garden City, NY: Doubleday, 1964), p. 307.

23. See Chapter II.

24. Smith, *Lucius D. Clay*, pp. 414–20.

25. Deighton, *The Impossible Peace*, pp. 207–22.

26. London Conference communiqué, 7 June 1948, *FRUS: 1948*, ii. 314–15. See also, on the significance of the London Conference, Turner, *The Two Germanies*, pp. 23–4.

27. Frank A. Ninkovich, *Germany and the United States: The Transformation of the German Question since 1945*, updated edn. (New York: Twayne, 1994), pp. 61–2.

28. Clay to William Draper, 3 Nov. 1947, quoted in Smith, *Lucius D. Clay*, p. 445.

29. Turner, *The Two Germanies*, pp. 29–30; Thomas Alan Schwartz, *America's Germany: John J. McCloy and the Federal Republic of Germany* (Cambridge, Mass.: Harvard University Press, 1991), p. 32.

30. Farquharson, "The Essential Division," p. 40; Ninkovich, *Germany and the United States*, pp. 62–3.

31. Tiul'panov report to CPSU Central Committee Commission Evaluating the Propaganda Administration of the SVAG, 16 Sept. 1946, Central Party Archives, Moscow, in CWIHP *Bulletin* 4 (Fall 1994), 46.

32. Naimark, *The Russians in Germany*, p. 326.

33. Ibid. 467.

34. See Raack, "Stalin Plans His Postwar Germany," pp. 66–7; also Gerhard Wettig, "All-German Unity and East German Separation in Soviet Policy, 1947–1949," CWIHP conference paper, Essen, June 1994, pp. 15–16.

35. *Khrushchev Remembers: The Glasnost Tapes*, trans. and ed. Jerrold L. Schecter with Vyacheslav V. Luchkov (Boston: Little, Brown), p. 165. See also Turner, *The Two Germanies*, p. 66.

36. Dietrich Staritz, "The SED, Stalin, and the German Question: Interests and Decision-Making in the Light of New Sources," *German History* 10 (Oct. 1992), 278.

37. Quoted in Ra'anan, *International Policy Formation in the USSR*, p. 94.

38. Staritz, "The SED, Stalin, and the German Question," pp. 278–80.

39. Djilas, *Conversations with Stalin*, p. 153.

40. A. Smirnov to Molotov, 12 Mar. 1948, quoted in Michael Narinsky, "Soviet Policy and the Berlin Blockade," CWIHP conference paper, Essen, June 1994.

41. PPS-37, "Policy Questions Concerning a Possible German Settlement," 12 Aug. 1948, *FRUS: 1948*, ii. 1289. See also PPS-37/1, "Position To Be Taken by the U.S. at a CFM Meeting," 15 Nov. 1948, ibid. 1321.

42. John Lewis Gaddis, *Strategies of Containment: A Critical Appraisal of Postwar American National Security Policy* (New York: Oxford University Press, 1982), pp. 86–8.

43. PPS-37, 12 Aug. 1948, *FRUS: 1948*, ii. 1296. For more on Kennan's thinking with respect to Germany, see Kennan, *Memoirs: 1925–1950*, pp. 415–26; also Wilson

D. Miscamble, *George F. Kennan and the Making of American Foreign Policy, 1947–1950* (Princeton: Princeton University Press, 1992), pp. 141–7.

44. The definitive version of Program A is PPS-37/1, 15 Nov. 1948, *FRUS: 1948*, ii. 1320–8.

45. Gaddis, *Strategies of Containment*, pp. 55–65.

46. See Kennan, *Memoirs: 1925–1950*, pp. 442–6.

47. Robert Murphy memorandum, conversation with Acheson, 9 Mar. 1949, *FRUS: 1949*, iii. 102.

48. Acheson to US Embassy, London, 11 May 1949, ibid. 873. See also, for a good discussion of Acheson's position at this time, Miscamble, *George F. Kennan*, pp. 158–69.

49. Smith, *Lucius D. Clay*, p. 536.

50. Schwartz, *America's Germany*, pp. 36–7.

51. Miscamble, *George F. Kennan*, pp. 169–71.

52. West Germans were discussing a "magnet" strategy as early as 1946–7. See Farquharson, "The Essential Division," pp. 41–2.

53. Paul H. Nitze, with Ann M. Smith and Steven L. Rearden, *From Hiroshima to Glasnost: At the Center of Decision: A Memoir* (New York: Grove Weidenfeld, 1989), p. 70.

54. Farquharson, "The Essential Division," p. 39.

55. Schwartz, *America's Germany*, p. 114; also Ernest R. May, "The American Commitment to Germany, 1949–55," *Diplomatic History* 13 (Fall 1989), 442–3.

56. Chester J. Pach, Jr., *Arming the Free World: The Origins of the United States Military Assistance Program, 1945–1950* (Chapel Hill: University of North Carolina Press, 1991), pp. 219–26.

57. NSC-68, "United States Objectives and Programs for National Security," 14 Apr. 1950, in Thomas H. Etzold and John Lewis Gaddis, eds., *Containment: Documents on American Policy and Strategy, 1945–1950* (New York: Columbia University Press, 1978), p. 411.

58. Schwartz, *America's Germany*, pp. 116–19.

59. Ibid. 118–19. See also Laurence W. Martin, "The American Decision to Rearm Germany," and Theodore J. Lowi, "Bases in Spain," both in Harold Stein, ed., *American Civil–Military Decisions: A Book of Case Studies* (Birmingham: University of Alabama Press, 1963), pp. 643–705. The Taiwan question is discussed in Chapter III.

60. Schwartz, *America's Germany*, p. 122.

61. Quoted ibid. 125.

62. Quoted ibid. 128.

63. May, "The American Commitment to Germany," pp. 446–7; also Gaddis, *Strategies of Containment*, pp. 109–15.

64. See Chapter II.

65. May, "The American Commitment to Germany," p. 446.

66. Ibid. 432–3.

67. Ibid. 456.

68. Stalin's last years are summarized in Adam Ulam, *Stalin: The Man and His Era* (New York: Viking, 1973), pp. 700–41; and in Werner G. Hahn, *Postwar Soviet Politics: The Fall of Zhdanov and the Defeat of Moderation, 1946–53* (Ithaca: Cornell University Press, 1982), pp. 136–56. For Kennan's expulsion, see George F. Kennan, *Memoirs: 1950–1963* (Boston: Atlantic, Little Brown, 1972), pp. 145–67.

69. The note is published in *FRUS: 1952–4*, vii. 169–72. I have particularly benefited, in the discussion that follows, from Gerhard Wettig, "Stalin and German

Reunification: Archival Evidence on Soviet Foreign Policy in the Spring of 1952," *Historical Journal* 37 (1994), 411–19; and a careful study by one of my students, Ruud van Dijk, "The 1952 Stalin Note Debate: Myth or Missed Opportunity for German Unification?" CWIHP Working Paper 14 (May 1996).

70. Acheson, *Present at the Creation*, pp. 629–30; Schwartz, *America's Germany*, pp. 265–6; Ann L. Phillips, *Soviet Policy Toward East Germany Reconsidered: The Postwar Decade* (Westport, Conn.: Greenwood Press, 1986), pp. 120–1. See also Central Intelligence Agency National Intelligence Estimate 17, "Probable Soviet Reactions to a Remilitarization of Western Germany," 27 Dec. 1950, in Scott A. Koch, ed., *CIA Cold War Records: Selected Estimates on the Soviet Union, 1950–1959* (Washington: CIA, 1993), pp. 111–16.

71. Schwartz, *America's Germany*, pp. 263–4, 267.

72. See Phillips, *Soviet Policy Toward East Germany Reconsidered*, pp. 120–1.

73. Acheson summary of Eden's views, 14 Mar. 1952, *FRUS: 1952–4*, vii. 176–7. See also Schwartz, *America's Germany*, pp. 264–5.

74. Acheson to US Embassy, London, 30 Apr. 1952, *FRUS: 1952–4*, vii. 218–19.

75. Van Dijk, "The 1952 Stalin Note Debate," pp. 27–35. Also useful, on the "battle of the notes," has been James C. Van Hook, "Schach: The United States and the German Question, 1949–1955" (Ohio University Honors Tutorial College and Contemporary History Institute thesis, June 1990).

76. See, for examples of this argument, Adam B. Ulam, *The Communists: The Story of Power and Lost Illusions, 1948–1991* (New York: Scribner's, 1992), pp. 72–3; Henry Kissinger, *Diplomacy* (New York: Simon & Schuster, 1994), pp. 497–500. For a more skeptical interpretation, see Marshall D. Shulman, *Stalin's Foreign Policy Reappraised* (Cambridge, Mass.: Harvard University Press, 1963), pp. 191–4.

77. One of the first studies to raise this issue was Coral Bell, *Negotiation From Strength: A Study in the Politics of Power* (New York: Knopf, 1963), pp. 103–6; but it was particularly vigorously debated in West Germany following the publication of Rolf Steininger's *Eine vertane Chance: Die Stalin-Note vom 10. März 1952 und die Wiedervereiningung* (Berlin: J. H. W. Dietz, 1985), which argued that Adenauer had persuaded the British and the Americans not to pursue the Stalin proposal.

78. Naimark, *The Russians in Germany*, pp. 266, 270–1; Staritz, "The SED, Stalin, and the German Question," p. 281; Van Dijk, "The 1952 Stalin Note Debate," p. 20.

79. Staritz, "The SED, Stalin, and the German Question," p. 283; also Phillips, *Soviet Policy Toward East Germany Reconsidered*, pp. 207–9; A. James McAdams, *Germany Divided: From the Wall to Reunification* (Princeton: Princeton University Press, 1993), pp. 24–7; and Wilfrid Loth, *Stalins ungeliebtes Kind: Warum Moskau die DDR nicht wollte* (Berlin: Rowohlt, 1994).

80. Quoted in Wettig, "Stalin and German Reunification," pp. 417–18.

81. Van Dijk, "The 1952 Stalin Note Debate," p. 26.

82. Alexei Filitov, "The Soviet Policy and Early Years of Two German States, 1949–1961," CWIHP Conference paper, Essen, June 1994, p. 6.

83. The Western note is in *FRUS 1952–4*, vii. 189–90.

84. Minutes, Stalin conversation with Pieck, Ulbricht, and Grotewohl, 7 Apr. 1952, Soviet Foreign Ministry Archives, in CWIHP *Bulletin* 4 (Fall 1994), p. 48. This source also prints Pieck's cryptic notes of the same meeting.

85. Staritz, "The SED, Stalin, and the German Question," pp. 287–90.

86. Kennan to State Department, 25 May 1952, *FRUS: 1952–4*, vii. 252–3.

87. Kennan, *Memoirs: 1950–1963*, pp. 108–9.

88. Marc Trachtenberg, *History and Strategy* (Princeton: Princeton University Press, 1991), p. 173.

89. Vladislav M. Zubok, "Soviet Foreign Policy in Germany and Austria and the Post-Stalin Succession Struggle, 1953–1955," CWIHP Conference paper, Essen, June 1994, pp. 9–10.

90. Quoted in Robert V. Daniels, ed., *A Documentary History of Communism*, rev. edn. (Hanover, NH: University Press of New England, 1984), ii. 172.

91. Albert Resis, ed., *Molotov Remembers: Inside Kremlin Politics: Conversations with Felix Chuev* (Chicago: Ivan R. Dee, 1993), p. 336.

92. Carlton Savage to Paul Nitze, 1 Apr. 1953, *FRUS: 1952–4*, viii. 1138.

93. Bohlen to State Department, 25 Apr. 1953, ibid. 1165. Eisenhower's 16 Apr. speech, made to the American Society of Newspaper Editors, is reprinted in ibid. 1147–55.

94. Phillips, *Soviet Policy Toward East Germany Reconsidered*, pp. 120–1; James Richter, "Reexamining Soviet Policy Towards Germany During the Beria Interregnum," CWIHP Working Paper 3, June 1992, p. 9.

95. *Molotov Remembers*, p. 334. See also Knight, *Beria*, pp. 191–2.

96. Pavel Sudoplatov and Anatolii Sudoplatov, with Jerrold L. Schecter and Leona P. Schecter, *Special Tasks: The Memoirs of an Unwanted Witness—A Soviet Spymaster* (Boston: Little, Brown, 1994), pp. 363–4. A long-time associate of Beria's, Sudoplatov was arrested and imprisoned for many years after Beria's downfall. For an assessment of Sudoplatov's evidence on this matter, see Zubok and Pleshakov, *Inside the Kremlin's Cold War*, pp. 159–60.

97. *Molotov Remembers*, p. 334. See also Andrei Gromyko, *Memoirs*, trans. Harold Shukman (New York: Doubleday, 1990), pp. 317–18, who provides a similar account.

98. Knight, *Beria*, pp. 183–91.

99. See Pipes, *The Russian Revolution*, pp. 74–5, 249; also Knight, *Beria*, pp. 226–7, citing the subsequent example of Yuri Andropov.

100. *Molotov Remembers*, p. 336. See also Knight, *Beria*, p. 191; Zubok and Pleshakov, *Inside the Kremlin's Cold War*, pp. 160–2.

101. Quoted in James G. Richter, *Khrushchev's Double Bind: International Pressures and Domestic Coalition Politics* (Baltimore: Johns Hopkins University Press, 1994), pp. 36–7.

102. Phillips, *Soviet Policy Toward East Germany Reconsidered*, pp. 131–4; Knight, *Beria*, pp. 192–3.

103. The best account is now ibid. 194–224.

104. Phillips, *Soviet Policy Toward East Germany Reconsidered*, pp. 150–3; Zubok, "Soviet Foreign Policy in Germany and Austria and the Post-Stalin Succession Struggle," pp. 16–18.

105. For Stalin's use of this tactic during the 1920s, see Alan Bullock, *Hitler and Stalin: Parallel Lives* (New York: Knopf, 1992), pp. 187–8. Khrushchev would do something similar when he endorsed Malenkov's ideas on the impossibility of winning a nuclear war having arranged the latter's retirement.

106. Kennan, *Memoirs: 1950–1963*, p. 161.

107. See Trachtenberg, *History and Strategy*, pp. 174–5.

108. Cutler memorandum, conversation with Eisenhower, 13 Aug. 1953, *FRUS: 1952–4*, vii. 510. Cutler's reference to stars and driftwood paraphrased a recent speech by General Omar Bradley.

109. NSC-160/1, "United States Position With Respect to Germany," 17 Aug. 1953, ibid. 518.

110. Dulles memorandum, 6 Sept. 1953, ibid. ii. 457–60.

111. NSC meeting minutes, 25 Mar. 1953, ibid. 260. For the Eisenhower adminis-

tration's emphasis on economy, see Gaddis, *Strategies of Containment*, pp. 132–6.

112. Trachtenberg, *History and Strategy*, pp. 185–6; also Saki Dockrill, "Cooperation and Suspicion: The United States' Alliance Diplomacy for the Security of Western Europe, 1953–54," *Diplomacy and Statecraft* 5 (Mar. 1994), 148–50. Dockrill points out that the United States was spending 15% of its gross national product on defense in 1952, while the figures for Great Britain were 13.2%, France 11.8%, the Netherlands 8.1%, and Belgium 7.6%.

113. Martin Gilbert, *Winston S. Churchill: "Never Despair," 1945–1965* (Boston: Houghton Mifflin, 1988), p. 831. See also Peter G. Boyle, ed., *The Churchill–Eisenhower Correspondence: 1953–1955* (Chapel Hill: University of North Carolina Press, 1990), pp. 41–55.

114. James G. Hershberg, " 'Explosion in the Offing'; German Rearmament and American Diplomacy, 1953–1955," *Diplomatic History* 16 (Fall 1992), 528–31; Hans-Jürgen Grabbe, "Konrad Adenauer, John Foster Dulles, and West German–American Relations," in Richard H. Immerman, ed., *John Foster Dulles and the Diplomacy of the Cold War* (Princeton: Princeton University Press, 1990), p. 125.

115. Eisenhower to Dulles, 8 Sept. 1953, *FRUS: 1952–4*, ii. 460–1 (emphasis in original).

116. Trachtenberg, *History and Strategy*, pp. 176–7.

117. Conant to Dulles, 28 Oct. 1953, *FRUS: 1952–4*, vii. 551–2. See also Hershberg, "Explosion in the Offing," pp. 536–44; and Rolf Steininger, "John Foster Dulles, the European Defense Community, and the German Question," in Immerman, ed., *John Foster Dulles and the Diplomacy of the Cold War*, pp. 93–4.

118. Hershberg, "Explosion in the Offing," p. 544; Grabbe, "Konrad Adenauer, John Foster Dulles, and West German–American Relations," pp. 112–14.

119. Dulles to Eisenhower, 5 Feb. 1954, *FRUS: 1952–4*, vii. 962. See also Phillips, *Soviet Policy Toward East Germany Reconsidered*, pp. 169–71.

120. Schwartz, *America's Germany*, pp. 282–3.

121. Dwight D. Eisenhower, *The White House Years: Mandate for Change* (Garden City, NY: Doubleday, 1963), p. 523. See also McAdams, *Germany Divided*, p. 28; and *Khrushchev Remembers*, trans. and ed. Strobe Talbot (Boston: Little, Brown, 1970), p. 505.

122. *Khrushchev Remembers: The Last Testament*, trans. and ed. Strobe Talbott (Boston: Little, Brown, 1974), p. 358.

123. Richter, *Khrushchev's Double Bind*, p. 116.

124. Steininger, "The EDC and the German Question," pp. 93–107, provides a good account.

125. May, "The American Commitment to Germany," p. 453.

126. Trachtenberg, *History and Strategy*, pp. 177–8. See also Norman Gelb, *The Berlin Wall: Kennedy, Khrushchev, and a Showdown in the Heart of Europe* (New York: Simon & Schuster, 1986), p. 92.

127. *Khrushchev Remembers: The Last Testament*, p. 361.

128. Quoted in Trachtenberg, *History and Strategy*, p. 179.

129. Ninkovich, *Germany and the United States*, p. 100.

130. NSC-160/1, 17 Aug. 1953, *FRUS: 1952–4*, vii. 512.

131. Turner, *The Two Germanies*, pp. 111–12.

132. *Khrushchev Remembers: The Glasnost Tapes*, pp. 164–5.

133. See Wolfgang Krieger, "Germany," in David Reynolds, ed., *The Origins of the*

Cold War in Europe: International Perspectives (New Haven: Yale University Press, 1994), pp. 151–3.

134. Naimark, *The Russians in Germany,* provides a clear and comprehensive account of how this happened. See also Turner, *The Two Germanies*, pp. 51–3, 99–108.

135. Ibid. 114.

136. Ibid. 127. See also Chapter VII.

137. May, "The American Commitment to Germany," pp. 454–6; Trachtenberg, *History and Strategy*, pp. 153–68, 180–91.

138. George F. Kennan, *Russia, the Atom, and the West* (New York: Harper, 1958), pp. 39–40.

139. Douglas Brinkley, *Dean Acheson: The Cold War Years, 1953–71* (New Haven: Yale University Press, 1992), pp. 81–3. "I am getting too respectable to be safe," a shaken Acheson commented.

140. Kennan, *Memoirs: 1950–1963*, p. 250. For Adenauer's reaction, see the memorandum of his conversation with Dulles, 7 Feb. 1959, *FRUS: 1958–60*, viii. 340; also, on the Reith Lectures controversy generally, Walter Hixson, *George F. Kennan: Cold War Iconoclast* (New York: Columbia University Press, 1989), pp. 171–93.

141. Beate Ihme-Tuchel, "The Soviet Union and the Politics of the Rapacki Plan," CWIHP Conference paper, Essen, June 1994.

142. Kennan, *Russia, the Atom, and the West*, pp. 40–1.

143. Gelb, *The Berlin Wall*, p. 63.

144. Khrushchev's 28-page note is summarized in *FRUS: 1958–60*, viii. 133. Extracts appear in United States, Department of State, *Documents on Germany: 1944–1985* (Washington: Government Printing Office, 1986), pp. 552–9.

145. P. Florin briefing for GDR ambassadors, 1–2 Feb. 1956, quoted in Hope Harrison, "Ulbricht and the Concrete 'Rose': New Archival Evidence on the Dynamics of Soviet–East German Relations and the Berlin Crisis, 1958–1961," CWIHP Working Paper 5, May 1993, pp. 4–5.

146. McAdams, *Germany Divided*, p. 29.

147. Pervukhin–Selyaninov report, "On the Situation in West Berlin," 24 Feb. 1958, quoted in Harrison, "Ulbricht and the Concrete 'Rose'," p. 6.

148. Trachtenberg, *History and Strategy*, pp. 180–91. See also Chapter VIII.

149. Smirnov comment at meeting with Ulbricht, 5 Oct. 1958, as reported in Pervukhin diary, 11 Oct. 1958, quoted in Richter, *Khrushchev's Double Bind*, p. 113.

150. Andropov to Central Committee, 28 Aug. 1958, quoted in Harrison, "Ulbricht and the Concrete 'Rose'," p. 17.

151. Ulbricht comment, 2 Oct. 1958, as reported in Pervukhin diary, 12 Oct. 1958, quoted in Harrison, "Ulbricht and the Concrete 'Rose'," pp. 15, 19–20.

152. Ibid. 6–7.

153. Ibid. 9–11.

154. Ibid. 20–1; also Richter, *Khrushchev's Double Bind*, p. 102; Zubok and Pleskakov, *Inside the Kremlin's Cold War*, pp. 194–8; and Hope M. Harrison, "New Evidence on Khrushchev's 1958 Berlin Ultimatum," CWIHP *Bulletin* 4 (Fall 1994), 35–9.

155. See, on Khrushchev's habit of impulsive improvisation, Michael R. Beschloss, *The Crisis Years: Kennedy and Khrushchev, 1960–1963* (New York: HarperCollins, 1991), pp. 380–1.

156. Valentin Falin, *Politische Erinnerungen* (Munich: Droemer Knaur, 1993), p. 336 I am indebted to Vladislav Zubok for this information. See also Richter, *Khrushchev's Double Bind*, p. 101.

157. Vladislav M. Zubok, "Khrushchev's Motives and Soviet Diplomacy in the Berlin Crisis, 1958–1662," CWIHP Conference paper, Essen, June 1994, pp. 20–1.
158. Ibid. 14–15, 38–9; Trachtenberg, *History and Strategy*, p. 171.
159. Dean Rusk, *As I Saw It*, as told to Richard Rusk (New York: Norton, 1990), p. 227. See also *Khrushchev Remembers: The Last Testament*, p. 501. Norman Gelb has provided a helpful catalog of Khrushchev's other favorite Berlin metaphors, most of which suggest that it was not only the West that felt pain: "a bone stuck in the throat which had to be disgorged," "a splinter that had to be extricated," "a cancer that had to be carved out," "a rotten tooth that had to be extracted" (Gelb, *The Berlin Wall*, p. 79).
160. Llewellyn Thompson to State Department, 3 Dec. 1958, *FRUS: 1958–60*, viii. 152.
161. Ibid. 195–6; William Burr, "Avoiding the Slippery Slope: The Eisenhower Administration and the Berlin Crisis, November 1958–January, 1959," *Diplomatic History* 18 (Spring 1994), 180, 185–91.
162. Dulles memorandum, conversation with Eisenhower, 30 Nov. 1958, *FRUS: 1958–60*, viii. 143.
163. John S. D. Eisenhower notes, Eisenhower–Dulles conversation, 29 Jan. 1959, ibid. 303.
164. Burr, "Avoiding the Slippery Slope," pp. 185–8. See also, on the West German "Hallstein Doctrine," McAdams, *Germany Divided*, p. 35.
165. James L. Richardson, *Germany and the Atlantic Alliance: The Interaction of Strategy and Politics* (Cambridge, Mass.: Harvard University Press, 1966), p. 40.
166. Burr, "Avoiding the Slippery Slope," pp. 199–200.
167. Memorandum, Dulles–Adenauer conversation, 8 Feb. 1959, *FRUS: 1958–60*, viii. 346–7.
168. Quoted in Trachtenberg, *History and Strategy*, p. 198; also Gelb, *The Berlin Wall*, p. 93. This comment does not appear in the sanitized official memorandum of this conversation, cited above, but Trachtenberg and Gelb got the quote from David Klein, who took the notes. The published document does cite Adenauer as insisting that "the situation should not be permitted to develop to any use of nuclear weapons" (*FRUS: 1958–60*, viii. 346).
169. Dulles meeting with Selwyn Lloyd, London, 5 Feb. 1959, *FRUS: 1958–60*, viii. 318. See also, on the British initiative, Trachtenberg, *History and Strategy*, pp. 198–201.
170. Memorandum, Eisenhower–Macmillan conversation, 20 Mar. 1959, *FRUS: 1958–60*, viii. 520–1.
171. Trachtenberg, *History and Strategy*, pp. 201–2.
172. Andrew Goodpaster notes, Eisenhower meeting with Douglas Dillon and Robert Murphy, 22 July 1959, *FRUS: 1958–60*, viii. 1032. There is some evidence, though, that Eisenhower staged this episode so as not to have to take personal responsibility for inviting Khrushchev. See Howard Campbell Craig, "The Thermonuclear Revolution and American Postwar Realism" (Ph.D. dissertation, Ohio University, 1995), pp. 210–12.
173. Harrison, "Ulbricht and the Concrete 'Rose'," p. 21.
174. Charles Thayer notes, Khrushchev–Harriman conversation, 25 June 1959, *FRUS: 1958–60*, viii. 941–3. Khrushchev's characterization of Adenauer, delivered on this occasion, is worth recording: "There is a current joke in Russia that if you look at Mr. Adenauer naked from behind, he shows Germany divided. If you look at him from the front, he demonstrates that Germany cannot stand."

The joke, apparently, was an old favorite. See Veljko Micunovic, *Moscow Diary* (Garden City, NY: Doubleday, 1980), p. 330.

175. Memoranda, Eisenhower–Khrushchev conversations, 26 and 27 Sept. 1959, *FRUS: 1958–60*, x. 462–7, 479–82.

176. Quoted in Jack M. Schick, *The Berlin Crisis: 1958–1962* (Philadelphia: University of Pennsylvania Press, 1971), pp. 121–2. See also Bohlen's memorandum of a conversation with Soviet ambassador to the United States Mikhail Menshikov, 8 July 1960, *FRUS: 1958–60*, x. 539.

177. Schick, *The Berlin Crisis*, pp. 17–20.

178. Pervukhin report, "On Several Issues regarding the Economic and Political Situation in Democratic Berlin," 10 Dec. 1959, quoted in Harrison, "Ulbricht and the Concrete 'Rose'," p. 26.

179. Soviet Foreign Ministry record of Khrushchev–Ulbricht meeting, 30 Nov. 1960, ibid., appendix A. See also Gelb, *The Berlin Wall*, pp. 63–70; and McAdams, *Germany Divided*, p. 48.

180. Khrushchev–Ulbricht meeting, 30 Nov. 1960, in Harrison, "Ulbricht and the Concrete 'Rose'," appendix A. See also Richter, *Khrushchev's Double Bind*, pp. 139–40; and Zubok and Pleshakov, *Inside the Kremlin's Cold War*, pp. 249–50.

181. O. P. Selyaninov diary, 5 Feb. 1960, quoted in Harrison, "Ulbricht and the Concrete 'Rose'," p. 27.

182. Ulbricht to Khrushchev, 18 Oct. 1960, quoted in ibid. 25.

183. Ibid. 32.

184. I follow here Hope Harrison's analysis, ibid. 28.

185. Khrushchev–Ulbricht meeting, 30 Nov. 1960, ibid., appendix A.

186. Ulbricht to Khrushchev, 18 Jan. 1961, in ibid., appendix B.

187. See Beschloss, *The Crisis Years*, pp. 63–5.

188. Memorandum, Kennedy–Brandt meeting, 13 Mar. 1961, *FRUS: 1961–3*, xiv. 26–7. See also Beschloss, *The Crisis Years*, pp. 174–6.

189. Thompson to State Department, 16 Mar. 1961, *FRUS: 1961–3*, xiv. 31–2.

190. Beschloss, *The Crisis Years*, pp. 77–8.

191. Ibid. 162–3, 176–7; also Harrison, "Ulbricht and the Concrete 'Rose'," p. 36. Khrushchev's comment is in *Khrushchev Remembers: The Last Testament*, p. 503.

192. See, on this important point, Harrison, "Ulbricht and the Concrete 'Rose'," p. 37.

193. Memorandum, Kennedy–Khrushchev meeting, 4 June 1961, *FRUS: 1961–3*, xiv. 93–4.

194. *Khrushchev Remembers: The Last Testament*, p. 503.

195. Memorandum, Kennedy–Khrushchev meeting, 4 June 1961, *FRUS: 1961–3*, xiv. 89, 94, 97–8. See also Beschloss, *The Crisis Years*, pp. 215–24.

196. Ibid. 224–5. See also James Reston, *Deadline: A Memoir* (New York: Random House, 1991), pp. 290–1.

197. Acheson report on Berlin, 28 June 1961, *FRUS: 1961–3*, xiv. 138–59.

198. See Beschloss, *The Crisis Years*, p. 258.

199. *Documents on Germany, 1944–1985*, p. 764.

200. Beschloss, *The Crisis Years*, pp. 257–8.

201. Thompson to State Department, 28 July 1961, *FRUS: 1961–3*, xvi. 233–4.

202. Transcript, Warsaw Pact meeting, 4 Aug. 1961, CWIHP *Bulletin* 3 (Fall 1993), 60.

203. See Richter, "Khrushchev, Domestic Politics, and the Origins of the Berlin Crisis," pp. 16–23; Robert M. Slusser, *The Berlin Crisis of 1961: Soviet–American Relations and the Struggle for Power in the Kremlin, June–November, 1961*

(Baltimore: Johns Hopkins University Press, 1973), pp. 10–18, 49–66, 68–75; also Chapter VII.

204. See Khrushchev to Ulbricht, 30 Jan. 1961, in Harrison, "Ulbricht and the Concrete 'Rose'," appendix C.
205. Pervukhin to Gromyko, 19 May 1961, ibid., appendix D.
206. Harrison, "Ulbricht and the Concrete 'Rose'," p. 39. See also Gelb, *The Berlin Wall*, pp. 97–9.
207. Harrison, "Ulbricht and the Concrete 'Rose'," p. 44.
208. For speculation about Ulbricht's intentions, see ibid. 39–40; also Gelb, *The Berlin Wall*, pp. 99–100.
209. Harrison, "Ulbricht and the Concrete 'Rose'," p. 35.
210. Zubok, "Khrushchev's Motives and Soviet Diplomacy," pp. 17–18; Gelb, *The Berlin Wall*, pp. 144–5.
211. Yuli Kvitsinsky, *Vor dem Sturm: Erinnerungen eines Diplomaten* (Berlin: Siedler Verlag, 1993), p. 179, quoted in Harrison, "Ulbricht and the Concrete 'Rose'," p. 47.
212. Ulbricht speech to Warsaw Pact leaders, 3 Aug. 1961, ibid., appendix H.
213. Ibid. 47; Gelb, *The Berlin Wall*, p. 140. See also Randall Bennett Woods, *Fulbright: A Biography* (New York: Cambridge University Press, 1995), pp. 315–16.
214. McAdams, *Germany Divided*, pp. 50–1.
215. W. W. Rostow, *The Diffusion of Power: An Essay in Recent History* (New York: Macmillan, 1972), p. 231. See also Gelb, *The Berlin Wall*, pp. 117–18.
216. Memorandum, Rusk meeting with ambassadors, 9 Aug. 1961, *FRUS: 1961–3*, xiv. 319.
217. Rusk to US embassy in Bonn, 12 Aug. 1961, ibid. 324.
218. Gelb, *The Berlin Wall*, pp. 242–58, provides a good account of these events.
219. Beschloss, *The Crisis Years*, p. 278.
220. Ibid. 334–5.
221. Khrushchev to Ulbricht, 28 Sept. 1961, quoted in Harrison, "Ulbricht and the Concrete 'Rose'," p. 52.
222. Quoted in Beschloss, *The Crisis Years*, p. 225.
223. *Khrushchev Remembers: The Glasnost Tapes*, pp. 169–70.

CHAPTER VI

1. Quoted in Richard Pipes, *Russia Under the Bolshevik Regime* (New York: Norton, 1994), p. 199.
2. Quoted from the notes of I. V. Kovalev in Sergei N. Goncharov, John W. Lewis, and Xue Litai, *Uncertain Partners: Stalin, Mao, and the Korean War* (Stanford: Stanford University Press, 1994), pp. 71–2.
3. ORE 29–49, "Prospects for Soviet Control of a Communist China," 15 Apr. 1949, in Michael Warner, ed., *CIA Cold War Records: The CIA Under Harry Truman* (Washington: CIA, 1994), p. 280.
4. The fact that we still use the term "third world" illustrates how thoroughly the Cold War experience shaped our perception of that highly diverse majority of humanity that had nothing whatever to do with the origins of that conflict, and often little to do with its subsequent evolution. We run the risk, now, of treating international relations rather in the way the English used to treat their railway carriages, with a "first" and a "third" class, but no "second." In the

absence of a generally accepted alternative, however, I have reluctantly perpetuated this antiquated practice.

5. Melvyn P. Leffler, *A Preponderance of Power: National Security, the Truman
Administration, and the Cold War* (Stanford: Stanford University Press, 1992), p.
147. For an interesting illustration, compare what George F. Kennan said about
colonialism in his top secret "long telegram" from Moscow of 22 Feb. 1946
(*FRUS: 1946*, vi. 705) with the language of President Harry S. Truman's highly
public "Truman Doctrine" address to the Congress, delivered 12 Mar. 1947
(*Public Papers of the Presidents: Harry S. Truman: 1947* (Washington: Government
Printing Office, 1963), pp. 178–9).

6. A good summary is Ole R. Holsti, "Models of International Relations and Foreign
Policy," *Diplomatic History* 13 (Winter 1989), 27–9. For a valiant effort to write
Cold War history from this perspective, see Thomas J. McCormick, *America's
Half-Century: United States Foreign Policy in the Cold War* (Baltimore: Johns
Hopkins University Press, 1989).

7. The Sino-Soviet alliance, as well as an array of treaty commitments the United
States maintained with its own Latin American, Middle Eastern, and Asian allies,
suggests the difficulty of using race as a determinant of Cold War alignments.

8. For a more general discussion of power disparities as prerequisites for empire, see
Michael Doyle, *Empires* (Ithaca: Cornell University Press, 1986), pp. 30–47.

9. Robert J. McMahon, "Credibility and World Power: Exploring the Psychological
Dimension in Postwar American Diplomacy," *Diplomatic History* 15 (Fall 1991),
455–71. See also, for background, Jack Snyder, *Myths of Empire: Domestic Politics
and International Ambition* (Ithaca: Cornell University Press, 1991); Frank
Ninkovich, *Modernity and Power: A History of the Domino Theory in the Twentieth
Century* (Chicago: University of Chicago Press, 1994); and Charles A. Kupchan,
The Vulnerability of Empire (Ithaca: Cornell University Press, 1994).

10. Douglas J. Macdonald, *Adventures in Chaos: American Intervention for Reform in the
Third World* (Cambridge, Mass.: Harvard University Press, 1992), pp. 67, 70–3,
89–90. See also Robert O. Keohane, "The Big Influence of Small Allies," *Foreign
Policy* 2 (Spring 1971), 161–82.

11. A point made clearly in NSC-68, "United States Objectives and Programs for
National Security," 14 Apr. 1950, printed in Ernest R. May, ed., *American Cold
War Strategy: Interpreting NSC 68* (New York: St. Martin's Press, 1993), p. 35. See
also Eric Hobsbawm, *The Age of Extremes: A History of the World, 1914–1991* (New
York: Pantheon, 1994), pp. 376–7; and Richard Crockatt, *The Fifty Years War:
The United States and the Soviet Union in World Politics, 1941–1991* (New York:
Routledge, 1995), p. 91.

12. The CIA emphasized this argument in ORE 25–48, "The Breakup of the Colonial
Empires and Its Implications for US Security," 3 Sept. 1948, in Warner, ed., *The
CIA Under Harry Truman*, pp. 219–34.

13. Warren F. Kimball, *The Juggler: Franklin Roosevelt as Wartime Statesman*
(Princeton: Princeton University Press, 1991), pp. 127–57; Peter W. Rodman,
More Precious Than Peace: The Cold War and the Struggle for the Third World (New
York: Scribner's, 1994), pp. 38–44. For American anti-colonialism generally, see
Scott Bills, *Empire and Cold War: The Roots of US–Third World Antagonism* (New
York: St Martin's Press, 1990), pp. 5–10; and Wm. Roger Louis, *Imperialism at
Bay: The United States and the Decolonization of the British Empire, 1941–1945*
(New York: Oxford University Press, 1978), pp. 147–58.

14. See ibid. pp. 259–73; Robert Dallek, *Franklin D. Roosevelt and American Foreign
Policy, 1932–1945* (New York: Oxford University Press, 1979), pp. 536–7; Gary

R. Hess, *The United States' Emergence as a Southeast Asian Power, 1940–1950* (New York: Columbia University Press, 1987), pp. 121–58; and Walter LaFeber, "Roosevelt, Churchill, and Indochina: 1942–45," *American Historical Review* 80 (Dec. 1975), 1277–95.

15. George McT. Kahin, *Intervention: How America Became Involved in Vietnam* (New York: Doubleday, 1986), pp. 14–15; William J. Duiker, *U.S. Containment Policy and the Conflict in Indochina* (Stanford: Stanford University Press, 1994), p. 29.

16. Bills, *Empire and Cold War*, p. 58; Hess, *The United States' Emergence as a Southeast Asian Power*, pp. 163–75; Piero Gleijeses, *Shattered Hope: The Guatemalan Revolution and the United States, 1944–1954* (Princeton: Princeton University Press, 1991), pp. 22–3; and Robert J. McMahon, *Colonialism and the Cold War: The United States and the Struggle for Indonesian Independence, 1945–49* (Ithaca: Cornell University Press, 1981), pp. 56–7.

17. H. W. Brands, *The Specter of Neutralism: The United States and the Emergence of the Third World, 1947–1950* (New York: Columbia University Press, 1989), pp. 17–20; also Robert J. McMahon, *The Cold War on the Periphery: The United States, India, and Pakistan* (New York: Columbia University Press, 1993), pp. 14–17. For Indonesia, see McMahon, *Colonialism and the Cold War, passim*.

18. Peter L. Hahn, *The United States, Great Britain, and Egypt, 1945–1956: Strategy and Diplomacy in the Early Cold War* (Chapel Hill: University of North Carolina Press, 1991), pp. 64–92. One of the best personal accounts of Truman's decision to recognize Israel is Clark M. Clifford, with Richard M. Holbrooke, *Counsel to the President: A Memoir* (New York: Random House, 1991), pp. 3–25.

19. Marshall to Caffery, 3 Feb. 1947, *FRUS: 1947*, vi. 77–8.

20. See, on this point, a CIA assessment, ORE 25–48, "The Breakup of the Colonial Empires and the Implications for US Security," 3 Sept. 1948, in Warner, ed., *The CIA under Harry Truman*, p. 232.

21. Gaddis, *The Long Peace*, pp. 158–64. See also the more detailed discussion in Wilson D. Miscamble, *George F. Kennan and the Making of American Foreign Policy, 1947–1950* (Princeton: Princeton University Press, 1992), pp. 178–246.

22. Bills, *Empire and Cold War*, pp. 82–90; Hess, *The United States' Emergence as a Southeast Asian Power*, pp. 169–84. For American activities in Europe, see Peter Coleman, *The Liberal Conspiracy: The Congress for Cultural Freedom and the Struggle for the Mind of Postwar Europe* (New York: Free Press, 1989), esp. pp. 1–79; and Sally Pisani, *The CIA and the Marshall Plan* (Lawrence: University Press of Kansas, 1991).

23. Acheson executive session testimony, 12 Oct. 1949, US Congress, Senate Committee on Foreign Relations, *Historical Series: Reviews of the World Situation, 1949–1950* (Washington: Government Printing Office, 1974), p. 87.

24. Acheson to US Consulate General, Hanoi, 20 May 1949, *FRUS: 1949*, vii. 29.

25. Andrew J. Rotter, *The Path to Vietnam: Origins of the American Commitment to Southeast Asia* (Ithaca: Cornell University Press, 1987) makes this argument most clearly; but see also Ronald McGlothen, *Controlling the Waves: Dean Acheson and U.S. Foreign Policy in Asia* (New York: Norton, 1993).

26. Duiker, *U.S. Containment Policy and the Conflict in Indochina*, pp. 23–8, 37, 48. See also, on the larger relationship between European security and "third world" stability, Leffler, *A Preponderance of Power*, pp. 312, 346–7.

27. I have adapted this terminology from Macdonald, *Adventures in Chaos*, pp. 12–15.

28. Duiker, *U.S. Containment Policy and the Conflict in Indochina*, pp. 90–5.

29. To use the title of Wendell L. Willkie's best-selling book, *One World* (New York: Simon & Schuster, 1943), one of the best contemporaneous sources for American attitudes, at the time, about colonialism.

30. Louis Fischer, *The Life of Lenin* (New York: Harper & Row, 1964), pp. 526–7; Pipes, *Russia Under the Bolshevik Regime*, pp. 198–200.
31. For more on this, see Chapter III.
32. Ulam, *Stalin: The Man and His Era*, p. 362; McMahon, *Cold War on the Periphery*, pp. 45–6; Anita Inder Singh, *The Limits of British Influence: South Asia and the Anglo-American Relationship, 1947–56* (New York: St. Martin's Press, 1993), pp. 37–8. For a more sympathetic view of Soviet policy toward India under Stalin, see Surendra K. Gupta, *Stalin's Policy Towards India, 1946–1953* (New Delhi: South Asian Publishers, 1988).
33. Kahin, *Intervention*, pp. 21–2. See also Duiker, *U.S. Containment Policy and the Conflict in Indochina*, pp. 38–9; Rotter, *The Path to Vietnam*, p. 101; and, for a confirmation of this point from Soviet archival sources, Igor Bukharkin, "Moscow and Ho Chi Minh, 1945–1969," paper delivered at the CWIHP–University of Hong Kong conference on "The Cold War in Asia," Jan. 1996, pp. 3–7. Mark Bradley's paper for the same conference, "Constructing an Indigenous Regional Political Order in Southeast Asia: Vietnam and the Diplomacy of Revolutionary Nationalism, 1946–1949," documents Ho's search for diplomatic recognition from India and Southeast Asia.
34. Stalin to the Democratic Party of Azerbaijan, 8 May 1946, quoted in Vladislav Zubok and Constantine Pleshakov, *Inside the Kremlin's Cold War: From Stalin to Khrushchev* (Cambridge, Mass.: Harvard University Press, 1996), p. 45.
35. Tanagawa Yoshiko, "The Cominform and Southeast Asia," in Yonosuke Nagai and Akira Iriye, eds., *The Origins of the Cold War in Asia* (Tokyo: University of Tokyo Press,1977), pp. 362–77. For a more recent assessment, Duiker, *U.S. Containment Policy and the Conflict in Indochina*, pp. 63–5; also Gavriel Ra'anan, *International Policy Formation in the USSR: Factional "Debates" during the Zhdanovschina* (Hamden, Conn.: Archon Books, 1983), pp. 111–15.
36. ORE-25–48, "The Breakup of the Colonial Empires," 3 Sept. 1948, in Warner, ed., *The CIA under Harry Truman*, p. 229.
37. The primary source is Shi Zhe, "With Mao and Stalin: The Reminiscences of Mao's Interpreter: Part II: Liu Shaoqi in Moscow," trans. Chen Jian, *Chinese Historians* 6 (Spring 1993), 82–6. For more on this meeting and its significance, see Chapter III.
38. I. V. Kovalev interview with S. N. Goncharov, "Stalin's Dialogue with Mao Zedong," *Journal of Northeast Asian Studies* 10 (Winter 1991), 61.
39. Quoted in Goncharov et al., *Uncertain Partners*, p. 105. See also ibid. 78.
40. Ibid. 105–8; also Shu Guang Zhang, *Deterrence and Strategic Culture: Chinese–American Confrontations, 1949–1958* (Ithaca: Cornell University Press, 1992), p. 172.
41. Ibid. 172–3. See also *Khrushchev Remembers: The Glasnost Tapes*, trans. and ed. Jerrold L. Schecter and Vyacheslav V. Luchkov (Boston: Little, Brown, 1990), pp. 155–6; Chen Jian, "China and the First Indo-China War, 1950–54," *China Quarterly* #133 (Mar. 1993), pp. 88–9; and Qiang Zhai, "Transplanting the Chinese Model: Chinese Military Advisers and the First Vietnam War, 1950–1954," *Journal of Military History* 57 (Oct. 1993), 692–3.
42. John W. Garver, "Polemics, Paradigms, Responsibility, and the Origins of the U.S.–PRC Confrontation in the 1950s," *Journal of American–East Asian Relations* 3 (Spring 1994), 13–14. Garver here is drawing on the influential work of Theda Skocpol, *States and Social Revolutions: A Comparative Analysis of France, Russia, and China* (Cambridge: Cambridge University Press, 1979), esp. pp. 169–71. See also, on the ideological roots of "third world" revolutions, Forrest D. Colburn,

The Vogue of Revolution in Poor Countries (Princeton: Princeton University Press, 1994).

43. Garver, "Polemics, Paradigms, Responsibility," p. 13 (emphases added).

44. See Chapter III.

45. Zhai, "Transplanting the Chinese Model," pp. 694–6; Chen, "China and the First Indo-China War," p. 90; Zhang, *Deterrence and Strategic Culture*, p. 174.

46. Quoted in Chen, "China and the First Indo-China War," p. 87. See also Zhai, "Transplanting the Chinese Model," pp. 690–2; Zhang, *Deterrence and Strategic Culture*, p. 170; and Duiker, *U.S. Containment Policy and the Conflict in Indochina*, pp. 88–9.

47. Chen, "China and the First Indo-China War," pp. 91–2. See also Zhang, *Deterrence and Strategic Culture*, pp. 174–6.

48. See Chapter III.

49. Zhai, "Transplanting the Chinese Model," pp. 698–707; Chen, "China and the First Indo-China War," pp. 93–7.

50. Quoted in Zhang, *Deterrence and Strategic Culture*, pp. 173–4.

51. Ibid. 181–2.

52. Quoted in Chen, "China and the First Indo-China War," pp. 102–3. See also Zhai, "Transplanting the Chinese Model," pp. 707–11; and Zhang, *Deterrence and Strategic Culture*, pp. 183–4.

53. Chen, "China and the First Indo-China War," pp. 105–6; Zhai, "Transplanting the Chinese Model," pp. 696–8, 712. Remarkably enough, Zhou Enlai admitted to Ho Chi Minh in July 1954 that the Chinese had only just learned that there were distinctive Vietnamese, Laotian, and Khmer peoples in Indochina. "We have all along believed that it was one country . . . and that [the] Khmer [were] a minority nation" (Zhou–Ho meeting, Liuzhou, 3 July 1954, quoted in Li Haiwen, "Restoring Peace in Indochina at the Geneva Conference," paper prepared for the CWIHP–University of Hong Kong conference on "The Cold War in Asia," Jan. 1996, p. 6).

54. See Duiker, *U.S. Containment Policy and the Conflict in Indochina*, p. 193; also Qiang Zhai, *The Dragon, the Lion, and the Eagle: Chinese–British–American Relations, 1949–1958* (Kent, OH: Kent State University Press, 1994), p. 143.

55. Chinese preparations for this conference are discussed in ibid. 139–40.

56. Ibid. 142–3; Zhang, *Deterrence and Strategic Culture*, pp. 184–5. The most thorough assessment of Eisenhower's actual intentions with respect to this situation is Melanie Billings-Yun, *Decision Against War: Eisenhower and Dien Bien Phu, 1954* (New York: Columbia University Press, 1988).

57. Chen, "China and the First Indo-China War," pp. 104, 107, 109; Zhai, *The Dragon, the Lion, and the Eagle*, pp. 140–1.

58. Transcript, Zhou Enlai–Ho Chi Minh meeting, Liuzhou, 3 July 1954, quoted in Li, "Restoring Peace in Indochina," pp. 6–7.

59. See Hahn, *The United States, Great Britain, and Egypt*, p. 90.

60. Bruce Robellet Kuniholm, *The Origins of the Cold War in the Near East: Great Power Conflict and Diplomacy in Iran, Turkey, and Greece* (Princeton: Princeton University Press, 1980), pp. 304–50, 383–99; Kuross A. Samii, *Involvement by Invitation: American Strategies of Containment in Iran* (University Park: Pennsylvania State University Press, 1987), pp. 69–94. New information on Soviet–Tudeh Party relations is contained in Natalia I. Yegorova, " 'The Iran Crisis' of 1945–1946: A View from the Russian Archives," CWIHP Working Paper 15 (May 1996).

61. Albert Resis, ed., *Molotov Remembers: Inside Kremlin Politics: Conversations with*

Felix Chuev (Chicago: Ivan R. Dee, 1993), p. 73. See also, on the Turkish crisis, Kuniholm, *The Origins of the Cold War in the Near East*, pp. 355–78; Zubok and Pleshakov, *Inside the Kremlin's Cold War*, pp. 92–3; and Melvyn P. Leffler, "Strategy, Diplomacy, and the Cold War: The United States, Turkey, and NATO, 1945–1952," *Journal of American History* 71 (Mar. 1985), 807–25.

62. Galia Golan, *Soviet Policies in the Middle East from World War Two to Gorbachev* (Cambridge: Cambridge University Press, 1990), pp. 29–34; Alexei Vassiliev, *Russian Policy in the Middle East: From Messianism to Pragmatism* (Reading, Berks.: Ithaca Press, 1993), pp. 16–19.

63. Quoted in Hahn, *The United States, Great Britain, and Egypt*, p. 50. For more on Henderson's concern about colonialism, see H. W. Brands, *Inside the Cold War: Loy Henderson and the Rise of the American Empire, 1918–1961* (New York: Oxford University Press, 1991), pp. 122–3.

64. PPS/21, "The Problem of Palestine," 11 Feb. 1948, *The State Department Policy Planning Staff Papers* (New York: Garland, 1983), ii. 84. See also David Schoen-baum, *The United States and the State of Israel* (New York: Oxford University Press, 1993), pp. 34–62.

65. Kennan memorandum, 21 May 1948, *FRUS: 1948*, v. 1021.

66. Aaron David Miller, *Search for Security: Saudi Arabian Oil and American Foreign Policy, 1939–1949* (Chapel Hill: University of North Carolina Press, 1980), pp. 177–84.

67. Hahn, *The United States, Great Britain, and Egypt*, pp. 52–4.

68. Ibid. 102. See also Alonzo L. Hamby, *Man of the People: A Life of Harry S. Truman* (New York: Oxford University Press, 1995), p. 537.

69. *Khrushchev Remembers*, trans. and ed. Strobe Talbott (New York: Little, Brown, 1970), p. 475. See also Hough, *The Struggle for the Third World*, pp. 36–7; and Vassiliev, *Russian Policy in the Middle East*, pp. 19–20.

70. Rami Ginat, *The Soviet Union and Egypt, 1945–1955* (London: Frank Cass, 1993), pp. 29, 41–2, 45–6.

71. Ibid. 38–9; Golan, *Soviet Policies in the Middle East*, pp. 34–41.

72. This summary reflects contemporary American assessments at the time, as e.g. in Philip Jessup to Marshall, 1 July 1948, *FRUS: 1948*, v. 1182–3; but see also the analysis in Ginat, *The Soviet Union and Egypt*, pp. 77–88.

73. Marshall memorandum of conversation, 12 May 1948, *FRUS: 1948*, v. 975.

74. Quoted in Ginat, *The Soviet Union and Egypt*, p. 85.

75. *Khrushchev Remembers*, p. 476. See also Ginat, *The Soviet Union and Egypt*, pp. 105, 119–20, 156–60; and Fawaz A. Gerges, *The Superpowers and the Middle East: Regional and International Politics, 1955–1967* (Boulder: Westview, 1994), pp. 23–4.

76. Quoted in ibid. 45.

77. Vladislav M. Zubok, "Soviet Intelligence and the Cold War: The 'Small' Committee of Information, 1952–53," *Diplomatic History* 19 (Summer 1995), 466–8. For earlier speculation on the reasons for Soviet coolness toward Mossadeq, see Golan, *Soviet Policies in the Middle East*, p. 177.

78. Samii, *Involvement by Invitation*, pp. 141–3. For Egypt, see Joel Gordon, *Nasser's Blessed Movement: Egypt's Free Officers and the July Revolution* (New York: Oxford University Press, 1992), pp. 161–8.

79. The phrase, attributed to Sir James Mackintosh (1765–1832), is a slightly more elegant restatement of the old British principle of "muddling through." There is, at times, much to be said for it. The difficulty, of course, is determining which times those are.

80. Policy Planning Staff memorandum, 21 May 1952, *FRUS: 1952–4*, ix. 233.
81. Minutes, State Department–Joint Chiefs of Staff meeting, 18 June 1952, ibid. 237.
82. The dilemma is perceptively analyzed in Macdonald, *Adventures in Chaos*, pp. 249–57, although I am skeptical about his argument that Republicans tend more often to try to bolster overseas allies while Democrats tend to try to reform them.
83. Hahn, *The United States, Great Britain, and Egypt*, pp. 109–16. See also Peter L. Hahn, "Containment and Egyptian Nationalism: The Unsuccessful Effort to Establish the Middle East Command, 1950–53," *Diplomatic History* 11 (Winter 1987), 23–40.
84. Hahn, *The United States, Great Britain, and Egypt*, pp. 122–30; Amin Hewedy, "Nasser and the Crisis of 1956," in Wm. Roger Louis and Roger Owen, eds., *Suez 1956: The Crisis and Its Consequences* (New York: Oxford University Press, 1989), pp. 163–4.
85. Quoted in Hahn, *The United States, Great Britain, and Egypt*, p. 159.
86. Roger Makins to Anthony Eden, 4 Oct. 1956, quoted in Wm. Roger Louis, "Dulles, Suez, and the British," in Richard Immerman, ed., *John Foster Dulles and the Diplomacy of the Cold War* (Princeton: Princeton University Press, 1990), p. 134. For the roots of Dulles's anti-colonialism, see Ronald W. Pruessen, *John Foster Dulles: The Road to Power* (New York: Free Press, 1982), pp. 409–10, 446–8, 504–6.
87. Dulles–Naguib conversation, 11 May 1953, *FRUS: 1952–4*, ix. 15–17 (emphasis in original).
88. Gerges, *The Superpowers and the Middle East*, pp. 54–5, provides a useful discussion of global vs. regional perspectives with respect to Egypt.
89. Dulles–Nasser conversation, 12 May 1953, ibid. 22–3 (emphasis in original).
90. Minutes, NSC meetings, 1 June and 9 July 1953, ibid. 381, 395.
91. Gordon, *Nasser's Blessed Movement*, pp. 191–7; Keith Kyle, *Suez* (New York: St. Martin's Press, 1991), pp. 54–6; and Ali E. Hillai Dessouki, "Nasser and the Struggle for Independence," in Louis and Owen, eds., *Suez 1956*, esp. pp. 31–7.
92. Hahn, *The United States, Great Britain, and Egypt*, pp. 184–5; Gerges, *The Superpowers and the Middle East*, p. 25.
93. Miles Copeland, *The Game of Nations: The Amorality of Power Politics* (New York: Simon & Schuster, 1969) pp. 177–8.
94. Dulles to US Embassy, Ankara, 26 Mar. 1955, and to US Embassy, Cairo, 30 Mar. 1955, ibid. 43, 45.
95. McMahon, *Cold War on the Periphery*, pp. 39–42, 162–76, 194–5. For more on American policy toward Yugoslavia, India, and the non-aligned movement, see Brands, *The Specter of Neutralism*, pp. 13–219.
96. Ibid. 264–5; Ginat, *The Soviet Union and* Egypt, pp. 191–4.
97. This document, along with the account of the Nasser–Zhou conversation, appears in the memoir of Nasser's confidant, Mohamed Heikal, *The Sphinx and the Commissar: The Rise and Fall of Soviet Influence in the Middle East* (New York: Harper & Row, 1978), pp. 57–9, who claims that the Chinese provided a copy to the Egyptians after the Sino-Soviet conflict broke out. Heikal is not always a reliable source, but this report seems consistent with what the Chinese were saying about support for national liberation movements elsewhere, as we have seen with respect to Indochina.
98. Golan, *Soviet Policies in the Middle East*, pp. 45–6; Ginat, *The Soviet Union and Egypt*, pp. 207–9.
99. Ibid. 160–90; Gerges, *The Superpowers and the Middle East*, p. 34.

100. *Khrushchev Remembers*, p. 477.
101. Ginat, *The Soviet Union and Egypt*, pp. 207–8; Hough, *The Struggle for the Third World*, pp. 37, 149–51, 228–9.
102. As it happened, Khrushchev did not actually make the visit until May 1964, only a few months before he was deposed. For a recent account, see Sergei Khrushchev, *Khrushchev on Khrushchev: An Inside Account of the Man and His Era*, ed. and trans. William Taubman (Boston: Little, Brown, 1990), pp. 58–62.
103. Hoover to Dulles, 11 July 1955, *FRUS: 1955–7*, xii. 132.
104. Dulles–Harold Macmillan conversation, 26 Sept. 1955, ibid. 517–19.
105. Hahn, *The United States, Great Britain, and Egypt*, p. 194.
106. Kyle, *Suez*, pp. 148–52. See also Macmillan's conversation with Dulles of 26 Sept. 1955, at which the British Foreign Secretary acknowledged that "[w]e could make life impossible for Nasser and ultimately bring about his fall by various pressures" (*FRUS: 1955–7*, xiv. 518). For growing American disillusionment, see Robert R. Bowie, "Eisenhower, Dulles, and the Suez Crisis," in Louis and Owen, eds., *Suez 1956*, pp. 190–2.
107. Dulles–Ahmed Hussein conversation, 19 July 1956, *FRUS: 1955–7*, xv. 867–73. See also Bowie, "Eisenhower, Dulles, and the Suez Crisis," pp. 192–6; and Diane B. Kunz, *The Economic Diplomacy of the Suez Crisis* (Chapel Hill: University of North Carolina Press, 1991), pp. 68–72.
108. Kyle, *Suez*, pp. 128–30.
109. Eisenhower Diary, 8 Mar. 1956, in Robert H. Ferrell, ed., *The Eisenhower Diaries* (New York: Norton, 1981) p. 319.
110. Dulles–Allen Dulles telephone conversation, 19 July 1956, *FRUS: 1955–7*, xv. 866.
111. For more on this, see John Lewis Gaddis, *The Long Peace: Inquiries into the History of the Cold War* (New York: Oxford University Press, 1987), esp. p. 192.
112. Ibid. 174–87. See also David Allan Mayers, *Cracking the Monolith: U.S. Policy Against the Sino-Soviet Alliance, 1949–1955* (Baton Rouge: Louisiana State University Press, 1986).
113. Kunz, *Economic Diplomacy of the Suez Crisis*, p. 194. The most comprehensive account is Kyle, *Suez*; but see also the shorter accounts by Kyle, Maurice Vaisse, and Mordecai Bar-Or in Louis and Owen, eds., *Suez 1956*, pp. 103–60, as well as Wm. Roger Louis, "The Tragedy of the Anglo-Egyptian Settlement of 1954," ibid. 43–71.
114. Bowie, "Eisenhower, Dulles, and the Suez Crisis," pp. 207–8; Kyle, *Suez*, pp. 300–1.
115. Gerges, *The Superpowers and the Middle East*, pp. 65–6, provides a good summary of the reasons why Eisenhower and Dulles took this position. For events in Eastern Europe, see Chapter VII.
116. See Rashid Khalidi, "Consequences of the Suez Crisis in the Arab World," in Louis and Owen, eds., *Suez 1956*, p. 378. For Washington's economic pressure, see Kunz, *Economic Diplomacy of the Suez Crisis, passim*.
117. John C. Campbell, "The Twin Crises of Hungary and Suez," in Louis and Owen, eds., *Suez: 1956*, pp. 246–7; Kyle, *Suez*, pp. 456–60. See also, for an Egyptian perspective, Heikal, *The Sphinx and the Commissar*, p. 72. There is a further discussion of Khrushchev's nuclear threat in Chapter VIII.
118. Gerges, *The Superpowers and the Middle East*, p. 79.
119. *Khrushchev Remembers*, pp. 475, 480.
120. Gerges, *The Superpowers and the Middle East*, p. 80. Kunz, *Economic Diplomacy of the Suez Crisis*, p. 179, makes the often-forgotten point that the United States also applied economic sanctions against Egypt.

121. Ibid. 170.
122. Dulles memorandum, 16 Nov. 1956, *FRUS: 1955–7*, xii. 330–1 (Emphases added).
123. Dulles conversation with Turkish, Iraqi, Iranian, and Pakistani ambassadors, 4 Dec. 1956, ibid. 370.
124. Kunz, *Economic Diplomacy of the Suez Crisis*, p. 158.
125. Eisenhower–Dulles telephone conversation, 6 Dec. 1956, *FRUS: 1955–7*, xii. 395–6. For the Eisenhower–Dulles relationship on Middle Eastern issues, see Bowie, "Eisenhower, Dulles, and the Suez Crisis," pp. 213–14.
126. *Public Papers of the President of the United States: Dwight D. Eisenhower, 1957* (Washington: Government Printing Office, 1958), pp. 6–16. For further background on the Eisenhower Doctrine, see Cecil V. Crabb, Jr., *The Doctrines of American Foreign Policy: Their Meaning, Role, and Future* (Baton Rouge: Louisiana State University Press, 1982), pp. 153–92; and Thomas G. Paterson, *Meeting the Communist Threat: Truman to Reagan* (New York: Oxford University Press, 1988), pp. 159–90.
127. Ibid. 180–2; Kunz, *Economic Diplomacy of the Suez* Crisis, p. 160. The vote was 72–19 in the Senate and 350–60 in the House.
128. NSC minutes, 11 Jan. 1957, *FRUS: 1955–7*, xii. 440.
129. NIE 30–2–57, "Near East Developments Affecting US Interests," 8 Oct. 1957, ibid. 609.
130. State Department Staff Study, "United States Objectives and Policies With Respect to the Near East," 30 Oct. 1957, ibid. 623.
131. Quoted in Heikal, *The Sphinx and the Commissar*, p. 82.
132. For the accounts of two jaded CIA agents, see Copeland, *The Game of Nations*, p. 239 and Wilbur Crane Eveland, *Ropes of Sand: America's Failure in the Middle East* (New York: Norton, 1980), pp. 293–5.
133. Gerges, *The Superpowers in the Middle East*, pp. 102–22, provides a recent review of the Lebanon crisis; but see also Stephen J. Genco, "The Eisenhower Doctrine: Deterrence in the Middle East, 1957–1958," in Alexander L. George and Richard Smoke, *Deterrence in American Foreign Policy: Theory and Practice* (New York: Columbia University Press, 1974), pp. 308–62, despite its age still a valuable account. There is also a brief but perceptive analysis in McMahon, "Credibility and World Power," pp. 464–5.
134. Eveland, *Ropes of Sand*, p. 299.
135. Minutes, NSC meeting, 31 July 1958, *FRUS: 1958–60*, xii. 129, 132.
136. NSC 5820/1, "U.S. Policy Toward the Near East," 4 Nov. 1958, ibid. 189.
137. Heikal, *The Sphinx and the Commissar*, p. 65.
138. See, on this important point, ibid. 16–17. I have also benefited from reading John Kevin Burns, "A Lesson in Nationalism: United States Relations with Egypt During the Eisenhower Presidency, 1953–1960" (MA Thesis, University of Maryland Baltimore County, 1994).
139. Gerges, *The Superpowers and the Middle East*, pp. 80–1.
140. Heikal, *The Sphinx and the Commissar*, p. 84.
141. For reasons to be discussed in Chapters VII and VIII.
142. *Khrushchev Remembers*, p. 488; Khrushchev, *Khrushchev on Khrushchev*, p. 58.
143. I have drawn these points primarily from Miller, *Soviet Relations with Latin America*, esp. pp. 1–50.
144. Gaddis Smith, *The Last Years of the Monroe Doctrine, 1945–1993* (New York: Hill & Wang, 1994), pp. 63–4.
145. Ibid. 61–2. See also Vernon A. Walters, *Silent Missions* (Garden City, NY:

Doubleday, 1978), pp. 150–69; Forrest C. Pogue, *George C. Marshall: Statesman, 1945–1959* (New York: Viking, 1987), pp. 385–93; and Robert E. Quirk, *Fidel Castro* (New York: Norton, 1993), pp. 25–6. I am also indebted to one of my students, Molly Smith, for her work on the *Bogotázo*.

146. Kennan's report is printed in *FRUS: 1950*, ii. 598–624. See also George F. Kennan, *Memoirs: 1925–1950* (Boston: Atlantic Little, Brown, 1967), pp. 476–84.

147. Here I differ with Smith, *The Last Years of the Monroe Doctrine*, pp. 65–90, who links the Kennan report to NSC-68 and sees in it a blueprint for subsequent American covert operations in Guatemala and elsewhere.

148. I am following here primarily Gleijeses, *Shattered Hope*, esp. pp. 140–8, 361–3, 380–1; but see also Richard H. Immerman, *The CIA in Guatemala: The Foreign Policy of Intervention* (Austin: University of Texas Press, 1982), and, for an account that attaches greater importance to the United Fruit Company's role, Stephen Schlesinger and Stephen Kinzer, *Bitter Fruit: The Untold Story of the American Coup in Guatemala* (Garden City, NY: Doubleday, 1982). Dulles's history lesson is quoted in Smith, *The Last Years of the Monroe Doctrine*, p. 87.

149. See Miller, *Soviet Relations with Latin America*, pp. 25–7.

150. Gleijeses, *Shattered Hope*, pp. 141, 147.

151. Ibid. 280–3, 295–304; also Herbert S. Dinerstein, *The Making of a Missile Crisis: October 1962* (Baltimore: Johns Hopkins University Press, 1976), pp. 10–13.

152. Ibid. 184–8.

153. Immerman, *The CIA in Guatemala*, p. 186.

154. The best recent account of these events is Quirk, *Fidel Castro*, pp. 87–209. But see also, for the impact of the Guatemalan affair on Castro's revolution, Dinerstein, *The Making of a Missile Crisis*, pp. 18–20; Immerman, *The CIA in Guatemala*, pp. 194–7; and Gleijeses, *Shattered Hope*, pp. 372–3.

155. Thomas G. Paterson, *Contesting Castro: The United States and the Triumph of the Cuban Revolution* (New York: Oxford University Press, 1994), pp. 108–10, 126–8, 137–8.

156. Walters, *Silent Missions*, pp. 313–37; Stephen E. Ambrose, *Nixon: The Education of a Politician, 1913–1962* (New York: Simon & Schuster, 1987), pp. 456–82.

157. Minutes, Cabinet meeting, 16 May 1958, *FRUS: 1958–60*, v. 238.

158. Dulles to Eisenhower, 7 Jan. 1959, ibid. vi. 347.

159. This memorable footage appears in part one of the 1992 BBC television documentary, "The Cuban Missile Crisis."

160. Eisenhower–Herter conversation, 18 Apr. 1959, *FRUS: 1958–60*, vi. 475.

161. Nixon memorandum, 19 Apr. 1959, ibid. 476. For a similar State Department assessment, dated 23 Apr. 1959, see ibid. 482–3.

162. I have borrowed the terms "balancing" and "bandwagoning" from international relations theory, although they are normally used there to characterize the behavior of states in an anarchic environment, not leaders in a relatively structured one. See Kenneth Waltz, *Theory of International Politics* (New York: Random House, 1979), pp. 125–6; and Stephen Walt, *The Origins of Alliances* (Ithaca: Cornell University Press, 1987), pp. 17–33. Walt goes on to discuss the role of ideology in the formation of alliances (ibid. 33–40), but he does not do so within the context of balancing and bandwagoning.

163. Quirk, *Fidel Castro*, esp. pp. 26–30, 54, 64, 160, 182. For Castro's addiction to baseball, see ibid. 199–201, 260; also Paterson, *Contesting Castro*, pp. 49–51.

164. One possibly apocryphal story from this period has Castro, having decided to take over the Cuban Bank, asking his advisers whether there was an economist

present. Guevara raised his hand, and Castro put him in charge of the bank. Later, Fidel commented: "I didn't know you were an economist." "Oh," Che replied, "I thought you said a communist." It is perhaps significant that this story was told in the National Security Council on 10 Mar. 1960 (*FRUS: 1958–60*, vi. 836); but that it also shows up in Andrei Gromyko, *Memoirs*, trans. Harold Shukman (New York: Doubleday, 1989), p. 183.

165. I am following, here, the analysis in Quirk, *Fidel Castro*, pp. 247–8; but see also *Khrushchev Remembers*, pp. 541–2.
166. Hough, *The Struggle for the Third World*, p. 72.
167. *Khrushchev Remembers*, p. 540. See also Dinerstein, *The Making of a Missile Crisis*, pp. 36–47; Quirk, *Fidel Castro*, pp. 290–1; and Paterson, *Contesting Castro*, pp. 28, 33, 71–2, 107–8, 142–6.
168. Quirk, *Fidel Castro*, pp. 273–4, 290–2; also *Khrushchev Remembers*, pp. 541–3.
169. Quirk, *Fidel Castro*, p. 292.
170. Quoted in ibid. 294.
171. Eisenhower to Harold Macmillan, 11 July 1960, *FRUS: 1958–60*, vi. 1003.
172. Dean Rusk, as told to Richard Rusk, *As I Saw It* (New York: Norton, 1990), p. 245. See also Richard Reeves, *President Kennedy: Profile of Power* (New York: Simon & Schuster, 1993), p. 105.
173. Herter to Selwyn Lloyd, 21 Feb. 1960, *FRUS: 1958–60*, vi. 806.
174. 5412 Committee memorandum, "A Program of Covert Action Against the Castro Regime," 16 Mar. 1960, ibid. 850–1.
175. Eisenhower to Macmillan, 11 July 1960, ibid. 1002–3.
176. Macmillan to Eisenhower, 22 July 1960, ibid. 1005.
177. See Kyle, *Suez*, p. 257.
178. Dinerstein, *The Making of a Missile Crisis*, pp. 82, 91; also Quirk, *Fidel Castro*, pp. 321–2; and Smith, *The Last Years of the Monroe Doctrine*, pp. 100–1.
179. Hough, *The Struggle for the Third World*, pp. 156–62.
180. Quirk, *Fidel Castro*, pp. 334–8, gives a vivid account. Khrushchev's own reminiscences appear in *Khrushchev Remembers: The Last Testament*, pp. 477–9.
181. Quirk, *Fidel Castro*, pp. 339–42. Gromyko's remark is in his *Memoirs*, p. 158.
182. Excerpts from Khrushchev's speech appear in Alvin Z. Rubinstein, ed., *The Foreign Policy of the Soviet Union*, 3rd edn. (New York: Random House, 1972), pp. 266–9.
183. Michael R. Beschloss, *The Crisis Years: Kennedy and Khrushchev, 1960–1963* (New York: HarperCollins, 1991), pp. 60–1.
184. *Public Papers of the Presidents: John F. Kennedy, 1961* (Washington: Government Printing Office, 1962), pp. 22–3.
185. See Beschloss, *The Crisis Years*, p. 63; also John Lewis Gaddis, *Strategies of Containment: A Critical Appraisal of Postwar American National Security Policy* (New York: Oxford University Press, 1982), pp. 198–9.
186. W. W. Rostow, *The Stages of Economic Growth: A Non-Communist Manifesto* (Cambridge: Cambridge University Press, 1960), esp. pp. 162–4. For a sharp critique of "development theory" as it evolved in the 1950s, see D. Michael Shafer, *Deadly Paradigms: The Failure of U.S. Counterinsurgency Policy* (Princeton: Princeton University Press, 1988).
187. The standard account has long been Peter Wyden, *The Bay of Pigs: The Untold Story* (New York: Simon & Schuster, 1979). But see also Richard M. Bissell, Jr., with Jonathan E. Lewis and Frances T. Pudlo, *Reflections of a Cold Warrior: From Yalta to the Bay of Pigs* (New Haven: Yale University Press, 1996), pp. 152–99.
188. Quoted in Reeves, *President Kennedy*, pp. 163–5.

189. See Chapter V.
190. *Khrushchev Remembers*, pp. 545–6. See also *Khrushchev Remembers: The Last Testament*, pp. 509–11; and *Khrushchev Remembers: The Glasnost Tapes*, p. 170.
191. "Ghost of a Kennedy–C.I.A. Plot Has Come Back to Haunt Clinton," *New York Times*, 30 Oct. 1994. See also Tim Weiner, "Keeping the Secrets That Everybody Knows," ibid.; and, for background on the Kennedy administration and British Guyana, Arthur M. Schlesinger, Jr., *A Thousand Days: John F. Kennedy in the White House* (Boston: Houghton Mifflin, 1965), pp. 773–9; and Cary Fraser, *Ambivalent Anti-Colonialism: The United States and the Genesis of West Indian Independence, 1940–1964* (Westport, Conn.: Greenwood Press, 1994), pp. 124–202. I am also indebted to a former Oxford student of mine, Jane Sillery, for information on this episode.
192. For reasons to be discussed in Chapter VII.

CHAPTER VII

1. Joseph Stalin, *Economic Problems of Socialism in the USSR* (1952), in Bruce Franklin, ed., *The Essential Stalin: Major Theoretical Writings, 1905–52* (Garden City, NY: Anchor Books, 1972), pp. 469–71. I am indebted, for this quotation, to Vladislav Zubok and Constantine Pleshakov.
2. Quoted in William J. Tompson, *Khrushchev: A Political Life* (New York: St. Martin's Press, 1995), p. 123.
3. Robert S. McNamara, with Brian VanDeMark, *In Retrospect: The Tragedy and Lessons of Vietnam* (New York: Random House, 1995), p. xvi. I have developed the metaphor of immunization more fully in *Strategies of Containment: A Critical Appraisal of Postwar American National Security Policy* (New York: Oxford University Press, 1982), p. 223.
4. For a valiant attempt to explain how such a view arose, see D. Michael Shafer, *Deadly Paradigms: The Failure of U.S. Counterinsurgency Policy* (Princeton: Princeton University Press, 1988), esp. pp. 43–132.
5. See Robert C. Tucker, *Stalin in Power: The Revolution from Above, 1928–1949* (New York: Norton, 1990) pp. 46–50, 345; also William Curti Wohlforth, *The Elusive Balance: Power and Perceptions During the Cold War* (Ithaca: Cornell University Press, 1993), pp. 77–8, and Tony Smith, *Thinking Like a Communist: State and Legitimacy in the Soviet Union, China, and Cuba* (New York: Norton, 1987), pp. 24, 45–8.
6. Robert A. Pollard, *Economic Security and the Origins of the Cold War, 1945–1950* (New York: Columbia University Press, 1985), pp. 7–9, 14–16; John Lewis Gaddis, *The United States and the Origins of the Cold War, 1941–1947* (New York: Columbia University Press, 1972), pp. 18–22; Eric Hobsbawm, *The Age of Extremes: A History of the World, 1914–1991* (New York: Pantheon, 1994), pp. 230–1.
7. See Martin Malia, *The Soviet Tragedy: A History of Socialism in Russia, 1917–1991* (New York: Free Press, 1994), p. 300.
8. Calculated in current prices, the United States GNP went from $126 billion in 1941 to $214 billion in 1945. Even in constant (1929) prices, the increase was impressive: from $139 billion to $181 billion (*The Statistical History of the United States from Colonial Times to the Present* (Stamford, Conn.: Fairfield Publishers, 1965), p. 139).

9. Malia, *The Soviet Tragedy*, pp. 201–9. See also Adam B. Ulam, *The Communists: The Story of Power and Lost Illusions, 1948–1991* (New York: Scribner's, 1992), pp. 6–7.

10. Gaddis, *The United States and the Origins of the Cold War*, pp. 12–14.

11. Pollard, *Economic Security and the Origins of the Cold War*, pp. 4, 10–11.

12. Quoted in Alfred E. Eckes, Jr., *A Search for Solvency: Bretton Woods and the International Monetary System, 1941–1971* (Austin: University of Texas Press, 1975), p. 127.

13. Henry R. Nau, *The Myth of America's Decline: Leading the World Economy into the 1990s* (New York: Oxford University Press, 1990), pp. 38–9, and Hobsbawm, *The Age of Extremes*, pp. 270–4, provide succinct overviews. For the Bretton Woods conference itself, see Eckes, *A Search for Solvency*, pp. 107–64.

14. Ibid. 141.

15. W. Averell Harriman and Elie Abel, *Special Envoy to Churchill and Stalin, 1941–1946* (New York: Random House, 1975), p. 384. See also Pollard, *Economic Security and the Origins of the Cold War*, p. 51; and Thomas G. Paterson, *Soviet–American Confrontation: Postwar Reconstruction and the Origins of the Cold War* (Baltimore: Johns Hopkins University Press, 1973), pp. 37–40.

16. Harriman and Abel, *Special Envoy*, p. 385.

17. Pollard, *Economic Security and the Origins of the Cold War*, pp. 50–3. See also, for the relationship of the Russian loan question to Lend-Lease, George C. Herring, Jr., *Aid to Russia, 1941–1946: Strategy, Diplomacy, the Origins of the Cold War* (New York: Columbia University Press, 1973).

18. Memorandum of 26 Dec. 1945, printed in Harold James and Marzenna James, "The Origins of the Cold War: Some New Documents," *Historical Journal* 37 (1994), 620–1.

19. Soviet foreign ministry memorandum, 29 Dec. 1945, printed ibid. 619. This document also raised the possibility that if it became a member, the Soviet Union might become liable for the debts of other participating states, and might not be able to control the uses of the gold it would have to contribute.

20. See Eckes, *A Search for Solvency*, pp. 141–6.

21. George F. Kennan, *Memoirs: 1925–1950* (Boston: Atlantic Little, Brown, 1967), pp. 292–3.

22. Ibid. 293. Kennan's actual telegram responded to another inquiry from the State Department, about the implications of Stalin's election speech of 9 Feb. 1946. He clearly had the inquiry about Bretton Woods in mind, though. For the relevant documentation, see *FRUS: 1946*, vi. 696 n.

23. Kennan to Byrnes, 22 Feb. 1946, ibid. 703.

24. Nau, *The Myth of America's Decline*, pp. 89–91. See also Dean Acheson, *Present at the Creation: My Years in the State Department* (New York: Norton, 1969), pp. 725–8.

25. For the influence of Bretton Woods on the Marshall Plan, see Warren I. Cohen, *America in the Age of Soviet Power, 1945–1991* (New York: Cambridge University Press, 1993), p. 42. The Soviet rejection of the Marshall Plan is discussed in Chapter II.

26. Malia, *The Soviet Tragedy*, p. 300.

27. Peter R. Beckman, *World Politics in the Twentieth Century* (Englewood Cliffs, NJ: Prentice-Hall, 1984), pp. 209, 236, 284. The Soviet Union's share of world steel production in these years went from 12% to 17% to 20%. See also Hobsbawm, *The Age of Extremes*, p. 258.

28. Nau, *The Myth of America's Decline*, p. 39. See also Geir Lundestad, *The American "Empire" and Other Studies of US Foreign Policy in a Comparative Perspective* (New

York: Oxford University Press, 1990), pp. 62–5; and David P. Calleo, "Since 1961: American Power in a New World Economy," in William H. Becker and Samuel F. Wells, Jr., eds., *Economics and World Power: An Assessment of American Diplomacy Since 1789* (New York: Columbia University Press, 1984), pp. 391–3.

29. I have borrowed this metaphor of "lubrication" from Fred L. Block, *The Origins of International Economic Disorder: A Study of United States International Monetary Policy from World War II to the Present* (Berkeley: University of California Press, 1977), pp. 4, 6.

30. Eckes, *A Search for Solvency*, pp. 237–71; Robert Solomon, *The International Monetary System, 1945–1976: An Insider's View* (New York: Harper & Row, 1977), pp. 176–215.

31. See Richard Crockatt, *The Fifty Years War: The United States and the Soviet Union in World Politics, 1941–1991* (New York: Routledge, 1995), pp. 11–13.

32. Preface to the French and German editions of "Imperialism: The Highest Form of Capitalism," in Robert C. Tucker, ed., *The Lenin Anthology* (New York: Norton, 1975), p. 207. See also Wohlforth, *The Elusive Balance*, pp. 67, 77–8.

33. Robert V. Daniels, ed., *A Documentary History of Communism*, rev. edn. (Hanover, NH: University Press of New England, 1984), ii. 137–8.

34. Vladimir O. Pechatnov, "The Big Three After World War II: New Documents on Soviet Thinking About Postwar Relations with the United States and Great Britain," CWIHP Working Paper 13 (June 1995), esp. pp. 18–19. See also Ambassador Nikolai Novikov's report, "U.S. Foreign Policy in the Postwar Period," 27 Sept. 1946, in Kenneth M. Jensen, ed., *Origins of the Cold War: The Novikov, Kennan, and Roberts "Long Telegrams" of 1946* (Washington: United States Institute of Peace, 1991), pp. 11, 13.

35. Wohlforth, *The Elusive Balance*, pp. 77–87, provides a clear account of the Varga "alternative" and what happened to it.

36. Quoted in Daniels, ed., *A Documentary History of Communism*, ii. 172. See also James G. Richter, *Khrushchev's Double Bind: International Pressures and Domestic Coalition Politics* (Baltimore: Johns Hopkins University Press, 1994) , pp. 32–3. For a different but unconvincing interpretation, see Hobsbawm, *The Age of Extremes*, pp. 232–3.

37. Kennan to Byrnes, 22 Feb. 1946, *FRUS: 1946*, vi. 701. See also Wohlforth, *The Elusive Balance*, pp. 95–9. Interestingly, though, Kennan attributed this problem as much to Russian national character as to Stalin himself or the nature of Marxist-Leninist ideology. "The very disrespect of Russians for objective truth— indeed their disbelief in its existence—leads them to view all stated facts as instruments for [the] furtherance of one ulterior purpose or another."

38. Robert A. Divine, *Second Chance: The Triumph of Internationalism in America during World War II* (New York: Atheneum, 1967) is still the best overall account.

39. Wohlforth, *The Elusive Balance*, pp. 78–9. See also Hobsbawm, *The Age of Extremes*, p. 271.

40. See Smith, *Thinking Like a Communist*, pp. 55–6; also John Lewis Gaddis, "International Relations Theory and the End of the Cold War," *International Security* 17 (Winter 1992/3), 38.

41. Wohlforth, *The Elusive Balance*, pp. 60–1, 65.

42. Lundestad, *The American "Empire"*, pp. 54–6, suggests this point. See also Thomas J. McCormick, *America's Half-Century: United States Foreign Policy in the Cold War* (Baltimore: Johns Hopkins University Press, 1989), pp. 46–53.

43. Block, *The Origins of International Economic Disorder*, pp. 12–14; Smith, *America's Mission*, p. 163.

44. One of my students, S. David Broscious, has documented a gradual shift from economic to geopolitical priorities in American postwar strategy in "From 'Peace and Prosperity' to 'Peace and Security:' The Marshall Plan and the Ideological Shift within U.S. Foreign Policy, 1947–1948," a paper delivered at the 1995 annual convention of the Society for Historians of American Foreign Relations.

45. Pollard, *Economic Security and the Origins of the Cold War*, pp. 156–61; Lundestad, *The American "Empire"*, pp. 72–3; Hobsbawm, *The Age of Extremes*, pp. 275–6; Lawrence S. Kaplan, *The United States and NATO: The Formative Years* (Lexington: University Press of Kentucky, 1984) p. 181; and Alfred E. Eckes, Jr., *Opening America's Market: U.S. Foreign Trade Policy Since 1776* (Chapel Hill: University of North Carolina Press, 1995), esp. pp. 157–77.

46. Smith, *America's Mission*, p. 172. See also, on American flexibility with respect to the Marshall Plan, Pollard, *Economic Security and the Origins of the Cold War*, pp. 133–6; Nau, *The Myth of America's Decline*, pp. 103–6; and Michael J. Hogan, *The Marshall Plan: America, Britain, and the Reconstruction of Europe, 1947–1952* (Cambridge: Cambridge University Press, 1987), pp. 434–5, 443–5.

47. Smith, *America's Mission*, pp. 160–3.

48. Lundestad, *The American "Empire,"* p. 65.

49. Wohlforth, *The Elusive Balance*, p. 80.

50. Or, as Tony Smith has put it with respect to West Germany, "the greatest outside force working against the socialists . . . was not the Americans but the Soviets" (*America's Mission*, p. 172). See also Jean Edward Smith, *Lucius D. Clay: An American Life* (New York: Henry Holt, 1990), p. 276.

51. Alan S. Milward, *The Reconstruction of Western Europe, 1945–51* (Berkeley: University of California Press, 1984) states this position forcefully with respect to Europe. But see also Hobsbawm, *The Age of Extremes*, pp. 275–6, which effectively challenges it for Europe as well as Japan.

52. The point is made both by Paul Kennedy, *The Rise and Fall of the Great Powers: Economic Change and Military Conflict from 1500 to 2000* (New York: Random House, 1987), p. 432, and by one of his chief critics, Joseph S. Nye, Jr., *Bound to Lead: The Changing Nature of American Power* (New York: Basic Books, 1990), pp. 72–3.

53. Hogan, *The Marshall Plan*, pp. 431–2.

54. Quoted in Daniels, ed., *A Documentary History of Communism*, ii. 172. For more on this, see Chapter V.

55. See Michael Doyle, "Kant, Liberal Legacies, and Foreign Affairs," *Philosophy and Public Affairs* 12 (Summer and Fall 1983), 205–35, 323–53; and Bruce Russett, *Grasping the Democratic Peace: Principles for a Post-Cold War World* (Princeton: Princeton University Press, 1993).

56. Michael Doyle, "An International Liberal Community," in Graham Allison and Gregory Treverton, eds., *Rethinking America's Security: Beyond the Cold War to New World Order* (New York: Norton, 1992), pp. 330–1.

57. Smith, *America's Mission*, pp. 286–7. See also Melvyn P. Leffler, *A Preponderance of Power: National Security, the Truman Administration, and the Cold War* (Stanford: Stanford University Press, 1992), pp. 52–3.

58. For more on this, see Chapter VIII.

59. Kennan, *Memoirs: 1925–1960*, p. 369; Gaddis, *Strategies of Containment*, pp. 30–1; Wilson D. Miscamble, *George F. Kennan and the Making of American Foreign Policy, 1947–1950* (Princeton: Princeton University Press, 1992), pp. 348–9.

60. Smith, *America's Mission*, p. 155. See also, for an intriguing discussion of how things might have gone the other way had Theodore Roosevelt's influence been

more durable than Woodrow Wilson's, Henry Kissinger, *Diplomacy* (New York: Simon & Schuster, 1994), pp. 29–55.

61. Quoted in Smith, *Lucius D. Clay*, p. 332. For Clay's handling of the press, see ibid. 365–6, 369–70.

62. D. Clayton James, *The Years of MacArthur: Triumph and Disaster, 1945–1964* (Boston: Houghton Mifflin, 1985), pp. 281–5.

63. Quoted in Smith, *America's Mission*, p. 146.

64. Ibid. 148–51.

65. For an extended demonstration, see David Hackett Fischer, *Albion's Seed: Four British Folkways in America* (New York: Oxford University Press, 1989). Another way of looking at the *Stunde Null* is to think of it as a "sensitive dependence on initial conditions" situation—to use the terminology of chaos theory—in which even slight shifts at the beginning of a process can profoundly affect its subsequent development. James Gleick, *Chaos: Making a New Science* (New York: Viking, 1987), pp. 11–31, provides a clear discussion.

66. Hugh Thomas, *Conquest: Montezuma, Cortéz, and the Fall of Old Mexico* (New York: Simon & Schuster, 1993), reconstructs the earlier moment brilliantly. But see also James, *MacArthur: Triumph and Disaster*, p. 4.

67. See Reinhold Wagnleitner, *Coca-Colonization and the Cold War: The Cultural Mission of the United States in Austria after the Second World War*, trans. Diana M. Wolf (Chapel Hill: University of North Carolina Press, 1994); also, for the prewar era, Frank Costigliola, *Awkward Dominion: American Political, Economic, and Cultural Relations with Europe, 1919–1933* (Ithaca: Cornell University Press, 1984).

68. See Chapter II.

69. David P. Calleo, *Beyond American Hegemony: The Future of the Western Alliance* (New York: Basic Books, 1987), pp. 28–39, summarizes Kennan's concerns well while relating them, interestingly, to those of Robert A. Taft.

70. Marc Trachtenberg, *History and Strategy* (Princeton: Princeton University Press, 1991), p. 167.

71. Kaplan, *The United States and NATO*, pp. 11, 100–1, 181.

72. Diane B. Kunz, *The Economic Diplomacy of the Suez Crisis* (Chapel Hill: University of North Carolina Press, 1991) provides the best account.

73. Three historians who have stressed comparisons to the American federal constitutional structure are Kaplan, *The United States and NATO*, pp. 60–1, 178; Ernest R. May, "The American Commitment to Germany, 1949–55." *Diplomatic History* 13 (Fall 1989), pp. 458–60; and Geir Lundestad, "The United States and European Integration, 1945–1995," forthcoming.

74. I have drawn these ideas primarily from Thomas Risse-Kappen, *Cooperation Among Democracies: The European Influence on U.S. Foreign Policy* (Princeton: Princeton University Press, 1995), pp. 12–41. But see also John Gerard Ruggie, "International Regimes, Transactions, and Change: Embedded Liberalism in the Postwar Economic Order," in Stephen D. Krasner, ed., *International Regimes* (Ithaca: Cornell University Press, 1983), esp. pp. 198–9; also the somewhat similar conclusions—reached by very different methods of analysis—in Kissinger, *Diplomacy*, pp. 79, 82–4, 103–4.

75. Lawrence S. Kaplan, *NATO and the United States: The Enduring Alliance*, updated edn. (New York: Twayne, 1994), pp. 24, 28–9, 37, 47. See also May, "The American Commitment to Germany," pp. 455–6.

76. See Chapter V. Lundestad, "The United States and European Integration,"

pp. 32–3, has a good discussion of how cool the Truman administration was initially to the idea of a European Defense Community.

77. Trachtenberg, *History and Strategy*, p. 159.
78. Risse-Kappen, *Cooperation Among Democracies*, pp. 42–82, provides a good case study.
79. These points are discussed in greater detail in Chapters III and IV, and in Kaplan, *NATO and the United States*, pp. 64–5, 67–8.
80. Philip Nash, "The Other Missiles of October: Eisenhower, Kennedy, and the Jupiters in Europe, 1957–1963" (Ph.D. Dissertation, Ohio University, 1994).
81. See Kaplan, *The United States and NATO*, pp. 14–29.
82. Stuart A. Kauffman, *The Origins of Order: Self-Organization and Selection in Evolution* (New York: Oxford University Press, 1993). See also M. Mitchell Waldrop, *Complexity: The Emerging Science at the Edge of Order and Chaos* (New York: Viking, 1992), pp. 275–323.
83. Kaplan, *The United States and NATO*, pp. 52–8. Although as yet unpublished, Lundestad's "The United States and European Integration, 1945–1995" is the best overview I have seen of American policies in this area, and their impact.
84. John W. Young, *Cold War Europe: 1945–1989* (New York: Routledge, Chapman, & Hall, 1991), pp. 28–53, provides a convenient overview.
85. Dulles to Macmillan, 10 Dec. 1955, *FRUS: 1955–7*, iv. 363. I am indebted to Geir Lundestad for this reference.
86. See Chapter II.
87. See Chapter V.
88. Leonid Ya. Gibiansky, "Problems of East European International-Political Structuring in the Period of Formation of the Soviet Bloc," paper prepared for a CWIHP conference, Moscow, Jan. 1993, p. 53.
89. Paul Marer, "Soviet Economic Policies in Eastern Europe," in John P. Hardt, ed., *Reorientation and Commercial Relations of the Economies of Eastern Europe* (Washington: Government Printing Office, 1974), p. 136. I am indebted to Vojtech Mastny for this reference. See also George Schöpflin, "The Stalinist Experience in Eastern Europe," *Survey: A Journal of East and West Studies* 30 (Oct. 1988), 126–8.
90. Sergei N. Goncharov, John W. Lewis, and Xue Litai, *Uncertain Partners: Stalin, Mao, and the Korean War* (Stanford: Stanford University Press, 1994), pp. 121–9. See also Shu Guang Zhang, "The Collapse of Sino-Soviet Economic Cooperation, 1950–1960: A Cultural Explanation," pp. 13–17, and Yang Kuisong, "On the Causes of the Changes in Mao Zedong's View of the Soviet Union," pp. 15–17, both papers prepared for the CWIHP–University of Hong Kong conference, "The Cold War in Asia," Jan. 1996.
91. Stalin to Shtykov, 30 Jan. 1950, CWIHP *Bulletin* 5 (Spring 1995), p. 9.
92. Tompson, *Khrushchev*, p. 229. See also pp. 1–2; as well as Malia, *The Soviet Tragedy*, pp. 317–20, 328; and Richter, *Khrushchev's Double Bind*, p. 56.
93. Ulam, *The Communists*, pp. 108–12; also Richter, *Khrushchev's Double Bind*, p. 32. For new evidence of Soviet concern about the East Berlin riots, see the report of 24 June 1953 prepared by V. Sokolovskii, V. Semyonov, and P. Yudin for Molotov and Bulganin, CWIHP *Newsletter* 5 (Spring 1995), 10, 17–21; also the accompanying commentary by Christian Ostermann.
94. See Malia, *The Soviet Tragedy*, p. 328; also Amy Knight, *Beria: Stalin's First Lieutenant* (Princeton: Princeton University Press, 1993), p. 227; and James M. Goldgeier, *Leadership Style and Soviet Foreign Policy: Stalin, Khrushchev, Brezhnev, Gorbachev* (Baltimore: Johns Hopkins University Press, 1994), pp. 17–21.

95. Tompson, *Khrushchev*, pp. 122, 184.
96. Ibid. 151. See also Fedor Burlatsky, *Khrushchev and the First Russian Spring* (London: Weidenfeld & Nicolson, 1991), pp. 82–3, 139–43, 145–9; Malia, *The Soviet Tragedy*, pp. 330–4; and Donald Filtzer, *The Khrushchev Era: De-Stalinisation and the Limits of Reform in the USSR, 1953–1964* (London: Macmillan, 1993), pp. 38–57.
97. Tompson, *Khrushchev*, p. 267.
98. *Khrushchev Remembers*, ed. and trans. Strobe Talbott (Boston: Little, Brown, 1971), p. 422.
99. Tompson, *Khrushchev*, pp. 130–1; Ulam, *The Communists*, pp. 114–18.
100. *Khrushchev Remembers*, p. 380.
101. Zhou Enlai to Mao Zedong, 24 Jan. 1957, CWIHP *Bulletin* 6 and 7 (Winter 1995/6), p. 153.
102. *Khrushchev Remembers*, pp. 373, 517. See also Ulam, *The Communists*, pp. 120–5.
103. *Khrushchev Remembers: The Glasnost Tapes*, trans. and ed. Jerrold L. Schecter with Vyacheslav V. Luchkov (Boston: Little, Brown, 1990), pp. 72–80, provides the fullest account; but see also *Khrushchev Remembers: The Last Testament*, trans. and ed. Strobe Talbott (Boston: Little, Brown, 1974), pp. 220–1, 493. Also useful, on the declining position of Molotov, is Richter, *Khrushchev's Double Bind*, pp. 64–8.
104. See Chapter V.
105. M. Steven Fish, "After Stalin's Death: The Anglo-American Debate Over a New Cold War," *Diplomatic History*, 10 (Fall 1986) 333–55. But see also John Lewis Gaddis, "The Unexpected John Foster Dulles," in Richard H. Immerman, ed., *John Foster Dulles and the Diplomacy of the Cold War* (Princeton: Princeton University Press, 1990), pp. 67–71.
106. See Chapter VIII.
107. Smith, *Thinking Like a Communist*, pp. 43–8; also Theodore S. Hamerow, *From the Finland Station: The Graying of Revolution in the Twentieth Century* (New York: Basic Books, 1990), p. 166; and Steven M. Goldstein, "Nationalism and Internationalism: Sino-Soviet Relations," in Thomas W. Robinson and David Shambaugh, eds., *Chinese Foreign Policy: Theory and Practice* (New York: Oxford University Press, 1994), pp. 230–1.
108. I have followed here Constantine V. Pleshakov, "Reform Versus Revolution: Khrushchev Deals With China," unpublished paper prepared for the Brown University Centennial Conference on Nikita S. Khrushchev, Dec. 1994, pp. 6–8.
109. Richter, *Khrushchev's Double Bind*, p. 74. See also ibid. 76.
110. Ibid. 102.
111. *Khrushchev Remembers*, pp. 375, 382. Khrushchev's speech, "On the Cult of Personality and Its Consequences," is reprinted in T. H. Rigby, ed., *The Stalin Dictatorship: Khrushchev's 'Secret Speech' and Other Documents* (Sydney: Sydney University Press, 1968), pp. 23–89. For the background of Khrushchev's attack on Stalin, see Filtzer, *The Khrushchev Era*, pp. 12–16.
112. Georgi Arbatov, *The System: An Insider's Life in Soviet Politics* (New York: Times Books, 1992), p. 49. See also Burlatsky, *Khrushchev and the First Russian Spring*, pp. 63–5.
113. Tompson, *Khrushchev*, pp. 153–61, provides a good summary of the Congress. See also Richter, *Khrushchev's Double Bind*, pp. 79–81.
114. Kissinger, *Diplomacy*, p. 519.
115. The Khrushchev–Gorbachev comparison is succinctly made in Filtzer, *The Khrushchev Era*, pp. 1–4, 82–4.

116. See Bernard S. Morris, *Communism, Revolution, and American Policy* (Durham: Duke University Press, 1987), pp. 3–4.
117. Burlatsky, *Khrushchev and the First Russian Spring*, pp. 132–3, makes this comparison effectively.
118. This proposition, of course, goes back to Tocqueville on the origins of the French Revolution. For a recent restatement, see Hamerow, *From the Finland Station*, pp. 19–35.
119. See Chapter V.
120. *Khrushchev Remembers*, pp. 382–3. See also Peter Grose, *Gentleman Spy: The Life of Allen Dulles* (Boston: Houghton Mifflin, 1994), pp. 419–27.
121. Polish Politburo protocol 129, meetings of 19, 20, and 21 Oct. 1956, CWIHP *Bulletin* 5 (Spring 1995), 40. See also, on this and other recently released documents, L. W. Gluchowski, "Poland, 1956: Khrushchev, Gomulka, and the 'Polish October,' " ibid. 1, 38–49; and Mark Kramer, "Hungary and Poland, 1956: Khrushchev's CPSU CC Presidium Meeting on East European Crises, 24 October, 1956," ibid. 1, 50–1. Also useful for background is Krystyna Kersten, "1956: The Turning Point," in Odd Arne Westad, Sven Holtsmark, and Iver B. Neumann, eds., *The Soviet Union in Eastern Europe, 1945–89* (New York: St Martin's Press, 1994), pp. 47–62.
122. *Khrushchev Remembers: The Last Testament*, p. 205.
123. Antonin Novotny notes, CPSU CC Presidium meeting, 24 Oct. 1956, CWIHP *Bulletin* 5 (Spring 1995), 54.
124. Ibid.
125. Quoted in Mark Kramer, "Khrushchev and Eastern Europe: De-Stalinization and Reconsolidation," paper prepared for the Khrushchev Centennial Conference, Brown University, Dec. 1994, p. 20. See also Burlatsky, *Khrushchev and the First Russian Spring*, pp. 85–6; and, for background on the Hungarian uprising, Charles Gati, *Hungary and the Soviet Bloc* (Durham: Duke University Press, 1986), pp. 127–55.
126. Quoted in Kramer, "Hungary and Poland, 1956," p. 51.
127. Ibid. 51–2; Tompson, *Khrushchev*, pp. 168–9.
128. Kramer, "Khrushchev and Eastern Europe," pp. 26–30. See also Burlatsky, *Khrushchev and the First Russian Spring*, pp. 88–92; and for a detailed contemporary account, Veljko Micunovic, *Moscow Diary*, trans. David Floyd (Garden City, NY: Doubleday, 1980), pp. 149, 170–4, 394–6.
129. Ibid. 92–3.
130. *Khrushchev Remembers: The Glasnost Tapes*, pp. 125–6.
131. Richter, *Khrushchev's Double Bind*, pp. 91–2.
132. *Khrushchev Remembers*, pp. 346–50.
133. Vasily Sidikhmenov, "Stalin and Mao Hearkened [*sic*] To Us," *New Times International* 5 (Feb. 1993), 31. I have benefited as well from reading an unpublished paper by M. Yu. Prozumenshchikov and I. N. Shevchuk, "Soviet–Chinese Relations, 1953–1959," prepared for a CWIHP conference, Moscow, Jan. 1993.
134. *Khrushchev Remembers: The Glasnost Tapes*, pp. 142–3. A similar admission appears in a report by the head of the Soviet foreign ministry's Far Eastern department, Mikhail Zimyanin, "The Political, Economic, and International Standing of the PRC," 15 Sept. 1959, printed in the CWIHP *Bulletin* 6 and 7 (Winter 1995/6), 178.
135. "The Greatest Friendship," 9 Mar. 1953, in Michael Y. M. Kau and John K. Leung, eds., *The Writings of Mao Zedong*, i: *September, 1949–December, 1955* (Armonk, NY: M. E. Sharpe, 1986), p. 329.

136. Transcript, Mao Zedong's conversation with a Yugoslavian Communist Union delegation, Beijing, Sept. 1956, CWIHP *Bulletin* 6 and 7 (Winter 1995/6), 151.
137. Soviet Ambassador P. F. Yudin report of a conversation with Mao, 31 Mar. 1956, ibid. 165; Mao conversation with Yugoslav delegation, Sept. 1956, ibid. 149.
138. Li Zhisui, *The Private Life of Chairman Mao*, trans. Tai Hung-chao (New York: Random House, 1994), pp. 115–18.
139. I have primarily followed, here, some of the implications of the discussion of "asynchronous" revolutionary development in Vladislav Zubok and Constantine Pleshakov, *Inside the Kremlin's Cold War: From Stalin to Khrushchev* (Cambridge, Mass.: Harvard University Press, 1996), pp. 214–15. But see also Hobsbawm, *The Age of Extremes*, pp. 465–8, and Frederick C. Teiwes, "Establishment and Consolidation of the New Regime," in Roderick MacFarquhar and John K. Fairbank, eds., *The Cambridge History of China*, xiv: *The People's Republic*, pt. 1: *The Emergence of Revolutionary China, 1949–1965* (New York: Cambridge University Press, 1987), p. 67; as well as the discussion of Liu Shao-qi's 1949 visit to Moscow in Chapter III.
140. See Chapter III.
141. Maurice Meisner, *Mao's China and After: A History of the People's Republic* (New York: Free Press, 1986), pp. 84–163, provides a good overview.
142. Mao Zedong speech, "On Sino-American and Soviet–American Relations," 27 Jan. 1957, CWIHP *Bulletin* 6 and 7 (Winter 1995/6), 152.
143. *Khrushchev Remembers*, p. 471; *Khrushchev Remembers: The Last Testament*, p. 252.
144. Li, *The Private Life of Chairman Mao*, p. 115.
145. "The Greatest Friendship," in Kau and Leung, eds., *The Writings of Mao Zedong*, i. 330. For Mao's adaptation of the Soviet model to Chinese conditions, see Teiwes, "Establishment and Consolidation of the New Regime," pp. 63–7, 129–42.
146. P. F. Yudin report of conversation with Mao Zedong, 22 July 1958, CWIHP *Bulletin* 6 and 7 (Winter 1995/6), 155–6.
147. Harrison Salisbury, *The New Emperors: China in the Era of Mao and Deng* (Boston: Little, Brown, 1992) emphasizes how easily China's revolutionary leaders developed imperial tendencies.
148. Li, *The Private Life of Chairman Mao*, p. 115; also Sidikhmenov, "Stalin and Mao," p. 32.
149. Yudin report, conversation with Mao, 31 Mar. 1956, CWIHP *Bulletin* 6 and 7 (Winter 1995/6), 166. Even Lenin, Mao acknowledged, had been capable of mistakes; after all he "crossed out and re-wrote some phrases . . . in his own works" (Ibid. 167; see also *Khrushchev Remembers: The Last Testament*, pp. 250–1).
150. Teiwes, "Establishment and Consolidation of the New Regime," p. 134. Mao later took credit for having helped Khrushchev solve the Polish crisis peacefully. See his conversation with P. F. Yudin, 22 July 1958, CWIHP *Bulletin* 6 and 7 (Winter 1995/6), 156.
151. Notes, meeting between Gomulka and Zhou Enlai, 11 Jan. 1957, CWIHP *Bulletin* 5 (Spring 1995), 43. See also Zhou's report to Mao Zedong, 24 Jan. 1957, ibid. 6 and 7 (Winter 1995/6) 153–4.
152. *Khrushchev Remembers: The Last Testament*, p. 254. For Khrushchev's distrust, see ibid. 245–6; also *Khrushchev Remembers*, p. 466.
153. Mao–Yudin conversation, 22 July 1958, CWIHP *Bulletin* 6 and 7 (Winter 1995/6), 155.

154. Yang, "On the Causes of the Changes in Mao Zedong's View of the Soviet Union," pp. 27–8.

155. Li, *The Private Life of Chairman Mao*, p. 220.

156. Mao's speech, made on 27 Feb. 1957, is in Roderick MacFarquhar, Timothy Cheek, and Eugene Wu, eds., *The Secret Speeches of Chairman Mao: From the Hundred Flowers to the Great Leap Forward* (Cambridge, Mass.: Harvard University Press, 1989), pp. 131–89.

157. Ibid. 201. For more on this sequence of events, see Merle Goldman, "The Party and the Intellectuals," in MacFarquhar and Fairbank, eds., *The Cambridge History of China*, xiv. 242–58.

158. *Khrushchev Remembers*, p. 467.

159. Li, *The Private Life of Chairman Mao*, p. 204.

160. Kenneth Lieberthal, "The Great Leap Forward and the Split in the Yenan Leadership," in MacFarquhar and Fairbank, eds., *The Cambridge History of China*, xiv. 293–359, provides an excellent overview.

161. Robert C. Tucker, *Stalin in Power: The Revolution From Above, 1928–1941* (New York: Norton, 1990), pp. 321–3. See also Donald S. Zagoria, *The Sino-Soviet Conflict, 1956–1961* (Princeton: Princeton University Press, 1962), pp. 81–2.

162. *Khrushchev Remembers: The Last Testament*, p. 273. See also Lieberthal, "The Great Leap Forward," p. 484.

163. Liu Xiao to Ministry of Foreign Affairs, Beijing, 20 Oct. 1958, quoted in Zhang, "The Collapse of Sino-Soviet Economic Cooperation," p. 35. Zagoria, *The Sino-Soviet Dispute*, pp. 77–141, provides a thorough discussion of the Soviet reaction to the Great Leap Forward.

164. *Khrushchev Remembers: The Glasnost Tapes*, p. 153. See also *Khrushchev Remembers*, p. 473.

165. Li, *The Private Life of Chairman Mao*, p. 225.

166. Lieberthal, "The Great Leap Forward," p. 306.

167. Nicholas R. Lardy, "The Chinese Economy Under Stress, 1958–1965," in MacFarquhar and Fairbank, eds., *The Cambridge History of China*, xiv. 366–7. See also Li, *The Private Life of Chairman Mao*, pp. 283, 290–1.

168. Ibid. 278, 291.

169. Lardy, "The Chinese Economy Under Stress," pp. 370–2. See also Basil Ashton, Kenneth Hill, Alan Piazza, and Robin Zeitz, "Famine in China, 1958–61," *Population and Development Review* 10 (Dec. 1984), 613–45.

170. I base this generalization on the estimate of 17–22 million deaths resulting from Stalin's pre-World War II policies, as cited in Chapter I, and on the generally accepted figure of 6 million deaths in the Holocaust. This yields a range of 23–8 million for Hitler and Stalin's combined domestic victims, as compared to the 16–27 million range for Mao cited above.

171. To be discussed in Chapter VIII.

172. Quoted in John Gittings, *Survey of the Sino-Soviet Dispute: A Commentary and Extracts from the Recent Polemics, 1963–1967* (London: Oxford University Press, 1968), pp. 347, 350

173. Ibid. 130–1.

174. Quoted in Zhang, "The Collapse of Sino-Soviet Economic Cooperation," pp. 38–9.

175. Tompson, *Khrushchev*, pp. 237–9. See also Richter, *Khrushchev's Double Bind*, pp. 103–5, 127.

176. Burlatsky, *Khrushchev and the First Russian Spring*, p. 130. For Soviet economic difficulties at the time, see Richter, *Khrushchev's Double Bind*, p. 127.

177. Michael Beschloss, *The Crisis Years: Kennedy and Khrushchev, 1960–1963* (New York: HarperCollins, 1991), pp. 165–7. Another successful example of leaping before looking is Franklin D. Roosevelt's public call, in May 1940, for the production of 50,000 airplanes a year at a time when existing production was less than a tenth of that number. See Doris Kearns Goodwin, *No Ordinary Time: Franklin and Eleanor Roosevelt: The Home Front in World War II* (New York: Simon & Schuster, 1994), pp. 44–5.
178. To be discussed in Chapter IX.
179. Gordon H. Chang, *Friends and Enemies: The United States, China, and the Soviet Union, 1948–1972* (Stanford: Stanford University Press, 1990), pp. 228–52.
180. One theorist who did anticipate this was the Yugoslav Edward Kardelj. See Burlatsky, *Khrushchev and the First Russian Spring*, pp. 117–18.
181. Allen S. Whiting, "The Sino-Soviet Split," in MacFarquhar and Fairbank, eds., *The Cambridge History of China*, xiv. 479.
182. *Khrushchev Remembers*, p. 466; *Khrushchev Remembers: The Last Testament*, pp. 245–6.
183. *Khrushchev Remembers*, p. 464.
184. Ibid. 466–7; Li, *The Private Life of Chairman Mao*, pp. 220, 222, 261–2. Khrushchev, however, does not appear to have been offended, and subsequently adopted the practice himself with visiting Western dignitaries.
185. For an excellent introduction to Gaullist thinking, see Philip H. Gordon, *A Certain Idea of France: French Security Policy and the Gaullist Legacy* (Princeton: Princeton University Press, 1993), esp. pp. 3–22. For the importance of personal animosities in Sino-Soviet relations, see Yang, "On the Causes of the Changes in Mao Zedong's View of the Soviet Union," pp. 6–7; and William Taubman, "Khrushchev vs. Mao: A Preliminary Sketch of the Role of Personality in the Sino-Soviet Dispute," paper prepared for the CWIHP–University of Hong Kong conference on "The Cold War in Asia," Jan. 1996.
186. Michael M. Harrison, *The Reluctant Ally: France and Atlantic Security* (Baltimore: Johns Hopkins University Press, 1981), pp. 134–68.
187. Gordon, *A Certain Idea of France*, pp. 79–160, provides a careful account.
188. For an early use of a similar metaphor, see John Foster Dulles, *War or Peace* (New York: Macmillan, 1950), p. 242.
189. *Khrushchev Remembers*, p. 477.
190. Both Hobsbawm, *The Age of Extremes*, po. 250–1, 259, 398–400, and Crockatt, *The Fifty Years War*, pp. 12–13, stress the significance of the late 1950s and early 1960s as the major turning-point in Cold War history.

CHAPTER VIII

1. Quoted in John Wilson Lewis and Xue Litai, *China Builds the Bomb* (Stanford: Stanford University Press, 1988), p. 37.
2. Memorandum, NSC meeting, 26 Jan. 1956, *FRUS: 1955–7* xx. 297.
3. See e.g. Philip E. Mosely, *The Kremlin and World Politics: Studies in Soviet Policy and Action* (New York: Vintage Books, 1960); and Donald S. Zagoria, *The Sino-Soviet Conflict, 1956–1961* (Princeton: Princeton University Press, 1962).
4. See Chapter IV.
5. John Mueller has developed this theme of the Cold War's end being the functional but peaceful equivalent of World War III. See his *Quiet Cataclysm:*

Reflections on the Recent Transformation of World Politics (New York: HarperCollins, 1995), esp. pp. 1–3.

6. George F. Kennan, "The Sources of Soviet Conduct," *Foreign Affairs* 25 (July 1947), 580.

7. John Foster Dulles, *War or Peace* (New York: Macmillan, 1950), p. 242. See also Dulles's speech to the Dallas Council on World Affairs, 27 Oct. 1956, *Department of State Bulletin* 35 (5 Nov. 1956), 695–9.

8. Robert A. Divine, *Foreign Policy and U.S. Presidential Elections: 1952–1960* (New York: Franklin Watts, 1974), pp. 32–6, 50–6.

9. I have discussed the "New Look" strategy in detail in John Lewis Gaddis, *Strategies of Containment: A Critical Appraisal of Postwar American National Security Policy* (New York: Oxford University Press, 1982), pp. 127–63. For an interesting comparison of the "New Look" with Khrushchev's strategic deception strategy, see Walter A. McDougall, *The Heavens and the Earth: A Political History of the Space Age* (New York: Basic Books, 1985), pp. 265–9.

10. Quoted in Richard Rhodes, *Dark Sun: The Making of the Hydrogen Bomb* (New York: Simon & Schuster, 1995), p. 510.

11. Andrei Sakharov, *Memoirs*, trans. Richard Lourie (New York: Knopf, 1990), p. 175.

12. David Holloway, *Stalin and the Bomb: The Soviet Union and Atomic Energy, 1939–1956* (New Haven: Yale University Press, 1994), pp. 307–8.

13. Eisenhower speech to the United Nations General Assembly, 8 Dec. 1953, *Public Papers of the Presidents of the United States: Dwight D. Eisenhower, 1953* (Washington: Government Printing Office, 1960), p. 817.

14. See Holloway, *Stalin and the Bomb*, pp. 227, 238, 327–8; also, on Hiroshima, David Callahan, *Dangerous Capabilities: Paul Nitze and the Cold War* (New York: HarperCollins, 1990), pp. 50–1.

15. Quoted in Rhodes, *Dark Sun*, pp. 508–9.

16. Quoted in Holloway, *Stalin and the Bomb*, p. 307.

17. Quoted ibid. 316–17.

18. Quoted ibid. 317.

19. An exception was Soviet Defense Minister and later Premier Nikolai Bulganin, whose hat was blown off by a Sept. 1954 air-dropped atomic bomb test. Chinese generals Peng Dehuai and Zhu De were also present. (Ibid. 327).

20. Nuel Pharr Davis, *Lawrence and Oppenheimer* (New York: Simon & Schuster, 1968), pp. 258. There are various other versions of this Truman–Oppenheimer conversation. See e.g. *The Journals of David E. Lilienthal*, ii: *The Atomic Energy Years, 1945–1950* (New York: Harper & Row, 1964), p. 118; also Merle Miller, *Plain Speaking: An Oral Biography of Harry S. Truman* (New York: G. P. Putnam, 1974), p. 228. Truman's thinking on nuclear weapons is discussed in Chapter IV.

21. Sakharov, *Memoirs*, pp. 192–5.

22. Charles Critchfield, quoted in Rhodes, *Dark Sun*, p. 543. For good recent discussions of the proceedings against Oppenheimer, see ibid. 530–59; also McGeorge Bundy, *Danger and Survival: Choices About the Bomb in the First Fifty Years* (New York: Random House, 1988), pp. 305–18.

23. Ibid. 541–3; also Robert A. Divine, *Blowing on the Wind: The Nuclear Test Ban Debate, 1954–1960* (New York: Oxford University Press, 1978), pp. 3–35; and Spencer Weart, *Nuclear Fear: A History of Images* (Cambridge, Mass.: Harvard University Press, 1988), pp. 183–214.

24. Press conference, 24 Mar. 1954, *Eisenhower Public Papers: 1954*, p. 346.

25. The 1 Apr. 1954, issues of the *New York Times* and *Washington Post* contain good accounts of the Eisenhower–Strauss 31 Mar. press conference.

26. Hagerty Diary, 31 Mar. and 1 Apr. 1954, in Robert H. Ferrell, ed., *The Diary of James C. Hagerty: Eisenhower in Mid-Course, 1954–1955* (Bloomington: Indiana University Press, 1983), pp. 36, 39.
27. For an example, see Rhodes, *Dark Sun*, photograph 76. Divine describes the international outcry resulting from the BRAVO test in *Blowing on the Wind*, pp. 6–35.
28. Notes, Eisenhower meeting with legislative leaders, 14 Feb. 1956, *FRUS: 1955–7*, xix. 198.
29. Memorandum, NSC meeting, 8 Dec. 1955, ibid. 172.
30. Churchill to Eisenhower, 9 Mar. 1954, in Peter G. Boyle, ed., *The Churchill–Eisenhower Correspondence, 1953–1955* (Chapel Hill: University of North Carolina Press, 1990), pp. 122–4. For Churchill's earlier advocacy of "atomic diplomacy," see Chapter IV.
31. Eisenhower to Churchill, 19 Mar. 1954, in Boyle, ed., *The Churchill–Eisenhower Correspondence*, p. 125.
32. See Boyle's concluding essay, ibid. 211–13; also M. Steven Fish, "After Stalin's Death: The Anglo-American Debate Over a New Cold War," *Diplomatic History* 10 (Fall 1986), 333–55.
33. Report by Panel of Consultants of the Department of State, "Armaments and American Policy," Jan. 1953, *FRUS: 1952–4*, ii. 1066. For more on this report, see Bundy, *Danger and Survival*, pp. 288–9.
34. Eisenhower speech to the UN General Assembly, 8 Dec. 1953, *Eisenhower Public Papers: 1953*, p. 817.
35. James Hagerty Diary, 27 July 1954, *FRUS: 1952–4*, xv. 1844–5. "I feel sorry for the old man," Eisenhower had told Hagerty beforehand: "He wants to get his country unified, but we cannot permit him to start a war to do it. The consequences would be too awful." (ibid. 1839).
36. Memorandum, NSC meeting, 3 Dec. 1954, ibid. ii. 804–5. See also Hagerty's diary entries for 3, 4 Jan. and 1 Feb. 1955, in *FRUS: 1955–7*, xix. 3–6, 39–40.
37. Memorandum, NSC meeting, 4 Aug. 1955, ibid. 101.
38. Dulles speech to the Council on Foreign Relations, 12 Jan. 1954, *Department of State Bulletin* 30 (25 Jan. 1954), 107–10. For the background and consequences of Dulles's speech, see Bundy, *Danger and Survival*, pp. 255–60; Gaddis, *Strategies of Containment*, pp. 145–61; and H. W. Brands, "The Age of Vulnerability: Eisenhower and the National Insecurity State," *American Historical Review* 94 (Oct. 1989), 972–3.
39. Memorandum, Dulles–Strauss telephone conversation, 29 Mar. 1954, *FRUS: 1952–4*, ii. 1379–80.
40. Memorandum, NSC meeting, 6 May 1954, ibid. 1428.
41. Dulles memorandum, "Basic National Security Policy (Suggestions of the Secretary of State)," ibid. 773. For more on the evolution of Dulles's thinking with respect to nuclear weapons, see John Lewis Gaddis, *The United States and the End of the Cold War: Implications, Reconsiderations, Provocations* (New York: Oxford University Press, 1992), pp. 66–73.
42. Holloway, *Stalin and the Bomb*, pp. 306, 336. See also Vladislav Zubok and Constantine Pleshakov, *Inside the Kremlin's Cold War: From Stalin to Khrushchev* (Cambridge, Mass.: Harvard University Press, 1996), pp. 164–6.
43. Quoted in Holloway, *Stalin and the Bomb*, pp. 338–9. See also, for a discussion of this episode, Arnold L. Horelick and Myron Rush, *Strategic Power and Soviet Foreign Policy* (Chicago: University of Chicago Press, 1966), pp. 19–22, 26–7; William Curti Wohlforth, *The Elusive Balance: Power and Perceptions During the*

Cold War (Ithaca: Cornell University Press, 1993), pp. 142–4; and James G. Richter, *Khrushchev's Double Bind: International Pressures and Domestic Coalition Politics* (Baltimore: Johns Hopkins University Press, 1994), pp. 48–51.

44. Quoted in Yuri Smirnov and Vladislav Zubok, "Nuclear Weapons after Stalin's Death: Moscow Enters the H-Bomb Age," CWIHP *Bulletin* 4 (Fall 1994), 14–15. See also, for the effect on Malenkov's thinking, Zubok and Pleshakov, *Inside the Kremlin's Cold War*, p. 169.

45. Quoted in Mohamed Heikal, *The Sphinx and the Commissar: The Rise and Fall of Soviet Influence in the Middle East* (New York: Harper & Row, 1978), p. 129. See also Holloway, *Stalin and the Bomb*, p. 339.

46. Horelick and Rush, *Strategic Power and Soviet Foreign Policy*, p. 26; William J. Tompson, *Khrushchev: A Political Life* (New York: St. Martin's Press, 1995), p. 143.

47. Memoranda, Eisenhower–Bulganin and Eisenhower–Zhukov conversations, 18 and 20 July 1955, *FRUS: 1955–7*, v. 376, 413.

48. Quoted in Michael R. Beschloss, *Mayday: Eisenhower, Khrushchev and the U-2 Affair* (New York: Harper & Row, 1986), p. 102.

49. *Khrushchev Remembers*, trans. and ed. Strobe Talbott (Boston: Little, Brown, 1970), p. 438.

50. Eisenhower United Nations speech, 8 Dec. 1953, *Eisenhower Public Papers: 1953*, p. 816.

51. Hagerty Diary, 3 Jan. 1955, *FRUS: 1955–7*, xix. 4. See also Hagerty's diary entry for 1 Feb. 1955, ibid. 40; and, for a more general comment on the tendency of top-level officials to stress nuclear *danger* over nuclear deterrence, Bundy, *Danger and Survival*, p. 380.

52. Technological Capabilities Panel (Killian) Report, 14 Feb. 1955, quoted in Brands, "The Age of Vulnerability," p. 974.

53. Eisenhower Diary, 23 Jan. 1956, *FRUS: 1955–7*, xix. 187.

54. Memorandum, Eisenhower meeting with Secretaries of State, Defense, and the Chairman of the Atomic Energy Commission, 23 Jan. 1956, ibid. 189; memorandum, NSC meeting, 26 Jan. 1956, ibid. xx. 297.

55. Report of the Central Committee to the 20th Party Congress, Feb. 1956, in Robert V. Daniels, ed., *A Documentary History of Communism*, ii: *Communism and the World* (Hanover, NH: University Press of New England, 1984), p. 225. See also Wohlforth, *The Elusive Balance*, pp. 144–5; Richter, *Khrushchev's Double Bind*, p. 80; and Zubok and Pleshakov, *Inside the Kremlin's Cold War*, pp. 184–5.

56. Statement Appended to the Report of the General Advisory Committee, 30 Oct. 1949, *FRUS: 1949*, i. 570–1. James G. Hershberg, *James B. Conant: Harvard to Hiroshima and the Making of the Nuclear Age* (New York: Knopf, 1993), pp. 470–8, has a careful discussion of Conant's thinking and its impact.

57. Kennan memorandum, "The International Control of Atomic Energy," 20 Jan. 1950, *FRUS: 1950*, i. 39.

58. Bradley to Louis Johnson, 23 Nov. 1949, *FRUS: 1949*, i. 595–6. See also Bundy, *Danger and Survival*, pp. 206–9; Rhodes, *Dark Sun*, pp. 387, 397–8; and David Alan Rosenberg, "American Atomic Strategy and the Hydrogen Bomb Decision," *Journal of American History* 66 (June 1979), 62–87. Bradley's ideas here paralleled those of Bernard Brodie. See Marc Trachtenberg, *History and Strategy* (Princeton: Princeton University Press, 1991), pp. 6–7.

59. For Conant's role in the drafting of NSC-68, see Hershberg, *James B. Conant*, pp. 499–502. See also, on the H-bomb decision generally, Herbert F. York, *The Advisors: Oppenheimer, Teller, and the Superbomb* (San Francisco: W. H. Freeman, 1976), pp. 41–74.

60. Memorandum, NSC meeting, 25 Mar. 1954, *FRUS: 1952–4*, ii. 639–41.
61. See e.g. Gaddis, *Strategies of Containment*, pp. 129–36.
62. Memorandum, NSC meeting, 23 June 1954, *FRUS: 1952–4*, ii. 1469. See also ibid. 1342.
63. Memorandum, NSC meeting, 24 June 1954, ibid. 696. See also Dulles to Eisenhower, 8 Sept. 1953, ibid. 461.
64. "We could stop the Soviets from overrunning Europe by resorting to the use of nuclear weapons, although, of course, this would kill millions of people. Moreover, we might have to give up our bases in Europe, and that was a hell of a problem" (memorandum, NSC meeting, 26 Jan. 1956, *FRUS: 1955–7*, xx. 297).
65. "The President said that the theory of retaliation falls down unless we can identify the aggressor. In many cases aggression consists of subversion or civil war in a country rather than overt attack on that country. In such cases it is difficult for us to know whom to retaliate against" (Memorandum, NSC meeting, 5 Aug. 1954, *FRUS: 1952–4*, ii. 708).
66. Memorandum, NSC meeting, 26 Jan. 1956, *FRUS: 1955–7*, xx. 297.
67. "[T]he United States cannot afford to preclude itself from using nuclear weapons even in a local situation, if such use will bring the aggression to a swift and positive cessation, and if, on a balance of political and military consideration, such use will best advance U.S. security interests" (NSC-5501, "Basic National Security Policy," approved by Eisenhower 7 Jan. 1955, ibid., xix. 33). For Eisenhower's nuclear threats during the first offshore island crisis, see Gordon H. Chang, *Friends and Enemies: The United States, China, and the Soviet Union, 1948–1972* (Stanford: Stanford University Press, 1990), pp. 131–42.
68. See Bundy, *Danger and Survival*, pp. 278, 283, 285, 377.
69. Carl von Clausewitz, *On War*, ed. and trans. Michael Howard and Peter Paret (Princeton: Princeton University Press, 1976), esp. pp. 75–80. See also Paret's introductory essay, "The Genesis of *On War*," ibid. 21–2; and Alan Beyerchen, "Clausewitz, Nonlinearity, and the Unpredictability of War," *International Security* 17 (Winter 1992/3), esp. p. 67.
70. See Christopher Bassford, *Clausewitz in English: The Reception of Clausewitz in Britain and America, 1815–1945* (New York: Oxford University Press, 1994), pp. 157–62.
71. Memorandum, NSC meeting, 7 Feb. 1957, *FRUS: 1955–7*, xix. 416. See also Eisenhower's comments at the NSC meetings of 20 Dec. 1956 and 11 Apr. 1957, ibid. 381, 473. For a particularly insightful discussion of Eisenhower's apparent contradictions and their probable Clausewitzian explanation, see Peter J. Roman, *Eisenhower and the Missile Gap* (Ithaca: Cornell University Press, 1995), pp. 65, 83–4, 111.
72. Ibid. 70–1. See also Brands, "The Age of Vulnerability," pp. 980–1; and Gaddis, *The United States and the End of the Cold War*, pp. 66–73.
73. Bundy, *Danger and* Survival, pp. 334–50; Callahan, *Dangerous Capabilities*, pp. 155–74; Douglas Brinkley, *Dean Acheson: The Cold War Years, 1953–71* (New Haven: Yale University Press, 1992), pp. 58–64. See also an older but still useful account, Richard A. Aliano, *American Defense Policy from Eisenhower to Kennedy: The Politics of Changing Military Requirements, 1957–1961* (Athens: Ohio University Press, 1975).
74. Trachtenberg, *History and Strategy*, pp. 40–2.
75. My rethinking of Eisenhower here follows the work of a former student, Campbell Craig, whose Ph.D. Dissertation, "The Thermonuclear Revolution and American Postwar Realism" (Ohio University, 1995), discusses these issues with great insight. See also Roman, *Eisenhower and the Missile Gap*, pp. 86–7.

76. It worked the other way as well, though: "[I]f we do not now have enough military strength to deter the Soviet Union from nuclear attack, the President said he could not be sure that 20 times as much military strength would succeed in deterring the Soviets" (Memorandum, NSC meeting, 21 Dec. 1956, *FRUS: 1955–7*, xix. 390).

77. Memorandum, NSC meeting, 27 Feb. 1956, ibid. 211. See also Eisenhower's comments on a Net Evaluation Subcommittee briefing, 23 Jan. 1956, ibid. 190–1.

78. Memorandum, Eisenhower conversation with Radford and Maxwell Taylor, 24 May 1956, ibid. 313. See also William Burr, "Avoiding the Slippery Slope: The Eisenhower Administration and the Berlin Crisis, November 1958–January 1959," *Diplomatic History* 18 (Spring 1994), 182.

79. Wohlforth, *The Elusive Balance*, p. 158; McDougall, *The Heavens and the Earth*, pp. 265–9; Zaloga, *Target America*, pp. 159–60; Tompson, *Khrushchev*, pp. 216–18.

80. Memorandum, NSC meeting, 8 Nov. 1956, *FRUS: 1955–7*, xxv. 419. I have benefited, here and in what follows, from reading the MA thesis of one of my students, Jason George, "Adapting to Circumstances: American Policy Toward Eastern Europe, 1953–1956" (Ohio University, 1995).

81. Memorandum, NSC meeting, 26 Oct. 1956, *FRUS: 1955–7*, xxv. 299. See also Stephen E. Ambrose, *Eisenhower: The President* (New York: Simon & Schuster, 1984), p. 368.

82. The relevant documentation is in *FRUS: 1955–7*, xxv. 305–7, 317–18, 321–2, 328, 347–8, 351–2. The Presidium meeting is confirmed in Mark Kramer, "Khrushchev and Eastern Europe: De-Stalinization and Reconsolidation," paper prepared for the Brown University Khrushchev Centennial Conference, Dec. 1994, p. 26.

83. Khrushchev mentioned, in a conversation with the Yugoslav ambassador on 12 Nov. 1956, that he had been aware of Eisenhower's reassurances and regarded them as a sign of weakness (Veljko Micunovic, *Moscow Diary*, trans. David Floyd (Garden City, New York: Doubleday, 1980), pp. 156–7). His detailed account of the decision to suppress the Hungarian uprising (*Khrushchev Remembers*, pp. 458–65) says nothing about fearing American or NATO involvement, although in a supplementary version there is a cryptic reference to Soviet troops having been deployed in such a way as to counter such interference, if it had come (*Khrushchev Remembers: The Glasnost Tapes*, trans. and ed. Jerrold L. Schechter and Vyacheslav V. Luchkov (Boston: Little, Brown, 1990), p. 125).

84. "Report of the President's Committee on International Information Activities," 30 June 1953, *FRUS: 1952–4*, ii. 1817. See also NSC 174, "United States Policy toward the Soviet Satellites in Eastern Europe," approved by Eisenhower on 23 Dec. 1953, ibid. viii. 116–28; and Bennett Kovrig, *Of Walls and Bridges: The United States and Eastern Europe* (New York: New York University Press, 1991), pp. 62–9.

85. Robert Cutler to Dulles, 3 Sept. 1953, *FRUS: 1952–4*, ii. 457.

86. Bulganin to Eden, 5 Nov. 1956, in Noble Frankland, ed., *Documents on International Affairs, 1956* (London: Oxford University Press, 1959), p. 289.

87. Richter, *Khrushchev's Double Bind*, p. 93; Keith Kyle, *Suez* (New York: St. Martin's Press, 1991). See also Chapter VI.

88. *Khrushchev Remembers*, p. 481. See also Horelick and Rush, *Stratregic Power and Soviet Foreign Policy*, pp. 31, 212; and Micunovic, *Moscow Diary*, pp. 148–9.

89. *Khrushchev Remembers: The Last Testament*, trans. and ed. Strobe Talbott (Boston: Little, Brown, 1974), p. 54. See also York, *The Advisors*, pp. 75–93.

90. General Curtis LeMay at the Naval War College, Apr. 1956, quoted in Rhodes, *Dark Sun*, p. 566. See also David Alan Rosenberg, " 'A Smoking Radiating Ruin at the End of Two Hours:' Documents on American Plans for Nuclear War with the Soviet Union, 1954–1955," *International Security* 6 (Winter 1981/2), 3–38.

91. Stephen J. Zaloga, *Target America: The Soviet Union and the Strategic Arms Race, 1945–1964* (Novato, California: Presidio Press, 1993), pp. 162–3.

92. See John Ranelagh, *The Agency: The Rise and Decline of the CIA* (New York: Simon & Schuster, 1986), pp. 306–7.

93. Memorandum, Eisenhower conversation with Sherman Adams and Herbert Hoover, Jr., 5 Nov. 1956, *FRUS: 1955–7*, xvi. 1000–1. For Bohlen and the intelligence estimates, see ibid. 995–6, 1018–20.

94. Memorandum, NSC meeting, 17 May 1956, ibid. xix. 307.

95. Memorandum, NSC meeting, 27 Feb. 1956, ibid. 211.

96. Memorandum, NSC meeting, 17 May 1956, ibid. 307.

97. Horelick and Rush, *Strategic Power and Soviet Foreign Policy*, p. 109. See also Sergei Khrushchev, *Khrushchev on Khrushchev: An Inside Account of the Man and His Era*, ed. and trans. William Taubman (Boston: Little, Brown, 1990), p. 106.

98. *Molotov Remembers: Inside Kremlin Politics: Conversations with Felix Chuev*, ed. Albert Resis (Chicago: Ivan R. Dee, 1993), pp. 226, 313.

99. Zaloga, *Target America*, pp. 121–4, 171–3.

100. For the Soviet and American uses of German rocket technology, see ibid. 115–21, 125–8; also McDougall, *The Heavens and the Earth*, pp. 41–55; and William B. Breuer, *Race to the Moon: America's Duel with the Soviets* (Westport, Conn.: Praeger, 1993).

101. *Khrushchev Remembers: The Last Testament*, p. 46.

102. *Khrushchev Remembers*, p. 444. See also Horelick and Rush, *Strategic Power and Soviet Foreign Policy*, p. 29.

103. Zaloga, *Target America*, pp. 145–6.

104. Here I can cite myself, an impressed teenager at the time, as a primary source.

105. Memorandum, NSC meeting, 1 Dec. 1955, *FRUS: 1955–7*, xix. 169.

106. Memorandum, Eisenhower meeting with scientific advisers, 15 Oct. 1957, ibid. 609 (emphasis added). See also James R. Killian, Jr., *Sputnik, Scientists, and Eisenhower: A Memoir of the First Special Assistant to the President for Science and Technology* (Cambridge, Mass.: MIT Press, 1977), pp. 14–15.

107. *Khrushchev Remembers: The Last Testament*, pp. 53–4.

108. *Khrushchev Remembers: The Glasnost Tapes*, p. 188.

109. *Khrushchev Remembers: The Last Testament*, p. 47.

110. See McDougall, *The Heavens and the Earth*, pp. 235–6; also Zubok and Pleshakov, *Inside the Kremlin's Cold War*, p. 197.

111. Horelick and Rush, *Strategic Power and Soviet Foreign Policy*, pp. 18, 27–9; also Allen W. Dulles, *The Craft of Intelligence* (New York: Harper & Row, 1963), p. 149; John Prados, *The Soviet Estimate: US Intelligence Analysis and Russian Military Strength* (New York: Dial Press, 1982), pp. 38–50; and Dino A. Brugioni, *Eyeball to Eyeball: The Inside Story of the Cuban Missile Crisis* (New York: Random House, 1991), pp. 8–10.

112. *Khrushchev Remembers: The Glasnost Tapes*, p. 187. See also Horelick and Rush, *Strategic Power and Soviet Foreign Policy*, pp. 29–30.

113. Micunovic diary, 12 Nov. 1956, in Micunovic, *Moscow Diary*, pp. 156–7.

114. See Horelick and Rush, *Strategic Power and Soviet Foreign Policy*, pp. 31, 212, 216; Richter, *Khrushchev's Double Bind*, pp. 93–4; and Zubok and Pleshakov, *Inside the Kremlin's Cold War*, pp. 191–2.

115. Memorandum, NSC meeting, 28 June 1957, *FRUS: 1955–7*, xxiv. 119–20. See also the transcript of a telephone conversation between John Foster Dulles and Allen Dulles, 8 July 1957, ibid. 146; also, for a similar analysis, Zubok and Pleshakov, *Inside the Kremlin's Cold War*, p. 177.

116. See Micunovic, *Moscow Diary*, p. 114.

117. Micunovic diary, 31 Oct. 1957, ibid. 311. See also Wohlforth, *The Elusive Balance*, pp. 157–60.

118. Horelick and Rush, *Strategic Power and Soviet Foreign Policy*, p. 42; Zagoria, *The Sino-Soviet Conflict*, pp. 156–7. For Khrushchev's subsequent acknowledgement of authorship, see *FRUS: 1958–60*, x. 365.

119. Horelick and Rush, *Strategic Power and Soviet Foreign Policy*, pp. 43–5, 49.

120. Zaloga, *Target America*, pp. 150–4, 191. See also *Khrushchev Remembers: The Last Testament*, pp. 46–8.

121. Quoted in Robert A. Divine, *The Sputnik Challenge* (New York: Oxford University Press, 1993), p. 44.

122. For the Gaither Committee report, see Prados, *The Soviet Estimate*, pp. 67–75; also Bundy, *Danger and Survival*, pp. 335–7; Roman, *Eisenhower and the Missile Gap*, pp. 31–4.

123. Divine, *The Sputnik Challenge*, p. 177. See also Joseph W. Alsop, with Adam Platt, *"I've Seen the Best of It": Memoirs* (New York: Norton, 1992), pp. 413–14; and Edwin M. Yoder, Jr., *Joe Alsop's Cold War: A Study of Journalistic Influence and Intrigue* (Chapel Hill: University of North Carolina Press, 1995), pp. 168–73.

124. Eisenhower radio-television address, 7 Nov. 1957, *Eisenhower Public Papers: 1957*, esp. pp. 789–94. For the reception of this speech, see Divine, *The Sputnik Challenge*, pp. 45–7.

125. Philip Nash, "The Other Missiles of October: Eisenhower, Kennedy, and the Jupiters in Europe, 1957–1963," (Ph.D. dissertation, Ohio University, 1994), pp. 12–57.

126. See Micunovic, *Moscow Diary*, pp. 327, 338, 340.

127. Nash, "The Other Missiles of October," pp. 13, 33. See also Zubok and Pleshakov, *Inside the Kremlin's Cold War*, pp. 159–60; and the careful discussion in Trachtenberg, *History and Strategy*, pp. 170–91.

128. I have borrowed this felicitous metaphor from Vladislav M. Zubok, "Khrushchev's Motives and Soviet Diplomacy in the Berlin Crisis, 1958–1962," paper prepared for a CWIHP conference on "The Soviet Union, Germany, and the Cold War," Essen, Germany, June 1994, p. 37.

129. Richter, *Khrushchev's Double Bind*, pp. 101–3; Zubok and Pleshakov, *Inside the Kremlin's Cold War*, pp. 195–6. See also Chapter V.

130. Horelick and Rush, *Strategic Power and Soviet Foreign Policy*, pp. 117–19.

131. Charles W. Thayer notes, Khrushchev–Harriman conversation, 23 June 1959, *FRUS: 1958–60*, viii. 941–2, x. 269–81. For a different interpretation of Harriman's reaction, see Rudy Abramson, *Spanning the Century: The Life of W. Averell Harriman, 1891–1986* (New York: William Morrow, 1992), pp. 573–4.

132. Quoted in Glenn T. Seaborg, *Kennedy, Khrushchev and the Test Ban* (Berkeley: University of California Press, 1981), p. 252. Bundy, *Danger and Survival*, p. 365, has a good discussion of Khrushchev's strange tendency to mix hair-raising threats with blowsy conviviality.

133. Memorandum, Harriman conversation with Christian A. Herter and other advisers, 10 July 1959, *FRUS: 1958–60*, x. 284–5.

134. Ann Whitman memorandum of Eisenhower comments, 1 July 1959, ibid.

295 n.; John S. D. Eisenhower memorandum, Eisenhower–Nixon conversation, 22 July 1959, ibid. 332. Nixon cannot be said to have followed this advice. See Beschloss, *Mayday*, pp. 180–4.

135. Memorandum, Eisenhower conversation with Herter and Allen Dulles, 8 July 1959, *FRUS: 1958–60*, x. 307.

136. Whitman memorandum, 1 July 1959, ibid. 295 n.

137. The circumstances of the invitation are summarized in an editorial note, ibid. 309–11. See also Chapter V.

138. For a good account of the Khrushchev visit, see Beschloss, *Mayday*, pp. 187–215. Khrushchev's own recollections are in *Khrushchev Remembers: The Last Testament*, pp. 368–416.

139. See the memorandum of Vice President Nixon's conversation with Khrushchev during his visit to the Soviet Union, 26 July 1959, *FRUS: 1958–60*, x. 360; also a memorandum of Eisenhower's conversation with Nixon and Under-Secretary of State Douglas Dillon, 5 Aug. 1959, ibid. 383.

140. See the CIA's internal history of the CORONA Project, written in 1973 by Kenneth E. Greer, in Kevin C. Ruffner, ed., *CORONA: America's First Satellite Program* (Washington: CIA, 1995), pp. 11–12. Khrushchev's recollection of the train trip, where he comments on the smoothness of the ride but not on what he might have seen from the windows, is in *Khrushchev Remembers: The Last Testament*, pp. 389–90.

141. Quoted in Horelick and Rush, *Strategic Power and Soviet Foreign Policy*, p. 58.

142. Zaloga, *Target America*, pp. 190–2; Roman, *Eisenhower and the Missile Gap*, pp. 175–92.

143. Lodge to Herter, 9 Feb. 1960, *FRUS: 1958–60*, x. 507.

144. Robert Amory, quoted in Peter Grose, *Gentleman Spy: The Life of Allen Dulles* (Boston: Houghton Mifflin, 1994), p. 350. For the defection of Lt. Col. Pyotr Popov, see ibid. 357–9; also Ranelagh, *The Agency*, pp. 255–6.

145. For these early reconnaissance operations, see Prados, *The Soviet Estimate*, pp. 29–30; Beschloss, *Mayday*, pp. 77–8; Zubok and Pleshakov, *Inside the Kremlin's Cold War*, p. 189; also Robert S. Hopkins III, "An Expanded Understanding of Eisenhower, American Policy, and Overflights," unpublished paper presented at the annual conference of the Society for Historians of American Foreign Relations, Annapolis, Md., June 1995, esp. pp. 3–5.

146. Memorandum, Eisenhower–Eden–Faure conversation, Geneva, 17 July 1955, *FRUS: 1955–7*, v. 350.

147. For the proposal, see ibid. 450–3.

148. See Beschloss, *Mayday*, pp. 98–105; McDougall, *The Heavens and the Earth*, pp. 118–20, 134; Divine, *The Sputnik Challenge*, pp. 4–6, 11–12; and John Lewis Gaddis, *The Long Peace: Inquiries into the History of the Cold War* (New York: Oxford University Press, 1987), pp. 198–9.

149. Memorandum, Eisenhower–Khrushchev conversation, Geneva, 22 July 1955, *FRUS: 1955–7*, v. 479–80. See also Eisenhower's comments on this exchange at an NSC meeting, 28 July 1955, ibid. 529–30.

150. Anatoly Dobrynin, *In Confidence: Moscow's Ambassador to America's Six Cold War Presidents (1962–1986)* (New York: Random House, 1995), pp. 147, 193–4, 424. Dobrynin claims that Khrushchev was prepared to accept "Open Skies," if for no other reason than to see if the Americans would allow Soviet overflights of their territory, but that the Politburo turned the idea down (ibid. 37–8). But this contradicts evidence from the Geneva summit, cited above, that Khrushchev rejected the idea on the spot.

151. Quoted in Beschloss, *Mayday*, p. 105.

152. Ibid. 80–93. See also Brugioni, *Eyeball to Eyeball*, p. 24; and Richard M. Bissell, Jr., with Jonathan E. Lewis and Frances T. Pudlo, *Reflections of a Cold Warrior: From Yalta to the Bay of Pigs* (New Haven: Yale University Press, 1996), pp. 94–110.

153. Ibid. 112–13; Brugioni, *Eyeball to Eyeball*, p. 302.

154. *Khrushchev Remembers: The Last Testament*, p. 444.

155. One earlier example may have been what we now know—and what American intelligence probably knew at the time—to have been the Soviet air force's extensive involvement in the Korean War. For more on this, see Chapter III.

156. Ranelagh, *The Agency*, pp. 172–3; Zaloga, *Target America*, p. 88.

157. Memorandum, Eisenhower–McElroy conversation, 12 Feb. 1959, *FRUS: 1958–60*, x. 260–2. Eisenhower presumably meant here a *unilateral* violation, not the mutually agreed overflights that would have been allowed under "Open Skies." See also, for earlier presidential expressions of skepticism on Soviet capabilities, Divine, *The Sputnik Challenge*, pp. 172–4.

158. Memorandum, Eisenhower–McElroy conversation, 12 Feb. 1959, *FRUS: 1958–60*, x. 261–2.

159. Greer, "Corona," in Ruffner, ed., *CORONA*, pp. 16–21. See also Prados, *The Soviet Estimate*, pp. 104–9.

160. Beschloss, *Mayday*, pp. 14–66, provides the best account, although there is new information on how the plane was shot down in Zaloga, *Target America*, pp. 158–9.

161. *Khrushchev Remembers: The Last Testament*, pp. 451, 455; also Zubok and Pleshakov, *Inside the Kremlin's Cold War*, pp. 202–5. Georgi Arbatov, however, claims that Khrushchev had done no serious preparation for the summit, and used the pretext of the U-2 to torpedo it (*The System: An Insider's Life in Soviet Politics* (New York: Times Books, 1992), p. 96).

162. Dobrynin, *In Confidence*, p. 42. See also Tompson, *Khrushchev*, p. 225; and Fedor Burlatsky, *Khrushchev and the First Russian Spring: The Era of Khrushchev Through the Eyes of His Advisor*, trans. Daphne Skillen (New York: Scribner's, 1991), p. 156–7.

163. *Khrushchev Remembers: The Last Testament*, p. 452.

164. See Tompson, *Khrushchev*, pp. 223–4; also Divine, *The Sputnik Challenge*, pp. 41–2.

165. Zubok and Pleshakov, *Inside the Kremlin's Cold War*, pp. 181–2.

166. *Khrushchev Remembers: The Last Testament*, pp. 449, 461.

167. Greer, "Corona," in Ruffner, ed., *CORONA*, pp. 21–2. The figure for ground resolution is in the Joint Mission Coverage Index for *Mission 9009: 18 August 1960*, ibid. 120.

168. NIE 11/8/1–61, "Strength and Deployment of Soviet Long Range Ballistic Missile Forces," 21 Sept. 1961, ibid. 130. See also Prados, *The Soviet Estimate*, pp. 117–18; and Fred Kaplan, *The Wizards of Armageddon* (New York: Simon & Schuster, 1983), pp. 286–90.

169. Quoted in Horelick and Rush, *Strategic Power and Soviet Foreign Policy*, p. 83. See also Alsop, *"I've Seen the Best of It,"* p. 415.

170. Zaloga, *Target America*, pp. 152–4.

171. See Brugioni, *Eyeball to Eyeball*, pp. 44–5.

172. Beschloss, *Mayday*, p. 288. See also, for Soviet attitudes on the legitimacy of satellite reconnaissance, Bundy, *Danger and Survival*, p. 351; and Gaddis, *The Long Peace*, pp. 203–6.

173. Quoted in Horelick and Rush, *Strategic Power and Soviet Foreign Policy*, p. 81.
174. Quoted in James G. Blight, Bruce J. Allyn, and David A. Welch, *Cuba on the Brink: Castro, the Missile Crisis, and the Soviet Collapse* (New York: Pantheon, 1993), p. 130.
175. The best discussion of this issue is in Bundy, *Danger and Survival*, pp. 338–44.
176. Zagoria, *The Sino-Soviet Conflict*, p. 160; also Adam B. Ulam, *The Communists: The Story of Power and Lost Illusions, 1948–1991* (New York: Scribner's, 1992), pp. 177–9.
177. *Khrushchev Remembers: The Last Testament*, pp. 255–7. See also Micunovic, *Moscow Diary*, p. 324; Lewis and Xue, *China Builds the Bomb*, pp. 67–8; and Li Zhisui, *The Private Life of Chairman Mao*, trans. Tai Hung-chao (New York: Random House, 1994), p. 125.
178. See Chapters IV and VI.
179. Lewis and Xue, *China Builds the Bomb*, p. 39. See also Gaddis, *The Long Peace*, pp. 184–5; Zubok and Pleshakov, *Inside the Kremlin's Cold War*, pp. 216–17; Shu Guang Zhang, *Deterrence and Strategic Culture: Chinese–American Confrontations, 1949–1958* (Ithaca: Cornell University Press, 1992), pp. 211–12.
180. For the American nuclear threats, see Chang, *Friends and Enemies*, pp. 131–7. For another general discussion of this crisis, see Qiang Zhai, *The Dragon, the Lion, and the Eagle* (Kent, Ohio: Kent State University Press, 1994), pp. 153–77.
181. See Lewis and Xue, *China Builds the Bomb*, p. 38.
182. Ibid. 39–45, 61–2.
183. Li, *The Private Life of Chairman Mao*, pp. 206–7. Presumably Li is describing Mikoyan's visit to Beijing at the time of the 8th Congress of the Chinese Communist Party in Sept. 1956. For more on this tense encounter, see Zagoria, *The Sino-Soviet Dispute*, pp. 55–6; also, for the aftermath, Micunovic, *Moscow Diary*, pp. 322–3, and the minutes of a conversation between Mao and Soviet ambassador P. F. Yudin, 22 July 1958, CWIHP *Bulletin* 6 and 7 (Winter 1995/6), 155.
184. Such is the view of Yang Kuisong, "On the Causes of the Changes in Mao Zedong's View of the Soviet Union," paper prepared for the CWIHP–University of Hong Kong conference on "The Cold War in Asia," Jan. 1996, pp. 27–9.
185. *Khrushchev Remembers*, p. 519.
186. Li, *The Private Life of Chairman Mao*, p. 262. Another source of grievance, on Mao's part, were proposals the Russians had made, earlier in the year, for joint naval cooperation and the construction of a long-wave radio facility for communicating with Soviet submarines, to be built on the Chinese coast. Mao reacted quite violently to these initiatives, regarding them as insults to Chinese sovereignty. See, on this issue, John Wilson Lewis and Xue Litai, *China's Strategic Seapower: The Politics of Force Modernization in the Nuclear Age* (Stanford: Stanford University Press, 1994), pp. 12–14.
187. Quoted in Zhang, *Deterrence and Strategic Culture*, p. 235. See also, for the connection between the Lebanon and Quemoy–Matsu crises, Xiao-bing Li, "Making of Mao's Cold War: The 1958 Taiwan Straits Crisis Revised," pp. 11–12; and Zheng Yongping, "Formulating China's Policy on the Taiwan Straits Crisis in 1958," p. 3, both papers prepared for the CWIHP–University of Hong Kong conference on "The Cold War in Asia," Jan. 1996. Traditional interpretations have assumed that Mao was responding to the failure of ambassadorial-level talks the Americans had been conducting with the Chinese since 1955, and to American plans for stationing nuclear-capable bombers and missiles on Taiwan. (See e.g. Robert Garson, *The United States and China Since 1949: A Troubled Affair* (Teaneck, NJ: Fairleigh Dickinson University Press, 1994), pp.

70–1). No doubt these developments did influence him, but it now looks as though the Lebanon crisis was the more immediate cause.

188. Li, *The Private Life of Chairman Mao*, pp. 237, 254.
189. Quoted in Zubok and Pleshakov, *Inside the Kremlin's Cold War*, p. 223.
190. Ibid. 224. See also the Soviet Central Committee's letter to the Chinese Central Committee, 27 Sept. 1958, CWIHP *Bulletin* 6 and 7 (Winter 1995/6), 226.
191. Andrei A. Gromyko, *Memoirs* (New York: Doubleday, 1989), pp. 251–2. The Chinese have denied that any such conversation, as Gromyko describes it, ever took place (Zhang, *Deterrence and Strategic Culture*, pp. 254–5). But the Zubok and Pleshakov account, cited above, is based on contemporaneous Soviet archival sources; Mao's physician recalls him outlining a similar strategy in the 1957 conversation quoted above; and so too does Khrushchev at the time of Mao's visit to Moscow later that year. (*Khrushchev Remembers: The Last Testament*, pp. 256–7).
192. Li, "Making of Mao's Cold War," pp. 12–13.
193. Mao speeches to the Supreme State Council, 5 and 8 Sept. 1958, CWIHP *Bulletin* 6 and 7 (Winter 1995/6), 216–19. See also, on the "noose" strategy, Li, "Making of Mao's Cold War," pp. 16–23; Zheng, "Formulating China's Policy on the Taiwan Straits Crisis in 1958," pp. 9–10; and Tao Wenzhao, "Relaxations and Tensions in Sino-American Relations, 1954–1958," paper prepared for the CWIHP–University of Hong Kong conference on "The Cold War in Asia," Jan. 1996, pp. 8–11.
194. Mao speech to the Supreme State Council, 5 Sept. 1958, CWIHP *Bulletin*, 6 and 7 (Winter 1995/6), 217. For the shelling figures, see Wu Xengxi, "Inside Story of the Decision Making during the Shelling of Jinmen," ibid. 210.
195. Ibid. 218.
196. Khrushchev to Eisenhower, 7 Sept. 1958, in Gillian King, ed., *Documents on International Affairs, 1958* (London: Oxford University Press, 1962), p. 187.
197. Zagoria, *The Sino-Soviet Dispute*, p. 214; Chang, *Friends and Enemies*, pp. 192–3. These interpretations as well as my own differ from that of Vladislav M. Zubok, who sees Khrushchev as "determined to stand with Beijing in a moment of crisis, and . . . prove that [he] remained loyal to the spirit and the letter of the Sino-Soviet Treaty of Feb., 1950" ("Khrushchev's Nuclear Promise," CWIHP *Bulletin* 6 and 7 (Winter 1995/6), 219).
198. Soviet Central Committee to Chinese Central Committee, 27 Sept. 1958, ibid. 226–7.
199. *Khrushchev Remembers: The Last Testament*, pp. 269–70.
200. Lewis and Xue, *China Builds the Bomb*, pp. 60–4.
201. Ibid. 308.
202. Quoted in Zagoria, *The Sino-Soviet Conflict*, pp. 278–9.
203. Ibid. 299–300.
204. *Khrushchev Remembers: The Last Testament*, p. 270.
205. See Chapter VII.
206. Zagoria, *The Sino-Soviet Conflict*, p. 300.
207. Tompson, *Khrushchev*, p. 194. See also Horelick and Rush, *Strategic Power and Soviet Foreign Policy*, p. 38, 65–6.
208. Quoted in Richter, *Khrushchev's Double Bind*, p. 140. See also Zubok and Pleshakov, *Inside the Kremlin's Cold War*, pp. 250–1; and Hope M. Harrison, "Ulbricht and the Concrete 'Rose': New Archival Evidence on the Dynamics of Soviet–East German Relations and the Berlin Crisis, 1958–1961," CWIHP Working Paper 5 (May 1993), pp. 22–5.

209. See Chapter V.

210. For anecdotal evidence to this effect, see the comments of former CIA official John Mapother in the Nuclear History Program Berlin Crisis Oral History Project *Transcripts* (College Park, Maryland: University of Maryland Center for International Security Studies, 1994), Interview 1, 9 Oct. 1990, p. 17.

211. Memorandum, Kennedy–Khrushchev conversation, 4 June 1961, *FRUS: 1961–3*, xiv. 89, 93. See also, on Khrushchev's attitude toward Kennedy, Burlatsky, *Khrushchev and the First Russian Spring*, p. 162.

212. *Khrushchev Remembers: The Last Testament*, pp. 256–7.

213. See Michael R. Beschloss, *The Crisis Years: Kennedy and Khrushchev, 1960–1963* (New York: HarperCollins, 1991), pp. 26–8, 65–6, 189–91, 202; also William D. Fahey, "The Best Intentions: The Origins of the Gilpatric Speech" (MA thesis, Ohio University, 1993), pp. 24–31.

214. See n. 168 above.

215. The flavor of these discussions is nicely captured in General Lyman Lemnitzer's abbreviated notes from the 7 Sept. 1961 meeting of the Berlin Steering Group, *FRUS: 1961–3*, xiv. 397–8. See also the interviews in the Nuclear History Program Berlin Crisis Oral History Project *Transcripts*.

216. *Public Papers of the Presidents: John F. Kennedy, 1961*, pp. 533–40. See also, on the differences between Eisenhower and Kennedy with respect to the defense of West Berlin, Bundy, *Danger and Survival*, pp. 371–8; also for a discussion of Eisenhower's and Dulles's relative flexibility on Berlin as compared to their own State and Defense Departments, Burr, "Avoiding the Slippery Slope," pp. 178, 199–205.

217. Llewellyn Thompson to State Department, 28 and 29 July 1961, *FRUS: 1961–3*, xiv. 233, 235.

218. Quoted in Beschloss, *The Crisis Years*, p. 263. See also Thompson to State Department, 28 July 1961, ibid. vii. 111–12.

219. Divine, *Blowing on the Wind*, pp. 213–40, provides a clear discussion of how this moratorium came about.

220. This issue is extensively documented in *FRUS: 1961–3*, vii. See also Seaborg, *Kennedy, Khrushchev, and the Test Ban*, pp. 29–85; and Richter, *Khrushchev's Double Bind*, pp. 146–7.

221. Viktor Adamsky and Yuri Smirnov, "Moscow's Biggest Bomb: The 50–Megaton Test of Oct. 1961," CWIHP *Bulletin* 4 (Fall 1994), 20.

222. See Sakharov, *Memoirs*, pp. 221, 229; also Zubok and Pleshakov, *Inside the Kremlin's Cold War*, p. 253.

223. Ibid. 215–18. Khrushchev's own account of this incident is in *Khrushchev Remembers: The Last Testament*, pp. 68–71.

224. Adamsky and Smirnov, "Moscow's Biggest Bomb," p. 20; Sakharov, *Memoirs*, p. 218.

225. Adamsky and Smirnov, "Moscow's Biggest Bomb," pp. 3, 19.

226. Sakharov, *Memoirs*, p. 215.

227. Hannes Adomeit, *Soviet Risk-Taking and Crisis Behavior: A Theoretical and Empirical Analysis* (London: Allen & Unwin, 1982), p. 214.

228. Adamsky and Smirnov, "Moscow's Biggest Bomb," p. 20.

229. United States Arms Control and Disarmament Agency, *Documents on Disarmament, 1961* (Washington: Government Printing Office, 1962), pp. 544–5.

230. Fahey, "The Best Intentions," p. 34.

231. I have followed, here, Fahey's thesis, cited above, which is based on interviews

with Gilpatric and Ellsberg. See also Bundy, *Danger and Survival*, pp. 381–2; Beschloss, *The Crisis Years*, pp. 329–32; Roger Hilsman, *To Move a Nation: The Politics of Foreign Policy in the Administration of John F. Kennedy* (New York: Dell, 1967), pp. 163–4; Gregg Herken, *Counsels of War* (New York: Knopf, 1985), pp. 140–2; and Richard Ned Lebow and Janice Gross Stein, *We All Lost the Cold War* (Princeton: Princeton University Press, 1994), pp. 36–8. Martin Hillenbrand has pointed out, in the Nuclear History Program Berlin Crisis Oral History Project *Transcripts*, that an additional effect was to reassure subordinates within the American government who, up to that point, had had no authoritative confirmation that the missile gap was not real (Interview 2, 22 Feb. 1991, p. 126).

232. L. Frank Baum, *The Wizard of Oz* (New York: Puffin Books, 1982), p. 135.
233. Quoted in Beschloss, *The Crisis Years*, p. 332. See also Fahey, "The Best Intentions," p. 82.
234. Quoted in Horelick and Rush, *Strategic Power and Soviet Foreign Policy*, p. 85 n.
235. Beschloss, *The Crisis Years*, p. 349.
236. Memorandum by Ambassador Josef Hegen and Counselor Werner Wenning, Beijing, 1 Dec. 1961, quoted in Harrison, "Ulbricht and the Concrete 'Rose,' " p. 53.
237. Scott D. Sagan, *Moving Targets: Nuclear Strategy and National Security* (Princeton: Princeton University Press, 1989), p. 25. See also Bundy, *Danger and Survival*, p. 322; and Roman, *Eisenhower and the Missle Gap*, p. 104.
238. Beschloss, *The Crisis Years*, p. 444.

CHAPTER IX

1. Both quotations appear in James G. Blight, Bruce J. Allyn, and David A. Welch, *Cuba on the Brink: Castro, the Missile Crisis, and the Soviet Collapse* (New York: Pantheon, 1993), p. 252.
2. Laurence Chang and Peter Kornbluh, eds., *The Cuban Missile Crisis, 1962: A National Security Archive Documents Reader* (New York: New Press, 1992), pp. 401–15, contains an extensive bibliography.
3. These new perspectives are most conveniently sampled in James A. Nathan, ed., *The Cuban Missile Crisis Revisited* (New York: St. Martin's Press, 1992). But see also Robert A. Divine, "Alive and Well: The Continuing Cuban Missile Crisis Controversy," *Diplomatic History* 18 (Fall 1994), 551–60.
4. George F. Kennan, *Memoirs: 1925–1950* (Boston: Atlantic Little, Brown, 1967), p. 368; John Lewis Gaddis, *Strategies of Containment: A Critical Appraisal of Postwar American National Security Policy* (New York: Oxford University Press, 1982), pp. 30–1.
5. William J. Tompson, *Khrushchev: A Political Life* (New York: St. Martin's Press, 1995), pp. 244–5; Vladislav Zubok and Constantine Pleshakov, *Inside the Kremlin's Cold War: From Stalin to Khrushchev* (Cambridge, Mass.: Harvard University Press, 1996), pp. 262–4.
6. This ratio is based on a 1962 estimate of 5,000 deliverable American nuclear warheads in 1962 against 300 for the Soviet Union, but as Robert McNamara has acknowledged the latter figure was probably an overestimate. (Blight et al., *Cuba on the Brink*, pp. 136–7; see also, for corroboration from the Russian side, Anatoli I. Gribkov and William Y. Smith, *Operation ANADYR: U.S. and Soviet Generals Recount the Cuban Missile Crisis* (Chicago: edition q, 1994), pp. 10–11).

Barton J. Bernstein, "Reconsidering the Missile Crisis: Dealing with the Problems of the American Jupiters in Turkey," in Nathan, ed., *The Cuban Missile Crisis Revisited*, p. 65, places the American advantage in ICBMs early in 1962 at about 9 : 1. For the 1952 estimate, see Chapter IV.

7. For recent assessments of Operation MONGOOSE, see Gribkov and Smith, *Operation ANADYR*, pp. 91–5, 105–7, 118–21; Raymond L. Garthoff, *Reflections on the Cuban Missile Crisis*, rev. edn. (Washington: Brookings Institution, 1989), pp. 6–9, 31–3, 122; and Richard M. Bissell, Jr., with Jonathan E. Lewis and Frances T. Pudlo, *Reflections of a Cold Warrior: From Yalta to the Bay of Pigs* (New Haven: Yale University Press, 1996), pp. 199, 203. Richard Reeves, *President Kennedy: Profile of Power* (New York: Simon & Schuster, 1993), pp. 263–7, 335–7, discusses Kennedy's awareness of the assassination plots against Castro. For a contemporary report on MONGOOSE and other related activities from Soviet Ambassador to Cuba Aleksandr Alekseev, dated 7 Sept. 1962, see the CWIHP *Bulletin* 5 (Spring 1995), pp. 63–4.

8. James G. Hershberg, "Before 'The Missiles of October': Did Kennedy Plan a Military Strike Against Cuba?" in Nathan, ed., *The Cuban Missile Crisis Revisited*, pp. 237–80.

9. "Notes Taken From Transcripts of Meetings of the Joint Chiefs of Staff, October–November 1962, Dealing with the Cuban Missile Crisis." I am indebted to Philip Nash for making available this document, recently released under a Freedom of Information Act appeal.

10. Blight et al., *Cuba on the Brink*, p. 41. See also Garthoff, *Reflections on the Cuban Missile Crisis*, p. 9.

11. Soviet transcript, Mikoyan–Castro conversation, 4 Nov. 1962, CWIHP *Bulletin* 5 (Spring 1995), 96.

12. *Khrushchev Remembers: The Glasnost Tapes*, trans. and ed. Jerrold L. Schecter and Vyacheslav V. Luchkov (Boston: Little, Brown, 1990), p. 170.

13. Quoted in Blight et al., *Cuba on the Brink*, p. 203. See also ibid. 124.

14. Soviet transcript, Mikoyan–Castro meeting, 4 Nov. 1962, CWIHP *Bulletin* 5 (Spring 1995), 96.

15. Gribkov and Smith, *Operation ANADYR*, p. 10. See also Richard Ned Lebow and Janice Gross Stein, *We All Lost the Cold War* (Princeton: Princeton University Press, 1994), p. 28.

16. Blight et al., *Cuba on the Brink*, p. 77. For two different interpretations that stress the strategic balance, see Garthoff, *Reflections on the Cuban Missile Crisis*, pp. 21–4; and Robert E. Quirk, *Fidel Castro* (New York: Norton, 1993), pp. 413–16.

17. Gromyko to CPSU Central Committee, 19 Oct. 1962, ibid. 66–7. See also Lebow and Stein, *We All Lost the Cold War*, p. 112; Andrei Gromyko, *Memoirs*, trans. Harold Shukman (New York: Doubleday, 1990), pp. 176–8; and Anatoly Dobrynin, *In Confidence: Moscow's Ambassador to America's Six Cold War Presidents (1962–1986)* (New York: Times Books, 1995), pp. 77–8.

18. *Time* 73 (13 Apr. 1959), 22. I owe this reference to Philip Nash, whose Ph.D. dissertation,"The Other Missiles of October: Eisenhower, Kennedy, and the Jupiters in Europe, 1957–1963" (Ohio University, 1994), pp. 1–57, provides the best account of the 1957 NATO MRBM-IRBM deployment decision.

19. Ibid. 58–191. The operational dates of the Turkish Jupiters are on pp. 170–1; also in Garthoff, *Reflections on the Cuban Missile Crisis*, p. 60. For documentation on Kennedy's decision to let the deployment proceed, see *FRUS: 1961–3*, xvi. 702–4.

20. Michael R. Beschloss, *The Crisis Years: Kennedy and Khrushchev, 1960–1963* (New York: HarperCollins, 1991), p. 444. See also Chapter VIII and, for an inspired

comparison to an episode in *Dr. Strangelove*, Nash, "The Other Missiles of October," pp. 193–4. The Jupiters were actually IRBMs, not MRBMs.

21. Memorandum, Nixon–Khrushchev conversation, 26 July 1959, *FRUS: 1958–60*, x. 363.

22. Quoted in Nash, "The Other Missiles of October," p. 165. Khrushchev was wrong if he thought there were American missiles in Iran. For a lengthy Gromyko–Rusk conversation on this subject, see Gromyko to the CPSU Central Committee, 20 Oct. 1962, CWIHP *Bulletin* 5 (Spring 1995), 67–9; also Gromyko, *Memoirs*, pp. 178–9.

23. The story is told by Khrushchev's son-in-law, Alexei Adzhubei, in the BBC television documentary "The Cuban Missile Crisis," pt. 1. See also Nash, "The Other Missiles of October," pp. 174–5.

24. *Khrushchev Remembers*, trans. and ed. Strobe Talbott (New York: Bantam, 1971), p. 547. See also Garthoff, *Reflections on the Cuban Missile Crisis*, pp. 12–16; Blight et al., *Cuba on the Brink*, p. 344; as well as the comments of Sergo Mikoyan in James G. Blight and David A. Welch, *On the Brink: Americans and Soviets Reexamine the Cuban Missile Crisis* (New York: Hill & Wang, 1989), p. 239; and Fedor Burlatsky, *Khrushchev and the First Russian Spring: The Era of Khrushchev Through the Eyes of His Advisor*, trans. Daphne Skillen (New York: Scribner's, 1991), p. 171.

25. Zubok and Pleshakov, *Inside the Kremlin's Cold War*, p. 260; Lebow and Stein, *We All Lost the Cold War*, pp. 48, 91; Nash, "The Other Missiles of October," pp. 176–7.

26. Blight et al., *Cuba on the Brink*, pp. 83, 198, 200; also pp. 242–3. Castro described his thinking in similar terms to a top Soviet official in a Jan. 1987 conversation. See Georgy K. Shakhnazarov, "Fidel Castro, Glasnost, and the Caribbean Crisis," CWIHP *Bulletin* 5 (Spring 1995), 88–9.

27. Gribkov and Smith, *Operation ANADYR*, p. 20. For a somewhat different interpretation of Castro's motives, see Blight et al., *Cuba on the Brink*, pp. 345–7.

28. Ibid. 254.

29. Ibid. 346–7; also Philip Brenner, "Thirteen Months: Cuba's Perspective on the Missile Crisis," in Nathan, ed., *The Cuban Missile Crisis Revisited*, pp. 193–4.

30. See Zubok and Pleshakov, *Inside the Kremlin's Cold War*, p. 260.

31. Blight et al., *Cuba on the Brink*, p. 254. See also Shakhnazarov, "Fidel Castro, Glasnost, and the Caribbean Crisis," p. 89.

32. Blight et al., *Cuba on the Brink*, p. 85; Blight and Welch, *On the Brink*, pp. 40–2; Garthoff, *Reflections on the Cuban Missile Crisis*, p. 24.

33. See Gromyko's account of an extended discussion of this matter with Dean Rusk on 18 Oct., after the Americans had discovered the Soviet IRBMs in Cuba but before they had revealed this information publicly (Gromyko to CPSU Central Committee, 20 Oct. 1962, CWIHP *Bulletin* 5 (Spring 1995), 68).

34. Soviet transcript, Mikoyan–Castro conversation, 4 Nov. 1962, ibid. 97. See also *Khrushchev Remembers: The Glasnost Tapes*, p. 171.

35. A point made well by Lebow and Stein, *We All Lost the Cold War*, p. 63.

36. See Chapter III.

37. Garthoff, *Reflections on the Cuban Missile Crisis*, p. 17; Beschloss, *The Crisis Years*, pp. 398–9. For the text of the treaty, see Gribkov and Smith, *Operation ANADYR*, pp. 185–8.

38. Ibid. 9, 17, 26–8. See also Blight et al., *Cuba on the Brink*, pp. 58–61; and Garthoff, *Reflections on the Cuban Missile Crisis*, p. 20.

39. Dino A. Brugioni, *Eyeball to Eyeball: The Inside Story of the Cuban Missile Crisis* (New York: Random House, 1991), pp. 56–217, provides a fine account of the

build-up and the discovery. For a sampling of CIA assessments, see Mary S. McAuliffe, ed., *CIA Documents on the Cuban Missile Crisis* (Washington: CIA, 1992), pp. 1–137.

40. Garthoff, *Reflections on the Cuban Missile Crisis*, pp. 35–6.
41. Gribkov and Smith, *Operation ANADYR*, pp. 15, 21, 55.
42. Soviet transcript, Mikoyan–Castro conversation, 4 Nov. 1962, CWIHP *Bulletin* 5 (Spring 1995), 97.
43. Gribkov and Smith, *Operation ANADYR*, pp. 51–2; Brugioni, *Eyeball to Eyeball*, pp. 197–9.
44. See Castro's acknowledgements of this point in Blight et al., *Cuba on the Brink*, pp. 199, 251; also Gribkov and Smith, *Operation ANADYR*, p. 70.
45. Blight et al., *Cuba on the Brink*, p. 200.
46. Beschloss, *The Crisis Years*, pp. 425–6, 500; Garthoff, *Reflections on the Cuban Missile Crisis*, pp. 29, 47–8. Bolshakov later claimed to have been unware of the missile deployment at the time he passed along Khrushchev's assurances that no offensive weapons were going into Cuba. See also Blight et al., *Cuba on the Brink*, pp. 207–8, where Castro acknowledges the artificiality of the distinction between "offensive" and "defensive" weapons.
47. Gribkov and Smith, *Operation ANADYR*, p. 15.
48. Lebow and Stein, *We All Lost the Cold War*, p. 87 (emphasis in original). See also ibid. 105.
49. Bernstein, "Reconsidering the Missile Crisis," p. 68; also McGeorge Bundy, *Danger and Survival: Choices About the Bomb in the First Fifty Years* (New York: Random House, 1988), p. 417.
50. Beschloss, *The Crisis Years*, pp. 442–3; Blight et al., *Cuba on the Brink*, pp. 136–7. See also Bundy, *Danger and Survival*, p. 448.
51. Lebow and Stein, *We All Lost the Cold War*, pp. 79, 95–8; Hershberg, "Before 'The Missiles of October'," pp. 260–1; Beschloss, *The Crisis Years*, pp. 414–15. Keating's sources have never been established, but for a plausible guess from a knowledgeable Washington insider, see Gribkov and Smith, *Operation ANADYR*, pp. 108–9.
52. Quoted in Chang and Kornbluh, eds., *The Cuban Missile Crisis*, p. 355. Kennedy made a similar statement on 13 Sept.
53. Dobrynin, *In Confidence*, pp. 79–80. "I've always believed—or at least I believed then—that we knew the Americans better than the Soviets," Castro commented in 1992 (Blight et al., *Cuba on the Brink*, p. 91). Raul Castro, however, did express confidence shortly before the crisis that Soviet *public* statements of support for Cuba in the face of American threats "will be very easy for ordinary Latin Americans and for the people of the USA itself to understand" (Alekseev to Soviet Foreign Ministry, 11 Sept. 1962, CWIHP *Bulletin* 5 (Spring 1995), 65).
54. Nash, "The Other Missiles of October," pp. 204–5.
55. See Donald Kagan, *On the Origins of War and the Preservation of Peace* (New York: Doubleday, 1995) p. 504, which notes the vehemence of British Prime Minister Neville Chamberlain's reaction—and the widespread popular support for it—when in Mar. 1939, Hitler violated the Munich agreement and took over all of Czechoslovakia. Beschloss, *The Crisis Years*, pp. 414–30, provides a good discussion of the domestic political pressures Kennedy faced on the eve of the missile crisis. See also Bundy, *Danger and Survival*, pp. 412–13; and Lebow and Stein, *We All Lost the Cold War*, pp. 95–8.
56. See, for an elaboration of these points, Scott Sagan, *The Limits of Safety: Organizations, Accidents, and Nuclear Weapons* (Princeton: Princeton University Press, 1993), pp. 53–5.

57. Bundy, *Danger and Survival*, p. 461. For Kennedy's estimate, see p. 453.
58. Sagan, *The Limits of Safety*, pp. 11–52, provides an excellent review of the theoretical literature on why accidents happen.
59. Soviet transcript, Mikoyan conversations with Castro and Guevara, 3 and 5 Nov. 1962, CWIHP *Bulletin* 5 (Spring 1995), pp. 93, 108. See also Lebow and Stein, *We All Lost the Cold War*, p. 116; Quirk, *Fidel Castro*, pp. 434, 443–5; and Vladislav M. Zubok, "'Dismayed by the Actions of the Soviet Union': Mikoyan's Talks with Fidel Castro and the Cuban Leadership, November, 1962," CWIHP *Bulletin* 5 (Spring 1995), pp. 59, 89–92.
60. Beschloss, *The Crisis Years*, pp. 544–5. See also Blight et al., *Cuba on the Brink*, p. 357; and Gribkov and Smith, *Operation ANADYR*, p. 176.
61. For some examples, in which he includes some of his own earlier writing, see Bernstein, "Reconsidering the Missile Crisis," p. 56.
62. Ibid. 57; Lebow and Stein, *We All Lost the Cold War*, pp. 123–5.
63. For the circumstances of the taping, see Marc Tractenberg, "White House Tapes and Minutes of the Cuban Missile Crisis: ExCom Meetings, October, 1962," in Sean M. Lynn-Jones, Steven E. Miller, and Stephen Van Evera, eds., *Nuclear Diplomacy and Crisis Management* (Cambridge, Mass.: MIT Press, 1990), pp. 283–9.
64. Transcript, ExComm meeting of 27 Oct. 1962, in Chang and Kornbluh, eds., *The Cuban Missile Crisis*, p. 216.
65. Dobrynin to Soviet Foreign Ministry, 27 Oct. 1962, CWIHP *Bulletin* 5 (Spring 1995), 79–80. See also Dobrynin, *In Confidence*, pp. 86–91; Bundy, *Danger and Survival*, pp. 432–3; and Lebow and Stein, *We All Lost the Cold War*, pp. 125–7. In another example of custodial historiography, Theodore Sorensen took it upon himself to rewrite Robert F. Kennedy's posthumous account of the crisis to obscure any suggestion that the President might have approved an explicit exchange of Cuban for Turkish missiles. See James G. Hershberg, "Anatomy of a Controversy: Anatoly F. Dobrynin's Meeting with Robert F. Kennedy, Saturday, 27 October 1962," CWIHP *Bulletin* 5 (Spring 1995), pp. 75–80.
66. Mikoyan's conversations with Castro early in Nov. 1962, make it very clear that he understood the Turkish missiles to be part of the settlement; indeed, he found himself having to explain why the Russians had insisted on the removal of the Jupiters and not the American naval base at Guantanamo. Mikoyan also suggests, though, that the Russians did not see the Turkish missiles *during the crisis itself* as having the importance Kennedy thought they did. Khrushchev got the idea of including them in the deal, Mikoyan claimed, from a Walter Lippmann column in the *Washington Post* on 25 Oct. (CWIHP *Bulletin* 5 (Spring 1995), pp. 98–9). Khrushchev later confirmed that he saw both the Turkish and Italian missiles, by this time, as having only "symbolic" importance because of their obsolescence (*Khrushchev Remembers: The Last Testament*, trans. and ed. Strobe Talbott (Boston: Little, Brown, 1974), p. 512). See also Lebow and Stein, *We All Lost the Cold War*, pp. 134–5.
67. Blight and Welch, *On the Brink*, pp. 83–4; Garthoff, *Reflections on the Cuban Missile Crisis*, pp. 95–6.
68. Bernstein, "Reconsidering the Missile Crisis," pp. 100–1; Lebow and Stein, *We All Lost the Cold War*, pp. 127–30.
69. Quoted in Nash, "The Other Missiles of October," p. 209.
70. Ibid. See also Bernstein, "Reconsidering the Missile Crisis," p. 90; Lebow and Stein, *We All Lost the Cold War*, pp. 119–20; and Gribkov and Smith, *Operation ANADYR*, p. 138.
71. See Elizabeth Cohn, "President Kennedy's Decision to Impose a Blockade in the

Cuban Missile Crisis: Building Consensus in the ExComm After the Decision," in Nathan, ed., *The Cuban Missile Crisis Revisited*, pp. 219–35.

72. Divine, "Alive and Well," p. 559.
73. Roberta Wohlstetter, *Pearl Harbor: Warning and Decision* (Stanford: Stanford University Press, 1962) is, of course, the classic work.
74. Sagan, *The Limits of Safety*, pp. 62–5, provides a clear discussion of the Defcon system. For the importance of the Pearl Harbor analogy, see Kagan, *On the Origins of War*, p. 506.
75. These points, as well as the next four paragraphs, draw heavily upon Sagan, *The Limits of Safety*, esp. chs. 2 and 3.
76. See Quirk, *Fidel Castro*, p. 417.
77. Garthoff, *Reflections on the Cuban Missile Crisis*, p. 46.
78. Gribkov and Smith, *Operation ANADYR*, pp. 26–7, 45–6. These figures correct earlier information provided by Gribkov in 1992. See Blight et al., *Cuba on the Brink*, pp. 58–65, 352–5.
79. Zubok and Pleshakov, *Inside the Kremlin's Cold War*, p. 265, claim that 164 nuclear "charges" were sent from the Soviet Union.
80. Quoted in Blight et al., *Cuba on the Brink*, p. 351.
81. Gribkov and Smith, *Operation ANADYR*, pp. 63–4. See also pp. 5, 27; and, for Khrushchev's own recollections of the proposed naval deployment, *Khrushchev Remembers: The Glasnost Tapes*, p. 172.
82. Gribkov and Smith, *Operation ANADYR*, pp. 139–41; Bundy, *Danger and Survival*, p. 425; Garthoff, *Reflections on the Cuban Missile Crisis*, pp. 37–40. See also, on the search for nuclear weapons in Cuba, Brugioni, *Eyeball to Eyeball*, pp. 538–48.
83. Gribkov and Smith, *Operation ANADYR*, p. 65.
84. For more counterfactual speculation, see ibid. 64–6, 173–8. "That fear and interest moves states to war will not surprise the modern reader," historian Donald Kagan has written, "but that concern for honor should do so may seem strange. If we take honor to mean fame, glory, renown, or splendor, it may appear applicable only to an earlier time. If, however, we understand its significance as deference, esteem, just due, regard, respect, or prestige we will find it an important motive of nations in the modern world as well" (*On the Origins of War*, p. 8).
85. Soviet transcript, Castro–Mikoyan conversation, 3 Nov. 1962, CWIHP *Bulletin* 5 (Spring 1995), p. 94.
86. Mark Kramer, "The 'Lessons' of the Cuban Missile Crisis for Warsaw Pact Nuclear Operations," ibid. 110, 112. See also Gribkov and Smith, *Operation ANADYR*, pp. 6, 43, 62–3, which claims that Pliyev did actually move the warheads; also Brugioni, *Eyeball to Eyeball*, pp. 547–8, which suggests on the basis of American reconnaissance photographs that some were actually mounted on missiles.
87. Gribkov and Smith, *Operation ANADYR*, p. 57; Blight et al., *Cuba on the Brink*, p. 86.
88. Castro to Khrushchev, 28 Oct. 1962, ibid. 484.
89. Gribkov and Smith, *Operation ANADYR*, p. 67. See also Gribkov's comments in Blight et al., *Cuba on the Brink*, pp. 104–5, 113–14; and Garthoff, *Reflections on the Cuban Missile Crisis*, pp. 82–5.
90. Blight et al., *Cuba on the Brink*, p. 108.
91. See, on Pliyev, Garthoff, *Reflections on the Cuban Missile Crisis*, pp. 18–19; Zubok and Pleshakov, *Inside the Kremlin's Cold War*, p. 264; Gribkov and Smith, *Operation ANADYR*, p. 25; and Kramer, "The 'Lessons' of the Cuban Missile Crisis for Warsaw Pact Nuclear Operations," pp. 110, 112.
92. Castro to Khrushchev, 26 Oct. 1962, ibid. 481.

93. Khrushchev to Castro, 30 Oct. 1962, ibid. 486–7. See also *Khrushchev Remembers: The Glasnost Tapes*, pp. 177, 182–3. For Castro's explanation of this message, which emphasizes translation difficulties, see Blight et al., *Cuba on the Brink*, pp. 121–2, 478–80.

94. Khrushchev to Castro, 28 Oct. 1962, in ibid. 482.

95. *Khrushchev Remembers: The Glasnost Tapes*, p. 183.

96. See Chapter VIII.

97. Beschloss, *The Crisis Years*, pp. 542–5. See also Reeves, *President Kennedy*, pp. 424–5.

98. John Lewis Gaddis, *Russia, the Soviet Union, and the United States: An Interpretive History*, 2nd edn. (New York: McGraw-Hill, 1990), p. 251. Khrushchev's admission is in *Khrushchev Remembers*, p. 553.

99. Ibid. 555.

100. *Khrushchev Remembers: The Glasnost Tapes*, p. 180.

101. Khrushchev to Castro, 30 Oct. 1962, in Blight et al., *Cuba on the Brink*, p. 488.

102. Soviet transcript, Mikoyan–Castro conversation, 4 Nov. 1962, CWIHP *Bulletin* 5 (Spring 1995), p. 97.

103. Zubok and Pleshakov, *Inside the Kremlin's Cold War*, p. 268; Gribkov and Smith, *Operation ANADYR*, p. 73; Tompson, *Khrushchev*, pp. 272–3; Khrushchev, *Khrushchev on Khrushchev*, pp. 156–7; Garthoff, *Reflections on the Cuban Missile Crisis*, p. 132.

104. For a convenient graphical representation of the post-Khrushchev Soviet strategic military build-up, see the CIA National Intelligence Estimate 11–3/8–76, "Soviet Forces for Intercontinental Conflict Through the Mid-1980s," 21 Dec. 1976, in Donald P. Steury, comp., *Estimates on Soviet Military Power, 1954 to 1984: A Selection* (Washington: CIA, 1994), p. 253.

105. Hershberg, "Before 'The Missiles of October,'" makes the strongest case for this possibility.

106. Garthoff, *Reflections on the Cuban Missile Crisis*, p. 127.

107. Blight et al., *Cuba on the Brink*, pp. 236–9; Quirk, *Fidel Castro*, pp. 480–3; also Carlos Lechuga, *In the Eye of the Storm: Castro, Khrushchev, Kennedy and the Missile Crisis*, trans. Mary Todd (Melbourne: Ocean Press, 1995), pp. 195–211.

108. John Lewis Gaddis, *The Long Peace: Inquiries into the History of the Cold War* (New York: Oxford University Press, 1987), pp. 215–45. The paragraph that follows draws on this essay.

109. A classic analysis of this system is Kenneth Waltz, *Theory of International Politics* (New York: Random House, 1979).

CHAPTER X

1. Warren I. Cohen, *America in the Age of Soviet Power, 1945–1991* (New York: Cambridge University Press, 1993), p. 261.

2. Eric Hobsbawm, *The Age of Extremes: A History of the World, 1914–1991* (New York: Pantheon, 1994), p. 614.

3. For an illustration of the errors that can arise from trying to guess the outcome of a historical event without knowing it, see John Lewis Gaddis, *The United States and the End of the Cold War: Implications, Reconsiderations, Provocations* (New York: Oxford University Press, 1992), pp. 133–54.

384 Notes for pages 282–7

4. Michael J. Hogan and Thomas G. Paterson, eds., *Explaining the History of American Foreign Relations* (New York: Cambridge University Press, 1991) provides a good introduction to these schools of interpretation; as does Anders Stephanson, "The United States," in David Reynolds, ed., *The Origins of the Cold War in Europe: International Perspectives* (New Haven: Yale University Press, 1994), pp. 23–52.

5. Two important exceptions were William H. McNeill, *America, Britain and Russia: Their Cooperation and Conflict* (New York: Johnson Reprint, 1970; originally published in 1953); and Louis J. Halle, *The Cold War as History* (New York: Harper & Row, 1967).

6. See Douglas J. Macdonald, "Communist Bloc Expansion in the Early Cold War: Challenging Realism, Refuting Revisionism," *International Security* 20 (Winter 1995/6), 152–88; and, for a more general set of complaints, John Lewis Gaddis, "International Relations Theory and the End of the Cold War," ibid. 17 (Winter 1992/3), 5–58. For another critique of realism from a different perspective, see John Gerard Ruggie, "The False Premise of Realism," ibid. 20 (Summer 1995), 62–70.

7. John Lewis Gaddis, "The Tragedy of Cold War History," *Diplomatic History* 17 (Winter 1993), 7–9, expands on this point.

8. See e.g. Halle, *The Cold War as History*, pp. 1–11.

9. Here the influence of Hans J. Morgenthau predominated, especially his *Politics Among Nations: The Struggle for Power and Peace* (New York: Knopf, 1948), which went through five subsequent editions. Other prominent "realist" analyses included Edward Hallett Carr, *The Twenty Years' Crisis, 1919–1939: An Introduction to the Study of International Relations* (New York: St. Martin's Press, 1939); Walter Lippmann, *U.S. Foreign Policy: Shield of the Republic* (Boston: Little, Brown, 1943); and George F. Kennan, *American Diplomacy: 1900–1950* (Chicago: University of Chicago Press, 1951).

10. Kenneth Waltz, *Theory of International Politics* (New York: Random House, 1979), pp. 183, 204.

11. For a similar metaphor used somewhat differently, see Marshall D. Shulman, "The Superpowers: Dance of the Dinosaurs," *Foreign Affairs* 66 ("America and the World, 1987/8"), 494.

12. Geir Lundestad, "Empire By Invitation? The United States and Western Europe, 1945–1952," *Journal of Peace Research* 23 (Sept. 1986), 263–77.

13. For an expanded argument, see John Lewis Gaddis, "On Moral Equivalency and Cold War History," *Ethics and International Affairs* 10 (1996), 131–48.

14. This section draws on ibid. 142–5, which in turn relies heavily upon Norman M. Naimark, *The Russians in Germany: A History of the Soviet Zone of Occupation, 1945–1949* (Cambridge, Mass.: Harvard University Press, 1995), pp. 69–140.

15. See the interviews with Red Army officers in pt. 1 of the British television series *Messengers From Moscow*; also Milovan Djilas, *Conversations with Stalin*, trans. Michael B. Petrovich (New York: Harcourt, Brace & World, 1962), p. 95.

16. Naimark, *The Russians in Germany*, pp. 120–1.

17. I have in mind, in particular, the treatment of Cold War history in the first draft of the National History Standards and the Smithsonian Institution's abortive effort to mount an exhibit on the dropping of the atomic bomb. Both are discussed more fully in my "Moral Equivalency" article, cited above. See also, for the argument that contemporary perceptions of good and evil are inappropriate in the writing of Cold War history, Michael J. Hogan, "State of the Art: An Introduction," in Hogan, ed., *America in the World: The Historiography of*

American Foreign Relations since 1941 (New York: Cambridge University Press, 1995), pp. 4–9.

18. See the works cited in n. 9 above.
19. Kennan, *American Diplomacy*, p. 66.
20. Kennan "long telegram" of 22 Feb. 1946, *FRUS: 1946*, vi. 709.
21. A point made by Tony Smith, *America's Mission: The United States and the Worldwide Struggle for Democracy in the Twentieth Century* (Princeton: Princeton University Press, 1994), p. 156.
22. Henry Kissinger, *Diplomacy* (New York: Simon & Schuster, 1994), pp. 332–3.
23. See John Mueller, *Retreat from Doomsday: The Obsolescence of Major War* (New York: Basic Books, 1989).
24. James Gleick, *Chaos: The Making of a New Science* (New York: Viking, 1987) provides a useful explanation.
25. See Melvyn P. Leffler, "New Approaches, Old Interpretations, and Prospective Reconfigurations," *Diplomatic History* 19 (Spring 1995), 187–8.
26. See the commentaries by Michael Hogan, Bruce Cumings, and (particularly surprisingly) Michael Hunt in Hogan, ed., *America in the World*, pp. 3–19, 127–39, 148–55.
27. A point made by Leffler with respect to my own work in "New Approaches, Old Interpretations, and Prospective Reconfigurations," p. 187; as well as in "Inside Enemy Archives: The Cold War Reopened," *Foreign Affairs* 75 (July/Aug., 1996), 121.
28. For more on this, see John Lewis Gaddis, "Peace, Legitimacy, and the Post-Cold War World: Where Do We Go From Here?" in Geir Lundestad, ed., *The Fall of Great Powers: Peace, Stability, and Legitimacy* (New York: Oxford University Press, 1994), pp. 351–68.
29. Or so Mueller argues in *Retreat from Doomsday*, esp. pp. 3–13.
30. I heard Gould make this point in a presentation at Ohio University in May 1994.

BIBLIOGRAPHY

I. DOCUMENTS

Boyle, Peter G., ed., *The Churchill–Eisenhower Correspondence, 1953–1955* (Chapel Hill: University of North Carolina Press, 1990).

Chang, Laurence, and Peter Kornbluh, eds., *The Cuban Missile Crisis, 1962: A National Security Archive Documents Reader* (New York: New Press, 1992).

Daniels, Robert V., ed., *A Documentary History of Communism*, rev. edn. (Hanover, NH: University Press of New England, 1984).

Etzold, Thomas H., and John Lewis Gaddis, eds., *Containment: Documents on American Policy and Strategy, 1945–1950* (New York: Columbia University Press, 1978).

Ferrell, Robert H., ed., *The Diary of James C. Hagerty: Eisenhower in Mid-Course, 1954–1955* (Bloomington: Indiana University Press, 1983).

——, *The Eisenhower Diaries* (New York: Norton, 1981).

——, *Off the Record: The Private Papers of Harry S. Truman* (New York: Harper & Row, 1980).

Frankland, Noble, ed., *Documents on International Affairs, 1956* (London: Oxford University Press, 1959).

Franklin, Bruce, ed., *The Essential Stalin: Major Theoretical Writings, 1905–52* (Garden City, NY: Anchor Books, 1972).

Genoud, François, ed., *The Testament of Adolf Hitler: The Hitler–Bormann Documents, February–April 1954*, trans. R. H. Stevens (London: Icon Books, 1961).

Jensen, Kenneth M., ed., *Origins of the Cold War: The Novikov, Kennan, and Roberts "Long Telegrams" of 1946* (Washington: United States Institute of Peace, 1991).

Kau, Michael Y. M., and John K. Leung, eds., *The Writings of Mao Zedong*, i: *September, 1949–December, 1955* (Armonk, NY: M. E. Sharpe, 1986).

Lih, Lars H., Oleg V. Naumov, and Oleg V. Khlevniuk, eds., *Stalin's Letters to Molotov, 1925–1936* (New Haven: Yale University Press, 1995).

Lilienthal, David E., *The Journals of David E. Lilienthal: The Atomic Energy Years, 1945–1950* (New York: Harper & Row, 1964).

MacFarquhar, Roderick, Timothy Cheek, and Eugene Wu, eds., *The Secret Speeches of Chairman Mao: From the Hundred Flowers to the Great Leap Forward* (Cambridge, Mass.: Harvard University Press, 1989).

McAuliffe, Mary S., ed., *CIA Documents on the Cuban Missile Crisis* (Washington: Central Intelligence Agency, 1992).

Millis, Walter, ed., *The Forrestal Diaries* (New York: Viking, 1951).

Public Papers of the Presidents of the United States: Dwight D. Eisenhower, 1953–61 (Washington: Government Printing Office, 1960–61).

——, *John F. Kennedy, 1961–63* (Washington: Government Printing Office, 1962–4).

——, *Harry S. Truman, 1945–53* (Washington: Government Printing Office, 1961–6).

Rigby, T. H., ed., *The Stalin Dictatorship: Khrushchev's 'Secret Speech' and Other Documents* (Sydney: Sydney University Press, 1968).

Rubinstein, Alvin Z., ed., *The Foreign Policy of the Soviet Union*, 3rd edn. (New York: Random House, 1972).

The State Department Policy Planning Staff Papers (3 vols., New York: Garland, 1983).

Steury, Donald P., comp., *Estimates on Soviet Military Power, 1954 to 1984: A Selection* (Washington: Central Intelligence Agency, 1994).

Tucker, Robert C., ed., *The Lenin Anthology* (New York: Norton, 1975).

——, *The Marx-Engels Reader*, 2nd edn. (New York: Norton, 1978).

US Bureau of the Census and the Social Science Research Council, *The Statistical History of the United States from Colonial Times to the Present* (Stamford, Conn.: Fairfield Publishers, 1965).

US Congress, Senate Committee on Foreign Relations, *Historical Series: Reviews of the World Situation, 1949–1950* (Washington: Government Printing Office, 1974).

US Department of State, *Foreign Relations of the United States* (Washington: Government Printing Office, 1861–).

——, *Foreign Relations of the United States: The Conferences at Cairo and Tehran, 1943* (Washington: Government Printing Office, 1961).

——, *Foreign Relations of the United States: The Conferences at Malta and Yalta, 1945* (Washington: Government Printing Office, 1955).

——, *United States Relations with China, with Special Reference to the Period 1944–1949* (Washington: Government Printing Office, 1949).

Warner, Michael, ed., *The CIA under Harry Truman* (Washington: Central Intelligence Agency, 1994).

II. BOOKS

Acheson, Dean, *Present at the Creation: My Years in the State Department* (New York: Norton, 1969).

Adams, Sherman, *Firsthand Report: The Story of the Eisenhower Administration* (New York: Harper, 1961).

Adomeit, Hannes, *Soviet Risk-Taking and Crisis Behavior: A Theoretical and Empirical Analysis* (London: Allen & Unwin, 1982).

Aliano, Richard A., *American Defense Policy from Eisenhower to Kennedy: The Politics of Changing Military Requirements, 1957–1961* (Athens: Ohio University Press, 1975).

Allison, Graham, and Gregory Treverton, eds., *Rethinking America's Security: Beyond the Cold War to New World Order* (New York: Norton, 1992).

Alperovitz, Gar, *Atomic Diplomacy: Hiroshima and Potsdam*, expanded and rev. edn. (New York: Penguin, 1985).

——, *The Decision to Use the Atomic Bomb and the Architecture of an American Myth* (New York: Knopf, 1995).

Alsop, Joseph W., with Adam Platt, *"I've Seen the Best of It:" Memoirs* (New York: Norton, 1992).

Ambrose, Stephen E., *Eisenhower: Soldier, General of the Army, President-Elect, 1890–1952* (New York: Simon & Schuster, 1983).

——, *Eisenhower: The President* (New York: Simon & Schuster, 1984).

——, *Nixon: The Education of a Politician, 1913–1962* (New York: Simon & Schuster, 1987).

Ambrosius, Lloyd E., *Woodrow Wilson and the American Democratic Tradition: The Treaty Fight in Perspective* (New York: Cambridge University Press, 1987).

Andrew, Christopher, and Oleg Gordievsky, *KGB: The Inside Story of its Foreign Operations from Lenin to Gorbachev* (New York: HarperCollins, 1990).

Arbatov, Georgi, *The System: An Insider's Life in Soviet Politics* (New York: Times Books, 1992).

Arendt, Hannah, *The Origins of Totalitarianism* (New York: Harcourt, 1951).

Arkes, Hadley, *Bureaucracy, the Marshall Plan, and the National Interest* (Princeton: Princeton University Press, 1972).

Banac, Ivo, *With Stalin Against Tito: Cominformist Splits in Yugoslav Communism* (Ithaca: Cornell University Press, 1988).

Barraclough, Geoffrey, *An Introduction to Contemporary History* (London: C. A. Watts, 1964).

Bassford, Christopher, *Clausewitz in English: The Reception of Clausewitz in Britain and America, 1815–1945* (New York: Oxford University Press, 1994).

Beard, Charles A., *President Roosevelt and the Coming of the War, 1941* (New Haven: Yale University Press, 1948).

Becker, William H., and Samuel F. Wells, Jr., *Economics and World Power: An Assessment of American Diplomacy Since 1789* (New York: Columbia University Press, 1984).

Beckman, Peter R., *World Politics in the Twentieth Century* (Englewoods Cliffs, NJ: Prentice-Hall, 1984).

Berezhkov, Valentin M., *At Stalin's Side: His Interpreter's Memoirs from the October Revolution to the Fall of the Dictator's Empire*, trans. Sergei I. Mikheyev (New York: Birch Lane Press, 1994).

Beschloss, Michael R., *The Crisis Years: Kennedy and Khruschev, 1960–1963* (New York: HarperCollins, 1991).

——, *Mayday: Eisenhower, Khrushchev and the U-2 Affair* (New York: Harper & Row, 1986).

Billings-Yun, Melanie, *Decision Against War: Eisenhower and Dien Bien Phu, 1954* (New York: Columbia University Press, 1988).

Bills, Scott L., *Empire and Cold War: The Roots of US–Third World Antagonism, 1945–47* (New York: St. Martin's Press, 1990).

Bissell, Richard M., Jr., with Jonathan E. Lewis and Frances T. Pudlo, *Reflections of a Cold Warrior: From Yalta to the Bay of Pigs* (New Haven: Yale University Press, 1996).

Blight, James G., Bruce J. Allyn, and David A. Welch, *Cuba on the Brink: Castro, the Missile Crisis, and the Soviet Collapse* (New York: Pantheon, 1993).

——, and David A. Welch, *On the Brink: Americans and Soviets Reexamine the Cuban Missile Crisis* (New York: Hill & Wang, 1989).

Bloch, Marc, *The Historian's Craft*, trans. Peter Putnam (New York: Vintage, 1953).

Block, Fred L., *The Origins of International Economic Disorder: A Study of United States International Monetary Policy from World War II to the Present* (Berkeley: University of California Press, 1977).

Bohlen, Charles E., *Witness to History: 1929–1969* (New York: Norton, 1973).

Bolkhovitinov, Nikolai N., *The Beginnings of Russian–American Relations, 1775–1815*, trans. Elena Levin (Cambridge, Mass.: Harvard University Press, 1975).

Borg, Dorothy, and Waldo Heinrichs, eds., *Uncertain Years: Chinese–American Relations, 1947–1950* (New York: Columbia University Press, 1980).

Borovik, Genrikh, *The Philby Files: The Secret Life of Master Spy Kim Philby*, ed. Philip Knightley (Boston: Little, Brown, 1994).

Borowski, Harry R., *A Hollow Threat: Strategic Air Power and Containment before Korea* (Westport, Conn.: Greenwood Press, 1982).

Brands, H. W., *Inside the Cold War: Loy Henderson and the Rise of the American Empire, 1918–1961* (New York: Oxford University Press, 1991).

——, *The Specter of Neutralism: The United States and the Emergence of the Third World, 1945–1950* (New York: Columbia University Press, 1989).

Breuer, William B., *Race to the Moon: America's Duel with the Soviets* (Westport, Conn.: Praeger, 1993).

Brinkley, Douglas, *Dean Acheson: The Cold War Years, 1953–71* (New Haven: Yale University Press, 1992).

Brodie, Bernard, ed., *The Absolute Weapon: Atomic Power and World Order* (New York: Harcourt, Brace & World, 1946).

Brugioni, Dino A., *Eyeball to Eyeball: The Inside Story of the Cuban Missile Crisis* (New York: Random House, 1991).

Buckley, Thomas H., *The United States and the Washington Conference, 1921–22* (Knoxville: University of Tennessee Press, 1970).

——, and Edwin B. Strong, Jr., *American Foreign and National Security Policies, 1914–1945* (Knoxville: University of Tennessee Press, 1987).

Buhite, Russell D., *Decisions at Yalta: An Appraisal of Summit Diplomacy* (Wilmington, Del.: Scholarly Resources, 1986).

——, *Soviet–American Relations in Asia, 1945–1954* (Norman: University of Oklahoma Press, 1981).

Bullock, Alan, *Ernest Bevin: Foreign Secretary, 1945–1951* (New York: Norton, 1993).

——, *Hitler and Stalin: Parallel Lives* (New York: Knopf, 1992).

Bundy, McGeorge, *Danger and Survival: Choices About the Bomb in the First Fifty Years* (New York: Random House, 1988).

Burlatsky, Fedor, *Khrushchev and the First Russian Spring* (London: Weidenfeld & Nicolson, 1991).

Callahan, David, *Dangerous Capabilities: Paul Nitze and the Cold War* (New York: HarperCollins, 1990).

Calleo, David P., *Beyond American Hegemony: The Future of the Western Alliance* (New York: Basic Books, 1987).

Carr, E. H., *The Twenty Years' Crisis, 1919–1939: An Introduction to the Study of International Relations* (New York: St. Martin's Press, 1939).

——, *What Is History?* (New York: Vintage, 1961).

Cassidy, David, *Uncertainty: The Life and Science of Werner Heisenberg* (New York: W. H. Freeman, 1992).

Chang, Gordon H., *Friends and Enemies: The United States, China, and the Soviet Union, 1948–1972* (Stanford: Stanford University Press, 1990).

Chen Jian, *China's Road to the Korean War: The Making of the Sino–American Confrontation* (New York: Columbia University Press, 1994).

Churchill, Winston S., *The Second World War: Triumph and Tragedy* (New York: Bantam, 1962).

Clausewitz, Carl von, *On War*, ed. and trans. Michael Howard and Peter Paret (Princeton: Princeton University Press, 1976).

Clifford, Clark M., with Richard M. Holbrooke, *Counsel to the President: A Memoir* (New York: Random House, 1991).

Cohen, Warren I., *The Cambridge History of American Foreign Relations*, iv: *America in the Age of Soviet Power, 1945–1991* (New York: Cambridge University Press, 1993).

Colburn, Forrest D., *The Vogue of Revolution in Poor Countries* (Princeton: Princeton University Press, 1994).

Coleman, Peter, *The Liberal Conspiracy: The Congress for Cultural Freedom and the Struggle for the Mind of Postwar Europe* (New York: Free Press, 1989).

Condit, Doris M., *History of the Office of the Secretary of Defense*, ii: *The Test of War, 1950–1953* (Washington: Government Printing Office, 1988).

Conquest, Robert, *The Great Terror: A Reassessment* (New York: Oxford University Press, 1990).

——, *The Harvest of Sorrow: Soviet Collectivization and the Terror-Famine* (New York: Oxford University Press, 1986).

——, *Stalin: Breaker of Nations* (New York: Viking Penguin, 1991).

Copeland, Miles, *The Game of Nations: The Amorality of Power Politics* (New York: Simon & Schuster, 1969).

Costigliola, Frank, *Awkward Dominion: American Political, Economic, and Cultural Relations with Europe, 1919–1933* (Ithaca: Cornell University Press, 1984).

Crabb, Cecil V., Jr., *The Doctrines of American Foreign Policy: Their Meaning, Role, and Future* (Baton Rouge: Louisiana State University Press, 1982).

Craig, Gordon A., and Francis L. Loewenheim, eds., *The Diplomats: 1939–1979* (Princeton: Princeton University Press, 1994).

Crockatt, Richard, *The Fifty Years War: The United States and the Soviet Union in World Politics, 1941–1991* (New York: Routledge, 1995).

Cumings, Bruce, *The Origins of the Korean War*, 2 vols., (Princeton: Princeton University Press, 1981–90).

Dallek, Robert, *Franklin D. Roosevelt and American Foreign Policy, 1932–1945* (New York: Oxford University Press, 1979).

Davis, Nuel Pharr, *Lawrence and Oppenheimer* (New York: Simon & Schuster, 1968).

Deighton, Anne, *The Impossible Peace: Britain, the Division of Germany, and the Origins of the Cold War* (New York: Oxford University Press, 1990).

Dinerstein, Herbert S., *The Making of a Missile Crisis: October 1962* (Baltimore: Johns Hopkins University Press, 1976).

Dingman, Roger, *Power in the Pacific: The Origins of Naval Arms Limitation, 1914–1922* (Chicago: University of Chicago Press, 1976).

Divine, Robert A., *Blowing on the Wind: The Nuclear Test Ban Debate, 1954–1960* (New York: Oxford University Press, 1978).

——, *Foreign Policy and U.S. Presidential Elections, 1940–1960*, 2 vols., (New York: New Viewpoints, 1974).

——, *The Reluctant Belligerent: American Entry into World War II*, 2nd edn. (New York: Knopf, 1979).

——, *Second Chance: The Triumph of Internationalism in America During World War II* (New York: Atheneum, 1967).

——, *The Sputnik Challenge* (New York: Oxford University Press, 1993).

Djilas, Milovan, *Conversations with Stalin*, trans. Michael B. Petrovich (New York: Harcourt, Brace & World, 1962).

Dobbs, Charles M., *The Unwanted Symbol: American Foreign Policy, the Cold War, and Korea, 1945–1950* (Kent, OH.: Kent State University Press, 1981).

Doyle, Michael, *Empires* (Ithaca: Cornell University Press, 1986).

Duiker, William J., *U.S. Containment Policy and the Conflict in Indochina* (Stanford: Stanford University Press, 1994).

Dulles, Allen W., *The Craft of Intelligence* (New York: Harper & Row, 1963).

Dulles, John Foster, *War or Peace* (New York: Macmillan, 1950).

Eckes, Alfred E., Jr., *Opening America's Market: U.S. Foreign Trade Policy Since 1776* (Chapel Hill: University of North Carolina Press, 1995).

——, *A Search for Solvency: Bretton Woods and the International Monetary System, 1941–1971* (Austin: University of Texas Press, 1975).

Eveland, Wilbur Crane, *Ropes of Sand: America's Failure in the Middle East* (New York: Norton, 1980).

Fawcett, Louise, *Iran and the Cold War: The Azerbaijan Crisis of 1946* (New York: Cambridge University Press, 1992).

Filene, Peter G., *Americans and the Soviet Experiment, 1917–1933* (Cambridge, Mass.: Harvard University Press, 1967).

Filtzer, Donald, *The Khrushchev Era: De-Stalinisation and the Limits of Reform in the USSR, 1953–1964* (London: Macmillan, 1993).

Fischer, David Hackett, *Albion's Seed: Four British Folkways in America* (New York: Oxford University Press, 1989).

Fischer, Louis, *The Life of Lenin* (New York: Harper & Row, 1964).

Foot, Rosemary, *A Substitute for Victory: The Politics of Peacemaking at the Korean Armistice Talks* (Ithaca: Cornell University Press, 1990).

——, *The Wrong War: American Policy and the Dimensions of the Korean Conflict, 1950–1953* (Ithaca: Cornell University Press, 1985).

Fraser, Cary, *Ambivalent Anti-Colonialism: The United States and the Genesis of West Indian Independence, 1940–1964* (Westport, Conn.: Greenwood Press, 1994).

Fried, Richard M., *Nightmare in Red: The McCarthy Era in Perspective* (New York: Oxford University Press, 1990).

Friedrich, Carl, and Zbigniew Brzezinski, *Totalitarian Dictatorship and Autocracy* (Cambridge, Mass.: Harvard University Press, 1956).

Gaddis, John Lewis, *The Long Peace: Inquiries into the History of the Cold War* (New York: Oxford University Press, 1987).

——, *Russia, the Soviet Union, and the United States: An Interpretive History*, 2nd edn. (New York: McGraw Hill, 1990).

——, *Strategies of Containment: A Critical Appraisal of Postwar American National Security Policy* (New York: Oxford University Press, 1982).

——, *The United States and the End of the Cold War: Implications, Reconsiderations, Provocations* (New York: Oxford University Press, 1992).

——, *The United States and the Origins of the Cold War, 1941–1947* (New York: Columbia University Press, 1972).

Gardner, Lloyd C., *Approaching Vietnam: From World War II through Dienbienphu* (New York: Norton, 1988).

——, *Spheres of Influence: The Great Powers Partition Europe, from Munich to Yalta* (Chicago: Ivan R. Dee, 1993).

Garthoff, Raymond L., *Reflections on the Cuban Missile Crisis*, rev. edn. (Washington: Brookings Institution, 1989).

Garton Ash, Timothy, *The Polish Revolution: Solidarity* (London: Penguin Books, 1983).

Gati, Charles, *Hungary and the Soviet Bloc* (Durham: Duke University Press, 1986).

George, Alexander L., and Richard Smoke, *Deterrence in American Foreign Policy: Theory and Practice* (New York: Columbia University Press, 1974).

Gerges, Fawaz A., *The Superpowers and the Middle East: Regional and International Politics, 1955–1967* (Boulder: Westview, 1994).

Gilbert, Martin, *Winston S. Churchill: Finest Hour, 1939–1941* (Boston: Houghton Mifflin, 1983).

——, *Winston S. Churchill: "Never Despair," 1945–1965* (Boston: Houghton Mifflin, 1988).

Ginat, Rami, *The Soviet Union and Egypt, 1945–1955* (London: Frank Cass, 1993).

Gittings, John, *Survey of the Sino-Soviet Dispute: A Commentary and Extracts from the Recent Polemics, 1963–1967* (London: Oxford University Press, 1968).

Gleason, Abbott, *Totalitarianism: The Inner History of the Cold War* (New York: Oxford University Press, 1995).

Gleick, James, *Chaos: Making a New Science* (New York: Viking, 1987).

Gleijeses, Piero, *Shattered Hope: The Guatemalan Revolution and the United States, 1944–1954* (Princeton: Princeton University Press, 1991).

Glynn, Patrick, *Closing Pandora's Box: Arms Races, Arms Control, and the History of the Cold War* (New York: Basic Books, 1992).

Golan, Galia, *Soviet Policies in the Middle East from World War Two to Gorbachev* (Cambridge: Cambridge University Press, 1990).

Goldgeier, James M., *Leadership Style and Soviet Foreign Policy: Stalin, Khrushchev, Brezhnev, Gorbachev* (Baltimore: Johns Hopkins University Press, 1994).

Goncharov, Sergei N., John W. Lewis, and Xue Litai, *Uncertain Partners: Stalin, Mao, and the Korean War* (Stanford: Stanford University Press, 1993).

Goodwin, Doris Kearns, *No Ordinary Time: Franklin and Eleanor Roosevelt: The Home Front in World War II* (New York: Simon & Schuster, 1994).

Gorbachev, Mikhail, *Perestroika: New Thinking for Our Country and the World* (New York: Harper & Row, 1987).

Gordon, Joel, *Nasser's Blessed Movement: Egypt's Free Officers and the July Revolution* (New York: Oxford University Press, 1992).

Gordon, Philip H., *A Certain Idea of France: French Security Policy and the Gaullist Legacy* (Princeton: Princeton University Press, 1993).

Gorodetsky, Gabriel, ed., *Soviet Foreign Policy 1917–1991: A Retrospective* (London: Frank Cass, 1994).

Gould, Stephen Jay, *Wonderful Life: The Burgess Shale and the Nature of History* (New York: Norton, 1989).

Graebner, Norman, ed., *The National Security: Theory and Practice, 1945–1960* (New York: Oxford University Press, 1986).

Greenfield, Keith Roberts, *American Strategy in World War II: A Reconsideration* (Baltimore: Johns Hopkins University Press, 1963).

Gribkov, Anatoli I., and William Y. Smith, *Operation ANADYR: U.S. and Soviet Generals Recount the Cuban Missile Crisis* (Chicago: edition q, 1994).

Gromyko, Andrei, *Memoirs*, trans. Harold Shukman (New York: Doubleday, 1989).

Grose, Peter, *Gentleman Spy: The Life of Allen Dulles* (Boston: Houghton Mifflin, 1994).

Gupta, Surenda K., *Stalin's Policy Towards India, 1946–1953* (New Delhi: South Asian Publishers, 1988).

Haglund, David G., *Latin America and the Transformation of U.S. Strategic Thought, 1936–1940* (Albuquerque: University of New Mexico Press, 1984).

Hahn, Peter, *The United States, Great Britain, and Egypt, 1945–1956: Strategy and Diplomacy in the Early Cold War* (Chapel Hill: University of North Carolina Press, 1991).

Hahn, Werner G., *Postwar Soviet Politics: The Fall of Zhdanov and the Defeat of Moderation, 1946–53* (Ithaca: Cornell University Press, 1982).

Halle, Louis J., *The Cold War as History* (New York: Harper & Row, 1967).

Hamby, Alonzo L., *Man of the People: A Life of Harry S. Truman* (New York: Oxford University Press, 1995).

Hamerow, Theodore S., *From the Finland Station: The Graying of Revolution in the Twentieth Century* (New York: Basic Books, 1990).

Hammond, Thomas T., ed., *Witnesses to the Origins of the Cold War* (Seattle: University of Washington Press, 1982).

Harbutt, Fraser, *The Iron Curtain: Churchill, America, and the Origins of the Cold War* (New York: Oxford University Press, 1986).

Harding, Harry, and Yuan Ming, eds., *Sino-American Relations, 1945–1955: A Joint Reassessment of a Critical Decade* (Wilmington, Del.: Scholarly Resources, 1989).

Hardt, John P., ed., *Reorientation and Commercial Relations of the Economies of Eastern Europe* (Washington: Government Printing Office, 1974).

Harriman, W. Averell, and Elie Abel, *Special Envoy to Churchill and Stalin, 1941–1946* (New York: Random House, 1975).

Harrison, Michael M., *The Reluctant Ally: France and Atlantic Security* (Baltimore: Johns Hopkins University Press, 1981).

Haslam, Jonathan, *The Soviet Union and the Struggle for Collective Security in Europe, 1933–39* (New York: St. Martin's Press, 1984).

Heikal, Mohamed, *The Sphinx and the Commissar: The Rise and Fall of Soviet Influence in the Middle East* (New York: Harper & Row, 1978).

Heinrichs, Waldo, *Threshold of War: Franklin D. Roosevelt and American Entry into World War II* (New York: Oxford University Press, 1988).

Herken, Gregg, *The Winning Weapon: The Atomic Bomb in the Cold War, 1945–1950* (New York: Knopf, 1980).

Herring, George C., Jr., *Aid to Russia, 1941–1946: Strategy, Diplomacy, the Origins of the Cold War* (New York: Columbia University Press, 1973).

Hershberg, James G., *James B. Conant: Harvard to Hiroshima and the Making of the Nuclear Age* (New York: Knopf, 1993).

Hess, Gary R., *The United States' Emergence as a Southeast Asian Power, 1940–1950* (New York: Columbia University Press, 1987).

Heuser, Beatrice, *Western "Containment" Policies in the Cold War: The Yugoslav Case, 1948–53* (New York: Routledge, 1989).

Hixson, Walter, *George F. Kennan: Cold War Iconoclast* (New York: Columbia University Press, 1989).

Hobsbawm, Eric, *The Age of Extremes: A History of the World, 1914–1991* (New York: Pantheon, 1994).

Hochman, Jiri, *The Soviet Union and the Failure of Collective Security, 1934–1938* (Ithaca: Cornell University Press, 1984).

Hodgson, Godfrey, *The Colonel: The Life and Wars of Henry Stimson, 1867–1950* (New York: Knopf, 1990).

Hoff Wilson, Joan, *Ideology and Economics: U. S. Relations with the Soviet Union, 1918–1933* (Columbia: University of Missouri Press, 1974).

Hogan, Michael J., *Informal Entente: The Private Structure of Cooperation in Anglo-American Economic Diplomacy, 1918–1928* (Columbia: University of Missouri Press, 1977).

——, *The Marshall Plan: America, Britain, and the Reconstruction of Europe, 1947–1952* (New York: Cambridge University Press, 1987).

——, ed., *America in the World: The Historiography of American Foreign Relations since 1941* (New York: Cambridge University Press, 1995).

——, ed., *Hiroshima in History and Memory* (New York: Cambridge University Press, 1996).

——, and Thomas G. Paterson, eds., *Explaining the History of American Foreign Relations* (New York: Cambridge University Press, 1991).

Holloway, David, *Stalin and the Bomb: The Soviet Union and Atomic Energy, 1939–1954* (New Haven: Yale University Press, 1994).

Hoopes, Townsend, and Douglas Brinkley, *Driven Patriot: The Life and Times of James Forrestal* (New York: Knopf, 1992).

Hopkirk, Peter, *The Great Game: The Struggle for Empire in Central Asia* (New York: Kodansha International, 1992).

Horelick, Arnold L., and Myron Rush, *Strategic Power and Soviet Foreign Policy* (Chicago: University of Chicago Press, 1966).

Hough, Jerry, *The Struggle for the Third World: Soviet Debates and American Options* (Washington: Brookings Institution, 1986).

Howard, Michael, *The Lessons of History* (New Haven: Yale University Press, 1991).

Hunt, Michael H., *The Genesis of Chinese Communist Foreign Policy* (New York: Columbia University Press, 1996).

Iatrides, John O., and Linda Wrigley, eds., *Greece at the Crossroads: The Civil War and Its Legacy* (University Park: Pennsylvania State University Press, 1995).

Immerman, Richard, H., *The CIA in Guatemala: The Foreign Policy of Intervention* (Austin: University of Texas Press, 1982).

——, ed., *John Foster Dulles and the Diplomacy of the Cold War* (Princeton: Princeton University Press, 1990).

Iriye, Akira, *The Cambridge History of American Foreign Relations, iii: The Globalizing of America, 1913–1945* (New York: Cambridge University Press, 1993).

James, D. Clayton, *The Years of MacArthur: Triumph and Disaster, 1945–1964* (Boston: Houghton Mifflin, 1985).

Kagan, Donald, *On the Origins of War and the Preservation of Peace* (New York: Doubleday, 1995).

Kahin, George McT., *Intervention: How America Became Involved in Vietnam* (New York: Doubleday, 1986).

Kaplan, Karel, *The Short March: The Communist Takeover in Czechoslovakia: 1945–1948* (New York: St. Martin's Press, 1987).

Kaplan, Lawrence S., *The United States and NATO: The Formative Years* (Lexington: University Press of Kentucky, 1984).

Kauffman, Stuart A., *The Origins of Order: Self-Organization and Selection in Evolution* (New York: Oxford University Press, 1993).

Kaufman, Burton I., *The Korean War: Challenges in Crisis, Credibility, and Command* (New York: Knopf, 1986).

Keegan, John, *A History of Warfare* (New York: Knopf, 1993).

Kennan, George F., *American Diplomacy: 1900–1950* (Chicago: University of Chicago Press, 1951).

——, *The Decision to Intervene* (Princeton: Princeton University Press, 1958).

——, *Memoirs: 1925–1950* (Boston: Atlantic Little, Brown, 1967).

——, *Memoirs: 1950–1963* (Boston: Atlantic Little, Brown, 1972).

——, *Russia and the West under Lenin and Stalin* (Boston: Little, Brown, 1961).

Kennedy, Paul, *The Rise and Fall of the Great Powers: Economic Change and Military Conflict from 1500 to 2000* (New York: Random House, 1987).

Keohane, Robert O., ed., *Neorealism and Its Critics* (New York: Columbia University Press, 1986).

Kersten, Krystyna, *The Establishment of Communist Rule in Poland, 1943–1948*, trans. John Micgiel and Michael H. Barnhart (Berkeley: University of California Press, 1991).

Khong, Yuen Foong, *Analogies at War: Korea, Munich, Dien Bien Phu, and the Vietnam Decisions of 1965* (Princeton: Princeton University Press, 1992).

Khrushchev, Nikita, *Khrushchev Remembers*, trans. and ed. Strobe Talbott (Boston: Little, Brown, 1971).

——, *Khrushchev Remembers: The Glasnost Tapes*, trans. and ed. Jerrold L. Schecter with Vyacheslav V. Luchkov (Boston: Little, Brown, 1990).

——, *Khrushchev Remembers: The Last Testament*, trans. and ed. Strobe Talbott (Boston: Little, Brown, 1974).

Khrushchev, Sergei, *Khrushchev on Khrushchev: An Inside Account of the Man and His Era*, ed. and trans. William Taubman (Boston: Little, Brown, 1990).

Killian, James R., *Sputnik, Scientists, and Eisenhower: A Memoir of the First Special Assistant to the President for Science and Technology* (Cambridge, Mass.: MIT Press, 1977).

Kimball, Warren F., *The Juggler: Franklin Roosevelt as Wartime Statesman* (Princeton: Princeton University Press, 1991).

Kindleberger, Charles P., *The World in Depression: 1929–1939* (Berkeley: University of California Press, 1973).

Kissinger, Henry A., *Diplomacy* (New York: Simon & Schuster, 1994).

Klehr, Harvey, John Earl Haynes, and Fridrikh Igorevich Firsov, *The Secret World of American Communism* (New Haven: Yale University Press, 1995).

Knight, Amy, *Beria: Stalin's First Lieutenant* (Princeton: Princeton University Press, 1993).

Knock, Thomas, *To End All Wars: Woodrow Wilson and the Quest for a New World Order* (New York: Oxford University Press, 1992).

Kofsky, Frank, *Harry S. Truman and the War Scare of 1948: A Successful Campaign to Deceive the Nation* (New York: St. Martin's Press, 1993).

Kolko, Joyce and Gabriel, *The Limits of Power: The World and United States Foreign Policy, 1945–1954* (New York: Harper & Row, 1972).

Kovrig, Bennett, *Of Walls and Bridges: The United States and Eastern Europe* (New York: New York University Press, 1991).

Krasner, Stephen D., ed., *International Regimes* (Ithaca: Cornell University Press, 1983).

Kuhn, Thomas S., *The Structure of Scientific Revolutions*, 2nd edn., enlarged (Chicago: University of Chicago Press, 1970).

Kuniholm, Bruce Robellet, *The Origins of the Cold War in the Near East: Great Power Diplomacy in Iran, Turkey, and Greece* (Princeton: Princeton University Press, 1980).

Kunz, Diane B., *The Economic Diplomacy of the Suez Crisis* (Chapel Hill: University of North Carolina Press, 1991).

Kupchan, Charles A., *The Vulnerability of Empire* (Ithaca: Cornell University Press, 1994).

Kyle, Keith, *Suez* (New York: St. Martin's Press, 1991).

Larrabee, Eric, *Commander-in-Chief: Franklin Delano Roosevelt, His Lieutenants, and Their War* (New York: Harper & Row, 1987).

Larson, Deborah Welch, *Origins of Containment: A Psychological Explanation* (Princeton: Princeton University Press, 1985).

Lasch, Christopher, *The American Liberals and the Russian Revolution* (New York: Columbia University Press, 1962).

Lechuga, Carlos, *In the Eye of the Storm: Castro, Khrushchev, Kennedy and the Missile Crisis*, trans. Mary Todd (Melbourne: Ocean Press, 1995).

Leffler, Melvyn P., *The Elusive Quest: The American Pursuit of European Stability and French Security, 1919–1933* (Chapel Hill: University of North Carolina Press, 1979).

——, *A Preponderance of Power: National Security, the Truman Administration, and the Cold War* (Stanford: Stanford University Press, 1992).

——, *The Specter of Communism: The United States and the Origins of the Cold War, 1917–1953* (New York: Hill & Wang, 1994).

Levering, Ralph B., *The Cold War: A Post-Cold War History* (Arlington Heights, Ill.: Harlan Davidson, 1994).

Levin, N. Gordon, Jr., *Woodrow Wilson and World Politics: America's Response to War and Revolution* (New York: Oxford University Press, 1968).

Lewis, John Wilson, and Xue Litai, *China Builds the Bomb* (Stanford: Stanford University Press, 1988).

Li Zhisui, *The Private Life of Chairman Mao,* trans. Tai Hung-chao (New York: Random House, 1994).

Lippmann, Walter, *U.S. Foreign Policy: Shield of the Republic* (Boston: Little, Brown, 1943).

Loth, Wilfried, *The Division of the World: 1941–1945* (New York: St. Martin's Press, 1988).

Louis, Wm. Roger, *Imperialism at Bay: The United States and the Decolonization of the British Empire, 1941–1945* (New York: Oxford University Press, 1978).

——, and Roger Owen, eds., *Suez 1956: The Crisis and Its Consequences* (New York: Oxford University Press, 1989).

Lundestad, Geir, *The American "Empire" and Other Studies of US Foreign Policy in Contemporary Perspective* (New York: Oxford University Press, 1990).

——, *The American Non-Policy towards Eastern Europe, 1943–1947* (New York: Columbia University Press, 1978).

——, ed., *The Fall of Great Powers: Peace, Stability, and Legitimacy* (New York: Oxford University Press, 1994).

Lynn-Jones, Sean M., Steven E. Miller, and Stephen Van Evera, eds., *Nuclear Diplomacy and Crisis Management* (Cambridge, Mass.: MIT Press, 1990).

Macdonald, Douglas J., *Adventures in Chaos: American Intervention for Reform in the Third World* (Cambridge, Mass.: Harvard University Press, 1992).

MacFarquhar, Roderick, and John K. Fairbank, eds., *The Cambridge History of China*, xiv: *The People's Republic*, pt. 1: *The Emergence of Revolutionary China, 1949–1965* (New York: Cambridge University Press, 1987).

Maier, Charles S., *In Search of Stability: Explorations in Historical Political Economy* (Cambridge: Cambridge University Press, 1987).

——, *Recasting Bourgeois Europe: Stabilization in France, Germany, and Italy in the Decade after World War I* (Princeton: Princeton University Press, 1975).

——, *The Unmasterable Past: History, Holocaust, and German National Identity* (Cambridge, Mass.: Harvard University Press, 1988).

Malia, Martin, *The Soviet Tragedy: A History of Socialism in Russia, 1917–1991* (New York: Free Press, 1994).

Massie, Robert K., *Dreadnought: Britain, Germany, and the Coming of the Great War* (New York: Random House, 1991).

Mastny, Vojtech, *Russia's Road to the Cold War: Diplomacy, Warfare, and the Politics of Communism, 1941–1945* (New York: Columbia University Press, 1979).

Matray, James Irving, *The Reluctant Crusade: American Foreign Policy in Korea, 1941–1950* (Honolulu: University of Hawaii Press, 1985).

May, Ernest R., *"Lessons" of the Past: The Use and Misuse of History in American Foreign Policy* (New York: Oxford University Press, 1973).

——, *American Cold War Strategy: Interpreting NSC-68* (Boston: St. Martin's Press, 1993).

Mayer, Arno, *Political Origins of the New Diplomacy, 1917–1918* (New Haven: Yale University Press, 1959).

Mayers, David Allen, *Cracking the Monolith: U.S. Policy Against the Sino-Soviet Alliance, 1949–1955* (Baton Rouge: Louisiana State University Press, 1986).

McCormick, Thomas J., *America's Half-Century: United States Foreign Policy in the Cold War* (Baltimore: Johns Hopkins University Press, 1989).

McCullough, David, *Truman* (New York: Simon & Schuster, 1992).

McDougall, Walter A., *The Heavens and the Earth: A Political History of the Space Age* (New York: Basic Books, 1985).

McGlothen, Ronald, *Controlling the Waves: Dean Acheson and U.S. Foreign Policy in Asia* (New York: Norton, 1993).

McMahon, Robert J., *The Cold War on the Periphery: The United States, India, and Pakistan* (New York: Columbia University Press, 1993).

——, *Colonialism and the Cold War: The United States and the Struggle for Indonesian Independence, 1945–49* (Ithaca: Cornell University Press, 1981).

McNamara, Robert S., with Brian VanDeMark, *In Retrospect: The Tragedy and Lessons of Vietnam* (New York: Random House, 1995).

McNeill, William H., *America, Britain, and Russia: Their Cooperation and Conflict* (New York: Johnson Reprint, 1970).

——, *The Pursuit of Power: Technology, Armed Force, and Society since A.D. 1000* (Chicago: University of Chicago Press, 1982).

Meisner, Maurice, *Mao's China and After: A History of the People's Republic* (New York: Free Press, 1986).

Messer, Robert, *The End of an Alliance: James F. Byrnes, Roosevelt, Truman, and the Origins of the Cold War* (Chapel Hill: University of North Carolina Press, 1982).

Miller, Aaron David, *Search for Security: Saudi Arabian Oil and American Foreign Policy, 1939–1949* (Chapel Hill: University of North Carolina Press, 1980).

Miller, James Edward, *The United States and Italy, 1940–1950: The Politics of Diplomacy and Stabilization* (Chapel Hill: University of North Carolina Press, 1986).

Miller, Merle, *Plain Speaking: An Oral Biography of Harry S. Truman* (New York: G. P. Putnam, 1974).

Miller, Nicola, *Soviet Relations with Latin America, 1959–1987* (Cambridge: Cambridge University Press, 1990).

Milward, Alan, *The Reconstruction of Western Europe, 1945–51* (Berkeley: University of California Press, 1984).

Miner, Steven Merritt, *Between Churchill and Stalin: The Soviet Union, Great Britain, and the Origins of the Grand Alliance* (Chapel Hill: University of North Carolina Press, 1988).

Miscamble, Wilson D., *George F. Kennan and the Making of American Foreign Policy, 1945–1950* (Princeton: Princeton University Press, 1992).

Molotov, Vyacheslav, *Molotov Remembers: Inside Kremlin Politics; Conversations with Felix Chuev*, ed. Albert Resis (Chicago: Ivan R. Dee, 1993).

Morgenthau, Hans J., *Politics Among Nations: The Struggle for Power and Peace* (New York: Knopf, 1948).

Morris, Bernard S., *Communism, Revolution, and American Policy* (Durham: Duke University Press, 1987).

Mosely, Philip E., *The Kremlin and World Politics: Studies in Soviet Policy and Action* (New York: Vintage Books, 1960).

Mosley, Nicholas, *Hopeful Monsters* (New York: Vintage, 1993).

Mueller, John, *Quiet Cataclysm: Reflections on the Recent Transformation of World Politics* (New York: HarperCollins, 1995).

——, *Retreat from Doomsday: The Obsolescence of Major War* (New York: Basic Books, 1989).

Murray, Robert K., *Red Scare: A Study in National Hysteria, 1919–1920* (Minneapolis: University of Minnesota Press, 1955).

Nagai, Yonosuke, and Akira Iriye, eds., *The Origins of the Cold War in Asia* (Tokyo: University of Tokyo Press, 1977).

Naimark, Norman N., *The Russians in Germany: A History of the Soviet Zone of Occupation, 1945–1949* (Cambridge, Mass.: Harvard University Press, 1995).

Nathan, James A., ed., *The Cuban Missile Crisis Revisited* (New York: St. Martin's Press, 1992).

Nau, Henry R., *The Myth of America's Decline: Leading the World Economy into the 1990s* (New York: Oxford University Press, 1990).

Newman, Robert P., *The Cold War Romance of Lillian Hellman and John Melby* (Chapel Hill: University of North Carolina Press, 1989).

——, *Owen Lattimore and the "Loss" of China* (Berkeley: University of California Press, 1992).

Ninkovich, Frank, *Germany and the United States: The Transformation of the German Question since 1945*, updated edn. (Boston: Twayne, 1995).

——, *Modernity and Power: A History of the Domino Theory in the Twentieth Century* (Chicago: University of Chicago Press, 1994).

Nitze, Paul H., with Ann M. Smith and Steven L. Rearden, *From Hiroshima to Glasnost: At the Center of Decision—A Memoir* (New York: Grove Weidenfeld, 1989).

Nye, Joseph S., Jr., *Bound to Lead: The Changing Nature of American Power* (New York: Basic Books, 1990).

Offner, Arnold A., *American Appeasement: United States Foreign Policy and Germany, 1933–1939* (Cambridge, Mass.: Harvard University Press, 1969).

Orwell, George, *Animal Farm* (New York: Harcourt, 1946).

——, *Homage to Catalonia* (New York: Harcourt, 1952).

——, *1984* (New York: Harcourt, 1949).

Paterson, Thomas G., *Contesting Castro: The United States and the Triumph of the Cuban Revolution* (New York: Oxford University Press, 1994).

——, *Meeting the Communist Threat: Truman to Reagan* (New York: Oxford University Press, 1988).

——, *Soviet–American Confrontation: Postwar Reconstruction and the Origins of the Cold War* (Baltimore: Johns Hopkins University Press, 1973).

——, ed., *Cold War Critics: Alternatives to American Foreign Policy in the Truman Years* (Chicago: Quadrangle Books, 1971).

Perlmutter, Amos, *FDR & Stalin: A Not So Grand Alliance, 1943–1945* (Columbia: University of Missouri Press, 1993).

Phillips, Hugh D., *Between the Revolution and the West: A Political Biography of Maxim M. Litvinov* (Boulder: Westview Press, 1992).

Pipes, Richard, *The Formation of the Soviet Union: Communism and Nationalism, 1917–23* (Cambridge, Mass.: Harvard University Press, 1954).

——, *Russia Under the Bolshevik Regime* (New York: Knopf, 1994).

——, *The Russian Revolution* (New York: Knopf, 1990).

Pisani, Sally, *The CIA and the Marshall Plan* (Lawrence: University Press of Kansas, 1991).

Pogue, Forrest C., *George C. Marshall: Statesman, 1945–1959* (New York: Viking, 1987).

Pollard, Robert A., *Economic Security and the Origins of the Cold War, 1945–1950* (New York: Columbia University Press, 1985).

Polvinen, Tuomo, *Between East and West: Finland in International Politics, 1944–1947*, ed. and trans. D. G. Kirby and Peter Herring (Minneapolis: University of Missouri Press, 1986).

Powers, Thomas, *Heisenberg's War: The Secret History of the German Bomb* (New York: Knopf, 1993).

Prados, John, *The Soviet Estimate: U. S. Intelligence Analysis and Russian Military Strength* (New York: Dial Press, 1982).

Pruessen, Ronald W., *John Foster Dulles: The Road to Power* (New York: Free Press, 1982).

Quirk, Robert E., *Fidel Castro* (New York: Norton, 1993).

Raack, R. C., *Stalin's Drive to the West, 1938–1945: The Origins of the Cold War* (Stanford: Stanford University Press, 1995).

Ra'anan, Gavriel, *International Policy Formation in the USSR: Factional "Debates" during the Zhdanovschina* (Hamden, Conn.: Archon Books, 1983).

Rabinowitch, Alexander, *The Bolsheviks Come to Power: The Revolution of 1917 in Petrograd* (New York: Norton, 1978).

Ranelagh, John, *The Agency: The Rise and Decline of the CIA* (New York: Simon & Schuster, 1986).

Reeves, Richard, *President Kennedy: Profile of Power* (New York: Simon & Schuster, 1993).

Remnick, David, *Lenin's Tomb: The Last Days of the Soviet Empire* (New York: Random House, 1993).

Resis, Albert, *Stalin, the Politburo, and the Onset of the Cold War* (Pittsburgh: University of Pittsburgh Center for Russian and East European Studies, 1988).

Reynolds, David, ed., *The Origins of the Cold War in Europe: International Perspectives* (New Haven: Yale University Press, 1994).

——, Warren F. Kimball, and A. O. Chubarian, eds., *Allies at War: The Soviet–American, and British Experiences, 1939–1945* (New York: St. Martin's Press, 1994).

Rhodes, Richard, *Dark Sun: The Making of the Hydrogen Bomb* (New York: Simon & Schuster, 1995).

——, *The Making of the Atomic Bomb* (New York: Simon & Schuster, 1986).

Rich, Norman, *Hitler's War Aims: Ideology, the Nazi State, and the Course of Expansion* (New York: Norton, 1973).

Risse-Kappen, Thomas, *Cooperation Among Democracies: The European Influence on U.S. Foreign Policy* (Princeton: Princeton University Press, 1995).

Roberts, Frank, *Dealing with Dictators: The Destruction and Revival of Europe, 1930–70* (London: Weidenfeld & Nicolson, 1991).

Robinson, Ronald, and John Gallagher, with Alice Denny, *Africa and the Victorians: The Climax of Imperialism* (New York: St. Martin's Press, 1961).

Robinson, Thomas W., and David Shambaugh, eds., *Chinese Foreign Policy: Theory and Practice* (New York: Oxford University Press, 1994).

Rodman, Peter W., *More Precious Than Peace: The Cold War and the Struggle for the Third World* (New York: Scribner's, 1994).

Roman, Peter J., *Eisenhower and the Missile Gap* (Ithaca: Cornell University Press, 1995).

Rostow, W. W., *The Stages of Economic Growth: A Non-Communist Manifesto* (Cambridge: Cambridge University Press, 1960).

Rotter, Andrew J., *The Path to Vietnam: Origins of the American Commitment to Southeast Asia* (Ithaca: Cornell University Press, 1987).

Russett, Bruce, *Grasping the Democratic Peace: Principles for a Post-Cold War World* (Princeton: Princeton University Press, 1993).

Sagan, Scott D., *The Limits of Safety: Organizations, Accidents, and Nuclear Weapons* (Princeton: Princeton University Press, 1993).

——, *Moving Targets: Nuclear Strategy and National Security* (Princeton: Princeton University Press, 1989).

Said, Edward, *Culture and Imperialism* (New York: Knopf, 1993).

Salisbury, Harrison, *The New Emperors: China in the Era of Mao and Deng* (Boston: Little, Brown, 1992).

Sakharov, Andrei, *Memoirs*, trans. Richard Lourie (New York: Knopf, 1990).

Samii, Kuross A., *Involvement by Invitation: American Strategies of Containment in Iran* (University Park: Pennsylvania State University Press, 1987).

Saul, Norman E., *Conflict and Concord: The United States and Russia, 1867–1914* (Lawrence: University Press of Kansas, 1996).

——, *Distant Friends: The United States and Russia, 1763–1867* (Lawrence: University Press of Kansas, 1991).

Schaller, Michael, *The American Occupation of Japan: The Origins of the Cold War in Asia* (New York: Oxford University Press, 1985).

——, *The U.S. Crusade in China, 1938–1945* (New York: Columbia University Press, 1979).

Schilling, Warner R., Paul Y. Hammond, and Glenn H. Snyder, *Strategy, Politics, and Defense Budgets* (New York: Columbia University Press, 1962).

Schlesinger, Arthur M., Jr., *A Thousand Days: John F. Kennedy in the White House* (Boston: Houghton Mifflin, 1965).

Schlesinger, Stephen, and Stephen Kinzer, *Bitter Fruit: The Untold Story of the American Coup in Guatemala* (Garden City, NY: Doubleday, 1982).

Schoenbaum, David, *The United States and the State of Israel* (New York: Oxford University Press, 1993).

Schrecker, Ellen W., *No Ivory Tower: McCarthyism and the Universities* (New York: Oxford University Press, 1986).

Schwartz, Thomas Alan, *America's Germany: John J. McCloy and the Federal Republic of Germany* (Cambridge, Mass.: Harvard University Press, 1991).

Shafer, D. Michael, *Deadly Paradigms: The Failure of U.S. Counterinsurgency Policy* (Princeton: Princeton University Press, 1988).

Sheinis, Zinovy, *Maxim Litvinov* (Moscow: Progress Publishers, 1990).

Shelden, Michael, *Orwell: The Authorized Biography* (New York: HarperCollins, 1991).

Sherry, Michael S., *Preparing for the Next War: American Plans for Postwar Defense, 1941–1947* (New Haven: Yale University Press, 1977).

——, *The Rise of American Air Power: The Creation of Armageddon* (New Haven: Yale University Press, 1987).

Sherwin, Martin J., *A World Destroyed: Hiroshima and the Origins of the Nuclear Arms Race* (New York: Vintage Books, 1987).

Shlaim, Avi, *The United States and the Berlin Blockade, 1948–1949: A Study in Crisis Decision-Making* (Berkeley: University of California Press, 1983).

Simmons, Robert R., *The Strained Alliance: Peking, P'yongyang, Moscow, and the Politics of the Korean Civil War* (New York: Macmillan, 1975).

Singh, Anita Inder, *The Limits of British Influence: South Asia and the Anglo-American Relationship, 1947–56* (New York: St. Martin's Press, 1993).

Skocpol, Theda, *States and Social Revolutions: A Comparative Analysis of France, Russia, and China* (Cambridge: Cambridge University Press, 1979).

Smith, Gaddis, *The Last Years of the Monroe Doctrine, 1945–1993* (New York: Hill & Wang, 1994).

Smith, Jean Edward, *Lucius D. Clay: An American Life* (New York: Henry Holt, 1990).

Smith, Tony, *America's Mission: The United States and the Worldwide Struggle for Democracy in the Twentieth Century* (Princeton: Princeton University Press, 1994).

——, *The Pattern of Imperialism: The United States, Great Britain, and the Late-Industrializing World since 1815* (Cambridge: Cambridge University Press, 1981).

——, *Thinking Like A Communist: State and Legitimacy in the Soviet Union, China, and Cuba* (New York: Norton, 1987).

Snyder, Jack, *Myths of Empire: Domestic Politics and International Ambition* (Ithaca: Cornell University Press, 1991).

Solomon, Robert, *The International Monetary System, 1945–1976: An Insider's View* (New York: Harper & Row, 1977).

Solzhenitsyn, Alexander, *The Gulag Archipelago* (3 vols., New York: Harper & Row, 1974–8).

Spence, Jonathan D., *God's Chinese Son: The Taiping Heavenly Kingdom of Hong Xuiquan* (New York: Norton, 1996).

——, *The Search for Modern China* (New York: Norton, 1990).

Stephanson, Anders, *Kennan and the Art of Foreign Policy* (Cambridge, Mass.: Harvard University Press, 1989).

Stone, I. F., *The Hidden History of the Korean War* (New York: Monthly Review Press, 1952).

Stueck, William, *The Korean War: An International History* (Princeton: Princeton University Press, 1995).

——, *The Road to Confrontation: American Policy toward China and Korea, 1945–1950* (Chapel Hill: University of North Carolina Press, 1981).

Sudoplatov, Pavel, and Anatolii Sudoplatov, with Jerrold L. Schechter and Leona P. Schecter, *Special Tasks: The Memoirs of an Unwanted Witness—A Soviet Spymaster* (Boston: Little, Brown, 1994).

Tansill, Charles C., *Back Door to War: The Roosevelt Foreign Policy, 1933–1941* (Chicago: Regnery, 1952).

Taubman, William, *Stalin's American Policy: From Entente to Detente to Cold War* (New York: Norton, 1982).

Thomas, Hugh, *Armed Truce: The Beginnings of the Cold War, 1945–46* (London: Hamish Hamilton, 1986).

——, *Conquest: Montezuma, Cortéz, and the Fall of Old Mexico* (New York: Simon & Schuster, 1993).

——, *The Spanish Civil War* (New York: Harper, 1961).

Tocqueville, Alexis de, *Democracy in America*, ed. J. P. Mayer, trans. George Lawrence (Garden City, NY: Doubleday, 1969).

Tompson, William J., *Khrushchev: A Political Life* (New York: St. Martin's Press, 1995).

Toranska, Teresa, *"Them": Stalin's Polish Puppets*, trans. Agnieska Kolakowska (New York: Harper & Row, 1987).

Trachtenberg, Marc, *History and Strategy* (Princeton: Princeton University Press, 1991).

Travis, Frederick F., *George Kennan and the American–Russian Relationship 1865–1924* (Athens: Ohio University Press, 1990).

Truman, Harry S., *Memoirs: Year of Decisions* (Garden City, NY: Doubleday, 1955).

Tuchman, Barbara, *The Zimmermann Telegram* (New York: Viking, 1958).

Tucker, Nancy Bernkopf, *Patterns in the Dust: Chinese–American Relations and the Recognition Controversy, 1949–1950* (New York: Columbia University Press, 1983).

Tucker, Robert C., *The Soviet Political Mind: Stalinism and Post-Stalinist Change*, rev. edn. (New York: Norton, 1971).

——, *Stalin as Revolutionary, 1879–1929: A Study in History and Personality* (New York: Norton, 1973).

——, *Stalin in Power: The Revolution from Above, 1928–1941* (New York: Norton, 1990).

Tucker, Robert W., and David C. Hendrickson, *Empire of Liberty: The Statecraft of Thomas Jefferson* (New York: Oxford University Press, 1990).

Ulam, Adam B., *The Communists: The Story of Power and Lost Illusions, 1948–1991* (New York: Scribner's, 1992).

——, *Stalin: The Man and His Era* (New York: Viking, 1973).

Unterberger, Betty Miller, *The United States, Revolutionary Russia, and the Rise of Czechoslovakia* (Chapel Hill: University of North Carolina Press, 1989).

Van Creveld, Martin, *Technology and War: From 2000 B.C. to the Present* (New York: Free Press, 1989).

Vassiliev, Alexei, *Russian Policy in the Middle East: From Messianism to Pragmatism* (Reading, UK: Ithaca Press, 1993).

Volkogonov, Dimitri, *Lenin: A New Biography*, ed. and trans. Harold Shukman (New York: Free Press, 1994).

——, *Stalin: Triumph and Tragedy*, ed. and trans. Harold Shukman (New York: Grove Weidenfeld, 1991).

Wagnleitner, Reinhold, *Coca-Colonization and the Cold War: The Cultural Mission of the United States in Austria after the Second World War*, trans. Diana M. Wolf (Chapel Hill: University of North Carolina Press, 1994).

Waldrop, M. Mitchell, *Complexity: The Emerging Science at the Edge of Order and Chaos* (New York: Viking, 1992).

Walker, Martin, *The Cold War: A History* (New York: Henry Holt, 1993).

Walt, Stephen, *The Origins of Alliances* (Ithaca: Cornell University Press, 1987).

Walters, Vernon A., *Silent Missions* (Garden City, NY: Doubleday, 1978).

Waltz, Kenneth N., *Theory of International Politics* (New York: Random House, 1979).

Watt, Donald Cameron, *How War Came: The Immediate Origins of the Second World War, 1938–1939* (New York: Pantheon, 1989).

Weart, Spencer, *Nuclear Fear: A History of Images* (Cambridge, Mass.: Harvard University Press, 1988).

Weigley, Russell F., *The American Way of War: A History of United States Military Strategy and Policy* (New York: Macmillan, 1973).

——, *Eisenhower's Lieutenants: The Campaigns of France and Germany, 1944–1945* (Bloomington: Indiana University Press, 1981).

Weinstein, Allen, *Perjury: The Hiss–Chambers Case* (New York: Knopf, 1978).

Westad, Odd Arne, *Cold War and Revolution: Soviet–American Rivalry and the Origins of the Chinese Civil War, 1944–1946* (New York: Columbia University Press, 1993).

——, Sven Holtsmark, and Ivor B. Neumann, eds., *The Soviet Union in Eastern Europe, 1945–89* (New York: St. Martin's Press, 1994).

Williams, Robert Chadwell, *Klaus Fuchs: Atom Spy* (Cambridge, Mass.: Harvard University Press, 1987).

Williamson, Samuel R., and Steven L. Rearden, *The Origins of U. S. Nuclear Strategy, 1945–1953* (New York: St. Martin's Press, 1993).

Willkie, Wendell L., *One World* (New York: Simon & Schuster, 1943).

Wilson, Theodore A., *The First Summit: Roosevelt and Churchill at Placentia Bay, 1941* (Boston: Houghton Mifflin, 1969).

Wohlforth, William Curti, *The Elusive Balance: Power and Perceptions during the Cold War* (Ithaca: Cornell University Press, 1993).

Wohlstetter, Roberta, *Pearl Harbor: Warning and Decision* (Stanford: Stanford University Press, 1962).

Woods, Randall Bennett, *A Changing of the Guard: Anglo-American Relations, 1941–1946* (Chapel Hill: University of North Carolina Press, 1990).

——, *Fulbright: A Biography* (New York: Cambridge University Press, 1990).

Wyden, Peter, *The Bay of Pigs: The Untold Story* (New York: Simon & Schuster, 1979).

Yoder, Edwin M., Jr., *Joe Alsop's Cold War: A Study of Journalistic Influence and Intrigue* (Chapel Hill: University of North Carolina Press, 1995).

York, Herbert F., *The Advisors: Oppenheimer, Teller, and the Superbomb* (San Francisco: W. H. Freeman, 1976).

Young, John W., *Cold War Europe, 1945–1989: A Political History* (London: Edward Arnold, 1991).

——, *France, the Cold War, and the Western Alliance, 1944–49: French Foreign Policy and Post-War Europe* (Leicester: Leicester University Press, 1990).

Zagoria, Donald S., *The Sino-Soviet Conflict, 1956–1961* (Princeton: Princeton University Press, 1962).

Zaloga, Stephen J., *Target America: The Soviet Union and the Strategic Arms Race, 1945–1964* (Novato, CA: Presidio Press, 1993).

Zhai Qiang, *The Dragon, the Lion, and the Eagle: Chinese–British–American Relations, 1949–1958* (Kent: Kent State University Press, 1994).

Zhang, Shu Guang, *Deterrence and Strategic Culture: Chinese–American Confrontations, 1949–1958* (Ithaca: Cornell University Press, 1992).

——, *Mao's Military Romanticism: China and the Korean War, 1950–1953* (Lawrence: University Press of Kansas, 1995).

Zubok, Vladislav, and Constantine Pleshakov, *Inside the Kremlin's Cold War: From Stalin to Khrushchev* (Cambridge, Mass.: Harvard University Press, 1996).

III. ARTICLES

Alperovitz, Gar, and Kai Bird, "The Centrality of the Bomb," *Foreign Policy* #94 (Spring 1994), 3–20.

Armitage, John A., "The View from Czechoslovakia," in Thomas T. Hammond, ed., *Witnesses to the Origins of the Cold War* (Seattle: University of Washington Press, 1982), 210–30.

Ashton, Basil, Kenneth Hill, Alan Piazza, and Robin Zeitz, "Famine in China, 1958–61," *Population and Development Review* 10 (Dec. 1984), 613–45.

Bernstein, Barton J., "The Atomic Bombings Reconsidered," *Foreign Affairs* 176 (Jan.–Feb. 1995), 135–52.

——, "A Postwar Myth: 500,000 U.S. Lives Saved," *Bulletin of the Atomic Scientists* 42 (June–July 1986), 38–40.

——, "Reconsidering the Missile Crisis: Dealing with the Problems of the American Jupiters in Turkey," in James A. Nathan, ed., *The Cuban Missile Crisis Revisited* (New York: St. Martin's Press, 1992), 55–129.

Beyerchen, Alan, "Clausewitz, Nonlinearity, and the Unpredictability of War," *International Security* 17 (Winter 1992/93), 59–90.

Birt, Raymond, "Personality and Foreign Policy: The Case of Stalin," *Political Psychology* 14 (1993), 607–25.

Bo Yibo, "The Making of the 'Leaning to One Side' Decision," trans. Zhai Qiang, *Chinese Historians* 5 (Spring, 1992), 57–62.

Bowie, Robert R., "Eisenhower, Dulles, and the Suez Crisis," in Wm. Roger Louis and Roger Owen, eds., *Suez 1956: The Crisis and Its Consequences* (New York: Oxford University Press, 1989), 189–214.

Brands, H. W., "The Age of Vulnerability: Eisenhower and the National Insecurity State," *American Historical Review* 94 (Oct. 1989), 963–89.

Brenner, Philip, "Thirteen Months: Cuba's Perspective on the Missile Crisis," in James A. Nathan, ed., *The Cuban Missile Crisis Revisited* (New York: St. Martin's Press, 1992), pp. 187–213.

Buhite, Russell D., and Wm. Christopher Hamel, "War for Peace: The Question of an American Preventive War against the Soviet Union," *Diplomatic History* 14 (Summer 1990), 367–84.

Bunce, Valerie, "The Empire Strikes Back: The Evolution of the Eastern Bloc from a Soviet Asset to a Soviet Liability," *International Organization* 39 (Winter, 1985), 1–46.

Burr, William, "Avoiding the Slippery Slope: The Eisenhower Administration and the Berlin Crisis, November 1958–January 1959," *Diplomatic History* 18 (Spring 1994), 177–205.

Calleo, David P., "Since 1961: American Power in a New World Economy," in William H. Becker and Samuel F. Wells, Jr., eds., *Economics and World Power: An Assessment of American Diplomacy Since 1789* (New York: Columbia University Press, 1984), 391–457.

Campbell, John C., "The Twin Crises of Hungary and Suez," in Wm. Roger Louis and

Roger Owen, eds., *Suez 1956: The Crisis and Its Consequences* (New York: Oxford University Press, 1989), 233–53.

Chen Jian, "China and the First Indochina War, 1950–54," *China Quarterly* #133 (Mar. 1993), 85–110.

——, "China's Changing Aims during the Korean War," *Journal of American–East Asian Relations* 1 (Spring 1992), 8–41.

——, "The Ward Case and the Emergence of Sino-American Confrontation, 1948–1950," *Australian Journal of Chinese Affairs* 30 (July 1993), 149–70.

Chikov, Vladimir, "How the Soviet Intelligence Service 'Split' the American Atom," *New Times* #s16 and 17 (1991), 37–40, 36–9.

Christensen, Thomas J., "Threats, Assurances, and the Last Chance for Peace: The Lessons of Mao's Korean War Telegrams," *International Security* 17 (Summer 1992), 122–54.

Chubarov, Viacheslav, "The War after the War," *Soviet Studies in History* 30 (Summer 1991), 44–52.

Cohen, Warren I., "Acheson, His Advisers, and China, 1949–1950," in Dorothy Borg and Waldo Heinrichs, eds., *Uncertain Years: Chinese–American Relations, 1947–1950* (New York: Columbia University Press, 1980), 13–52.

Cohn, Elizabeth, "President Kennedy's Decision to Impose a Blockade in the Cuban Missile Crisis: Building Consensus in the ExComm After the Decision," in James A. Nathan, ed., *The Cuban Missile Crisis Revisited* (New York: St. Martin's Press, 1992), 219–35.

Cumings, Bruce, "'Revising Postrevisionism,' or, The Poverty of Theory in Diplomatic History," *Diplomatic History* 17 (Fall 1993), 539–69.

Dessouki, Ali E. Hillai, "Nasser and the Struggle for Independence," in Wm. Roger Louis and Roger Owen, eds., *Suez 1956: The Crisis and Its Consequences* (New York: Oxford University Press, 1989), 31–41.

Dingman, Roger, "Atomic Diplomacy During the Korean War," *International Security* 13 (Winter 1988/9), 50–91.

Divine, Robert A., "Alive and Well: The Continuing Cuban Missile Crisis Controversy," *Diplomatic History* 18 (Fall 1994), 551–60.

Doyle, Michael W., "An International Liberal Community," in Graham Allison and Gregory Treverton, eds., *Rethinking America's Security: Beyond the Cold War to New World Order* (New York: Norton, 1992), 307–33.

——, "Kant, Liberal Legacies, and Foreign Affairs," *Philosophy and Public Affairs* 12 (Summer and Fall 1983), 205–35, 323–53.

Dulles, John Foster, "A Policy of Boldness," *Life* 32 (19 May 1952), 146–60.

Farquharson, John, "'The Essential Division': Britain and the Partition of Germany 1945–9," *German History* 9 (Feb. 1991), 23–45.

Federenko, Nikolai T., "Stalin and Mao Zedong, (Part I)," *Russian Politics and Law*, 32 (July–Aug. 1994), 74–95.

——, "Stalin and Mao Zedong (Conclusion)," *Russian Politics and Law*, 33 (Jan.–Feb. 1995), 82–96.

Fish, M. Steven, "After Stalin's Death: The Anglo-American Debate Over a New Cold War," *Diplomatic History* 10 (Fall 1986), 333–55.

Foot, Rosemary, "New Light on the Sino-Soviet Alliance: Chinese and American Perspectives," *Journal of Northeast Asian Studies* 10 (Fall 1991), 16–29.

Gaddis, John Lewis, "The Emerging Post-Revisionist Synthesis on the Origins of the Cold War," *Diplomatic History* 7 (Summer 1983), 171–90.

——, "International Relations Theory and the End of the Cold War," *International Security* 17 (Winter 1992/3), 5–58.

Gaddis, John Lewis, "On Moral Equivalency and Cold War History," *Ethics and International Affairs* 10 (1996), 131–48.

——, "Peace, Legitimacy, and the Post-Cold War World: Where Do We Go From Here?" in Geir Lundestad, ed., *The Fall of Great Powers: Peace, Stability, and Legitimacy* (New York: Oxford University Press, 1994), 351–68.

——, "The Tragedy of Cold War History," *Diplomatic History* 17 (Winter 1993), 1–16.

——, "The Unexpected John Foster Dulles," in Richard H. Immerman, ed., *John Foster Dulles and the Diplomacy of the Cold War* (Princeton: Princeton University Press, 1990), 47–77.

Garver, John W., "Polemics, Paradigms, Responsibility, and the Origins of the U.S.–PRC Confrontation in the 1950s," *Journal of American–East Asian Relations* 3 (Spring 1994), 1–34.

Genco, Stephen J., "The Eisenhower Doctrine: Deterrence in the Middle East, 1958–1958," in Alexander L. George and Richard Smoke, *Deterrence in American Foreign Policy: Theory and Practice* (New York: Columbia University Press, 1974), 308–62.

George, Alexander L., "Ideology and International Relations: A Conceptual Analysis," *Jerusalem Journal of International Relations* 9 (1987), 1–21.

Gerber, Larry G., "The Baruch Plan and the Origins of the Cold War," *Diplomatic History* 6 (Winter 1982), 69–95.

"Ghost of a Kennedy–C.I.A. Plot Has Come Back to Haunt Clinton," *New York Times*, 30 Oct. 1994.

Gibiansky, Leonid, "The 1948 Soviet–Yugoslav Conflict and the Formation of the 'Socialist Camp' Model," in Odd Arne Westad, Sven Holtsmark, and Ivor B. Neumann, eds., *The Soviet Union in Eastern Europe, 1945–89* (New York: St. Martin's Press, 1994), 26–46.

Gluchowski, L. W., "Poland, 1956: Khrushchev, Gomulka, and the Polish October," Cold War International History Project [hereafter CWIHP] *Bulletin* #5 (Spring 1995), 1, 38–49.

Goldstein, Steven M., "Nationalism and Internationalism: Sino-Soviet Relations," in Thomas W. Robinson and David Shambaugh, eds., *Chinese Foreign Policy: Theory and Practice* (New York: Oxford University Press, 1994), 224–65.

——, "Sino-American Relations, 1948–1950: Lost Chance or No Chance?" in Harry Harding and Yuan Ming, eds., *Sino-American Relations: A Joint Reassessment of a Critical Decade* (Wilmington, Del: Scholarly Resources, 1989), 119–42.

Goncharov, S. N., "Stalin's Dialogue with Mao Zedong," *Journal of Northeast Asian Studies* 10 (Winter, 1991), 45–79.

Gorodetsky, Gabriel, "The Formulation of Soviet Foreign Policy: Ideology and Realpolitik," in Gorodetsky, ed., *Soviet Foreign Policy 1917–1991: A Retrospective* (London: Frank Cass, 1994), 30–44.

Grossman, Atina, "A Question of Silence: The Rape of German Women by Occupation Soldiers," *October* 72 (Spring 1995), 43–63.

Hahn, Peter L., "Containment and Egyptian Nationalism: The Unsuccessful Effort to Establish the Middle East Command, 1950–53," *Diplomatic History* 11 (Winter 1987), 23–40.

Hanhimäki, Jussi, "'Containment' in a Borderland: The United States and Finland, 1948–49," *Diplomatic History* 18 (Summer 1994), 353–74.

Haslam, Jonathan, "Litvinov, Stalin, and the Road Not Taken," in Gabriel Gorodetsky, ed., *Soviet Foreign Policy 1917–1991: A Retrospective* (London: Frank Cass, 1994), 55–62.

He Di, "The Evolution of the Chinese Communist Party's Policy toward the United States, 1944–1949," in Harry Harding and Yuan Ming, eds., *Sino-American*

Relations: A Joint Reassessment of a Critical Decade (Wilmington, Del.: Scholarly Resources, 1989), 31–50.

——, "'The Last Campaign to Unify China': The CCP's Unmaterialized Plan to Liberate Taiwan, 1949–1950," *Chinese Historians* 5 (Spring 1992), 1–16.

——, "The Most Respected Enemy: Mao Zedong's Perception of the United States," *China Quarterly* #137 (Mar. 1994), 144–58.

Hershberg, James G., "Anatomy of a Controversy: Anatoly F. Dobrynin's Meeting with Robert F. Kennedy, Saturday, October 27 1962," CWIHP *Bulletin* #5 (Spring 1995), 75–80.

——, "Before 'The Missiles of October': Did Kennedy Plan a Military Strike Against Cuba?" in James A. Nathan, ed., *The Cuban Missile Crisis Revisited* (New York: St. Martin's Press, 1992), 237–80.

Hewedy, Amin, "Nasser and the Crisis of 1956," in Wm. Roger Louis and Roger Owen, eds., *Suez 1956: The Crisis and Its Consequences* (New York: Oxford University Press, 1989), 161–72.

Hogan, Michael J., "State of the Art: An Introduction," in Hogan, ed., *America in the World: The Historiography of American Foreign Relations since 1941* (New York: Cambridge University Press, 1995), 3–19.

——, "The Vice Men of Foreign Affairs," *Reviews in American History* 21 (1993), 320–8.

Hollander, Paul, "Soviet Terror, American Amnesia," *National Review* 46 (2 May 1994), 28–39.

Holloway, David, "Soviet Scientists Speak Out," *Bulletin of the Atomic Scientists* 49 (May 1993), 18–9.

Holsti, Ole R., "Models of International Relations and Foreign Policy," *Diplomatic History* 13 (Winter 1989), 15–43.

Hunt, Michael H., "Beijing and the Korean Crisis, June, 1950–June, 1951," *Political Science Quarterly* 107 (Fall 1992), 453–78.

——, "Mao and the Issue of Accommodation with the United States, 1948–1950," in Dorothy Borg and Waldo Heinrichs, eds., *Uncertain Years: Chinese–American Relations, 1947–1950* (New York: Columbia University Press, 1980), 185–233.

James, Harold, and Marzenna James, "The Origins of the Cold War: Some New Documents," *Historical Journal* 37 (September 1994), 615–22.

Jehl, Douglas, "C.I.A. Opens Files on Cold War Era," *New York Times*, 1 Oct. 1993.

[Kennan, George F.] "X", "The Sources of Soviet Conduct," *Foreign Affairs* 25 (July 1947), 566–82.

Keohane, Robert O., "The Big Influence of Small Allies," *Foreign Policy* #2 (Spring 1971), 161–82.

Kersten, Krystyna, "1956—The Turning Point," in Odd Arne Westad, Sven Holtsmark, and Iver B. Neumann, eds., *The Soviet Union in Eastern Europe, 1945–89* (New York: St. Martin's Press, 1994), 47–62.

Khalidi, Rashid, "Consequences of the Suez Crisis in the Arab World," in Wm. Roger Louis and Roger Owen, eds., *Suez 1956: The Crisis and Its Consequences* (New York: Oxford University Press, 1989), 377–92.

Khariton, Yuli, and Yuri Smirnov, "The Khariton Version," *Bulletin of the Atomic Scientists* 49 (May 1993), 26–7.

Kramer, Mark, "Hungary and Poland, 1956: Khrushchev's CPSU CC Presidium Meeting on East European Crises, 24 October 1956," CWIHP *Bulletin* #5 (Spring 1995), 1, 50–1.

——, "The 'Lessons' of the Cuban Missile Crisis for Warsaw Pact Nuclear Operations," CWIHP *Bulletin* #5 (Spring 1995), 59, 110–15, 160.

Krátky, Karel, "Czechoslovakia, the Soviet Union, and the Marshall Plan," in Odd Arne Westad, Sven Holtsmark, and Ivor B. Neumann, eds., *The Soviet Union in Eastern Europe, 1945–89* (New York: St. Martin's Press, 1994), 9–25.

LaFeber, Walter, "Roosevelt, Churchill, and Indochina: 1942–45," *American Historical Review* 80 (Dec. 1975), 1277–95.

Lardy, Nicholas R., "The Chinese Economy Under Stress, 1958–1965," in Roderick MacFarquhar and John K. Fairbank, eds., *The Cambridge History of China*, xiv: *The People's Republic*, pt. 1: *The Emergence of Revolutionary China, 1949–1965* (New York: Cambridge University Press, 1987), 360–97.

Larsh, William, "W. Averell Harriman and the Polish Question, December, 1943–August, 1944," *East European Politics and Societies* 7 (Fall 1993), 513–54.

Leffler, Melvyn P., "Inside Enemy Archives: The Cold War Reopened," *Foreign Affairs* 75 (July/Aug. 1996), 120–35.

——, "New Approaches, Old Interpretations, and Prospective Reconfigurations," *Diplomatic History* 19 (Spring 1995), 173–96.

——, "Strategy, Diplomacy, and the Cold War: The United States, Turkey, and NATO, 1945–1952," *Journal of American History* 71 (Mar. 1985), 807–25.

Lenin, Vladimir, "On the Question of the Nationalities or of 'Autonomization'," in Robert V. Daniels, ed., *A Documentary History of Communism* (Hanover, NH: University Press of New Hampshire, 1984), I, 151–53.

Lieberthal, Kenneth, "The Great Leap Forward and the Split in the Yenan Leadership," in Roderick MacFarquhar and John K. Fairbank, eds., *The Cambridge History of China*, xiv: *The People's Republic*, pt. 1: *The Emergence of Revolutionary China, 1949–1965* (New York: Cambridge University Press, 1987), 293–359.

Louis, Wm. Roger, "Dulles, Suez, and the British," in Richard H. Immerman, ed., *John Foster Dulles and the Diplomacy of the Cold War* (Princeton: Princeton University Press, 1990), 133–58.

——, "The Tragedy of the Anglo-Egyptian Settlement of 1954," in Wm. Roger Louis and Roger Owen, eds., *Suez 1956: The Crisis and Its Consequences* (New York: Oxford University Press, 1989), 43–71.

Lundestad, Geir, "Empire by Invitation? The United States and Western Europe, 1945–1952," *Journal of Peace Research* 23 (Sept. 1986), 263–77.

Macdonald, Douglas J., "Communist Bloc Expansion in the Early Cold War: Challenging Realism, Refuting Revisionism," *International Security* 20 (Winter 1995/6), 152–88.

Mansourov, Alexandre Y., "Stalin, Mao, Kim, and China's Decision to Enter the Korean War, September 16–October 15, 1950: New Evidence from the Russian Archives," CWIHP *Bulletin* #s 6 and 7 (Winter 1995/6), 94–107.

McCormack, Gavan, "Kim Country: Hard Times in North Korea," *New Left Review* #198 (Mar.–Apr. 1993), 22–24.

McDermott, Kevin, "Stalinist Terror in the Comintern: New Perspectives," *Journal of Contemporary History* 30 (1995), 111–30.

McMahon, Robert J., "Credibility and World Power: Exploring the Psychological Dimension in Postwar American Diplomacy," *Diplomatic History* 15 (Fall 1991), 455–71.

Milward, Alan S., "Was the Marshall Plan Necessary?" *Diplomatic History* 13 (Spring 1989), 231–53.

Miner, Steven Merritt, "His Master's Voice: Viacheslav Mikhailovich Molotov as Stalin's Foreign Commissar," in Gordon A. Craig and Francis L. Loewenheim, eds., *The Diplomats: 1939–1979* (Princeton: Princeton University Press, 1994), 65–100.

Murray, Brian, "Stalin, the Cold War, and the Division of China: A Multi-Archival Mystery," CWIHP *Working Paper* 12 (June 1995).

Narinsky, Mikhail, "Soviet Foreign Policy and the Origins of the Marshall Plan," in Gabriel Gorodetsky, ed., *Soviet Foreign Policy 1917–1991: A Retrospective* (London: Frank Cass, 1994), 105–10.

Nash, Philip, "The Use of Counterfactuals in History: A Look at the Literature," Society for Historians of American Foreign Relations *Newsletter* 22 (Mar. 1991), 2–12.

Norris, Robert S., and William M. Arkin, "Nuclear Notebook: Estimated U.S. and Soviet/Russian Nuclear Stockpile, 1945–94," *Bulletin of the Atomic Scientists* 40 (Nov./Dec. 1994), 58–9.

Pechatnov, Vladimir O., "The Big Three after World War II: New Documents on Soviet Thinking about Post War Relations with the United States and Great Britain," CWIHP *Working Paper* 13 (July 1995).

Pennacchio, Charles F., "The East German Communists and the Origins of the Berlin Blockade Crisis," *East European Quarterly* 24 (Sept. 1995), 294–314.

Petrov, Vladimir, "Soviet Role in the Korean War Confirmed: Secret Documents Declassified," *Journal of Northeast Asian Studies* 14 (Fall 1994), 42–67.

Poggiolini, Ilaria, "Italy," in David Reynolds, ed., *The Origins of the Cold War in Europe: International Perspectives* (New Haven: Yale University Press, 1994), 121–43.

Pollack, Jonathan D., "The Korean War and Sino-American Relations," in Harry Harding and Yuan Ming, eds., *Sino-American Relations, 1945–1955: A Joint Reassessment of a Critical Decade* (Wilmington, Del.: Scholarly Resources, 1989), 213–37.

Popov, V. P., "State Terror in Soviet Russia, 1923–1953: Sources and Their Interpretations," *Russian Social Science Review* 35 (Sept. 1994), 48–70.

Pozdeeva, Lydia A., "The Soviet Union: Territorial Diplomacy," in David Reynolds, Warren F. Kimball, and A. O. Chubarian, eds., *Allies at War: The Soviet, American, and British Experiences, 1939–1945* (New York: St. Martin's Press, 1994), 355–85.

Puchala, Donald J., "The History of the Future of International Relations," *Ethics and International Affairs* 8 (1994), 177–202.

Raack, R. C., "Stalin Plans his Post-War Germany," *Journal of Contemporary History* 28 (Jan. 1993), 53–73.

Ravindranathan, T. R., "The Legacy of Stalin and Stalinism: A Historiographical Survey of the Literature, 1930–1960," *Canadian Journal of History* 29 (Apr. 1994), 113–46.

Reynolds, David, "Great Britain," in Reynolds, ed., *The Origins of the Cold War in Europe: International Perspectives* (New Haven: Yale University Press, 1994), 77–95.

——, *et al.*, "Legacies: Allies, Enemies, and Posterity," in David Reynolds, Warren F. Kimball, and A. O. Chubarian, eds., *Allies at War: The Soviet–American, and British Experiences, 1939–1945* (New York: St. Martin's Press, 1994), 417–40.

Roberts, Geoffrey, "Moscow and the Marshall Plan: Politics, Ideology, and the Onset of the Cold War, 1947," *Europe-Asia Studies* 46 (1994), 1371–96.

Roesler, Jörg, "The Rise and Fall of the Planned Economy in the German Democratic Republic," *German History* 9 (Feb. 1991), 46–61.

Roman, Peter J., "Curtis LeMay and the Origins of NATO Atomic Targeting," *Journal of Strategic Studies* 16 (Mar. 1993), 46–74.

Rosenberg, David Alan, "American Atomic Strategy and the Hydrogen Bomb Decision," *Journal of American History* 66 (June 1979), 62–87.

——, "The Origins of Overkill: Nuclear Weapons and American Strategy," in Norman Graebner, ed., *The National Security: Theory and Practice, 1945–1960* (New York: Oxford University Press, 1986), 123–95.

Rosenberg, David Alan, "'A Smoking Radiating Ruin at the end of Two Hours': Documents on American Plans for Nuclear War with the Soviet Union, 1954–1955," *International Security* 6 (Winger 1981/2), 3–38.

Ruggie, John Gerald, "International Regimes, Transactions, and Change: Embedded Liberalism in the Postwar Economic Order," in Stephen D. Krasner, ed., *International Regimes* (Ithaca: Cornell University Press, 1983), 195–231.

Sagan, Scott D., "The Perils of Proliferation: Organization Theory, Deterrence Theory, and the Spread of Nuclear Weapons," *International Security* 18 (Spring 1994), 66–107.

Sagdaev, Roald, "Russian Scientists Save American Secrets," *Bulletin of the Atomic Scientists* 49 (May 1993), 32–6.

Schilling, Warner R., "The Politics of National Defense: Fiscal 1950," in Warner R. Schilling, Paul Y. Hammond, and Glenn H. Snyder, *Strategy, Politics, and Defense Budgets* (New York: Columbia University Press, 1962), 1–266.

Schlesinger, James, "The Impact of Nuclear Weapons on History," *Washington Quarterly* 16 (Autumn 1993), 5–12.

Schöpfin, George, "The Stalinist Experience in Eastern Europe," *Survey: A Journal of East and West Studies* 30 (Oct. 1988), 124–47.

Shakhnazarov, Georgy K., "Fidel Castro, Glasnost, and the Caribbean Crisis," CWIHP *Bulletin* #5 (Spring 1995), 83, 87–9.

Sheng, Michael M., "America's Lost Chance in China? A Reappraisal of Chinese Communist Policy toward the United States before 1945," *Australian Journal of Chinese Affairs* 29 (Jan. 1993), 135–53.

Shi Zhe, "With Mao and Stalin: The Reminiscences of a Chinese Interpreter," trans. Chen Jian, *Chinese Historians* 5 (Spring 1992), 35–46.

——, "With Mao and Stalin: The Reminiscences of Mao's Interpreter: Part II: Liu Shaoqi in Moscow," trans. Chen Jian, *Chinese Historians* 6 (Spring 1993), 67–90.

Shulman, Marshall D., "The Superpowers: Dance of the Dinosaurs," *Foreign Affairs* 66 ("America and the World, 1987/8"), 494–515.

Sidikhmenov, Vasily, "Stalin and Mao Hearkened [*sic*] To Us," *New Times International* #5 (Feb. 1993), 31.

Smirnov, Yuri, and Vladislav Zubok, "Nuclear Weapons after Stalin's Death: Moscow Enters the H-Bomb Age," CWIHP *Bulletin* #4 (Fall 1994), 14–15.

Soutou, Georges-Henri, "France," in David Reynolds, ed., *The Origins of the Cold War in Europe: International Perspectives* (New Haven: Yale University Press, 1994), 96–120.

Staritz, Dietrich, "The SED, Stalin, and the German Question: Interests and Decision-Making in the Light of New Sources," *German History* 10 (Oct. 1992), 274–89.

Stephanson, Anders, "The United States," in David Reynolds, ed., *The Origins of the Cold War in Europe: International Perspectives* (New Haven: Yale University Press, 1994), 23–52.

Swain, Geoffrey, "The Cominform: Tito's International?" *Historical Journal* 35 (1992), 641–63.

Takhnenko, Galina, "Anatomy of a Political Decision: Notes on the Marshall Plan," *International Affairs* (Moscow) (July 1992), 111–27.

Tanagawa, Yoshiko, "The Cominform and Southeast Asia," in Yonosuke Nagai and Akira Iriye, eds., *The Origins of the Cold War in Asia* (Tokyo: University of Tokyo Press, 1977), 362–77.

Teiwes, Frederick C., "Establishment and Consolidation of the New Regime," in Roderick MacFarquhar and John K. Fairbank, eds., *The Cambridge History of China,* xiv: *The People's Republic*, pt. 1: *The Emergence of Revolutionary China, 1949–1965* (New York: Cambridge University Press, 1987), 51–143.

Trachtenberg, Marc, "White House Tapes and Minutes of the Cuban Missile Crisis: ExCom Meetings, October, 1962," in Sean M. Lynn-Jones, Steven E. Miller, and Stephen Van Evera, eds., *Nuclear Diplomacy and Crisis Management* (Cambridge, Mass.: MIT Press, 1990), 283–89.

Trani, Eugene P., "Woodrow Wilson and the Decision to Intervene in Russia: A Reconsideration," *Journal of Modern History* 48 (Sept. 1976), 440–61.

Tumanov, Georgy, "How the Great Leader Was Made," *New Times* #17 (Apr. 1993), 24–6.

Walker, J. Samuel, "The Decision to Use the Bomb: A Historiographical Update," *Diplomatic History* 14 (Winter 1990), 97–114.

——, "History, Collective Memory, and the Decision to Use the Bomb," *Diplomatic History* 19 (Spring 1995), 319–28.

Weathersby, Kathryn, "Korea, 1949–50: To Attack or Not to Attack? Stalin, Kim Il-sung and the Prelude to War," CWIHP *Bulletin* #5 (Spring 1995) 1, 2–9.

——, "New Findings on the Korean War," CWIHP *Bulletin* #3 (Fall 1993) 1, 14–18.

——, "New Russian Documents on the Korean War," CWIHP *Bulletin* #s 6 and 7 (Winter 1995/6), 30–5.

——, "Soviet Aims in Korea and the Origins of the Korean War, 1945–1950: New Evidence from the Russian Archives," CWIHP *Working Paper* 8 (Nov. 1993).

——, "The Soviet Role in the Early Phase of the Korean War: New Documentary Evidence," *Journal of American-East Asian Relations* 2 (Winter 1993), 425–58.

Weiner, Tim, "Keeping the Secrets That Everybody Knows," *New York Times*, 30 Oct. 1994.

West, Philip, "Confronting the West: China as David and Goliath in the Korean War," *Journal of American–East Asian Relations* 1 (Spring 1993), 5–28.

Westad, Odd Arne, "Unwrapping the Stalin-Mao Talks: Setting the Record Straight," CWIHP *Bulletin* #s 6 and 7 (Winter 1995/6), 23–4.

Whiting, Allen S., "The Sino-Soviet Split," in Roderick MacFarquhar and John K. Fairbank, eds., *The Cambridge History of China*, xiv: *The People's Republic*, pt. 1: *The Emergence of Revolutionary China, 1949–1965* (New York: Cambridge University Press, 1987), 478–538.

Xu Yan, "The Chinese Forces and Their Casualties in the Korean War: Facts and Statistics," *Chinese Historians* 6 (Fall 1993), 45–58.

Yaffe, Michael D., "'A Higher Priority than the Korean War!': The Crash Programmes to Modify the Bombers for the Bomb," *Diplomacy and Statecraft* 5 (July 1994), 358–70.

Yang Kuisong, "The Soviet Factor and the CCP's Policy toward the United States in the 1940s," *Chinese Historians* 5 (1992), 17–39.

Yegorova, Natalia I., "The 'Iran Crisis' of 1945–1946: A View from the Russian Archives," CWIHP *Working Paper* #15 (May, 1996).

Zhai Qiang, "The Making of Chinese Communist Foreign Relations, 1935–1949: A New Study from China," *Journal of American–East Asian Relations* 1 (Winter 1992), 471–7.

——, "Transplanting the Chinese Model: Chinese Military Advisers and the First Vietnam War, 1950–1954," *Journal of Military History* 57 (Oct. 1993), 689–715.

Zhang, Shu Guang, "In the Shadow of Mao: Zhou Enlai and New China's Diplomacy," in Gordon A. Craig and Francis L. Loewenheim, eds., *The Diplomats: 1939–1979* (Princeton: Princeton University Press, 1994), 337–70.

Zubok, Vladislav, "'Dismayed by the Actions of the Soviet Union': Mikoyan's Talks with Fidel Castro and the Cuban Leadership," CWIHP *Bulletin* #5 (Spring 1995), 59, 89–92.

——, "Soviet Intelligence and the Cold War: The 'Small' Committee of Information, 1952–53," *Diplomatic History* 19 (Summer 1995), 453–72.

——, " 'To Hell with Yalta!' Stalin Opts for a New Status Quo," CWIHP *Bulletin*, #s 6 and 7 (Winter, 1995/6), 24–7.

——, and Constantine Pleshakov, "The Soviet Union," in David Reynolds, ed., *The Origins of the Cold War in Europe: International Perspectives* (New Haven: Yale University Press, 1993), 53–76.

IV. UNPUBLISHED MATERIAL

Asada, Sadao, "The Shock of the Atomic Bomb and Japan's Decision to Surrender," paper presented at the Society for Historians of American Foreign Relations annual convention, Annapolis, Md., June 1995.

Bradley, Mark, "Constructing an Indigenous Regional Political Order in Southeast Asia: Vietnam and the Diplomacy of Revolutionary Nationalism, 1946–1949," CWIHP conference paper, Hong Kong, Jan. 1996.

Broscious, S. David, "From 'Peace and Prosperity' to 'Peace and Security:' The Marshall Plan and the Ideological Shift within U.S. Foreign Policy, 1947–1948," paper presented at the Society for Historians of American Foreign Relations annual convention, Annapolis, Md., June 1995.

——, "Longing for an International Police Force, Banking on American Superiority: Harry S. Truman's Approach to Nuclear Energy," paper presented at a Nuclear History Program–Contemporary History Institute conference, Ohio University, Sept. 1991.

Bukharkin, Igor, "Moscow and Ho Chi Minh, 1945–1969," CWIHP conference paper, Hong Kong, Jan. 1996.

Burns, John Kevin, "A Lesson in Nationalism: United States Relations with Egypt during the Eisenhower Presidency, 1953–1960," MA thesis, University of Maryland Baltimore County, 1994.

Craig, Howard Campbell, "The Thermonuclear Revolution and American Postwar Realism," Ph.D. dissertation, Ohio University, 1995.

Filitov, Alexei M., "The Soviet Administrators and Their German 'Friends',"
Norwegian Nobel Institute conference paper, Moscow, Mar. 1993.

George, Jason, "Adapting to Circumstances: American Policy Toward Eastern Europe, 1953–1956," MA thesis, Ohio University, 1995.

Gibiansky, Leonid Ya., "Problems of East European International-Political Structuring in the Period of Formation of the Soviet Bloc," CWIHP conference paper, Moscow, Jan. 1993.

Gobarev, Victor M., "Soviet Military Plans and Activities During the Berlin Crisis, 1948–1949," CWIHP conference paper, Essen, June 1994.

Kramer, Mark, "Khrushchev and Eastern Europe: DeStalinization and Reconsolidation," paper presented at the Brown University Centennial Conference on Nikita S. Khrushchev, Providence, RI, Dec. 1994.

Li Haiwen, "Restoring Peace in Indochina at the Geneva Conference," CWIHP conference paper, Hong Kong, Jan. 1996.

Lukes, Igor, "A Road to Communism: Czechoslovakia, 1938–1948," Norwegian Nobel Institute conference paper, Moscow, Mar. 1993.

Lundestad, Geir, "Empire by Integration: The United States and European Integration, 1945–1996," paper presented at the European Association for American Studies meeting, Warsaw, Mar. 1996.

Mansourov, Alexandre Y., "Did Conventional Deterrence Work? Why the Korean War Did Not Erupt in the Summer of 1949," CWIHP conference paper, Hong Kong, Jan. 1996.

Murray, Brian Joseph, "Western Versus Chinese Realism: Soviet–American Diplomacy and the Chinese Civil War, 1945–1950," Ph.D. dissertation, Columbia University, 1995.

Narinsky, Mikhail M., "Soviet Policy and the Berlin Blockade, 1948," CWIHP conference paper, Essen, June 1994.

——, "The Soviet Union and the Marshall Plan," CWIHP conference paper, Moscow, Jan. 1993.

Nash, Philip, "The Other Missiles of October: Eisenhower, Kennedy, and the Jupiters in Europe, 1957–1963," Ph.D. dissertation, Ohio University, 1994.

Parish, Scott D., "The Turn Towards Confrontation: The Soviet Reaction to the Marshall Plan, June 1947," CWIHP conference paper, Moscow, Jan. 1993.

Pleshakov, Constantine V., "Reform Versus Revolution: Khrushchev Deals With China," paper presented at the Brown University Centennial Conference on Nikita S. Khrushchev, Providence, RI, Dec. 1994.

Prozumenshchikov, M. Yu., and I. N. Shevchuk, "Soviet–Chinese Relations, 1953–1959," CWIHP conference paper, Moscow, Jan. 1993.

Sheng, Michael M., "Ideology and Chinese Communist Foreign Policy: Mao Deals with Superpowers, 1935–50," unpublished book manuscript.

Taubman, William, "Khrushchev vs. Mao: A Preliminary Sketch of the Role of Personality in the Sino-Soviet Dispute," CWIHP conference paper, Hong Kong, Jan. 1996.

Westad, Odd Arne, "Losses, Chances, and Myths: The United States and the Creation of the Sino-Soviet Alliance," forthcoming in *Diplomatic History*.

Yang Kuisong, "On the Causes of the Changes in Mao Zedong's View of the Soviet Union," CWIHP conference paper, Hong Kong, Jan. 1996.

Yegorova, Natalia I., "From the Comintern to the Cominform: Ideological Dimensions of Cold War Origins (1945–1948)," CWIHP conference paper, Moscow, Jan. 1993.

Zhang, Shu Guang, "The Collapse of Sino-Soviet Economic Cooperation, 1950–1960: A Cultural Explanation," CWIHP conference paper, Hong Kong, Jan. 1996.

Zubok, Vladislav, "Eastern Europe's Place in the Priorities of Soviet Foreign Policy, 1945–1947," Norwegian Nobel Institute Working Paper, Jan. 1994.

——, "Khrushchev's Motives and Soviet Diplomacy in the Berlin Crisis, 1958–1962," CWIHP conference paper, Essen, June 1994.

INDEX